Daniel Reconsidered

Daniel Reconsidered

The Key to the Divine Timetable

J. Allen

Scripture Teaching Library

ISBN: 978-1-909789-11-1

Published by
SCRIPTURE TEACHING LIBRARY
Cookstown, Northern Ireland.

www.scriptureteachinglibrary.com

Printed by Kingsbridge Press Ltd, Cookstown, Northern Ireland.
Cover image: Stephen Allen

Contents

To the precious memory of my youngest son,
STEPHEN,
who began this project by the questions he kept asking.
Now he has all the answers in the presence of
the Sovereign of Whom Daniel wrote.

Foreword

MANY READERS OF *Daniel Reconsidered* will already be indebted to Mr Allen's work through his commentaries on 1 Timothy and Revelation in the John Ritchie *What the Bible Teaches* series. Given the acclaim that those commentaries received, such will come to this volume with high expectations. They will not be disappointed.

Mr Allen has been appreciated in many parts of the world for his meticulous Bible expositions, not least for his handling of prophetic themes. This work represents the mature thinking of one whose mind has considered these matters in over sixty years of careful Bible study.

We are privileged to now have from his pen a commentary on the book of Daniel, which robustly defends the historical accuracy of Daniel as well as being unashamedly pre-millennial. Both of these aspects of Daniel's prophecy have been challenged over recent decades. Many liberals deny the predictive element in Old Testament prophecy and, flying in the face of compelling evidence, attempt to establish a second century BC date for Daniel. This work takes a firm stance against such an approach.

Others with equal force seek to explain Daniel within the paradigm of amillennial thinking but such a perspective is rigorously rejected in this commentary. The very clear prophetic outline given in these pages demands the establishment of the Kingdom of the Lord Jesus in this world when the 'times of the Gentiles' have run their course.

In this regard, particularly noteworthy is Mr Allen's explanation of the vision of chapter 7. Here the author navigates the reader through a most challenging and key prophecy and sets forth an interpretation that is carefully argued and will prove to be deeply instructive and thought provoking to every careful student. The same can be said for the careful exegesis of the landmark prophecy of the seventy weeks in chapter 9.

Another feature of *Daniel Reconsidered* is the careful harmonising of the material presented in Daniel with its New Testament counterpart, the book of Revelation. This commentary demonstrates how closely connected these two major prophetic works are in the Divine library.

The reader will find in these pages painstaking attention to detail – this includes matters historical, archaeological, doctrinal, textual, and dispensational. This collection of material is presented in a manner that is clear, accessible, and analytical. At the same time there is a pastoral application of pertinent lessons wherever appropriate, which gives the commentary a freshness that can, at times, be lacking in works of a more technical nature.

This book is not a superficial summary of Daniel's message. Here is a work of depth and breadth, a work of spiritual insight and penetrating analysis. Where debated issues are considered, the author is very fair in his handling of differing viewpoints, setting forth the various alternatives and giving clearly articulated reasons for the conclusions reached. This furnishes the reader with the necessary material enabling him or her to come to an informed decision on any given point.

The Lord Jesus, when speaking of the book of Daniel the prophet in Mark 13:14, could exhort his audience 'let him that readeth understand'. Daniel's prophecy has not always been easy to understand but I am assured that anyone who is willing to take up this commentary and, with Bible in hand, to consider or re-consider Daniel chapter by chapter, will find Mr Allen's work an invaluable aid in the understanding process.

DAVID GILLILAND
August 2013

Preface

Why another book on Daniel?

I HAVE READ MANY BOOKS on Daniel over the years and I stand indebted to many authors. Some informed me, some interested me, some intrigued me, and some irritated me. However, all have contributed in some way to my enjoyment of Daniel – the man and the book. While valuing the information of one author, enjoying the stimulation of another, even responding to the irritation of another, a unique picture of Daniel has been building up in my mind.

Daniel was a man whose long life (almost a century) was lived at Babylon – the capital of the world empire – under the men who ruled the world of their time – a Nebuchadnezzar and a Cyrus. Against this background of transient earthly empires, Daniel, a highly placed civil servant in both empires, is used of God to tell of a *coming King* Who would be entrusted by God with an *everlasting Kingdom*, which would never pass away. While most expositors mention this central theme, few seem to stress the unique way that the whole book centres exclusively, both historically and prophetically, on this coming King. The preparation for Him, the programme before Him and the power displayed in Him are contrasted with what has preceded Him on earth. This present study will attempt to convey Daniel's preoccupation with this Sovereign. On occasions when ministering on this book my subtitle has been *'The Coming King'*.

Why a *Commentary* on Daniel?

The answer is simple. This is the form I personally have found most helpful and useful in study. My favourite commentaries on the books of the Bible have been those that, having first outlined the book, have then gone through it chapter by chapter, then paragraph by paragraph, down to a verse by verse, phrase by phrase, exposition. In this way, no significant points can be left out or skipped over. Every problem must be faced, even if it means the confession that the author has no answer.

Another feature I look for in a commentary is the clear setting out of the positive truth of Scripture. This must come first. If alternative views need discussion, as they often do, then the scriptural reasons for their rejection can be made clear. I have sought to take this approach with the difficult passages in Daniel – with what success the reader will be able to judge. There is one exceptional case in this book, where the reader will see I had to take the very opposite approach, for a special reason. I had to write it, as it had come to me, step by step, as I pondered what I had been taught by highly respected, godly, men. It has not been an easy path. I would meet what was, to me, a problem of interpretation in Daniel's writing – something did not fit. Seeking help from trusted expositors, I found that which seemed to meet the case – then, on reconsideration, saw that this interpretation was not doing justice to the text. So, back to Scripture, and it soon became clear that what was needed was a major shift in perspective ('paradigm' is the word theologians use). Such a shift is not so easily done as we grow older. But that shift in viewpoint often brings a more satisfactory solution to specific problems, as the picture jigsaw falls into place. I confess that I have not, on every occasion, been able to follow the path to this happy conclusion – but, stopped by additional problems not previously seen, have had to leave the original problem without a solution. It will be clear in the exposition when this has occurred.

Why *another* Commentary on Daniel?

Beyond the reasons given for the appearance of this commentary there lies a more personal journey – almost a personal odyssey. While writing on the book of Revelation,[1] I was compelled to study the book of Daniel for the necessary background of prophetic truth. Being unable to find, at times, in the commentaries available to me on Daniel, the information I needed, I promised myself that I would try some day to fill that gap when opportunity occurred. Seventeen years later this commentary is the result. What had I failed to find in many commentaries on the book of Daniel? Four things troubled me: (a) insufficient detail of the historical background in which Daniel lived; few commentaries dated events in Daniel's writings, so they did not seem to carry much local colour; (b) inadequate references to the ministry of contemporary writers – Jeremiah and Ezekiel – who ministered to the same nation at the same time as

[1] Allen, *What the Bible Teaches, Revelation.*

Daniel, each prophet having a different audience; (c) indifferent attention given to showing Daniel as the seedbed of the book of Revelation; and (d) insufficiently clear identification between the men spoken of in Daniel, like the 'Little Horn', and the men mentioned in the NT. Constantly, as I studied, I wondered which figure depicted which man in the prophetic passages in the NT. Out of these considerations grew the title *Daniel – Reconsidered: The Key to the Divine Timetable*. Whether this book meets any or all of these criteria only the reader will be able to judge.

From discussions and arguments down the years, I owe much to brethren (and sisters informally) who have discussed matters arising from the book of Daniel. I have learned a lot from able ministers of the prophetic Word and I owe them deep gratitude for their help and guidance.

When it came down to this writing then my special thanks are due to:

1. My wife, for her patience during the hours when Daniel made a third party in the home, a constant companion on our travels, and even intruded into family visits. I do appreciate the patience of my wife and the whole family circle. The grandchildren were invaluable when the word processor displayed tantrums.

2. Simon Lafferty, grandson of my wife, for his researches into history in the background study and his invaluable assistance in the checking of dates as well as keeping an eye on the grammar. Another grandson, Richard Morrison, was often summoned at short notice to rescue the manuscript from computer ills due to my technological ineptitude. In the same field, when the technological problems got out of hand, there was also the readily given first aid of the expert David Clulow, who came repeatedly to my aid when all seemed lost. My thanks to all for the assistance so cheerfully given.

3. Special thanks are due also to the following brethren for their invaluable assistance in the preparation of the manuscript:

(a) David Gilliland, for his willingness to go through the manuscript and, with critical eye, view the theology, as well as checking the logic of the arguments. His suggestions were invaluable, and the book is much better for his help. He was also kind enough to write the Foreword.

(b) All the committee members of Scripture Teaching Library. Robin McKeown, for his encouragement and support and Walter Boyd, Mark Sweetnam, and David McAllister for their help in many fields, not least the checking of the manuscript for printing. They have spent many hours in this task, and I owe them many thanks for their help.

(c) Colin Glendinning, of Kingsbridge Press Ltd, who guided me through the preparation of the manuscript and facilitated the printing of the book.

While thus expressing my very deep appreciation for the help given, I must carry the ultimate responsibility and accept the blame for any mistakes.

Except where otherwise indicated, all quotations from Scripture are taken from the Authorised (King James) Version (Newberry edition).

ABBREVIATIONS

TEXTS

Translations used or referred to are abbreviated as follows:

AV	Authorised Version
RSV	Revised Standard Version
JND	New Translation by J.N. Darby
LXX	The Septuagint: Greek Translation of the Old Testament
ESV	English Standard Version, Collins, 2002
NET	NET BIBLE, First Edition, 2009 (www.bible.org)
MT	Masoretic Text: ancient rabbinic text of the Hebrew Bible
NAS	New American Standard Version
NIV	New International Version, 1979
New.	The AV as edited by Thomas Newberry. Known as 'The Englishman's Bible'
NT	New Testament
OT	Old Testament
RV	Revised Version (*AV* revised and published in England, 1885)
Sp	Translation of OT from Hebrew into English by Helen Spurrell, 1985

Standard Works are referred to under the following abbreviations:

CBD	*The Cambridge Biographical Dictionary* ed. David Crystal, (Cambridge: CUP, 1994).
OCD	*The Oxford Classical Dictionary* ed. Hornblower and Spawforth, (Oxford: OUP, 2012).
OHCW	*The Oxford History of the Classical World* ed. Boardman, Griffin and Murray, (Oxford: OUP, 1986).
ODCW	*The Oxford Dictionary of the Classical World* ed. Roberts, (Oxford: OUP, 2005).
UBD	Merrill F. Unger, *Unger's Bible Dictionary,* (Chicago, IL: Moody Press, 1957).
DOTW	Aaron Pick, *Dictionary of Old Testament Words for English Readers,* (Grand Rapids, MI: Kregel, 1977).

OTWS William Wilson, *Old Testament Word Studies*, (Grand Rapids, MI: Kregel Publications, 1978).

TWOT *Theological Wordbook of the Old Testament* ed. Harris, Archer and Waltke, (Chicago, IL: Moody Bible Institute, 1981).

WSD Baker and Carpenter, *The Complete Word Study Dictionary*, OT, (Chattanooga, TN: AMG Publishers, 2003).

Introduction

Section 1
The Author and his Times

A. Personal Circumstances

A most remarkable feature of this book is that amongst the first group of captives transported to Babylon by Nebuchadnezzar from Jerusalem was a young man, Daniel, who was to become the author of this book. So, from the first day of the captivity period allowed of God to fall on the nation of Israel, God had His man at the centre of world affairs – in Babylon. Transported to Babylon from Nebuchadnezzar's first invasion of Israel, in the year 606 BC, Daniel remains there, at the centre of the empire, throughout the seventy-year captivity – indeed, Scripture makes a special note of this fact, as is recorded – 'Daniel continued even unto the first year of king Cyrus' (1:21). It is perfectly clear that this year does not mark his death, since he records the date of his last vision as 'in the third year of Cyrus' (10:1). The emphasis is simply that God's man was in Babylon for the entire span of the captivity. Following his capture of Babylon Cyrus issued the decree (2 Chron. 36:22–23) that allowed captive Jews to return to Judah, thus marking the end of the captivity period. Obedience to that decree led the first returnees to Judah under Zerubbabel (536 BC). God had set the period of discipline as seventy years (Jer. 29:10) and this is exactly the period of servitude experienced by the nation (606–536 BC). However, the author of this book not only experienced the entire period of national captivity in Babylon, but, most significantly, did not return with any of the companies that went back to Jerusalem, but was permitted of his God to continue for some years under the new Medo-Persian rule.

Daniel, whose name means 'God is my Judge', is a man whom God used mightily as a witness for Him. He is assuredly one of the most remarkable men in Scripture. Blameless in personal life, addressed by the archangel Gabriel as 'greatly beloved' (9:23), found faultless as to his public life when scrutinised by bitter enemies in an unsympathetic environment (6:4), Daniel stands out as a moral and spiritual giant. Rudely snatched from his homeland by a conquering army when but a teenager he was brought to Babylon – the very centre of pagan idolatry. That Babylon was called the 'golden city' was due to that idolatry. Gold, paid as tribute to the gods in Babylon by its world-conquering army, was used to decorate the multitude of temples there. Family, friends, and the fellowship of kindred hearts left far behind, Daniel and fellow-deportees had to make life-changing choices, under threat to their lives, in this totally pagan environment.

Within days certainly, possibly within hours, of arrival in Babylon (1:8), this teenager faces the first test – so simple yet so vital. The result will show whether as boy or man he can be a fit witness for God. So simple – whether to eat the food from the king's table or not? The demanding education programme, in anticipation of which they had been selected and then transported so swiftly to Babylon, required keenness of intellect. That, in its turn, demanded the best in food – and the best would be on the king's table. The logic is clear. For the young deportees the reasoning was equally clear and simple – first, no scriptural diet laws were observed in Babylon; secondly, some portion of the best dishes was routinely offered to the idol. To eat would make them ceremonially unclean – they would be defiled. So the issue for these youths was a simple question for each soul – did the Word of God have authority over them in Babylon or not? Some it might not worry – see how, at a later date, King Jehoiachin acted when in Babylon (2 Kgs 25:27–30) – but these young men were prepared to risk their lives and obey God.

From this first test it is clear that God can trust this young man to represent Him – even in Babylon. This testing process continues over Daniel's lifetime as God takes him deeper into His counsels. The final test, in the den of lions (6:1–27), takes place when he is eighty-eight years old, and, passed with honours, as was the first test, God can entrust Daniel with the key prophecy of Scripture that will include the date for the coming of the Messiah.

Though he records the events that befell him and his friends, it is to be noted that Daniel does not name himself as the author in the first six chapters of his book. However, in the second part of the book he identifies himself twelve times as the recipient of the visions (7:2, 15, 28; 8:1, 15, 27; 9:2, 22; 10:2, 7, 11, 12) and then, as if adding his signature, he identifies himself for the thirteenth and last time (12:5). This personal identification, 'I Daniel', follows the Divine instruction, 'Shut up the words and seal the book'. The book of Daniel is thus to be viewed as a unit with a single author. The first six chapters, so vivid and graphic in presentation, are so closely interwoven with the final visions, in the last six chapters, that the unity of the book has never been seriously questioned by conservative scholarship. For the link between the chronology of the book and the life of Daniel, see Table 1 (below).

TABLE 1

Chronology of the Life of Daniel in the Dating of the Chapters

Chapter	Date BC	Daniel's Age	
1	606	18	(see note (c) below)
2	603	20	
3	601	23	
4	571	53	
5	539	84	
6	537	86	
7	553	70	
8	551	72	
9	538	85	
10–12	536	88	

From the sequence of the chapters and the dates, so carefully recorded, there is presented a young man, showing spiritual development, under Babylonian conditions, from simple obedience to the Word of God to the communication of the Scripture of Truth (10:21). Daniel will be entrusted to deliver the key prophecy of the seventy weeks (9:24–27) – the only prophecy in Scripture that links the coming of Christ to a specific, readily identified date in earth's history. The study of a man growing old in the service of his God can best be viewed in table form, as shown for easy reference. The chapters describing events in the book are dated, and the corresponding age of Daniel noted for each event.

(a) The chapters are dated directly in the text or by the events recorded there. The last three chapters present one vision, covered by the date given on its opening (10:1).

(b) We know that Daniel was taken captive to Babylon at the time of the first Babylonian invasion of Israel (606 BC) as a teenager (1:1).[1] There is no record of his year of birth or of his parentage. To be selected for training by Nebuchadnezzar would suggest that he must have belonged, if not to the royal line, at least to a leading family in Judah.

(c) Expositors have made their own judgements (guesses!) as to his age when deported. Some commentators have questioned the possibility of King Nebuchadnezzar prostrating himself before a boy of thirteen years (2:46). In his most helpful commentary, Keil[2] suggests that the Hebrew word 'children' (1:4, 10) was used of youths from fifteen to nineteen years old. He points out that the same word is translated 'young men' when it is said of Solomon, 'he forsook the counsel of the old men ... and consulted with the young men that were grown up with him and which stood before him' (1 Kgs 12:8). Many commentators have favoured the age of fifteen, but there seems to be an increasing number of more recent scholars who opt for eighteen. Three years is the difference between a boy and a man standing before the Babylonian Court (2:48); also between boys and men in their promotion to the administration of Babylon (3:30). For these entirely subjective reasons it seems best suited to see Daniel as an eighteen-year-old youth when carried captive to Babylon. That age is adopted in this commentary and used in Table 1.

B. National Conditions

It has been made clear that the author is possibly the teenage scion of the royal house of Judah or a closely-related family (Table 1 Note (b)) who becomes, first, a senior administrator in the Babylonian Empire, then the Senior President of the Satrapy (Province) of Babylonia under King Darius in the Medo-Persian Empire. First

[1] See Appendix 1, The History of Judaea.

[2] Keil and Delitzsch, *Commentary on the Old Testament*, Vol.9, p.2

trained and then tested, Daniel can be trusted by God to deliver His message. He does this by recording selected events in history in the first part of his book, (chapters 1–6), and, in the last six chapters (chapters 7–12) by revealing the visions given to him.

It will be shown that the message of this book will have immediate instruction for the nation of Israel now under the discipline of their God in captivity under pagan rule. That nation, called of God for a Divine purpose, had not been a united people since the division of the kingdom in the fifth year of King Rehoboam (930 BC).[3] Now both the ten tribes (Ephraim) and the two tribes (Judah) were united – but in captivity. Israel had been taken captive by Assyria in 722 BC, and now the people of Judah, and among them Daniel, would join the captives in the Babylonian Empire. The Assyrian Empire had fallen to Babylon after the total destruction of their capital city, Nineveh (615 BC), by Nebuchadnezzar. Now in captivity, under the most terrible of conditions, two matters must have burdened the hearts of faithful Israelites who believed their Scriptures and put confidence in Jehovah: they might reasonably ask – does God still care for us? Or, has God a future for us? Daniel's book will answer the questions. (See Section 2 E. Purpose of the book).

C. Chronological Data

Since the book embraces the lifetime of Daniel and the conditions under which he and his fellow-captives lived, it is useful to have reference to the changing conditions during that period, with the relevant dates. For easy reference, the key dates in the life of Daniel are set out in Table 2.

TABLE 2

Key Dates in the Life of Daniel
(Against the background of the history of Israel)

Event	Date (BC)	Age of Daniel
Daniel born	c. 624/623*	
Battle of Megiddo	609	14
King Jehoahaz reigns 3 months	609	
King Jehoiakim placed as king	609	
Nebuchadnezzar takes Jerusalem	606	

[3] Thiele, *A Chronology of the Hebrew Kings*. Consult Appendix 1, The History of Judaea.

Daniel taken captive	606	18 (Table 1, Note (c))
Captivity of Israel Commences	**606**	
Battle of Carchemish (Egyptian bid for world power ended)	605	19
Rebellion of Jehoiachin (Jerusalem taken – Ezekiel taken captive)	597	27
Rebellion of Zedekiah (Jerusalem destroyed)	586	37
Desolations of Jerusalem dated	586	
Fall of Babylon to Cyrus	539	84
Edict of Cyrus authorising return	539	84
Return of captives led by Zerubbabel	536	87
Captivity of Israel ends	536	87
Death of Daniel	c. 530	c. 93/94 (tradition)
Return of the Remnant of Israel to Jerusalem		
Return under Zerubbabel	536	
Ministry of Haggai and Zechariah	520	
Temple Rebuilt	516	
Return under Ezra	458	
Return under Nehemiah	445	
Decree to restore and to build Jerusalem	1st *Nisan*, 445 BC	

*Assuming Daniel was 18 when deported.

Table 1 and Table 2

From the dates outlined in Table 1 and in Table 2, it is clear that Daniel lived in a key period of OT history. That key period was the seventy years between the carrying away of Israel to Babylon and the return of the remnant to Jerusalem. This book takes the trouble to emphasise that Daniel lived through the whole period of this Babylonian captivity (1:21) and into the time of the Medo-Persian Empire, which replaced Babylon on the world stage. He lived to see the return of the exercised remnant of Israel to Jerusalem under Zerubbabel (536 BC). Tradition places his death around 530 BC, which gives him a life span of ninety-plus years.

SECTION 2
THE BOOK AND ITS CHARACTER

A. Date

(a) The Credibility of the Date

Once Daniel is accepted as the author, then the question of date is settled. The last vision is given to Daniel in the year 536 BC. Scripture does not record his death, but tradition places it around 530 BC, making him a man of c. 93 or 94 years. It is a reasonable assumption that Daniel completed his writing around 536 BC. The writing would then be deposited amongst the sacred archives of Israel and copied for distribution throughout the Jewish *diaspora*. When the visions were completed Daniel was instructed 'shut up the words, and seal the book' (12:4). It will be shown in the comments (*in loc.*) that the verbs used do not mean to prevent men from seeing it, but to preserve it securely for the blessing of generations to come. One of the immediate purposes of this prophecy was to assure the nation under discipline that God had not finished with it.[4] If the nation repented, as Daniel prayed it would (9:1–19), then there was a glorious future for it. This message was therefore designed to cause immediate exercise in the captive people of Israel to return to Jerusalem. This means that the book would likely be in circulation before or shortly after the death of Daniel – which is generally given by conservative scholarship as 530 BC. So the book dates itself as *c.* 530 BC.

It must be pointed out that God had placed Daniel in Babylon, the capital of the Babylonian Empire, for a purpose. He would be used of God to unfold the purposes of God, centred on the Person of the Messiah, in a programme involving the nations of the earth. God had also brought another man to this same city, who did not move in the social circles that surrounded Daniel, but who was simply one of the captives. This was Ezekiel, who was carried captive on Nebuchadnezzar's second invasion (597 BC); he was to play a vital role in the preservation of the Israelites over this same period. God had also a third man in touch with Him over the same period. This, of course, was Jeremiah, who was with the company of those left in the land after the deportation to Babylon. God would preserve individuals who trusted in Him, even in these darkest of

[4] See Section 2 E: Purpose

days, if there was an acknowledgement of sin. It is of spiritual interest to note how God had an effective witness in each centre where the people of Israel were scattered in these years of captivity. Note that these three witnesses were contemporaneous.

Prophet	Location	Date of Ministry
Jeremiah	Jerusalem and Egypt	Began 627 BC (Jer. 1:1–3) Ended death *c.* 580 BC Ministered 47-plus years
Ezekiel	Babylon (from 597 BC)	Began 592 BC (Ezek. 1:2) Last message 571 BC (Ezek. 29:17) Ministered 22-plus years
Daniel	Babylon (from 606 BC)	Jeremiah ministering in Jerusalem from 627 BC Did Daniel hear Jeremiah in years 623–606 BC? Ezekiel began ministry in Babylon in 592 BC Daniel died *c.* 530 BC

(b) The Reliability of the Date

It should not be forgotten that this Daniel has two unimpeachable witnesses, one indeed infallible, who vouch for his authenticity:

Witness 1 Ezekiel was a captive priest carried to Babylon in the second invasion of Israel by Nebuchadnezzar (597 BC) and called by God to a ministry directed to the captive people of Israel. Ezekiel, contemporary with Daniel and of about the same age, did not move in the exalted circles in which Daniel lived and worked as a high official in the empire. Yet in three passages in his book (Ezek. 14:14, 20; 28:3) Ezekiel speaks of Daniel as one who was well-known for his righteousness (Ezek. 14:14, 20) and wisdom (Ezek. 28:3). It would have been very strange if a contemporary prophet of the Lord in the land of exile had had no knowledge of one who was so prominent in Babylon and used of God as a mighty witness. The reverse does not apply: Daniel, in the palace, lived in a world far apart from the ordinary captives, most of whom were treated as mere slaves.

Witness 2 The second Witness makes the authenticity of author and book unassailable. The Lord Jesus Christ puts the stamp of Divine authority upon both when He says, 'When ye therefore shall see the abomination of desolation, spoken of by Daniel the prophet, stand in the holy place' (Mt. 24:15). The importance of this authentication will be discussed when the attack of critical scholarship on this book is examined.[5] When any question as to the historicity, authenticity, or reliability of the man Daniel, or the book of Daniel, arises, we do well to recall that both man and book have the imprimatur of Deity upon them both – the Lord Jesus Christ spoke of him as 'Daniel the prophet'. The book of Daniel is to be seen as a sixth century BC writing of this Daniel the prophet in the city of Babylon.

B. Place of the Book in the Hebrew Canon

In any Bible translated into the English language the book of Daniel is invariably placed as the last of the Major Prophets – Isaiah, Jeremiah, Ezekiel and Daniel. Since this order is clearly chronological, the placing of Daniel can readily be understood. It is also the order found in the Septuagint, in the Vulgate, and, strangely enough, in Josephus. It should, however, be observed that Josephus reduces the twenty-four books of the canon to twenty-two by including Ruth with the Judges and including Lamentations with Jeremiah.

The Hebrew canon counts twenty-four books and divides them into three categories:

1. The Law (5 books), comprising: Genesis, Exodus, Leviticus, Numbers, and Deuteronomy.
2. The Prophets, comprising:
   (a) The Former prophets (4 books): Joshua, Judges, Samuel, Kings.
   (b) The Latter prophets (4 books): Isaiah, Jeremiah, Ezekiel, The Twelve.
3. The Writings (11 books), comprising: Psalms, Proverbs, Job, Song of Songs, Ruth, Lamentations, Ecclesiastes, Esther, **Daniel**, Ezra-Nehemiah, Chronicles.

The reason why Daniel was added to the third division, instead of the second, was not because of any doubt as to its authenticity. If there had been any doubt, it would never have been placed amongst the sacred books in any category. Placing it amongst these books was the acknowledgment by Israel that it was from God. All the books in the canon were so acknowledged and all three divisions carried equal authority – no extra authority was given, even to the

[5] Introduction, Section 2 C.

Law. Neither had this placing anything to do with its date in the sixth century BC. Malachi (one of 'The Twelve') was later than Daniel. The reason for placing Daniel amongst 'The Writings' was pointed out some years ago by the highly-respected scholar Robert Dick Wilson[6] (1856–1930), and it is still valid: 'It is more probable that the book was placed in this part of the Hebrew canon, because Daniel is not called a *nabhi* (prophet) but rather a *hozeh* (seer) and a *hakim* (wise man). None but the works of the *nebhim* (prophets) were put in the second part of the Hebrew canon.' As already emphasised, this has nothing do with inferiority; all three divisions were held in equal respect. It is simply a matter of nomenclature – and Daniel never calls himself a prophet!

Daniel never writes of himself as prophet, and, in fact, in many respects he stands apart from the prophets. Daniel gives no record of any call to prophetic ministry as did Ezekiel (Ezek. 2:1–8), Jeremiah (Jer. 1:4) and Isaiah (Isa. 6:1–8). Daniel was never instructed to preach to the people or plead with them publicly, as the other prophets were. He does not even make public statements to the nation. There is also a very clear difference in the way the prophecies came to him – mainly through the interpretations of dreams (his own or others') or of visions granted to him. A new genre of prophetic ministry is brought to light in Daniel, which will later be described as 'apocalyptic'. This book answers to OT prophecy the way the book of Revelation relates to NT prophecy.

Daniel is to be seen as a captive Jew who becomes a civil administrator in Babylon. Personally tested by his God, he was fitted to deliver his God-given messages in the presence of the mightiest of earthly monarchs during the Babylonian and Medo-Persian Empires. As already emphasised, the Lord Himself gives Daniel prophetic status when He speaks of him in the Olivet Discourse as 'Daniel the prophet' (Mt. 24:15; Mk 13:14) – thus placing the stamp of Divine authority upon the ministry of Daniel for all time. This Divine imprimatur by the Lord Himself takes on added significance when it is realised that this is the very book that in recent years has come under relentless sceptical attack by liberal critics, who find its message unpalatable.[7]

[6] Wilson, *Book of Daniel*, Vol. 2, p. 783.
[7] See Introduction, Section 2 E: Purpose.

C. Attack of the Critics

Neither the Jewish Sanhedrin in OT times nor the earliest of Christian writings in NT times raise the slightest doubt about the historicity of Daniel, or raise a question about the authenticity of this book as a document dating from the sixth century BC. At the very least, no record has ever been found that any question was ever raised about the place of the book in the canon of Scripture. It seems to have gained immediate acceptance in Israel and was placed amongst the sacred books. Even this apocalyptic type of prophetic communication (through dreams and visions) does not seem to have raised any serious questions.

It was only after eight hundred years that any question was raised about Daniel and his book. In fact it was a pagan philosopher called Porphyry (c. AD 234–305) who tried to discredit Daniel. This was just a side issue in his venomous attack on Christianity. He wrote fifteen books under the title *Against the Christians*, since he scoffed at the idea of believing that a sixth century BC prophet could predict so accurately what actually occurred in the second century BC. As a result, he had to question the existence of a real historical Daniel, and suggested that the author was a second century Maccabean writer who took the name of Daniel and wrote history, as if it were prophecy, for the encouragement of the Maccabean warriors. He had no evidence whatever to support his theory. It was based on his refusal to accept the reality of miracles and the accuracy of Divine prophecy. Able scholars of his day, and very particularly Jerome (AD 347–420), answered him fully.[8] Writing in the introduction to his *Commentary on Daniel*, Jerome remarks, 'And because Porphyry saw that all these things had been fulfilled and could not deny that they had taken place, he overcame this evidence of historical accuracy by taking refuge in this evasion, contending that whatever is foretold of Antichrist at the end of the world was actually fulfilled in the reign of Antiochus Epiphanes, because of certain similarities to things which took place at this time. But his very attack testifies to Daniel's accuracy. For so striking was the reliability of what the prophet foretold, that he could not appear to unbelievers as a predictor of the future, but rather a narrator of things already past.' Jerome thus testifies to the fact that the attack upon Daniel was not motivated by any historical inaccuracies, but

[8] Walvoord, *Daniel the Key to Prophetic Revelation*. See page 16 for Jerome's answers to Porphyry.

by the prejudice of an unbelieving mind that refused to accept the accuracy and inerrancy of God-given prophecy. To explain the evidence, Porphyry sought to discredit the writing by introducing the author as a pseudo-Daniel – a Maccabean author, writing in the second century BC, and claiming the name of Daniel to give him some credibility. So the critical evaluation of Daniel is very straightforward and can be summarised very briefly – it is a fraud!

It is a remarkable fact that nothing more was heard of this pagan attack on Daniel until the rise of 'Higher Criticism' in the eighteenth century. This term 'Higher Criticism' was first used by J.G. Eichhorn in 1787 to distinguish it from 'Lower Criticism'. 'Lower Criticism' dealt with the text of ancient documents – to determine, by comparison of copies, the true text – to present exactly what was written. 'Higher Criticism' included discussion on such topics as literary form, date, authorship, and purpose of the document. These 'higher critics', notably in German universities, had an overall approach to Scripture that questioned the traditional authorship of many books. They claimed that many of the books of Scripture had multiple authors and went through many redactions before assuming the form that we have today. Their basic approach was to deny biblical inerrancy and infallibility and thus to deny the plenary verbal inspiration of Scripture. Their attack on Daniel was but a part of their attack on the whole of Scripture.

Based on the denial of the inspiration of Holy Scripture (2 Tim. 3:16; 2 Pet. 1:20–21) it follows that such critics would deny the reality of miracles and the possibility of detailed prophecy. Both miracles and accurate prophecy are features of this book of Daniel, and so they had to discredit it. The Lord, of course, knew very well that, especially towards the end of the age, this book would come under sustained attack. He knew that the very existence of such a Hebrew Daniel would be questioned and that this book would be ascribed to a pseudo-Daniel, otherwise unknown, living in the times of the Maccabees in the latter half of the second century BC. This pseudo-Daniel, in the views of such sceptics, wrote history until the time of the death of Antiochus Epiphanes (164 BC). Then, using his imagination, he made prophetic statements that history has shown to be very far wide of the mark. Thus the critics would parade the evidence against the historic Daniel. They pointed to the anachronisms, the use of Persian and Greek loan words that, they insisted, were of later borrowing, as well as historical inaccuracies that they claimed would not have been made by any writer of the sixth century BC. The answer to these charges, and the proof that they have no basis in fact, will show that they have arisen from the unwillingness of the natural heart to accept the fact that the God of the Bible can work miracles and predict the future accurately. It will be shown that in recent years archaeological and historical research has completely shattered every sceptical objection and vindicated Daniel in a most remarkable way. Any remaining problems fade into insignificance as it is remembered that the Lord Himself said: 'Daniel the prophet'.

The critics attacked the book in four particular areas:

(a) The Place of the Book in the Canon of Scripture. The question as to why this book is not placed in the canon amongst the Prophets but amongst the Writings. This has already been answered in the Introduction, under Section 2 B.

(b) 'Philological Peculiarities', a term coined by Sir Robert Anderson[9] to describe the attack of one sceptical critic who had written: 'the Hebrew is pronounced by the majority of experts to be of a later character than the time assumed for it.'[10] The Aramaic is supposed to be marked by idioms taken from later than the sixth century BC. Further, not only are Persian words used in the book, but it also contains Greek words, which, the critics assert, could not have been in use in Babylon during the Exile'. One of the major points of attack has been the use of three words in the list of six musical instruments in the orchestra of Nebuchadnezzar (3:5) that are claimed by critics to be of Greek derivation. The words are 'cornet' (in Aramaic 'zither'), 'psaltery' (in Aramaic 'harp') and 'dulcimer' (in Aramaic 'pipes'). On this the *NET* Bible has an interesting textual comment: 'Though much has been made of this in terms of suggesting a date in the Hellenistic period for the writing of the book, it is not surprising that a few Greek cultural terms, all of them the names of musical instruments, should appear in this book. As a number of scholars have pointed out, the biggest surprise (if in fact the book is to be dated in the Hellenistic period) may be that there are so *few* Greek loan words in Daniel'. This sums the matter up very concisely.

(c) Historical Errors. Typical of the charges made in earlier days, when archaeological research was in its infancy, were problems like: (a) there was no record of any deportation from Jerusalem in the

[9] Anderson, *Daniel in the Critic's Den*, p. 15.
[10] Wilson, *Studies in the Book of Daniel*. Vol. 1, p. 324.

third year of King Jehoiakim (1:1); (b) there was no King Belshazzar to be found in Babylonian records – Nabonidus was the last ruler as far as the record went; (c) there was no such person as Darius the Mede.[11] All these questions will be dealt with as they arise in the commentary, and it will be clearly shown that modern research has either solved the problem fully or, in a few cases, suggested possible solutions perfectly in keeping with Divine inspiration of the book without conflict with fragmentary human records.

(d) Prophetic Accuracy. In later years liberal criticism has subjected these prophecies of Daniel to another point of attack. They have refused to accept the careful dating of the coming of the Messiah presented in the 'seventy weeks prophecy' (9:24–27), which is arrived at by simply taking Scripture as it stands, in the normal historical-grammatical-literal way that is applied in the understanding of all Scripture. Critics in recent years, bringing their own spiritualising schemes of prophecy to Daniel have sought to make Scripture fit their anti-millennialism. This leads to a denial of the literal millennial Kingdom. To rule this out of Daniel, the four empires, represented by the metals in the image of Nebuchadnezzar's dream, must be made to fit the four empires of the past – Babylon, Media, Persia and then Greece. This takes prophecy out of the picture, and Antiochus Epiphanes is looked upon as the covenant confirmer of verse 27, and the history ends with him. In interpreting the passage in this way, the pseudo-Daniel of the second century BC is seen as writing history. This means that the whole point of the prophecy is missed and the seven-year covenant has been fulfilled in the rise and fall of Antiochus Epiphanes in the second century BC.[12] When this is carried to its logical conclusion it robs us of the prophetic identification of the Messiah and it raises a most serious question as to the validity of the endorsement of the Lord for 'Daniel the Prophet'. These questions do not even arise when the normal method of scriptural interpretation (historical-grammatical-literal) is used in the interpretation of the prophecies of Daniel.

These problems will be answered in the commentary as they arise in the text. Historical research in the cuneiform archives and evidence from modern archaeological digs have answered, it is fair to say, every one of the queries raised by the sceptical mind. It can,

[11] See ibid (note 6), 12.

[12] Montgomery, *The International Critical Commentary, Daniel*, p. 385ff.

with perfect honesty, be claimed that there is very convincing evidence for the total reliability and accuracy of every statement in Daniel. Full details are presented in the writings of John F. Walvoord[13] and Sir Robert Anderson.[14] Summarising the result of much research, it can be said that in every case where investigations have been carried out, in archaeological digs and in philological examinations of inscriptions on buildings and on tombs, not one critical objection has been sustained. Daniel was right! Giving the answers in detail to these attacks, unfortunately, falls outside the scope of this commentary, but the student is directed to the careful and clear examination of these critical questions in the writings of the authors mentioned and, of course, in the writings of others.[15]

In any case, the battle lines are drawn. Either this book must be what it claims to be: the writing of a sixth century administrator in the kingdom of Babylon, with its record of miracles and God-breathed prophecy, or the book is a fraud (however 'pious' the motive). Those who accept the critic's case see the book as written by one of the Hasidim party in the time of the Maccabees (164–37 BC) to encourage his brethren in the faithfulness of their God Who would bring them through this time of suffering in triumph and would still fulfil His purpose in His persecuted people. Wishing to conceal his identity and claim authority he did not have, the writer calls himself Daniel as a captive in Babylon. The charge of the critics, then, is that the book is a 'forgery'. They argue that the practice of attributing one's own writing to a great figure of earlier history was an accepted and respectable fashion at this time. Charles Boutflower sums up the critics' view when he writes: 'The critics look upon the book of Daniel as a religious novel, resting upon a shadowy background of history, written about 164 BC in the troubled days of the Maccabees, and written with this noble intention, *viz.* to encourage the faithful in a time of persecution and to support them under very severe trials.'[16] Boutflower further explains: 'But, all the same it is in their eyes a mere work of imagination, cleverly put together, but containing not a few historical inaccuracies owing to its having been written three or four hundred years after the times which it describes. To them, therefore, its great

[13] Walvoord, *Daniel: The Key to Prophetic Revelation*, p. 16–27.

[14] Anderson, *Daniel in the Critics Den*, p. 15.

[15] Wilson, *Studies in the Book of Daniel; A Discussion of the Historical Questions*, Vol. 1 & 2 should be consulted.

[16] Boutflower, *In and Around the Book of Daniel*, p. 2.

facts are pure fancies; its mighty miracles, mere feats of imagination; its so-called prophecies, past history clothed with the garb of prophecy.'[17] However, modern research has shown that Daniel can be relied upon in every detail so far investigated.

The Apocalyptic Genre

In connection with the 'apocalyptic' genre of Divine communication, most critics allow that Daniel, in the OT, and Revelation, in the NT, stand alone. Even the casual reader can detect the difference between the scriptural and non-scriptural works. The pseudo-graphic books linked with Daniel show how this inspired writing is totally distinguished from such books as (a) The Song of the Three Holy Children; (b) The History of Susanna; (c) Bel and the Dragon; (d)The Prayer of Manasses.[18] Even casual reading will assure any open mind that these writings cannot be classed as Scripture. At two critical junctures in scriptural history God has used the apocalyptic genre to convey truth with a contextual setting that allows the interpretation to be gleaned from that setting without human imagination being involved. The book of Daniel and the book of the Revelation both fall into this apocalyptic genre; they convey truth through dream or vision. The point to be made is that the symbols used in this kind of communication must be interpreted from Scripture alone and not the imagination of the reader. The links between Daniel and Revelation are remarkable and attention will be drawn to parallels in these two books as they arise in the text.

Summary

Daniel the man is to be accepted as a historical person living in Babylon in the sixth century BC.

Daniel the book is to be accepted as an accurate and authentic writing inspired of God, accepted as authentic Scripture, and placed amongst The Writings – the third division of the Hebrew canon – in the sixth century BC.

D. The Structure of the Book

A somewhat unusual feature of this book is the fact that two languages are used in the writing. While unusual, it is not unique. The same feature occurs in the book of Ezra – where two small

[17] Boutflower, *In and Around the Book of Daniel*, p. 2, n. 9.

[18] The Apocrypha includes 14 books, of which the final six are these four books followed by I and II Maccabees. For the history of the Maccabees see Appendix 6.

sections (4:8–6:18 and 7:12–26) are in Aramaic. In the prophecy of Jeremiah there is one verse (Jer. 10:11) in Aramaic. Here a whole section of the book is in Aramaic – from the fourth verse of chapter 2 to the closing verse of chapter 7 (2:4–7:28). In the court scene in chapter 2, Daniel draws attention to the fact that the Chaldeans reply to King Nebuchadnezzar in their own tongue: 'in Syriack' (*AV*), translated as 'the Syrian language' (*RV*), or as 'Aramaic' (*RV* marg). This is not surprising, as this is the native language of both Nebuchadnezzar and the Chaldeans. What is surprising is that Daniel continues to use Aramaic until the end of chapter 7. At the close of this section Daniel switches, without any break or explanation, into the Hebrew language.

It should be clearly understood that Aramaic was the *lingua franca* of the period and used throughout the whole area by the people. It was the language in which official, commercial and political business was transacted over the whole region. Thus Aramaic was the language, broadly speaking, of the Gentile world while Hebrew was the national language of Israel. The question arises naturally in the circumstances: why did Daniel use two different languages for his record?

1. Linguistic Structure

A study of the sections in which the languages are used will provide the answer to the above question:

Section	Language	Subject	Concerns
1:1–2:4	Hebrew	Private life of Daniel	Israel
Conditions faced by Jews under the first Gentile king.			
2:4–7:28	Aramaic	Public life of Daniel	Gentile nations
Concerns Gentile nations 2:4–7:28			
8:1–12:13	Hebrew	Visions of Daniel	Israel, the nations
Conditions faced by Jews under later Gentile Kings, Antiochus Epiphanes, *The Portrait*, (8:9–14), Antichrist, *The Person*, (11:36–45)			

This language division offers a very valid and inbuilt way of handling the structure of this book. This, in fact, marks out the people who are the main concern of each part of the prophecy. There are really only two parties to be addressed – the Jews and the Gentiles – and these are identified by the languages they used in that day.

The nature of the Aramaic used in these passages has been used by liberal commentators to attack the authenticity of Daniel. It has been argued by James A. Montgomery[19] that the Aramaic in this book is Western Aramaic, used in Israel, but it was Eastern Aramaic that was current in Babylon – thus supporting the thesis of a pseudo-Daniel writing in Israel in the second century BC. More recent research by R.D. Wilson on the ancient documents has shown that the difference between the Eastern and Western Aramaic did not exist in pre-Christian times. In this respect Daniel has been completely vindicated and critical voices have been silenced on this issue.[20]

A similar attack has been made on the Hebrew used in the book[21] – it was claimed that the Hebrew used by Daniel demanded a second century date, particularly as it was too rough to belong to a pre-exilic date. Other scholars have denied this claim and shown that the Hebrew is similar to that used in Ezekiel, Ezra, and Chronicles. More recent scholarship has found the same Hebrew in the Dead Sea Scrolls. Again Daniel has been vindicated, in that there is not the slightest evidence in the Hebrew used to support a second-century date and very much that demands a sixth-century date, as suggested by the vast majority of conservative scholars.

While the principles upon which the book is divided into the various sections are often discussed, there never has been any serious challenge to its unity. Only the liberal commentators who deny the historical Daniel and a sixth-century BC date make any attempt to attribute portions of the book to different writers. Although the two parts of Daniel show differences in character, there is such an obvious continuity that few have seriously questioned the unity of the book. The Daniel of chapter 1 is the same Daniel identified three times (12:4,5,9) in the final paragraph of the book.

[19] Montgomery, *The International Critical Commentary, Daniel*, p. 15ff.

[20] Wilson, *Studies in the Book of Daniel*, Vol. 1 &2.

[21] Driver, *The Cambridge Bible for Schools and Colleges, in loc.*

2. Literary Structure

There are two distinct parts to the book:

Part 1	**Daniel's Ministry in Babylon**	**Ch. 1–6**
Section A	**Daniel and his Friends**	**Tests of Faith**
Ch.1	The King's Demand and the Word of God	
Ch.2	The King's Dream and the Wisdom of God	
Ch.3	The King's Decree and the Worship of God	
Section B	**Daniel and his Foes**	**Triumphs of Faith**
Ch.4	A King's Pride Humbled	Nebuchadnezzar
Ch.5	A King's Profanity Judged	Belshazzar
Ch.6	A King's Presumption Exposed	Darius

Lesson of Part 1

God can and will preserve a remnant faithful to Himself through the darkest days of Gentile dominion.

As well as the perennial lessons for all times of persecution for saints, these passages will have a special application for saints in the Tribulation.

Part 2	**Daniel's Visions in Babylon**	**Ch. 7–12**
	Ch.7 – Vision 1	
The Character of the Future		The Powers (World Rule)
	Ch. 8 – Vision 2	
The Conflicts in the Future		The Personalities (World Rulers)
	Ch. 9 – Vision 3	
The Control of the Future		The Programme (Chronology and Christ)
	Ch. 10–12 – Vision 4	
The Consummation in the Future		The Person (Christ)

Lesson of Part 2

God will allow the pride, profanity and presumption of man to go to great lengths: his will be seen in the manifestation of earth's man – The Antichrist. God replaces him with the manifestation of God's Man – The Christ.

This literary structure will be followed in the exposition.

E. The Purpose of the Book

It was the dark hour of Israel's captivity. They had been dragged away from a burning city; their memory carried an unforgettable picture – the Temple of God a smouldering ruin. Carried, in the train of a conquering army, six hundred miles to the centre of world idolatry – Babylon; these souls must have asked themselves searching questions. Questions about the power of God – it certainly looked as if the power of the idols had triumphed! Was God impotent? Questions about the purpose of God – it certainly looked as if, with the nation of Israel, that purpose had failed miserably; had God finished with His people? Was their God intransigent and unforgiving? Was God indifferent?

These captives knew very well the cause of the captivity. The ministry of Isaiah had been pointed, plain, and practical (Isa. 1:18) – their own sin had brought this upon them. They knew the sentence on that sin – the ministry of Jeremiah had been equally plain as he announced the seventy years of captivity (Jer. 25:8–11). Now it had all come to pass! Down in Babylon there is no longer any distinction between the captives from the ten tribes, carried captive down to Assyria in 722 BC, and the captives from Judah, brought down in 606 BC. Both groups are under the heel of mighty Babylon. The Assyrian Empire had been taken over by Babylon after Nebuchadnezzar had destroyed Nineveh, the Assyrian capital, in 615 BC. Now, listening to the gibes of the pagans amongst whom they now were living, two types of question in particular must have weighed on every faithful heart in the nation. One reason at least behind Daniel's writing must be a Divine answer to these questions arising in the hearts of His own people. Does this book answer the questions?

Questions arising in the hearts of faithful concerned men and women in Israel would be:

1. National Questions

Question 1 – The Power of God

Was the God of Israel impotent?

The idolaters of Babylon would delight to point out the lesson of the past – on the battlefield, your God failed! Our gods triumphed! Are you sure that your God is truly God and the only God – the Most High – as you claim? God's answer through Daniel is in Part 1 of his book: The God of Israel is the only God. Nebuchadnezzar learns that He is 'God of gods' (2:47), Belshazzar learns that he is 'Lord of heaven' (5:23) and Darius learns that He is 'the living God' (6:26). The God of Daniel is the only God – He is omniscient (Ch. 2), omnipresent (Ch. 3) and omnipotent (Ch. 6). God exercises His sovereignty over persons and nations. This brings in a parallel note that will be further unfolded in Part 2 of the book, in the Covenant and in the Kingdom that were specially linked with Israel and with earth. These promises would not be abandoned, but fulfilled to both Israel and the nations. God is not only almighty; He is eternal. When all earthly kings and kingdoms are replaced by God's King and Kingdom, pictured in the 'stone cut out without hands' (2:44–45), this Kingdom will stand 'for ever and for ever' (7:18).

Question 2 – The Purpose of God?

Was the God of Israel indifferent?

Again the idolaters of Babylon, drawing upon their knowledge of their idols, would gleefully point out – you have failed your God, so your God is finished with you! Our gods have triumphed – had you not better pay tribute to these new victorious gods? Otherwise you have no future as a nation! Reasoning of this kind would be the atmosphere in which they existed and the flesh would ask – is this not reasonable and logical?

God's answer through Daniel is recorded in Part 2 of his book. The God of Israel working out His purpose, had made Israel a covenant people. But this God is a holy God and their sin demanded discipline, hence the captivity with a view to their repentance and recovery (9:3–19). That was one aspect of the character of the God Who had called their nation. But God was not only a holy God, Who must judge sin, He was a faithful God Who will keep His word. This God would keep His promises given to Abraham (concerning the land), to David (concerning the throne) and through Jeremiah (concerning the covenant). Daniel's message is that the promises will be fulfilled. Their God is not only holy and faithful but He is also gracious – a God Who will forgive. As Daniel learns and conveys his message to his nation he makes clear that there is to be opened a way, through repentance, to recovery and restoration. However, this way back to God rests entirely upon God acting through the Person identified in this book as Messiah (9:25). Because God was holy, it was only through this Messiah, His coming and then His 'cutting off' (9:26), that blessing could be enjoyed. The acceptance of this Messiah would be the path to blessings temporal and eternal. In the national acceptance of Him all the promises would be made good to Israel. A Divine provision for their sin ('Messiah be cut off' (9:26)) would enable a Divine programme to be brought to its consummation by a God – holy, faithful, and gracious. The purpose of God would be fulfilled in the blessing of the nation of Israel, through which, as God had planned, blessing would flow to all mankind. His purpose could not fail! Unlike the temporal kingdoms of earth, Daniel learned of the Sovereign One – the Most High 'Whose kingdom is an everlasting kingdom' (7:27). Daniel's mission was to convey this message of hope to a people suffering a faith-shattering captivity under Gentile rule. Israel had failed their God but their God would neither forget them nor fail them.

Israel would learn, through this book, that God had not finished with them as a nation. On repentance of their sin and the acceptance of this Messiah they had before them a glorious future – an everlasting Kingdom. What a glorious hope to gladden saints in the still darker days of the Tribulation yet to come.

But there would be other questions, too, in the minds of individually-exercised saints.

2. Personal Questions

Question 1

Does God care for me under captivity in Babylon?

Beyond the national questions discussed above, there would be, in the heart of every exercised Israelite, who had responded to his God through the Scriptures, utter dismay at what had happened, and many questions would press upon the heart. First, they would need to know how they, as lonely believers in the true God surrounded by the absolute paganism of an alien society, should behave. They, and of course the children born there, would learn in the behaviour of Daniel and his three friends in Babylon how they should react when faced with choices that emphasised their difference from idolaters. Such a choice as Daniel and the young men faced as soon as they arrived in Babylon – obedience to the Word of God or defilement (Ch. 1); when faced with a second choice concerning worship – worship the image or die (Ch. 3); when faced with a third choice in witness for God – disavow your God or face the lions (Ch. 6). These challenges were inherent to living in Babylon.

This book of Daniel would certainly bring a challenge as to how they were living in an idolatrous society. These would be real tests in Babylon, and believers would need reassurance as to whether God cares for His own when nationally they are under Divine discipline. The answer from Daniel is a resounding affirmative – the God of Daniel and the God of those who trust Him is the God Who cares! God cares – when four Hebrew boys are under the death sentence (2:17–18); when three Hebrew boys are thrown into the furnace (3:21); when Daniel is abandoned to the lions (6:16). Every believer can be completely reassured that God can and will take care of His own. This truth must also have brought fresh strength to persecuted believers in Maccabean times, as it will do again in Tribulation days.

Question 2

Can I still trust God in Babylon?

This book will testify to a God Who could and Who would preserve those who trusted Him through the darkest of trials. The lesson is there! A lesson learned in the fiery furnace and amongst the lions would tell that God can still be trusted in the darkest of circumstances in life. This book of Daniel would be a great comfort to believers in the times of the Maccabees (174–150 BC). It is a worthwhile exercise to study the NT confirmation of the faith of so many believers in those times in the Epistle to the Hebrews (Heb. 11:33–40). It would be impossible to assess what measureless comfort has been brought to troubled saints facing similar circumstances down the ages from this book of Daniel.

While bringing comfort, this book has always offered a challenge to believers. The opening verses of the book give witness to the sovereignty of God in the statement, 'And the Lord gave Jehoiakim king of Judah into his hand' (1:1–2). Thrones and empires do not depend on military prowess, political skills or the might of an idol – God is in absolute control amongst the nations. His purposes will be fulfilled on the world stage, and, the earlier this lesson is learned by each world power, the better for that power. The challenge is not only national – and Nebuchadnezzar and Cyrus and Darius represent rulers who, at least in part, learned this lesson. It also carries a personal challenge, and those who, like Daniel and his friends, learn the lesson, can be used of God and richly blessed, even under the most compromising of conditions. The character of Daniel is shaped under these conditions, so that he can be addressed by heaven as 'greatly beloved'. One could readily challenge the heart as to the term heaven would use in addressing each believer today.

Not alone does the book bring comfort and challenge to believers; it reveals the character of our God to each believing heart. It shows Him to be faithful and covenant-keeping, Who, while absolutely holy, will, through grace, righteously restore His banished ones. It shows that God is omnipresent and able to be with His own in every trial; omnipotent, in that no power, either human or satanic, can hinder the working out of His purposes. Our God is omniscient. God alone can make known the future – all the resources of satanic power cannot look beyond the present. In this book, God does just that, and gives the prophetic programme for the expected Redeemer – the Messiah. Through Daniel comes the seventy weeks prophecy (9:24–27), which unfolds a timetable for earth – touching upon what lies ahead for this world. Through the coming of the Messiah, by way of the cross ('shall Messiah be cut off') to His crowning in the Kingdom will the purpose of a holy, faithful, and gracious God be worked out on earth. For this programme God has given us the key date through Daniel. From our vantage point, close to the end time, it can be seen how God has worked out His programme in the past, and this gives us absolute confidence that the same God will bring it to the consummation as planned. This book of Daniel has enriched and enlightened the saints down the ages as to what He is doing amongst the nations; as saints of today we would be so much poorer in our understanding of what God is doing now if we did not have this book. God has given us a chart to mark stages in the Divine plan. With the complete revelation of Daniel in our hand, and the further light of the NT revelation shining on Israel and the nations, we can agree with Nebuchadnezzar at his stage of apprehension, and acknowledge: 'Now I Nebuchadnezzar praise and extol and honour the King of heaven, all whose works are truth, and His ways judgment: and those that walk in pride He is able to abase' (4:37).

Chapter 1

The King's Demand and the Word of God

THIS CHAPTER PROVIDES the historical background to the entire book. It is a fascinating and moving story of how a young man from the land of Israel, Daniel by name, came to be in Babylon and the conditions that he faced there. A vital part of the story will be to see how these very conditions contributed to the development of his character so that this young man can be used of God to stand and speak for Him in the presence of the great monarchs of earth. In Daniel's case an unusual insight is permitted of how God develops the character of a servant through the circumstances of life so that He can use him. God does this with every key servant He uses – Moses the legislator, David the sovereign and Paul the apostle are outstanding examples. Yet in each of these cases God made the training years silent years – the case of Daniel is exceptional. God plans to use the man Daniel, not only as a channel to communicate prophetic truth, but as a pattern for believers of any age called to live for God in uncongenial circumstances, so for these two reasons he must be publicly tested. Entrusted with the unfolding of a programme concerning the people of Israel, and given a key date (9:25) – not given even to an Isaiah or a Jeremiah – that would govern prophetic chronology concerning the Christ, Daniel stands forth as an honoured servant of God. Such trust demands a man of a certain character. Hence the opening scenes of this book record the careful training and testing of Daniel. While Babylonian training may fit a man for a high position in a Babylonian Empire, it will not do for the Kingdom of God. God takes up that same man and develops in him a spiritual fitness to become the spokesman of heaven in Divine things. The experience set out in this chapter shows the first stage in that training. The basic test for Daniel, as for any true servant of God, is a simple one – will the servant obey God or man? Perhaps a more pointed question is – will the servant obey his God at any cost? This chapter provides the answer.

There are three sections to the chapter:

1. Daniel's Circumstances — vv. 1–7
2. Daniel's Conviction — vv. 8–16
3. Daniel's Character — vv. 17–21

1. DANIEL'S CIRCUMSTANCES – VERSES 1–7

Verses 1–2 Historical Setting

Verse 1 In the simple statements of the first verse the stage is set for the drama of the book. The story begins in the reign of King Jehoiakim in Judah, where the Chronicler (2 Chron. 36:5) gives the length of his reign as eleven years (609–597 BC). King Josiah, the last King of Judah to walk in the ways of David his father (2 Chron. 34:1–2), had died of his wounds received at the Battle of Megiddo in 609 BC (2 Chron. 35:20–24). Josiah had unwisely interfered in the politics of earth and had gone to war to stop Pharaoh Necho, the ruler of Egypt, from going to the aid of Assyria against the rising power of Babylon. On the death of Josiah, the people of Judah replaced him with his twenty-three year old son, Jehoahaz. However, Jehoahaz occupied the throne for only three months. Pharaoh, on his way back from his northern campaign, incensed by Josiah's refusal to allow his army safe passage on his way north, marched into Jerusalem, replaced Jehoahaz as king with his older brother Eliakim, and placed the city under heavy tribute. As a final insult, and as an indication that he claimed the rights of deity, Pharaoh changed the name of the king from Eliakim, meaning 'God will set up' to Jehoiakim meaning 'whom the Lord will set up'. Jehoahaz was taken to Egypt as hostage for his brother's good behaviour. Judah became a tribute state to Egypt. The reign of Jehoiakim is summarised and evaluated by the Chronicler in one sentence: 'He did that which was evil in the sight of the LORD his God' (2 Chron. 36:5).

During the years following Egypt's intervention in Judah, the rising power of the Neo-Babylonian Empire, led by the rebel Nabopolassar, a Chaldean self-proclaimed King of Babylon, was attacking the crumbling Assyrian Empire. By a clever move in diplomacy and masterly use of his well-trained veteran army he besieged Nineveh, the Assyrian capital city, captured it, and then destroyed it. Nabopolassar left Nineveh a smouldering ruin in the desert in 612 BC. This left him free to deal with Egyptian power, which, under Pharaoh Necho, deeply suspicious of the ambitions of this new power on the world scene, had been supporting Assyria. Early in the year 606 BC, King Nabopolassar, now ailing in health, sent his son Nebuchadnezzar,[1] who had already proven himself an outstanding leader on the battlefield, at the head of a powerful army to bring all parts of the old Assyrian Empire, including the nations paying tribute to Egypt, under the control of Babylon. It was particularly important for Babylon to control the states lying on the corridor along the Mediterranean coast – and Judaea was just such a nation. As a consequence, the Babylonian army, under the crown prince Nebuchadnezzar, swept into Judah and surrounded Jerusalem. There is no description of any prolonged siege, or any destruction of the city, or brutality to the defenders. Jerusalem under Jehoiakim simply surrendered.

Daniel records the date as 'the third year of the reign of King Jehoiakim king of Judah' – a date he would never forget. Since Pharaoh had made Jehoiakim king in 609 BC, the invasion year must be 606 BC – the year before the final defeat of Egypt by Nebuchadnezzar, at the Battle of Carchemish on the banks of the Euphrates. The date of this battle is well attested in history as 605 BC.[2] It was when Nebuchadnezzar was in Jerusalem that he received the news of his father's death. Such was his hurry to get to Babylon that, instead of taking the normal and safer route northwards to the Euphrates then down the river, he set out with a small bodyguard directly 'across the desert'. Berosus[3] the Babylonian historian presents a record of this hurried dash back to Babylon to make sure no usurper seized the throne.[4] Crowned in Babylon, he then led his armies to finally settle the issue of world hegemony with Egypt at the Battle of Carchemish on the Euphrates. The evidence supports the fact that the subjugation of Judaea dates from 606 BC.

The question is often raised as to why Jeremiah dates this invasion in 'the fourth year of Jehoiakim the son of Josiah king of

[1] The spelling in English Bibles is generally 'Nebuchadnezzar'. In the Hebrew Bible it is sometimes given as 'Nebuchadrezzar'. The spelling with the 'n' is the Aramaic form and means 'Nebo god of fire', or 'Prince of the god Nebo' (Newberry Reference Bible *in loc.*).

[2] For a full discussion of records that fix the date of this first invasion of Judah as 606 BC see Appendix 1. It is shown there that historical records, when fairly considered, give Daniel their full support in dating this first Babylonian invasion under Nebuchadnezzar in 606 BC and before the Battle of Carchemish (605 BC).

[3] Berosus (or Berossus) lived *c.* 260 BC. A priest in Babylon who used Temple of Bel archives to write three books of Babylonian history in Greek. Only parts of these writings have been preserved, in Josephus and Eusebius.

[4] Anderson, *Daniel in the Critic's Den*, p. 17.

Judah' (Jer. 25:1; 46:2). There is no discrepancy; in fact they corroborate each other when it is remembered that Daniel counts regnal years from the date of accession to the throne, which was the method used in Babylon. The Hebrew method, as used by Jeremiah in Jerusalem, was to count the accession year up to the beginning of the sacred year – the month *Nisan* – as year one, and then add the following years of the reign. Hebrew dates thus often included an extra year.[5]

The further question is sometimes raised as to why Daniel speaks of Nebuchadnezzar as 'King of Babylon', when he was only crowned on his return, after capturing Jerusalem. This is spoken of as the proleptic, or anticipative, use of a title.[6] This occurs often both in common practice and in Scripture as, for example, in the genealogy of the Lord Jesus – the text reads 'And Jesse begat David the king' (Mt. 1:6). Transported to Babylon, Daniel had never known Nebuchadnezzar by any other title.[7]

The year 606 BC can thus be accepted with all certainty as the year when the first attack on Jerusalem by Nebuchadnezzar was made, and as the year when Daniel was taken to Babylon, and as the year when the seventy-year captivity in Babylon began (Jer. 25:9–12).[8]

Verse 2 To Judah and Jerusalem, the invasion of the land by King Nebuchadnezzar and the capture of Jerusalem must have been an unbelievable shock. To the faithful Israelite, such a terrible blow would raise fundamental questions about their God. Was Israel not the chosen nation (Deut. 7:6–8)? Was not Judah the godly remnant of Israel (Isa. 1:9)? Was not Jerusalem the city where Jehovah had put His Name (Deut. 12:5)? Was this not the city of the throne of David (2 Sam. 5:6–7)? Did not the Temple of Solomon stand in this city? The questions in every exercised mind in Judah would surely be – why did their God permit this deportation of His people and the capture of His city? What weight could be given now to the promises made to Abraham – with reference to the land (Gen. 15:18–

[5] For a full discussion of the issue see Walvoord, *Daniel*, p. 32.

[6] A prolepsis is defined as 'the taking of something future as already done or existing' (*OED*).

[7] Sir Robert Anderson points out that, when reporting the unveiling of a statue to Queen Victoria in the palace grounds, contemporary reporters spoke of her as having lived in Kensington Palace. The world of that day knew that Queen Victoria never did live there but, as a girl, she had been brought up there. There was no mistake. Anderson, *Daniel in the Critics Den*, p. 20.

[8] For further details see Appendix 1.

21), and in the promises made to David – with respect to the throne (2 Sam. 7:16)?

Daniel answers those burning questions in this verse – and in one simple sentence – 'and the Lord gave Jehoiakim king of Judah into his hand'. Unbelieving hearts may look for political causes, or weigh up the balance of military forces, but these are only secondary matters. The issue is that God delivered His people into the hand of an invading army, at a time when every believing heart might have expected a miraculous deliverance, as had happened on occasions in the past (2 Kgs 19:35). The deliverance of this same city from the mighty Assyrian army a century before (701 BC) would have been in the mind of many (2 Kgs 19:35). But this time there was no deliverance. It is significant that the word 'Lord' in this verse is not the translation of *Jehovah* but of *Adonay*, a word meaning 'owner', 'ruler', or 'sovereign', and which stresses the absolute sovereignty of God. The translation of the verb as 'gave' seems to fit the context exactly. It was neither the might of his army, nor the undoubted military skill of Nebuchadnezzar, that brought Jerusalem under his power. It was a deliberate disciplinary act of their sovereign God.

There was no excuse for Judah not to know this truth. God had forewarned the nation of Israel, on its deliverance from Egypt, of the consequence of disobedience to His Word, (Deut. 28:36–37, 49–68). The prophets down the years had warned repeatedly against such departure. Isaiah had pointed out their evident disobedience to the commandments of the Lord (Isa. 24:1–6); Jeremiah had pointed to their disregard of the Sabbath and, particularly, the ignoring of the Sabbatical years (Jer. 34:12–22). Finally, the inroads of idolatry with the accompanying immorality, made plain by Jeremiah in the closing years of the monarchy (Jer. 7:24–8:3; 44:20–23), rendered direct Divine discipline inescapable. This invasion by Nebuchadnezzar in the third year of the reign of Jehoiakim was the first instalment of Divine discipline. Having, in disobedience to the Scriptures and defiance of His servants the prophets, become worshippers of idols, God must deal with His people. To do this, God allowed His people to be carried down to the very home of the idol – Babylon itself – the most idol-worshipping city in the world at that time. Israel would learn a very bitter lesson; so bitter indeed that, subsequent to the seventy-year captivity, pagan idol worship of this kind would never trouble them again as a nation. With his people Daniel will go through the seventy years of national discipline in Babylon.

As a sign of Divine displeasure with the nation God also gave into Nebuchadnezzar's hand 'part of the vessels of the house of God'. Another translation reads, 'with some of the vessels in the house of God' (*ESV*). Doubtless the ill-advised display of these treasures to the ambassadors of Babylon by Hezekiah, one hundred years before (Isa. 39:2–4), had left covetous memories in Babylon. Isaiah had predicted the deportation (Isa. 39:6) of all these vessels. Now Scripture is partially fulfilled – notice the stress on 'part' or 'some' – but not 'all'. This was a clear warning from God, yet still leaving the way open for repentance, under the ministry of Jeremiah. Due to the nation rejecting this warning and showing no sign of repentance, God allows the invader to return. The second Babylonian invasion, in 597 BC, brought about by the rebellion of Jehoiakim, and then the third invasion, in 586 BC, brought about by the rebellion of Zedekiah, brought the fulfilment of Isaiah's prophetic words, 'nothing shall be left' (Isa. 39:5–6). All the vessels of the sanctuary and all the valuable things from the city of Jerusalem had been carried to Babylon; city and sanctuary were totally desolated. Truly God was patient with His people during these last twenty-three years, from Josiah until the destruction of the city (609–586 BC), as the Chronicler records:

> And the LORD God of their fathers sent to them by his messengers, rising up betimes, and sending; because he had compassion on his people, and on his dwelling place: but they mocked the messengers of God, and despised his words, and misused his prophets, until the wrath of the LORD arose against his people, till there was no remedy' (2 Chron. 36:15–16).

In giving Jehoiakim into the hand of Nebuchadnezzar, God allowed him, not only to seize part of the sacred vessels to display as war trophies in the house of Marduk, his favoured idol in Babylon, but also to deport many of the leaders of the nation, including their family members, to Babylon. Isaiah had spoken plainly: 'And of thy sons that shall issue from thee, which thou shalt beget, shall they take away; and they shall be eunuchs in the palace of the king of Babylon' (Isa. 39:7). The Babylonian historian Berosus writes: 'He [Nebuchadnezzar] committed the captives he had taken from the Jews to the charge of others while he went in haste over the desert to Babylon'.[9] As already explained, Nebuchadnezzar, summoned by

[9] Josephus, *Complete Works*, p. 613.

news of his father's death, took a small escort and hastened to Babylon by the much shorter, but more hazardous, route, across the desert. This extract from Berosus, who is reckoned by antiquarians to be generally dependable in his records, shows that Nebuchadnezzar committed the young men seized in Jerusalem to the care of an army escort, with instructions to follow the usual route – northwards to the Euphrates and then downriver to Babylon.

Nebuchadnezzar now did something most striking and unusual – he left Jehoiakim on the throne of Judah! Certainly he was but a vassal prince, not to Egypt now, but to Babylon. Perhaps these captives from the important families in Judaea were meant to be hostages against the good behaviour of his subject king. Daniel was amongst this first group of captives taken to Babylon.

The invasion of Judah[10] in 597 BC was a direct response to the rebellion of Jehoiakim (2 Kgs 24:1), who looked once again to Egypt for support. At first Babylon sent only army units to suppress the rebellion but, eventually, in 598 BC Nebuchadnezzar himself set out with an army to deal with the rebels. Before he arrived, Jehoiakim had died and been replaced by his 18-year-old son – Jehoiachin. No Egyptian help arrived, and Nebuchadnezzar took the city once again, in March 597 BC. Jehoiachin was carried to Babylon along with the queen mother, much spoil, and all of the Temple vessels previously left behind (2 Kgs 24:8–16). This deportation is said to be 'in the eighth year' of King Nebuchadnezzar's reign, thus in 597 BC. Jehoiachin had only reigned three months. It was in this second deportation that Ezekiel was carried to Babylon (Ezek. 1:1–3) along with ten thousand of the prominent citizens, and all the craftsmen and smiths (2 Kgs 24:14–16). Nebuchadnezzar placed Mattaniah, uncle of Jehoiachin, on the throne and changed his name to Zedekiah.

Jeremiah urged Zedekiah to accept, as under Divine sovereignty, the yoke of Babylon (Jer. 27:1–22). Nevertheless, Zedekiah listened to false counsellors and false prophets (Jer. 28:2–4) and allowed himself to be persuaded that Egypt would come to his aid. With this idea of Egyptian support in his mind, Zedekiah revolted against the suzerainty of Babylon. The result was total disaster. Nebuchadnezzar took Jerusalem again (2 Kgs 25:1–12), in 586 BC. Most of the remaining citizens joined their compatriots in Babylon, and the city of Jerusalem was totally devastated. The great Temple of Solomon, which had stood for four hundred years, was razed to

[10] See Appendix 1.

the ground. Zedekiah, attempting to flee, was captured and compelled to watch the slaying of his sons, before his own eyes were put out and he was carried down to Babylon.

The vessels that Nebuchadnezzar brought back in 606 BC he carried into the 'land of Shinar'. This is a term, somewhat archaic, even in Daniel's day, for Babylon (see Isa. 11:11). Doubtless Daniel uses the name deliberately, to reflect that fact that this area had been the centre of rebellion against God from earliest times. An earlier despot, called Nimrod, who may well have been an ancestor of Nebuchadnezzar (Gen. 11:1–9), held sway there, and built an empire there, in defiance of God's command to scatter and populate the earth. It is also subsequently to be identified by the prophet Zechariah as the place where 'wickedness' had its base, from which it had spread over the world, and the place to which it would return (Zech. 5:11). In these days of Nebuchadnezzar, Babylon was recognised worldwide as the centre of idolatry and iniquity. This was the place to which God allowed His people to be taken as captives.

The vessels were carried from the 'House of God' in Jerusalem and placed by Nebuchadnezzar in the 'house of his god' in Babylon. This was the common religious response of a victorious army to signify that the victory was due to the superior power of their gods. 'His god' probably refers to the god (idol) Marduk, the chief god of Babylon, who was worshipped by the king. While the name 'Nebuchadnezzar' has the name of the god 'Nebu' in it, this may well have been his father's god, while Nebuchadnezzar worshipped Marduk. This seems to be confirmed by archaeology, where the majority of Nebuchadnezzar's inscriptions refer to Marduk. There is also the additional fact that he called his own son 'Evil-Merodach' (Jer. 52:31–34; 2 Kgs 25:27–30), which means 'man of Marduk'.[11] E.J. Young, the Hebrew scholar, points out that the expression 'the House of God' in Scripture should read 'the House of the true God', since Daniel prefixes the word 'God' with the definite article, as if to distinguish the true God of Judah from the false gods of Babylon.[12] These vessels were placed in the treasure house of Nebuchadnezzar's god, and would remain there for sixty-six years, until the night of King Belshazzar's feast (5:2), when they would be desecrated afresh in drunken revelry.

[11] Miller, *New American Commentary, Daniel*, p. 59.

[12] Young, *Daniel*, p. 38.

Verses 3–7 Personal Situation

Verse 3 It would appear from this Scripture that only a small specially-selected group of captives was carried to Babylon in this first act of deportation. As suggested earlier, they may have been hostages for the good behaviour of King Jehoiakim. Ashpenaz, a senior court official of King Nebuchadnezzar, who attended upon the king personally, was specifically ordered to select certain young men for deportation to Babylon. The verb 'should bring' is the same verb used in the previous verse ('brought') in connection with the vessels, and thus implies that these boys were brought from Jerusalem to Babylon at the same time as the vessels. Ashpenaz is described as 'the master of his eunuchs'. However, the word 'eunuch' may fasten too rigorously upon one meaning of the Hebrew word '*saris*'. The word was, of course, used of a eunuch in the literal sense (Isa. 56:3), but it was also extensively used in a more general sense, to designate a 'court official'. It is the word used of Potiphar, who was married (Gen. 37:36). Isaiah had warned Hezekiah, after his indiscretion with the ambassadors from Babylon, 'And of thy sons that shall issue from thee, which thou shalt beget, shall they take away; and they shall be eunuchs in the palace of the king of Babylon' (Isa. 39:7). The Jewish translation of the word in this passage is 'nobles'.[13] Even if Josephus[14] hints that these Hebrew boys were made eunuchs in Babylon, there is no scriptural evidence to support this suggestion. In fact, the statement 'no blemish' in the next verse must mean 'no physical defect', as it does when used in connection with an Aaronic priest (Lev. 21:17). This expression could hardly be used to describe a eunuch in the literal sense. Some authorities suggest that only those court officials who were in charge of the harem were eunuchs physically.

The first qualification that Nebuchadnezzar demanded in the chosen youths related to their ancestry. They were to belong to Israel. This is reference, not to the northern ten tribes, which had already been carried into captivity by Assyria, in 722 BC, but to the fact that they must be direct descendants of Jacob. They were also to be linked with royalty ('of the king's seed') and thus be of the nobility in Judah ('of the princes' AV). While there is no supporting scriptural evidence, Josephus[15] states without question that Daniel

[13] Walvoord, *Daniel: The Key to Prophetic Revelation*, p. 3.

[14] Josephus, *Complete Works*, p. 222.

[15] See evaluation of Josephus as a historian in Appendix 6.

belonged to the family of King Zedekiah. These youths of high social standing would serve (a) as hostages for the good behaviour of his puppet kings in Jerusalem – Jehoiakim, Jehoiachin, and Zedekiah; (b) as a reminder to Nebuchadnezzar and the empire of his military exploits and how many kingdoms he controlled; and (c) when trained, they would be equipped as candidates to fill suitable positions in administration of the kingdom, particularly in Jewish affairs.

Verse 4 The young men selected had to be of a certain age. Instead of the word 'children' (*AV*), the word closest in meaning in English would seem to be 'youths' (*RV*) – the word in Hebrew in general use to cover the teenage years. However, E.J. Young pointed out some years ago that it is the same word translated 'young men', who were contemporary with, and had become counsellors of, King Rehoboam (1 Kgs 12:8–9). It is most unlikely that these young men would be in the early teens; they were much more likely to have been, at the very least, in their late teens. These captives from Judah, who were to commence an intensive educational programme, would most likely be in their late teens. Without additional evidence, many commentators opt for fifteen as the age of Daniel and his friends. Taking into account the etymology suggested by Young, and keeping in mind the events that follow the training, it would seem that the age of eighteen would be a better fit for the criteria. Age and date calculations in this commentary will be based on the assumption that Daniel was eighteen when taken captive to Babylon. This would give Daniel a birth date of 623 BC. If further evidence on the matter comes to light, suitable adjustments can readily be made.

In addition to their ancestral links, these youths had to have a certain physical appearance. Two terms are used:

(a) 'in whom was no blemish' indicates that they were to be without any physical defect. This is the term used for the physical completeness of the priest in Israel – no organs missing or mutilated (Lev. 21:17–21). As argued above, these particular youths could not be eunuchs in the literal sense.

(b) 'well favoured' could be translated 'of good appearance' (*ESV*). There was to be nothing in their outward appearance that would be in any way repulsive – they were to be attractive young men.

The next qualification deals not with their physical health but their mental ability – no time was to be wasted on slow learners. Three terms are used:

(a) 'skilful in all wisdom' would point to their ability to absorb information ('ability' comes from the adjective 'skilful'); 'in all wisdom' covers every field of knowledge required. In modern terms, their intelligence quotient (IQ) must be high. As pointed out by Hebrew scholars,[16] the word 'wisdom' is not to be confined to religious matters, but includes instruction in all areas.

(b) 'cunning in knowledge' ('endowed with knowledge' *ESV*) conveys the idea of 'well-informed'. Thus, as far as their education had already progressed, they were to be chosen from the top class.

(c) 'understanding science' carries the idea of 'quick to understand', and this would point to the more recondite areas of knowledge – in fact, the science of their day. The Chaldeans of Babylon were amongst the leading thinkers – the mathematicians and astronomers of world fame.

The concluding qualification sums up the personality of the chosen youths. They had to have the 'ability in them to stand in the king's palace'. The word 'ability' (basically 'power') describes their comportment, their poise, their general carriage, that would be suitable for the highest offices attached to the royal court. 'To stand in the king's palace' is an idiomatic way of describing the service of the king in whatever job he allocates to the individual (1 Kgs 10:8; 12:8).

The first part of the instruction to Ashpenaz has to do with the standards governing the choice of the youths. This second part defines what was to be done with those chosen. 'That he should teach them the learning and the tongue of the Chaldeans' (*RV*) is clear, while another translation is yet more specific: 'to teach them the language and the literature of the Chaldeans' (*ESV*). Daniel and his friends would already know, at the very least, two languages. As well as Hebrew (their mother tongue), they would be familiar with Aramaic the *lingua franca* of the day and the international language of commerce and diplomacy. Now they were to be taught a version of Akkadian, known as Neo-Babylonian. This was written in cuneiform script made up of wedge-shaped characters written on clay tablets. Archaeologists have uncovered thousands of these tablets in the desert sands of Iraq. The discovery of these tablets allows us an insight into the wealth of literature with which Daniel

[16] Miller, *New American Commentary, Daniel*, p. 61.

and his friends were expected to become conversant. This was an advanced society, where records of trade, business transactions, and legal transfers were kept as routine; governmental orders, statements, and reports were all filed for reference. Added to this, there was the scientific material relating to the heavens, then the religious material from the temples, and the omens and prophecies of previous ages, as well as the writings of the philosophers. Babylon was the university centre of the day, and boasted the great library of Ashurbanipal the Assyrian king (669–626 BC), which had but recently been transported to Babylon.

For the first time in the book, mention is made of the Chaldeans. The term is used by Daniel, as it was used in his day, in two different ways – the specific meaning each time it is used depends on the context. Sometimes its use is simply ethnic, and it describes the people whose home is in Chaldea (Babylon); thus, in this context, it is simply another word for Babylonians; it is used in this way in this book (5:30; 9:1). However, in other places (as in 2:2), it identifies a special class amongst the learned men (*kasdim*) of Babylon. The special field of these men was religion – they were acquainted with all the religious lore, going back to Nimrod and his wife, Semiramis. They have been identified as the priests of the Babylonian mystery cult. In this first occurrence of the term, the context indicates that the wider meaning should be accepted. These youths were to be taught 'the language and literature of the Babylonians'.

Verse 5 The chosen young men were soon faced with their very first challenge. It may be assumed, quite rightly, that the educational programme for which they had been selected would pose a challenge to their faith. The Babylonian story of creation and the flood would stand out in contrast to the simple splendour of the creation account in Genesis. However, even before they began the programme, the young men were faced with an immediate challenge that would form their character. It was an oriental custom to feed officers of the royal court the choice food and wine from the table of the king – thus the king's men were assured of the very best of food. Now, as a great privilege, these trainee courtiers were granted this same privilege by the king himself. Food was 'appointed', in the sense of 'assigned' (the idea is the quantitative distribution), to these youths; it is called 'a daily provision of the king's meat and of the wine which he drank'. The *RV* margin for 'meat' gives 'dainties', which reflects the Persian loan word used here, and while it would certainly include many exotic dishes, perhaps a more mundane translation would be more accurate – 'rich food'. The term 'daily provision', which comes from a literal translation of the Hebrew – 'a portion of the day in its day',[17] hints that there were no 'warm ups' – there was fresh food every day. The purpose behind this provision was to ensure that these young men, kept in the best of health by the best of food, were physically able to undertake this intensive study course. The word 'nourishing' is the word used for the development of children in the home (Isa. 1:2) and includes both their physical and mental health. At the completion of this three-year programme these youths were expected to be fit to stand before the king. The idiom to 'stand before the king' means that, at that point, they would enter upon their service and responsibilities in the court of the king. It is implied that individual postings would be made as result of this royal examination (vv. 19–20).

Verses 6–7 The trainees selected for the programme, who would have the new diet coming directly from the king's table, must now have new names. Their birth names from the past, linking them with *El* and *Jehovah*, would not do in Babylon. New names, reflecting their new location and the victorious gods of Babylon, must be found for them. This is attended to immediately by 'the prince of the eunuchs', likely a subordinate officer to Ashpenaz, and he gives them their Babylonian names. In Scripture a new name reflects a new relationship; an Abram becomes Abraham, a Sarai becomes Sarah, and a Simon becomes Cephas, to show that each had an encounter with the Lord. This was accepted practice in Babylon and meted out to all captives. It was fully intended as a deliberate insult to the god of the captive peoples. Also, pragmatically, it was a very effective way of cutting people off from their past. In their acceptance of the Babylonian names by the four Hebrew boys, there is no suggestion that their faith in Jehovah was abandoned. This was not their choice; it was done to them. After all, Joseph was given an Egyptian name by Pharaoh (Gen. 41:45) and Hadassah was known by her foreign name – Esther (Es. 2:7). While making no verbal objection, these young men must have felt the implications of this very deeply.

[17] Walvoord, *Revelation*, p. 35.

The significance of the name changes can be seen when it is realised that the new names are linked with the gods of Babylon:

- Daniel means 'God is my judge' or 'my judge is God'. He now becomes Belteshazzar, meaning 'Bel protect his life' or 'Bel's prince'. Bel is identified with Nebo, son of Marduk.
- Hananiah means 'Jehovah is gracious'. He now becomes Shadrach, meaning 'command of Aku'. Aku was the moon god.
- Mishael means 'who is what God is?' He now becomes Meshach, meaning 'who is what Aku is?'
- Azariah means 'helped of the LORD' or 'Jehovah hath helped''. He now becomes Abed-nego, meaning 'servant of Nego'. Nego is a corruption of Nebo, the second great god in the Babylonian pantheon.

It will be noted that each Hebrew name contains a reference to either God *(El)* or LORD *(Jehovah)* and indicates that these boys came from godly homes in Israel: their early knowledge of the things of God would now bear fruit. This may explain why these young men, in contrast to others in the captivity, remained true to their God through the severest trials. It will also be noted that each Babylonian name contains a reference to one or other of the gods in the Babylonian pantheon. Daniel identifies himself in his later writings by his Hebrew name.

2. DANIEL'S CONVICTION – VERSES 8–16

Verse 8 Resolve in the Heart

There is no doubt that the food provided from the table of the king was both delicious and generous. Its very provision indicated the high favour and interest of the king. However, it posed a basic moral problem to Daniel and the other youths. The problem was really twofold:

(a) The food would not have been prepared in accordance with the directions of the Mosaic Law. First, the blood might not have been drained from the meat in keeping with the meat offering (see Lev. 17:13–14). Second, the meat may have been from animals banned under that same Law (see Leviticus 11 and Deuteronomy 14 for the distinction between 'permitted' and 'proscribed' animals). Historical records indicate that pork and horseflesh were common ingredients in the meals of Babylon. To knowingly eat such, for an

Israelite, would be sin. This would make the individual ceremonially unclean.

(b) While there is no absolute prohibition in the Mosaic Law for the drinking of wine, it is clear from the history of the period, reflected in Babylonian practice, that the meat and wine (as represented in token portions) would both have been dedicated to an idol. This rule was absolute when the meals were prepared for the king. For an Israelite, to eat such food would be, to a sensitive conscience, to acknowledge the idol to which the food was offered. This would render the individual morally unclean.

With this conviction, Daniel purposed in his heart that he would not 'defile' himself with the king's meat or the king's wine. The word 'defile' is used eleven times in the OT of ceremonial defilement and is often translated 'pollute' or 'polluted' (see, for example, Ezra 2:62; Neh. 7:64; Isa. 59:3). It made no difference to him that others of the Israelite captives may well have found no problem in eating from the king's table. They could well have reasoned that, being in Babylon, at least six hundred miles from Jerusalem, and under such alien conditions, they were relieved from the strict letter of the Law. They could also have reasoned that to object would enrage the king, jeopardise their comfortable billet, and endanger their lives. At a later date (562 BC), yet under the same conditions, King Jehoiachin did not seem to have the slightest conscience about eating the same food (2 Kgs 25:27–30). For Daniel the issue was plain – was the Word of God to be obeyed or not? He had settled it in his heart that he, for one, would obey the Word of the Lord. His example obviously influenced his three companions, who joined him in his protest (v. 12). Daniel had clearly understood that disobedience to the Word of God was the very reason why God had allowed His people, Israel, to be brought into these dire straits. The lesson had to be learned that, if there was to be a genuine spiritual recovery, there could be no compromise in this matter. There can be no doubt – this simple action of eating or not eating the king's meat was the supreme test of fidelity to the Word of the Lord for Daniel. His response demonstrated the character of a man whom God could trust to speak for Him before King Nebuchadnezzar. It also served the very practical purpose of distinguishing Daniel and his companions from others willing to compromise with the lifestyle of Babylon.

Daniel is not only revealed as a young man of principle; in the latter part of the verse he is seen as a young man marked by courtesy. He is shown as handling a very delicate and dangerous situation well. Instead of stirring up animosity and inviting punishment by brusquely refusing the dishes provided, he courteously asks the prince of the eunuchs if, on the ground of conscience, he might be excused from the eating of these dishes.

Verses 9–14 Requests on the Tongue

Verses 9–10 Daniel makes his first request to Ashpenaz the prince of the eunuchs, and is denied. The tense given in the translation 'Now God made Daniel to find favour and compassion in the sight of the prince of the eunuchs' (*RV*) translates correctly the Hebrew text, according to grammarians.[18] The present tense is understood to mean that it is the courteous approach of Daniel to the eunuch in charge of the dietary programme that allows God, at this moment, to touch the heart of this court official. The word 'favour' means 'kindness' or 'goodwill'; while the word 'tender love' is a plural word indicating 'sympathetic understanding'. So he got a sympathetic answer, even if it was a refusal to comply with the request.

The master of the eunuchs (v. 3) and the prince of the eunuchs in this verse (v. 8) would seem to be the same official, whose name is given as Ashpenaz (v. 3). He was certainly speaking rightly, and, indeed, understating the case, when he answered 'I fear my lord the king'. The absolute despotism of Nebuchadnezzar is seen in the sentencing of his wise men to death in the next chapter (2:13); he certainly would not have hesitated to deal in summary fashion with any failure, even in a senior court official. Ashpenaz knew that any failure would mean, not merely loss of his position, but likely the loss of his head. The king's orders had been explicit. Ashpenaz dared not change such a royal command. If he did, and this group of captives showed any ill effect, any enquiry would place the blame firmly on him. 'Worse liking' (the Hebrew root of the word means 'to be sad or upset') does not mean any serious illness, but simply that they did not show the same robust health as their companions – they would look pale or undernourished! Ashpenaz did not grant Daniel's request, yet, strangely enough, he did not reject it out of hand. In fact, in his attempt to explain his personal dilemma, he opened the way for Daniel to make his second proposal.

[18] *OTWS*, p. 159.

Verses 11–14 Daniel makes his second request to the steward to whom the young Hebrews had been entrusted and this time it is granted. Having settled the matter to his own satisfaction at least, Ashpenaz leaves the care of the captives in the hand of his 'steward' (*RV*). The word *Melzar*, transliterated in the *AV* as a proper name, carries the Hebrew article, which, a number of grammarians suggest, makes it more likely to describe a steward charged with the care of the four Hebrew captives (other translations give 'overseer' or 'guardian'). Knowing that the steward has been a witness to the foregoing conversation, Daniel takes advantage of the particular door that the chief of the eunuchs has opened for him. Daniel puts his second proposal directly to the steward and suggests to the steward a test – a test that had three elements to it that would eliminate any risk to his life – a risk that Ashpenaz could not take. The three elements can be seen thus: (a) A different diet. Daniel suggests that, in place of the king's meat, the four boys should be placed on a diet of 'pulse', or 'vegetables' (*ESV*). The Hebrew word means 'that which grows from seed.'[19] The word includes vegetables, but also fruits, grains, and bread that is made from grains; this food would in our day be labelled 'vegetarian' or 'healthy' diet, or 'going green'. It is clear that Daniel excluded meat from the diet, for the reasons given earlier (v. 8). Instead of the wine from the king's table, he suggested water; (b) A limited time. Daniel suggests a period of ten days to try the vegetable diet. This, of course, would be the key factor for the steward. First, it is certainly a reasonable time in which to give a diet a fair trial. Furthermore, the steward could likely see that any weakness in the captives resulting from the diet could rapidly be repaired without incurring the notice or the wrath of the king; (c) A personal responsibility. The issue of the test would be in the hand of the steward, who could check their physical condition daily. If they looked healthy, they could then be allowed to continue on their diet. Any deterioration in their condition would have to be dealt with immediately. The decision was his to make. The steward agreed to the suggestion. 'Listened to them in this matter and tested them for ten days' (*ESV*) is a good translation. It also shows that the three companions of Daniel were standing with him in the request and the subsequent trial.

[19] Miller, *New American Commentary, Daniel*, p. 69.

Verses 15–16 Result Seen in the Face

The result of the test is clearly written in the faces of the young men. At the end of the ten-day trial period, it is no surprise that Daniel and his friends appeared 'fairer' (literally 'better') and 'fatter in flesh' (better nourished), than those who had continued to eat the king's food. That the vegetarian diet contributed substantially to this healthy condition there cannot be any doubt. However, it is not to be questioned that God honoured the confidence of those four youths who implicitly obeyed His word – even in Babylon. His added blessing made them stand out in any company. Daniel and his friends had proved their point, and without further ado the steward, on his own responsibility, no longer demanded that they eat the king's rich food, but continued their vegetable diet for the whole period of training.

3. DANIEL'S CHARACTER – VERSES 17–21

Verse 17 This closing section of the chapter is a summary of the three-year training course and a record of their examination before the king. These four young men had shown that they were prepared to obey the Word of God at any cost – even at the cost of risking their lives. God could trust these young men. In their turn they had proved in their own experience that their God could be trusted. Mutual confidence between God and His servants is the result. In this paragraph, God shows His confidence in them. While achieving the required educational standards demanded in Babylon, these young men received from God gifts not achievable in pagan educational establishments. Now in their early twenties, God equipped them with special endowments, as trustworthy servants, for the tasks they would soon have to face in witness for Him. 'Knowledge and skill' implies not only the factual knowledge of the Chaldeans, but the insight (skill) to use that knowledge in the circumstances to spiritual profit. This ability to distinguish the true and the false would be a vital matter in keeping them from being carried away with the religious superstitions of Babylon. 'In all learning and wisdom' refers to the body of literature available to them and the wisdom to assess its worth. As Moses was learned in the wisdom of Egypt (Acts 7:22), so Daniel and his friends were learned in the wisdom of Babylon. God used both Moses and Daniel, each man against his own background, to show that true wisdom was not found in either Egypt or Babylon, but in the knowledge of God (1 Cor. 2:7).

While all four youths shared in the gift of keen intellectual insight that gave them a true appreciation of all the culture of Babylon, Daniel had a special gift bestowed upon him by God. 'But Daniel' is the translation suggested by an eminent Hebrew scholar,[20] and shows that Daniel had a very special gift that set him apart even from his three companions. This gift is described as 'understanding in all visions and dreams'. This clearly indicates that he had: (a) the ability to receive visions from God, which is the mark of a true prophet (1 Sam. 3:1); and (b) the ability to interpret dreams. Daniel will be called upon to use both aspects of his gift in his service for God. Here God stamps approval upon this method of communication with men, later called 'apocalyptic' – the use of dreams and visions. Modern criticism blames Daniel for this new method of communication, but God had used it previously, in connection with Job (Job 33:14–16), and now gives warning, in this gift to Daniel, that He will use it again. Daniel is given the ability to interpret the dreams. He is being fitted for the service for which God intends to use him.

Against the Babylonian background, this special God-given ability of Daniel was vitally important. The Chaldeans believed in dreams and visions and spent much ingenuity in interpreting them as they looked for future guidance. Daniel will be used of God to show that the God of Israel, and He alone, can truly be the 'revealer of secrets' (2:47).

Verse 18 The Examination of the Trainees

The appointed period of training completed, the trainees must face a rigorous and most daunting examination before no lesser judge than King Nebuchadnezzar himself. 'At the end of the days' refers to the close of the three-year period of training (v. 5). If the three years are to be understood in a strict sense then this would be the year 603 BC. The importance of the occasion is seen in that the prince of the eunuchs, Ashpenaz, in his official capacity, introduces the whole company under training to the king.

[20] Miller, *New American Commentary, Daniel*, p. 70.

Verse 19 The Appointment of the Officers

An informal oral examination by the king was no small matter. It is clear from Scripture that Nebuchadnezzar was a very astute and well-taught man, with a very sharp mind. The courtiers with whom he surrounded himself would have to measure up to very high intellectual standards. As the king talked (the simple verb 'talked' is more accurate than 'communed')[21] with these trainees, it soon became clear that four stood out from the rest of the company. It would almost seem that, as the questions became more and more searching, and the discussion moved to a more scholarly level, one by one the candidates left the audience chamber until only four were left standing in the king's presence. These four are named, using their Hebrew names, as Daniel, Hananiah, Mishael and Azariah.

It would seem that these remaining four candidates are immediately appointed to the king's service. The 'therefore' refers to the fact that the examination is over and they are still standing in his presence. But the expression 'stood they before the king' has more in view than surviving the dismissal of others. It is in fact the normal expression for admission to the king's service (see comments on v. 5). Their responsibilities are not defined as yet, but it is clear that their appointments to high office will follow; at this moment their names are placed on the imperial payroll. From the statements that follow, no probation period is required, and they are very soon involved in giving advice to the king – which implies senior administrative posts.

Verse 20 The Assessment of the Administrators

This verse: (a) summarises the administration of these new appointees to the king's service; and (b) covers a period of time, as various matters come before the king and his advisory council for action. In every situation, Nebuchadnezzar found that these Hebrews gave sound advice based on 'wisdom and understanding'.[22] High intelligence allied to keen discernment, with the background knowledge gained in their studies, made them indispensable to the king. Could there be any greater commendation than the approval of King Nebuchadnezzar summarised in the statement 'he found them ten times better than all the magicians and astrologers that were in all his realm'. This

[21] *OTWS*, 88.

[22] See comments under v. 7 for explanation of these terms.

statement is not hyperbolic, but conveys the fact that these men were outstandingly better than all the other counsellors around Nebuchadnezzar.

The particular group of counsellors named here is that comprising 'magicians-astrologers'. The word 'magician' in English involves trickery and deception and makes the word synonymous with 'conjuror'. However, the root word from which 'magician' comes in Hebrew is a word that means 'to cut, carve, engrave' and, in the Babylonian context, would refer to cuneiform writing on clay tablets. In light of this, most grammarians suggest that they were the 'sacred writers', who recorded and preserved the materials used in religious activities. This is interesting when linked here with the next word, 'astrologers', which stands alongside it without any conjunction. Clearly they formed one group, best shown in English with a hyphen, and which in some translations is given as 'enchanters-sorcerers'. The movements of heavenly bodies was meticulously chronicled and, based on these astronomical calculations, a whole body of knowledge, so-called, was recorded that allowed incantations and spells to be developed, purportedly based on communication with the spirit world. Thus men, and even empires, were controlled by men with such training. This is not so very different from our day, when many seek to order their lives by predictions based on astrological charts, or consult mediums as channels to the occult. In Babylon, these men represented the occult practices of that day. The verse is showing clearly that Daniel and his friends, who believed the Word of God, were better counsellors than all the agents of the occult.

Verse 21 This summary verse is added to show that Daniel outlived the Babylonian Empire. Liberal critics have seized upon it as a mistake and point out that Daniel received a vision in the third year of King Cyrus of Medo-Persia (10:1). However, this verse does not say that Daniel died in the first year of Cyrus, but simply that he 'continued even unto the first year of king Cyrus'. Since this was the year when the rule of Babylon ended (539 BC), this verse is simply stressing the fact that Daniel survived throughout the whole period of the Neo-Babylonian Empire, and, more important, from the scriptural point of view, he was a captive in Babylon for the whole period of the seventy-year captivity of Israel.

Neither the date of Daniel's birth nor the date of his death is given in Scripture. It is a fair assumption, from the facts recorded in his book, that he was born around 623 BC, in Judah, possibly in Jerusalem. This would make him around 18 at his deportation in 606 BC. The last recorded date in this book is the third year of King Cyrus, 535 BC (10:1), which would make him 88 years old at that time. The year of his death cannot be given exactly, but many reliable historians place it around 530 BC, which means he lived until he was around 93 years old.

Chapter 2:1–30

The King's Dream and the Wisdom of God

THE FIRST TEST FOR DANIEL and his friends in Babylon having been passed successfully with honours, it is but a short time after the completion of their training course that they are faced with an even more searching test.

The chapter may be divided as follows:

1. The King and his Dream — vv. 1–3
2. The Wise Men and their Dismay — vv. 4–13
3. Daniel and his Dependence upon God — vv. 14–30
4. The Dream and its Interpretation — vv. 31–49

1. The King and His Dream – Verses 1–3

Verse 1 The careful dating of this dream is to be observed. The dream that God gave to Nebuchadnezzar was given in the second year of his reign, and this dating would be in line with the Babylonian method of calculating regnal years. This begins the count from the New Year following the accession of the king. On the death of his father, Nabopolassar, Nebuchadnezzar ascended the throne in September 605 BC.[1] The first year of his reign would therefore be counted from the following New Year; in the Hebrew calendar the month was called '*Nisan*' (March-April in our calendar) and is dated 604 BC. So the second year of Nebuchadnezzar would run from the month of *Nisan* 603 BC to *Nisan* 602 BC. That this would coincide with the time when Daniel and his three friends had completed their three-year training course can be seen from a study of the following table:

[1] Nabopolassar rebelled against his Assyrian overlord and was the founder of the Neo-Babylonian Empire. See Appendix 2.

Year of Nebuchadnezzar's Reign	**Training Years of Daniel and his Three Friends**
Accession Year, Sept 605 BC – March-April (*Nisan* 604 BC)	Daniel's first year
First Year, *Nisan* 604 BC – *Nisan* 603 BC	Daniel's second year
Second Year, *Nisan* 603 BC – *Nisan* 602 BC	Daniel's third year

Daniel and his three friends were brought to Babylon near the close of the year 606 BC.[2] Sometime after their arrival, which would be into the year 605 BC, they were appointed a three-year course of training (1:5). Their final examination (1:19) and official installation in office (1:20) would then be near the end of the year 603 BC or just into 602 BC, which, in either case, would be King Nebuchadnezzar's second year.

So it would appear that God gave this dream to Nebuchadnezzar just after the young men had finished their three-year training course. This passage makes it clear that Daniel and his three friends, having passed their examinations with honour, were reckoned amongst the counsellors of the king. At least their names must have been on the official list, since Arioch, the captain of the king's guard, was searching for them to put them to death (2:13). The fact that they were not present at the first interview throws no doubt on their competency or experience – in fact, the very opposite! It may well suggest that, on previous occasions of consultation, these four had so far outshone their colleagues in giving counsel to the king (1:20) that, through jealousy, the older men quietly left them in bed when came this unexpected late-night summons to the royal presence. Grey-haired, grey-bearded, patriarchal figures did not need these lads in their early twenties.

The sleep of Nebuchadnezzar, the King of Babylon, had been disturbed – he 'dreamed dreams'. Much learned discussion has centred on the use of the plural in this expression. Some commentators suggest that the dream was repeated on several nights, and this view appears to be supported by the repetition of the plural in the next verse.[3] However, an able Hebrew scholar, Stephen R. Miller, points out that the Hebrew expression is

[2] See Appendix 1.

[3] Stuart, *A Commentary on the Book of Daniel, in loc.* discusses various ways to understand the plural.

idiomatic, and means simply that he was in 'a state of dreaming', rather than that he dreamed several dreams.[4] The record only presents one dream, and the use of the singular (twice in v. 3) is conclusive. The tense is pluperfect and should be translated 'had dreamed', as if it was the troubled state of his mind after the dream, and not just dream itself, that bothered him. Whatever it was, it had robbed him of sleep, not simply for the remainder of one night, but possibly the trouble had returned when he had sought sleep for several nights in succession. The word 'troubled' is graphic. Its basic meaning is 'to strike as with a hammer',[5] and it describes the pounding of a troubled heart as a result of extreme agitation. Nebuchadnezzar might be described as 'thunderstruck'– apprehensive and agitated. The result is that 'his sleep brake from him'. Again the verb is graphic, and pictures the king chasing sleep – trying to catch it. His concern would deepen as one sleepless night followed another.

The monarch of the greatest empire of his day lies sleepless. Victor on so many battlefields, commander of armies with courtiers innumerable awaiting his wish, yet he cannot enjoy a restful night. Shakespeare was right when he wrote, 'uneasy lies the head that wears a crown.'[6] Accustomed to intrigue and murder, even within his own court, and needing a watchful eye on all the conquered nations, Nebuchadnezzar must have had many a fear for himself and for the future of the empire his father, King Nabopolassar,[7] and he had built; a far greater empire than Assyria or Egypt had ever ruled. Now a dream leaves him sleepless. In Chaldean thinking – and this was his ethnic background – a dream was a message from the unseen world; indeed, a message from the gods. For Nebuchadnezzar, to the cares of the day was added the restlessness of sleepless nights. It is scarcely surprising that Nebuchadnezzar tossed and turned restlessly on his gilded couch – this particular night Nebuchadnezzar's patience snaps.

The cultural background of Nebuchadnezzar, where dreams were treated as messages from the gods, would create within him a deep unease.[8] He would fear that this awesome dream carried some ominous message, which he feared to decipher. From the scriptural

[4] Miller, *New American Commentary, Daniel*, p. 77.
[5] *OTWS*, p. 455.
[6] Shakespeare, *King Henry IV* Part 2, Act 3, Sc. 1, l. 31.
[7] See Appendix 2.
[8] Miller, *New American Commentary, Daniel*, p. 78.

point of view, there is no problem with the fact that God was the author of Nebuchadnezzar's dream. God used this method of communication before the Divine revelation in Scripture was available to men. He used dreams to communicate with believers – thus He spoke to Joseph (Gen. 37:5–8). He used dreams to speak to unbelievers – thus He spoke to King Abimelech (Gen. 20:3) and to Pharaoh (Gen. 41:1–8).[9] As he has done in so many holy things, Satan imitates what God does, but with the intention of deceiving mankind. In this present age, the believer has the complete revelation of the mind of God in the Word of God, and nothing more is needed for our instruction. Attempting to peer into the future by interpretation of drug-induced dreams and visions, the use of astrological charts, or indeed by any other means, is to leave the individual open to satanic deception.

Verses 2–3 Thoroughly upset and worried, King Nebuchadnezzar summons his counsellors. Autocratic monarchs consult only at their own convenience. Whatever time of day or night it might be, the inner court of the Babylonian Empire is called into immediate session. Collectively the group is called 'the wise men of Babylon' (v. 12). Four classes within this group are mentioned:

(a) The Magicians. As discussed in comments under 1:20, this word indicates, not so much workers of magic or masters of trickery, but the scholarly recorders of the court. The root of the word is 'stylus', or 'pen', and they could well have been those responsible for the keeping of the official records of happenings and discussions in the king's presence. They were also responsible for the keeping of the record of astronomic observations that became the basis of astrologic prediction. In the six listings of the various grades of counsellors (1:20; 2:10, 27; 4:7; 5:7, 11) the magicians are mentioned in all but one. Their absence from the list on the night that Babylon fell to the Medo-Persian army may be significant.[10]

(b) The Astrologers. Again, a reference to comments on 1:20 will show that, while the word is often translated 'enchanters', as those who are in touch with the dead through the power of necromancy, the *AV* is a more exact translation. The word 'astrologers' suggests those who, from a study of the stars, seek to predict the future. This was a special skill built on accurate astronomical observations but,

[9] See also Job 33:14–16 in this connection.
[10] See commentary at 5:7.

from that basis, going off into pagan speculation as to the influence of the stars on men and events on earth. In this area lies the whole deception of astrology that Satan would use down the ages, and still uses, to control the lives of individuals. The reputation of Babylon as a world authority on astronomy was well founded – their skill and proficiency were recognised worldwide.[11] It is sobering to think that Satan hijacked this centre of astronomical observation and made it a tool for his deceptive purposes by the use of astrology.

(c) The Sorcerers. This word is a borrowing from the Akkadian language and means 'to practise magical arts, sorcery, charms, with an intent to do harm to men and beasts'[12] (translated 'witchcraft' in Nah. 3:4). This describes the incantations, derived from occult practices, to secure a blessing on friends, or to bring a curse on enemies. In all pagan kingdoms those skilled in these practices were given an honoured place as indispensable to the wellbeing of the kingdom.

(d) The Chaldeans. This is the most significant term, as clearly they are the leaders and spokesmen for the whole group (v. 4 and v. 10). As discussed in the previous chapter (see comments at 1:4), this term is used in two distinct ways. First, it identifies ethnically the original inhabitants of southern Babylonia (note the term 'Chaldees' in Gen. 11:28), who conquered all of Babylonia. It was in this ruling race that Nabopolassar and his son Nebuchadnezzar had their ethnic background and their culture. The term is used in this ethnic sense in 1:4; 5:30; 9:1. Second, the Chaldees as a race were traditionally famous for their astronomical observations down ages past, as noted by Unger:

> As scientists the Chaldeans founded the exact science of astronomy. For over almost four hundred years they had kept meticulous astronomical records. One of their astounding contributions was to reckon the length of the year as three hundred and sixty five days, six hours, fifteen minutes, and forty-one seconds; a calculation that reproduces within thirty minutes what modern instruments have given.[13]

However, these very accurate astronomical observations were but the foundation upon which was built the whole false structure of

[11] Whitcomb, *Daniel*, p. 36.

[12] *OTWS*, p. 404.

[13] *UBD*, p. 187.

astrological prognostication, including all the satanic deception embraced under this term. As noted above, the term in this book can point to the ethnic background, but on this occasion it points to this special group, within the general class of 'wise men' (v. 12), who have not only an ethnic link with the king, but who have made a special study of astrology. These two factors would add weight to their counsel to King Nebuchadnezzar. In this case they take the lead in answering the king.

While the broad groupings of the counsellors are marked out, it would be unwise to press the technical distinctions too far. Very probably each individual would contribute to any discussion from his specific area of expertise, but they certainly appear to have responded to any question as a group. It is this group that is summoned to stand before the king to do what they very likely had done many a time before – use their combined expertise to interpret a dream.

The purpose of the calling of this august council is stated explicitly by Nebuchadnezzar – 'for to shew the king his dreams'. The verb 'to shew' is given in the lexicon as 'to bring to light; to shew, to exhibit before any one, to shew openly', and the root suggests the removal of a veil from the eye.[14] In reply, the wise men (v. 4, 11) and Daniel (v. 24) use a synonym, though it is still translated into English as 'shew', but the root of this word means 'to breathe', and seems to suggest a verbal unfolding through the ear. Perhaps the king anticipates, in his more specific verb, the problem he is about to set his counsellors!

Obedient to the king's command, the counsellors file into the presence of their autocratic master and await his pleasure. Nebuchadnezzar explains concerning the dream that has troubled him and his anxiety to know what it means. It is interesting to note his carefulness in the language he uses. Nebuchadnezzar does not say that he wants to 'know the interpretation of the dream'. His language is more specific – he wants to 'know' the dream. One cannot help but feel that this wily monarch has something more on his mind than just the meaning of a dream.

2. The Wise men and their Dismay – verses 4–13

This section is studied under the following headings:

The Confidence of the Wise Men v. 4

[14] *OTWS*, p. 388.

The Confrontation with the King	vv. 5–7
The Challenge of the King	vv. 8–9
The Confession of the Wise Men	vv. 10–11
The Condemnation of the King	vv. 12–13

As the 'Chaldeans' begin their answer to the king, Daniel adds a little note that gives ground for thought. The note is just a single word in the Hebrew, but translated as 'in Syriac' (*AV*) or 'in the Syrian language' (*RV*) changed in the margin to 'in Aramaic'. It seems best to take it as a note written by Daniel in the margin of his record. There is no confusion here. The Arameans were essentially the same people as the Chaldeans; an ethnic minority in Chaldea, to which both Nabopolassar and his son Nebuchadnezzar belonged. They had brought their language to Babylon, where it was variously known as Syriac or Aramaic. This language was the language of the court, the language of diplomacy, and the language of trade. It was spreading rapidly through the empire. Daniel's note here indicates that, when the counsellors replied to the king, in the normal court language, Daniel takes the opportunity of changing the language of his record from Hebrew to Aramaic. Daniel continues the record in this language until the end of chapter seven. This is neither incidental nor accidental, but by Divine permission for the scriptural record.[15] It is sufficient to note, at this point, that it gives a remarkable example of Divine supervision in the way Scripture has been brought to us. A simple matter is obvious. These chapters in the Aramaic language deal particularly with Gentile nations in a period that will later be identified by the Lord Himself as the 'times of the Gentiles' (Lk. 21:24). It is therefore most fitting, and of Divine mercy, that they are written in the language that the Gentile nations of the day could understand directly. Had Daniel written these chapters in Hebrew, the message would have been more restricted in circulation. When the message reverts to the Hebrew language, in the final chapters of the book (chapters 8–12), the nation of Israel is the focus of the prophecies.

Verse 4 The Confidence of the Wise Men

After the customary Babylonian greeting to the king in formal audience – 'O king, live for ever,' the wise men invite the king to tell them his dream and assure him with complete confidence, 'we will

[15] For the significance and implication of the change of language see Introduction, Part 2 D.

shew the interpretation'. This assurance stemmed from the training they had received from the 'dream manuals' of Babylon, where every facet of dreams – the symbols and the actions – had specific rules of interpretation. Standard meanings, based on these rules, could then be added, using further tested lines of deduction – it was quite a formidable 'science' in the hands of experts.[16] When able to pool their knowledge, these men knew that any dream would pose little problem to their presentation of a reasonable interpretation. They knew this, and hence their absolute confidence before the king – 'tell [us] ... and we will shew the interpretation'.

Verses 5–7 The Confrontation with the King

In his reply, King Nebuchadnezzar shocked and dismayed the wise men of Babylon. He simply refused to tell them his dream. The translation 'the thing is gone from me' (*AV*) has led to a misunderstanding of the situation. In the English language it is easy to interpret 'thing' (without an article) as the dream, because the words come close together. Taken thus, it states bluntly that Nebuchadnezzar had forgotten the dream. This is not so, and, as the story unfolds, the idea that Nebuchadnezzar had forgotten the dream becomes completely untenable. The verb 'gone from me' is a Persian word meaning 'sure'.[17] Another translation of 'the thing' is 'the command' (as in *JND*). This opens the way for the link with that which follows and the verse would now read, 'The word from me is sure: if you do not make known to me the dream and the interpretation ...' (*RSV*). The *NET* translation is similar: 'My decision is firm. If you do not inform me of both the dream and its interpretation, you will be dismembered and your homes reduced to rubble!' Nebuchadnezzar's meaning is clear – he is not going to tell the dream to the wise men. His mind was made up irrevocably (it was 'sure'); he had decided that they must present before him both dream and interpretation. The 'ifs' that follow present the possibilities of their choice: if they did not tell the dream and interpretation (v. 5), then the awful penalty was spelled out: their persons and their possessions would suffer. If they did tell the dream and interpretation (v. 6), then the prospects were delightful.

[16] Miller, *New American Commentary, Daniel*, p. 80. Archaeological references in support are given.

[17] Wood, *A Commentary on Daniel*, p. 32.

Is it not possible to feel sympathy for men, even pagan priests, faced with such an ultimatum?

The retribution announced on failure was dire. Their persons would be dismembered and their homes desecrated. The verb translated 'cut in pieces' describes a practice, widespread at this time in the east, in which the body of a criminal was either hacked to pieces by knives or pulled apart by horses. 'Made a dunghill' was another eastern practice, in which dwellings were completely destroyed and the site used as garbage dumps or public latrines. Sentences of this type were routine in the Babylonian Empire, as witnessed by the treatment of King Zedekiah of Judah, when his sons were slain and his eyes put out (2 Kgs 25:7), and the treatment of the two rebels whom 'the king of Babylon roasted in the fire' (Jer. 29:22). In Babylon such punishments would have been routine. Repulsive as the sentence on failure would certainly be, so success would be the very opposite, and most attractive to the natural heart; 'gifts' and 'rewards' are both collective singular nouns, virtually synonymous, to indicate that the rewards would be showered on the whole group. An extra special award surely lies in the 'great honour' promised here. Stephen R. Miller intriguingly suggests, from the word origin of 'honour', that this may be either promotion or marriage to one of the king's daughters.[18] This again would be in keeping with imperial practice of the time.

A pertinent question must be asked – why did the king present his closest advisors with such an unreasonable demand at this time? Scripture does not suggest any explicit reason; it simply states the fact. There is no question that such a capricious and arbitrary action is perfectly in keeping with the character of Nebuchadnezzar, as history reveals it. However, that this is but a moment of strange caprice on the part of the king cannot be the whole story. As the scene is pondered, other factors come into focus. Nebuchadnezzar was a warrior of no mean ability, with a splendid record of military conquest behind him; this is not disputable. He was also a young man who, during the years of his father's illness, was frustrated by the aged counsellors of the realm limiting his ambitions and publicly calling upon their gods to restrain him. They had used the full range of omens, augurs, and oracles within their power to warn him of impending disaster if he pursued the course he was taking in the expansion of the empire. Further, in his pursuit of power, he

[18] Miller, *New American Commentary, Daniel*, p. 82.

was well aware of the back-room diplomacy, the intrigue, and the bribery that lurked just under the surface. In the earlier years, following his father's practice, he had used some of these very men who stood before him to incite and expose traitors to the realm. Now, this dream had given him such a tremendous opportunity to test his counsellors. Were they dependable counsellors, in touch with the gods, or not? If they had real contact with the gods, as they claimed, surely they could relate the dream. If they could not relate the dream, then the question in his mind would be could he have confidence in their interpretation? This consideration of the motive of the king might explain why the king made no mention of the absence of the young Hebrews from this gathering – King Nebuchadnezzar had the men he wanted before him. Now that he had issued his demand, Nebuchadnezzar was implacable. At stake is the ability and credibility of the wise men of Babylon.

Verse 7 The wise men were obviously shaken by this demand of the king. They had not a shadow of doubt that the king remembered the dream and thus was putting them to a test. Two things support this conclusion. First, they plead with the king to tell them the dream. Notice they do not suggest any stimulus to his memory, nor do they make suggestions to try to stimulate his memory, as psychologists would do today. These men knew it was the king who had taken the decision not to tell the dream. Secondly, if they had really believed that the dream was truly gone from the king's memory they could, had they so wished, soon have produced a dream, and then used their many arts to convince the king he had dreamt this very thing. However, they seem to have realised that this would be of little use, and that the king was deliberately withholding the information. In these circumstances to attempt such a subterfuge would invite instant death. They had to temporise.

Verses 8–9 The Challenge of the King

The king will not listen to their pleading. His reply shows he has evaluated these men rightly. He knew they would plead for time. 'Know of certainty' or 'know for sure' (*NET*), as the first word in the Aramaic sentence, expresses his conviction! He is absolutely certain that their hesitation and their further request for the dream are simply an attempt to gain time. 'Buy the time' is a good translation (*RV* marg.). He knows they cannot do what he asks, unless their claims to speak for the gods are true, and yet they cannot be honest, and admit their inability to do so. The wise men know that to admit that they cannot do this is to lose their credibility forever. So the natural response is to call for time – the situation may change, inspiration may come, or the king may come to his senses. This interpretation is demanded by the repetition of the expression from verse 5 with the same meaning: 'because ye see the order from me is sure'. In challenging the wise men in this way, it is clear that the king knows the dream, and no invented dream and subsequent interpretation will deceive him. Further, the wise men know this too.

The next statement of the king reinforces this interpretation. His point is clear, and his reply may be paraphrased thus: 'If ye will not make known unto me the dream, there is but one decree for you'. If they cannot tell the dream, they must die – the emphasis in the verse is upon the dream. Nebuchadnezzar has taken the measure of these men and knows full well what a tissue of lies would come out if he recounted the dream to the wise men – the interpretation would be no problem. Nebuchadnezzar also knows, facing this crisis, what they will likely do. As had happened in difficulties on occasions in the past, they were ready, with lying and corrupt words, to talk endlessly 'till the time be changed'. The wise men seem to have quickly grasped what the king was doing, and had seen that they must try to weather the storm, by talking until he was in a better and more reasonable frame of mind. This was a familiar tactic, which had worked in the past. This time the king is determined it will not work. The king speaks bluntly: 'Tell me the dream, and I shall know that ye can shew me the interpretation thereof.' The recounting of the dream would be the proof that the interpretation was valid. It is thus made very clear that the king is very deliberately putting his counsellors to the test.

Verses 10–11 The Confession of the Wise Men

Alarmed and furious at such an unexpected demand, it is obvious that the counsellors struggle to keep their temper and be courteous to the king. It is clear that only the consciousness of standing in the presence of an absolute despot, notorious for his terrible rages, with his bodyguards lining the hall, restrains their fury and moderates their language. First, they argue that such a request is totally unreasonable, because it lies outside human ability; they use plain language too – 'There is not a man upon the earth that can shew the king's matter.' Again, they claim that, not only is such a request unreasonable, but it is completely unprecedented. No king, however powerful or mighty – 'king, lord, nor ruler' – has ever asked any counsellor, however trained or skilled – 'magician, or astrologer, or Chaldean' – to do such a thing. There is subtle flattery here, as they imply that King Nebuchadnezzar is too great a man as to expect from his counsellors what has never been asked before. The scorn of the wise men takes them a step further – and a step they must have deeply regretted later. This request, according to the wise men, is not only (a) unreasonable, (b) unprecedented, but their final claim should settle the matter – it is (c) impossible. Confessing that such a thing was 'rare' (AV), 'precious',[19] and 'difficult',[20] the wise men admitted it was beyond human ability. Their logic carried them to the next step – they confessed that this was a matter that could only be revealed by the gods. The idols were on earth but behind these idols were entities 'whose dwelling is not with flesh'. Such a statement from these wise men not only shows the limitation of human ability, of which they were fully aware, but it shows too, with absolute clarity, that they feared the impotence of satanic powers. It can scarcely be doubted that, if they had been able, such demonical powers would have come to the aid of their earthly spokesmen at this critical juncture. The fact that they kept strangely silent at this crisis bears testimony to satanic impotence. It is obvious that Satan did not know the dream that God gave to Nebuchadnezzar until Daniel revealed it. The stage is being set, in a palace audience chamber in the idol capital of the world, where Satan had his throne at this time,[21] for the confrontation, not simply between a king and his counsellors, but between the power of Satan and the power of God. What Satan cannot do, God can. Already God has His spokesman in place.

Verses 12–13 The Condemnation of the King

Verse 12 The wording of the reply of the wise men, to what they judged to be a most unreasonable, unprecedented, and impossible request of the king, had been as cautious and as courteous as they could possibly manage. Nevertheless, it was certainly blunt and virtually charged Nebuchadnezzar with being totally unreasonable, in asking such an impossible thing. It is scarcely to be wondered at that this autocratic despot, unaccustomed as he was to any

[19] *OTWS*, p. 340.
[20] Walvoord, *Daniel: The Key to Prophetic Revelation*, p. 53.
[21] Compare Rev. 2:13. It would seem Satan moved his centre of earth operations with changing times.

opposition to his will, was 'angry and very furious'. He simply flew into a rage (*cf.* Pharaoh, Gen. 40:2; 41:10) and ordered the execution of all the wise men of Babylon. The term 'wise men of Babylon' must cover, not only the men present before the king, but all those embraced by the four groups mentioned (v. 2). It is at this point that Daniel and his three friends come under the edict of the angry king.

That Nebuchadnezzar was prepared to kill all the wise men of Babylon demands some explanation beyond the rage of a frustrated despot who was accustomed to having his own way on every occasion. This becomes more urgent as it is recognised that he deliberately withheld the dream. First, it is perfectly clear that he is testing them. He has given them a challenge that they admit needed acquaintance with the gods. Did they not claim to be in touch with the gods, through their priestly sacrifices and astrological charts? Clearly failure in this case would cast doubt on any prior predictions they had made, and Nebuchadnezzar would hardly be willing to ask for further routine predictions if they were not found trustworthy in this case. A second consideration that must be taken into account is that Nebuchadnezzar is obviously worried about the future, and may not feel very secure on his recently acquired throne. One reason for his hasty return from Jerusalem across the desert in 606 BC was that he knew there were those with seditious intention behind the scenes. In fact, his father was a usurper,[22] who had used intrigue and bribery to secure the succession of his son. His previous acquaintance with most, or perhaps all, of these wise men, during the time he was 'King-Designate' as his father's heir, would have raised questions in his mind as to their trustworthiness. The desire to weaken the power of these older counsellors could lie behind the sudden addition of four Hebrews to their number (1:20). Doubtless, Nebuchadnezzar had intended to test them when an opportunity would arise. Now the opportunity had arisen, and he seized it. Adding to the underlying uneasiness of a new king was the dream itself, the main feature of which was the fact that a very imposing man-like statue is smashed by a sudden and unexpected blow. Nebuchadnezzar knew enough of the interpretation of dreams to have feared what this foretold – maybe for him personally. Familiar with the endless intrigues of an oriental court, he may well have been wondering if some of these wise men were actually

[22] Oates, *Babylon*, p. 127.

planning his assassination. He showed not the slightest reluctance to rid himself of them altogether.

Verse 13 The decree goes forth from the throne, and there can be no delay. The verb 'should be slain' translates an Aramaic participle that could be literally translated 'were being killed',[23] suggesting that the execution had already begun. However, in the context of the passage, it is much better to understand it as the first step in the process of assembling the whole company of the wise men for official execution – and this gathering had already begun. The names of the Hebrews must already have been entered in the official register, and, in response to the king's order, Daniel and his three friends are sought by Arioch, captain of the guard.

3. DANIEL AND HIS DEPENDENCE UPON GOD – VERSES 14–30

There is a remarkable symmetry in the five sections of this part of the chapter:

Before the King	vv. 14–16
Before the Throne of God	vv. 17–19
Praise to God for an Answer	vv. 20–23
Before the King	vv. 24–26
From the Throne of God	vv. 27–30

Verses 14–16 Before the King

The day is breaking in Babylon, and Daniel is already at his desk, possibly in the library quite close to the royal apartments. Suddenly he is interrupted, as the door bursts open and Arioch, the captain of the king's bodyguard, well known of course to Daniel, stands before him. Abruptly he learns of the death sentence pronounced *in absentia* upon him and his three Hebrew friends. Even under such a blow, Daniel's equanimity does not desert him; he remains as calm as he did in a previous crisis (1:9–10); dignity and courtesy still mark him as he stands before his designated executioner. That Daniel answered Arioch with 'counsel and wisdom', which translates as 'prudence and discretion' (ESV), indicates remarkable poise in a young man unexpectedly faced with summary execution. The 'answered' of Daniel shows that Arioch had given him the

[23] Miller, *New American Commentary, Daniel*, p. 84.

explanation for this sudden arrest. Daniel would be perfectly aware of the role of Arioch. The word 'guard', found in other writings outside Scripture, is understood generally as 'slaughterer' or 'executioner'.[24] This task, in the Babylonian Empire, belonged to the bodyguards of the king; the captain of the bodyguard was also the king's official executioner. Arioch, whose name means 'mighty lion', would be the officer responsible for making sure that the whole company under sentence was executed.

Arioch must have had a very high respect for Daniel. That he even explained to Daniel the reason for his arrest indicates that respect. That he allowed Daniel to go further and ask, 'Why is the decree so hasty from the king?' is most remarkable. It suggests a very unusual man holding this particular office. Linguists dispute whether the Aramaic word should be translated as 'hasty' or 'harsh'.[25] Contextual arguments can be made for both translations, but the weight of evidence supports 'harsh', indicating that such a severe judgment was hardly justice for those who had not been given any opportunity to defend themselves before the king. Not that fairness or justice carried much weight in Babylon under such a despot but, at the very least, it caused Arioch to pause for a moment's consideration and to explain what had happened to Daniel – he 'made the thing known to Daniel'.

After Arioch explained the situation, it is clear that our record only contains the necessary outline of what occurred. Daniel would not dare to approach the king unannounced and without the correct procedure. On the other hand, Arioch must have been a very trusted courtier, to hold the post he did and to have such an unusual right of access to the king. Daniel also must have convinced Arioch, in a very short space of time, that he could interpret the dream – if only he were given time. There is no doubt that, in the action he took, Arioch risked his life. Taking full advantage of his trusted status, Arioch arranged for Daniel to have an audience with the king. It must have been an awe-inspiring, nerve-racking, moment for Daniel as, with due ceremony, he was ushered into the presence of the most feared man in the world. Courtiers, attendants, and guards, in splendid formal dress or uniform, surrounded his majesty. As a mere stripling entered the

[24] *OTWS*, p. 203.

[25] *OTWS*, p. 209. Wilson opts for 'harsh, severe'; A. Pick, *Dictionary of Old Testament Words*, p. 189, opts for 'hasten, hurry in all passages'. The same word is used in 3:22: 'the king's commandment was urgent'.

audience hall and approached the king, even with Arioch by his side, the silence must have been palpable. High officials of empire must have held their breath as a young Jewish lad, even if he is a respected officer high up the civil service list, moved toward the king who, just a few moments before, had issued the death sentence on the wisest men in the kingdom. Having denied the request of the wise men for a delay, the courtiers would know that King Nebuchadnezzar would be in no mood to listen to any appeal. However, strange as it appears, the king did listen.

The cooling of his temper, the appeal of his trusted Arioch, something very special in the demeanour of Daniel, would all have helped, but, above everything else, the absolute assurance of Daniel that his God was able to give the interpretation of the dream must have carried weight with Nebuchadnezzar. Added to this, he certainly wanted to hear what the dream portended. Doubtless to the absolute amazement of the court circle, Nebuchadnezzar granted the request of Daniel. As far as the record goes, no time limit is given to Daniel – but the whole scene presents urgency. If this was the early morning of the day following the night of confrontation, the implicit time granted could possibly be until the same time the next morning – a twenty-four-hour stay of execution (see v. 19).

Often overlooked in this episode is the faith of Daniel. He did not know what the king had dreamed. He knew only that the wisest men in the kingdom had shown inability to recall it – so Daniel would know that the power behind the idol was completely stymied as well. Yet he had promised the king to return with the information – possibly within twenty-four hours. Thus he was placing implicit confidence in his God. Few men or women have ever demonstrated faith like this – and known, at the same time, that their life was at stake.

Verses 17–19 Before The Throne of God

Petition to God for an Answer vv. 17–19

Verses 17–18 Although no time limit had been set by the king, Daniel did not delay. The apartments where he and his friends lived, according to modern archaeological sketches, were close to the royal apartments, so Daniel hastened there and briefed his three friends on the situation. Where we might have expected panic, Daniel proposed prayer. So, in the capital city of idolatry, four young men – Daniel, Hananiah, Mishael, and Azariah – not long out of their teens, get on their knees before the God of heaven. Babylonians worshipped the heavens, but four young men knew the 'God of the heavens' (literal reading). Already they had put Him to the test in their faithfulness to His Word (1:8) and He had proven absolutely dependable. Now they were to put Him to the test in the fearlessness of their witness for Him before the mightiest monarch on earth. While the title 'God of heaven' can be traced back to Abraham (Gen. 24:7), and is used as he contemplates the idolatrous background from which he was delivered, it came into particular use in Israel during and after the Babylonian exile (Ezra 1:2; Neh. 1:5). It presents God as Creator, outside and apart from created things – such are simply the work of His hands. Idolaters are defined in Scripture as those 'who changed the truth of God into a lie, and worshipped and served the creature more than the Creator' (Rom. 1:25). It should be remembered that the Babylonians worshipped the sun, the moon, and the stars, but Daniel and his three friends, bowed together in the capital city of idolatry, go beyond the created realm, and wait upon the Creator.

The petition of the young men in the hour of their need is for 'mercies'; a word derived from a verb meaning 'to show tender love and compassion'. These young men were learning a bitter truth of Scripture: 'The tender mercies of the wicked are cruel' (Prov. 12:10), but they would confess with a repentant King David: 'His [God's] mercies are great' (2 Sam. 24:14). Daniel would echo this sentiment in later life, when he would acknowledge 'to the Lord our God belong mercies' (9:9). Daniel was fully aware that any answer from God would not be on the basis of worth, as if God owed them a response, but on the ground of His mercy and infinite compassion. The particular mercy they desired at this moment was the revelation of 'this secret'. The Persian word used is 'mystery,' which to the Babylonians meant simply 'something unknown'. This word 'secret' is translated in the Septuagint (Greek) version as *musterion*, which in the NT means 'that which, being outside the range of unassisted human apprehension, can be known only by Divine revelation'.[26] In this case, the secret was the dream God gave to Nebuchadnezzar and its interpretation.

These young men knew their lives were at stake. Failure to honour the commitment that Daniel had given King

[26] Vine, *An Expository Dictionary of New Testament Words*, p. 97.

Nebuchadnezzar would mean their death, along with the wise men of Babylon. That they did not fear death is clear in this passage, and shown publicly when they face the fiery furnace about a year later (3:16–18). The latter part of verse 18 and the tense in verse 24 make clear that the assembling of the wise men for the public official execution was still in progress. Failure would mean that they would join that condemned company. Four young men on their knees before their God stand between the wise men of Babylon and execution.

Verse 19 Between the petition (vv. 17–18) and the praise (vv. 20–23) lies the moment when God answered their prayer. To this answer to prayer Daniel responds in praise. There is no indication of how long the young men prayed – they prayed, indeed, until God answered their cry. It was when they heard Daniel burst into praise that they knew their prayer had been answered.

Daniel was given the information in a 'night vision'. Had the day slipped away in prayer and a further night had fallen? Perhaps it is the method of revelation – a 'night-vision' type of communication – rather than the timing that is here given. As suggested above (v. 16) there may well have been an implicit twenty-four-hour time limit in the response of the king, so this would now be the morning following the confrontation. Knowing that he had been allowed to view what God had shown to Nebuchadnezzar, Daniel cannot be silent; he bursts out in notes of thanksgiving to his God.

That God did use dreams to convey His mind in certain situations to both believers and to sinners has already been shown (v. 1). The word 'vision' demands something that filled the eye but was given directly by God. Later in this book God will use this method of communication to convey His mind to Daniel (7:2; 9:23); whether it comes by night or day makes no difference; it comes directly from God, and the recipient is awake and not asleep. Since both an image and its interpretation are involved, the vision had to include both the visual (to see) and the aural (to hear). What a moment it must have been for Daniel to view the image and receive the explanation! What a note of praise bursts from his lips to the God of heaven!

Praise to God for an Answer vv. 20–23

Verse 20 The Aramaic participle here translated 'blessed' simply means 'praise'; the verb is used by Daniel in the previous verse, and is repeated in this verse. It is remarkable that Nebuchadnezzar uses the same word in praise to God after the restoration of his mental faculties (4:34). Both Daniel and Nebuchadnezzar have recognised that the God Whom they have come to know through His dealings with them is worthy of their adoration. Three notes stand out in Daniel's song of praise: the God of Daniel is omnipresent, omniscient and omnipotent.

1. His Name. This is articulated by Daniel, but his three friends join in – notice the first person plural (v. 23). Heartfelt thanksgiving reveals deep appreciation of the God they had to come to know. Daniel's acquaintance with this God begins with the 'God of heaven' (v. 19) and ends with the 'God of my fathers' (v. 23). He recognises their experience, but repeats what Scripture recorded of believers who had gone before – like Abraham, Isaac and Jacob. Daniel was treading in the footprints of others who had trusted the same God. The God of Daniel is omnipresent in every age.

2. His Wisdom. What the wise men of Babylon, with the powers of darkness behind them, were unable to do, God allows a lad from among the Jewish captives to do – to show the dream. The wisdom of men has limitations, but the wisdom of God has none – He knows all. The Aramaic word for 'wisdom' covers both the knowledge itself and the capacity to utilise that knowledge in taking a right decision. No limitation can be placed on the knowledge and wisdom of the God of Daniel. He is omniscient.

3. His Might. As the meaning of the image is interpreted to Daniel, there seems to have dawned upon his soul the consciousness the power of One Who, in absolute sovereignty, is in control of history. Daniel will come to know that it is neither the skill of the diplomat nor the size of the army that shapes national destinies, but the will of the 'God of heaven' (v. 18). The nations, which in the eyes of men look so powerful and mighty, are but pawns moving on the board of earth under the hand of a Master. The God of Daniel is omnipotent.

His mind overwhelmed with the consciousness of such a God, Daniel moves from adoration to a fresh appreciation of how distinct is his God from the no-gods, the idols of Babylon. Men come and men go – omnipresent throughout time, He belongs to eternity! Men boast of their knowledge and wisdom – He is the giver of both wisdom and knowledge, He knows what is in the light, and the darkness can hide nothing from His eye. He is omniscient. Kings rise and kings fall – He removes one and He sets up another. He is omnipotent – history is but the outworking of absolute sovereignty. The God of heaven is absolutely supreme.

Verses 21–22 This supremacy and superiority of this God above the idols of Babylon seems to absorb Daniel as he continues to pour out his soul in wondering worship. Five areas of supremacy are mentioned:

1. Historically. 'He changeth the times and the seasons.' Both 'times' and 'seasons' refer, in this context, not to the annual seasonal changes, but to the turn of events in history. This God is the One Who controls events in all the eras and epochs of history, either directly or indirectly. The present participle used indicates the continuing direct intervention of God in historical time. Men have sought this control down the ages. It is hardly surprising therefore that the final world emperor, as pictured in the 'Little Horn' out of the fourth beast, will aspire 'to change times and laws' (7:25). This man is claiming that which belongs to Deity alone.

2. Nationally. 'He removeth kings, and setteth up kings.' Nebuchadnezzar had acted in this way with the kings of Judah (2 Chron. 36:6–21), as indeed he had done in all the conquered and vassal states of his empire. Now he would learn that there is Another, Who is in supreme control. Kings, however great they imagined themselves to be, were but puppets in His hand.

3. Individually. 'He giveth wisdom unto the wise, and knowledge to them that know understanding.' God deals with nations and He deals with kings, but the glorious facet of His Deity, which brings Him so near to men, is that He condescends to deal with the individual. He gave wisdom and understanding to Solomon (1 Kgs 4:29). He does the same for all those who seek Him with the same humble spirit. Daniel has personally proved the truth of this and, seeing through all the superstitions and idolatries of Babylon, is now open to the understanding that God gives to His own. The wisdom of Babylon belongs to earth and the wise men were denied understanding. Daniel received the wisdom given of God and therefore had the capacity to understand the visions (see the use of the word 'understanding' in 9:22; 10:1).

4. Prophetically. 'He revealeth the deep and secret things.' The two words 'deep' and 'secret' complement each other in defining what is inaccessible to man. There are matters that are beyond man's ability to uncover; most likely the reference here is to the depth revealed in the cosmos that is beyond the mind of man to

fathom. Every fresh discovery by man leads to a further question, and then another question, *ad infinitum*. There is a depth to the cosmos that man has not yet fathomed. The evolutionary lie, despite being opposed to all true science, is being used of Satan in our day, to satisfy man's feeble intellect and hold the minds of men in absolute thraldom – a chain difficult to break. Yet God reveals Himself in the Scriptures as the Creator. The 'secret' things are the 'hidden' things that God has kept in His own counsel – to men one of these secrets is the future. It is here that Satan steps forward again and professes, through his agents, to tell the future. The witchdoctors, magicians and astrologers are satanic agents in the attempt to unfold what God has placed in His own power. Babylon had available a variety of useful tools in the service of Satan but, at the moment, they are under sentence of death. Their satanic master is shown as powerless to help. Daniel's God alone can reveal the secret.

5. Essentially. 'He knoweth what is in the darkness, and the light dwelleth with him.' 'Darkness' physically is the absence of light. In the spiritual realm, it is that which fills the mind of natural man untouched by the light of Divine revelation. God knows exactly what is there, and all the debasement of humanity in idolatrous Babylon does not surprise Him. By contrast 'light dwelleth with Him' as if it essentially makes its home with Him Who is light (1 Jn 1:5). In simple language, all true revelation is from God. Since Christ speaks of Himself as 'The light of the world' (Jn 9:5) some expositors[27] see a very interesting reference to the One Who dispels the darkness that sin has brought into the world; and He does dwell with God. Wood writes, 'Since Christ is particularly "the Light" of God (Jn 1:4–8), numerous expositors see an intended secondary reference to Him, as the One Who dispels the darkness of sin; and Christ does indeed dwell with the Father.'[28]

Verse 23 The joyous response of Daniel is evident in this note of personal thanksgiving to God for His answer to their cry. It should be noted that the first word in the Aramaic text is 'Thee' – God gets all the glory! 'Thank' and 'praise' are virtually synonymous in this context, though it could be argued that Daniel moves from appreciation of this direct answer to his prayer to the appreciation of the God Who has answered the prayer. Daniel acknowledges too

[27] Carson, *The Gospel according to John*, p. 362.
[28] Wood, *A Commentary on Daniel*, p. 61.

that the 'God of my fathers' has now condescended to honour him as He honoured the patriarchs of old with Divine revelation. 'Wisdom' and 'might' that belong essentially to Deity (v. 20) have now been granted to God's servant. In the context, 'wisdom' must be interpreted as the knowledge of the dream and 'might' as the ability to interpret it. Daniel further acknowledges that this answer of God has been in direct response to the united prayers of the four young men who bowed together before God. Note the first person plural in the 'we' and the 'us'. As a group they prayed and, though the answer came to Daniel, it was in response to their united prayer.

Verses 24–26 Before the King

Verse 24 If 'night vision' is interpreted literally then the twenty-four-hour stay of execution is nearly at an end (v. 19). However, as shown, the expression may be interpreted as simply the type of communication, and not linked to a time of day. Whatever view is taken, there is clearly no time to be lost. Daniel presents himself before Arioch – the man charged with his execution. Arioch stands out in this story as one who has the confidence of the king and yet who has come to have great respect for Daniel. In turn, Daniel has a mutual respect for Arioch, in his role as intermediary with the king. Daniel had two requests to make of Arioch at this point. The first – 'Destroy not the wise men of Babylon', and the second – 'Bring me in before the king.' The first is quite surprising, and shows the calibre and thoughtfulness of Daniel, who, in spite of his own dire situation, could think of others. At the same time, it also displays his fearless courage – courage to directly countermand a command of the king of Babylon. This shows that the gathering of all the wise men was still proceeding but the executions had not yet begun. Daniel obviously feared that they would die before any counter-order could come from the throne. Daniel's second request shows fearless conviction: 'Bring me in before the king' displays no hesitation at the thought of facing that fearsome monarch once more. The second part: 'I will show unto the king the interpretation' displays not a trace of hesitation or doubt. Daniel is now fully conscious that his God has arranged the whole situation. Daniel is content to move in step with his God.

Verse 25–26 No time is lost. The word 'in haste' could be translated 'quickly', or 'at once' (*NIV*), and, according to a well-regarded linguist,[29] comes from a root meaning 'to be alarmed'; its use here shows the emotional involvement of the apparently calm Arioch. Any delay in the execution of the wise men would be laid to his charge. So without delay arrangements are made, and Daniel stands again before the king. With much more conviction this time, and identifying himself more closely with Daniel, Arioch presents Daniel to the king as the man who can interpret the dream. Anxious to preserve his own life, and, possibly, to bolster his standing with the king, he claims the credit for finding Daniel. The verb 'found' implies a personal search, and the location – among the captives of Judah – suggests the idea of a very exhaustive search. Much credit is due to Arioch for not dismissing Daniel brusquely on either of the occasions when he approached him; he also deserves further credit for the risk he took in trusting Daniel to do what he claimed to be able to do. He certainly risked his reputation, his job, and most likely his life, on Daniel's credibility. But Arioch had not 'found' Daniel in any meaningful sense: God had arranged matters so that Daniel as the servant of God was to stand before this earthly sovereign. Arioch had been used of God as the intermediary for this important confrontation.

Daniel's presentation before the king is strangely formal, in light of the fact that he had stood there such a short time before. It is necessary to think in terms of the formality and the protocol of such an oriental court, as well as to keep in mind the busy life of a monarch of such a great empire – there was always a queue of persons to have an interview with the king. As far as Nebuchadnezzar was concerned, he had likely dismissed Daniel from his mind and expected that the execution decree on the wise men was being carried out. But the king's attention is arrested by the arrival of Arioch and his dramatic announcement – 'I have found a man of the captives of Judah, that will make known unto the king the interpretation.' It is easy to imagine every head turning and every eye swinging round to fasten upon Daniel. It would seem that the king recognised him immediately under his Babylonian name Belteshazzar (1:7) and acknowledged him before the court, before he put his question to him – otherwise Daniel would not have been allowed to address the king. The shock, the disbelief, in that royal gathering must have been severe: questions, doubts, mutterings, can be imagined – 'He's only a lad! A Jew as well! A

[29] Wood, *A Commentary on Daniel*, p. 62.

slave too! Is the king mad? Is the great King Nebuchadnezzar of Babylon really going to listen to this peasant?' Mighty Babylon has lessons to learn! The blunt, direct, no-nonsense question of the king breaks the stunned silence that has fallen on the gathering: 'Art thou able to make known unto me the dream ..., and the interpretation thereof?' It should be noted that the wording is exactly that same as that in the question he had put to the wise men of Babylon (v. 6). Arioch may leave out the word 'dream', and fasten upon the word 'interpretation' (v. 25), but the king has every intention of standing by his original demand for dream and interpretation. The question hangs in the air as every eye fastens upon Daniel.

Verses 27–30 From the Throne of God

Daniel, now the centre of attention, and with every eye fixed upon him, with three masterly touches ensures that all recognise that it is the God in heaven (*cf.* v. 18) Who has acted in this matter. Glory is to be ascribed to this God alone. Notice Daniel points out the three actors in this drama in the Babylonian Court:

(1) One who Reveals

God in heaven	'That revealeth Secrets'	vv. 27–28

(2) One who Receives

Nebuchadnezzar	'As for thee, O King'	v. 29

(3) One who Interprets

Daniel	'As for me'	v. 30

1. One Who Reveals – God in heaven

First, Daniel reminds the king that the wise men of Babylon have failed to declare 'the secret', which, as explained above (v. 19), includes both the dream and the interpretation. Daniel mentions the three groups of counsellors designated 'wise men' by the king. Two groups have been previously listed (astrologers and magicians (1:20; 2:2)) but he includes, for the first time, another category, whom he calls 'soothsayers'. This term is derived from a verb with two meanings – 'to cut' and 'to decide' – and it described men whose advice and prophecies were based upon the study of the entrails of an animal slain as sacrifice to a particular god – a synonym would be 'diviner' or 'fortune teller'.[30] Daniel's point is that the whole class of 'wise men', whatever their particular area of

[30] Wood, *A Commentary on Daniel*, p. 63.

expertise, has been publicly exposed as helpless in this matter. The implicit deduction is that the gods of Babylon, of whom the wise men professed to be the spokesmen, were equally helpless. Their helplessness calls into question the very reality of such gods. In the thinking of Nebuchadnezzar this point would not be lost, but Daniel lays emphasis on it – Nebuchadnezzar must not miss the implication of what has happened.

In contrast to the many gods of Babylon, Daniel sets over against them the God in heaven. The singular word used for God (*Elah*) sets this God in contrast to the multitude of gods in the Babylonian pantheon. 'God of heaven' (v. 18), a title used in the mouth of a believing Israelite, speaks of His power as the One Who has brought the created heavens (dual number) into existence. Here the title 'God in heaven', used in the presence of a pagan king, points to the place where He dwells. Thus, at one stroke, the magnificent temples of Babylon, whereon Nebuchadnezzar has bestowed many fortunes, are effectively rendered pointless – empty buildings! This is the God Who characteristically is the Revealer of secrets, and now this God has condescended to reveal one of those hidden things, which otherwise are not accessible to men, to Nebuchadnezzar, through Daniel. The secret that this God in heaven makes known to King Nebuchadnezzar is defined by Daniel as 'what shall be in the latter days'.[31]

The term 'latter days' goes back to Jacob (Gen. 49:1), which passage sets the meaning for the fourteen times it is used in the OT. It always makes reference to the closing portion of the time under consideration. In Genesis 49:1 it refers to the closing stages of the history of the tribes of Israel; here it clearly refers to the later stages of Gentile rule on earth, preceding the millennial Kingdom of Christ; later in the book (10:14) it refers to the closing stages of Israel's history as a nation (see also Num. 24:14; Deut. 4:30; 31:29). The NT uses a similar phrase, with similar meaning (*cf.* 1 Tim. 4:1; 2 Tim. 3:1; 1 Pet. 1:5; 2 Pet. 3:3; Jude 18). Daniel makes it plain to Nebuchadnezzar that 'thy dream, and the visions of thy head upon thy bed' are a direct revelation from God, directed to a particular period of earth history. This revelation is granted to Nebuchadnezzar for a particular purpose.

[31] As Daniel's God is presented as 'God in heaven' it must be remembered that Nebuchadnezzar claimed to be the personal representative of the god 'Bel', the patron god of the city of Babylon. In addition to this, he claimed to be the spokesman for the supreme god 'Marduk', the head of the Babylonian pantheon (see Appendix 2).

2. One Who Receives – King Nebuchadnezzar

Verse 29 Daniel reminds King Nebuchadnezzar of the night of the dream. Tossing from side to side, restless and uneasy upon his bed, he was looking into the future, wondering and worrying about what lay ahead for his mighty empire, so recently carved out of the dying Assyrian Empire by his father, and now under his control. Daniel crystallised the burden on the heart of Nebuchadnezzar that night in one phrase: 'what should come to pass hereafter'. The term 'hereafter' clearly refers to the concern of the king for himself and his kingdom in the immediate future, and very likely within his own lifetime. Was Nebuchadnezzar thinking of Babylon itself and the intrigues within the palace that he knew were presently afoot – the likely reason for the challenge with which he faced his counsellors? Perhaps he was pondering the world scene, and worrying about the diplomatic exchanges he knew were taking place, between the Medes, the Persians, and the Egyptians, for an alliance against Babylon. Nebuchadnezzar's rise had been meteoric, and he knew full well the resentments and intrigues that surrounded his throne. Further afield, he knew the resentment in the recently subdued nations was growing. Medes, on one border, and Egyptians, on the other, were ready at any time to invade his empire. Daniel shows the king that God has reacted to his concern and, for His own purpose, is prepared to reveal that which must humble the proudest monarch on earth – King Nebuchadnezzar. He would learn that the mightiest monarch on earth is a mere tool in the working out of the purpose of the God in heaven.

It is essential to keep in mind that the Babylonian Empire under King Nebuchadnezzar comes into prophetic Scripture as the instrument in the hand of Jehovah to discipline the disobedient nation of Israel. Babylon's earlier – and indeed later – history is largely irrelevant to the story, but from the capture of Jerusalem (606 BC) to the fall of Babylon to Cyrus (539 BC), Babylon has a place in the prophetic timeline. King Nebuchadnezzar was the first Gentile king to bring the city of Jerusalem under his control. He was not aware of it, but he was introducing a period that the Lord Jesus would later speak of as the 'times of the Gentiles' (Lk. 21:24) – the period when God, because of their sin, could not be publicly identified with His people (Israel) or His city (Jerusalem). God would allow both to be brought under Gentile dominion. Thus God, to the first Gentile king over Jerusalem, would, in His grace, give an outline of the period of the 'times of the Gentiles'. This period commenced with King Nebuchadnezzar, and continues through succeeding kingdoms, until it closes with coming of Christ to set up the Kingdom of God on earth.

3. One Who Interprets – Daniel

Verse 30 With absolute humility, Daniel claims no credit whatever. His wisdom is as useless as that of the wise men; he can claim no special knowledge above any living person. It is God Who reveals; it is God Who interprets and he is but the channel whom God has chosen to use. No glory attaches to Daniel. The reason that God has used him in the matter is given clearly: 'to the intent that the interpretation may be made known to the king' (RV). God is desirous of giving Nebuchadnezzar a glimpse of what lies ahead for his nation, and other nations as well, and has chosen Daniel as the channel. All glory must be given to God. The response of Nebuchadnezzar to this Divine revelation will show whether he believes in the God of heaven or the gods of Babylon. This response will show the king where he stands – it will reveal 'the thoughts of thy heart'.

CHAPTER 2:31–49

4. THE DREAM AND ITS INTERPRETATION – VERSES 31–49

The Image	Description	vv. 31–33
	Destruction	vv. 34–35
The Interpretation	Metals and their Meaning	vv. 36–40
	The Stone and its Message	vv. 41–45
The Impression		
	The Reaction of the King	v. 46
	The Response of the King	vv. 47–49
Excursus	**Question 1 – Teaching in the Image**	
	What is portrayed in the image?	
	Question 2 – Time in the Image	
	What period is surveyed in the image?	

Verses 31–33 The Image – Description

Verse 31 Majesty of the Image

The moment has come. The wise men of Babylon have been silenced. All the resources of idolatry having proven inadequate to reveal the secret of Nebuchadnezzar's dream, God (*Elah*) has His man in place. The silence in the audience chamber must have been palpable, as every eye focussed upon Daniel, who begins without the slightest hesitation – 'Thou, O king, sawest, and behold....' The king would relive the moment when, terrified, he stood before a majestic image, overawed by its very size. His startled surprise is recalled in the word 'behold'! The present participle in the verb 'sawest' could be translated 'while you were watching'.[1] The same participle, repeated in the next verse, shows the king totally unable to shift his gaze from the scene. Daniel draws attention to three things about the image that filled his vision. First, the sheer size of

[1] Miller, *New American Commentary, Daniel*, p. 91.

the image – no measurements are given – but the word 'great', sometimes translated 'mighty', is here used in the sense of 'overpowering'. A man before that image is rendered insignificant. Nebuchadnezzar's image (3:1), ninety feet high, made a short time later, was meant to reproduce the same effect – overpowering indeed. The second thing that strikes Daniel about the image is its 'brightness' – the descriptive word, often translated 'excellent', carries the idea of 'exceeding any other', and so comes to mean 'pre-eminent' – outshining all others. This word is repeated, in connection with this same empire, when God restores the kingdom to Nebuchadnezzar after his period of insanity (4:36). The polished metal reflects the sunlight with dazzling splendour. The expression 'stood before thee' suggests the idea of confrontation; this huge figure towering over the king is described by the third word, 'terrible', which, coming from a verb whose root means 'to fear', is better translated 'terrifying'.[2] Intrepid warrior, as on many a battlefield he had shown himself to be, Nebuchadnezzar, overawed, seems to shrink back from this great image – overpowering, dazzling, and terrifying.

Verses 32–33 Materials of the Image

Daniel now describes the unique feature of this image – its composition. Babylon was crowded with images, yet few would have more than one metal in them; this image is made up of four metals. Each metal is distinct, and confined to specified parts of the image, but together they form one image. Then into this four-metal image is introduced one surprising non-metallic material – clay. Daniel describes the image by the metals as follows:

Gold The head of the image was 'fine gold', identifiable by its own golden sheen, which in the sunlight would draw the eye of the beholder. This splendour would hold the eye and shroud the image with light.

Silver Below the neck in the human frame is the breast with the arms. The metal in this section is identified as silver, and it too catches the eye with its own special sheen.

Brass Below the breast, the belly and thighs form the third division, which would have the darker glow of bronze. The Aramaic word describes an alloy made from copper and zinc, which is generally translated 'brass'. However, more recent scholarship and

[2] Walvoord, *Daniel*, p. 63.

archaeological artefacts suggest that in the sixth century BC the word described an alloy of copper and tin, so perhaps 'bronze' (*RSV*) is a more correct rendering.

Iron The legs of the image are the fourth division of the image, and Daniel presents them as of the metal iron. This would make the legs of the image black in colour. Automatically the eye of the beholder will follow the intensity of the light from the top to the bottom – from head to feet; from the bright head to the dark feet. No wonder Nebuchadnezzar was alarmed.

As the eye follows Daniel's description down to the feet of the image, something unexpected catches the attention – the black colour of the iron is interspersed with a bluish tinge that hints of a different material. Daniel explains this when he identifies the material of the feet as 'part of iron and part of clay'. The clay here is not to be understood as the malleable clay, or simply mud, taken directly from the ground. The word used here and translated 'clay' describes clay baked as pottery and then glazed. All Daniel's audience would be familiar with the word. Material of this kind was to be seen in all the temples, palaces and monuments that crowded the city of Babylon. Iron and glazed pottery may look well together and, perhaps, give the appearance of strength, but it is only an outward appearance for decorative purposes. It can bear very little weight. The word 'broken', or 'brittle', describes it very well (v. 42).

Verses 34–35 The Image – Destruction

The repetition of the participle translated 'thou sawest' (v31) shows the king totally absorbed in the unfolding drama of the dream; to catch that drama it may be translated 'while you were watching'. Nebuchadnezzar was watching the total destruction of the great image. Daniel articulates the picture – a stone smites the image on the feet – obviously the weakest point. The iron and the clay pottery are smashed and the image begins to collapse. The metals, in the reverse order of iron, bronze, silver and gold, are pounded to pieces and carried away, just as chaff is blown from a threshing floor, when the winnowing wind sweeps through. The site is cleared completely – the image is gone. Under the gaze of a fascinated audience, Daniel recalls the final scene granted to Nebuchadnezzar. The stone, the agent of destruction, now begins to grow. From being a stone, originally torn from a mountain without human agency – 'cut out without hands' – it became 'a great mountain, and filled the whole earth'.

Even before Daniel began the interpretation, the impact of the dream on his Babylonian audience must have been considerable, not only upon the king, as it would recall all his anxieties, but also upon all the others who were hearing it for the first time. Familiar with the making of magnificent idols, these men would see in the image what man could achieve. Something made by man with infinite patience and adequate resources – an idol that man could worship – could be so readily wiped out and replaced. This dream showed that such a human achievement was doomed. It would be brought to nothing – made like chaff of a threshing floor – by a simple stone. In fact, the stone had the capacity to completely replace the image. No wonder the spirit of Nebuchadnezzar was troubled and sleep fled on the night he had the dream. The image was certainly terrifying, but what must have worried him was the stone. Arriving, unheralded and unannounced, from no recognisable, identifiable, source, this stone smashed the image and replaced it on the earth. It is speculation, but Nebuchadnezzar must have pondered the power and origin of the stone. This would be a sensible concern for a man recognised as a world leader.

It may be pointed out at this stage that there are four unusual features that mark out this stone as supernatural, and which must have weighed with the king as he pondered the dream. These may be listed for convenience of reference:

(a) The Origin of the Stone: it is described as 'cut out without hands'. In a later verse the words 'out of the mountain' are added (v. 45). 'Without hands' is an expression used to show that no human activity or agency brings this about (Mk 14:58; 2 Cor. 5:1; Col. 2:11); in other words, Divine action is involved.

(b) The Mission of the Stone: it flies through the air as a missile and is aimed directly at the feet of the image. The feet, clearly the weakest part of the image, as composed of iron and clay (pottery), are smashed on the impact of the stone. This is obviously no accident but the result of Divine purpose.

(c) The Power of the Stone: the smashing of the feet opens the way for the total destruction and pulverisation of the whole image. Note the order of the pulverisation: the iron, the clay, the brass, the silver and the gold are smashed in pieces, and the image is no more. The total destruction of the image into the tiniest particles is emphasised by using the familiar figure of the threshing-floor: when the threshed grain is tossed against the wind, the heavy grain falls to the floor, while the useless chaff is blown away by the wind.

The very materials of the image, seen now as chaff, are thus symbolised as worthless and are swept away without trace. There is no doubt about this – Divine power is seen.

(d) The Growth of the Stone: this amazing and supernatural stone, its destructive work done, now grows to become a great mountain and fill the whole earth. Clearly a Divine plan is to be recognised behind the action.

Verses 36–40 The Interpretation – Metals and their Meaning

Verse 36 In the stillness of the audience chamber the voice of Daniel falls silent. As Daniel has recounted the dream, King Nebuchadnezzar and the court have been absorbed in the unfolding drama, and not a sound has broken the silence. Now, amid that breathless hush, he gives the interpretation.

As a side issue, yet important for the understanding of the matter, much scholarly debate has been centred on the use of the plural 'we' by Daniel in the phrase 'we will tell the interpretation'. Did he mean to include his three companions who had joined with him in prayer? This seems unlikely, since King Nebuchadnezzar knows nothing of the part his friends have played in the story, and to introduce them now might suggest conspiratorial collaboration. The public limelight throughout has fallen on Daniel and upon him alone. It should remain focussed on him. Some commentators suggest that Daniel meant to include God (as the Source) and himself (as the channel) of the communication.[3] This appears out of character for Daniel and far too pretentious a claim for a man like Daniel. Perhaps the best interpretation is to see it as an editorial plural designed to reduce the impact of a proud personal 'I'. This was originally suggested by E.J. Young[4] some years ago and is supported by J.F. Walvoord,[5] who writes, 'Of the various interpretations, the editorial plural, which would denote more humility than 'I', seems to be the best explanation'.

Verses 37–38 The Head of Gold

As the dream has been presented to the court there must have been an almost eerie stillness and an absolute silence. From the stillness

[3] Wood, *A Commentary on Daniel*, p. 67.
[4] Young, *The Prophecy of Daniel*, p. 72.
[5] Walvoord, *Daniel: The Key to Prophetic Revelation*, p. 64.

of the king, it is clear to all that he is reliving the moments when he first saw the dream and watched its drama. Tension mounts as Daniel says simply, 'we will tell the interpretation'. Courteous, yet with authority, he turns and addresses the king. His direct 'Thou, O king ...' would cause every eye to focus on King Nebuchadnezzar. Then, into the stillness comes a tremendous accolade, as Daniel addresses him with a startling title: 'king of kings'! There cannot be the slightest doubt that this address acknowledges King Nebuchadnezzar as the outstanding king of his time. Nebuchadnezzar would, of course, have fully acquiesced in this assessment. On battlefields round the known world he had shown outstanding military skills; around the council tables of earth he had shown rare ability as a diplomat handing international affairs; as a ruler of his people he had proved to be an autocratic but, in the main, a just ruler. It is of interest that this same title is given to Nebuchadnezzar by Ezekiel when he captured the Phoenician city of Tyre (Ezek. 26:7). Yet it must be clear that none of these considerations lie behind the title here given of God. Military skill, diplomatic acumen, or governmental justice may win the approbation of men, but it is on other grounds completely that this title is given by the God of heaven to Nebuchadnezzar. Fearlessly, and without the traditional compliments, Daniel gives the reason why Nebuchadnezzar is addressed in such a way. Daniel's words are incisive: 'the God of heaven hath given thee a kingdom'. In pagan pride you imagined that your ability on the battlefield, your skill around the council table, and your lavish gifts to Marduk have won you this position – no such thing – it is the God of heaven Who has entrusted it to you. Humiliating to the king before his courtiers and, assuredly, dangerous for Daniel, it was yet absolutely essential. Nebuchadnezzar must be brought to see that he owes his throne and all the authority, prestige and honour that goes with it, to the sovereign will of 'the God of heaven'. This God, of His own sovereign will, has brought Nebuchadnezzar to the throne; He had given him 'a kingdom' – a word better translated here as 'dominion'. Dominion belongs to Deity, and God had entrusted Babylon to the care of Nebuchadnezzar. With that kingdom came what Daniel spells out in three words: (a) 'power' – the root of the word lies in 'riches'; (b) 'strength' – the root comes from 'authority'; and (c) 'glory' – the word could be translated 'honour', or 'majesty'. Nebuchadnezzar knew full well that he had riches incalculable, authority indisputable, and majesty incomparable. What he did not know was that these were all gifts of the God of heaven. 'Humbled' must be the word to describe Nebuchadnezzar at this juncture – and by the words from a young Judaean captive. Nebuchadnezzar must have cringed.

The scope of this dominion given of God to Nebuchadnezzar is outlined as 'wheresoever the children of men dwell, the beasts of the field and the fowls of the heaven'. Words could not be plainer to express a universal dominion over lands where men, beasts or birds lived. The phrases 'given into thine hand' and 'ruler over them all' indicate that Nebuchadnezzar had absolute power in lands where men, beasts and birds lived. It does not mean that he could give orders to birds or beasts, but that where these lived his authority ran. That Nebuchadnezzar is addressed as 'king of kings' and that such dominion has been given to him indicate the important place he fills in Divine purpose at this time. God allows him to fill this place and play his part in earth history but he must bear responsibility for his own actions, for which he will answer to God.

'Thou art this head of gold' is the Divine interpretation of this part of the image. Frequently in Scripture the terms 'king' and 'kingdom' are employed interchangeably by use of metonymy; the kingdom is personified in the ruler, and he is seen to be the embodiment of the kingdom. It will be easily recalled, for example, that 'Pharaoh' stands generally for 'Egypt', as in a later day 'Caesar' stands for 'Rome'. However, on this occasion the language is so emphatic that it is clear that the head of gold points to Nebuchadnezzar personally, and not to the Babylonian Empire. This becomes clear when history unfolds and we recognise that there was a Babylonian empire before Nebuchadnezzar became king, and there was a Babylonian empire after Nebuchadnezzar, but neither is mentioned here, and the phrase 'after thee' (v. 39) leads directly to Cyrus, the king of Medo-Persia.[6]

The material in the head is gold, the most valuable metal in the image. It reflects God's estimate of the Babylonian Empire, as embodied in Nebuchadnezzar personally, compared with the empires that followed. Gold was a fitting and recognisable symbol for Babylon. This city, in general conversation of the day, was linked with gold. It is called 'The golden city' in Scripture (Isa. 14:4); Marduk, the heathen god of Babylon, was called 'the god of gold', very likely because the majestic idol in his magnificent temple was

[6] See Appendix 2.

solid gold. Herodotus, the traveller and historian who visited Babylon within ninety years of Nebuchadnezzar's time, was astonished at the amount of gold there – walls and even buildings were overlaid with gold.[7]

Notes

1. 'King of kings'

The capture of Jerusalem is an important time mark in prophetic teaching. The identification of Nebuchadnezzar as the head of gold marks the opening of the period called the 'times of the Gentiles' by the Lord Himself (Lk. 21:24). This is the period in which God has permitted the sovereignty He had given to Israel, as head of the nations (Deut. 28:13), to be lost, and for Jerusalem to come under Gentile authority. The first Gentile nation entrusted with this sovereignty is Babylon, as embodied in King Nebuchadnezzar. The people of Israel were carried as captives to Babylon. The nation that God had chosen for the working out of His Divine purpose and the bringing in of the Redeemer had failed, and, as a consequence, was scattered through other nations. Despite partial recoveries, at various times, down to this present day, it is clear that they will remain scattered until God reclaims Jerusalem and establishes the Messianic Kingdom under the Son of Man, as anticipated in this book (7:13). This specific time period, from the first Gentile king in Jerusalem (King Nebuchadnezzar) until the final Gentile king in Jerusalem (7:26), is known as the 'times of the Gentiles', and this four-metal image represents the kingdoms and their kings who will be permitted by God to hold the sceptre over the city where Jehovah had placed His Name – Jerusalem. Only four will be allowed to do this until God introduces His King – the One spoken of in this book as the 'Son of Man' (7:13). Nebuchadnezzar, as the first of these kings, is addressed as 'king of kings'; an honour that God permits for a time. The title belongs inherently, exclusively, and eternally to the Son of Man in Kingdom power (Rev. 19:16).

2. 'This Head of Gold'

It has already been suggested that the title 'Head of Gold' identifies King Nebuchadnezzar personally. If that is so, then this adds to the significance of the date of the capture of Jerusalem by

[7] Showers, *The Most High God*, p. 18.

Nebuchadnezzar in 606 BC (2 Chron. 36:6–7). This is where Nebuchadnezzar comes into the Divine programme as 'head of gold'. After the death of his father, Nabopolassar, in 605 BC, Nebuchadnezzar was crowned King of the Neo-Babylonian Empire, which he ruled with skill and ability for forty-three years (605–562 BC). The empire outlived him by only twenty-three years, and in the time of King Belshazzar the city of Babylon fell to Cyrus (539 BC). The post-Nebuchadnezzar period of the empire is ignored in the timeline of the image.[8]

Verse 39 (a) The Breast and the Arms of Silver

As a first reaction, Nebuchadnezzar must have been immensely flattered to be identified as the head of gold. Doubtless, it was satisfying to his ego, but second thoughts may have brought some serious reality to mind. This was a deathblow to his worship of 'Marduk' ('Bel' was his Babylonian name); the wealth lavished upon this god had been a waste of treasure. Again, if the God of heaven had given him his throne, that same God could take it away again. This must have struck Nebuchadnezzar just about the moment Daniel was speaking of the replacement of the great Babylonian Empire by another. This was hard to understand. That Nebuchadnezzar would be replaced by his son, at least by a successor from his family, would be the natural course of things. Perhaps Nebuchadnezzar had been already considering the succession and whom he would choose to succeed him. Now he learns that he has no choice in the matter. The same God Who had given the kingdom to him would replace, not him alone, but the kingdom. The Babylonian Empire would be replaced in world dominion by another kingdom, and one described as 'inferior to thee'. A more literal translation is, 'after you shall stand another kingdom lower than you'.[9] E.J. Young comments on the tense of the verb and writes: 'The future "shall stand" is a more accurate translation than "shall arise", for there is nothing mobile in the scene.'[10] It would be after Nebuchadnezzar that another kingdom would rule from Babylon and dominate the nations of their world. The words of Daniel are clear: 'which shall bear rule over all the earth'. Noticing the metals, the 'golden kingdom' was to be replaced

[8] See Appendix 2.
[9] Wood, *A Commentary on Daniel*, p. 67.
[10] Young, *The Prophecy of Daniel*, p. 74.

by 'the silver kingdom'. The sobering fact for Nebuchadnezzar was that this kingdom was to be 'inferior to thee'.

While this second kingdom is not named at this point – it will be named later in the book (5:31; 8:20) – yet history provides the answer: the power that followed Babylon on the world scene was the Medo-Persian Empire, ruled by the dynamic Cyrus the Great. In the image, this empire is symbolised in the silver breast and arms. The two arms suggest the two parts of the empire (the Mede and the Persian) cooperating as one, by the skill and diplomacy of Cyrus. This empire dominated the world for over two hundred years, from the capture of Babylon, in 539 BC, until the rise of Alexander the Great, in 331 BC. This identification of the second metal is supported by the later prophecy, where the ram is the symbol of the Medo-Persian Empire (8:3–4, 20). This fact in itself would scarcely be a surprise to Daniel. He would be familiar with the clear prophetic warnings, through Jeremiah the prophet, to Babylon, and the specific mention of the Medes (Jer. 51:11, 28) as the agent of their doom. Jeremiah was only adding his voice to the judgement announced by earlier thundering of Isaiah, when he cried, on behalf of Jehovah against Babylon, 'Behold, I will stir up the Medes against them' (Isa. 13:17).

The Medo-Persian Empire was not inferior to the Babylonian in military might – it conquered Babylon. It was not inferior in size – in acreage the Medo-Persian Empire was far greater than the Babylonian Empire.[11] Nor can the inferiority be related to wealth. While gold was plentiful in Babylon, silver was the currency of the trading world, the medium of exchange over the known world, and its possession was the measure of wealth of that day. Medo-Persia was recognised in its own day as the 'silver empire'. The taxes demanded from each satrapy (province) in the empire had to be paid to the imperial treasury in silver coinage. The whole tax system was extensive and efficient (11:2; Ezra 4:13). Medo-Persia accumulated vast resources in silver, upon which it drew for its extensive military campaigns. Silver was thus a most appropriate metal to represent this empire – and readily recognised in its day. The inferiority is indicated in the value of the metals: as silver is inferior to gold in value, where value reflects God's perfect standard, so Medo-Persia

[11] See maps, p. 682–683.

is inferior to Babylon in the nature of its rule.[12] In Babylon, rule was centred in one man, despotic and autocratic it is true, nevertheless, centralised and unified. The very fact that Medo-Persia embraced two disparate peoples, who were scattered over 127 provinces governed by 127 princes (satraps), virtually independent rulers (6:1; Est. 1:1), showed that it lacked the central control evidenced in Babylon. Autocratic rule, when in the hands of God's man, is the ideal – Babylon portrayed this in principle, but in practice, in the hands of man, it was always a failure. The oligarchic rule of Medo-Persia, where the power was in the hands of a few ruling families, did not even approach the ideal of God – it was inferior to Babylon in the type of rule exercised.

Verse 39 (b) The Belly and Thighs of Brass

It has been pointed out, from recent archaeological research, that the Aramaic word used here indicates bronze (an alloy of copper and tin).[13] This is the third kingdom in the sequence, and the prophecy is 'shall bear rule over all the earth'. Little is said about this kingdom here, but it will be identified later, under the portrayal of the rough he-goat (8:21). History leaves us in no doubt that the third world-empire is the Grecian Empire, under Alexander the Great. Alexander came from the land of Macedonia, a little known mountain region in Northern Greece, and, in one swift campaign, brought the mighty Medo-Persia under his personal control. Crossing the Hellespont in 334 BC with not more than 50,000 infantry and 5,500 cavalry he attacked the mighty empire of Medo-Persia under Darius III.[14] A superb tactical genius on the battlefield, Alexander, in eight decisive battles, defeated every army raised against him, buried Darius, and brought the constituent parts of that great empire under his sway. Babylon, still the capital of Babylonia, but now under Persian rule (see comments at 6:1), surrendered to Alexander in 331 BC. A Greek Empire appears in the Divine timeline when Jerusalem is captured.

That this empire should be represented by the metal alloy bronze is entirely fitting. The Greeks used this metal extensively and had

[12] Accepting the literal translation 'lower than you' could point to a lower status in dignity. Some have tried to interpret this in the moral realm, some in the economic realm. Keil gives the best interpretation describing it as 'lack of inner unity', which agrees with the suggestion in the comments above. See Keil *in loc.*

[13] 'Brass', *UBD*, p. 733.

[14] *OCD*, p. 86.

trained a highly-skilled workforce to produce it. Greek soldiers wore bronze armour. They had bronze helmets, breastplates, shields and swords. The Greek phalanx, a wheeling line of bronze-clad warriors, sometimes with interlocked shields, led by Alexander, his armour shining in the sun, put the might of Medo-Persia to the sword. The Greek Empire was far more extensive than the Medo-Persian, as Alexander pushed his army, not only to the limit of its endurance, but beyond it, to conquer Asia and penetrate as far as the Indus River in India. Only the near mutiny of his Macedonian veterans prevented him from pushing further west.[15]

It is interesting to see that not only the belly was of bronze, but the thighs as well. God was surely indicating that this empire, in its later stages, would be divided. This was exactly what happened. Alexander scarcely survived his conquest of Persia, and returned to Babylon, where he died when 33 years of age. His kingdom, as will be shown,[16] was eventually divided after twenty years of warfare, among four of his warring generals (8:22), who each established his own empire. Only two of these empires are important to scriptural history, and the interesting point is that they were located east and west of Babylon. The one to the east of Babylon had its base in Syria; the one to the west of Babylon was centred in Egypt. If the base is switched to Jerusalem, as will be the case when the history of Israel is in view (as in chapter 11), then these two enemies become the King of the North (Syria) and the King of the South (Egypt).

Verse 40 'And the fourth kingdom shall be strong as iron'

While the legs are mentioned in the description (v. 33), here the emphasis falls on the material – 'strong as iron'. In the light of history again, the fourth empire must be identified as Rome, and iron is certainly a very fitting representation of the Roman Empire. From its arrival on the prophetic stage, by the subjugation of the last vestiges of Alexander's Grecian Empire by 146 BC, until the fall of the Western Roman Empire to the Ostrogoths in AD 476 or, especially if we go on to the fall of the Eastern Roman Empire (Byzantine) the better part of a thousand years later, in AD 1453, it displayed an implacability in the early years, and a durability in later years, but rarely seen in world-dominating empires. Rome replaced the bronze weapons of the Persian and Grecian armies by the much

[15] Fox, *Alexander the Great*, p. 364.
[16] See Appendix 5.

more durable and harder metal. Iron was used for the shields, the swords and the helmets of its legions. In fact the *pilum* (both pike and javelin) was a distinctive Roman weapon, and consisted of a stout iron head, with a long iron collar, fitted to a wooden shaft.[17] The deliberate double emphasis in this passage is striking, and leaves not a doubt as to the power of Rome. 'Forasmuch as iron breaketh in pieces and subdueth all things: and as iron that breaketh all these, shall it break in pieces and bruise.' It takes but a little imagination to hear, in this statement, the tramp, tramp, tramp of the iron-clad legions of Rome, swinging along the straight Roman highways of the empire, followed by the clash of the iron-pointed *pilum* on the iron shields, as the legions marched into battle in *testudo* formation, on the battlefields of the expanding empire. This would be followed by the shrieks of the nations, crushed by the power of Rome moving to world dominion. At that period the strength of Rome shattered every opposing nation, and its strength was evidenced by its durability. Babylon and its empire dominated the world for little over 100 years. The Medo-Persian Empire stood for around two hundred years and the Grecian Empire not much more than 130 years, while Rome, before the east-west division, as Republic and Empire, ruled the world for over five hundred years.

What has been revealed by God through the image and the interpretation was all prophecy: from this year (603 BC), the events lie in the future. From our perspective this part, from the Babylonian Empire to the Roman Empire, has become history, and what an accurate history it is. Four world empires have followed each other on the world stage – the Babylonian Empire, the Medo-Persian Empire, the Grecian Empire and the Roman Empire.

However, it is now necessary for the understanding of this chapter to pose two questions. The first question concerns the teaching of the image – what exactly is portrayed in the image? The second question concerns the timing in the image. For us, prophecy in the image has already become history; at what point, for us, does the image become prophetic again? The question concerns the time period presented in the image. If it does become prophetic for us, then there must be a time break in the image, but where does it fall? Since the answers to these two questions must come from communications given to Daniel subsequent to this date (for example chapter 9, in 538 BC) or from NT Scriptures, it has been

[17] Boutflower, *In and Around the Book of Daniel*, p. 32.

when she writes, 'Some commentators have thought that the division of the legs and toes in this last kingdom should be interpreted, but again these are part of the symbolism of the human figure, which would not be complete without them.'[18] This seems reasonable, until it is pointed out that the two arms of silver have significance with regard to the Medes and the Persians in that empire. Also, the division in both the Grecian and Roman empires (see comments on v. 39) do have a real significance in history. In connection with the ten toes, it is enough to point out that the final ruler of this empire is described as a beast with ten horns (7:7; Rev. 13:1). It is therefore a very valid inference, and perfectly justifiable, that the numbers, though not stressed, have an interpretative significance. The Grecian Empire has the two thighs that become two legs in the Roman Empire, and these two legs end in five toes on each foot.

Not observing the necessary time break in the image, expositors have tried to interpret the clay in terms of the Roman Empire, and interpretation has varied as the years have brought a variety of factors to light. Some expositors have suggested that the metals of the image reflect four different kinds of leadership, which is true – autocracy in Babylon, oligarchy in Medo-Persia, democracy in Greece and imperial in Rome.[19] They suggest that each form of leadership has weaknesses, and, when tensions arise internally, the nations can fracture. Every one of these nations suffered from internal dissension and was divided for political reasons.[20] This is perfectly correct, and this fact alone rules out political differences as an interpretation of the clay. These differences have been present in all the previous empires; the clay must represent something not present in the earlier empires.

In more recent years, other sources of weakness in empires have been suggested as interpretation of the clay. Some have suggested that the clay-iron picture should be interpreted as the attempted cohesion between: (a) dictatorship and democracy, or (b) conservatism and socialism, with socialism moving to communism. Some have suggested that the iron and clay could possibly represent different peoples; in the advocacy of this view the expression 'mingle themselves with the seed of men' has been interpreted as

[18] Baldwin, *Daniel*, p. 104.
[19] Ironside, *Daniel*, p. 24.
[20] Wood, *A Commentary on Daniel*, p. 70.

intermarriage between different races.[21] However, an eminent Hebrew scholar insists that the word 'seed' must be taken here in its agricultural meaning.[22] When the seed sown in the field is mixed, the end result is a crop that is impossible to separate at harvest and thus is good for nothing. With this in mind, it is better to see in the clay, not two peoples, but two cultures, brought together in an unnatural union. A union being eventually forged, the iron and the clay (tile) are presented together in such a way as makes an onlooker think they have been successfully joined. From the outside it appears attractive and decorative, but inherently it carries a fatal weakness.

Coming down to the present time, the great interest of many governments, particularly in western lands today, is to develop an integrated society, embracing every culture from round the world. Most will admit that, despite tremendous efforts, this policy has very largely been a failure; men are trying to integrate elements that are so fundamentally different that they cannot merge. When sown together (v. 43) the result is a product that is pleasing to the eye, but very fragile. From the perspective of the twenty-first century, this seems a very reasonable interpretation of the clay, and throws an interesting sidelight on the efforts, in our day, in Britain, to form a multicultural society, with Islam as one of the cultures. It is suggested that Islam may be represented in the clay. Most assuredly Islam in recent years has become a power on the world stage. Existing quietly from the seventh century AD until the twentieth century, suddenly it has emerged in recent years as a force that, while crossing national boundaries, yet remains distinct, and cannot be assimilated into any existing culture. It is suggested that here it appears for the first time in the prophetic picture.

This suggestion is made with due caution, recalling the failed suggestions of earlier years, and recognising that things can change rapidly in world affairs. Yet the recent history of Islam seems to fit the picture. Mohammed, the founder of Islam, lived and taught in the seventh century AD (c. 570–c. 632). This was therefore long after the gospel had gone round the earth. For over thirteen hundred years it has been in the background of world affairs. The point of change came when Israel was recognised as an independent nation, on May 14, 1948, by the decree of the United Nations – passed by the General Assembly six months before (November 1947). Since then,

[21] Young, *The Prophecy of Daniel*, p. 77

[22] Keil and Delitzsch, *Commentary on the Old Testament*, Vol. 9, p. 109.

a terrifying militancy has stirred Islamic lands, so that their one declared interest is to wipe this nation of Israel off the world map. Israel never has been on the maps published in Islamic countries – they recognise no such nation. Militant Islam in the political realm has been followed by cultural Islam in the area of emigration – most recently to the lands in the west. The Islamic population figures for many European countries, the United Kingdom included, as well as Canada and the USA, are so high percentage-wise that governments in democratic nations have to take these voters into their calculations. The strength of firm government (the iron) has to be modified by the need to adjust to that which will splinter when pressure is applied (the potters' clay). The geographical division of east and west has given way to a cultural division that divides peoples, not ethnically or politically, but so radically that they cannot merge, and to mingle is impossible. Any outward appearance of strength is, like the pottery of Babylon, just an outer façade, and liable to shatter under external impact. It is important to notice that clay seems to predominate in the toes. The significance of this will be shown in the interpretation, and will stress the fact Islam has developed under two terms: 'militant' and 'moderate', and these two identities of the same Islam are dealt with at different points in the timeline.

Verses 44–45 There would be a strange stillness in the audience chamber as Daniel reached the dramatic climax of the dream. Nebuchadnezzar must have been wondering about that stone that smote the image on the feet. Had he wondered about: (a) the origin of the stone: where did it come from? He would reason that the description 'cut out without hands' suggests the supernatural; Deity must be involved; (b) the mission of the stone: the deliberate destruction of that which represented the dominion of man; (c) the destiny of the stone: the stone that became a great mountain to fill the whole earth; it would seem to take over the world.

All the questions of Nebuchadnezzar are answered in one brief statement: 'In the days of these kings shall the God of heaven set up a kingdom.' The fifth mention of the God of heaven in the chapter indicates the One Who now steps in to introduce a Person symbolised as a 'stone', Who will arrive unexpectedly, to smash the final manifestation of kingship on earth and replace it with a 'mountain', symbolising the Kingdom of God. This one statement shows the origin, the power and the destiny of the stone. Four prophetic statements distinguish this Kingdom from all the earthy kingdoms that have gone before:

(a) It 'shall never be destroyed'. No invader will ever overthrow it. This takes note of its protection.

(b) It 'shall not be left to other people'. No successor will ever be required for the throne. There can never be any diminution of its acreage through dividing the inheritance. This speaks of its preservation.

(c) 'It shall break in pieces and consume all these kingdoms'. All the ten kingdoms that, under the Man of Sin, had opposed the returning King will be dealt with judicially. Their kingdom structures will be destroyed, their citizens judged; they can never again rebel against heaven. This precedes the establishment of the Kingdom of God. This shows its power.

(d) 'It shall stand for ever'. It will never fade nor fall, as other kingdoms have done down the ages. This Kingdom goes into the eternal state. What a destiny lies before its citizens. This tells of its permanence.

The time of the arrival of this Kingdom is given as 'in the days of these kings'. The trouble is that no king or kings have been specifically mentioned in the chapter. Some commentators suggest that this looks back and refers to the kings of the four empires mentioned. This is not reasonable, as the only king mentioned is King Nebuchadnezzar, and to introduce the others at this point neither makes sense nor fits the context. The only logical and contextual explanation is to remember, as shown, that the feet and ten toes of the image represent the end-time kingdom of earth. It has already been shown that this links this end-time empire with the ten-horned beast that Daniel saw come out of the sea (7:7) and the ten-horned beast that John saw come out of the sea (Rev. 13:1). The ten horns in each picture speak of ten kings reigning simultaneously. Thus our thoughts are directed again to the end-time kingdom, and that eschatological moment when Christ comes back to earth (Rev. 20:11) to overthrow all earthly kingdoms and set up His Kingdom – the Kingdom of God. In the days when ten kings are aligned behind the mighty emperor, the leader of end-time rebellion, this Stone will strike to establish the Kingdom of God. In the destruction effected by the Stone every vestige of dominion that men wielded, whether as iron, bronze, clay, silver, or gold (note the order in the text) will be totally smashed and removed. While the King is seen as a 'stone'; the Kingdom of God is seen as a 'mountain'.

Those who would deny a literal Kingdom on earth, known under the broad title of 'amillennialists', fail to see that, as the four preceding kingdoms have been literal earthy kingdoms, this final Kingdom must be of the same character. It cannot be spiritualised; it too must be a literal Kingdom on earth; otherwise words can be made to mean anything we like. Further, this Kingdom arrives dramatically, by the literal coming of Christ to earth and the literal destruction of the armies of earth (Rev. 19:11–21). The Kingdom thus established is the literal Kingdom that has been the subject of the prophecies of Scripture down the ages and the subject of the prayers of saints when they have cried, under the despotic rule of men, 'Thy kingdom come!' Then it will have arrived, in the fulfilment of prophecy, for the pleasure of saints, and graced by the presence of the Sovereign – where God will find delight in His people. John F. Walvoord sums up the chapter concisely: 'Only the premillennial position, which assigns this event as coinciding with the second advent of Christ, gives literal fulfilment to the symbolism involved in the destruction of the image.'[23]

In his final word, Daniel ends as he began, by assuring the king that neither the dream nor the interpretation came from him, but from 'the great God'. Daniel is only His spokesman. He assures the king that the dream is 'certain' – true, and the interpretation 'sure' – trustworthy. By stressing the authenticity and the reliability of the revelation in the dream and the interpretation, Daniel wants Nebuchadnezzar to face up to the implications of what has been disclosed to him. One can imagine the stillness in the audience chamber, as every eye moves from Daniel to the king as they await his response.

Verses 46–49 The Impression

Verse 46 The Reaction of the King

That stillness would deepen as, with total shock, the court sees that mighty monarch of Babylon prostrate himself before a youth – and not just any youth – but a Jewish captive at that! Unbelievable! The word 'worshipped', as shown by the usage of the same word in the next chapter (3:3–7, 28), must not be reduced to the weaker 'showed respect for'. It is the Aramaic word for the worship of deity, and this usage is supported by the command of the king to offer an

[23] Walvoord, *Revelation*, p. 76

'oblation' – a bloodless sacrifice (Ezra 7:17) and 'sweet odours' (incense) to Daniel. Both of these offerings were, in Babylonian practice, reserved for deity. Many commentators take the view that Daniel should have refused these honours, but that is to misunderstand the situation. Daniel recognised that the king was honouring him simply as the spokesman for his God, and, on this ground, accepted the offering as the genuine acknowledgement by the king of the God of Daniel. This becomes absolutely clear from what the king says in the next verse. There is not the slightest suggestion of Daniel being acknowledged as God.

Verses 47–49 The Response of the King

Verse 47 Confession of the King

Doubtless, Daniel must have felt some disappointment that the king has not shown repentance and asked questions about his own future. However, it must have been with thankfulness that he heard the mightiest of earthly monarchs at that time recognise, to a surprising degree, the God of Israel. The king had learned, in an unforgettable way, that the God Whom Daniel served could reveal secrets (mysteries) beyond the reach of men, but, more importantly, he had recognised His supremacy ('God of gods') and His Sovereignty ('Lord of kings'). The king admitted that Daniel's God was absolutely unique and outranked the pantheon of gods worshipped in Babylon. What Nebuchadnezzar failed to see, and it would take further dealings of God with him before he would bow the knee and admit it, was that Daniel's God was the only God.

Verse 48 Gratitude of the King

The king kept the public promise he had made in the presence of his court (v. 6). 'The king made Daniel a great man' may be rightly translated as 'placed Daniel in a high position' (*NIV*). This could be nothing other than an honoured place in the inner court of the Babylonian Empire. In our day we would speak of his promotion to cabinet rank. In keeping with this instant promotion there would be so many things needed by one who was moving from obscurity to prominence. The king, with lavish hand, bestowed these additional gifts upon this former captive. Two responsibilities were attached to this rank. One was administrative – 'ruler over the whole province of Babylon'. The other was advisory – 'chief of the governors over all the wise men of Babylon'. This latter role was the logical result of the part Daniel had just played in the unfolding and interpretation of the dream, and, incidentally, in doing this, saving the lives of these very men over whom he is now promoted. God could trust a man who had shown such purpose of heart (1:8) to bear witness for Him in the capital of the pagan world.

Verse 49 Request of Daniel

Recognising the part his three companions had played in the drama of this chapter and their fellowship in prayer, Daniel now asks for appointments for Shadrach, Meshach, and Abed-nego in the province of Babylon. Two things may be noted: (a) Daniel has accepted the promotion by the king and acts immediately in the confidence of its reality; (b) Daniel ensures that the appointment of his three friends is seen to come directly from the king. He does not wish to be accused of favouritism at some later stage. The statement that 'Daniel sat in the gate of the king' simply means that Daniel exercised his cabinet rank at the royal court, in constant attendance upon the king.

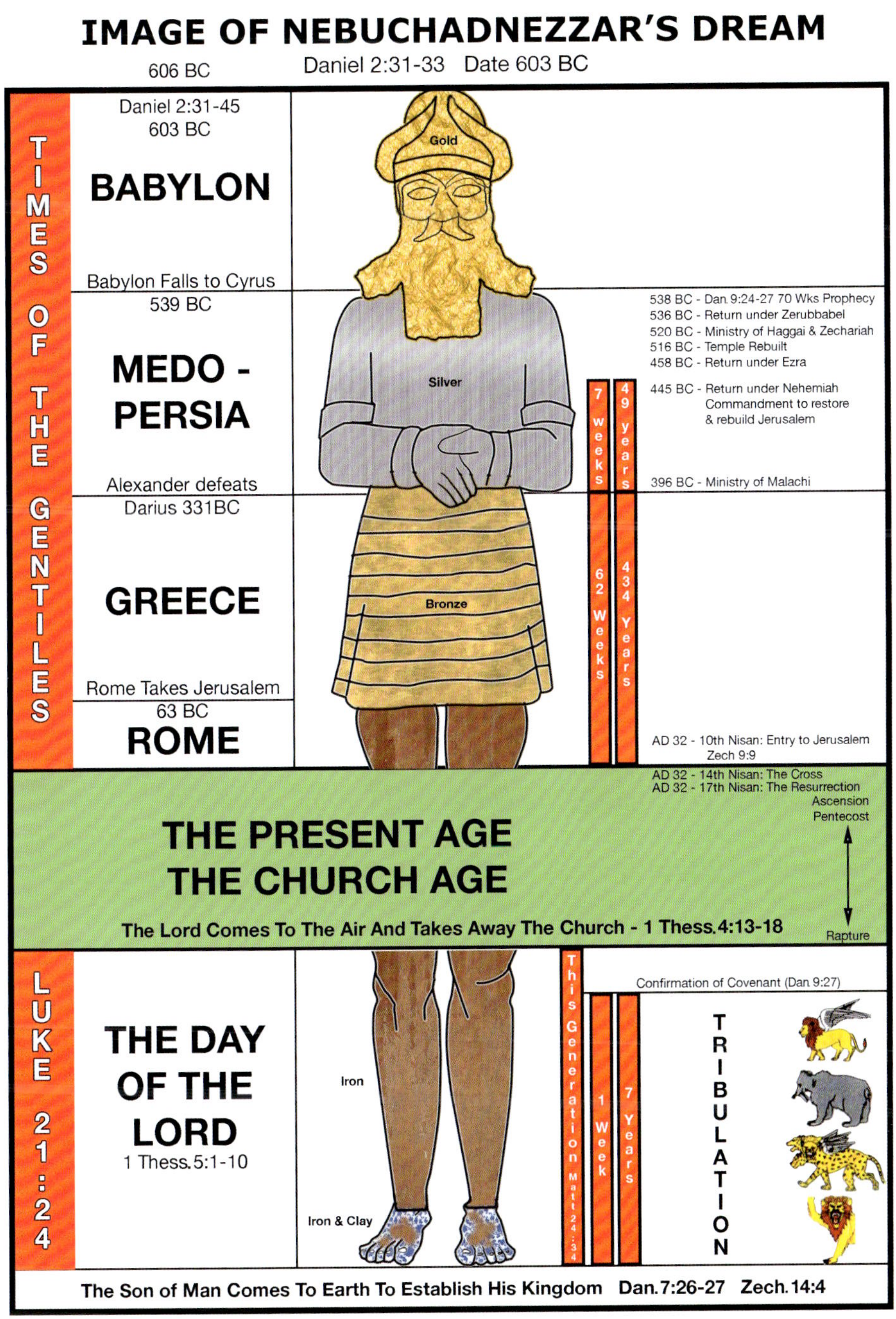
IMAGE OF NEBUCHADNEZZAR'S DREAM
606 BC
Daniel 2:31-33 Date 603 BC
TIMES OF THE GENTILES
Daniel 2:31-45
603 BC
BABYLON
Babylon Falls to Cyrus
539 BC
MEDO - PERSIA
Alexander defeats
Darius 331BC
GREECE
Rome Takes Jerusalem
63 BC
ROME
Gold
Silver
Bronze
7 Weeks
49 years
62 Weeks
434 Years
538 BC - Dan 9:24-27 70 Wks Prophecy
536 BC - Return under Zerubbabel
520 BC - Ministry of Haggai & Zechariah
516 BC - Temple Rebuilt
458 BC - Return under Ezra
445 BC - Return under Nehemiah
Commandment to restore
& rebuild Jerusalem
396 BC - Ministry of Malachi
AD 32 - 10th Nisan: Entry to Jerusalem
Zech 9:9
AD 32 - 14th Nisan: The Cross
AD 32 - 17th Nisan: The Resurrection
Ascension
Pentecost
Rapture
THE PRESENT AGE
THE CHURCH AGE
The Lord Comes To The Air And Takes Away The Church - 1 Thess.4:13-18
LUKE 21:24
THE DAY
OF THE
LORD
1 Thess.5:1-10
Iron
Iron & Clay
This Generation Matt 24:34
1 Week
7 Years
Confirmation of Covenant (Dan 9:27)
TRIBULATION
The Son of Man Comes To Earth To Establish His Kingdom Dan.7:26-27 Zech.14:4

EXCURSUS

Question 1 Teaching in the Image: What is portrayed in the Image?

A number of points must be kept in mind if the image is to be properly understood:

(a) The dream is given to King Nebuchadnezzar, who himself is symbolised in the head of gold, so what is presented must be thought of in terms of 'rule'. His personal replacement by another, who is followed by another, and so on, directs our thought, beyond individuals, to the abstract idea of 'rule', or 'kingship'. It soon becomes clear that these rulers are supreme in the aspect of 'rule' they exercise, for they control more than one nation, so the thought expands to the idea of 'dominion'. The 'dominion' is held by a man over the nations of the world of his day. So it is suggested that the image must represent the abstract idea of 'kingship', or 'dominion', vested in a man.

(b) It is also to be noted that it is kingship within a certain limited period. The period in view is when Israel and Jerusalem are under Gentile domination. The intention of Jehovah was that the nation of Israel should be 'head of the nations' (Deut. 28:13). When Israel was such a nation, then a king of the line of David would reign, with Jerusalem as the capital city – the only geographic place on earth where God had put His Name (Deut. 12:4–7). The purpose of God has never changed: that through David's line in Israel there would come a King into Whose hand God would commit the sovereignty of earth. This is evident in the prophetic word through Balaam: 'He hath not beheld iniquity in Jacob, neither hath he seen perverseness in Israel: the LORD his God is with him, and the shout of a king is among them' (Num. 23:21), and again: 'There shall come a Star out of Jacob, and a Sceptre shall rise out of Israel' (Num. 24:17). Because of their disobedience to the Word of God, the nation of Israel has been removed from the map, the citizens deported, and the city of Jerusalem destroyed. God has allowed a Gentile king to hold a sovereignty that includes Jerusalem but is exercised on a worldwide scale. The first Gentile king to exercise such authority is King Nebuchadnezzar, from Babylon. The image shows that he will be followed by three others in succession – the four metals represent four rulers and their kingdoms. It will also cover the period of the rule – the specific period in which God will permit such worldwide dominion. The period therefore runs from

Nebuchadnezzar's capture of Jerusalem (606 BC) until God reclaims kingship through the Messiah, Whom He will send into the world. These four metals therefore represent the four kingdoms that God allows to exercise this worldwide dominion until Christ returns as King, to claim His crown. This time period will be identified by the Lord Jesus Christ as the 'times of the Gentiles' (Lk. 21:24).

(c) There are, therefore, but four empires that will exercise this dominion within this limited time period. The length of each reign runs from the capture of Babylon until its loss to their successor empire within the period. When they come into this Divine timeline (by taking control of Babylon) they are represented in the image by different metals. This will have important implications for the final empire, which has a metal with an alien material in it – clay.

(d) The differing nature of the metals suggests that these kingdoms differ from each other in significant ways. The following features indicate some of the differences suggested by the metals:

Value of the Metals The most valuable of the metals is in the head – gold. There is evident depreciation in the series as silver replaces gold, the silver gives way to the alloy bronze, and this in turn is replaced by iron. The teaching to be drawn from this can be noticed in the phrase 'inferior to thee' (v. 39), spoken to Nebuchadnezzar. It cannot mean size, as a glance at the maps provided at the end of this volume will show; in fact, each succeeding empire is far more extensive than its predecessor; the fourth empire is by far the largest in area. So the value cannot lie in the area of the empire geographically, nor, it might be added, in the fields of demography or economy.

As suggested in the comments on the text (v. 39), Scripture makes it plain that the Divine ideal of kingship is autocracy – rule in the hands of one man. This is reflected in the first Adam (Ps. 8:5), who failed so grievously, but it will be manifest fully in the second Man, the last Adam (1 Cor. 15:45), when God commits all into His hand. Thus it must be the quality of the rule, as measured by a Divine standard, that is emphasised in the deteriorating value of the metals.

The following table is of interest in consideration of the quality of the rule in the four kingdoms:

Gold	Babylon	Autocratic rule	Rule in the hands of one (5:18 – One Autocrat) A Personality – sent of God
Silver	Medo-Persia	Oligarchic rule	Rule in the hands of a few (6:1 – Twelve princes) Privilege – privileged families

(Aristocratic families controlled royalty by dynastic marriages)

Bronze	Greece	Democratic rule	Rule in the hands of people (8:21 – the Great Horn) People – elected by parliament

Copying the democratic policies of the Greek cities Thebes, Sparta, Athens and Corinth, an elected Government of Macedonia sitting in Aegae (on the central plain of Macedonia) had, in theory, to approve the nomination of Alexander in place of his murdered father. Since Alexander had been nominated by the whole of the army, there was never any question about their acceptance of him as king.

Iron	Rome	Imperialistic rule	Rule based on military power (v. 40 – Power) Power of armed force

(From the days of Julius Caesar (c. 101–44 BC), the crossing of the Rubicon, and the passing of the Roman Republic into the Roman Empire, the authority for rule was undoubtedly the allegiance of the legions – military power ruled in Rome.)

Weight of the metals The heaviest metal is at the top. The specific gravity measurements are as follows: gold (19), silver (11), bronze (8.5), and iron (7.8). With decreasing specific gravity in the metals there would be a tendency for the image to be top heavy – an inherent instability. Dominion in the hands of fallen man seems generally to carry less authority, or the 'inherent dignity' that each empire commands, as empire succeeds empire. This is readily observed even in the histories of each of these empires.

Hardness of the metals Decreasing values and decreasing weights are countered by an increasing hardness of the metals. Iron is by far the hardest. This would suggest that, as empire gave way to empire, the lot of the subject peoples became increasingly hard to endure. The life of subject peoples became increasingly difficult as world dominion passed from Babylon to Medo-Persia, to Greece, and finally to Rome. The captives in Babylon from Nebuchadnezzar's time, with brief intermissions of more kindly rule, passed through increasing subjection, until they were slaves without any rights, under the Roman Empire. Dominion in the hands of man becomes increasingly cruel.

Brightness of the Metals There can be little question that the polished gold has the highest reflecting power of all the metals – in the sunlight it would be a blaze of light. This blaze of light from the image diminishes considerably as the eye moves from gold to silver to bronze to iron. The decreasing brightness may suggest the diminishing respect given to the Word of God in these empires. The dealings of God with Nebuchadnezzar left a testimony with the whole nation (4:1–3). Darius of the Medo-Persian Empire (6:25–27) witnessed to the God of Daniel as the living God. Josephus bears witness to the effect of Daniel's prophecy upon Alexander the Great, the founder of the Grecian Empire, and even Herod the Great, in the Roman Empire, believed what the Word of God said about the birth of Christ (Mt. 2:16). This brightness of the Word diminishing can be viewed in the opposite way – the decreasing light of faith in Scripture would permit the increasing darkness of unbelief as empire gives way to empire. Study, for example, the way Daniel was honoured in Babylon and how he was respected under Darius the Mede. Compare how the saints in Israel were treated in the later stages of the Grecian Empire under Antiochus Epiphanes and in the times of the Maccabees. Study how faithful Jews were treated under the Roman Empire and we stand before the cross of Calvary under the Roman Governor. A little further consideration takes us into the final end-time kingdom of the Antichrist and the treatment meted out to the saints of that age (Rev. 13:7). Decreasing light and increasing darkness are featured in this image.

Note (a) The Clay

Since clay is not a metal, it is strangely out of place in this list. In all the features mentioned above, except weight, it is obvious that the clay would rate close to zero. The interpretation of the clay is discussed in the comments at verses 41–43.

Note (b) The Deterioration

As kingdom succeeded kingdom down the time period under consideration, suggested as the times of the Gentiles, each king would fall increasingly short of the Divine ideal, and become less and less representative of what God intended. This will be seen when the final end-time ruler comes onto the scene. He will be the embodiment of dominion committed to man, but by that time the deterioration seen in this table will have reached its low point and will be fully displayed in the man identified as the 'Man of Sin' (2 Thess. 2:3–4). This man will be the very antithesis of what God intended man to be, as reflected in the Second Man – Christ. This earthy man is the one who will be replaced by the Second Man Who 'is from heaven' (1 Cor. 15:47, *NET*) – identified in this book as Son of Man (7:13–14). The dominion God intended will be fully displayed in a man, but that Man will be God's Man. With such a King there can be no deterioration in the Kingdom, and it is revealed – 'whose kingdom is an everlasting kingdom' (7:26–27).

Question 2 Time in the Image: What period is surveyed in the Image?

It has already been stressed that this image shows the dominion of earth allowed of God to be exercised by Gentile nations, from the capture of Jerusalem by Babylonian power, in the person of King Nebuchadnezzar, until the Son of Man takes the Kingdom (7:27) and rules earth from Jerusalem. This is the consummation of the purpose of God for earth in time. That consummation is depicted graphically by the stone in Nebuchadnezzar's dream, first striking the image on the toes and then smashing the whole image, to replace it on earth. The implicit timeline runs from 606 BC to the coming of Christ as the Son of Man to take the Kingdom. So the image covers the time referred to by the Lord as the time when Israel had lost sovereignty and earth has a Gentile ruler – the 'times of the Gentiles'.

Since Daniel had identified Nebuchadnezzar as the head of gold he would realise that this period of Gentile dominion over Israel must begin with the capture of Jerusalem in 606 BC. This is the moment when Nebuchadnezzar comes into the Divine timeline. For Daniel this is history. The further kingdoms seen in the image are prophecy to Daniel. As the image is viewed from this age, of the Church, over two and a half millennia later, it must be recognised that the period represented from the head of gold (Nebuchadnezzar) down to the legs of iron (Roman Empire) is now history. It can be followed down the years with a history book in hand – the rise and fall of the empires of Babylon, Medo-Persia and Greece, until the Roman Empire comes on to the scene and brings to an end the Seleucid dynasty, the last remnant of the Grecian Empire, about 64 BC.

In Daniel's third vision (9:24–27), Daniel is given another prophetic timeline, which would date the coming to the nation of the promised Messiah – the prophecy of the 'seventy weeks'. This prophetic timeline runs from a fixed date, given as 'the going forth of the commandment to restore and build Jerusalem'. From this date in history, the time span is given as 490 years, until all the promises of a coming King and a coming Kingdom are fulfilled in the Person of the expected Messiah. That means that from the given starting date – shown in the comments *in loc.* to be the 1st *Nisan* in the year 445 BC – to the consummation is a period of 490 years. The consummation is when the Messiah deals with the desolator (9:27), the last of the Gentile kings, and takes the Kingdom. This must be exactly the same point at which the image is smashed by the stone.

Thus both these timelines (one implicit in this image, related to the Kingdom, and the other explicit in the seventy weeks prophecy, related to the King), while commencing from two different dates in history (the image timeline at 606 BC and the seventy weeks prophecy timeline at 445 BC) both conclude at the same point – the establishing of God's King in God's Kingdom on earth.

The timelines may be summarised thus: (a) the image timeline is from 606 BC to the realisation of the Kingdom; (b) the seventy weeks prophecy timeline is from 445 BC to the recognition of the King.

Conclusions

1. Since the seventy weeks prophecy, given as 490 years, is to commence in 445 BC and close with God's Kingdom under God's King, there must be a lengthy time break in the period. This time break has been carefully marked by Gabriel the angelic messenger in the revelation of the seventy weeks prophecy to Daniel (9:24–27). It is made clear that the time break must fall between the sixty-ninth and the seventieth week. Having marked the close of the sixty-ninth week as the presentation of the Messiah, two events are mentioned – the cutting off of Messiah and the destruction of the city and sanctuary (Jerusalem and the Temple) – both of which are

STRUCTURE IN THE BOOK OF DANIEL

Chapter 1	Chapter 2	Chapter 3	Chapter 4	Chapter 5	Chapter 6	Chapter 7	Chapter 8	Chapter 9	Chapter 10	Chapter 11	Chapter 12
Daniel and Friends Tests of Faith			Daniel and Foes Triumphs of Faith			Vision 1	Vision 2	Vision 3	Vision 4		
A King's Demand	A King's Dream	A King's Decree	Nebuchad-nezzar Pride	Belshazzar Profanity	Darius Presumption	FOCUS: Little Horn	FOCUS: King of fierce countenance	FOCUS: Time of consummation	'The Time of the End' (Dan.8:17; 11:35,40; 12:4)		
Hebrew	Aramaic	Aramaic	Aramaic	Aramaic	Aramaic	Aramaic	Hebrew	Hebrew	Hebrew		
HISTORY FORESHADOWS PROPHECY						PROPHECY FORETELLS HISTORY					

Hebrew Indicates chapter written in Hebrew

Aramaic Indicates chapter written in Aramaic

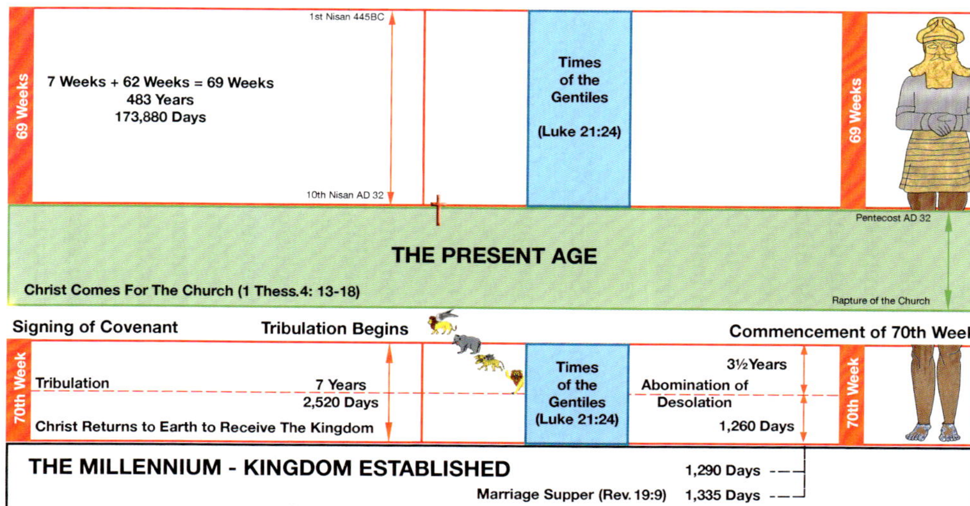

The present age closes at the Rapture, when the Lord comes to the air and the Church is called away (1 Thess. 4:13–18).

The seventieth week of Daniel's prophecy is the final period of seven years, before Christ comes back to the earth to establish the Kingdom. In the NT this period is called the Tribulation. In Daniel it is the seventieth week of the prophecy, and is divided thus:

	The Tribulation
The Commencement	The confirmation of a covenant with Israel
The Crisis	The 'Abomination of Desolation' in Jerusalem
The Consummation	The Son of Man takes the Kingdom

Right Side of Chart

The Image

Consider now the image, which to Daniel in Nebuchadnezzar's reign was all prophetic. For us, in the Church age, everything up to the point where the metal iron (symbolic of the Roman Empire) comes into the image has now become history. From the time of the taking of Jerusalem by King Nebuchadnezzar (606 BC), four empires have succeeded each other in rule over that city. These have been Babylon, followed by Medo-Persia, then Greece (through Alexander the Great), and finally the fourth kingdom, Rome, took over from the successors of Alexander the Great in the Greek Empire. This means that now the timeline has reached Messiah, in the time of the Roman Empire. As shown above, the last day of the sixty-ninth week of the prophecy was the tenth day of the month *Nisan* in AD 32. On this very day Christ rode into Jerusalem upon the ass, in fulfilment of the prophecy of Zechariah (Zech. 9:9) – presenting Himself as King.

Time Gap in the Image

This is where the time gap must begin also in the image. The clock of prophecy stopped at the close of the sixty-ninth week. This surely must mean that all that follows from AD 32 in the Roman Empire is irrelevant from the prophetic point of view. The time gap in the seventy weeks prophecy runs, as already shown, from AD 32 to a date in the future, when, the Church having been 'caught up' by her Lord (1 Thess. 4:17), the way is open for the confirmation of a covenant in Israel (9:27) that was intended to bring peace to that troubled land. The prophetic clock is restarted with the countdown of the seven-year Tribulation, until Christ takes the Kingdom.

The implication is that the period in the image from the timeline of the cross in AD 32 is not history for our time, but is still prophecy – from the legs to the feet and then to the toes is referring to conditions that will pertain in the period after the removal of the Church and the confirmation of the covenant and be evident before the Coming of Christ in glory in the Consummation. This prophecy points to the period around about the time of the signing of the covenant in Israel, when Israel comes back into the prophetic timeline and the clock of prophecy has been restarted! Therefore, there is no need to search for any correspondence in the history of the old Roman Empire for the 'legs' and then the 'feet and the toes' of the image. The interpretation of these three features lies in the future. This means that what is unfolded in verse 41 is not history – it has not yet been fulfilled – it is prophetic.

Failure to see exactly where the time gap must fall in the image has led to much speculation as to the historical significance of the legs and feet and toes. Identifying the iron correctly as the Roman Empire, it is assumed (reasonably) that it stands on two legs, even though this fact is not mentioned, nor is any interpretive point drawn from it. Many expositors conclude that this depicts the division of the Roman Empire when the Emperor Theodosius ruled. This emperor had left instructions that, on his death, the Roman Empire be divided between his two sons. A glance at dates will show that Theodosius died on January 17, AD 395, and left his son Honorius in charge of the Western Empire, with capital Rome, and his son Arcadius in charge of the Eastern Empire, with capital in Constantinople. Rome fell to the Ostrogoths in AD 476 – a date most historians agree marks the fall of the Western Roman Empire. Constantinople survived as capital of the Byzantine Empire until AD 1453. However interesting this division of the Roman Empire is, or however attractive it may be, as interpretation of the legs of the image, it simply cannot be the interpretation of what is envisaged here. If this political split in the Roman Empire is pictured in the two legs of the image, it might well be asked why then does the image not stand on one foot? If this line of interpretation is pursued, two further things must be looked for in the Roman Empire. First, the emergence of ten divisions of the empire under ten rulers, which must answer to the ten toes of the image. A second point is that history will have to show the entry of some alien and weakening factor into the Roman Empire, to interpret the clay. It is sufficient to make a commentator careful when it is realised that, no matter how painstakingly the history of the Roman Empire is researched, there are no clear indications of the evidence for either of these features in the history of that empire. Some have tried to either: (a) identify the clay as the moral degradation of the empire – such as portrayed by Gibbon;[24] or (b) contend that the rise of democracy in conflict with Roman imperialism weakened the empire before the invading Gothic armies. These interpretations carry little weight and savour of special pleading. When Scripture is compared with Scripture and permitted to speak for itself no special pleading is needed.

If the suggestion made above as to the timeline of the image – that it stops at the cross of Christ – is accepted, then it becomes clear that the two legs of the image do not, and cannot, reflect the political division of the later Roman Empire. The question then arises as to their interpretation – if any is needed. A clue to a possible interpretation lies in the fact that the division clearly begins in the Grecian Empire, with the mention of the thighs of bronze, and this same division pertains to the Roman Empire and becomes more evident in the feet and toes of the final stages of this empire. There never was any political division in Alexander's empire but, after his death, there arose a very clear geographic division in the Greek Empire. It is suggested that this is the division that is pictured in the image. John F. Walvoord, a valued expositor, supports this view and writes:

> the upper part of the legs represented the twofold stage of the last period of the Alexandrian Empire which specially concerned the Jews, namely Syria and Egypt. This was two-legged because it embraced two continents, or two major geographic areas, the East and the West – since the image is in Babylon. Rome continued to embrace lands that took the empire both eastwards to India and westwards to Britain.[25]

Thus the suggestion is that the two legs represent, not empires, but two geographic divisions in one empire, that began in Alexander's empire, was continued into the Roman Empire, and, by implication,

[24] Gibbon, *History of the Decline and Fall of the Roman Empire.*

[25] Walvoord, *Daniel: The Key to Prophetic Revelation*, p. 34.

will be continued into the last stages of the final world empire, seen in the feet and the ten toes. This final stage of empire will thus have two divisions, represented by the two legs, two feet, and then the divisions are seen finally as ten toes distributed geographically east and west of Jerusalem. In a further revelation granted to Daniel (10:1–12:4) it will be seen how vital this part of the image becomes in our understanding of this final empire under the last world leader.

Summary

Thus the conclusion can be summarised: when the moment arrives for the confirmation of the peace covenant in Israel, the moment indeed when the clock of prophecy is restarted, there will then be on earth a superpower seen under a super-man, of whom Nebuchadnezzar, Cyrus, Alexander and Caesar were but faint portraits. This empire will have certain particular features reminiscent of the Roman Empire, but going far beyond Rome. In this empire there will be present, first, an inherent east-west division that runs through, not just a continent, but the world scene – neither politically nor racially nor economically, but culturally. The dividing line would run through Babylon, where the image stood. Babylon has always been a centre of division. The second distinguishing feature of this empire will be that under the king or emperor will be ten kings or nations, united seemingly under one man. Yet this professed unity is so fragile – like pottery tile – that it will not stand the blow. This unification or globalisation in the latter times may well begin as an economic cooperation committee or confederation that then gives rise to a political unification of the constituent nations. This could lead to a global empire that excludes all the conflict arising from the nationalism of earth history. Whether economic or political, this empire has a built-in weakness that will be the third identifying feature that sets this empire apart from its predecessors. This weakness will be the interpretation of the clay in 'the feet and toes' (v. 41) and replicated in 'the toes of the feet' (v. 42). The suggested interpretation of the clay has been given in the comments under vv. 41–43.

Chapter 3

The King's Decree and the Worship of God

Nebuchadnezzar's Image – Preliminary Notes

1. The Dating of the Chapter – 601 BC

Many expositors take the view that the time interval between chapter 2 and chapter 3 is around twenty years.[1] The evidence for this is quite tenuous and rests entirely upon the Septuagint – the Greek translation of the OT – and especially upon the revision of that translation by Theodotion (second century AD), which links this chapter with the destruction of Jerusalem (2 Kgs 25:8–10), under Zedekiah. This took place in the nineteenth year of Nebuchadnezzar's reign, thus in 586 BC. On balance, all the evidence is against such a late dating and it is better to place it about two years or less after chapter 2, and thus in the year 601 BC. Daniel would then have been a youth of twenty-three years of age. The reasons for this earlier date are: (a) the chronological order of the chapters has never been questioned; (b) it follows, very naturally, the promotion of the three young men recorded in the last verse of chapter 2; (c) it is a reasonable inference that the king conceived the idea of the image from his dream, and it is most unlikely he would take twenty years to erect it; and (d) it is also possible, since the image demanded implicit and visible obedience to the king's command, that Nebuchadnezzar meant to use it as a loyalty test in his new administration. Had he not put his counsellors to a severe test as to their credibility? The early date in 601 BC, about four years into his reign, seems to fit the picture much better.

2. The Purpose of the Chapter

A. For the Saints

God always allows those who would testify for Him to be tested. These Hebrew boys were to testify for the living God in Babylon,

[1] Walvoord, *Daniel: The Key to Prophetic Revelation*, p. 80.

the city of dead idols. In chapter 1 they have been shown to be men of purpose (1:8); in chapter 2 they are clearly men of prayer (2:17–23); now they were to be tested as to whether they were mere time-servers in Babylon or men of principle, who would never break under pressure. These boys, now young men in their twenties, were to be faced with a terrifying test to reveal the calibre of their faith. The outcome would determine their usefulness to God in Babylon. The guiding principle of such a useful life must be obedience to the Word of God whatever the cost – even if that cost was a blazing fiery furnace. It will be seen how these young men came triumphantly through the test.

B. For the Sovereign

It soon becomes clear that there is a second purpose behind the events recorded in this chapter. In the events around the fiery furnace, God continues His gracious dealings with this idol-worshipping king. He has to learn, in real experience, not only of the ignorance, but now the impotence, of every idol. Already the king has learned that the God of Daniel is a Revealer of Secrets (2:47) – He is omniscient. Now he will learn that this same God is the Deliverer of Servants (3:28) – He is omnipotent. The spiritual education of King Nebuchadnezzar will be complete in chapter 4, when God has further dealings with him and he finally bows the knee in the presence of the Most High (4:34).

3. The Message of the Chapter

A. For all Time

Written clear and plain for all time is the message that God is able to deliver His people who put their confidence in Him. When, to the natural eye, the case appears hopeless, God can deliver those who trust Him. Yet God does not always answer His people with the kind of deliverance expected. That same confidence in their God enables true believers to accept dreadful disappointment, knowing that the ultimate result will be for their blessing and God's glory. This is clearly expressed by the young men in the words 'but if not' (v. 18). They are perfectly content to leave the outcome in the hand of their God. The twin truths of comfort in the power of God and confidence in the purpose of God stand out clearly in the chapter for any believer in any age. How often must believers have turned to this passage in the age of the Maccabean persecution, in the persecution under pagan Rome, and in the persecution under papal Rome, down to the times of the Covenanters, and even more recent persecutions, under communist regimes?

B. For a Particular Time

It has been pointed out in the Introduction that in Part 1 of this book there is no direct prophecy. What is recorded is history, but the events chosen for selection carry lessons for the future. There can be little question that in the seven-year Tribulation period, which comes into view in Part 2, there will be a time of terrible persecution and awful pressure upon believers in that day. A major issue in that period will be an image of a man erected on the wing of the Temple in Jerusalem (Rev. 13:13–17). Replicas of this image will be erected in parliament buildings, mayoral palaces and company board rooms across earth, as worship is demanded for a man. The Lord identifies this as 'the abomination of desolation'; a title first used in this book and quoted by the Lord (12:11; Mt. 24:15). Failure to yield worship to that image will mean death (Rev. 13:15) – it is unlikely to be a fiery furnace, but believers will face the block, or possibly the guillotine. Scripture speaks clearly: 'I saw the souls of them that were beheaded for the witness of Jesus, and for the word of God, and which had not worshipped the beast, neither his image' (Rev. 20:4). Conditions under Nebuchadnezzar foreshadow this time, and the lessons from this chapter will be a source of comfort and confidence to the saints of that future day; in the rest of this book much will be learned about the personality and the power of the despotic end-time ruler. For believers of that day to see their circumstances so clearly pictured in this prophetic book will be a source of great strength, knowing that their God is still the same omnipotent and omniscient God. This truth will be a stay to souls in a darker day yet to come.

C. A Particular Test

It may seem somewhat strange, but there is no record of any Babylonian king claiming deity. Alexander the Great in his later years was moving in that direction,[2] and the later Seleucids – the Greek dynasty that followed Alexander, with their capital in Antioch, demanded worship, as did the later Caesars. However,

[2] O'Brien, *Alexander the Great: The Invisible Enemy*, p. 201.

Nebuchadnezzar, even after all his victories and conquests, never personally demanded worship but gave the honour to the gods. After the fall of Jerusalem, he built a new temple at tremendous expense for his favourite god – Marduk. The inference is that while the word 'worship' occurs a number of times times in the chapter, it is not worship to him personally that is demanded. The image in the mind of Nebuchadnezzar represented the state – mighty Babylon. In subsequent years his building projects would transform the city (4:30), but already it filled his mind; this image is certainly his representation of 'the golden city' – the name well known in the world of that day. To worship the image would be to acknowledge Nebuchadnezzar as the embodied representative of the state, and to glorify the patron god of Babylon – Marduk. With this understanding, it becomes clear that King Nebuchadnezzar is presenting the act of obeisance to the image, not as a religious act of worship, but as a political act of homage to the state; and of course to him as representative of the state. Individuals were free to worship whatever god they chose, but as loyal subjects they must show their submission to the state – and by extension to King Nebuchadnezzar.

It can scarcely be doubted that the man of the end-time, mentioned above, whose image will stand on the wing of the Temple in Jerusalem in the Tribulation period, will use that image in exactly the same way – as a test of loyalty to him and to the state. An incidental link between history in Nebuchadnezzar and prophecy in 'the Man of Sin' is the recurrence of the number six. It is seen in the dimensions of the image – sixty cubits high and six cubits wide. Six is associated with man in his greatness, and Goliath comes to mind (1 Sam. 17:4), yet the six always falls short of the seven that in many cultures speaks of perfection. The image on the Temple wing in Jerusalem in the day yet to come embodies the world empire of the last days, representing an emperor of whom Nebuchadnezzar is but a portrait. Associated with this end-time emperor is the treble six – 666 (Rev. 13:18).

To summarise the story – in this chapter is disclosed, in the clearest light, what living under a dictatorship may mean for those who worship the one true God. Totalitarian states have varied in character down the ages but they have had one thing in common – the worship of God must take second place to the worship of the state. Worship of God may be permitted, as it was under fascism, or it may be banned, as it was and is under communism, but both demanded an uncompromising subservience to the state. As will become clear, this is what is presented in the image of Nebuchadnezzar, and this carries a special lesson and special encouragement for the Tribulation days, when the Man of Sin will demand worship for himself (2 Thess. 2:3–4) and his image (Rev. 13:11–17). Believers in that day will be faced with a very similar challenge to that faced by Shadrach, Meshach and Abed-nego.

4. The Absence of Daniel

The absence of Daniel from the drama of this chapter needs explanation. This is very likely the result of two factors in the situation: (a) his duties, and (b) the location of the image. After the interpretation of Nebuchadnezzar's dream, Daniel was appointed to Cabinet rank (2:49) and was made responsible for the administration of the city of Babylon. On occasions, when the rest of the court would move with the king, it would be most likely that Daniel would be required to stay behind in the city. As will be shown in discussion, the mention of 'the plain' (v. 1) shows that the location could not have been within the city: historical research is adamant there were no plains within the city walls. Thus the location itself lay outside Daniel's jurisdiction. If the 'plain of Dura, in the province of Babylon' (v. 1) is to be linked, as many archaeological authorities do, with the ruins identified as 'Tulul Dura' excavated in recent years, then this is a plain in the province of Babylon about twelve miles south east of the city.[3] Thus, when the court moved there, and all the officials of the empire were summoned to attend the dedication of the image, Daniel's responsibilities would most likely have detained him in the city.

The chapter falls readily into the following paragraphs:

The Dedication of the Image	vv. 1–3
The Proclamation of the King	vv. 4–7
The Accusation of the Chaldeans	vv. 8–12
The Investigation of the Charges	vv. 13–18
The Verdict of the King	vv. 19–23
The Deliverance of the Hebrews	vv. 24–27
The Decree of Nebuchadnezzar	vv. 28–30

[3] See map, p. 682.

Verses 1–3 The Dedication of the Image

Verse 1 The Erection

There is no doubt that the memory of his remarkable dream would remain with King Nebuchadnezzar for a considerable time. Soon the thought of reproducing the image of the dream as an impressive golden statue would seem a reasonable undertaking and, at the same time, it would be visible evidence of his wealth and power. Further, since he personally had been identified in the interpretation as the head of gold, it would be impressive to have the whole image of gold, as if to banish any thought as to the passing away of his kingdom. Such a statue would be most impressive as a representation of the 'golden city'. Despite the questions of some expositors, arising from the fact that no direct description is given, there can be no doubt but that this image is that of a man.[4] As an alternative, one commentator suggests an obelisk and writes: 'The size of the image and its shape are both remarkable. In height it vied with the date palms that still grow in the plains of Iraq to approximately the height of this image (90 feet), and it was almost as slender, at nine feet in width. It must have been more like an obelisk than a statue, and stylised if it resembled a human being at all'.[5] The problem of the height and proportions of the statue has been answered by recent archaeology, which shows that such images were generally placed on a wide platform base, possibly a third of the overall height of the statue. An eminent archaeologist[6] has recently claimed to have uncovered what could be the very base of this image in 'Tulul Dura', an archaeological site sixteen miles south of Babylon.[7] Thus this image would be a magnificent statue of a man, in normal proportions, raised on a thirty-feet-high platform. These figures are based on the normal Babylonian cubit of eighteen inches. The use of the sexagesimal system (dividing something into sixty equal parts, for example a 'minute', an 'hour', or a 'circle' – the base is six), was normal practice in Babylon at this time, and was based on their astronomical studies

[4] Montgomery, *The International Critical Commentary, Daniel*, p. 196.

[5] Baldwin, *Daniel*, p. 100.

[6] Montgomery, *The International Critical Commentary, Daniel*, p. 197, speaks of an archaeologist called Oppert who thought he had discovered the base of the image in excavations near *Tul^ul D^ura* (mounds of Dura).The river Dura flows into the River Euphrates six miles south of Babylon.

[7] Miller, *New American Commentary, Daniel*, p. 111.

and measurements. Such a structure – ninety feet high – would dominate the plain. In the king's dream the head alone was of gold, but the pride of Nebuchadnezzar's heart, allied with the wealth of Babylon, would demand that the whole image be presented of gold. Even in Babylon it would be very unlikely that the whole image was solid gold. Rather, in keeping with the practice of the time, the image would be of some less costly material overlaid with gold. The fact that it is spoken of as 'an image of gold' presents no problem. The altar in the court of the tabernacle is called 'the brasen altar' (Exod. 38:30), yet we know it was made of shittim wood overlaid with brass (Exod. 27:2). In this image there lurks a glorification of man that comes perilously near deification. With the sun shining on this magnificent statue it must have been an awesome sight dominating the Plain of Dura.

Whether the image was made ready in sections in different locations or prepared on site is not clear but, at last, it is set up in the Plain of Dura. It would seem there is some significance in the verb 'set up', which is repeated eight times in the first eighteen verses, and on each occasion of its use King Nebuchadnezzar is the subject. It appears that Daniel understands that the king personally supervised the erection of this image.

Verses 2–3 The Edict

Then comes the day of dedication – a word defined by Wilson[8] as follows: 'describing the first use of anything as of a house, the Temple, an altar etc., by setting them aside in a solemn manner'. A scriptural example of this is the dedication of the altar to God in the book of Ezra (Ezra 6:16–17). For the dedication of the image, King Nebuchadnezzar assembled all the principal officials of the empire. Seven different classes of officials are named, and it is a reasonable assumption that they are listed in order of seniority, beginning with the most senior. The Aramaic words are difficult to translate into terms meaningful to us. In this respect the research of John F. Walvoord[9] has presented convincing evidence to understand them as follows:

1. Princes: administrators of the empire – direct representatives of the king.
2. Governors: commanders or military chiefs.

[8] *OTWS*, p. 112.

[9] Walvoord, *Daniel: The Key to Prophetic Interpretation*, p. 83.

3. Captains: presidents or governors in civil government.
4. Judges: counsellors or advisers.
5. Treasurers: superintendents of the public treasury.
6. Counsellors: lawyers or guardians of the law.
7. Sheriffs: magistrates who applied the law.

The concluding statement 'all the rulers of the provinces' would embrace all lesser dignitaries of a province subject to the governor. Amongst this latter group would be Shadrach, Meshach and Abed-nego (lesser officials under Daniel in the province of Babylon).

From this comprehensive list of the officials of the Babylonian Empire, and the repetition of the same list in the next verse (v. 3), it becomes clear that the king is using the image, not only for the aggrandisement of himself, but for another, more crucial purpose. If the date of 601 BC for this chapter is correct, then King Nebuchadnezzar, crowned only four years before, in 605 BC, might feel it absolutely essential to assess the loyalty of key officials in the new civil administration. The small number of Chaldeans and the ethnic culture of Nebuchadnezzar meant that his key officials were often men of other races controlling 'people, nations, and languages' (v. 4), held together only by the power of his army. This explains his personal interest in this dramatic day.

Verses 4–7 The Proclamation of the King

Verses 4–5 The Herald Summons

The use of a herald seems to have been a particular Babylonian institution used for public proclamations issued by the king. It should be observed that, while no authority is quoted, the entire gathering knows well whose command lies behind the voice of the herald. Again, it is noted that the gathering represented the entire empire with its many peoples, cultures and languages. The herald would cry in Aramaic, the *lingua franca* of the empire, and all representative officials would be conversant with this language. The herald addresses the company as 'O people, nations, and languages', thus embracing the many lands, some recently brought under the sway of Babylon and subjected its iron rule. The announcement itself was simple. There would be a signal given – the sound of the Babylonian orchestra – at which sound the whole company was commanded to fall down and worship the image. No other option was available, no excuse acceptable – everyone must bow. The consequence of not bowing as ordered was made abundantly clear – it would mean the cruellest of deaths – a burning fiery furnace! To encourage (ensure?) loyalty and to explain the burning, the herald would likely point to one of the smelting furnaces used in the construction of the image, that was clearly visible in the hillside nearby. The smoke and the blaze of that furnace – with the door flung dramatically open at this strategic moment – would carry a very clear warning to every official. Nebuchadnezzar demanded the loyalty and obedience of each official in his empire.

The orchestral signal was made up of six types of instruments, doubtless chosen to blend harmoniously and provide a proper sensual atmosphere for this act of national submission. It is a somewhat thankless task to try to translate the Aramaic names into instruments familiar to us, but the generally accepted equivalents may be noted.[10] 'Cornet' is generally understood as a horn of some kind, since the same word is used of an animal's horn. 'Flute' comes from a verb that means 'to hiss or whistle', so it is best understood as probably made from reeds and maybe similar to our fife. 'Harp', sometimes translated 'lyre' (*NRSV*), is certainly a stringed instrument, with the number of strings varying from three to twelve. 'Sackbut' was also a stringed instrument, but triangular in shape and having four strings. 'Psaltery' seems to have been another type of stringed instrument, but with the strings stretched over a drum and plucked with a small pick. 'Dulcimer' seems to have been a wind instrument of some kind; in one translation it is rendered 'bagpipe'.[11]

Much has been made at times of the number six in the six instruments mentioned, as reflecting the efforts of man after perfection, but this interpretation is not supported by the concluding phrase, 'all kinds of musick'. Perhaps this could be counted as number seven. These six were only representative of the full orchestra, and assuredly, Nebuchadnezzar would have the best available music from all over the empire on this august occasion. The stateliness and the solemnity of the occasion are highlighted by the repetition of the list of musical instruments (vv. 7, 15).

The fact that three of the names of these musical instruments are of Greek derivation – 'harp', 'psaltery' and 'dulcimer' – has been used by critics to support a date for the book in the second century BC.

[10] *NET in loc.* The text notes are most helpful in the identification of these instruments.

[11] *NAS.*

This claim has already been examined and found to be without substance.[12]

Verses 6–7 The Orchestra Sounds

One can only imagine the hush that must have fallen over that great company – conservative estimates place the numbers gathered at around three hundred thousand persons – as the voice of the herald faded. Every ear would be listening for the sound of the signal, and every eye would be fixed on the image, with perhaps an apprehensive glance at the blaze of the nearby furnace. Then it happened! The music sounded. This great congregation fell on their faces, prostrating themselves before the image. That this was an act of worship to the image itself is debatable, as already discussed. Older commentators and Aramaic scholars[13] do not see this act as acknowledging a new deity, but as recognising, in symbolic form, the power of the empire and emperor. In a secondary way, those accustomed to worshipping idols would go beyond this and see the image as representing the god behind the empire. Thus, the different races in the empire, no matter which god they worshipped, would have had no problem whatever in bowing before the symbol of the empire in which they lived. In this act, they were acknowledging the god who stood behind the empire. Even Jews, Nebuchadnezzar would argue, should have no problem. The destruction of Jerusalem was indisputable evidence of the superiority of the gods of Babylon over Jehovah. Nebuchadnezzar would surely argue that all of his subjects must be quite willing to: (a) acknowledge the indisputable greatness of his kingdom, and (b) acknowledge him as their god-given ruler in this act of homage. Nebuchadnezzar would argue that this was not a religious issue but simply a political matter. Now, surveying this vast company stretching over the plain, prostrate at his feet, he must have felt fully satisfied that he was in command. Everyone was now aware, by this demonstration of his authority, that all power in the Babylonian Empire belonged to him – not a dissident could be seen.

Verses 8–12 The Accusation of the Chaldeans

Suddenly the self-congratulation of the king is somewhat rudely interrupted by a group of Chaldeans. These men, because of their

[12] See Introduction, Section 2C, 'Critical Attack'.
[13] Keil and Delitzsch, *Commentary on the Old Testament*, Vol. 9, p. 124.

race and status, having the right of direct access to the king, had a very grave charge to make against three important officials of the province of Babylon. As previously explained (2:2), these Chaldeans were the leading group amongst his counsellors. Having the same ethnic background as Nebuchadnezzar (from Chaldea), they had special recognition as counsellors of the inner court and also, it appears from the record, would seem to have been granted privileged access to the king. Using the formalised courteous language necessary in approaching the king – 'O king, live for ever' – they reminded him of his decree regarding the image and the synchronised act of worship he had demanded at the musical signal. As could be expected, they were very careful to remind him of the penalty for disobedience. With this introduction, they then formally charge three officials of the province of Babylon with deliberate defiance of the king's command. The charge is specific and the names are given – Shadrach, Meshach, and Abed-nego. Whether Nebuchadnezzar recognised the names or not it is difficult to be sure. He may well have done and this, we can imagine, would add to his fury. It is obvious that the king himself had not observed this act of defiance, and these officials, zealous in his honour, were not going to allow such an affront to the king to be treated lightly. Despite the courteous language, there is an implied criticism of the king, which he would certainly catch. Having shown their carefulness of his honour, they went a step further and clearly implied that the appointment of these Jews to such high office in the province had not been a very wise action. The sting lies in the fact, as these guardians of his honour reminded the king, that he was the one who had appointed them. As unsleeping guardians of the throne, they were watching the situation very carefully, and here was a danger signal. While the thousands around them prostrated themselves before the image these three officials stood erect and defiant. The implications are clear in the minds of the Chaldeans – could this affront to the person of the king be allowed to pass unreported? These Chaldeans, as wise and dependable counsellors, dare not allow such a blatant insult to the throne to pass unreported!

Enemies of the Hebrews since their promotion by the king, the Chaldeans had likely been investigating their administrative work in the province (2:49). Now, suddenly, this courageous act of the three Hebrews had given them the opportunity they had awaited to denounce them to the king. These Chaldeans would have known the sincerity and responsibility with which these Hebrews discharged their duties in the province. They could make no charges against them in their work. They would also be aware of their uncompromising stand against idolatry, so it must have been with great relief that they realised that this was now the opportunity to get rid of these interlopers, who had been given such rapid promotion in their city. The verb 'accused' is a very strong word, which, in its literal usage, means 'to eat the pieces of, devour' (Job 19:22), and shows the malicious intent behind the accusation. The specifics of the charge are spelt out to the king: (a) disrespect for the person of the king –they 'have not regarded thee'; (b) disregard for the practice of the king – 'they serve not thy gods'; and (c) disobedience to the proclamation of the king – 'nor worship the golden image which thou hast set up'. Presented in this way the charges are certainly more than enough to stir a quick-tempered monarch to fury. These courtiers thought they knew well how King Nebuchadnezzar would react to such charges.

Verses 13–18 The Investigation of the Charges

Verse 13 The Command of the King

The result of their charge was all that the Chaldeans could have expected. 'In his rage and fury' is a hendiadys, translated 'furious with rage' (*NIV*), that highlights the paroxysm of anger of this proud despot as he commanded the Hebrews to be brought before him. This was an order that allowed no delay.

Verses 14–15 The Challenge by the King

What the accusers may not have expected was that, instead of acting on their word and passing the death sentence instantly, the king initiated his own investigation and even offered the accused a second chance. The question 'Is it true?' in some translations is rendered –'Is it of purpose?'(*JND*). If this is accepted, then the king is asking the question, not simply to confirm a fact already well supported by the evidence before him, but to enquire if these men have some justification to give for their action. In other words, had they not heard the order? Or had they misunderstood what was demanded? He would allow the accused an opportunity to explain. As the three young men are presented before him, Nebuchadnezzar would possibly remember how grateful he had been to Daniel for the interpretation of the dream image, and how, at the request of Daniel, he had promoted these three Hebrews. Their faces would recall their record of faithful service and make them unlikely rebels. At any rate, he is prepared to give them another chance. It is interesting that the king omits the first charge the Chaldeans had made against the Hebrews – disrespect for his person – and repeats only the second and third charges, relating to his gods and the image.

Some have suggested that it is possible the worship of the image was a daily act at this festive gathering, over the days of the dedication. Read in this light, the king was giving them a day's delay and another chance to bow. However, this is most unlikely. It seems clear that this is a one-day festal gathering for the dedication of the image. The ceremony of the day is interrupted when the king orders a special and immediate sounding of the music again! This would mean that every eye in that great gathering would be focussed on three lonely Hebrew youths arraigned before the king. The incentive to obey is clear when Nebuchadnezzar repeats the threat to 'cast [them] the same hour into the midst of a burning fiery furnace'.

The scene can be pictured in graphic terms. The centrepiece is the enthroned king on the raised platform. Three lonely figures stand before the king; guards stand behind them and behind the king. To one side of the platform is the majestic image, and around that dais is the massed orchestra of Babylon. On the other side of the platform, built into the hill, is a limestone furnace with the lower door, about the height of man, standing open, with flames belching out from it. Smoke pours from the open top, where a ramp allows the rock to be wheeled up to, and then tipped into, the furnace. The great company of many thousands stands silently with hushed breath as three men make their choice – to obey or not to obey; to live or to die – to bow or to burn!

King Nebuchadnezzar now raises the issue at stake. It is not an issue between a king and his subjects. Rather, the challenge is between the gods of Babylon, as represented in the image, and the unseen God of the Hebrews. This is exactly where Nebuchadnezzar places the emphasis: 'Who is that God that shall deliver you out of my hands?' That the God of Daniel was able to reveal secrets the king had been forced to acknowledge (2:47), but a God able to deliver from that fiery furnace? Impossible! The proud king felt he was on sure ground here! These stubborn Hebrews must bow. What a triumph this will be for him as the representative of the gods of Babylon! If they will not bow, it is still his victory; there is no God able to deliver from such a blazing furnace. Either way he wins!

Verses 16–18 The Confidence of the Three Hebrews

Verse 16 Amid that hushed gathering in the presence of the greatest monarch on earth at that time, the answer was given by three lonely Hebrews – courteously, directly and forthrightly. Courteously, even though some commentators would like to add the word 'king' to their answer, since they judge the direct vocative of the Masoretic[14] pointing of the text, 'O Nebuchadnezzar,' lacks courtesy. E.J. Young, a noted Hebrew scholar, gets over that problem by omitting the pointing and reading the text: 'Shadrach, Meshach, and Abed-nego answered and said to the king, "O Nebuchadnezzar, we have no need to answer thee in this matter"' (*RV*). He argues that it is Daniel who, in the writing of the account and in the heat of the moment, omits the formal introduction the Hebrews would normally use. Using the translation quoted (*RV*), which seems to catch the thought of the Aramaic original, the stand taken by the three young men needs no explanation from them. Nebuchadnezzar has had sufficient dealings with the people of Israel to know they were forbidden by God to bow to idols – the Law was clear, 'Thou shalt not make unto thee any graven image ... thou shalt not bow down thyself to them, nor serve them' (Exod. 20:4–5). As those who sought to obey the God of heaven (2:44), they had no option but refuse the command of Nebuchadnezzar.

Verse 17 The Power of Their God

Since they had no option in the matter of their obedience to their God, they had no option with regard to the commandment of the king – they must refuse to bow! That conclusion must still stand even if the consequence of this refusal is the burning fiery furnace. It is of interest to note that there is no article before 'burning fiery

[14] See Osterley and Robinson, *An Introduction to the Books of the Old Testament*, (London: S.P.C.K., 1953), p. 13: 'The task of preserving and handing down the sacred text fell to a body or class of men who are commonly known as *Masoretes*. The name is derived from the Hebrew term *Masorah*, which means "tradition". But the work of the *Masoretes* went much further than merely copying the text accurately and seeing that it was provided with the proper vowel signs. They studied it with the utmost diligence, counting the verses in each book, identifying the middle word, and appending in the margin countless notes, calling attention to anything unusual or remarkable in the text. Even such variations as an abnormally large or small letter were faithfully copied, and a note showed that the peculiarity was traditional not arbitrary'.

furnace'; the implication of this is simply 'any fiery furnace'. It will not matter whether the fiery furnace is the normal one, or a special fiery furnace heated 'seven times more than it was wont' – that makes not the slightest difference – they are prepared to face any fiery furnace. The absolute confidence of these young men in their God must have radiated through the great company. 'If it be so' – defines the reality – if the king's penalty for our refusal to bow stands, and we are found guilty as charged, then, from any fiery furnace, our God is able to deliver us. The simple confidence of these young men is awe-inspiring. Assuredly they were acquainted with the ministry of Isaiah: 'When thou passest through the waters, I will be with thee; and through the rivers, they shall not overflow thee: when thou walkest through the fire, thou shalt not be burned'(Isa. 43:2). So they had complete confidence in their God; they can state: '[He] ... is able to deliver us' with absolute conviction. Such confidence should have been a warning to King Nebuchadnezzar.

Verse 18 The Purpose of Their God

Fully aware of the power of their God to deliver them, the faith of these Hebrews rises to a new height as they ponder another relevant factor. Perchance their God has another end in view. Perhaps He wishes to show idol worshippers how His people die. If this is so, their case still stands – God is to be obeyed. That is not negotiable; it is their responsibility, so there will be no bowing! Then the issue is in the hands of God – either they live as witnesses to His power or they die as witnesses to His purpose at this time. They trust Him still! At this point they join the patriarchal Job in his supreme confidence in God, when he cried through the tears, 'Though He slay me, yet will I trust in Him' (Job 13:15). Walvoord sums the matter up very concisely: 'These men ask for no miracle; they expect none'.[15] There is not a hint of compromise in their absolute loyalty to their God and their confidence in His unchanging word. One look into the blazing fury reflected in the face of Nebuchadnezzar would tell the Hebrews that there was no possibility of compromise on his part.

[15] Walvoord, *Daniel: The Key to Prophetic Revelation*, p. 89.

Verses 19–23 The Verdict of the King

Verse 19 First Order – The Fiery Furnace

It may be pointed out at this point that other factors are clearly at work in the whole situation. The Chaldean plotters have been unbelievably successful. They had seized the opportunity provided by the dedication to bring about a personal confrontation between the king and the three Hebrew officials, whose promotion in the province of Babylon they had so deeply resented. They doubtless revelled in the blow to the self-esteem of the king who had humbled them by his appointment of these Hebrews. They knew exactly what the king was doing in his loyalty test, and as long-standing servants to the throne, they resented this testing. They had used the king's demand to their advantage and would now be rid of these troublesome Hebrews. Now that the confrontation had been achieved, the plotters could be satisfied that either the king or the three Hebrew officials must be humiliated before the representatives of the empire; in either case they would be the winners.

Now King Nebuchadnezzar, enraged beyond measure and infuriated beyond reason at such intransigence, reveals uncontrollable temper. The inward fury is seen outwardly, in his face. Scripture sums it up: 'the expression of his face was changed' (*RSV*) – any tolerance is gone and sheer hatred blazes in the eyes of the king. The result can be seen in the foolish order he gives merely to vent his rage: he orders the furnace to be heated seven times more than normal. If it is his intention to increase the suffering of his victims, this is a very foolish order. Surely for this purpose he should have ordered a slow-burning fire! But reason gives way to fury, and the crowd, absorbed in the drama, watch, as more and more is added, and the roar of the flames drowns speech. Here is the tangible evidence of the incandescent fury of Nebuchadnezzar. 'Seven times' is a proverbial expression (Prov. 24:16; 26:16), but in this context it simply means 'as hot as possible'.

Verse 20 Second Order – The Special Forces

The term 'the most mighty men that were in his army' describes exactly King Nebuchadnezzar's bodyguard. Chosen by the king and trained to the limits of human endurance, members of this elite corps were marked out by their character and their courage; they would have laid down their lives for the king, if required to do so.

Standing now by the side of the podium, they are charged with the execution of the king's sentence. At a command, they bind these stubborn youths and move toward the ramp that leads to the top of the fiery furnace. As described earlier, archaeological research makes it clear that this was a perpendicular limekiln set against the hillside, with an opening at the top to which a ramp led. Rock was added through this top opening. At the bottom, where the fuel was added, there would be a door with a grill where air was drawn in, and which could also be used for the extraction of the lime.

Verses 21–23 The Execution – The Searing Flame

The urgency of the king's command brooked no delay – not even the normal delay to strip the criminal. Unusual is the fact that these Hebrew youths were bound in 'their coats, their hosen, and their hats, and their other garments'. This unusual action, meant to hasten their death, would become additional testimony to Divine preservation in the flame. Fully clothed and bound with ropes is the graphic picture as we see them bundled up the ramp to the blazing mouth of the super-heated furnace. Every eye in that crowd would follow as they were thrown one by one into the open mouth of the furnace. We can visualise these bound and helpless men falling down the central shaft, through the flames.

The urgency of the king's command, the hasty summons with no warnings given, and being under the gaze of the elite of the empire, may have led these picked and seasoned men of the king's bodyguard to take undue risks with such a furnace far above its normal temperature. Whatever happened, we may attempt to explain or to rationalise – a sudden addition of fuel, a bursting furnace, no flameproof uniforms – these are possibilities, but as they hurled their victims into the furnace the executioners died. Scripture is plain: 'the flame of the fire slew those men'. A just God deals righteously with those who would so treat His servants. Orders from a superior officer are no valid excuse. That swirl of flame engulfing the executioners was no accident. Bodies lie along the ramp and teach a solemn lesson to all who understand. The final glimpse of the young men is of three bound figures falling down the shaft of the furnace into the heart of the flames.

Verses 24–27 The Deliverance of the Hebrews

Verses 24–25 What Nebuchadnezzar Saw

His rage subsiding as his orders are executed, the king seats himself on his throne to enjoy the carrying out of his royal command and the display of his despotic power. This will be a lesson to any would-be dissidents amongst his officials of empire. Through the opened lower door of the furnace he doubtless expects to see bodies fall as flaming torches to the floor of the furnace. Instead, to his utter consternation, he sees, not bound men, but bond-free men; men not writhing in agony but walking about freely; not scrambling for the exit but seemingly at ease in the midst of the flame. And counting... one, two, three, but there is Another! King Nebuchadnezzar cannot believe what he is seeing. Calling for confirmation that only three men were cast into the furnace, the king fastens his eyes on the fourth and identifies him as '[one] like the Son of God' (*AV*). Hebrew scholars point out that the Aramaic word for 'God' is plural and in this section of the prophecy generally refers to heathen gods. Hence the translation should be 'a son of the gods' (*RV*). As far as his understanding goes, Nebuchadnezzar grasps the fact that, in the preservation of these men, his action has been repudiated and reversed by a divine power – rather, it seems to dawn on him, by a divine person. This fourth figure confirms the intervention of supernatural power and is identified by him as 'a son of the gods'. It would be unlikely that his understanding went beyond this at the moment. Nevertheless, the impact on the king is devastating. 'Astonied' is too weak to convey in English the terror in the Aramaic word, which means 'to be astonished, terrified, tremble from fear'.[16] With our fuller revelation in Scripture, there is no doubt that the One in the furnace with the three young men was 'the Angel of the LORD' (note the word angel in v. 28), even Christ Himself, in a pre-incarnate Theophany.

Verses 26–27 What Nebuchadnezzar Did

The shock and fear at such a manifest Divine intervention to frustrate the command of the king soon gives way, very naturally, to a certain curiosity. To see more clearly, the king approaches the door of the burning fiery furnace. The word translated 'mouth' (*AV*) is the Aramaic word for 'door' (*RV* marg.). This is, of course, the

[16] *OTWS*, p. 24.

lower opening in the furnace, through which the lime was drawn when the fire had done its work. With courtesy now, he calls for the Hebrews to come out. In addressing them as 'servants of the Most High God' the king is: (a) accepting the miracle of their deliverance as those favoured of their God; and (b) owning the absolute supremacy of Jehovah, the God of Israel. He knows full well that none of the gods of Babylon could deliver his worshippers in this way. Such gods have been completely out-ranked now, in Nebuchadnezzar's estimation, by this undeniable demonstration of Divine power. The great image, too, has been discredited before the whole nation; in fact it is never heard of again.

Obedient to the king, yet showing no haste, the three young men come out of the furnace. The most important men of Babylon, the elite of the empire (v. 2), crowd round to examine them. Not a shred of evidence could be found that they had been in any furnace: their bodies were not burned, their hair was not singed, their clothing was intact, and there was not even the smell of burning upon them. What a testimony to the God of heaven (2:44).

Verses 28–30 The Decree of Nebuchadnezzar

Verse 28 The King's Confession – Praise

In his praise to the God of the Hebrews, Nebuchadnezzar publicly acknowledges two things. First, he recognises the pre-eminence and the power of the God Who could preserve His servants through the furnace. The supremacy of this God is absolute – so King Nebuchadnezzar has been brought to acknowledge, 'there is no other god that can deliver after this sort' (v. 29). It is to be noticed that, while this is a major concession, it is far from confessing this God as the only God. Again, there is no suggestion of his turning to this God from the idols and putting a personal confidence in Him. God as the Revealer of secrets (chapter 2), and God as the Preserver of His people (chapter 3), he has, perforce, to acknowledge. The God Who is the Saviour of men is even yet a stranger to him. That revelation will require the personal dealings of the next chapter.

The expression 'sent his angel' is used in many cultures as the usual way to describe an appearance or interference of the gods in human affairs, either by appearing themselves or sending a representative. It interprets Nebuchadnezzar's earlier words, 'a son of the gods'. He knew divine intervention had taken place. He had yet to know, in His fulness, the God Who had intervened. The second thing that Nebuchadnezzar acknowledges is that it was the personal confidence these three young men had placed in their God that led to their defiance of the king's command. They 'defied the king's command' (*NIV*); the consequence was yielding their bodies to the flame rather than bowing the knee to the idol. It would seem that Nebuchadnezzar envied the trust these men could place in their God. He knew full well that no god in Babylon could inspire such trust!

Verse 29 The King's Decree – Publication

Arising out of these events, King Nebuchadnezzar sends out a decree throughout the empire. It might have been expected that he would have commanded the worship of Jehovah the God of the Hebrews. Not so! It was simply to the effect that the God Who could deliver His people as these Hebrews had been delivered was worthy of the greatest respect. Nebuchadnezzar commands that the God of the Hebrews, Who had so displayed His power, must not be spoken against. The persons who would do so would be 'cut in pieces, and their houses ... made a dunghill' – summary judgement for such profanity. Judaism was to be placed amongst the permitted religions of Babylon. This decree was used of God for the physical preservation of the nation of Israel during the years of captivity, and they enjoyed the benefits of it right up to the fall of Babylon. Such was the outcome of the faithful and fearless witness of three young men in Babylon. The purpose of God behind the crisis they had faced was worked out through a fiery furnace. Their part was simply to obey His Word, put their trust in Him, and leave matters in His hand.

Verse 30 The King's Reward – Promotion

The final act of King Nebuchadnezzar on this momentous day was the promotion of the very men he had cast into the furnace. Recognising that his best interests before this mighty God demanded reparation, he heaped his rewards on these faithful servants of God and promoted them to more responsible posts in the province of Babylon. The very plot of Satan had rebounded on his agents in Babylon, and the very men they had sought to remove from the province have now been promoted to positions of greater power. The Chaldean plotters must have been much chagrined. They would know to tread warily in the administration of King Nebuchadnezzar – he must have pondered long on the part his court circle had played on this memorable day.

CHAPTER 4

Daniel and his Foes   Triumphs of Faith   Chapters 4–6

THE INCIDENTS SELECTED for the Divine record in this section of the book focus, not upon the testing of the servants whom God would use, but rather upon the triumphs granted to His servants in testimony. God used their faith to bring kings to acknowledge Him. The testimony of faithful Daniel is used to humble three proud despots of earth. When the three chapters are considered together as a unit this becomes very clear.

1. PLAN OF SECTION B

Ch. 4	King Nebuchadnezzar	571 BC	Daniel is 53 years
	Pride of a king		Humbled
	Ignored Deity – despite earlier dealings of God		

God had revealed Himself to Nebuchadnezzar as omniscient (chapter 2) and omnipotent (chapter 3). Through Daniel, Nebuchadnezzar had been told thirty-two years before – in 603 BC – that 'the God of heaven hath given thee a kingdom' (2:37). Yet he ignored this God (v. 30).

Ch. 5	King Belshazzar	539 BC	Daniel is 84 years
	Profanity of a king		Judged
	Defied Deity – despite the dealings of God with his father, Nebuchadnezzar.[1]		

King Belshazzar knew why King Nebuchadnezzar had carefully preserved the vessels from the Temple in Jerusalem. His calling for these vessels, and their use in the drunken orgy in a feast of the god Marduk, was a deliberate act of defiance of the God Whom Nebuchadnezzar had been brought to know.

[1] See comments under 5:10–12.

Ch. 6	King Darius	537 BC	Daniel is 86 years
	Presumption of a King		Exposed
	Claimed Deity – despite the witness of Daniel		

King Darius dared not deny the request of his courtiers, who were offering him the status, claimed and evidenced in court protocol, that the king was the specially-favoured of deity, and this was but a step to recognising in him the representative of deity. Thus no law could ever be altered. This idea, suggested by his courtiers, seems to have appealed particularly to this Median king; he regarded himself as being under the special protection of his god *Ahuramazda* (an amalgamation of names of several gods).[2] Especially favoured by his god, he could be the channel of blessing to others.[3] The courtiers were asking Darius to act, as he was supposed to act from his cultural background, by the very nature of his office as king.

2. PURPOSE OF SECTION B

The Practical Purpose

Two lessons may be learned.

Lesson 1 God, in absolute sovereignty, may permit ungodly men to hold responsible positions on earth, but He is still a holy and a just God. In the incidents recorded, areas of weakness in three mighty kings are shown that led to failure. Failure leads to wickedness that, unless there is genuine repentance, will bring certain retribution from a holy and righteous God. How God dealt with these men carries lessons for every age – for sovereigns and for sinners.

Lesson 2 A further general lesson to be observed is not only the failure of man, but over against this stands the faithfulness of a God Who can be trusted to deliver all that He promises to those who put their trust in Him. In each case considered, a failing sovereign is humbled and a faithful saint is honoured. This carries encouragement for believers in every age.

The Prophetic Picture

Since the Lord spoke of 'Daniel the prophet' (Mt. 24:15), it would be expected that the historical episodes Daniel selects for his record have prophetic overtones. This is to be noted in this section.

[2] Cook, *The Persians*, p. 221, footnote.
[3] Cook, *The Persians*, p. 218.

In the interpretation of the image in King Nebuchadnezzar's dream (2:28) God has shown that in the latter days there would be a world empire – represented by the feet and toes of the image to be destroyed on the arrival of God's King and Kingdom – represented by the stone. In the direct prophecies in Part 2 of this book, the ruler of this mighty empire comes into focus as 'The Little Horn' (7:8) and 'the coming prince' (9:26 *NET*). It is suggested that the predominant characteristics of this world ruler are to be found foreshadowed in the composite picture presented of despotic rule in the three kings – Nebuchadnezzar, Belshazzar and Darius. Adumbrated in these three kings, these very features will be seen clearly in this final ruler of the end-time. The man dominating the world scene of that future day will undoubtedly manifest the pride of a Nebuchadnezzar, the profanity of a Belshazzar and the presumption of a Darius – only on a far greater scale and to a far greater degree. The lesson written large is simple: God has dealt with men showing these very features in the past, so all can be assured that He can and will deal fully and finally with this ruler to arise in the future.

CHAPTER 4 – A KING'S PRIDE HUMBLED

PRELIMINARY NOTES

1. The Date of the Chapter 571 BC Daniel aged 53 yrs

While Daniel does not date the chapter, there are sufficient indications to show that a large time gap occurs after chapter 3. The clues are as follows:

(a) Peace and prosperity are enjoyed throughout the empire (v. 4).

(b) The building operations of the king had been completed in Babylon (v. 30).

(c) Nebuchadnezzar's 'mental derangement' followed a year of grace after the dream (v. 29).

(d) Nebuchadnezzar's 'mental derangement' lasted seven years.

(e) There is a time period after the 'mental derangement' when Nebuchadnezzar ruled competently again. Thus if Nebuchadnezzar died in 562 BC[4] (the date accepted by most historians), the dream must have been given at least eight, and possibly nine, years before his death, and thus about 571BC, when

[4] See Appendix 2.

Daniel would be about 53 years old. Thus between chapter 3 and chapter 4 there is a gap of around thirty years.

2. The Distinctive Character of the Chapter

This chapter stands alone in Scripture. This is the record of a state document, issued by the mightiest monarch in the world of his day, from the world-renowned royal palace of Nebuchadnezzar, in the 'golden city' of Babylon. Neither place is mentioned in the document itself, but every slave in the empire would know where this proclamation came from. In this unique document, King Nebuchadnezzar speaks to all the peoples of his empire of God's dealings with him. Unashamedly, and without qualification, he sets out, in this public way, how he was brought very low, his pride judged by the Most High God. For any man this would be a most remarkable confession, but for King Nebuchadnezzar, the mightiest of monarchs, 'remarkable' is too weak a word – 'unparalleled', or even 'unprecedented', would be a better word. Again, instead of being buried in the archives of Babylon, possibly until his death, the king himself decides to publish it now, while he is still alive. This speaks of a Divine superintendence. Liberal critics of a past day scoffed at the possibility of such a proclamation being made in Babylon. However, more recent archaeology,[5] from inscriptions recovered from the desert sands, would agree that both the vocabulary and the form of expression in this document belong to Nebuchadnezzar. For the believer in the Divine inspiration of Scripture the inclusion of this document here by Daniel settles the matter; it is the authentic record of God dealing with Nebuchadnezzar.

This is Nebuchadnezzar's third encounter with God. In chapter 2, Nebuchadnezzar had to acknowledge before Daniel 'your God is a God of gods, and a Lord of kings, and a revealer of secrets' (2:47). The omniscience of Deity overwhelms him. In chapter 3 he had to confess before the leaders of his empire: 'there is no other God that can deliver after this sort' (3:29). The omnipotence of Deity convicts him. At the close of this third encounter with God Nebuchadnezzar, his pride gone, bows the knee in worship: 'Now I Nebuchadnezzar praise and extol and honour the King of heaven' (4:37). This God manifests His omnipresence in a very real way with His own people – whatever their circumstances. There seems little

[5] Wilson, *Studies in the Book of Daniel*, p. 402.

doubt that God has wrought a miracle of grace in this pagan king. This chapter is the personal testimony from King Nebuchadnezzar of the dealings of God with him.

3. The Plan of the Chapter

Because of the unusual character of this event, and also the fact that the king himself tells the story, it will be helpful to observe the balanced way in which the story is presented. This balance can be observed in the following overview:

Prologue	vv. 1–3	A Royal Declaration
A. The Dream Recounted	vv. 4–18	Nebuchadnezzar Speaks
B. The Dream Interpreted	vv. 19–27	Nebuchadnezzar Listens
C. The Dream Realised	vv. 28–33	Nebuchadnezzar Recalls
Epilogue	vv. 34–37	A Royal Confession

Verses 1–3 Prologue: A Royal Declaration

The chapter carries the personal and authoritative note of the first person singular – 'I Nebuchadnezzar' – used three times (vv. 4, 34, 37). Archaeologists and archivists who have studied such historical documents from this period point out their surprise that Nebuchadnezzar uses none of the grandiose titles customarily attached to such a document. Would this be a hint that he has really learned one lesson, at least, from the experience? The main point of the chapter lies not in any mandate – for there is none – but in the message it brings to all the peoples of his empire. Nebuchadnezzar issues no command, but makes a confession. It records a personal encounter with God that had left a deep impression on the mighty Nebuchadnezzar. He addresses 'all people, nations, and languages, that dwell in all the earth', to retell his story, that they too may be impressed by the dealings of God with an individual. The hyperbolic language, similar to the all-inclusive language of his previous decree (3:29), is a feature of edicts issued in Babylon, whose monarchs claimed universal sovereignty. Archaeologists have deciphered gravestones where these claims are made – one describes himself as 'king of the four quarters of the earth'. While the hyperbolic titles are missing, it may still be admitted that, after such dealings of God with him, a humbler note might have been expected. However, he was still, without question, in the eyes of men, the mightiest monarch on earth. Nebuchadnezzar would know well that meekness, in these circumstances, might be interpreted as weakness, and that could be dangerous. The expression 'I thought it good' is translated by Miller[6] as 'It is my pleasure', thus indicating that the king had real joy in telling of the signs and wonders by which God had made Himself known to him. A 'sign' would describe the disclosure of Divine purpose in a dream; as shown in such as was the image in chapter 2. A 'wonder' would point to the display of Divine power; as was shown at the furnace in chapter 3. What Nebuchadnezzar is now about to disclose will add both a sign – Divine judgement, in the period of the king's insanity – and a wonder – Divine grace, in the king's restoration. The plurals may be plurals of emphasis – these events are out of the routine – they are designed to speak to men.

Nebuchadnezzar makes clear that the God Who has shown such personal interest in him is not some god of the Babylonian pantheon, but The Most High God. This God *(Elahah)* has a Kingdom that is timeless and called 'an everlasting kingdom'; it is also boundless, and spoken of as 'from generation to generation' (4:3, 34). Men come and men go, national boundaries change through the generations, but the supremacy of this God is absolute – He is the Supreme One – immeasurable. Yet the startling truth is that this God has a personal interest in individual men – even in a proud king. Nebuchadnezzar marvels and yet rejoices at such grace.

Neither the city nor the province of Babylon is mentioned as the place of origin of this remarkable document. This is not necessary: the people who heard this proclamation would not have the slightest doubt of its origin. Public proclamations were official proclamations: through the voice of the herald was heard the voice from the throne.

Verses 4–18 A. The Dream Recounted: Nebuchadnezzar Speaks

Verses 4–5 The King's Distress

The formal introduction gives place now to the personal, as the king reverts to the first person singular 'I Nebuchadnezzar'. First, he describes the conditions enjoyed at this time. If the date is 571 BC, as suggested, and thus about thirty years after the erection of the great image (3:1), then historical records suggest that the Babylonian Empire was enjoying a good measure of prosperity and peace.

[6] Miller, *New American Commentary, Daniel*, p. 129.

Scripture makes two statements. The first describes personal domestic circumstances – 'at rest in mine house'. The noun translated as 'at rest' means to be 'free from apprehension or fear'. This is somewhat unusual. We know from history that any monarch of those days had often very good reason to be afraid of home-based treachery and family betrayal. Happy with his beautiful and faithful wife, Nebuchadnezzar had no fears in this respect. The second statement – 'flourishing in my palace' – points to public and official matters of state. The participle 'flourishing' comes from a verb that means 'the growing green of a tree'[7] (Ps. 52:8). On the political scene, as on the domestic front, there was not an enemy in sight, and all plans and programmes seemed, as far as Nebuchadnezzar could see, to be going well. Peace at home and abroad – what a fortunate king! Recent archaeological discoveries from cylinders recovered from excavated tombs, as well as the congratulatory statements on monuments, have confirmed this statement about the kingdom at this time. This gave to Nebuchadnezzar both the time and the resources he needed to complete his tremendous building programme in Babylon, even to the famous hanging gardens he had built for his Median wife.[8]

This sense of peace was suddenly disturbed by a dream. His first dream disturbed his sleep (2:1), but this dream terrified him: 'made me afraid' (*AV*) is a good translation of the first verb, but 'troubled' is too weak for the second verb. A better translation is 'alarmed me' (*ESV*), but 'terrified me' (*NIV*) gets closest to the effect on the king. Between the two verbs comes what Nebuchadnezzar describes as 'the thoughts upon my bed' and the 'the visions of my head'. Obviously alarmed at what the dream showed, his imagination had begun to run riot, and he recognised that the dream clearly portended some terrible catastrophe. Nebuchadnezzar's thoughts would range over all sorts of disasters, and most likely dwell much upon the supernatural element so prominent in the dream. It is no wonder he was troubled! It seems his peace and prosperity were about to be rudely shattered.

[7] Wood, *A Commentary on Daniel*, p. 103.
[8] Clayton and Price, *The Seven Wonders of the Ancient World*, p. 38.

Verses 6–7 The King's Disappointment

Using the language of absolute authority,[9] King Nebuchadnezzar records his immediate reaction – 'made I a decree'. The wise men were to report immediately – no excuses would be permitted. Everyone belonging to this class must appear before the king. The urgent note in this decree makes the late arrival of Daniel of special interest. The four categories mentioned here: 'the magicians, the astrologers, the Chaldeans, and the soothsayers'[10] would embrace all those responsible for interpreting omens and advising the king. Included would be those who were experts in the interpretation of dreams. In addition to the standard interpretations, familiar to most, it would seem that Babylon had what could be called an interpretative rule book for more recondite matters. When Nebuchadnezzar refused to tell them his earlier dream (2:5), these men were clearly at a complete loss; the rules did not allow for such an eventuality. This meant that their usual claim of direct contact with the gods – part of their stock-in-trade – was put to the test and failed miserably. They were saved from the king's wrath by the revelation that God gave through Daniel. It appears that now, thirty years later, these wise men, or their successors, had regained some measure of the king's confidence. Here, the matter is urgent, and the king pushes any doubts of their competence to the back of his mind and tells them the dream.

The outcome, at first glance, is somewhat surprising. Nebuchadnezzar records it thus: 'they did not make known unto me the interpretation [of the dream]' (*AV* and *JND*). Another translation reads: 'they could not interpret it for me' (*NIV*), which is supported by the *NET* translation: 'they were unable to make known the interpretation to me.' However, looking closely at the context it would appear that the *AV* (supported by *JND*) has caught the thought, with its translation 'did not', more accurately than those using 'could not'. It seems also to reflect the thinking of the king at this time. With their well-understood, clear-cut, rules for dream interpretation, it would appear these wise men could easily have given the king a feasible interpretation of the dream. Thus 'could not' is an unlikely explanation of their failure. It is far more likely that, realising, by their own rules of interpretation, the imminence of a terrible disaster for the king or his kingdom, they were terrified

[9] See 'decree' in 2:13; 3:29.

[10] See interpretation of the different terms under 2:2 and 2:27.

for their lives. To tell a despot of King Nebuchadnezzar's reputation that disaster was coming was more than their lives were worth. They judged it safer to remain silent. The king certainly seems to have arrived at the same conclusion, and places the emphasis on the unwillingness of his counsellors to give the interpretation. Once again the courage of Daniel is underlined. Even as he gave the interpretation, Daniel must have known full well that he was placing his life at risk. In this document, to be publicised throughout the empire, the king, wisely perhaps, makes no mention of his reaction to this patent act of defiance on the part of his senior counsellors.

Verses 8–9 The King's Desire

Many and varied are the reasons suggested for the late arrival of Daniel in the audience hall – the wise men have already heard the account of the king's dream, and have had time to talk it over, and announce their decision to the king, before Daniel appears. The simplest explanation comes from the fact that Daniel held two posts: he was 'master of the magicians', as Nebuchadnezzar acknowledges (v. 9), but also 'ruler over the whole province of Babylon' (2:48). As a worshipper of the true God, Daniel would probably spend as little of his time as possible with the wise men in their special quarters, near to the audience chamber – he would have very little of common interest with these key personnel of the idol-gods. As a collegiate group living close to the audience hall, they were readily summoned before the king. Daniel would normally be at work in the administrative section of the palace, some distance from the audience chamber. While the wise men simply walked down a short corridor, Daniel had to be specially summoned from a distant office. It is to be noted that Daniel suffers no rebuke from the king for his later arrival but, strange as it may seem, one can sense in the king something approaching relief as Daniel appears. The expression 'at last' (*RSV*) seems to suggest the king was watching the door for Daniel to arrive. When at last he appears, the face of Nebuchadnezzar seems to light up: Daniel is instantly recognised and warmly greeted by the king. However explained, his late arrival in the audience hall was arranged by God to allow the recalcitrance of the wise men to be exposed.

In the record, the king refers to Daniel by his Hebrew name, but in this public document he identifies him by his Babylonian name, Belteshazzar, which he had given him (1:7). He points out that this name incorporates the name of his god, 'Bel': they would know that 'Belteshazzar' means 'Prince of Bel', and 'Bel' is the Hebrew name for the idol 'Marduk'. The name of Belteshazzar would be familiar to those living in the province and Nebuchadnezzar uses it to address Daniel three times in this proclamation (vv. 9, 18, 19). Yet, in using his Hebrew name, Nebuchadnezzar pays a tribute to Daniel and his God. The difference between Daniel and the wise men is clearly understood by the king, and pointed out in the words 'in whom is the Spirit of the holy gods'. While the language is drawn from a pagan idol-worshipping background, it indicates that Nebuchadnezzar has recognised, at last, that Daniel speaks for the Most High (v. 34) – in fact, the only God.

In the greeting with which Nebuchadnezzar welcomes Daniel he acknowledges:

(a) Daniel's primacy in the knowledge of Babylonian mythology – this is best understood as knowing exactly what he was talking about when dealing with the pagan myths. He speaks to him as 'master of the magicians'. It is suggested by Leupold, a Dutch commentator, that 'magicians' should be translated 'scholars', to avoid any idea that they were simply involved with dark arts.[11]

(b) Daniel's intimacy with the gods – the expression 'the Spirit of the holy gods is in thee' can be understood from Nebuchadnezzar's polytheistic background as simply an admission that Daniel is in communication with the supernatural. Other scholars[12] consider the word 'gods' (*elahin*) to be singular and a reference to Daniel's God – one different from the many Babylonian gods. There is some support for this view in the adjective 'holy', which seems to be used mainly of persons and things set apart for use of Deity, rather than simply related to moral purity. From the evidence available, it seems a valid inference that the king had a very high respect for Daniel's God. At the very least, he admits that Daniel serves a different god, who might even be the true God.

(c) Daniel's ability to reveal secrets lies in the admission of the king: 'and no secret troubleth thee'. A remarkable confirmation of a widespread appreciation of Daniel's ability is seen in the ironic challenge that his contemporary Ezekiel offers to the Prince of Tyre: 'Behold, thou art wiser than Daniel; there is no secret that they can hide from thee' (Ezek. 28:3). Daniel's fame had already spread

[11] Leupold, *Exposition of Daniel*, p. 178.

[12] Montgomery, *Critical and Exegetical Commentary on the Book of Daniel*, p. 225.

through every stratum of Babylonian society. In addressing Daniel like this, it is clear that Nebuchadnezzar had not fully grasped the lesson of chapter 2 – that God alone was omniscient. Nebuchadnezzar ascribes to Daniel that which he had personally disclaimed (2:27–30), and that which belonged only to Daniel's God (2:29–30).

In his brusque command to Daniel, 'tell me the visions of my dream that I have seen, and the interpretation thereof,' Nebuchadnezzar seems to be repeating the problem he had set the wise men in the early days of his monarchy (2:5) – to recount the dream and then give the interpretation. But this cannot be so, for, in the next verse, Nebuchadnezzar immediately begins to recount his dream. It is better to understand it as simply the king's way of acknowledging the past experience in light of the present problem. This interpretation of an admittedly grammatically-difficult statement is supported by the literal translation of Leon Wood: [13] 'The visions of my dream that I have seen, even its interpretation declare.'

Verses 10–18 The King's Description

Verses 10–12 The Tree: Greatness and Glory

At first glance, there was nothing really dramatic in Nebuchadnezzar's dream. A tree – a solitary tree it would seem – standing out in the landscape; above normal height, and still growing. The isolation of the tree means there is nothing, not even another tree, to catch the eye – it stands alone 'in the midst of the earth'. Leon Wood's translation of the statement: 'I saw and behold,'[14] seems to catch the implication of both the verb and tense – 'looking, I was looking'. The height of the tree marks it as unusual but, even as the king looked, it was visibly still growing, until it seemed to reach unto heaven – it could be seen over all the earth. This visibility is emphasised in the translation by H. C. Leupold from the Aramaic, 'its visibility was to the extremity of the whole world.'[15] What a magnificent, eye-catching, tree! An amazingly sturdy tree, and yet aesthetically so pleasing – its leaves were 'fair', or 'beautiful' (*NIV*); nutritionally satisfying in the quality and quantity of its fruit – described as 'much', or 'abundant' (*NIV*), and 'for all'. This tremendous tree provided shelter and food for the

[13] Wood, *A Commentary on Daniel*, p. 107.
[14] Wood, *A Commentary on Daniel*, p. 108.
[15] Leupold, *Exposition of Daniel*, p.179.

beasts of the field, as well as a home for the birds of the air. Whether the expression 'for all' includes mankind is debatable, but certainly the 'all flesh' that follows could be so explained. Symbolically it portrays, in a tree, the greatness and glory of a person – measured, in this instance, by the number of dependants who live under its shade. Nebuchadnezzar could hardly fail to see himself in the picture.

From the Scriptures available to him, Daniel would know very well that a tree was used figuratively to depict individual men. The godly man is described as 'a tree planted by the rivers of water' (Ps. 1:3); the wicked is described as 'spreading himself like a green bay tree' (Ps. 37:35). King Amaziah of Israel uses the figure of the 'cedar' as a fitting picture of himself (2 Kgs 14:9), and a similar figure is used of kings among the nations – the king of Assyria (Ezek. 31:3) and the king of the Amorites (Amos 2:9). These very words must have recalled, for Daniel at least, and possibly Nebuchadnezzar as well, what God had promised him as the head of gold in the earlier dream of the image. There is an echo of the earlier promise: 'And wheresoever the children of men dwell, the beasts of the field and the fowls of the heaven hath He given into thine hand, and hath made thee ruler over them all' (2:38).

Verses 13–18 The Tree: Government and Grace

Verse 13 Suddenly there is action. The note of surprise is indicated by the exclamation 'behold'. A figure has appeared in the vision – called 'a watcher and a holy one'. This expression is a hendiadys, and describes, not two persons, but a single individual. This is supported by the singular verb 'came down', and the conjunction can readily be treated as explanatory, and translated 'even a holy one'. The word for 'watcher' is sometimes translated 'messenger' (*NIV*), as is also the word 'angel', but the second word 'holy one' seems to indicate a messenger, or an angel of a special class, charged with the supervision of affairs on earth. That there is a class of such angels is suggested by the plurals used in both words (v. 17). The words that Nebuchadnezzar used to describe this heavenly visitor were possibly coloured by his own cultural background (where they are found frequently in inscriptions), but the Holy Spirit has endorsed their usage as descriptive of this class of angels – 'watchful and holy'. That they are agents of the Most High is shown clearly (v. 17): they carry out His will. The word 'watcher' occurs only in this chapter (vv. 13, 17, 23), and would recall the eyes of the living creatures (Ezek. 1:18) and 'the eyes of the LORD' (Zech. 4:10). Earth is always under Divine surveillance. As a consequence, there is always the possibility of Divine intervention in the affairs of men and of nations.

Verses 14–17 The loud voice of the watcher carries absolute authority. That authority is exercised over unseen servants or agents – the plural is demanded by the plural form of the verbs. First, there is a peremptory command to unseen workers – 'Hew down the tree'. The command is instantly executed and further action follows: the branches are cut off, the leaves shaken off, and the fruit scattered. The tree can no longer provide the shelter and food formerly available for beasts and birds and men. Yet, even in the judgement, something unusual comes into the picture. The tree is not to be uprooted or totally destroyed. Normally, when the stump of a tree is left in the ground exposed to the air it splits and rots and, very soon, every trace of the tree has gone. Not so in this case – the stump is to be left in the ground, with a band of iron and brass tightened around it. Some commentators argue that 'band' should be translated 'fence',[16] and see it as an encircling fence protecting the tree stump. However, the context demands more than this: it demands that the essential life of this tree is to be preserved by means of a tight band of iron and brass fastened around the stump. The band allows the life of the tree to be arrested but preserved; it cannot develop as a tree. Despite judgement, the tree itself is to survive in the banded stump left alone in the open field. Thus, while the sentence upon this individual is both just and severe (inflicted by God), there is a hint of Divine grace in it, with the possibility of recovery in future days. Both iron and brass in Scripture carry the idea of 'hardness', which can be interpreted in two ways. The 'good' sense is associated with God and the 'evil' sense with the sinner.[17] The stubborn pride of Nebuchadnezzar displays 'hardness' in its evil sense, shown in a man opposing God. This can be dealt with by the grace of God, even through the 'hardness' of discipline. The sovereign purpose of God is achieved when the 'hardness' in discipline recovers the sinner to his gracious God.

[16] Miller, *New American Commentary, Daniel*, p. 133.

[17] See iron in Jer. 1:18 and Is. 48:4, and brass in Deut. 28:23 and Lev. 26:19.

Again, it should be observed that from the second part of verse 15 the impersonal pronoun 'it' (with antecedent 'tree') is replaced by the personal pronoun 'him', so clearly the picture now focuses on the man symbolised by the tree. No name has yet identified the individual, but Nebuchadnezzar, as a very intelligent man, must already have had dark forebodings of what was to come. The condition and the company of this person under Divine judgement are both clearly set out: 'Let him be drenched with the dew of heaven, and let him live with the animals among the plants of the earth' (*NIV*). This is the consequence of the inward change decreed by the 'watchers' and demanded by 'the holy ones' – 'Let his mind be changed from that of a man and let him be given the mind of an animal' (*NIV*). Here 'heart', or 'mind', is not the 'seat of emotion' but the 'seat of reason' – the controlling factor in the personality (outward) and character (inward) of any man. Formerly, he thought as a man thinks; this individual can now think only as an animal thinks. As he thinks, so is he, and, as a result, the man shows animal behaviour. In psychiatry this condition is termed 'lycanthropy', and is defined as 'a delusion in which a person believes he or she is a wolf'. Medical studies show that, when afflicted with this mental condition, persons believe themselves to be an assortment of animals – wolves, gerbils, dogs, birds, cats, rabbits, tigers, etc. The 'werewolf' superstition lies in the etymology of the word. In this particular case a time limit is placed on the condition – it is imposed by Divine action and will be removed by the same power. The time limit is set until 'seven times pass over him'. Standing alone the word 'times' means 'sevens', or, in Latin, 'heptads', and could mean a heptad (a seven) of days, weeks, months, or years. However, in this context, days or weeks or even months would make little sense, and most certainly do not fit the chronology of Nebuchadnezzar's reign, so the period must be seven years. This is supported by the use of the same word in a context where it must be interpreted as years (7:25). It is so translated in the Greek text (*LXX*).

The decision taken by this Divine council of watchers and holy ones (clearly acting as an executive council for God) has both the words 'decree' (watchers) and 'demand' (holy ones) attached to it. The first word (decree) reflects acceptance of Divine righteousness, and the second word (demand) reflects acquaintance with Divine holiness. What holiness demands righteousness will execute. Divine purpose behind this action means that living men know, by His actions, that God has both the right and the power to deal with men, individually or nationally, in absolute sovereignty. No-one may argue when He raises even the 'lowliest' (*RSV*) of men to the place of rule or authority. The expression 'the kingdom of men' is clearly the 'realm where men can hold authority', but even in this realm God has the final say in the persons who fill that role of authority. This means He may pass over the proud man, whose pride renders him unfit for Divine purpose, and take up the humble man to fill the place of authority. The 'basest' of men (*AV*) could be misunderstood in English, as the perception of the meaning of the word has changed since 1611. The Hebrew word (*shepal*) is more accurately translated 'lowliest' (*RSV*). The word reflects a principle that runs through Scripture and is expressed in the statement that 'God resisteth the proud but giveth grace to the humble' (Prov. 3:34 *LXX*). Exemplified in the life of Hannah (1 Sam. 2:6–8), and of Mary (Lk. 1:52), it is quoted in the NT on two occasions (Jas 4:6; 1 Pet. 5:5), and shows that the pride of man carries no weight with God. The mention of the 'Most High' in the second part of the verse makes clear that there is no suggestion of any council of 'watchers and holy ones' acting independently of Him. It is abundantly clear that they are but the agents who execute His will.

At this decree, the very heart of Nebuchadnezzar must have trembled. It is very relevant at this point to remember that in the early years of his reign Nebuchadnezzar was never afraid to acknowledge his humble origins – through his family, he had no claim to royalty or nobility. It is of interest that the archaeologist and commentator Charles Boutflower points out that Nebuchadnezzar's father, Nabopolassar, in various inscriptions in Babylonian temples and tombs that archaeologists have unearthed in recent years, had described himself as being 'of very humble origin'.[18] Nebuchadnezzar would have known this, and would also vividly recall that Daniel had already pointed out that he owed his kingdom to the God of heaven (2:36–38). Now, the very lowliness that, in the earlier part of his reign, had allowed God to entrust him with the kingdom was gone. Lowliness had been replaced by pride in his own power and achievements, with no acknowledgement of God. In fact he personally was ripe for judgement. Yet God in grace would give him one further chance, if he was prepared to accept the warning in the dream. The very insanity with which he would be smitten would be an object lesson for men to see that God ruled in

[18] Boutflower, *In and Around the Book of Daniel*, p. 37.

the kingdom of men. The 'living' (plural) must include not only Nebuchadnezzar himself but many others, who would see or hear of God's dealings with him. The lesson stands for all time.

Verse 18 This final word from Nebuchadnezzar assures Daniel of three matters: (a) The reliability of the report; it is his own personal experience, given in his own words; (b) The inability of the wise men to interpret it – in the discussion earlier (v. 7), the view was taken that they were frightened even to attempt to interpret the dream; the king here simply accepts their refusal as reflecting the same inability as they showed in connection with his former dream thirty years before (2:10–11); (c) The confidence that the king had in the ability of Daniel to interpret the dream, in keeping with the link he believed Daniel to have with Deity. This is the third time Nebuchadnezzar refers to the 'Spirit of the holy gods' being in Daniel (vv. 8, 9, 18). Nebuchadnezzar recognised, at the very least, that Daniel was dependent on supernatural power. In fact, Daniel was only the channel for his God to communicate with men. So the stage is set for Daniel to interpret the dream.

Verses 19–27 B. The Dream Interpreted: Nebuchadnezzar Listens
Verse 19 The Hesitation of Daniel

It is essential to remember that this document is for public proclamation throughout the empire. Thus the change from the first person (biographic) to the third person (narrative) by the king can be justified, as Daniel now becomes the focus of the action, and the king describes the scene as an observer. Two matters are significant. First, it is worthy of note that Nebuchadnezzar introduces Daniel into his narrative using both Hebrew and Babylonian names. In the second matter, the king is obviously shocked, perhaps alarmed, by the reaction of Daniel to the dream when, clearly upset, Daniel remains silent. The dismay in the face of Daniel, and his subsequent silence as the king ended his recapitulation of the dream, must have increased immeasurably the apprehension gripping Nebuchadnezzar. The king records it clearly: 'Daniel, whose name was Belteshazzar, was astonied for one hour.' Different translations show the range of meaning in the verb 'astonied' (*AV* and *RV*): it is translated 'dismayed' (*RSV* and *ESB*), 'perplexed' (*NIV*), and 'upset' (*NET*). Daniel's silence added solemnity to that moment. The word for 'hour' can mean an exact hour, but when used idiomatically in Aramaic, as here, and in light of the four other occurrences in this book (3:6, 15; 4:33; 5:5), the best translation would seem to be 'upset for a brief time' (*NET*). To those in that audience hall, held by the drama of the moment, it may not have been an hour, but it surely felt like it. It is the king who breaks the silence. Knowing intuitively, as he must have done, that the dream revealed some judgement on him or his kingdom, Nebuchadnezzar seems to fear that Daniel might hesitate to break such news to him. Lest Daniel deny him the interpretation, as the wise men have just done for fear of his anger (v. 7, see comments), he speaks to reassure Daniel. The king, of course, has misunderstood the situation completely – Daniel's hesitation is not due to fear of Nebuchadnezzar – it is due to fear for him! Absolute dismay must have filled his heart as the dream unfolded: coming judgement on a king who, with all his failings, had responded positively to God and, in many ways, had shown himself a wise and fair ruler over his people. Now, with this personal judgement revealed by God, Daniel's heart was troubled as he pondered the consequences for the captive people of Israel.

In the stillness Daniel speaks, not because of any reassurance of personal safety from the king, but because he knows his message is from God – and the same God Who had spoken to this same man thirty years before (chapter 2). God is speaking again, not in grace this time, but in government! In his introductory remarks, Daniel's affection for the king is clear. This dream would delight those in his kingdom defined as 'them that hate thee' and then Daniel renames them as the king's 'enemies'. Within the kingdom, or outside it, the enemies of Nebuchadnezzar would rejoice at his humbling. Thus, in this brief introduction to the interpretation, Daniel: (a) dispelled any question of perplexity over the interpretation of the dream; (b) denied any notion that he had hesitated out of fear of the reaction of the king to an unpleasant interpretation; and (c) disclosed that his sympathy and support would be with Nebuchadnezzar if he responded positively to the Divine revelation.

Verses 20–22 The Interpretation of the Tree

The repetition of Nebuchadnezzar's description of the tree shows the care with which Daniel had listened to the king. Daniel recognised that he had no authority to add to what God had given; it was his only to interpret. He did this so pointedly and plainly that it is not difficult to see the accusing finger pointed at the king –

'Thou, O king'. No question now! Nebuchadnezzar had doubtless feared the interpretation, but now he must face it. The king of great Babylon, he personally is to be the subject of Divine action. Now all the features of the tree would fall into place. That great tree depicted the growth, the greatness, and the grandeur of the world dominion of Nebuchadnezzar, as seen in his empire, and he was the very embodiment of the empire. An interesting fact is recorded by Boutflower[19] concerning this great king. An inscription on a tomb in Babylonia records that Nebuchadnezzar loved the mighty cedars of Lebanon. On one of his military expeditions into Israel (possibly the one in 597 BC, against the rebel King Jehoiachin) he had himself depicted as the royal woodcutter cutting down one of those mighty cedars. This was to be transported to Babylon, to be used in the building of the tower of Babylon – one of his earliest works. A royal woodcutter he might have considered himself with respect to other kings, but now a Divine Woodcutter would soon be at work on him.

Verses 23–26 The Interpretation of the Judgement

Verses 23–24 Daniel continues the careful recounting of Nebuchadnezzar's dream in the action of a 'watcher and a holy one', but making two changes: (a) After the instruction to 'hew the tree' down, instead of the details given previously (v. 14), he uses the simple statement 'and destroy it'. This verb does not mean to destroy the material of the tree – it is frequently translated 'spoil'– but simply to spoil its usefulness as a tree to provide food or shelter. The same verb is used five times in this book, but the other four occurrences are always with a positive sense, to describe the Kingdom of God that will never be destroyed – never spoiled (2:44; 6:22, 26; 7:14); (b) The statement regarding the change of heart (v. 16) from that of a man to that of a beast is omitted, since it is clearly self-interpreting and needs no further elucidation.

Verse 25 Now it is plainly stated that this decree is from the Most High and there can be no conflict with 'the decree of the watchers' (v. 17): they are simply the executive agents of the Most High. The person to be affected is 'my lord the king' – King Nebuchadnezzar himself. When the judgment on his pride falls he is to:

(a) be driven, not only from the palace, but from men;

[19] Boutflower, *In and Around the Book of Daniel*, p. 83.

(b) have the company of beasts of the field;
(c) find pasture there – 'eat grass as oxen';
(d) be exposed, without a shelter, to the elements – 'they shall wet thee with the dew of heaven'.

The impersonal plural in the pronoun ('they') does not identify the persons or agents who would take the action against the king. The passive voice indicates what is done to him by others, and is well-presented in the translation: 'You will be driven away from people and will live with the wild animals; you will eat grass like cattle and be drenched with the dew of heaven' (*NIV*). Since the king is under a Divine sentence, it is clear that the agents are not important, and this use of the passive voice indicates that God has ordered it. One authority[20] gives the word for 'grass' (v. 15, second usage) as 'an herb', and suggests that, when used in the plural 'herbs', it means fodder for manger or table. Perhaps 'herbage' would be a better rendering. This same word is used for 'grass' on five occasions in the book (v. 15 (second usage) v. 25, v. 32, v. 33; 5:21), while a different word, meaning 'tender grass', is used twice (v. 15 (first usage), v. 23). Lonely, hungry and cold are words that spring to mind to describe the picture of that human figure eating grass and loping along with animals when driven away from the dwellings of men.

This condition was to continue for seven years (v. 16). It would take this period of time for the stubborn heart of Nebuchadnezzar to learn the simple lesson that the Most High ruled in the kingdom of men. In this special case, the lesson in Divine supremacy is personal to Nebuchadnezzar, but there stands a lesson for all proud hearts amongst those called 'the living' (v. 17). World rulers, who seem to be especially prone to such megalomania as beset Nebuchadnezzar, should take note; indeed, all should take heed.

Verse 26 In the final word of interpretation, Daniel explains that the protection of the stump left in the ground, by use of the band of iron and brass, carries a note of hope. The binding of the stump was an assurance that this bestial state, however painful and humiliating, was but for a time, and the essential life would be preserved through this time. There was really more than a hope; it was virtually a promise of the possibility of a recovery! The condition for that recovery is spelt out in the words 'till thou know'

[20] *OTWS*, p. 199.

of the previous verse. Now, in anticipation of this repentance, the statement from the watchers is 'thou shalt have known'. Repentance has brought acknowledgement of the Most High; now the promise grants a full recovery of his humanity and a full restoration of his imperial status. This was assured as soon as Nebuchadnezzar realised that 'the heavens do rule'. Babylonian deities had temples built, at tremendous expense, on earth; the God of Israel needed no such earthly dwelling: He dwelt in the heavens. Many translations (based on textual evidence) give the singular 'that Heaven rules' (*RSV*, *ESV*, *NIV*, *NET*), and this may well be the basis of the use of the phrase 'Kingdom of heaven', an expression used in the Gospel of Matthew as synonymous with 'Kingdom of God'.

Verse 27 Counsel to the King

Astonished as he must have been at the revelation of Divine judgement upon the king, Daniel would know that he was not only an interpreter of dreams but he was a spokesman for his God. With God-given courage, he places before King Nebuchadnezzar the real issue. Courteously, and yet with plainness of speech, Daniel points to him the reason for Divine discipline – 'thy sins' and 'thine iniquities' – words no-one normally would have dared use to this despotic ruler. 'Let my counsel be acceptable unto thee' is a courteous way of demanding a positive response. The message of the dream was humiliating, but, if accepted, that message opened the way to blessing. Two actions were required:

(a) 'Break off thy sins by righteousness'. The verb 'break off', which is used (literally) of breaking off golden earrings (Exod. 32:3), or (metaphorically) of breaking the yoke of bondage (Gen. 27:40), is used here spiritually – of breaking a pattern of life; in other words, to stop sinning. Accepting the standards of heaven, and so acting righteously, would mean his actions would in the future reflect Divine standards. The actions of an autocratic monarch, springing from the selfish pride, would suddenly be changed. The standards of heaven would mark him. What a change!

(b) 'Break off … thine iniquities by shewing mercy'. The same verb governs this statement. Pride had led Nebuchadnezzar to act in defiance of Divine standards. The same evil in the heart had led to the mistreatment of many of the captive peoples he had transported to Babylon as slaves, to whom no mercy had been shown. Nebuchadnezzar's building projects, in particular, had led to thousands upon thousands of slaves suffering and dying under extreme conditions for the sake of his pride. He was to show mercy to the 'poor' – this company would be readily identified in Babylon. Wilson[21] points out that this is the only time this particular word for 'poor' is used in this book. The more usual translation of the word is 'meek', or 'humble', and it implies 'patient submission to suffering and trouble'. This definition describes admirably the many peoples crushed by imperial power to gratify the pride and self-aggrandisement of the king.

This is not salvation by works, but, when these works would be manifest in Nebuchadnezzar's life, they would be indisputable evidence of true repentance toward God, in Whom he had believed. He would be a Divinely-changed man! A man who had been brought to the knowledge of the Most High (v. 25); of whom, in NT language, it could be said that he was 'born again'. The whole nation would be aware of such a change. What a testimony for God.

The expression 'lengthening of thy tranquillity' points to the escape from the impending judgement. This statement, however, is introduced by the expression 'if it may be'. In other words, if Nebuchadnezzar acts immediately there is just a possibility (not a promise, for the Divine patience had reached its limit with Nebuchadnezzar) that the sentence could be suspended. It would be a fair deduction – from the careful language used by Daniel – that Nebuchadnezzar had gone almost too far. Daniel makes it clear that the way of escape from the Divine sentence is open – immediate repentance and faith in the God speaking to him. Any other response invites instant judgement.

Nebuchadnezzar records no immediate personal response to the interpretation. He must have been shocked and upset, and the absence of any angry denunciation of Daniel suggests he was not so much angered as suddenly sobered. On the other hand, the absence of any mention of reward for Daniel, as compared with the honours heaped upon him after the interpretation of the first dream (2:48), may suggest his displeasure.

Verses 28–33 C. The Dream Realised: Nebuchadnezzar Recalls

The following six verses tell of the fulfilment of the dream in the experience of Nebuchadnezzar. It did not come immediately, as God allowed him a period of reflection – indeed God seems to wait

[21] *OTWS*, p. 318.

2. 'For the house of the kingdom'

The *RV* translates it: 'for the royal dwelling place', and another commentator interprets it: 'as a royal residence'.[25] The implication is that his inordinate pride could not be satisfied with any more humble dwelling. This is the only suitable place where such a king, as he thought himself to be, could dwell. Pride in his city!

3. 'By the might of my power'

Behind such a person ensconced in such a majestic palace lay power! With no acknowledgement of the God Who had previously revealed Himself as the God Who can reveal the future (2:47), and deliver His people in the present (4:25), he will now have to learn, by bitter experience, that He is a God Who 'resisteth the proud' (1 Pet. 5:5). Nebuchadnezzar was proud of his military campaigns that had brought the known world to his feet and the political skill that had enabled him to weather all the subsequent storms and enjoy peace. Failing to recognise that it was God Who had given all this: 'for the God of heaven hath given thee a kingdom, power, and strength, and glory' (2:37), he claimed it for himself. King Nebuchadnezzar was proud of his achievements. He was proud of his city. He was proud of his palace. He was proud of his power!

4. 'For the honour of my majesty'

A study of the usage of this word 'honour' in the OT seems to limit it to the honour that men give to men. It is used in this way in Esther – ten times (Est. 1:4, 20; 6:3, 6 (twice), 7, 9 (twice), 11; 8:16) – and three times in the Psalms (45:9; 49:12, 20). On the two occasions it is used in this book it is in the same sense. Nebuchadnezzar promises 'great honour' to the man who could interpret the dream (2:6). In this verse Nebuchadnezzar claims that he has reached that place of supreme honour amongst men. The city contributes to the place of honour he holds in the estimation of men as the greatest king on earth at this time.

Verses 31–32 The Penalty of Heaven Falls

The moment has arrived; the patience of heaven is exhausted, and the judgement is executed. While the proud words are in his mouth, the voice from heaven falls on his ear. Pride and its

[25] Leupold, *Exposition of Daniel*, p. 197.

punishment go together. Whether the voice is that of the watcher (v. 13), or simply a supernatural voice from heaven, we are not told. The message is addressed to Nebuchadnezzar alone. 'O king Nebuchadnezzar, to thee it is spoken' is more accurately translated, 'O Nebuchadnezzar they do declare'.[26] The plural may refer to the 'watchers', whose spokesman has just been heard, who now execute the sentence that has been passed (v. 17). The verb is in the passive voice and perfect tense – as if it had already been carried out – we read, 'The kingdom is departed from thee.' In the purpose of God it is completed action. Within the hour, his behaviour will show him to be mentally unstable and unfit to rule. What follows is the result. Driven from that splendid palace, not merely to live with commoners, but driven even from human habitation, to find his home among the beasts of the field and to share their herbage ('eat grass as oxen'). Seven years is the length of his sentence. In the moments before his mind toppled Nebuchadnezzar must have trembled.

Verse 33 The opening words of this verse, in 'the same hour', remind us of the time period between sentence and execution with respect to the fiery furnace (3:6). On that occasion, Nebuchadnezzar set the time; now heaven sets it and there is no appeal. It befell him exactly as threatened. It is not easy to imagine the consternation that rocked the council halls of Babylon as senior figures were hastily summoned to deal with such an unbelievable crisis. The king, having ripped off those magnificent robes, moving on hands and feet as an animal and uttering animal sounds, presented a major crisis in the council chambers of Babylon. The fulfilment happened precisely as prophesied in the dream, and interpreted by Daniel, with two added details that came to light with the passage of time. His hair, untended, grew long and, with exposure to the elements, matted into eagle-like feathers. His nails, uncut, grew and curled up like the claws of a bird. Thus how quickly this man of military skill and brilliant mind is brought down to the level of a beast. Nebuchadnezzar faithfully records the depth of his humiliation.

This condition has been identified down the years, and recognised as a type of insanity, rare indeed, but not unknown, in many countries. While in this particular case it was an affliction from God, natural causes seem to have produced the same

[26] Wood, *A Commentary on Daniel*, p. 120.

condition of men, thinking of themselves as a beast and imitating the behaviour of an animal. E.J. Young, in his commentary (published in 1949 and, it may be said, fully in accord with medical opinion of recent times), supports his thinking, and writes: 'The disease which came upon the king is known technically as *Lycanthropy*, in which the sufferer imagines himself to be changed into an animal and, to a certain extent acts like that animal. Apparently Neb (*sic*) had that form of the disease which would be called *Boanthropy*, i.e. he thought himself to be an ox, and so ate grass like an ox.'[27] Young goes on to quote E.B. Pusey who, after a study of a large number of cases, writes interestingly; 'Not even the extreme form of insanity interferes with the inner consciousness, or, consequently, with the power to pray. The inner consciousness remains unchanged, while up to a certain point, the sufferer thinks, speaks, acts as if he were another.' This is remarkably like this case of Nebuchadnezzar and, in particular, his obviously conscious action when he records, 'at the end of the days I Nebuchadnezzar lifted up mine eyes unto heaven.' The active voice indicates a conscious action that showed: (a) acceptance of the judgement of God; and (b) repentance for that which had brought the judgement. For the first time he acknowledges the God he had ignored. As a consequence of that evident repentance Nebuchadnezzar acknowledges, 'mine understanding returned unto me.'

Verses 34–37 Epilogue: A Royal Confession

(a) Repentance toward God

Nebuchadnezzar, not surprisingly, makes no reference to his experiences during the period of his insanity. That God protected him there cannot be the slightest doubt. That he was left unmolested, when in any other kingdom of the world a manifestly insane monarch would have been either locked out of sight or murdered, and a successor appointed, is clear evidence of Divine protection. The band of iron and brass round the trunk on the tree was the symbolic presentation of the same fact. In practical terms, it is clear that his close counsellors, possibly influenced by Daniel, must have agreed to cooperate in the care of the king in this condition and ensure that he was confined in the palace gardens, away from public scrutiny. The dream and Daniel's interpretation

[27] Young, *The Prophecy of Daniel*, p. 112.

of it, and, very especially, the time limit of seven years, must have been major factors in their thinking. A further important factor would be the preservation of the kingdom for Nebuchadnezzar, and with that, of course, would come their jobs. The public may not even have been aware of the king's condition. Public appearances were rare for a king in that day; only special occasions demanded his attendance. The absence of the king from a particular function could be explained, and the normal routine of government would be handled by the same officials, in their usual fashion.

The fact that such an interregnum in the reign of Nebuchadnezzar is not mentioned in the chronicles of Babylon is a major point with liberal critics, who dispute the authenticity of the record. It seems to be forgotten that this omission from the records is only to be expected. The history of the period comes from inscriptions on memorial plaques and tombstones, and, of course, only the king could authorise such works. The main objective in these inscriptions was to memorialise their victories. Defeats and disasters were not for the records, the chronicles and mural inscriptions; they were to be forgotten. It is most unlikely that such a humiliation of the greatest king of the Neo-Babylonian Empire would be put into these official records. The fact that Nebuchadnezzar issued this unique proclamation throughout the empire was doubtless due to Divine supervision.

(b) Restoration of Mental Health

Nebuchadnezzar reverts again to the first person to continue his personal testimony to the dealings of God that led to that look of repentance heavenward and the consequent restoration of his mental faculties. Then from heart and lips burst words of praise to the One Who had dealt so graciously with him – notes of praise that included the public acknowledgement of the aspects of the character of the God he has been brought to know. These considerations show the greatness of God set over against the 'nothingness' (vanity) of the idol:

1. His Supremacy. 'I blessed the Most High' – the gods of Babylon are displaced forever from his heart – even if they existed, they are of an infinitely lower order and other Scriptures show that any other supernatural power is satanic in character.

2. His Eternity. 'I praised and honoured Him that liveth for ever, whose dominion is an everlasting dominion, and His kingdom is from generation to generation' – kingdoms may rise and fall and

mighty monarchs come and go on the world stage. Kings come and go; generations rise and pass – this God exists eternally.

3. His Sovereignty. '[Who] doeth according to His will in the army of heaven, and among the inhabitants of the earth.' His sovereign right to command is seen not only in heaven, where the angels act on His command, but He has the same rights over mankind. 'Nothing' is the Divine assessment of men and the nations (Isa. 40:17). In this sovereignty both Divine omniscience and Divine omnipotence are clearly seen. It has been clearly demonstrated in the dealings of God with this mighty monarch of earth. There was no person, nor any power, able to oppose this Mighty God and ask 'what doest Thou?'

(c) Restoration of his Kingdom

At the same time as his mental powers were restored to Nebuchadnezzar, his position and powers in the kingdom were restored to him. King Nebuchadnezzar is absolutely clear that he owes it all to his God. He speaks of three vital matters restored to him:

1. 'The glory of my kingdom'. The word 'glory' means 'excellence' – an attraction to draw every eye. It was a mighty kingdom, yet in the pride of his heart he had forgotten it was given to him by God. Now he can glorify God that He has allowed nothing to be diminished of the glory he had before the period of insanity; in fact, 'excellent majesty was added' to him.

2. 'Mine honour and brightness'. The word 'honour' has been used before (v. 30), to indicate what man can give. It draws attention to the respect that men have for a person or thing. In the eyes of men he had not lost any of that dignity. In fact, his subsequent rule will show that this honour had grown. The word 'brightness' means 'splendour' and is used of the image – 'whose brightness was excellent' (2:31). It might have been expected that in the seven years of his absence these glories would have waned. This was not so; his empire shone as brightly as before. God saw to it that there was a complete restoration.

3. 'My counsellors and my lords sought unto me'. These counsellors had attended the king in the exercise of his power with regard to the fiery furnace (3:24, 27); now, surprisingly, they, or their successors, gather around him again. Did they recognise that Nebuchadnezzar had had dealings with God? 'Lords' does not point to specific offices, but describes the 'officials' necessary for the administration of the kingdom. Nebuchadnezzar had neither to fight nor scheme to regain authority. Willingly, the leading men of the kingdom sought him out. This may well be a testimony to the acumen he had shown in his previous years, but it is more likely to be the evidence of the hand of God in the full restoration as promised.

4. 'I was established in my kingdom, and excellent majesty was added unto me'. Greatness and glory had marked his earlier reign, from 605 BC to the date of the dream in 571 BC – a period of thirty-four years. With the year of probation taking him to 570 BC, the seven years of insanity would bring him to 563 BC. History records his death in 562 BC, so he only lived after his restoration less than two years – a short period, it is true, but long enough for the added peace and prosperity to testify to blessing from God. Nebuchadnezzar has learned his lesson well. He does not ascribe these new honours to himself, as he would have done in days gone by, but admits they come from God. History testifies to the honour in which he was held at the end of his reign.

(d) A Royal Testimony

Verse 37 In the final note of testimony in this remarkable and unique document published during the great days of the Babylonian Empire, King Nebuchadnezzar gives unqualified testimony to the King of heaven. Three present participles show the movement of his heart towards the God he has been brought to know. 'Praise' speaks of the exercise of the heart; 'extol' tells of the testimony of his lips; and 'honour' reflects the work of his hands in sacrifice and service. Together they present the elements of true worship. Nebuchadnezzar has been brought to recognise the reality of the works of God (truth) in a man's life and the righteousness of the ways of God (judgement) with men. His personal testimony lends weight to the final statement – 'those that walk in pride He is able to abase'.

The debate amongst commentators as to whether we shall meet Nebuchadnezzar in heaven still goes on. Men like Calvin, Keil, and Pusey point out that Nebuchadnezzar makes no reference to mercy, and think the evidence is insufficient to prove his salvation. On the other hand, there is in his life what many can see as a very definite conversion from the idols of Babylon to the Most High God (v. 24) – King of heaven (v. 37). There is sincere repentance in the acknowledgement of God (v. 34). There are notes of worship in his response to God's dealings with him (v. 37). More recent commentators, including some of those quoted from in this book, like J.F. Walvoord,[28] Leon Wood,[29] Stephen Miller, and many others, believe that we shall meet Nebuchadnezzar in the glory, as he by faith responded to the revelation of God given through Daniel. Miller puts the case concisely: 'One cannot be dogmatic, but the language of the text suggests that Nebuchadnezzar did have a saving encounter with the true God.'[30] As Nebuchadnezzar moves off the stage of scriptural history, there could scarcely be a clearer testimony to his relationship with God than the final verse of this chapter. It certainly seems like a confession of true faith in the living God.

PROPHETIC NOTE

The character and conduct of Nebuchadnezzar may be studied so as to compare and contrast him – the first Gentile king in the 'times of the Gentiles' (Lk. 21:24) – with the last Gentile king of that same period, who will be described later to Daniel. In the second part of this book he will be shown to be a Gentile who rules the ten-power kingdom of the end-time (7:23–25). Nebuchadnezzar, in his pride, was brought low by God's dealings with him in grace. This final king, named in the NT and called the 'man of sin ... son of perdition' (2 Thess. 2:3–4), having long ago rejected every gracious appeal, will display Nebuchadnezzar's pride, but magnified to the utmost. That overweening pride will lead this man to a profanity that goes far beyond the profanity of Belshazzar (chapter 5), in the introduction of his image into the holy place (2 Thess. 2:4). This in turn will lead him to a presumption of Deity that will go far beyond that of Darius (chapter 6). Pride, profanity and presumption will be the marks of that final Gentile world-ruler. The later visions of Daniel will identify this man as the 'Little Horn' (7:23–25) and the 'prince that shall come' (9:26). Of this last ruler in the 'times of the Gentiles' Nebuchadnezzar in all his pride is but a feeble portrayal.

[28] Walvoord, *Daniel: The Key to Prophetic Revelation*, p. 112: 'It is entirely possible that Nebuchadnezzar will be numbered among the saints'.

[29] Wood. *A Commentary on Revelation*, p. 138: 'No doubt that Nebuchadnezzar's knowledge of God at this point was meager (sic), but it seems that what he had he held sincerely and that he did experience a change of heart'.

[30] Miller, *New American Commentary, Daniel*, p. 142.

CHAPTER 5

THE SETTING OF CHAPTER 5 WITHIN SECTION B

Chapter 4	A King's Pride Nebuchadnezzar	Humbled 571 BC
Chapter 5	A King's Profanity Belshazzar	Judged 539 BC
Chapter 6	A King's Presumption Darius	Exposed 539 BC

AS A RECORDER OF HISTORICAL EVENTS in these chapters, Daniel has proved to be a most accurate and reliable historian. This has already been pointed out in the Introduction (Section 2 C). This chapter will bear further testimony to the reliability of Daniel in this record. Yet a point made in earlier chapters must be emphasised: Daniel is not just a recorder of past events, but, under Divine inspiration, he is doing something far beyond the ability of any uninspired historian; he is recording events from his own experience, yet placing them in such a particular order, that what was history becomes a shadow of something to come. This is the reason why the Lord spoke of him as 'Daniel the prophet' (Mt. 24:15). This is a vital part of his prophetic ministry, so that the Pride of a Nebuchadnezzar, the Profanity of a Belshazzar and the Presumption of a Darius are shadows of the substance that will be seen *par excellence* in the personality of an end-time ruler whose political rise, autocratic rule, and utter ruin will be seen in Part 2 of this book.

CHAPTER 5 – A KING'S PROFANITY JUDGED
PRELIMINARY NOTES

1. The Date of the Chapter 539 BC Daniel aged 84 yrs

In the study of chapter 4, the year of the restoration of Nebuchadnezzar to the throne after his seven-year period of disciplinary insanity was shown to be the year 563 BC. The chapter now before us records the fall of the city of Babylon to the Medo-Persian army, under Cyrus the Great. The date of that event is well established in secular history as taking place on the night of 13 October 539 BC. On this night, King Belshazzar had decided to hold the great Feast of Bel (Aramaic name 'Marduk') – the patron deity of the city. Thus, between chapter four and chapter five there is a period of twenty-three years and some months.[1]

A survey of these years will show them as being marked with civil unrest, military setbacks, and political intrigues that often ended in murder and usurpation. The historic landmarks may be summarised thus:

(a) Nebuchadnezzar died in 562 BC, having reigned for forty-three years (605–562 BC). An absolute autocrat, yet, by the standard of his times, he was, on the whole, a just and a fair ruler for his people.

(b) Evil-Merodach, the son of Nebuchadnezzar, took the throne. An evil man, he was murdered within two years and his brother-in-law, Neriglissar, seized the throne

(c) Neriglissar was murdered after four years and replaced by his teenage son, Labashi-Marduk, who was but a puppet for military leaders who wanted some legitimacy for their control of the empire. During this period, powerful factions competed for place and power. Usurpations and murder within the royal household were reflected in weakness in the administration of the empire. This opened the way for rebels to rise up and seize power in many areas. To deal with these insurrections, the available defence forces were woefully inadequate. The consequence was that there was a growing despair in the face of the rising might of the Medo-Persian alliance that was being forged by Cyrus the Great.

(d) At last an able man called Nabonidus appeared on the political stage. He was one of the generals in Nebuchadnezzar's army – a scholar, yet a most capable strategist on the battlefield. Deeply religious and of priestly lineage, he did not worship Bel, the patron god of Babylon, but the god Sin, whose temple – in Haran – he excavated, rebuilt, and adorned most lavishly. Backed by powerful figures in the administration, Nabonidus seized the throne in 556 BC and brought some stability to the empire for the final seventeen years of its existence. An unusual man for the times, he was deeply interested in early Babylonian history and archaeology, so that, engaged with these pursuits, he was absent

[1] See Appendix 2 for historical detail and dates.

from Babylon for extended periods of time. At one such site, the oasis of Taima in Arabia, he spent so much time that he built a royal residence there.

The fragmentary records available to scholars, until well into the twentieth century, were all agreed in naming Nabonidus as the last king of Babylon before Cyrus took the city. These inscriptions and dedicatory tablets, on temples, buildings, and gravestones, made no mention of any son of Nebuchadnezzar called Belshazzar. The name could not be found in any of the records, and the confirmed dates for the reign of Nabonidus left no room for any king to follow him before the fall of Babylon. Sceptical and liberal commentators joined forces to declare Belshazzar unhistorical and to label Daniel inaccurate. Such critics insisted that Daniel had made a grave error in his reference to Nebuchadnezzar as the father of Belshazzar (v. 2). In recent years, in the deciphering of newly translated cuneiform inscriptions, the name Belshazzar has come to light – in triumphant vindication of Daniel's accuracy. Three special texts, from different areas of Babylon and deciphered by three different archaeologists,[2] confirm that Belshazzar was the eldest son of Nabonidus. In further vindication of Daniel, it has been learned that Nabonidus, during the last ten years of his reign – from c. 549 BC – made this son Belshazzar co-regent with him in the empire, with complete authority to deputise for him as King of Babylon during the periods of his absence.[3] While a further point still requires confirmation, it is generally conceded amongst historians that there is evidence to suggest that Nabonidus, to consolidate his claim to the throne, had married Nitocris, the daughter of Nebuchadnezzar, who became the mother of Belshazzar.[4] Confirmation is still being sought as more documents are discovered and deciphered. When King Nabonidus left Babylon, with the declared purpose of gathering a sufficiently powerful army to confront the invading Median army under Cyrus, he left his son Belshazzar in control of the city of Babylon, with the title of King. The fact that Belshazzar was co-regent with his father

[2] Pusey, *Daniel the Prophet*, p. 344.

[3] For the historic references see Wood, *A Commentary on Daniel*, p. 130. Wood quotes from Sidney Smith, *Babylonian Historical Texts, Relating to the Downfall of Babylon* (London: Methuen & Co Ltd., 1924). One of the texts is *A Persian Verse Account of Nabonidus* which reads 'He freed his hand; he entrusted the kingship to him. Then he undertook a distant campaign.'

[4] Wood, *A Commentary on Daniel*, p. 140.

explains why he could only offer to the interpreter of the writing on the wall the place of 'Triumvir' (third ruler) in the kingdom (v. 29).

2. The Feast of Belshazzar

The thoughtful reader will seek the reason for the celebration of such a feast in a beleaguered city with the enemy at the gates. Within the past days, not only had the Medo-Persian army brought up heavy siege engines and catapults, but Cyrus, the victorious Medo-Persian general, had arrived to take control of the siege. The outlook for Babylon was certainly far from secure. Should not the king and counsellors in this besieged city be seeing to the defences, rather than holding such a feast? Why did Belshazzar hold the feast? There has been a variety of suggestions:

(a) Some commentators think that Belshazzar intended the feast to display a vainglorious contempt for the Medo-Persian army encamped around the city – an act of defiance in the presence of the enemy. The difficulty is that there is little evidence in this chapter, and little support from historical records, that the city was ablaze with light and revelry. However, there is one notable exception to this statement: Herodotus, the historian and famous traveller, tells a different story,[5] and while some doubts arise about his sources, his history is generally dependable – see quotation at verse 3. This quotation does not agree with the idea of a city asleep while the king and his lords were reveling in an inner hall of the palace, but shows a city engrossed in drinking and dancing in a festive mood.

(b) Other commentators have suggested that it was possibly to celebrate some minor victory in the continuing siege, and thus keep up the hearts of the people of the besieged city. Again, however, there is no evidence that the revel was taking place in the city and no record of any victory, even a minor one, can be found in historical records. The latest news had been of disaster to the Babylonian army, led by Nabonidus.

(c) The Greek historian Xenophon (435–354 BC), writing in the next century, has an interesting suggestion that is helpful. He suggests that this feast was the annual celebration of the god 'Bel' held at this time of the year (October 13 in our calendar). Bel was the head of the Babylonian pantheon and the patron god of the city, whom Nebuchadnezzar had worshipped under his Accadian name, 'Marduk'. Nebuchadnezzar had impoverished other territories to

[5] Herodotus, *The History of Herodotus*, Book 1, para. 191, p. 43.

rebuild the great temple of Esagila in his honour; in fact he had made the temple of Marduk the richest and most magnificent temple in the city. Since Belshazzar had been named in honour of this god – Belshazzar means 'Prince of Bel' – there is no doubt he would, in normal circumstances, be expected to lead the celebration. Some historians doubt this and find good reason to think this feast should have been allowed to drop out of the religious calendar, as it had in the previous few years. There is no doubt that, since Nabonidus had seized the throne, Marduk had lost some credibility! Consider the blows Babylon had received: (a) The city is in dire peril – the Medo-Persian attack is expected daily; (b) King Nabonidus has left Belshazzar his son as King-Regent, but with a reduced garrison, as he had taken an army into Arabia with the design of confronting Cyrus in the desert; (c) the latest news from the army of Nabonidus is disastrous – the Babylonian army totally routed and King Nabonidus taken captive.

One would have thought that King Belshazzar would have been better seeking the God Whom his grandfather had been brought to know, than playing host to this Bacchanalian orgy to a discredited idol, in besieged Babylon! However, as will be shown in the comments (v. 2), there were very compelling reasons why, in the judgement of King Belshazzar, this particular feast must be held!

Chapter five divides readily under three headings:

Drunken Revelry in Babylon's Hall	vv. 1–4
Divine Revelation on Babylon's Wall	vv. 5–24
Dread Retribution in Babylon's Fall	vv. 25–30

Verses 1–4 Drunken Revelry in Babylon's Hall

As a preliminary to our discussion, the following points should be noted:

1. Except for the mention of his name in the dating of two of the visions given to Daniel (7:1; 8:1), this is the only place in Scripture where King Belshazzar is mentioned.

2. For additional detail in the history of the times and support for the identifications made with reference to 'King Belshazzar' (v. 1), 'The Queen' (v. 10), and 'Darius the Median' (v. 31), see Appendix 2.

Verses 1–2 A Great Feast

Verse 1 'Belshazzar the king made a great feast to a thousand of his lords' is the simple statement that introduces a dramatic scene. First the host – King Belshazzar – is clearly the instigator of this feast which, since Nabonidus took the throne, had been rather neglected – he had given priority to another god, named Sin. King Belshazzar acts to call this feast. Then the question arises – why call such a feast at this time? In the introduction to this chapter, reference has been made to a suggestion made by Xenophon, a Greek historian writing a century later, that this feast was the annual celebration in honour of the patron god of Babylon, called Bel-Marduk. Most historians accept this suggestion, since the dates coincide. The feast falls on 13 October, and this is the night Babylon fell to the army of Cyrus. Since King Belshazzar had been named in honour of this god (Belshazzar means 'Prince of Bel'), there is no doubt that he was the one who would be expected to host the feast.

That he called a thousand of his lords is an indication of the importance and scale of the celebration. The word 'lords' would cover the higher officials in government – all those who by the nature of their office would be closest to the king. The word is used to describe the men around Nebuchadnezzar (4:36). Another point of interest comes from archaeology: recent excavation of a great hall (60 feet wide and 172 feet long) in the ruins of Babylon may well point to the very site of this feast. This hall could readily have accommodated a thousand of Belshazzar's lords, and, in addition, it has a special recess, where the king would be elevated above the crowd, and yet able to play a leading part in the festivities. The walls are of plaster and decorated with painted stucco designs, including lions and leopards – an art form peculiar to Babylon. One would wonder if this was the very plaster ('plaister' in *AV*) upon which Babylon's doom was written!

To celebrate this feast in the year when the city was under siege, the Babylonian army in the field in precipitate retreat, and King Nabonidus, Belshazzar's father, taken captive by the Medo-Persian army, may seem strange. Nevertheless, Belshazzar had very weighty reasons for the celebration; it would almost seem as if he did not dare cancel it. Consider the following:

(a) The city of Babylon was adjudged by every military strategist of the day to be absolutely impregnable.[6] Added to its inherent strength of double walls, with one hundred watchtowers, was a twenty-year supply of food already in store. The people of Babylon were totally confident that the city could not be taken. Josephus bears testimony to the total assurance of the citizens that even Cyrus could not capture Babylon. Obviously Belshazzar was not worried about this possibility.

(b) The feast was in honour of the patron god of the city of Babylon. King Nebuchadnezzar had worshipped this god in earlier years and been lavish in his donations to the Temple of Marduk, an old Sumerian sun god always associated with Babylon.[7] King Belshazzar bore his name with pride and worshipped him. The Babylonian people worshipped Bel. It would have been impiety most deplorable to ignore this feast for another year. In fact, in this disastrous year, when deliverance by supernatural aid was urgently needed, it was essential that Bel be honoured as he had been in the past.

(c) A further factor that would weigh heavily on the mind of King Belshazzar was that his own father, King Nabonidus, though he had given him the name Belshazzar, in honour of Bel, had in these last ten years lavished much more wealth on the moon god, Sin, than he had on Marduk. He had built a temple for the moon god in Taima,[8] where he was often based when absent from Babylon. It fact there seems to be the feeling, in the history work quoted, that this feast had been at least neglected, if not omitted, in the previous few years.

(d) But something more seems to have been weighing heavily on the mind of Belshazzar. He revelled in the fact that, seventy years before this, Bel had shown himself more powerful than even the Hebrew God, Jehovah. The Temple of Jehovah in Jerusalem had been destroyed and the people of Israel deported to Babylon. But in more recent times the god of Babylon, so mighty in the past, had been most grievously insulted. Within two years of the end of his forty-three year reign, during the greater part of which he had worshipped Bel, Nebuchadnezzar had issued an empire-wide edict praising Jehovah as King of heaven (4:1–37), and, inferentially, downgrading Bel. Belshazzar would certainly point out that from

[6] See Appendix 2 for references.

[7] Saggs, *The Babylonians*, p. 120. This is a reprint of *The Greatness that was Babylon*, first published in 1962.

[8] Saggs, *The Babylonians*, p. 121 ff., for the story of war between the sun-god (Marduk) and the moon-god (Sin).

Persians came upon them by surprise and took the city. Owing to the vast size of the place the inhabitants of the central parts (as the residents at Babylon declare) long after the outer portions of the town were taken, knew nothing of what had chanced, but as they were engaged in a festival, continued dancing and revelling until they learnt the capture but too certainly. Such then were the circumstances of the first taking of Babylon.' It is only fair to say that some question his accuracy at this point, as there is little support from other authorities – and many accept that the city was asleep.

Such drunken revelry soon breaks down every normal barrier and abandons every normal restraint. A crescendo of shouts of exultation, screams of lechery, and songs of debauchery join in the frenzy of unrestrained festivity. Idolatry and immorality, happily joined together, carry the royalty and nobility of Babylon into an orgy of sin. Babylon lives up to its name.

Verses 5–24 Divine Revelation on Babylon's Wall

Verses 5–9 A Great Fear

Verse 5 The expression 'in the same hour' has been used on two occasions already in this book (3:6, 15) to show that two things follow quickly upon each other without delay. Here, it indicates that heaven responded to this behaviour quickly. Just as the revelry reached a crescendo, heaven acted. Dramatically (the *NIV* translates the phrase as 'suddenly'), the 'fingers of a man's hand' appeared – the Hebrew reads 'came forth' (*AV*) – and might suggest that part of the hand came through the wall to write 'over against the lampstand'. The literal reading is 'end part of human hand'; the word 'fingers' is not in the text, but it interprets accurately 'end part of a hand', which writes on the plaster of the wall, beside the lampstand, close to the king. Here it could not be missed. Archaeologists have pointed out that many walls in Babylon's palaces are plastered with a lime-based white plaster, to take the paintings of animals with which they are decorated. Part of a human hand – no writing instrument is mentioned – begins to write on the plaster of the palace wall. Any observer would realise that this was supernormal and supernatural.

It is clear that the king's eye was the first to catch the movement on the wall. Likely turning to see the cause of the movement, he sees part of a man's hand writing on the wall. Startled, and then stunned, his gaze riveted on the hand slowly writing, possibly a goblet of wine slipping from his own hand, to crash on the floor – the king's face changes. Every eye in the hall swivels to gaze at the king, then, following the direction of his look, every eye is caught, as the hand continues to write. As one reveller after another turns and catches sight of the moving hand, voices fall silent, one by one. Wine goblets are put down, or drop from nerveless fingers; the shouting fades; the ribald song dies away – an eerie silence grips the banquet hall. In absolute silence, king and courtiers watch as the message on the wall is completed and the hand fades from sight.

Verse 6 Every eye in that great hall, at first fixed on the moving hand, would then swivel to fasten on the king's face. The change can only be described as shocking. Disaster and doom are written large in the reaction of the king. The statement is brief but telling: 'the king's countenance was changed'. 'Turned pale' (*NIV*) is far too weak. The word 'countenance' is not the usual word for 'face'. The same word is used of Nebuchadnezzar (4:36) and translated 'brightness' or 'splendour'. A few minutes earlier, flushed with royal pride and lit up in alcoholic euphoria, he had looked every inch a king in control of the feast. What a change! Filling the same throne, there is now the pale wreck of a man, shaking in every limb, his knees knocking one against another. It is obvious to everyone in the hall that he is a desperately frightened man. The word 'loins' in Scripture is synonymous with the seat of manly strength (Job 40:16; Ps. 66:11; Prov. 31:17); the expression 'to gird up the loins' (Job 38:3; 40:7, etc.) means 'to summon all the reserves of strength'. So the 'joints of his loins ... loosed' describes the absolute weakness that had descended upon King Belshazzar; he had no further resources upon which he could draw; he was a man shaken to the very core of his being. No longer in control of his body, 'his knees smote one against another' (see also Nah. 2:10) – an expression that today speaks of trembling fear. We are told the reason for these physical signs – 'his thoughts troubled him'. On the battlefield, history holds no record of cowardice against Belshazzar, so it can hardly be any thought of the coming assault on the city that made him a trembling wreck. This was very different: the touch of the supernatural had undoubtedly brought him to face an inescapable fact. He was acting in deliberate defiance of a mighty God – the God of Israel – the God of his grandfather Nebuchadnezzar! Now he knew that he was face-to-face with the God he had defied. Fear gripped him, and the very same fear – the fear of the supernatural – brought stillness into this crowded banquet hall of sycophantic, drink-sodden courtiers. This is a moment of truth, when the whole company almost forgets to breathe, as it awaits the response of the king. No-one dare speak – not even a whisper – the silence must have been absolute! Then, suddenly, the silence is shattered! A voice – a shout – a rising note that, becoming shrill, ends up almost a scream!

Verse 7 Across that silent hall, the voice of the king would seem to rise to a pitch that justifies 'scream' as, imperiously, he demands the presence of the wise men of the kingdom. The adverb 'aloud' used to describe the cry wrenched from the throat of the king would be accurately translated as 'in earnest', or 'in strength' (*NET* note). It demanded instant action; the king was not acting. No delay was allowed; the king meant the wise men to be there – now! 'To bring in' could be literally translated 'cause to enter' (*NET* note). It can be imagined how urgently that summons would be carried through the corridors of the palace to the quarters of the wise men.

While only three groups of the wise men are mentioned here – astrologers, Chaldeans and soothsayers – out of the four groups listed earlier in the book (2:2), it seems clear that all the men on duty answered this imperial summons. 'Then came in all the king's wise men' is a comprehensive statement, and any suggestion that the fourth group, 'magicians', have been omitted through subtle satanic action to close out Daniel is without foundation. It is true that Daniel had been promoted by Nebuchadnezzar, who addressed him as 'master of the magicians' (4:9), but that was over thirty years in the past; Daniel is now an old man of eighty-four, and most likely retired from normal duties. This would mean he was in his own quarters and the king's summons did not reach him.

Doubtless, pointing with shaking hand to the writing on the wall, the king demanded two things of his hastily-summoned counsellors: (a) read this writing; and (b) show me the interpretation thereof. That plea – for the language suggests he was almost pleading – is followed immediately by the promise of incredible reward for the person doing this. It is perfectly clear, from the reward promised, that the king was acutely aware that he was asking something inordinately difficult. So unusual are the circumstances that the king seems to grasp that the future of the kingdom, and even his personal survival, is at stake. With the city under siege, the urgency in his demand, as well as the profligacy of his reward, are readily understood.

Why the writing required the attention of the wise men to read it has been a problem for commentators. From Daniel's reading of the message it could be argued that the writing was in Aramaic, with which the wise men would be familiar. The answer usually given is that, while Aramaic is the language used, the characters used for the words are those of the Western Phoenician Script. With this particular script Daniel would be perfectly familiar, as these characters were used in Israel.[13] The wise men, it is argued, would only be accustomed to Aramaic written in the Eastern Phoenician Script. This is a plausible explanation but, very rightly, not all commentators are happy with it, and E.J. Young[14] writes scathingly: 'However, this is to interpret the miracle on naturalistic principles.' This is a perfectly justifiable criticism – able men, with their combined scholarship, would hardly be stymied by an unusual script. The fact that the wise men did not make the slightest attempt to read the writing would suggest that the characters employed must have been so unusual that they knew instantly that this writing demanded more than erudition could bring to it – it required Divine illumination. For the third time, publicly and comprehensively (2:47; 3:29; 4:34), at the world centre of idolatry, there is displayed, for all to see, the helplessness of the spokesmen for the idol-gods and the power behind them. The summons must go out for the spokesman of Jehovah.

Into that silent hall the voice of the king brings a promise to whoever can: (a) read the writing; and (b) show the interpretation thereof. The reward is three-fold and, indeed, most impressive: (a) Shall be clothed with 'scarlet', or 'purple' (*RV*). Herodotus (*c.* 484–420 BC), the traveller, and writer of a valued historical narrative, asserts that the purple robe in Babylon and in Persia was reserved for royalty. No-one else was permitted to wear this colour (see Est. 8:15); (b) Have a chain of gold about his neck. Again, Herodotus insists that, at this period, only those personally honoured by the king in this way for their fidelity to the throne were allowed to wear a golden chain (see Gen. 41:42); (c) Shall be the third ruler in the kingdom. To offer as a reward such a place of authority in the city of Babylon is beyond comprehension. Some special factors, apart from

[13] Wood, *A Commentary on Daniel*, p. 139.

[14] Young, *The Prophecy of Daniel*, p. 122.

alcohol, must be at work here. The 'third ruler' (AV) translates the Aramaic as an ordinal number and means the third ruler in order of authority: Nabonidus, Belshazzar, and then the promoted interpreter. E.J. Young, a world authority in the language, writes, 'The Aramaic could more precisely mean "a third-ling or triumvir, one of three".' This could mean each would have equal authority in a group of three.

The unbelievable honour that Belshazzar holds out to the interpreter of the writing on the wall shows: (a) how deeply the king was moved! (b) how serious the situation was; and (c) how accurately Belshazzar spoke, and how carefully Daniel has recorded his words, without feeling any necessity to explain why it is a number three position in the kingdom and not a number two position that is promised. As explained in the preliminary notes to this chapter, King Belshazzar is but co-regent with his father. To bring in another would make him a 'triumvir' – a third ruler of equal status with the first two. It also shows, from the perspective of history, how Scripture vindicates itself when all the facts are known. Scripture remains trustworthy in every statement.

Verses 8–9 So unprecedented has been the summons, and so impatient the king, that some of the wise men still seem to be gathering while the king is speaking, but now, it would seem, they are all here, their eyes fixed on the writing on the wall. Silence still reigns and not a voice is raised to read or interpret the writing. It is clear that the king, not in the least reassured by the reaction of the wise men, is now terrified. Compare 'troubled' (v. 6) with 'greatly troubled' (v. 9); his countenance grows even more pale; the lords are 'perplexed' (RV) – they are totally at a loss to know what to do. That perplexity is accentuated by the low murmur of voices, as they frantically seek from each other the meaning of this strange writing on the wall. A real feeling of impending calamity broods over this interrupted banquet.

Verses 10–12 A Great Fame

At this moment of high drama, there steps into the hall a dignified figure identified by Daniel simply, without any introduction or explanation, as 'The queen'. It is possible to deduce from the language (AV) that the noises from the feast in the great hall carried to the secluded quarters of the queen – first the uproar and then the silence. These sounds and, especially, the ensuing silence, would give cause for concern or curiosity, so the queen decided to see what was happening. However, a close study of the wording suggests a different reason for her arrival at this point. It would appear that messengers were keeping her in touch, both with the events, and the reactions to those events, in the banquet hall. Now, when the news reaches her of the failure of the wise men to read the mysterious writing, she must have realised her moment had come! Having heard the cause of the silence, she would recognise that she alone had the answer to the king's dilemma. No stranger to the king, and certainly well-known to the lords, she steps into the banquet hall with an inherent dignity and a confident step that must have drawn every eye and stilled every tongue.

The identity of this lady has given historians ground for much painstaking research and commentators much ground for speculation and debate. However, simply accepting the scriptural account as Daniel gives it, pondering her dramatic appearance at this crucial moment, and, finally, listening to her most pointed advice to the king, would point in one direction in her identification. Historical records may then be searched for confirmation. In this search the following points need to be given weight:

(a) This lady cannot be the wife of Belshazzar as might be the expected deduction from the title 'queen' that Daniel uses. Her demeanour before the king and her language as she addresses him rule out this possibility. Further evidence against this view is the fact that all wives were already in the banquet hall (v. 2). Either she had not been invited or she had refused to go. For the wife of King Belshazzar neither possibility is tenable.

(b) Yet this lady can move unhindered through the palace and walk into this banquet hall seemingly unattended; she even dares to come into the king's presence without a direct summons; few men in Babylon, never mind a woman, would have dared to do that. Their life would have been immediately forfeit.

(c) She addresses the king courteously, yet absolutely fearlessly and without a trace of obsequiousness, as if she has every right to be heard.

(d) She is listened to with deep respect by all the courtiers and courtesans. Not one voice of protest is raised, and, more impressive still, the king acts on her advice without the slightest hesitation.

(e) She shows a close and detailed knowledge of the history of Babylon, and, in her very words about Daniel, there are echoes of the words of Nebuchadnezzar. Words that the great king had used come easily to her tongue.

(f) She identifies Daniel, not simply as the man to answer the need of the moment, but as the only man in the kingdom who could interpret the writing. She makes this assertion without the slightest hesitation or reservation. She is so sure of his ability to meet this emergency that there is not a single qualifying doubt, beginning with 'maybe' or 'perhaps', as she 'advises' or – perhaps a more accurate word – 'orders' the king to call Daniel.

(g) Her words, too, seem to carry a rebuke, as if Belshazzar was to be blamed for Daniel's present obscurity in the kingdom. Perhaps she knew that Belshazzar, at the very least, had taken no action to keep this honoured counsellor of Nebuchadnezzar near the throne. It is most likely, as was customary in all the kingdoms of the day, when there was a change of dynasty by *coup d'état*, that all the counsellors of the previous regime were compulsorily retired, if not executed. The reasoning behind this action was straightforward – they had obviously failed their king and were thus unlikely to be of any help under a new regime. This could have happened in 562 BC when King Nebuchadnezzar died. It is more likely to have happened in 556 BC, seventeen years before this moment, when Nabonidus – one of Nebuchadnezzar's generals, who himself had no ancestral link with Nebuchadnezzar, seized the throne. The wise men would all be compulsorily retired and replaced by others. This retirement is assuredly the reason why he was not called with the present company of wise men. Despite his age, Daniel possibly still retained his other administrative responsibility as ruler in Babylon (8:2, 27) and thus his home would be in quarters in the administrative building. It would be someone very sure of her privileged position who would speak thus to King Belshazzar.

(h) She speaks of Nebuchadnezzar as his 'father', but this term in Aramaic, as already discussed (v. 2), is a very wide term and can mean 'grandfather', or in some cases, more generally, 'ancestor',[2] or even 'predecessor'. This lady gives King Belshazzar a very secure status as a successor in the direct line of the great Nebuchadnezzar, and close enough to know intimately how God had dealt with this proud monarch.

Earlier expositors relying largely upon Josephus[15] have identified this 'queen' as the widow of King Nebuchadnezzar and the mother of Belshazzar[16] – and their arguments carry much weight. However, no evidence from any cuneiform text has come to light to support the identification of Belshazzar as a son of Nebuchadnezzar. An alternative suggestion was that one of his generals in the army, Nabonidus by name, had married Nebuchadnezzar's widow, and Belshazzar was their son. A beautiful woman, younger than Nebuchadnezzar, there is little doubt that such a diplomatic marriage would have given Nabonidus a legitimate claim to the throne. Little evidence again being found in the records, it was thought that Nabonidus had married Nebuchadnezzar's widow but brought into the marriage his own son by a previous marriage – Belshazzar.[17] However, in more recent studies this suggestion too has presented too many problems to be fully satisfying. The biggest problem arises in this chapter – her message to Belshazzar appears much more intimate than stepmother speaking to a stepson who could have been about her own age. In recent years, some cuneiform texts[18] have supported an alternative suggestion that has gained wide acceptance amongst conservative commentators. It is suggested that this queen is a daughter of Nebuchadnezzar. It would seem she married Nabonidus when he was one of Nebuchadnezzar's generals. If this suggestion is accepted, despite the lack of unqualified support from historical research – and the records are still very fragmentary – then the picture becomes much clearer. Summing up a long argument Miller writes: 'Most likely she was the wife of Nabonidus, and a daughter, not a widow, of Nebuchadnezzar. If so, she may be the famous Nitocris. At any rate, this woman displayed first-hand information concerning the affairs of Nebuchadnezzar that would not have been known by a younger wife of Belshazzar, and she seems to have observed Daniel's ministry in Nebuchadnezzar's court.'[19] Accepting this suggestion as best fitting the evidence available to us, this queen is seen as the

[15] Josephus, *Complete Works*, p. 225. He speaks of this woman as 'the king's grandmother'.

[16] Keil & Delitzsch, *Commentary on the Old Testament*, Vol. 9 p. 185. Keil is forthright 'By [queen] interpreters rightly understand the mother of the reigning king, the widow of his father Nebuchadnezzar, since according to verse 2f, the wives of the king were present at the festival, and the *Queen* came in before the king as only a mother could do'.

[17] Oates, *Babylon*, p. 131.

[18] Miller, *New American Commentary, Daniel*, p. 160 for references to the cuneiform texts (Footnote 73).

[19] Miller, *New American Commentary, Daniel*, p. 160.

wife of King Nabonidus and she is also the mother of Belshazzar.[20] This makes Belshazzar a grandson of Nebuchadnezzar through his mother. Thus this lady can speak to Belshazzar as only a mother can speak, and he listens. The fact that she is a daughter of the great Nebuchadnezzar – the founding father of the empire – lends weight to her words, and the lords listen. It is suggested that these deductions fit the picture and link up with the fragmentary records available from Babylonian archaeological research.[21] It is further suggested that, thus identified, this lady fulfils the eight conditions given above. Her dramatic entry, personal dignity, and matronly advice as an older lady give added weight to this conclusion. Her personal memories of God dealing with her father accounts for her clear recollection of Daniel. Her absence from the feast is not therefore due to age, but to the fact that her husband is a prisoner in Persian hands, which meant that her presence would have outraged accepted protocol. It would also explain her close contact with what was going on in the banquet hall. Her watchful eye on the proceedings in the hall, on behalf of husband and son, would be a routine measure, and would arise from the ever-present threat of conspiracies, especially now when things were going wrong in the empire.

Verses 10–11 Message to the King

Her address to the king – 'O king, live for ever' is the normal, formal, and respectful greeting to a monarch. However, in this particular case, it must carry a shade of unintentional irony, when we know that this king has only hours to live. Her next words are an accurate reading of the furrowed brow and the pallid face. The translation is dramatic but it catches the thought: 'Don't be alarmed! Don't look so pale!' (*NIV*). While the inability of the wise men to read the writing is the ostensible reason for the king's distress, did the queen recall her father's reaction to the dream (2:1) and the very human reaction to the supernatural – fear? Did she see the same fear in Belshazzar's face? At least she knew where the

[20] See Appendix 2 for detail.

[21] The fact that Nabonidus was an antiquarian and when on duty on behalf of Nebuchadnezzar in the field with an army used the opportunity of deciphering cuneiform texts of the previous era would have kept him out of the disturbed times until the murder of his brother-in-law, in which some suggest he had a part, allowed him to put in his claim. He confessed himself 'I am Nabonidus who have not the honour of being somebody – kingship is not in me' (See Oates, *Babylon*) – but someone overcame his diffidence, possibly his wife.

answer was to be found. In a direct response to her son's obvious perplexity she gives her advice.

She speaks bluntly: 'there is a man in thy kingdom'; a man, she implies, whom you have demoted, ignored and forgotten, yet he continues to serve you faithfully. With absolute conviction the queen gives the identification marks that made this man different:

(a) He was distinguished from other men in the time of the great king Nebuchadnezzar by 'the Spirit of the holy gods' (the very language of Nebuchadnezzar, 4:8, 18).

(b) He possessed the 'wisdom of the gods' expressed in 'light' – meaning an insight into matters – and 'understanding' – meaning a readiness to act on the insight given, and 'wisdom' – as if he was walking in step with the gods (expressed practically in 4:27). Couched in language Belshazzar would understand, it would seem that this lady shared the light her father had enjoyed through the dealings of God with him. This daughter of Nebuchadnezzar, having learned of God from her father, must surely have passed some knowledge of this God to Nabonidus her husband and Belshazzar her son.

It is very interesting to know that there seem to be indications in the inscriptions left by Nabonidus that he showed at least respect for Nebuchadnezzar's testimony; there had been no obvious response in Belshazzar except that he seems to be fully acquainted with what the queen has recalled. Clearly he had tried to lose himself in the profligate lifestyle of Babylon and put such things out of mind. The challenge of his grandfather's day, put by the queen, is now before the king – to do what Nebuchadnezzar had done – call for Daniel. Just to put the matter beyond doubt, the queen then backed up her personal testimony to Daniel with the weighty fact that Nebuchadnezzar had thought so highly of him as to make him master of the magicians, astrologers, Chaldeans and soothsayers. It is to be noted that all four terms are used (as in 4:7), Daniel was supreme head amongst the wise men of Babylon (compare 1:20; 2:2, 27; 5:7).

Verse 12 The queen ends with a very high commendation of Daniel as the only man who could solve this problem. She expresses not the slightest doubt of his ability to read and interpret the writing on the wall. She seems almost to fear that Belshazzar will hesitate and not accept her advice. Daniel stands out by:

(a) 'an excellent spirit' which must refer, not to his attitude to life, but to the 'Spirit of the holy gods', mentioned earlier, which gives him ability beyond others in the area of –

(b) 'knowledge', which implies that he had already the relevant background information to reach the right conclusion, summed up in the next word –

(c) 'understanding', which is already used (v. 11) for the illumination required for any matter not clear. In the next statement –

(d) 'interpreting of dreams' is the area where knowledge and understanding are put to good use, as she herself can testify from the experiences of her father already recorded by Daniel (chapter 2 and chapter 4) –

(e) 'shewing of hard sentences' and 'dissolving of doubts' would be better translated 'the explaining of riddles' and 'the solving of difficult problems'.[22] These statements may refer either to Daniel's interpretation of the dreams for Nebuchadnezzar or additional experiences of which we have no record – it makes little difference.

Now she names the man as Daniel – his Hebrew name; then she adds the name given to him by Nebuchadnezzar – Belteshazzar. At this point the language of the queen is still courteous but becomes peremptory: 'let Daniel be called'; she is not desiring a favour but giving an order. She has absolute confidence that Daniel 'will shew the interpretation'. The fact that she uses his Hebrew name, in preference to his Babylonian name, tells of her deep respect for the man God has used to bring her father, and, one would be tempted to add, herself as well, to the knowledge of the true God. Startling in its abruptness and striking in its confidence, the challenge rings through the banquet hall – 'Now let Daniel be called, and he will shew the interpretation.' The queen knew she had the answer to King Belshazzar's problem.

Verses 13–16 Mandate from the King

It must have been a moment of sheer drama when the aged man of God, now 84 years old, steps into that banquet hall. What a contrast with the drink-sodden yet suddenly silenced crowd. As far as the evidence goes, he may still have held office in the city of Babylon. Since there is no mention of any delay after the summons, this suggests that his quarters were known to the officers and not very

[22] Miller, *New American Commentary, Daniel*, p. 161.

far away. The reference to the king's business (8:27) in the third year of Belshazzar (551 BC) is twelve years before, and thus too far away for absolute proof, but shows, at least, that he was still at his desk when aged 72. The fact to be noted is that he was not at this feast of Belshazzar. Whether as already retired he was not invited, or being outside Belshazzar's favoured ring of younger officials he was ignored, is not made clear, but the fact remains that he was not there. Much more likely is that the conviction about defiling food, which had marked him out as a young man (1:8), marked him still in his later years as the line of separation from the idolatry of Babylon.

Verses 13–14 The king's question using his Hebrew name shows he knew all about Daniel but had never met him. No answer is expected; the king would know none other would be allowed to present himself before him. The interrogative is best rendered as a statement: 'thou art that Daniel'. The king's next words carry a hint of intimidation as he reminds Daniel that he is only a Judaean captive brought to Babylon by King Nebuchadnezzar. It is very obvious that Belshazzar knew more about Daniel than he had admitted to the queen. He reveals that he knew of the captivity (not mentioned by the queen); he knew that Daniel came from the very land whose God he had defied in a very public way this very night. The sacred vessels of Daniel's God were on the table before him and possibly one was in his hand. Already God is dealing with Belshazzar. The very lampstand illuminating the handwriting had, almost certainly, been carried down to Babylon from the Temple of Solomon in Jerusalem in 597 BC.[23]

His knowledge of Daniel, the king confesses, comes not from his own experience but from that of others; nevertheless his fame has reached even to the throne. 'I have even heard of thee' – although some translations omit the word 'even' (*RV*), as being without significant manuscript authority, but it does express the idea more clearly – you are well known in most circles – even as far as the palace. He then repeats the warm words of the queen, with some slight emendations. He acknowledges 'the Spirit of the gods is in thee'. Nebuchadnezzar had acknowledged this (4:8, 9, 18) and it has just been repeated by the queen (v. 11). However, Belshazzar drops the word 'holy' from his statement. Was his conscience already at work? He repeats the words used by the queen – 'light',

[23] The *LXX* uses 'lampados' in all the passages, Exod. 38:16; Zech. 4:4 and *in loc.*

'understanding' and 'excellent wisdom'. Belshazzar gives Daniel full credit for his ability before he poses the problem.

Verses 15–16 The king summarises the situation:

(a) The problem: It is right in front of you Daniel; it is the matter of this writing on the wall. The dramatic circumstances around the writing show its vital importance but no-one can read it!

(b) The perplexity: I expected my wise men and astrologers to be able to read and to interpret it – but they cannot! Two groups only are mentioned at this point (compare v. 7) but this could be a short-hand way of referring to the whole corpus of wise men.

(c) The plea: now your reputation tells me you can 'make interpretations' and 'dissolve doubts'. These two expressions are a repetition of two of the three statements made by the queen (v. 12). Again the abbreviation of the statements brings a sense of urgency. Time is passing and the desperation of the king becomes more apparent. He leaves the problem with Daniel.

(d) The promise: It is to his credit that as he presented the problem to Daniel, whatever he personally thought of this captive from Israel, he did not renege on the promise he had made to the one who could read and interpret the writing on the wall (v. 7). The same three-fold promise is held out to Daniel. He would carry the mark of royalty (the purple), the mark of fidelity (the gold necklace), and the mark of authority (third ruler in the kingdom).

Verse 17 Moments before the King

Daniel responds immediately, without the slightest hesitation, as if, indeed, he had been patiently waiting for this God-arranged moment. Almost brusquely, as if he was aware that time was running out, yet with absolute confidence in his God, he assures the king this message is from his God. There was no need for incentive or bribe; Daniel will interpret the writing as a loyal servant of God and in the interests of the king. As to the 'gifts' and 'rewards' promised to the interpreter, these may be retained ('to thyself') or bestowed (on others), as pleased the king, but he does not require, nor will he accept, any gratuity of this kind. Implied in this blunt, but perfectly courteous, refusal is the fact that he is acting now, not merely as a loyal servant of the throne of Babylon, but as a spokesman for the Most High God. Daniel dare not allow his words to appear to be biased by any expectation of reward. He did not want the king to think he could be bribed.

The message of Daniel is divided into three sections by two direct appeals to the king. Each appeal is introduced by the use of the second person singular pronoun 'thou'. These are to be seen as follows:

Verses 18–21 A Recognition History Demands

Verse 18 Appeal 1: 'O thou king ...'

The first thing Belshazzar has to learn is that behind history stands The Most High God. This is the God of Whom Nebuchadnezzar had to learn (3:26; 4:2); it was now the turn of Belshazzar. Men, especially kings, ignorant of this truth, are apt to think the position of power they hold is due to their own merit or a credit to their ability. In Babylon the name of King Nebuchadnezzar stood high for the greatness of the kingdom which God gave him. In Daniel's message to King Nebuchadnezzar in the interpretation of the dream (2:37) the kingdom given to him was associated with 'power and strength and glory' but, as Daniel made absolutely plain, this was given of God. It is just here that failure arose. Nebuchadnezzar heard Daniel's warning but did not take the truth seriously enough; he accredited the majesty, glory, and honour of the kingdom to himself (4:30). **The majesty** – the dominion that God gave him over 'all people, nations and languages' (3:4, 7, 29) – he misused. Instead of acting as a regent for God he became a despot, before whom men trembled and died. Such was the power at his disposal that it was the will of the king, not the will of God, that was done, irrespective of righteousness or justice. The expression 'whom he would' – repeated four times – covers the life and death of many of his subjects. God never intended that a king should act in this way. **The glory** associated with the throne he made his own. 'His heart was lifted up, and his mind hardened in pride' is the Divine revelation of the moment when, looking across the city, Nebuchadnezzar claimed, 'Is not this great Babylon, that I have built' (4:30) and God's judgement fell upon him. Instantly he lost the majesty of the throne; instead of ruling he was driven from the sons of men; he was allowed no contact with mankind. The glory claimed as his own filled his heart with pride. It was taken from him. Now his actions were reminiscent of the behaviour of a beast: his dwelling was with wild asses (the lowest, shyest and wildest of domesticated cattle, Job 39:5–8); his food, instead of the richness of Babylonian cuisine, was the grass the oxen chewed; his body, instead of enjoying the luxury of the palace, was 'wet with the dew of heaven'. **The honour** in which he had been held was stripped from him and he was driven away from mankind. God took away what He had bestowed and the man was a pitiable creature. This remained so until that moment when he acknowledged that 'the most High ruleth in the kingdom of men'. The lesson for every human heart is still the same – the blessings of earth are not ours by right; they are allowed of God. Daniel spells out the lesson for Belshazzar.

Belshazzar must have sat mesmerised as Daniel rehearsed a history he knew so well. Nebuchadnezzar's experience had been proclaimed throughout the empire but he, most likely, had learned of it at his mother's knee. Daniel's words are aimed at the conscience of the king as he reminds him, 'though thou knewest all this'. Daniel's message was crystal clear: kings ruled by Divine permission and were accountable to God as to how they ruled. God could readily strip away what He had given. Belshazzar must surely have trembled at this truth. He stood in that banquet hall, suddenly sobered, amid the ruins of a licentious orgy where profligacy and profanity had cried for judgement. Now it had come! To add to his terror, in his grandfather's story he would recall the moment when the judgement fell. Pride in the splendour of Babylon, claimed for self as expressed by Nebuchadnezzar (4:30), was the signal for the judgement. Was history not being repeated: Belshazzar in this feast was boasting not in Babylon's splendour but in Babylon's security? Little did Belshazzar realise that, as God stripped the splendour of Babylon from Nebuchadnezzar, at this very moment God was stripping away the security of Babylon from Belshazzar. Cyrus was in the process of diverting the waters of the Euphrates River and within hours Medo-Persian soldiers would be within the city. Belshazzar seemed to be conscious that the key lay in the writing on the wall – hence his anxiety to get the interpretation.

Verses 22–24 A Responsibility History Brings

Verse 22 Appeal 2: 'And thou his son, O Belshazzar'

For the second time Daniel uses the pointed 'thou', not with 'king' but, more pointedly still, with his personal name: 'O Belshazzar'. This must have startled the courtiers – not one of them would dare speak to the king in this way, and Daniel just a Judaean captive! What impudence! But Daniel would surely point his finger at Belshazzar as he cried, 'Thou – his son'. As already pointed out (see comments on v. 10), the word 'son' in Aramaic can have a wider meaning than normal. It can mean 'son' or 'grandson' or even 'predecessor' (in filling the throne), just as the parallel word can mean 'father' or 'grandfather'. If the identification of the queen as the daughter of Nebuchadnezzar is correct (see comments on v. 10) then Belshazzar is not the son of Nebuchadnezzar, but the son of his daughter Nitocris, and thus Nebuchadnezzar's grandson. From childhood Belshazzar would have known all that Daniel has just recalled. But this knowledge of the dealings of God with his grandfather had not made the slightest difference to Belshazzar; he had never learned the lesson he was meant to learn. The result is summed up in the charge laid against him of personal guilt before God. Daniel is but the spokesman as he challenges, 'thou ... hast not humbled thine heart, though thou knewest all this.' In fact, far from humbling himself, Belshazzar had done the very opposite and gone much further in pride and arrogance than Nebuchadnezzar ever dared. One can visualise Daniel pointing to the sacred vessels on the table as he charges, 'thou ... hast lifted up thyself against the Lord of heaven' in your sacrilegious act of using the vessels from the House of the Lord in idolatrous worship. Daniel would recognise those sacred vessels from the Temple.

The gods in the pagan world were represented by idols made of different materials. Six materials are mentioned twice in the chapter (vv. 4, 23) – silver, gold, brass, iron, wood and stone. The lists differ only in the order of the gold and silver. Whether they are representations of different gods or different representations of one god – the latter is most likely on this occasion – makes no real difference. Daniel challenges this idolatrous gathering as he brings the full light of Scripture to bear upon the scene. Using quotations, one from the Pentateuch (Deut. 4:28); one from the Writings (Ps. 115:5–7); and one from the Prophets (Isa. 44:9), Daniel shows the utter futility of such idolatry. Idols see not, nor hear, nor know – in truth they are dead idols. Not an easy truth to set before the idol worshipper who, at the same time, is an imperious despot with a temper easily roused. It was assuredly dangerous to speak so disparagingly of the gods Belshazzar had worshipped throughout his life. Daniel goes even further. Idolatry is one thing, when behind it is ignorance, but when idolatry is linked with deliberate defiance of the God Who has made Himself known in creation and providence, then Divine judgement is invited. Belshazzar stands guilty on both counts. As the God of Creation; does Belshazzar not know that his life is in God's hand –'in whose hand thy breath is' (v. 23)? As the God of Providence; does Belshazzar not know that God has allowed his grandfather's testimony as witness to him personally – 'whose are all thy ways' (v. 23) is Daniel's word? He refused to learn from the majesty of God in creation, or the grace of God seen in His dealings with his grandfather (v. 22), which were designed of God for Belshazzar's blessing. This God Who has spoken to you, Daniel charges, 'hast thou not glorified'. To paraphrase: 'Never has it occurred to you, O King Belshazzar, to bow the knee to this God!' The word 'glorify' in this context means 'to honour in light of majesty'. Instead of giving God the honour and majesty due to Him, Nebuchadnezzar had claimed it as his own (4:30) and suffered for that sin. Belshazzar, knowing how God had dealt with his grandfather, bears the guilt of deliberate defiance of the God Who has spoken to him – this feast highlights that defiance of his grandfather's God. Mercy can no longer stay the sentence – the handwriting is on the wall. The sentence is from the throne.

Now, absorbed and fascinated, every eye would follow the eyes of Daniel as he turns from gazing at the king and turns to the writing on the wall. The sin of King Belshazzar has been fully exposed. Refusing to listen to the voice of the Creator God; rejecting the dealings of a gracious God through the testimony of his grandfather; persisting in the profligacy of the idolatrous Babylonian life-style; the climax has been reached in the profanity of this feast. Guilty before the 'Lord of heaven' (v. 23), the moment has arrived for the sentence to be read – just four Aramaic words. The stillness can be imagined as Daniel reads the sentence upon that sin: *Mene, Mene, Tekel, Upharsin.*

Verses 25–30 Dread Retribution in Babylon's Fall

Verse 25 The Sentence

Quoting Jewish rabbis, E.J. Young suggests that part of the difficulty of reading the words may have arisen because the characters, while written in Aramaic, may have been written vertically instead of horizontally.[24] Since only the consonants would have been written, and if some unfamiliar script was used (possibly Western

[24] Young, *The Prophecy of Daniel*, p. 126.

Phoenician), the writing would appear very different and difficult. The human side of the story is interesting, but somewhat irrelevant; the main issue is that human intelligence cannot interpret this writing and Daniel, the spokesman for God, is equipped to do this. With these suggestions in mind, what was written on the wall may have been something of this kind:

P T M M
R K N N
S L ‘ ‘

Which, transliterated into English, becomes, when reading right to left *Mene* , *Mene*, *Tekel*, *Upharsin*.

Verses 26–29 The Interpretation

The interpretation given by Daniel is succinct and clear – just as clear as the sentence itself.

Daniel interprets the three words as Aramaic past participles in the passive voice as follows:

Mene – God hath numbered thy kingdom and finished it!

Mene – God hath numbered thy kingdom and finished it!

(All authorities agree that the repetition of the word makes it emphatic – this matter is settled – no change is possible.)

Tekel – Thou art weighed in the balances and found wanting!

Peres –Thy kingdom is divided and given to the Medes and Persians!

Mene comes from a verb meaning ‘to number’ which Wilson[25] explains as meaning ‘to allot, to appoint, to number out or to count’ and suggests it always indicates a specific allocation, as shown by its usage. It is used of persons (Gen. 13:16); of horses (1 Kgs 20:25); of tribes (Ezra 6:17); and of days (Ps. 90:12). A passive participle indicates that the numbering has been done by another, and in this case the person Who does the numbering is God; since God does the numbering there can be no alteration – it is final. It is a final count – complete. God has finished ticking off the days of Belshazzar’s kingdom. It is over. Not another day can be added to the tally.

[25] *OTWS*, p. 289.

Tekel comes from a verb 'to weigh'. It shows the action of God with regard to the assessment of His individual creatures. His balances are just and his weights are true (see Lev. 19:36; Prov. 16:11); Job desired to be weighed in an even balance (Job 31:6); God weighs actions (1 Sam. 2:3) and spirits (Prov. 16:2). God hates a false balance (Prov. 20:23) and the balances of deceit. His balances are just (Prov. 16:11) and the result is declared in Scripture: 'All have sinned, and come short of the glory of God' (Rom. 3:23). The figure of weighing here implies weighing against a Divine standard; the result is that each individual has been found 'wanting'. No-one can reach the Divine standard and therefore must seek mercy. Nebuchadnezzar sought and found such mercy; Belshazzar was found wanting; in spite of God's dealings with him he never sought mercy. Hence the verdict of heaven stands: 'found wanting'. A righteous God must deal with recalcitrant man!

Upharsin as read by Daniel includes the letter 'u', which is the simple enclitic that links one phrase to the phrase before and should be translated as 'and'. 'Pharsin' is the passive participle plural of the verb 'to divide', meaning 'something already divided'. The verb does not carry the idea of dividing into two equal parts; rather it means divided into pieces, or shattered.[26] So the idea is not that half of the kingdom would go to the Medes and the other half to the Persians but that the Medo-Persian Empire, under Cyrus, would shatter the Babylonian Empire into pieces. In naming the Medes before the Persians, as Daniel does, there is historical accuracy (6:8, 12) for up to the time of Cyrus the Medes were always named before the Persians. From the time of Cyrus and his exploits the Persians were named before the Medes.[27] Cyrus was a Persian and he married a Median princess. Cyrus had united Medes and Persians so it was a unified political entity with a united army when Babylon was captured'.[28] When interpreting the writing, Daniel uses the singular form 'peres', which may point to the decisive blow that shattered the whole empire. The blow was the fall of Babylon that night. Also, in the use of the word 'peres' there is an evident bonus for Daniel in use of paronomasia.[29] In Aramaic the word 'Paras' is

[26] Young, *The Prophecy of Daniel*, p. 127. Miller, *New American Commentary, Daniel*, p. 165.
[27] Young, *The Prophecy of Daniel*, p. 127.
[28] Young, *The Prophecy of Daniel*, p. 284.
[29] 'Paronomasia' is defined as 'to draw attention to some additional point by the sound of the word'.

the word for Persians. If the vowels (Masoretic pointing) are omitted each word reads 'prs' – and the one can stand for the other. So Daniel draws attention to both the act itself – the shattering of the kingdom – and the perpetrator of that act of destruction – the Persians.

It is to be observed that the sentence is passed on King Belshazzar personally. For the condition of the nation he is held responsible as the king and judged accordingly. The kingdom will be affected because it is under his authority; it is spoken of as 'thy kingdom'. The next verse will simply record the result of the sentence: 'In that night was Belshazzar the king of the Chaldeans slain.'

The voice of Daniel falls silent. Before anyone can move the king speaks. With surprising composure, and perhaps with a certain bravado to hide any fear in the presence of the whole court, King Belshazzar commands that the high honours promised to the reader and interpreter (v. 7) of the writing be heaped upon Daniel. Daniel has done what was asked of him. In an attempt to treat the occasion as a normally as possible the king orders the carrying out of his promise. Daniel is honoured immediately with: (a) the purple robe; (b) the chain of gold about his neck; and (c) the proclamation that made him the third ruler in the kingdom (see commentary on v. 16 for the implications of these gifts). Some commentators have raised doubts as to how quickly these things could be carried out, but a little consideration will suggest that a purple robe and a gold necklace would be readily available in the royal palace in Babylon. On the third matter, an immediate proclamation by the king to this gathering of the promotion of Daniel to 'Triumvir' would be recognised throughout the empire. All would know that a more formal declaration would be issued officially in the morning. Little did they realise what the next dawn would bring.

A more intriguing question to many a reader must be as to why Daniel, who earlier with a measure of brusqueness had refused the promised honours, raises no word of protest now, as he is clothed in the purple robe, adorned with the golden necklace, and listens to the royal proclamation. Our first reaction would be that Daniel, knowing they would be very short-lived and be of no value in the morning, when the Medo-Persian army took the city, accepted the honours. This is a mistake. The passage makes no mention of the immediate fall of Babylon nor is there any evidence to suggest that Daniel was aware of this. The answer lies in the change of situation. The interpretation of the writing and the honours to Daniel that followed immediately at the king's command brought a major change of atmosphere in that hall. In the earlier situation (v. 17) Daniel dared not allow the king to think that he could be bribed to interpret the writing or that he had to be rewarded to speak for his God. That is in the past. At this point Daniel is not even consulted. The king has promised, and now he commands that the promises be carried out. To reject the honours, in the fevered atmosphere of this hall, and in the circumstances facing the city, would bring Daniel, and with him all the people of Israel, under grave suspicion of treachery or betrayal. Another thought may also have been in the mind of Daniel as he received the honours: with the change of empire, announced in the writing on the wall, God could be fitting him for a testimony for Him in that new empire. That this is how it works out becomes abundantly clear in the next chapter. For these cogent reasons Daniel submits and accepts the honours of Babylon.

The effect upon the audience of the interpretation and the subsequent honouring of Daniel in that once festal hall are not given to us. The meaning of the writing had been given; a shocked king had attempted to bring normality into the hall; but for each individual present the issue is personal. Their response to this announcement will fix their destiny. The issue before each soul is clear – do I believe the message or not? Belief in the God revealed through Daniel is set over against the idolatrous Babylon they know. One can only imagine the arguments around the tables, the tempers lost, the voices raised – for and against accepting the writing on the wall. Upon the king, the sentence was explicit and, even though nothing has been said about his death that night, the numbered days of the kingdom would mean death for him – if Daniel was to be believed! As to the city, the two-year siege of Babylon by the Medo-Persian army must result in its fall – if Daniel was to be believed! As leaders of that nation, their future was dark; death itself stared them in the face – if Daniel was to be believed! One could well imagine the senior military commanders, red in the face, defending the impregnability of the defences of Babylon, then in a temper storming out of the hall to go round the checkpoints once again, and inspect the sentries at the gates and the guards in the towers. This was a fortress city and they were proud of their defences. Voices would be raised; emotions stirred; charges made one against another, while the unbelievers mocked and scoffed at such credulity and superstition as they got on with the party.

Verse 30 Daniel's terse record of this remarkable night in history draws attention because of its solemnity, its clarity and its brevity. It stands out as the night when the capital city of the mightiest empire of that day fell to an invader – yet such an earth-shattering event is dismissed in one line of Scripture. Daniel records no battle, no thunder of the siege weapons with which the Medo-Persian army was now equipped, no slaughter or looting, which usually followed the fall of capital cities – Jerusalem and Nineveh are tragic examples. The one fact recorded is the death of King Belshazzar. All the rest is passed over in silence. In the very next verse the record moves to another empire and a new king is in place. *Sic transit gloria mundi.*

The capture of Babylon was the final act of the march to greatness of the Medo-Persian power under Cyrus.[30] The facts relative to Babylon are summarised here for convenience of reference.[31]

The Date

The vast majority of scholars agree that this was the night of the great festival in honour of the patron deity of Babylon – the god Bel (Akkadian name) called also Marduk (Aramaic name).[32] This night was October 13, 539 BC, when the festivities were led by King Belshazzar, who was left to defend the city of Babylon while his father, Nabonidus, led an army into Arabia to try to hinder the march of Cyrus toward Babylon.

The Man

The leader of the attacking force was a dynamic military leader called Cyrus, who for twenty years had been binding the Medes and the Persians into one united power. He commenced his conquests by overthrowing Astyages, the last king of Media, and absorbing Media into the Persian Empire. Cyrus married a Median princess – the daughter of the deposed king. His next military campaign was to deal with Croesus, the king of Lydia, whose realm embraced almost the whole of what is now known as Asia Minor. Cyrus defeated Croesus and brought his empire, with its rich resources, under his control. With his now battle-hardened army of veterans he began the systematic conquest of the Babylonian Empire. This

[30] Appendix 3, History of the Medo-Persian Empire.
[31] Appendix 2, History of the Neo-Babylonian Empire.
[32] *UBD*, p. 414.

campaign has brought his army to the gates of the capital city – Babylon.

To the God of Daniel this is no surprise. One hundred and fifty years before this night God had already marked out His man for dealing with Babylon. Isaiah had cried, 'Thus saith the LORD to His anointed, to Cyrus, whose right hand I have holden, to subdue nations before him; and I will loose the loins of kings, to open before him the two leaved gates; and the gates shall not be shut' (Isa. 45:1). Isaiah speaks again: 'That saith of Cyrus, "He is My shepherd, and shall perform all My pleasure"'(Isa. 44:28). This is the man whom God used to execute the sentence upon Belshazzar.

The City

Every military strategist of the day knew that Babylon was impregnable. Strongly fortified, its double walls of earth and brick were over three hundred feet high and eighty-five feet broad and strengthened with two hundred and fifty watch towers and with one hundred gateways made of brass. The River Euphrates ran through the middle of the city but it also was enclosed with massive stone quays protected from any access from the river with brass gates and locking cross-bars (Jer. 50:15; 51:53). At this time it was already stored with enough food for twenty years. No wonder the Babylonian lords felt secure that festal night. Everyone was aware that Babylon was impregnable.

No-one was more aware of the impregnable nature of the defences of Babylon than Cyrus. He knew well that even the heavy siege batteries and all the normal methods used to attack fortified cities would be unlikely to succeed. So he devised an abnormal means of attack. His key to Babylon was the river Euphrates and the way the river ran right under the massive walls. This was the point where Cyrus took action. God had actually forewarned proud Babylon of this point of weakness. Over a century and a half earlier his prophets had spoken: 'A drought is upon her waters; and they shall be dried up' (Jer. 50:38; Isa. 45:1–2). Out of sight of the citizens, Cyrus had his engineers dig channels from the River Euphrates to by-pass the city. On this night of the feast, when Belshazzar and his lords were carousing, the Persian engineers broke the bunds and diverted the water of the Euphrates away from its normal channel.[33] When the water level in the main channel had become low enough

[33] Herodotus, *The History of Herodotus*, Book 1, para. 191, p. 43.

to allow men to wade through it, Cyrus ordered his army into the riverbed and marched them into the city. The brass gates were forced – some sources hint at bribery, and others of betrayal by some disaffected priests of the old mystery cult going back to Nimrod, but the outcome was that the army of Cyrus was in the city with scarcely a blow having to be struck. There was no raging battle and no major destruction. Medo-Persian soldiers moved to seize the royal palace and attacked the guards. The noise drew the attention of those still in the banquet hall; King Belshazzar ordered the great door to be opened to see what was happening. On this, the soldiers of Cyrus rushed into the great hall where, cutting through the lightly-armed courtiers, they found King Belshazzar, sword in hand, ready to defend himself. There in the banquet hall, possibly on the very spot where he had heard his sentence from God through Daniel, he was cut down and died.

Despite the alleged impregnability of Babylon God had said of the kingdom – 'numbered … finished'. There was no appeal. God had already named the man and arranged the method of dealing with the defences of Babylon. Cyrus did what God had said he would do. King Belshazzar fell under His personal judgement and died, while the Babylonian kingdom was numbered and finished. Isaiah had already announced concerning Babylon, 'But these two things shall come to thee in a moment … the loss of children, and widowhood: they shall come upon thee in their perfection for the multitude of thy sorceries, and for the great abundance of thine enchantments' (Isa. 47:9). Babylon, judged of God, lost its sovereign and its sovereignty in one night.

Historical records, like those of Herodotus (*c*.484–*c*.425 BC), Xenophon (*c*.435–354 BC), Berossus (wrote *c*.260 BC) and the Nabonidus Chronicle, all generally are in agreement, with some disparity on minor points, that great Babylon was taken by Cyrus the Persian general using the strategy outlined above. There was no major assault. Guards died at their posts but there was little destruction. The city awoke to find itself under a new regime. The records all agree that King Belshazzar died when the city was taken.

The Empire

With the death of Belshazzar the mighty empire of Babylon disappeared off the world map. King Nabonidus, the father of Belshazzar, already made captive by Cyrus, was treated kindly by Cyrus after the fall of Babylon and given a small principality in

Carmenia, in which to live out his days. The city Babylon was incorporated into the Persian Empire and became the local capital of Babylonia. It is clear that the destruction of the city, as announced by Jeremiah in chapters 50 and 51, did not take place at this time.

The Medo-Persian Empire established by King Cyrus covered a far greater land area than the Babylonian Empire had ever known.[34] This empire was to endure for over two hundred years, from the fall of Babylon (539 BC) until the arrival of Alexander the Great upon the world scene (332 BC). With the weight of empire upon him, Cyrus could only remain in Babylon a few months after the conquest. There were many calls for his presence, especially in Susa, the capital city of the empire. However, there was one problem in Babylon that had to be solved immediately – the administration of the city. Conquering the city had taken place so quickly and so relatively quietly that it is not surprising that the Babylonian administrative machinery was taken over almost intact. This made it easy to quickly reorganise it on Persian lines. Cyrus commenced this reorganisation, then left it to his appointee to complete the job. Before he left Babylon Cyrus appointed Darius the Median to rule Babylon, with title of King of Babylon.

Verse 31 In the Hebrew Bible the chapter division places this verse as the first verse of chapter 6, which, *prima facie*, would seem the logical place for it, since it introduces a new person in charge of the city of Babylon. Four things are stated about this person in this one sentence:

(a) His name – Darius – a name unknown in any record of secular history available to us of this period.

(b) His race – the Mede – there is no problem with this, since it was the known and avowed policy of Cyrus to place the ablest men of subjected peoples in as high positions as they were capable of filling; a very astute policy that repaid Cyrus with peace in subject states where else there had arisen many a rebel.

(c) He 'took the kingdom' – another translation, which reads 'took control of the kingdom' (*NET*), seems to get close to the meaning. Since it is Cyrus who captured Babylon, this man was clearly appointed by Cyrus to rule over the kingdom of Babylonia as king in his absence (6:6).

[34] See maps, p. 682–683.

(d) His age – 62 years. An advanced age, one would think in that day, to take over a kingdom. However, it cannot but be noticed that in the next chapter he appoints a man over twenty years his senior as first president of the three in control of the city of Babylon.

Much discussion has centred on the identity of this man, arising mainly out of a seeming desire to try to fit him into incomplete fragmentary records from archaeological research that do not agree with cach other. No-one of this name is known from secular history and the records show that Cyrus remained the supreme ruler until his death nine years later. An added complication is that different records from different sources give different names to persons who must be the same. In the study of the identity of Darius much time and energy has been given to argument and counter argument, with tremendous interest, it is true, but with little spiritual gain. Three main views lead the field with respect to the identification of 'Darius the Median':

(a) A Median general called Gubaru – whom Cyrus appointed as governor

The commentator generally associated with view is J.C. Whitcomb Jr.[35] He shows that in the *Nabonidus Chronicle*[36] two names are linked with Babylon: Ugbaru and Gubaru. Ugbaru commanded the army on the night that Babylon was captured. Whitcomb points out that he died within three weeks of the capture of the city and was replaced by another Median general called Gubaru who remained governor of the city for fourteen years. After a very thorough examination of the cuneiform text of the Nabonidus Chronicle[37] and comparison with other textual fragments unearthed over recent years, Whitcomb writes: 'It is our conviction that Gubaru the Governor of Babylon and the region beyond the river appears in the book of Daniel as Darius the Mede, the monarch who took charge of the Chaldean kingdom immediately following the death of Belshazzar.'[38] Whitcomb goes on to point out that, while the Median name of this person was Gubaru, when promoted after the capture of Babylon he was given the honourable title 'Darius King of Babylon' by Cyrus himself. This is the only name that Daniel

[35] Whitcomb, *Darius the Mede*.
[36] Appendix 2, History of the Neo-Babylonian Empire.
[37] See explanation of the *Nabonidus Chronicle* in Appendix 2, History of Neo-Babylonian Empire.
[38] Whitcomb, *Darius the Mede*, p. 24.

would have known, while writers away from the city – it is from further away regions that the majority of the textual fragments originate – still gave him his old name. This seems to answer most of the problems and, it may be said, the majority of present day commentators seem to favour this identification. When all the arguments are weighed, pro and con, it seems this simple solution solves most of the problems. Whitcomb sums the matter up quite concisely from this perspective as follows:

> It is true that the name 'Darius the Mede' has not yet been found in any extra-Biblical inscription of pre-Christian times. Nevertheless, Gubaru the governor of Babylon fits the biblical description of Darius the Mede so remarkably that the writer believes he will be recognised in due time as the monarch who played such an important role in the life of Daniel after the fall of Babylon.[39]

Many will agree with this statement.

(b) A son of Cyrus called Cambyses

The commentator and historian who sets forth the claim of Cambyses, the son of Cyrus, who served under him during this campaign and was present at the fall of Babylon, is Charles Boutflower.[40] He presents his case most ably, drawing upon many ancient archives, to show what Cyrus intended to do for Cambyses, his son – he intended to make him king in Babylon. There is missing, however, any solid reliable and corroborative evidence historically that Cyrus ever carried out what he, with all honesty, intended to do. The main objections in his case are: (a) his age – Cambyses could not have been 62 years old; and (b) no record gives him the title 'king of Babylon' until after the death of Cyrus.[41] Not many expositors now advance the claim of Cambyses to the throne of Babylon.

(c) Cyrus himself under a different name – Darius the Mede

This claim rests on the understanding that Cyrus used both names, as it can be readily shown that many kings in those days did, to emphasise different facets of their rule in different areas. This view

[39] Whitcomb, *Darius the Mede*, p. 66.
[40] Boutflower, *In and Around the book of Daniel*, pp. 142–167.
[41] Boutflower, *In and Around the book of Daniel*, p. 65.

is strongly supported by D.J. Wiseman, of the British Museum, who points out that the Aramaic reading of the last verse of chapter 6 should be 'in the reign of Darius even in the reign of Cyrus the Persian' (6:28), where the conjunction 'and' is translated epexegetically.[42] This view is popular, as it appears simple, and is also supported by the Septuagint and Talmudic readings. However, it faces a major problem that has never been satisfactorily resolved. This lies in Daniel's statement 'Darius the son of Ahasuerus, of the seed of the Medes' (9:1), when every other source insists that Cyrus, on the paternal side, was Persian. Few expositors today support this identification (however, see note at end of chapter).

Historical and archaeological research has vindicated Daniel in each case where sceptical minds have challenged his statements. Historians admit that the archival record is very fragmentary and incomplete, and there is not the slightest doubt that further evidence, as it comes to light, will show the accuracy of his statements with respect to Darius the Mede. While the archaeological and historical investigations are useful and interesting, yet Scripture stands unchallenged. When all the scriptural references are considered together, a clear picture begins to emerge of the man whom God allowed to fill a certain place in Divine records at a critical time for God's chosen nation. There are five scriptural references to this Darius, all of them in the book of Daniel:

1. 5:31 – 'And Darius the Median took the kingdom, being about threescore and two years old.'
2. 6:1 – 'It pleased Darius to set over the kingdom a hundred and twenty princes.'
3. 6:28 – 'So this Daniel prospered in the reign of Darius, and in the reign of Cyrus the Persian.'
4. 9:1 – 'In the first year of Darius the son of Ahasuerus, of the seed of the Medes, which was made king over the realm of the Chaldeans.'
5. 11:1 – 'Also I in the first year of Darius the Mede, even I, stood to confirm and to strengthen him.'

The name Darius is a dynastic name and is borne by several kings[43] of Medo-Persia. This Darius cannot be identified with any of the

[42] Wiseman, 'The Last Days of Babylon' in *Christianity Today*, Vol. II, No.4, (Nov. 25, 1957).
[43] See Appendix 3, The History of the Medo-Persian Empire.

kings listed, nor can his father, called Ahasuerus (9:1); he must also be clearly be distinguished from a later Darius (Hystaspes), who came to the throne seventeen years later (521 BC). It seems that Darius could be 'an old Iranian royal title',[44] with which Cyrus honoured this able general. Concerning this king of Babylon Scripture presents a most interesting portrait:

1. His Appointment (5:31)

Immediately after Babylon was taken, and Scripture and History agree that Cyrus took the city, he appointed Darius the Median, of somewhat advanced age, to rule the city. Born in 601 BC, this Median would still be over twenty years younger than Daniel, who had been promoted by King Belshazzar in his last act of civil administration, to be the a 'triumvir' – a third ruler in the kingdom of Babylon. That he was of Median race, while Cyrus was a Persian, is perfectly in keeping with the conciliatory policy of Cyrus displayed in all his conquests. The policy of Cyrus was to share the spoils of victory, and thus to keep Media and Persia united under his control. This policy, adopted throughout the empire, brought able men from the Median race into government, contributed to the peace of the empire, and pre-empted any rebellion from a disgruntled defeated enemy. Here Babylon is one of the 'spoils of victory'. For Cyrus to appoint a man of his age to such a prestigious post speaks highly of Darius. His record bears out the confidence of Cyrus.

2. His Administration (6:1)

The first duty laid upon this king by his overlord Cyrus was clearly the task of bringing the administrative machinery of Babylon into line with the structure practised in the Medo-Persian Empire. Cyrus had begun this work but, having to leave for his capital Susa within a few weeks of the conquest, left the completion of the reorganisation to Darius. It is the exercise of this responsibility that brings Daniel to the notice of the king and sets the stage for the subsequent events of chapter 6.

[44] Albright, 'The Date and Personality of the Chronicler', *Journal of Biblical Literature*, XL, (1921), pp. 104–124.

3. His Action (6:28)

Chapter 6 records this restructuring and the resulting plot involving the den of lions, as a result of which Daniel is promoted again in the city of Babylon. Darius had determined to set Daniel over the whole city (6:3) as president of the three-member ruling council of Babylon. The hierarchal order is clear – Cyrus the Great was in overall command; Darius, his special appointee, addressed as King; followed by Daniel, as chief administrator. This verse notes the prosperity of Daniel throughout the reign of Darius in Babylonia while Cyrus was the overall ruler in the empire. Daniel seems to have lived until 530 BC and died shortly before Cyrus the Great, who died in 529 BC.

4. His Authority (9:1)

The unusual statement made about this king is 'which was made king over the realm of the Chaldeans'. This is a most unusual way to describe the receiving of a kingdom. The passive voice indicates a higher authority. It has already been shown that Darius was appointed by Cyrus, who had just taken the city of Babylon. This may also be the explanation behind the verb 'took' in the statement 'took the kingdom' (5:31). 'Taken' because 'given', is a summary statement that covers the appointment of Darius by Cyrus. Nevertheless, this giving goes further: his reign is so crucial in Divine purpose that Divine aid is given to Darius (see 11:1). The extent of his kingship is defined as 'over the realm of the Chaldeans'. As will be shown (see comments at 9:1), this kingship of Darius extended from Babylon, the capital city, and included the ancient territory of Chaldea in southern Babylonia. This was almost the old Babylonian Empire. The Medo-Persian Empire, with its capital at Susa, was far more extensive. The empire, including Babylonia, was still under Cyrus the Great.

5. His Assistance (11:1)

In chapter 10 Daniel is allowed to see the forces at work behind the political scenes of earth. Most conservative scholarship places this verse as the closing verse of chapter 10. The reasons are convincing and it readily falls into place. In the unseen spiritual battle behind earthly events special attention is drawn to Darius, who in this first year needed Divine assistance. It becomes clear that his kingship is crucial to the purposes of God on earth and thus Darius is divinely

The empire yet to come will exercise a greater power than any of these empires.

(B) The picture of an emperor yet to come who will outdo all previous rulers in:

(a) Pride, yet he will be humbled, as Nebuchadnezzar was humbled (chapter 4);
(b) Profanity, yet he will be judged, as Belshazzar was judged (chapter 5);
(c) Presumption, yet he will be shown to be as impotent as Darius (chapter 6).

The empire yet to come will be ruled by a charismatic personality who will display a far greater pride, profanity and presumption than any of these kings.

Lesson of Part 1 God can and will preserve a remnant of His people under the trying conditions of the Tribulation period that lies ahead for Israel and the world (12:1–2; Mt. 24:21–22). The final empire and its emperor are foreshadowed in these chapters.

CHAPTER 6 – A KING'S PRESUMPTION EXPOSED 538 BC

PRELIMINARY NOTES

1. The Language of the Chapter

That Daniel continues to use the Aramaic language in this chapter (he has done so since 2:4) reminds the reader that Israel is under Gentile rule. The character and conditions of that rule are revealed in these chapters as Israel has experienced it in the past. The prophetic note is that this Gentile rule over Israel will be repeated in the future, under a more powerful personality, with greater power than any who belong to history. The corollary is easily seen: the God, able to preserve those who trusted Him in these difficult times in the past, will certainly be the same for believers in a future day.

2. The Date of the Chapter: early 538 BC

The fall of the city of Babylon to Cyrus the Great can be dated precisely in secular history to the thirteenth of October 539 BC – that dramatic night when the masterly strategy of a true military genius delivered what men had judged to be an impregnable fortress into his hands without a real battle and with very minimal destruction. Very few died that night with King Belshazzar (see comments at 5:30).

Not only was the city of Babylon captured without serious destruction but the whole administrative machinery of state was still in place albeit with a new man at the head of the administration. In keeping with his usual practice when bringing a subject people under his control, Cyrus first examined the civil structures still available to him in the conquered territory then selected a suitable man to run the territory in his interests. To retain the allegiance of his Median allies his usual policy was to appoint a suitable man of that race to be governor. He did just this in the city of Babylon and chose Darius the Median. The identity of this man has been discussed in detail in the previous chapter (see comments on 5:31). After a study of various historical possibilities from individuals named in the Babylonian records – and remembering the fact that the records are so fragmentary and incomplete – it is best to leave him with the name given by Daniel: Darius the Median. As Daniel has proven reliable in every previous matter of historical investigation there is no doubt that, as further archaeological research into the records becomes available, Daniel will be totally vindicated. John C. Whitcomb suggests a possible candidate is known in secular records by his Median name, Gubaru, a general with King Cyrus on the night that Babylon fell. Having to leave Babylon within months Cyrus, in keeping with his usual policy, put a reliable Median in charge and gave him the honoured title – King of Babylon. Some detail has already been presented as to the abilities that fitted Darius for this very responsible role given him by Cyrus. Having appointed Darius, Cyrus left Babylon to return to Susa, his capital city, where urgent matters awaited him. This very remarkable man, to whom Cyrus entrusted a large part of his empire with the title 'King of Babylon', is mentioned five times in this book (5:31; 6:1, 28; 9:1; 11:1). See comments at 5:31. Appointed by Cyrus and assuming that he took over control of Babylon within weeks or months, this becomes the first year of his reign. The year can be dated as 538 BC. This chapter, therefore, comes after Daniel had received the visions recorded in chapter 7 and chapter 8 but before the key prophecy of chapter 9. To place this experience in its chronological setting the dates are shown thus:

Ch.7	First year of Belshazzar	553 BC	Daniel aged 70	Vision 1
Ch.8	Third year of Belshazzar	551 BC	Daniel aged 72	Vision 2
Ch.5	Final year of Belshazzar	539 BC	Daniel aged 84	
Ch.6	First year of Darius	538 BC	Daniel aged 85	
Ch.9	First year of Darius	538 BC	Daniel aged 85	Vision 3

Since the dating of the 'Den of Lions' experience places it in the same year as the vision of chapter 9, it is difficult to decide from the context which experience came first in that year. The order of the chapters cannot be accepted as conclusive since the purpose and subject matter demand a place in Part 1 of the book. There are two valid reasons that suggest the 'Den of Lions' episode comes before the vision of chapter 9:

(a) The obvious resentment of the senior civil servants for Daniel shown in the chapter. King Darius has shown his preference for him in the intended promotion of this ex-Babylonian civil servant, Daniel, to the most senior post in his realm. Senior administrators, familiar with the procedures of their civil service, had doubtless been assured that they would fill all the top posts in this conquered territory. Now for one of the conquered people to be promoted over their heads was too much – and very particularly distasteful because he was a Jew! It is suggested that a confrontation as presented in this chapter would occur as soon as the administration was set up – thus early in the year 538 BC.

(b) If God was going to allow His servant to be tested one last time then, it is suggested, the test would surely come before God entrusts to him the key prophecy that introduces the Messiah, in chapter 9.

It is suggested that these two reasons present a logical case for the den of lions experience to be dated early in the year 538 BC, and so before the vision of chapter 9. Daniel is now an old man of 85 years.

3. The Outline of the Chapter

As shown below, Daniel was:

vv. 1–3	Favoured of Darius	Promotion of Daniel
vv. 4–9	Framed by his enemies	Plot against Daniel
vv. 10–15	Faithful to his God	Prayers of Daniel
vv. 16–22	Fed to the lions	Preservation of Daniel
vv. 23	Freed by the king	Power of the king
v. 24	Fate of the accusers	Penalty upon evil men
vv. 25–27	Faith honoured	Proclamation of the king

Verses 1–3 Favoured of Darius – Promotion of Daniel

Verses 1–2 The records of Babylon show that within a few months of taking Babylon Cyrus had placed it under the control of a Median governor and returned to Mesopotamia and his capital city, Susa. The Median ruler is identified in chapter 9:1 as 'Darius the son of Ahasuerus, of the seed of the Medes, which was made king over the realm of the Chaldeans'. The expression 'made king' shows that Darius owed his appointment to Cyrus King of Persia, whom he would own as overlord. His authority or dominion is restricted to the 'realm of the Chaldeans' – which is, effectively, the old Babylonian Empire. This was a major area, or 'satrap' (province), within the great Persian Empire. As explained under comments on chapter 5:31, this Median was likely one of Cyrus' generals, who had been at his side as Babylon was taken and is now honoured with the specific title 'King of Babylon' and left with absolute authority.

As discussed earlier (see comments at 5:30–31) it would seem that the fall of Babylon had occurred with only minor physical destruction in the city, and the main structures of the civil administration of the Babylonian Empire would still exist. However, control of the new administration was vital and it is clear that Cyrus had just the man to do this in Darius. Wasting no time he set about the reorganisation of his realm on the Persian pattern with enthusiasm. Darius appointed one hundred and twenty princes (*AV*) or 'satraps' (*RV* transliterates the Persian word '*satraps*'), and over these he placed three presidents, of whom Daniel was one. The word '*satrap*' is the Persian word to describe an official having control over a province (*satrapy*). This is the Persian structure of empire as seen with reference to King Ahasuerus in the book of Esther: 'This is Ahasuerus which reigned, from India even unto Ethiopia, over a hundred and seven and twenty provinces' (Es. 1:1). Darius copied this structure on a smaller scale and appointed his own men. It is not really surprising that he appointed Daniel. A distinctive mark of Persian policy when taking over a kingdom was to disrupt the previous organisation as little as possible and retain the control of influential men who were familiar with the administration. These officials had two main tasks. One was the administration of law and the maintenance of order and the second was the collection of revenues for the state. The word 'president' ('head', or 'chief') is unknown outside this chapter and Darius may be here establishing a precedent. An interesting and accurate translation gives, 'The satraps were made accountable to them so that the king might not suffer loss' (*NIV*). It is clear the presidents were appointed to scrutinise the work of the satraps. This new code of conduct may have played a part in the happenings of this chapter.

Verse 3 The Context of the Plot

Into this situation a new factor is introduced by the outstanding character and competence of Daniel. This is very well expressed by the translation: 'Now Daniel so distinguished himself among the administrators and the satraps by his exceptional qualities' (*NIV*). 'An excellent spirit' (*AV*) is the same expression as used of him by the queen (5:12) and could be translated 'a commendable attitude'. Such an outstanding administrator of ability and affability, combined with integrity and honesty, could not fail to catch the eye of the king. Darius would certainly be aware of Daniel's interpretation of the writing on the wall and his promotion under Nebuchadnezzar. At this point Darius planned to place Daniel in control over the whole kingdom; Daniel would then be indeed the third ruler in the Persian kingdom. It would seem that this was another new post created by Darius for the improvement of the administration of his realm. Once appointed to this post, Daniel would be over the other two presidents and all the satraps and have direct access to the king.

It is clear that it is this projected promotion which sets the stage for the supreme test that Daniel must face. This becomes the incentive for the plot by the other two presidents and the satraps to find a reason to disqualify Daniel. They were not going to allow Daniel, a Jewish captive, to hold such an influential position in the kingdom. The fact that he had shown himself a man of integrity must have added fuel to their fury, since he would then be in a position to scrutinise their shady dealings. This conclusion is supported by noting the sequential repetitions of the word 'then' in verses 3, 4, and 5. The concern at the news of Daniel's promotion (v. 3) prompts a conference (v. 4) that leads to an unpalatable conclusion (v. 5). This in turn is followed a further 'then' (v. 6), when the plan to discredit Daniel becomes a plot to destroy him. This tight sequential action is characteristic of this chapter, in which the events take place over a very short period of time: from v. 6 most of the action takes place in one twenty-four-hour day. Fourteen times the word 'then' is used from this first occurrence – 'Then this Daniel was preferred above the presidents and princes' (v. 3) – to the final one as Darius concluded the whole matter with a decree – 'Then king Darius wrote unto all people, nations, and languages' (v. 25).

Verses 4–9 Framed by his Enemies: Plot against Daniel

Verse 4 The Conference about the Plot

The translation of the first word, 'then', in this verse as 'at this' (*NIV*), dramatises the conjunction, but rightly so. The intention of Darius gave the other two presidents (in the plural) and satraps (also in the plural) deep concern. How many satraps were involved there is no way of knowing. Only a relatively small number would live within the city, and perhaps only a small number of these may have been involved. That Daniel should be promoted, and thus able to scrutinise their work, was something they could not allow to happen. A conference was called to find some way to discredit Daniel in the eyes of the king. They sought to find occasion against Daniel. The word 'occasion' is more accurately translated 'grounds for charges' (*NIV*). Originating in jealousy, the bitterness towards Daniel prompting this search would grow rapidly on account of his age and of his race. An old man and a captive Jew – their indignation can almost be felt in the passage – for this man to be promoted above able young Persians! Perhaps, too, they had already felt the rebuke and restriction of the presence of this incorruptible man in their meetings and they would know how different their life would be should he be placed in control.

It soon became obvious that Daniel's work was above reproach. They left no stone unturned, as they investigated the records, interviewed the secretaries and inspected the books under the control of Daniel, but they found no error. 'Error' indicates the thought of 'neglect', or 'failure to act' (see Ezra 4:22), which might be called negligence (*NIV* does translate it as 'negligent'). They found no 'fault' (from the root 'to corrupt'); no trace of a corrupt, underhand dealing in his own interest could be found in all his official work. He was a 'faithful' man, which, in this context, demands the translation 'trustworthy'; the king could place absolute confidence in him, as one who would guard the king's interests unselfishly.

Verse 5 The Conclusions of the Plotters

The plotters were confounded and possibly conscience-smitten as their search revealed a man of impeccable probity. Their emergency conference comes to two conclusions. The first conclusion is that they were wasting time. The absolute integrity of Daniel ruled out any possible ground for a charge against him in his official life; no hint of any corrupt dealing was to be found. Bent on their purpose to discredit him, they came to a second conclusion: that the only possible way was to go further, and destroy him through his religious life. Being well aware of Daniel's devotion to the Law of his God, they judged that if they could entrap him in a conflict with Medo-Persian Law they could not merely discredit him, but they could totally destroy him. Their hesitation in adopting such a course is understandable in that they well knew the life-threatening risk involved in tampering with Medo-Persian Law. They would only take this course as a last resort. However, so incensed are some of them with Daniel that they are prepared to take this risk, which, the sequel shows, was very real. They fasten on Daniel's daily practice of praying to his God – a practice well known throughout the city – as a possible key to his destruction. Without ostentation, and yet with true devotion, Daniel waited three times daily upon his God, in the midst of Babylon. What a testimony in an idolatrous city. The conspirators also seem to take for granted that a man faithful to the king, as their present investigations have just shown him to be, will also be faithful to his God. In other words, Daniel would be unlikely to change his daily practice, even under threat of a gruesome death. The word 'law' is used in this book of the decree of the king (2:13, 15) but also of God's law (7:25). Thus Babylonian interpretation of Daniel's devotion to his God presented it as the keeping of a decree. Having reached these two conclusions, the conference may have gone on to discuss what action to take or possibly it was adjourned, to study ways and means. While we are not allowed to be privy to all these discussions, the sequel shows what they had to do. They had to arrange a specific course of action; they had to draw up the wording of the statute to be presented to the king; and finally they had to apply for an audience with the king. This last matter they would fix as early as possible – perhaps for the next morning. These men could not have been unaware of the dangers they faced in initiating such an action before such an autocratic despot. All this will come out in the sequel.

Verse 6 The Confrontation with the Plotters

The connective 'then' shows that, having focussed on the area of Daniel's life to attack, the conspirators wasted no time. In twenty-four hours, as the repetition of 'then' shows from v. 6 to v. 25, the action would take place – from sunrise of one day to sunrise of the next. Within this time frame, the matter would be settled. It has been suggested already that the previous evening the conspirators had sought to arrange this audience with the king. The reading 'Then these presidents and princes assembled together to the king' is too weak a translation. The reading 'came tumultuously to the king' (*RV* marg.) does justice to the word as used in other contexts, but here it is somewhat strong, suggesting an unruly crowd, which in this empire would have been dealt with immediately by the palace guard. The Aramaic scholar Montgomery[1] shows that here the word should be rendered 'in concert', as suggesting a group of delegates. This is supported by other translators – 'by agreement' (*RSV*) and 'as a group' (*NIV*). These readings support the suggestion that permission had already been sought from the king for the presentation of a petition. This same group of men is found acting in concert on two further occasions in this chapter. In the first they act 'in concert' (v. 11) to gather under Daniel's windows to gather evidence for their accusation and in the second they act 'in concert' (v. 15) to demand the execution of the Medo-Persian law upon Daniel. With permission granted, it must have been quite impressive to see the two remaining presidents and princes (satraps) solemnly present themselves before the king. It is most unlikely that 120 satraps were present; most of these were scattered throughout the empire. A small group from Babylon – the headquarters of the branches of administration – would likely claim to speak representatively for the whole civil service.

Verses 7–9 The Claim of the Plotters

The spokesman for the group greets the king courteously with the formal address usual to kings. Claiming to speak for all, with delegated authority, he gives an impressive list of offices in the kingdom and then presents the decree, with what amounts to almost a demand for the signature of the king. His claim to speak for 'all the presidents of the kingdom, the governors (deputies), and

[1] Montgomery, *The International Critical Commentary, Daniel*, p. 272.

the princes (satraps), the counsellors, and the captains' is patently false. Only two presidents out of three are present, and we know, even if the king did not, that there would not have been time since Daniel's proposed promotion to consult all the satraps, especially the more distant ones, and get their approval. If this is an honest claim, why is Daniel not present? Then the question arises in the mind – why did not the king ask the reason for the absence of Daniel from this special delegation?

The delegation requires the king to sign the document they have prepared. His signature on this document would 'establish a royal statute' and 'make a firm decree'. The verb 'to establish' comes from the root 'to arise' and means 'to stand firm and upright'.[2] Only the signature of the king is required to establish this document as a 'royal statute', carrying his personal authority. The verb 'to make' means 'to set forth strongly',[3] and such a signature would set this document above any ordinary administrative document of empire.

This document – 'A royal statute' and 'A firm decree' – to be publicised throughout the empire declared that 'whosoever shall ask a petition of any God or man for thirty days, save of thee, O king, he shall be cast into the den of lions.' Clear and concise it is – and the penalty for breaking it is just as concise. To the western mind this is simply absurd nonsense, and some critics have so labelled it, pointing out that the Septuagint omits the request. However, in the context of idolatrous nations where the king is seen as the representative of deity, as was the case in Babylon, it is not something to be dismissed as a fairy tale. King Darius was accustomed to being addressed as deity and for his officials to flatter him in this way would appeal to his vanity. The word 'petition' points, not to ordinary requests like 'lend me a loaf', but 'prayer-type' requests that demand the bended knee and outstretched hands. Since Darius was recognised as sole representative of deity, but was also a man, a petition to any other man had to be excluded as well. This clearly would severely restrict the petitions that were constantly being offered to the priests in the idol temples with suitable gifts (bribes?).[4] Darius was to be

[2] *OTWS*, p. 149.

[3] Wood, *A Commentary on Daniel*, p. 160.

[4] As a side issue, neither Darius nor the officials would worry about this unduly. The arrogant and greedy priests from the major temples were a constant source of trouble to both the king and the official administration in any empire. From time to time action had to be taken to

recognised as the sole mediator between man and god. Vanity and pride must have filled the heart of Darius as he pondered how much his officials thought of him; they had assuredly designed this petition to honour him and recognise his divine powers. Perhaps also in the mind of the king this could be a test for the new administration, as well as a uniting bond in his diverse empire. That the period of the decree was to be restricted to thirty days was reasonable. It would do honour to the king, on whom every eye in the kingdom would be fixed. Only through Darius could any man approach his god. What the king did not know was that his officials assumed that a month gave adequate time to trap Daniel. At the same time, its limited duration should not antagonise the priests unduly or jeopardise the revenues to the temples. This time factor balance had to be observed, or there could be serious discontent, and even disorder, led by disgruntled priests.

To be thrown into a den of lions was a gruesome death but in perfect keeping with the Persian mind, which, historians point out, revelled in devising horrible death sentences.[5] The Hebrew word means 'pit', or 'den', and this was simply either a natural cave or one specially dug into a hillside, with a door from ground level into a two-compartment chamber. The wall dividing the two compartments would have a door controllable through an overhead ventilation shaft. This overhead shaft through the hill was not only for ventilation – through it food or victims could be thrown in to the beasts. Access to this vertical shaft would normally be covered with a large and heavy stone. This fits the picture given here of Daniel being 'cast into' (v. 16) and 'taken up' (v. 23) again from the den. This threat of such a gruesome death, under the flashing claws and teeth of hungry lions, was meant to make men tremble and think again about their actions. It normally did.

The skill of these conspirators is to be acknowledged. With flattering words of insincere adulation and pretended goodwill, they so present their case and suggest the benefits of such a decree to a clearly sensible man that one can almost see him reaching for the stylus. Agreed, the king is vain, and his vanity has been played upon, and this brings about his downfall. Nevertheless, the skills of these officials are clearly devilish in their origin. The very haste

curb their rapacity. Probably Darius thought this was as good a time as any to show them their proper role.

[5] Cook, *The Persian Empire*, p. 142.

with which they urge upon the king the signing of the decree has been calculated, lest the king has time for consideration. Reflecting on it might allow him to question the reason for this most unusual proposal. No time is allowed and, seizing the stylus, King Darius signs 'the writing even the binding decree'.[6] The translation 'even' shows there is only one document signed and the description repeats the words used previously (v. 8). The word 'sign' is literally 'inscribe', which implies putting his personal imprimatur on the writing placed before him. Once signed, Darius' decree became law. Such a law in Medo-Persia could not be altered. The conspirators had won!

Verse 9 Commandment of the King

There would be no time lost in the issue of this decree through all the normal publicity channels open to the king; these officials would see to it with alacrity. Post – the famous 'pony express', the original postal couriers across the empire – was known throughout the world. Posts, travelling quickly, handed it to town-criers in every city reached by the speeding ponies; news would spread quickly across the kingdom. Public announcements in every satrapy would be heard on the steps of every city hall. From city halls criers and posts would make it known in public places and in temples. Honour to the king would be the theme. Even if his secretaries had not already kept him informed of the meetings, from which he had been excluded, now Daniel must be fully aware of the stratagem concocted for his downfall. He would know, with absolute clarity, that this was the result of the jealousy and of the bitterness he had already felt amongst his colleagues, and could likely have named the conspirators. This declaration has cleared the air and he knows where he stands. Daniel was to be either discredited or destroyed depending on how he responded to the challenge.

Verses 10–15 Faithful to his God – Prayers of Daniel

Verse 10 Decision of Daniel

This presented Daniel with a very simple yet very vital decision. Should he outwit the conspirators by praying in secret? He could readily do this and let them feel foolish at the end of the month. Or should he continue to pray, as he had done for many years, in that

[6] Wood, *A Commentary on Daniel*, p. 161.

specially set-apart room on the housetop where the windows had been placed 'open toward Jerusalem' (RSV)? This reading suggests that those windows had been constructed in such a way as to be always open toward Jerusalem. If Daniel failed to keep to his well-known daily routine then the conspirators would claim that Daniel's devotion to his God was but a matter of convenience and routine, as they worshipped their idols; it did not really matter. The question then to be answered was whether such a man could be trusted to be truly faithful to his king. Would such a man be fit for such a high office as Darius planned?

With calm deliberation, at the accustomed hour the spies of the conspirators, or possibly some of their own number, would see Daniel emerge from his office, cross the courtyard to his home, mount to the second floor, and enter that room where 'he kneeled upon his knees' and 'prayed, and gave thanks before his God'. The decree of Darius made not the slightest difference. This was what he had done for years ('previously', RSV). There is thus revealed, incidentally, in this record something of the spiritual discipline in the life of such a busy official as Daniel. Here is the key to the success of the testimony of Daniel in Babylon. Summarised in three participles – 'kneeled' (showed his respect); 'prayed' (made his requests); 'gave thanks' (rendered his thanks for answers received). The use of the participles shows this is what he did continually as he came into the presence of God. The 'three times a day' reflects the practice of David, as revealed in the Psalms: 'Evening, and morning, and at noon, will I pray, and cry aloud: And He shall hear my voice' (Ps. 55:17). Daniel bows the knee and, as advised by Solomon in his prayer at the dedication of the Temple, has the windows open towards Jerusalem. Solomon, foreseeing that God would have to discipline His people, prayed for their recovery and cried, 'If they pray toward this place, and confess thy name, and turn from their sin, ... then hear thou in heaven, and forgive' (1 Kgs 8:35–36). Daniel did exactly this, with the conscious knowledge of the encouragement of his contemporary prophet, Jeremiah: 'then shall ye call upon Me, and ye shall go and pray unto Me, and I will hearken unto you' (Jer. 29:12). It is clear that the prophecy of Jeremiah was in Daniel's hands and, at this special time (538 BC), very much in his mind (see comments at 9:2.). So Daniel, having weighed the issues, makes his decision absolutely clear. Undismayed, undeterred and unafraid, he moved to keep his noon rendezvous with his God.

Verse 11 Discovery by the Conspirators

Doubtless alerted by their spies, these men assembled. This is the second time the word 'assembled' (see v. 6) is used and it should be translated 'met in concert', or 'by agreement'; so the men involved gather again – possibly under Daniel's window. They wanted to be able to bear personal testimony to Daniel's defiance of the royal decree. One cannot help but wonder if the conspirators heard their names mentioned before God as Daniel would doubtless open his heart about the conspiracy before his God. On this occasion, to 'prayers' is added, for the first time, the word 'supplication', meaning 'to show favour', or 'have mercy'. Its inclusion might suggest that Daniel had a special request this day for Divine intervention on the part of God. He knew his need in light of the conspiracy gathering around him. Hearing themselves prayed for, these eavesdroppers showed no trace of repentance. Far from repenting, they likely rejoiced that they now had Daniel in their net.

Verse 12 With the sixth sequential 'then' moving the action from under Daniel's window to the palace they 'came near' – approached the dais whereon the King sat, and received that nod from the king that allowed men to approach him with petitions at certain hours. They presented their case. First they reminded the king of his decree – restating its terms and reminding him of the signature and the sentence incurred in the breaking of it. The king, doubtless wondering why they are dwelling on this matter of yesterday, agreed that 'The thing is true'. In effect, he admits, 'I did sign and thus the law stands'. The vain man seems to have thought that it was all in his honour they were going over this matter, to emphasise his influence with the gods.

Verse 13 Denunciation of Daniel

With the seventh sequential 'then' in the story the charge is detonated! Now the subject is Daniel and in bitter words the charge is laid against him. 'That Daniel' – the bitterness is conveyed in the demonstrative adjective – the man from a captive people shows not the slightest regard for the king. The implication is clear: surely the king did not know that Daniel is a mere captive from Judah, or, surely he would not have thought of promoting him to such a responsible position. The charge is formulated in the paraphrase 'Let us (your reliable presidents and satraps) tell you O king! Your trust is totally misplaced and this man neither respects you nor your decree so recently issued. Our test of loyalty has shown up the first traitor. The evidence – three times a day Daniel prays to his God!'

In laying the charge before the king it is possible that the composure of these men gave way to a note of triumph, as they presented what they thought was an unanswerable case; a case on which the king must act. Perhaps they did not realise that, in their implication of the king's ignorance of Daniel's background, they were making a serious charge of royal incompetence in selecting Daniel for this high office.

Verse 14 Dismay of the King

With the eighth sequential 'then' in the story the conspirators got the shock of their lives. Perhaps they expected Darius to react as Nebuchadnezzar had reacted over forty years previously, when the same kind of charge was laid against the three Hebrew young men (3:8–12). In his fury Nebuchadnezzar had ordered that they be tested again, but this time in the light of the fiery furnace. Perhaps they expected Darius to summon Daniel for a test in their presence, for indeed their charge was serious. The statement 'the king ... was sore displeased with himself' (*AV*) is perhaps a little strong. The verb seems to be used impersonally and should be translated 'was much distressed' (*RSV*), or, as in the literal, if a little cumbersome, translation given by Wood: 'there was sore displeasure upon him'.[7] The displeasure may, indeed, partly have been with himself. His own gullibility and pride had allowed him to accept the insincere flattery of his officials and be carried away with his own vanity. But the charge, as presented against Daniel, within hours of its proclamation, and the way it was presented, had allowed the veil to drop from his eyes. The whole plot was open to him. He could see their jealousy of Daniel and question the reason. Darius seems to be assured in his own mind of the utter probity of Daniel in office, and would wonder if this cast doubt upon the trustworthiness of these conspirators. Then the way these men had used him as simply a tool in their plot cast him in the role of simpleton. This showed little respect for him or for the impartiality of Medo-Persian law. If these men could conspire on this scale the question must have arisen in his mind: was his position safe? No wonder he was displeased.

[7] Wood, *A Commentary on Daniel*, p. 165.

deliver. Here, King Darius openly confesses to a trust – not in his idol, but assuredly in Daniel's God. Daniel's testimony to the king had been so faithful that now he is willing to acknowledge that God openly. Conscious of his own helplessness, and that of his idol, he must now leave the matter in the hands of Daniel's God. There are two ways of understanding the imperfect tense in the verb 'deliver'. One is to translate it as a wish (the jussive sense) as in 'May your God, whom you serve continually, deliver you' (*RSV*); the other is to translate it as a prediction: 'Thy God whom thou servest continually, He will deliver thee' (*AV*). The weight of scholarship lies with the latter translation, though Walvoord[9] would modify it somewhat by suggesting it is better translated, 'He must deliver thee' as standing in contrast to his own failure. But, whether a wish or a prediction, the statement by the king shows the testimony of Daniel had carried sufficient weight to influence the thinking of a mighty king.

The final scene tells of the king's defeat, doubtless to the delight of the plotters, as Daniel, faithful to his God and to his king, is cast into the den of lions. The Aramaic verb 'to cast' simply means 'to throw' and does not necessarily mean us to think of Daniel being hurled down into the den through the ventilation shaft. More likely the lions had been drawn, by some food let down through the shaft, into the inner compartment and a partition lowered by chains through the ventilation shaft to keep them in. Now the side entrance could be opened, Daniel hastily thrust through it, and the door slammed. The partition would then be withdrawn on its chains through the ventilation shaft, leaving Daniel at the mercy of the lions.

Verse 17 Now an unusual event marked these final proceedings. It is clear that neither the king nor his officials trusted each other. A stone was called for, to block the side entrance door, and, more unusual still, a seal was placed so as to link the stone and the rock face. This seal would be either melted wax or wet clay and covered the join so that if the stone, for any reason, were moved, the seal would be broken. A double control was then demanded. The wax or clay was impressed with the personal signet of the king; this was normally carried on a ring and used only on documents personally authorised by the king himself. No other had this seal or was even

[9] Walvoord, *Daniel: The Key to Prophetic Revelation*, p. 140.

permitted to use it. Now, on behalf of the officials present, the official government seal was stamped into the wax. This seal would only be available to these men, now identified as 'his lords' (a word used of men close to the throne, 5:23). This double sealing meant that the approval of both the king and his lords was required before that stone could be moved and the door opened. The distrust was clearly mutual. The officials feared that the king could come to Daniel's rescue if only his seal was on the tomb. The king feared that the officials might kill Daniel, if God preserved him from the lions, if only their seal was on the tomb. The concluding statement of the verse shows that the purpose of the action against Daniel – his death – was not to be frustrated by any human hand. The tomb was sealed! Silence seems to descend on that dark hillside as the groups move back toward the palace. Did neither the king nor the officials wonder why those lions had suddenly fallen silent?

Verse 18 Distress of the King

The verse takes most readers by surprise. Nebuchadnezzar showed not the slightest concern as he ordered the three Hebrews to be flung into the furnace (3:19–23). It might be thought that Darius would show just as little concern over what must have been quite a routine affair in Persia. A shrug of the shoulders and the night's programme of entertainment could begin! But not this night! This story is different!

Returning to the palace, there followed a night the king would never forget. Normally tables would be spread with special delicacies for the royal palate, with suitable guests summoned to share the banquet and entertainment. Tonight the king fasts; very likely, having eaten nothing from midday, he disregards the delicacies, cancels all visitors, and dismisses the 'instruments of music', a term which included not just a variety of musical instruments but singing girls and dancing groups. The king cancels every arrangement. Perhaps the blunt translation 'no diversions were brought to him' (*RSV*) reflects just how he felt.

But this is only part of the story. Fasting and alone, something more is added to his troubles. He has anticipated the oblivion enjoyed in sleep. Now sleep escapes him – the reading is graphic – 'sleep fled from him' (*RV*). Using the Aramaic equivalent of the Hebrew verb 'to flee', sleep is pictured flying from the king as he pursues her. It is obvious the king is tossing and turning in his bed, but sleep does not come tonight; his mind is not at rest and his conscience is uneasy. King Darius has reason, rather reasons, for a sleepless night: (a) His naivety in signing such a document; (b) His impotence to deliver a trusted counsellor whom he knew had done no wrong; (c) The perfidy of senior officers who could plot in this way – can he trust them again? Whatever the reason, concern-ridden or conscience-stricken, there is no sleep for King Darius. He must have watched for the tardy dawn with impatience, and yet with a deep fear of what it would bring. Recalling the roars of those hungry lions, and then their silence, his faith in Daniel's God does not seem as robust in the cold morning light.

Verses 19–22 As the eastern horizon brightens at the dawn of a new day the sleepless king hastens to the den. Though he cannot see down the ventilation shaft, he knows he can easily be heard, and calls out to Daniel. His voice betrays him – 'in a tone of anguish' (*RSV*) – for that tone does not seem to show the same confidence as on the previous night. King Darius is anticipating a terrible silence as he cries piteously, 'O Daniel, servant of the living God, is thy God, whom thou servest continually, able to deliver thee from the lions?' Still, there are positives about King Darius and the testing of his faith: (a) He came personally to the den; (b) He uses Daniel's language and speaks of 'the living God'; which, in itself, is a tribute to Daniel's testimony. Knowing that the many gods in Babylon could not help in this situation, the king is crying out for assurance that Daniel's God is different. Much depends on the next few moments.

In light of what is to happen within the next hour some have suggested a different reason for the haste of the king in the early dawn to reach the den of lions. Ancient Babylonian law demanded that one who had been tortured during the night and survived must be set free the next morning. The suggestion is that the king wanted to be there at the earliest possible moment, to have the best chance of saving Daniel's life. This suggestion has little merit – even Darius would be aware that a wounded and bleeding Daniel would have been no testimony for his God. A still alive but desperately savaged Daniel would not be an answer to faith in the living God. How much better is the ringing testimony to the power of God in the words – 'no manner of hurt was found upon him' (v. 23).

The voice of Daniel, rising through the shaft, brings the usual courteous words of greeting from Daniel: 'O king, live for ever' – a benediction used a number of times in this book (2:4; 3:9; 5:10; 6:21) but carrying special warmth on this occasion. Is there on this special occasion a connection between the king's use of the term 'living God' and the wish expressed by Daniel for the 'life' of the king? This is the man, albeit a king, who through his folly had ordered Daniel thrown to the lions. Without any doubt, the absolute serenity of Daniel shines through the next statement – as if it was a usual happening and only to be expected: 'My God hath sent His angel, and hath shut the lions' mouths, that they have not hurt me.' Grammarians point out that the verb translated 'said' is unusual, and generally used to introduce a public statement delivered with authority, deliberation and care.[10] Daniel shows no perturbation whatever. Undismayed by the night with the lions, he speaks calmly, clearly and with authority, seeking blessing on the man who put him there. He speaks of 'my God'; he speaks of His presence through His angel; he speaks of His power in dealing with the lions. But Daniel speaks not only of Divine preservation; this meant Divine vindication for all to see. The charges laid against him are false.

Daniel explains why a holy God could act so and deliver His servant. He gives two reasons, and the second arises from the first. The first reason is that before God 'innocency was found in me'. This means far more than any charge men had brought. The word 'innocency' comes from the same root as the verb 'to cleanse' (Hebrew). Simply stated, it means he was cleared judicially before God of every charge. He does not tell us how this came about but, without a doubt, it was on the same basis as King David when he rejoiced in the same consciousness: 'Blessed is he whose transgression is forgiven, whose sin is covered. Blessed is the man unto whom the LORD imputeth not iniquity, and in whose spirit there is no guile' (Ps. 32:1–2). Daniel was not claiming sinlessness or perfection but he was claiming that, before God, there was no sustainable charge demanding death. He was cleared; no charge of unfaithfulness to his God or to his king could be maintained against him. The second reason comes out of the first: clear before God; before the king he is equally clear! Daniel knew how carefully the conspirators had searched his record for any suggestion of failure in his official duties. The fact that they had found none is not enough; Daniel's service to the king is subject to a closer scrutiny – that of his God. Now his God, through the deliverance

[10] Wood, *A Commentary on Daniel*, p. 165.

from the lions, shows to the world that the record of Daniel is absolutely clear.

That God used an angel as His agent in Daniel's deliverance is perfectly in keeping with Scripture, which teaches that angels are servants of God entrusted with service to mankind as set forth in the comprehensive statement, 'Are they not all ministering spirits, sent forth to minister for them who shall be heirs of salvation?' (Heb. 1:14; Ps. 34:7; 91:11). Daniel may well have revelled in the consciousness of David's experience: 'The angel of the LORD encampeth round about them that fear Him, and delivereth them' (Ps. 34:7). Though called simply an angel, this heavenly visitant might well have been the 'Angel of the LORD' – the term used when Jehovah showed His presence in pre-incarnate Theophany. Daniel would be reminded of the Angel of the LORD, Who brought deliverance to Abraham, to David, and to Gideon, and to many others at strategic times. Daniel would rejoice in the presence of the angel, and, with the lions' mouths stopped, what converse Daniel could have enjoyed with His Lord. The Spirit of God has put the experience of Daniel into the records of faith as 'stopped the mouths of lions' (Heb. 11:33). In the presence of this holy messenger the whole beast is clearly subdued; the record stands: 'no manner of hurt was found upon him'. A lion could cause a lot of hurt with paws and claws. The comparison with what happened to the three Hebrews thrown into the furnace is to be noticed. Nebuchadnezzar, as he viewed the Hebrew boys in the furnace, had to confess, 'they have no hurt', and when delivered they were found to be without even 'the smell of fire' (3:24–28). It is of interest that the Septuagint interprets the text without reference to the angel, simply noting that God saved Daniel from the lions. With the light of NT Scripture we can well understand our Lord, in Theophany experience, sharing the fire with His own saints (3:24–26), and we can see Him now facing the lions with His aged servant. It is open to us to meditate on this night of fellowship in the lions' den. It would seem Daniel spent a more relaxed night than the king.

Verse 23 Freed by the King – Power of the King

Gladness and not surprise is the king's immediate reaction. Glad that his respected counsellor was alive, relieved that his foolish pride had not resulted in the death of such a counsellor, and doubtless delighted that the plot had failed. It is clear that by this time the king has been joined at the ventilation shaft by all his officials and one can only imagine the chagrin and dismay of the conspirators. Now, before them all, the king orders that 'they' take up Daniel out of the pit. The 'they' must be the conspirators. What a sight, to see the very men who had plotted such a death for Daniel now forced to draw him up out of the den of lions. The verb itself is used in the active voice of vertical movement in later references ('came up' in 7:3, 8, 20). Here the same verb is used in the passive voice, so it is clear that ropes are lowered and Daniel is drawn up out of the den through the vertical shaft. The unsealing of the main entrance, requiring the lions to be drawn into the other compartment, would have taken too long for an impatient king. To the further discomfit of the conspirators, the keenest scrutiny showed that 'no manner of hurt was found upon him'. There was not even a scratch or the mark of a claw. This is not about the miraculous survival of a man under strange circumstances but a miracle that must be of God. Even Daniel's enemies are made to testify to that. Daniel's confidence in his God is fully recompensed. Daniel's God can be safely trusted.

Verse 24 Fate of the Accusers – Penalty upon Evil Men

For the third time in this story the king gives a direct order – he commands. He had commanded, however reluctantly, the deliverance of Daniel to the den of lions (v. 16) and, doubtless with delight, he had commanded the drawing up of Daniel from the den (v. 23). Now, it would almost seem with relief, he orders the death of the men who had accused Daniel, and not only the men, but their wives and children too. The verb 'accused' literally translated means 'who had eaten his pieces';[11] an idiom that means they had spoken maliciously, with evil intent, in falsely accusing Daniel of disloyalty to the king. Now the death they had plotted for Daniel was to be their death. There was no doubt of their disloyalty in seeking to use the king as a tool in their dark plot. Darius could never trust them again. As explained previously, there is no need to think of all the presidents (2) and all the satraps (120) being thrown into the den. The story centres upon a small group of ringleaders, most likely from within Babylon itself, who claimed to speak for all. Clearly they spoke only for themselves. That their wives and children (the word used is 'sons') are included in this terrible death seems barbaric to us in our day but this was written into Persian law

[11] Miller, *New American Commentary, Daniel*, p. 187.

THE PROPHETIC LESSON

While few commentators draw attention to it, the location of this chapter as the final chapter in Part 1 of the book, to which has been given the subtitle 'Prophecy through History', makes us look for a deeper lesson than merely a historical happening with moral overtones. Certainly that is precious, but there is a deeper lesson which is not difficult to find or to interpret. Like chapter 3, the parallel chapter in Part 1, it foreshadows the ultimate deliverance of the people of Israel from a dark personage and a dark period that still lies in the future. This persecutor brings fearful persecution upon all who would witness for God, and particularly the people of Israel in the Tribulation period at the end of the 'times of the Gentiles'. This persecutor will be a person claiming sovereignty over earth, with the pride of a Nebuchadnezzar (chapter 4), the profanity of a Belshazzar (chapter 5) and the presumption of a Darius (chapter 6). This persecution will take the form of: (a) a furnace for anyone who will not engage in prevailing idolatry (chapter 4); (b) a feast that combines idolatry and immorality, over which sentence is pronounced (chapter 5); and (c) a foe who will claim absolute deity over every citizen, under the threat of something more dreadful than the den of lions (chapter 6), possibly something akin to the guillotine.

God will deliver His faithful and bring them into His literal Kingdom on earth, which will be shown to be an everlasting Kingdom (7:27). As Daniel sees in the next chapter, this will take place when the Son of Man comes in the clouds of heaven, 'and there was given Him dominion, and glory, and a kingdom, that all people, nations, and languages, should serve Him: His dominion is an everlasting dominion, which shall not pass away' (7:13–14). The Son of Man will deal with this persecutor and deliver His people as He establishes this everlasting Kingdom.

CHAPTER 7

INTRODUCTION TO CHAPTER SEVEN

THIS CHAPTER WILL BE DIVIDED into four sections:

1. Introduction to Part 2 of the book
2. Introduction to chapter 7
3. Commentary on chapter 7:1–8
4. Commentary on chapter 7:9–28

INTRODUCTION TO PART 2 OF THE BOOK

With respect to subject matter, the book of Daniel divides into two parts. Before moving into Part 2, a summary of Part 1 may be helpful in keeping the whole picture in view as well as stressing the unity of the book:

A Backward Look

Summary of Part 1	Prophecy through History	Ch. 1–6
Section 1	Daniel and his Friends	Ch. 1–3
Section 2	Daniel and his Foes	Ch. 4–6

The experiences related in this first part of this book have the city of Babylon as background for the stories centred on the Jewish captives in that city at the time when it appeared that Israel as a nation had been wiped off the world map. These stories show the Divine protection that God can give and will give His people who trust Him. The fury of a despot (2:12), the flame of a furnace (3:4–6), or the ferocity of lions (6:16) become but the occasions for God to display His power to deliver those who put trust in Him. Direct prophecy in this section is confined to the dream of Nebuchadnezzar, which is the key to the understanding of the later prophecies in the book. Nevertheless, the stories of the first section carry a prophetic message when we come to Part 2 of this book and see how the nation of Israel and the saints who trust God will be treated by empires and world rulers yet to come. These stories, perfectly historical in their setting, become prophetic as it becomes clear that Nebuchadnezzar, Belshazzar and Darius, who appear at the commencement of a period when Israel had lost its national identity, furnish character portraits of rulers who are yet to come onto the world stage at the close of the period. This special period is identified by the Lord as the 'times of the Gentiles' (Lk. 21:24), which period commenced with the capture of Jerusalem by Nebuchadnezzar in 606 BC and will close with the deliverance of Jerusalem by the Son of Man at His return to earth (7:13–14; Zech. 14:3–4).[1] The sovereignty lost by Jerusalem in 606 BC to a Gentile monarch will be regained by the Son of Man as He destroys the last Gentile monarch and establishes His Kingdom in Jerusalem. This final Gentile monarch, from whom the Son of Man will personally deliver the city of Jerusalem, the nation of Israel and the persecuted saints, will be such a despotic character under satanic control that Nebuchadnezzar, Belshazzar and Darius can offer but faint portrayals of aspects of his character. The persecution of the nation of Israel, and all who dare accept the claims of the Messiah in that time yet future, will be so cruel that the 'search and destroy edict' (2:13), the 'fiery furnace' (3:19) and the 'lions' den' (6:16–17) of Babylon will fade into relative insignificance (12:1). Believers in that day of awful tribulation – especially during the last three-and-a-half years before the Son of Man comes – will draw courage and confidence from these records. There will emerge many a Daniel in that day. Trust in the living God will be *sine qua non* – without which testimony for God cannot exist.

These records hold important lessons for believers in every age. Even in the present day of Church testimony many believers have suffered – and in some lands continue to suffer – for Christ, so these very chapters remain a source of strength and assurance to believers. Even after this age of grace is closed by the coming of the Lord to the air to take away the Church (1 Thess. 4:13–18), the believers of that coming day will find this history even more precious as they go through the Tribulation. The coming of the Lord for the Church opens the 'day of the Lord' (1 Thess. 5:1–3), which climaxes in the seven-year Tribulation period before the Son of Man takes the Kingdom (7:13–14). It is in this Tribulation period, when 'transgressors are come to the full' (8:23), that faith will be so severely tried, and this is also the time when these chapters will provide their greatest comfort to believers. The night of the

[1] See Appendix 7, 'The Times of the Gentiles'.

Tribulation will give way to the dawn of Kingdom glory as Jehovah promised through Malachi: 'But unto you that fear My name shall the sun of righteousness arise with healing in His wings' (Mal. 4:2).

In Part 1 Daniel's background is given and his credentials are examined for the responsibility of prophetic ministry to God's people. To fill this prophetic office in Babylon, the capital city of world idolatry, where Satan ruled, God used a man whom He allowed to be put to the test that he might be shown to be of unimpeachable character, of impeccable conduct, and a man who placed absolute, unswerving confidence in the Word of his God. Only then could God trust him with the vital prophecies of the end-time. No wonder the Lord added that stamp of Divine approval when He spoke of him as 'Daniel the prophet' (Mt. 24:15). Nothing more is needed or could be granted to authenticate the reliability of Daniel. In Part 1 Daniel has been shown that God can deliver His own; now in Part 2 Daniel will be shown that God can foretell the future.

A Forward Look

1. Summary of Part 2 – History through Prophecy Ch. 7–12

Ch.7	First year of Belshazzar	553 BC	Daniel aged 70	Vision 1
Ch.8	Third year of Belshazzar	551 BC	Daniel aged 72	Vision 2
Ch.9	First year of Darius	538 BC	Daniel aged 85	Vision 3
Ch. 10–12	Third Year of Cyrus	536 BC	Daniel aged 88	Vision 4

God permitted His servant Daniel to go through the various tests of Part 1 before He entrusted him with the prophetic visions of Part 2. As will be noted from the dates, all the visions fall in the later years of his life. The one exception is the test before the third vision (chapter 9). Before entrusting to Daniel this key prophecy God permitted him to face this final test in chapter 6 – the lion's den experience under Darius in early 538 BC when Daniel was 85.

At different dates in the latter part of his life God gave Daniel four visions that revealed future happenings on earth, set forth in chronological order as shown. Given to Daniel in the sixth century BC (within the seventy year period of Israel's captivity, 606–536 BC), some of these prophecies had their fulfilment in the years immediately after Daniel (note chapter 8 *inter alia*). From Daniel's perspective they were prophetic; from our perspective they have become history. So detailed are these particular prophecies, and so exactly have some of them been fulfilled, that this part of the book has been used to support the attack of liberal criticism upon the authenticity of Daniel. By definition, liberalism denies that God can reveal the future; so such critics are driven to deny the veracity of Daniel's prophetic statements. To accuse Daniel of mistakes in history or error as to a fact has been the norm for liberal criticism down the years. Further detailed and more recent historical and archaeological research has shown, in every case examined, that the 'mistakes' and 'errors' charged to Daniel are readily explicable, and, by raising the question, the critic has shown his own mind. In every case cited Daniel has been triumphantly vindicated.[2] However, so opposed is the sceptical mind to a God Who can reveal the future, that such sceptics insist that these events could not have been put on record in the sixth century by Daniel (623–530 BC). With this *a priori* assumption they further assume, without a single scrap of supporting evidence, that these prophecies must have been written by some pseudo-Daniel (unknown to history) in the second century BC. Some ready scribe – so they allege – living in the time of the Maccabees would have seen these things actually taking place and, to encourage his brethren, wrote them into a prophetic setting of four centuries earlier. To gain acceptance for the writing he put the name of Daniel to it. This deception, a figment of the sceptical mind, is without a vestige of historical support. It simply shows how far unbelief in a God Who can reveal the future will go in defence of its scepticism.[3]

In Part 2 Daniel changes from using the third person to speaking in the first person. This shift emphasises that he is not now interpreting the dreams of another but that he has been taken into the confidence of his God and given that which he can personally unfold. Twelve times in these six chapters Daniel uses the emphatic 'I Daniel'. There is one strange exception, when he reverts to the third person for one statement (10:1).

2. The Setting of the Visions

Vision 1 and Vision 2

These visions are given in the early years of the last king of the Babylonian Empire: the first and third years of Belshazzar.

[2] See Introduction, Section 2C.
[3] Anderson, *Daniel in the Critic's Den*, p. 23.

Vision 3 and Vision 4

These visions are given in the early years of the first king of the Medo-Persian Empire: the first year of Darius, and the third year of Cyrus. Since it will be shown that these dates are the same, Cyrus ruled the empire, while, under him, Darius ruled the old Babylonian Empire.

3. The Period Covered by the Visions

So that the matter is clear, it will be restated that these four visions given to Daniel unfold the history of the nation of Israel while under Divine discipline, as well as the history of other nations as each comes into contact with Israel – God's key nation on earth. The time span is from the conquest of Jerusalem by Nebuchadnezzar to the liberation of that same Jerusalem (Rom. 11:25–26) by the Messianic Prince identified as the Son of Man (7:13). In other words, these visions cover the period identified by the Lord Himself by the title of the 'times of the Gentiles' (Lk. 21:24). This period commenced when God permitted Nebuchadnezzar to conquer Jerusalem, the only city on earth with which Jehovah, the covenantal God of Israel, has ever identified His Name. He had placed His Name there (Deut. 12:5) as the centre of His relationship with earth. The period will close when Jehovah's Sovereign deals with the final Gentile king, takes the city of Jerusalem, sets up His Kingdom and rules in person 'from the River even to the ends of the earth' (Zech. 9:10). The Church is not the subject of prophecy. Even though it has been in the counsels of God eternally (Eph. 3:1–13), the Church has not been revealed at this point, so it is not seen in OT prophetic Scripture. The Church comes into the programme of God after the Messiah has been presented to, and rejected by, the nation of Israel. It will be shown in the commentary, at the relevant points, that in the prophetic outline provision is made for the entry of the Church into the Divine programme, but this can only be seen in the light of history. This is why the Lord Himself only begins to speak of the Church after He has seen that His ministry has been rejected by the Jewish leaders (Mt. 16:18) – the rejection of the ministry of Christ was followed, as the Lord knew it would be, by the rejection of the Person of Christ.[4]

[4] See Appendix 7, 'The Times of the Gentiles'.

4. The Languages Used in the Visions

Two languages are used in this book, as shown:

Hebrew Chapter 1:1–2:3 Private Life of Daniel
Concerns the Hebrew Nation

Aramaic Chapter 2:4–7:28 Public Life of Daniel
Concerns the Gentile Nations

Hebrew Chapter 8:1–12:13 Visions of Daniel
Concerns Israel and the Nations

It will be important to note that chapter 7 is written in **Aramaic** and chapters 8–12 are written in **Hebrew,** so Vision 1 is recorded in **Aramaic** and Visions 2, 3, and 4 are recorded in **Hebrew.** This language difference will have a bearing on the interpretation of the visions.

5. The Development in the Visions

The emphasis in each vision complements and develops that of the previous vision. It will be pointed out that chapters 7–12 deal exclusively with the consummation of the 'times of the Gentiles'. The development of this theme in each vision is clear from the following summary:

Vision 1

Chapter 7 deals with the emergence of a final world power politically, and the emergence of a final world ruler personally. Since this will be a Gentile empire – with a Gentile ruler – the language is **Aramaic**. This empire will be a confederation of ten powers ruled by the by the '*prince that shall come*' (9:26).

Vision 2

Chapter 8:1–22 presents the emergence of a world power prophetically for Daniel, and historically for readers today.
Chapter 8:23–26 deals with the emergence of a final religious ruler in Israel – the Antichrist (See also 11:36–45). Since Israel is in view, the language is **Hebrew**.

Vision 3

Chapter 9 presents the Divine programme for the 'time of the end', and outlines a distinct period for the Consummation – the seventieth week (v. 27).

Vision 4

Chapters 10–12 outline the different powers at work in the 'time of the end' and Divine patience as saints await the Consummation. Since Israel is the key nation at the 'time of the end' the language is **Hebrew**.

The contrast in purpose between Part 1 and Part 2 may be summarised thus:

Part 1 God **can** preserve His people *individually* for the Kingdom – His Power.

Part 2 God **will** preserve His people *nationally* for the Kingdom – His Promise.

6. The Method of Revelation in the Visions

A careful reader notes immediately that in this part of the book truth is presented by the use of picture and symbol in the visions. The most obvious example is the use of animals to represent nations. Commentators refer to this type of writing as 'apocalyptic'. The book of the Revelation is the prime example of this genre of biblical writing. It must be kept in mind in the study of this kind of revelation that, while symbols play a major part in such writing, the symbols will be interpreted by the immediate context, but if this is not so, then they will be interpreted by other Scriptures. Free rein cannot be given to the imagination of the interpreter; to do this can lead to unscriptural conclusions, which can become the basis of false teaching. Further, it must be understood that this method of communication is not a drama conceived in the mind of the author to convey truth. In Scripture it is what the author has seen and heard that is conveyed to the reader. Since what he sees and hears comes from God, the author is simply the channel of communication. This is how inspiration is defined in Scripture: 'For the prophecy came not in old time by the will of man: but holy men of God spake as they were moved by the Holy Ghost' (2 Pet.

1:21). A golden rule in the interpretation of apocalyptic prophecy that would have preserved from much unscriptural teaching can be summarised thus: 'A valid principle for interpreting prophecy is to accept the plain sense of the text unless there is a good reason to adopt some other meaning.'[5] This can be summarised in a brief statement: 'When the literal sense makes good sense, seek no other sense lest you end up with nonsense.' This is the rule underlying interpretation in this commentary.

INTRODUCTION TO CHAPTER SEVEN

Vision 1

Ch. 7:1–28 First Year of Belshazzar 553 BC Daniel is 70 yrs

A. The Setting of the Chapter

This is the final chapter in the Aramaic language section of the book, which, as previously noticed, deals with the relationship of the nations of the world with Israel – the nation through whom God would bring the Messiah. Further, it is to be particularly observed that this vision is given in the year following the accession of Belshazzar to the throne of Babylon. A third point, relevant to the dating of the vision, is to note that Belshazzar's reign did not follow immediately upon the death of Nebuchadnezzar (562 BC) as one might assume from a casual reading. There was an interval of nine troubled years when three claimants to the throne were murdered.[6] Some measure of stability had come with the seizure of the throne by an able general called Nabonidus, who had campaigned with Nebuchadnezzar in earlier years. A group of army conspirators, tired of the years of murderous chaos since the death of Nebuchadnezzar (562 BC), removed Labashi-Marduk, a young grandson of Nebuchadnezzar, and replaced him with one from their number. Nabonidus' claim to the throne was his marriage to a daughter of Nebuchadnezzar. In addition to his military experience – he was a capable army general – he was a man with an absorbing interest in the ancient history of Babylon going back as far as the eighteenth century BC. He delighted to search out monuments, gravestones and buildings with inscriptions dating back to the great Babylon of Hammurabbi (c. 1792–1750 BC)[7] with his codification of

[5] Miller, *New American Commentary, Daniel*, p. 193.
[6] See Appendix 2, The History of the Neo-Babylonian Empire.
[7] *CBD*, p. 420.

law.[8] In his pursuit of these archaeological records of past greatness recorded in the inscriptions on buildings and tombs, King Nabonidus seemed to regard Babylon as of secondary importance and was often absent for long periods. Under cover of posing a threat to the rising power of Cyrus the Persian, he led an army from Babylon to Harran and camped near the oasis of Taima in north-west Arabia, where he had planned to investigate some archaeological sites. Before setting out, he appointed his son Belshazzar as co-regent in the empire, with the title 'King of Babylon'. Records show that this was done in the third year of his reign (553 BC). Most historians agree that Daniel is perfectly accurate and uses the title correctly when he writes of Belshazzar as 'King of Babylon'.[9]

In his interpretation of the vision of the image, given to Nebuchadnezzar (2:36–45), Daniel told of the four empires that would rule over the nation of Israel during the time of Divine discipline for sin when Jerusalem, their capital city, would be under Gentile rule. These four empires would exercise sovereignty during the 'times of the Gentiles' (Lk. 21:24). Daniel explained that these four empires would successively replace each other. In the image of the dream the first empire was pictured as the head of gold, which is interpreted by Daniel, not as the Babylonian Empire, but as King Nebuchadnezzar personally. This vision in chapter 7 was given to Daniel when Nebuchadnezzar had been dead nine years (562–553 BC) and seventeen years of captivity (from 553–536 BC) still stretched before Israel (Jer. 25:11–12). Those Jewish captives with a spiritual exercise were doubtless pondering what lay ahead for their people. God is now going to answer that exercise of heart through these four visions and, in doing so, give much more detail of what lay ahead for Israel. These prophecies would be: (a) a stimulus to those Israelites exercised to return to Jerusalem; and (b) a stay to such Israelites when problems arose. The books of Ezra and Nehemiah give the history of this return. The reading of this prophecy would show to those exercised believers that Israel and Jerusalem would once again be the centre of Divine interest, and would continue to be so, until the arrival of the Messiah.

The time frame of the chapter is therefore set in a period when the glory of Babylon had begun to wane and concern was abroad as

[8] Oates, *Babylon*, pp. 60–82. Historians in recent years spell the name as 'Hammurapi'.

[9] See Appendix 2, History of the Neo-Babylonian Empire.

to what the future held. This concern was deepened as men could see that, on the political horizon, there was a man rising to world prominence through his military exploits – Cyrus the Persian. The mighty Median kingdom had fallen to him; the wealthy Lydian kingdom had followed and now it seemed he planned to capture great Babylon.

B. The Interpretation of the Chapter

(a) The Generally Accepted View

Except for a few lonely voices, the generally accepted view of this chapter goes back to the publication in the mid-nineteenth century of the ten-volume *Commentary on the Old Testament* by the well-known and respected conservative commentators C.F. Keil and F. Delitzsch. C.F. Keil contributed Daniel to the series (c. 1859). Keil writes: 'In this vision the four world-monarchies which were shown to Nebuchadnezzar in the form of an image are represented under the symbol of beasts; and there is a further unfolding not only of the nature and character of the four successive world kingdoms, but also of the everlasting Kingdom of God established by the judgment of the world-kingdoms'.[10] This interpretation, it may be said, is followed by the majority of conservative commentators and has found almost universal acceptance amongst those who are prepared to accept Daniel's prophecy as given of God. The following quotation, even if a little lengthy, from Leon Wood, an able conservative commentator, sums up the matter concisely. He writes:

> As noted in chapter two, the dream-image, in its four divisions, symbolised the four great empires – the Babylonian, the Medo-Persian, the Grecian, and the Roman. The same is true in respect of the four beasts seen in the first vision. There are two main differences, however. First the dream-image, by its nature, pictures the unity of history running through these empires, in that the image is one whole, having related symbolic parts; whereas the four beasts, being each fully distinct from each other, depict the diversity of history exhibited by the empires. Second, the human-like dream-image, seen by the pagan Nebuchadnezzar, represented these empires from the viewpoint of man as each having intrinsic value, corresponding

[10] Keil and Delitzsch, *Commentary on the Old Testament*, Vol. 9, p. 220.

> to the descending values of the metals of the image; whereas the four beasts, seen by the godly Daniel, show these empires from God's viewpoint, each being beastly in nature and value.[11]

This is the view taken by most conservative scholars. While some expositors have expressed serious reservations, arising from various problems in their studies, few have given these points the study they deserve – with the consequence that another aspect of the vision seems to have been missed. In the early nineteenth century, before archaeological research and the reading of the cuneiform inscriptions had ruined their sceptical case against Daniel, any dissident voices would have come from liberal-minded critics. Such saw the same parallel between the metals of the image and the beasts from the sea but, to keep to their dating scheme for a 'Pseudo-Daniel' writing in the second century BC, they would re-label both the metals and the beasts as representing Babylon, Media, Persia and Greece.[12]

(b) Problems with the Generally Accepted View

However, a few voices down the years have raised problems with this interpretation. Amongst the best known in this group of conservative commentators are G.H. Lang,[13] Sir Robert Anderson,[14] and Geoffrey R. King.[15] They have highlighted some of the difficulties presented by the usual interpretation and, unlike many, were prepared to face the implications and look for another answer. Each problem requires an answer and, in light of that answer, it is necessary to consider whether the problems are sufficiently serious to encourage the search for an alternative interpretation. And, most vital of all, do other Scriptures support either interpretation? Scripture must be the standard by which any interpretation is assessed.

Seven problems can be identified with the generally accepted view:

1. Concerning the Storm (vv. 1–3)

The very first problem confronting the reader of this chapter is often ignored by commentators. This is a time problem: In the

[11] Wood, *A Commentary on Daniel*, p. 178.
[12] See Introduction and Background, Section 2 C.
[13] Lang, *The Histories and Prophecies of Daniel*.
[14] Anderson, *Daniel in the Critic's Den*.
[15] King, *Daniel*.

vision the four beasts all emerge from the same sea and clearly from the same storm when 'the four winds of the heaven strove upon the great sea'. The storm is generally understood, quite reasonably, to symbolise a period of international turmoil. This means that the four beasts arise from one specific period of international tension amongst the nations. This certainly does not fit with the emergence of the kingdoms in chapter 2, where kingdom succeeds kingdom on the world stage, as it is perfectly clear that the kingdoms represented in the four metals cannot be on the world stage at the same time. That the term 'the great sea' is used as a proper noun in the OT when it is speaking of the Mediterranean Sea is not disputed (Num. 34:6–7; Josh. 1:4; 9:1; 15:11–12; 15:47; 23:4 etc.); particularly when the Scripture is dealing with the borders of the land promised to Israel. Whether, in this passage, the term applies to the Mediterranean Sea particularly, or simply refers to any stormy sea, is a matter of interpretation. G.H. Lang[16] makes it a major point in his interpretation and insists that four emerging nations must have land links with the Mediterranean Sea. However, since this is a symbolic presentation, to tie one feature to a literal place without contextual support is hardly fair exegesis. Further, in going beyond what Scripture presents, unnecessary exegetical questions are raised. However, Lang is one of the few commentators who see that some modification in the general interpretation of this chapter is required. It is perfectly clear that these four beasts represent empires that, while arriving successively, are all on the world stage at the same time (*cf.* v. 7 with v. 12).

2. Concerning the Tense of the Verb 'shall arise' (v. 17)

The angel interprets the four beasts as 'four kings, which *shall arise* out of the earth'. We must remember that the date for this vision is 'the first year of Belshazzar', which in our chronology is 553 BC. Nebuchadnezzar, identified as the head of gold of the image, had died in 562 BC, nine years before this vision was given, and the Babylonian Empire was in serious decline. To say the least, Nebuchadnezzar hardly seems to fit into the class of four kings 'which shall arise'. Many commentators slip over this point without dealing with it. Walvoord[17] deals with it by drawing attention to a side issue – the textual variation preferred by liberal critics, and

[16] Lang, *The Histories and Prophecies of Daniel*, p. 78.
[17] Walvoord, *Daniel: The Key to Prophetic Revelation*, p. 172.

simply ignores it thereafter. Wood is forthright and admits the difficulty but offers a somewhat recondite explanation. He writes:

> The form of the verb "shall arise" (root *qu^m*), is imperfect, designating incomplete action. Some expositors have objected that this fact makes impossible the idea that the first beast represents Babylon, particularly Nebuchadnezzar, since he was already dead at the time of the vision. The history of the four empires, however, is taken as a unit, which is incomplete until the fourth empire is destroyed and the form of the verb can only be imperfect, even though one aspect of the verb has begun well before.[18]

So at least there seems to be a possible grammatical answer to this particular problem. However, it appears a little strange that an important point in prophetic interpretation should depend, for its proper interpretation, on the knowledge of a very obscure point of Aramaic grammar, readily grasped only by Aramaic-speaking folk. Would this grammatical point have been clear to those who read the passage in Daniel's day?

3. Concerning the Transformation in the First Beast

It is granted that the Babylonian Empire could readily be represented by a lion with wings. This motif has been found displayed in terracotta murals on the walls of various palaces in Babylon, even though the wings are not the wings of the eagle but the wings of the buzzard – a motif which, it must be pointed out, had much more in common with the Assyrian Empire than with the Babylonian Empire. Much is often made of the changes brought about in the first beast – stated thus: 'I beheld till the wings thereof were plucked, and it was lifted up from the earth, and made stand upon the feet as a man, and a man's heart was given to it' (v. 4). Defenders of the traditional interpretation point to what happened to Nebuchadnezzar as recorded: 'and he was driven from men, and did eat grass as oxen, and his body was wet with the dew of heaven, till his hairs were grown like eagles' feathers, and his nails like birds' claws' (4:33). However, a little consideration shows that what happened to this first beast is not what happened to Nebuchadnezzar – it is the very opposite. Nebuchadnezzar was reduced to a beast-like condition for a time. This ruler of beast-like character is

[18] Wood, *A Commentary on Daniel*, p. 196.

transformed into something with man-like features: feet and heart. There is no suggestion that this is a temporary condition. The interpretation seems to be somewhat strained when it tries to match two things essentially different.

4. The Problem of the Bear (v. 5)

In the traditional interpretation the bear represents Medo-Persia – the second empire in the image. As already discussed, the silver metal is an ideal representation of this nation that accumulated silver and valued this metal as no nation has ever done, before or since. To find it represented now as a bear is very strange indeed. History and archaeology may be searched in detail but so far not a single reference has been found to link the bear with either the Median or the Persian Empire. The animal always associated with Media and Persia is the ram. This is the animal used in the next chapter and we are left in no doubt by the interpreting angel: 'The ram which thou sawest having two horns are the kings of Media and Persia' (8:20).

While having no historical support whatever to link the bear with Medo-Persia, many conservative commentators still spend considerable time in countering liberal critics who want to show that the bear represents the Median Empire. For liberalism this is a vital link in their theory of a 'pseudo-Daniel', writing history in the second century BC,[19] instead of the biblical Daniel writing prophecy in the sixth century BC. But, while countering their arguments, conservative commentators still insist on making the bear represent Medo-Persia. They see the features of a bear – its ungainly gait, its sheer body strength, its voracious appetite – note the three ribs in the mouth – as delineating the Medo-Persian Empire. Drawn in to support this thesis is the statement 'it raised up itself on one side', which they interpret as describing the fact that the Persian Empire, appearing on the scene later than the Median Empire became, in the end, the dominant partner. This is all perfectly true, and, as will be shown, this latter point is the correct interpretation of the two horns of the ram of which Scripture speaks: 'and the two horns were high; but one was higher than the other, and the higher came up last' (8:3). However, there is very considerable support amongst modern Aramaic scholars for translation of the statement in this chapter as in the *RV* margin: 'it made for itself one dominion',

[19] See Introduction. Section 2 C, 'Attack of the Critics'.

which, when the textual emendation is accepted by commentators, is made to point to the policies adopted by Cyrus to ensure both the Medes and the Persians were completely integrated in the Medo-Persian Empire, which Cyrus, with unparalleled diplomatic skill, had united under his leadership. It will be shown in the comments on verse 5 that a much more feasible interpretation can be offered for these features in the bear.

5. The Problem of the Leopard (v. 6)

In the generally accepted interpretation, the leopard is equated with the Grecian Empire, represented in the image as 'the belly and thighs were of brass'. The leopard is acknowledged as perhaps the fastest animal on earth and there is no difficulty interpreting this as a picture of the great Grecian (Macedonian) warrior, Alexander the Great (356–323 BC), who in eight years of military invasion and in eight victorious battles (334–331 BC) brought not only the Persian Empire, but the world, to his feet. He is the only military commander of whom it could rightly be said 'he never lost a battle'.[20] While the speed of conquest fits Alexander of the Grecian Empire, the rest of the description raises questions. Why did such a speedy beast need 'four wings of a fowl', which really have nothing to do with speed – in fact they would have undoubtedly, by wind resistance, have reduced the speed of the leopard. To what do these wings correspond in either Alexander personally or in the Grecian Empire? In reference to the four heads of the leopard, this beast has four heads when it arrives on the scene. In the case of Alexander, it was at least twenty years after his death that the division of his kingdom into four parts took place. This again offers a somewhat forced interpretation of the four wings to fit something that developed later and is described more clearly in later visions (8:23; 11:3–4).

6. The Problem of the Fourth Empire (v. 7)

Even if the problems with the first three beasts are ignored, as a link is sought with the empires represented by the metals in the image, there are still major problems if this fourth beast is seen as the Roman Empire. Questions might arise: (a) What made Rome so totally different from the kingdoms that preceded it?; (b) Even if the two legs are interpreted as the east-west division of the Roman

[20] See Appendix 4, History of the Grecian Empire. See quotation from Diodorus Siculus (first century BC) in *History in Quotations*, ed. M.J. Cohen and John Major, (London: Cassell, 2004).

Empire from the time of the Emperor Theodosius (379–395 BC) the question arises as to when Rome was ruled by ten contemporary kings. It will be shown in the commentary that there is a simple answer to these questions. But, for the moment, there is a bigger question in the traditional interpretation. It can be shown grammatically that in the statement 'diverse from all the beasts that were before it', the preposition 'before' should be interpreted, not as a preposition of time – 'preceded' it – but as a preposition of space – 'were standing in front of' it. In other words, while they had appeared in succession, they were now all together – the first three standing before the fourth one. This is supported by the statement of what Daniel observed when the fourth beast was destroyed: 'As concerning the rest of the beasts, they had their dominion taken away: yet their lives were prolonged for a season and time' (v. 12). On the traditional interpretation, this is impossible to explain in any logical way. It simply does not fit the given picture.

7. The Problem of Repetition

Those who see chapter 7 as paralleling the dream image of chapter 2 might well be asked: What is the purpose of repeating the prophecy of the four kingdoms? To answer that: (a) 'chapter 7 fills in certain details not given in chapter 2' seems somewhat inadequate; or (b) 'repetition underlines the certainty of the prophecy', seems a little like special pleading; or (c) 'to King Nebuchadnezzar it is given to see the glory of the Gentile kingdoms while godly Daniel is allowed to see their beastly character' is somewhat naïve and sounds as if God was accommodating His revelation to the recipient. It was God Who gave the dream and the vision – why should the recipient's viewpoint be of importance when God was revealing what He was going to do in the nations? There must be more behind the difference than this trivial point. On this very issue, Sir Robert Anderson wrote: 'Daniel 2 and Daniel 7 are both in the Chaldee [Aramaic] portion of the book, and are therefore bracketed together, and separated from what follows. This strengthens the presumption which would obtain in any case, that the latter vision is not a repetition of the earlier one. Repetition is very rare in Scripture.'[21] In fact, as Sir Robert Anderson surveys the traditional view of making chapter 7 repeat the sequence of the four kingdoms of the 'times of the Gentiles' given in chapter 2, he has this to say:

[21] Anderson, *The Coming Prince*, p. 274.

> So strong indeed is the *prima facie* case in support of this view that I have not felt at liberty to depart from it in the foregoing pages. At the same time I am constrained to own that the case is less complete than it appears to be, and that grave difficulties arise in connection with it; and the following observations are put forward tentatively to promote enquiry into the matter.[22]

These seven problems will have to be taken into account and resolved as this chapter is interpreted. The interpretation will require repetition in the refutation of some of these arguments.

C. The Focus of the Chapter

In light of the discussion on the problems mentioned, it might help in understanding the chapter if the main focus in each of the chapters is considered.

Chapter 2 The interpretation of Nebuchadnezzar's dream image presents the period of Gentile rule over Israel. It shows the commencement of this Gentile rule in Nebuchadnezzar, the course of Gentile rule in three successive kingdoms, and then a concise summary of the close of the period. That close of the period of Gentile rule over Jerusalem is pictured dramatically by a stone 'cut out of the mountain without hands' (v. 45), which 'smote the image upon his feet' (v. 34). The majority of the detail in the passage is given in connection with the first kingdom. The focus seems to fasten the attention upon the commencement of the period – the sceptre of dominion has been removed from Jerusalem and established in Babylon. The focus falls on the commencement of the period called the times of the Gentiles.

Chapter 7 The interpretation of the vision presents, without question, the close of Gentile rule over Israel. There are four kingdoms present, but not the same kingdoms as in chapter 2. The four are present together (v. 12) until one grows exceedingly powerful – 'dreadful and terrible' (v. 7) and, while absorbing aspects of the previous three empires, yet leaves them still in national existence. It will be learned in the interpretation (v. 25) that it is from this final empire that earth's final ruler will come, who will dominate earth for the last three-and-a-half years of history. He will

[22] The reference under footnote 18 opens a section dealing with some of the problems under discussion.

be the greatest (or the worst) ruler earth has ever produced; he will be Satan's man from whom the kingdom will be taken by a Divine decree, directly from 'His throne' (v. 9), and given to the Son of Man. So the focus falls on the close of the period called the times of the Gentiles.

So while there are very close links between these two dream scenes, chapter 7 is not merely a repetition of chapter 2 but deals with the close of the time period whose commencement was dealt with in chapter 2. It would seem that Daniel has this same terminus in mind when he sums up his interview with the interpreter in the statement, 'Hitherto is the end of the matter' (v. 28), or, as given in the Spurrell translation, 'Here is the conclusion of the subject-matter.' We would say 'This is the end of the story.'

D. The Outline of the Chapter

It is often useful to have an outline of the whole chapter as the backdrop to more detailed study. The following outline has been found helpful:

The Vision (Part 1) Background – The Sea

vv. 2–7 The Four Beasts
v. 8 The Little Horn

The Vision (Part 2) Background – The Throne

vv. 9–12 The Fiery Throne: The Scene in Heaven
vv. 13–14 The Future King: The Sovereign from Heaven
vv. 15–16 The Reaction of Daniel

The Interpretation (Part 1)

vv. 17–18 The Four Beasts and the Future Kingdom
vv. 19–22 The Fourth Beast and the Final Ruler

The Interpretation (Part 2)

vv. 23–25 Detail of the Fourth Beast and Final Ruler
vv. 26–27 Detail of the Kingdom of God and the King
v. 28 The Reaction of Daniel

COMMENTARY ON CHAPTER 7: 1–8

The Close of Gentile Dominion

Date of chapter 7 553 BC Daniel aged 70 yrs

Verse 1 This first verse gives the date and indicates the theme of the chapter. Daniel dates his vision in the first year of Belshazzar King of Babylon, which in our chronology is the year 553 BC. Daniel is now seventy years of age. So this vision is given to Daniel fourteen years before the death of Belshazzar (539 BC), of which we have the record in chapter 5, when Daniel was eighty-four years of age. It also places it fifteen years before the experience of Daniel in the den of lions, as recorded in chapter 6 (538 BC). So that when Daniel faced these two representatives of Gentile monarchy – Belshazzar in his final day on the throne and Darius in his first year on the throne – God had already revealed to His servant the end of all Gentile monarchy. Not only so, but God had already shown him that the sovereignty of earth belonged to the Son of Man (7:13–14). What a stay this prophetic foreknowledge must have been to the soul of Daniel in those testing hours! Prophetic truth is meant to do this for believers in every age.

To explain the dating here it is necessary to glance, for a moment, at the history of Babylon.[23] It will be recalled that from the death of Nebuchadnezzar, in 562 BC, there was a period of about nine years when three claimants to the throne were murdered. The final usurpation of the throne by Nabonidus in 555 BC brought some measure of stability. Nabonidus was a very able man from Nebuchadnezzar's staff who, while coming from a non-royal background, soon proved himself a very capable man in politics and also in military affairs. He brought a measure of stability to the empire, sorely needed in light of the military threat to Babylon posed by the alliance of Media with Persia and the rise of Cyrus the Great. To bolster his rather slender claim to the throne he had married Nitocris, the daughter of Nebuchadnezzar. In his third year he appointed Belshazzar, his son by Nitocris, as co-regent of the empire (second only to himself) and with the title King of Babylon. Babylonian records still spoke of Nabonidus as the last king of the empire. This would therefore be the year 553 BC, recorded by Daniel, quite correctly, as the first year of Belshazzar. Equally correctly Belshazzar is called King of Babylon.

[23] Appendix 2, History of the Neo-Babylonian Empire.

It can readily be understood that, with Nebuchadnezzar dead, and murderous usurpers laying claim to the throne, there would be deep anxiety amongst the captives from Judah as to what the future held for their nation. The remnant of the nation left in Judaea had been sustained by the prophetic ministry of Jeremiah. That this ministry was also available in Babylon in written form is clear from the reference by Daniel to the 'books' (9:2). In that passage God had given Jeremiah the length of the captivity period – seventy years. Israelites deported to Babylon had the ministry of Ezekiel to point out the necessity of repentance and confession of their sin before there could be any hope of forgiveness and restoration. The hearts of the spiritual in Israel must have been deeply concerned as to what was going to happen now that the mighty Nebuchadnezzar had gone. They still had twenty-six years of the captivity period before them (562–536 BC). At this point God gives Daniel a sight of the end of Gentile rule. Further, at this point of deep concern, God entrusts Daniel with a glimpse of 'the saints' entering into their Kingdom in the land promised to Abram and his seed (Gen. 15:18) under the promised King of the seed of David (2 Sam. 7:12–16). At this moment such a possibility seemed remote. This writing of Daniel, while presenting problems, must have been a real source of Divine strength and renewed stamina to exercised saints held, as yet, under Babylon's sway. The fact that Daniel continues to use the Aramaic language in this chapter before changing to Hebrew in the next chapter confirms the deduction that what it presents is, not the course, but the consummation and close of the 'times of the Gentiles'.

The link between 'visions' and 'dream' recalls the use of these same terms in chapter 2 (v. 28) and in chapter 4 (vv. 5, 13). On each occasion it is to be noted that the word 'visions' is in the plural while the word 'dream' is in the singular. It suggests that God gave the dream and then highlighted certain aspects by focussing on special features. In this passage, while the dream is one there are two visions – the great sea (vv. 1–8) and the Throne (vv. 9–14). When Daniel awoke he put the dream in writing and thus conveyed the 'sum of the matters'. The word 'sum' means 'head' or 'chief'[24] and would indicate that all that was necessary for the clear understanding of the message was in the writing.

[24] *OTWS*, p. 375.

The Vision (Part 1) Background – The Sea vv. 2–8

Verses 2–7 The Four Beasts

Verse 2 In this verse Daniel changes from the use of the third person to the first person as if to underline the fact that he, personally, is the channel of the revelation this time and not merely the interpreter, as was the case with the dreams of Nebuchadnezzar. Alternatively, the abrupt change may suggest simply that the first verse was added at a later date as an introduction to the record already written. The introductory verb 'I saw' is in participle form and should be translated 'I was looking'.[25] This verb is used repeatedly in this chapter, where Daniel's attention is so gripped it is as if he cannot lift his eyes from the scene. The participle is used nine times (vv. 2, 4, 6, 7, 9, 11 (twice), 13, 21) and leads frequently to the arresting cry 'lo' or 'behold'. Derived from the same verb, 'to see', this is a summons to 'stop and take a good look at this'. This exclamation occurs seven times (vv. 2, 5, 6, 7, 8 (twice), 13) and highlights unexpected happenings in the vision.

The vision focuses on what is called the 'great sea'. Scripture uses this term generally to refer to the Mediterranean Sea. This is clear when used in the identification of the land borders of Israel (Num. 34:6–7; Josh. 1:4; 9:1; 15:11–12; 15:47; 23:4). G.H. Lang writes: 'It is clear that from the time of Moses the term had one regular meaning, and this was still current in Daniel's day, as witnessed by its use by his contemporary Ezekiel' (Ezek. 47:10, 15, 19, 20; 48:28).[26] Lang is followed by a number of commentators, who insist on the geographic reference to the Mediterranean Sea and imply that all four beasts arise out of lands bordering this sea. It seems strange and somewhat illogical to tie a literal geographic area into a symbolic scene. Even if one accepts this interpretation, it is obvious that it does not fit the four kingdoms of chapter 2 – it was only by stretching history that either Babylon or Medo-Persia had any real connection with the Mediterranean Sea. It is suggested that, lacking the article, the expression may point to the sea most famous in the world of that day as setting the scene for a great storm. No additional significance should be attached to the term.

The 'four winds of heaven' – used on two further occasions in this book (8:8; 11:4) – symbolise natural forces that are operative in a

[25] Wood, *A Commentary on Daniel*, p. 180.

[26] Lang, *The Histories and Prophecies of Daniel*, p. 78.

well-ordered creation. As ordained by a Creator God they operate by Divine permission. The number 'four' speaks of universality; these agents of the Divine will operate throughout the world. On occasion, however, when required to do so, these four winds may operate, not under their normal laws as established by their Creator, but act under direct Divine order in an abnormal way for a Divine purpose. This is the case here, when the winds are set to oppose one another; they are behaving abnormally as they become agents of God's judgement on earth; this results in a storm stirred up on the great sea (as in Jonah 1:4).

In the book of Revelation there is a similar storm scene on earth (Rev. 7:1–3) but with an additional factor. The four winds, under orders to stir up the storm, are suddenly arrested and held back by four angels. It is clear that the interpretation of this symbolic scene shows that, while orders for the seven-year Tribulation period have already been given, now God, through grace, decides to delay the storm until the 144,000 of Israel have been sealed with 'the seal of the living God'. It is tempting to link the storm in this chapter with the storm in Revelation and see in each of them a picture of the same period – the seven-year Tribulation period. If this link is valid then Revelation chapter 7 precedes this chapter in time sequence. In Revelation the storm is delayed; here the storm has arrived.

In the symbolism of Scripture the sea, on occasion, symbolises the nations of earth (Isa. 17:12–13; Rev. 17:15). There can be little question that the sea, pulled in one direction by gravitational forces and, as here, driven in another direction by opposing winds, becomes a fitting symbol of nations in turmoil. The verb 'strove'[27] is a very dramatic verb and means 'to break forth, to rush forth as the winds do, as if to battle'. Miller suggests 'churning up the great sea'.[28] The use of this unusual verb in this connection rules out any suggestion that this is just the normal state of nations out of which each of the four nations mentioned arise in their own time down the ages. This is not the picture here. In fact, the very opposite is the case. Normal interpretation demands a tremendous storm to be interpreted as a time of turmoil from which the four beasts emerge in succession.

[27] *OTWS*, p. 424.
[28] Miller, *New American Commentary, Daniel*, p. 195.

Verses 3–8 This paragraph could readily be sub-titled 'The Four Great Beasts'. A number of features about these beasts must be noted:

(a) The word 'great' is a duplicated adjective in which attention is directed to sheer size and is translated by Spurrell as 'large'; they are notable for their outstanding size;

(b) They are linked in their origin – they all arise from the same storm in the great sea;

(c) They do not emerge from the sea together as a group at the same moment but successively, one following the other;

(d) There is no suggestion of each emerging beast devouring or defeating or overcoming its forerunner. In fact, the four are on the earth stage together. When the fourth one is destroyed (v. 11), the other three remain for a time;

(e) they differ one from another just as the animals which are used to personify them differ from one another.

To represent nations, or even individuals, as animals, as is done both in Scripture and other literature, is not necessarily derogatory but depends on context, and on the feature of the animal stressed. For example, the apostle Paul warned the assembly at Corinth against the subtlety of the serpent in the words 'as the serpent beguiled Eve through his subtilty, so your minds should be corrupted from the simplicity that is in Christ' (2 Cor. 11:3). Yet, on the other hand, it is to be noted that when the Lord sent forth His disciples as heralds of the Kingdom He commanded, 'Be ye therefore wise as serpents, and harmless as doves' (Mt. 10:16). It can also readily be recalled that the lion is used to highlight an aspect of Satan's behaviour (1 Pet. 5:8) and used also as a picture of the Saviour (Rev. 5:5). In this light, the features of these beasts will require careful exegesis.

Verse 4 The First Beast: The Lion with Eagle's Wings

The scant but very significant detail given of the first three beasts serves to emphasise the fact, already observed, that before us here are 'end-times' and it is the fourth beast on which the vision will focus. This fourth beast will fill the stage.

Most expositors have no doubt whatever that the lion represents the Babylonian Empire in general and Nebuchadnezzar in particular and align it directly with the head of gold in the image (2:32). This seems to be supported by the additional and unusual feature that this lion had eagle's wings. There is no doubt that the lion, as king of the animals, and the eagle, as king of the birds, in popular thought, provide an excellent symbol of the sovereignty of Nebuchadnezzar, in whom the strength of the lion and the speed of the eagle are clearly evident. When it is also pointed out that archaeologists have discovered many winged lions on the walls of the ruined palaces of Babylon the case seems complete. It would be a mere quibble to point out that the wings of the lion on Babylon's walls belong, not to the eagle, but to the vulture. However, they are both birds of prey and, in either case, the wings simply suggest speed in action and reaction. What clearer picture could be drawn of Babylon's mighty king, who had captured and destroyed the city of Jerusalem?

But keeping this interpretation in mind, the second part of this verse begins to pose some problems. Daniel's gaze is riveted upon this beast as he sees three things happen to it. The following translation is helpful here: 'I was gazing upon it, until its wings were plucked off wherewith it was lifted up from the ground; and upon its feet it rose up erect like a man, and a man's heart was given it.'(*SP*). Notice:

(a) Providential Retribution. Something dramatic happens to this beast. The beast lost its wings. The verb 'plucked off' or 'pulled out' is a dramatic word and used of tearing the hair from the beard (Isa. 50:6). Something takes place by the hand of some other who is not named, and this beast has suddenly lost its power to lift itself from the earth. The means of speedy action, an earlier characteristic of this unusual beast, have suddenly and roughly been stripped from it. The passive voice indicates this has been done to it. No indication is given as to as to the agent.

(b) Personal Response. The beast responds (note the active voice) by rising up and standing erect like a man. It has chosen, of its own accord, to display a change of role; it now behaves as a man and stands on two feet (the noun is dual).

(c) Public Recognition. As a consequence of the stroke that has grounded it and the subsequent repudiation of its beastly ways, it seems there is recognition of a change in character as described by the statement 'a human mind was given to it' (*NET*).[29] In the time under review (as Daniel 'was looking') he could see a very real change in this beast, which could only come by Divine action.

[29] *NET* translation is: 'and a human mind was given to it' with the textual note 'in *Aram* [Aramaic] "heart of a man"'.

The usual interpretation for this dramatic change is given by Leon Wood, who writes:

> The lion became a man outwardly and then inwardly; symbolising that Nebuchadnezzar, following his time of insanity became 'humanised' in this manner of rule. A humanitarian interest came to play a major role in his life, rather than a beastly lust for power.[30]

This is certainly worth close consideration, but when compared with the scriptural account it presents the very reverse of what happened to Nebuchadnezzar. Here a beast is made to stand on its feet and act as man and then is given a man's heart. In the case of Nebuchadnezzar (4:31–33) the opposite takes place. He was a man who, under Divine discipline, was made to go on all fours like a beast; his mind was reduced to the level of that of a beast. He recovered from that condition to become a man again. This beast became what it had never been. It is to be regretted that a superficial resemblance has been allowed to mislead many in the interpretation of this beast.

In reaching an interpretation of this beast the emphasis must fall first on the conditions from which the beasts emerge. It has already been noticed that it is an end-time storm when the nations of earth are in turmoil. What greater storm could there be than the one spoken of by the Lord when He said:

> And there shall be signs in the sun, and in the moon, and in the stars; and upon the earth distress of nations, with perplexity; the sea and the waves roaring; men's hearts failing them for fear, and for looking after those things which are coming on the earth: for the powers of heaven shall be shaken. And then shall they see the Son of man coming in a cloud with power and great glory' (Lk. 21:25–28).

What greater storm can arise than the Tribulation that precedes the coming of the Son of Man? It is suggested that this is the time Daniel has before him and this is one of four kings or kingdoms that will emerge from the storm. The second point to be emphasised is that the contemporaries of this first kingdom will be the three beasts who follow. While they are probably watching each other with distrust, building up their arsenals and threatening war

[30] Wood, *A Commentary on Daniel*, p. 182.

company of 'them that stood by' (v. 16), who would be the angelic superintendents of the nations. 'They' would, ironically, challenge this beast to carry on with its power-hungry policy of taking over neighbouring nations. We would possibly have said that this beast had 'bitten off more than it could chew'.

As already pointed out there is no scriptural support for using the symbol of the bear for the Medo-Persian Empire. Neither historical records nor archaeological research can offer any support in the matter. The scriptural symbol is the ram (8:3–4, 20) and this symbol can draw a wealth of support from history and archaeology: the ram is as well recognised historically as a symbol for Persia as the lion is recognised as the symbol for the British Empire. Even if the translation 'raised up itself on one side' is insisted upon (see v. 5), this seems a strange way to describe the relationship between Media and Persia, as if the kingdom had two geographic areas competing against each other for control. The wise policies of Cyrus precluded any such eventuality and this is absent from history.[33] Much more relevant and historically exact is the picture of the ram appearing with the two horns at the outset of conquest with the higher horn appearing last (8:3). This is a far more fitting picture of the rise of Cyrus the Great. It may also be said that it requires a very selective view of the history of Persia to see any correspondence with the next two statements: (a) 'it had three ribs in the mouth of it between the teeth' and (b) 'and they said thus unto it "Arise, devour much flesh"'. While the empire under Cyrus expanded at the expense of its neighbours and extended beyond Babylonia and Lydia and Egypt as far as Greece to become a world-dominating empire, it was never as voracious as some of the other empires.

Verse 6 The Third Beast: The Leopard

The traditional interpretation of this third beast is to see the leopard as a personification of the third kingdom to hold world dominance and have Jerusalem under its control. This was, of course, the Grecian Empire and very particularly under its founder and best known representative – Alexander the Great (356–323 BC). This is the kingdom represented in the image as the 'belly and ... thighs of brass' (2:32). This identification appears reasonable especially when the following points are considered:

[33] See Appendix 3.

(a) One thing associated with the leopard is speed and there is no question but that speed is associated with the personal rise of an obscure prince – Alexander, son of Philip II of Macedon – in an obscure province – Macedonia – despised by the sophisticated Greek city-states, in a minor political power – Greece – to world control in a lifetime that spanned only thirty-three years. Also to be considered is the speed of the conquest of the Persian Empire. From crossing the Dardanelles (Spring 334 BC) to the final defeat of Darius III at the Battle of Gaugamela (October 331 BC) took just over three years. Another factor to consider is the speed with which by the prowess of Alexander, backed by an original army of under fifty thousand Macedonian warriors brought the world to his feet in eight years (331–323 BC).

(b) Speed is emphasised in two ways in this symbol; firstly in the inherent speed of the leopard, and secondly in the addition of wings that would be expected to increase the speed. However, as will be pointed out, there is a considerable doubt as to whether the wings of a fowl would assist or hinder the speed of the leopard; (c) The four heads of this beast have lent support to the identification with Greece. History agrees that after twenty years of war among themselves after the death of Alexander came his 'successors' – their own term for the four generals of Alexander – who divided his empire into four parts.

On the face of it, the case seems complete and there seems to be no reason to question the identification. However, as with the previous animals, some important matters do not seem to have been taken into account. Consider the following points:

(a) A very relevant point is that the symbol of the leopard is never used elsewhere in Scripture or in historical records to represent Greece or the Grecian Empire. The scriptural symbol for Greece is the goat, used in the next chapter (8:5–8). The question then must arise as to why two symbols are used, in successive chapters, to depict one empire; a question to which it is difficult to find a satisfying answer. There can be no question that the goat is the universally accepted symbol for Greece.

(b) A further point is that the wings are the wings of a fowl, not the wings of the bird of prey as seen on the lion (v. 4). Instead of speed of conquest, what may be symbolised is the safety, shelter and security offered by those wings. The Lord used this symbol when He said 'O Jerusalem, Jerusalem ... how often would I have gathered thy children together, even as a hen gathereth her chickens under her wings, and ye would not!' (Mt. 23:37). There is certainly no evidence of Alexander's empire offering shelter and safety to anyone.

(c) Again it should be observed that this leopard has four wings right from its appearance on the world stage. It seems a little strange to interpret them as representing the four parts into which the Grecian Empire was finally divided, twenty years at least after the death of Alexander.

With the problems in regard to the identification of these animals with the nations symbolised in the metals of the image in mind, it might be reasonable to ask if there is any alternative view. The suggestions now put forward are presented with due respect for the many capable expositors and commentators who have been used of God to bring out the truths of prophetic Scripture over many years and to whom the present writer owes an incalculable debt. The suggestions are not meant to be controversial but constructive, taking into account the problems just reviewed. If the suggestions contribute to a clearer view of what Scripture presents then this will be beneficial for all. As always, the final court of appeal is Scripture – what Scripture presents must be final for every believer. In this light the following considerations are presented:

Reconsideration of the Generally Accepted Interpretation of the Four Beasts

Setting the Time Frame: The Sea and the Storm

If the sea (v. 2) has been rightly interpreted as presenting the nations of earth, then the statement that precedes it – 'the four winds of the heaven strove upon the great sea' – must depict storm conditions. This in the context must mean a time of international turmoil amongst the nations of earth. It has already been shown that the mention of the 'great sea' uses the acquaintance of men with a sea known to them, without tying the storm to a particular locality – for example linking the interpretation to the Mediterranean Sea. So these beasts must represent nations that emerge to play their part at one particularly turbulent period in earth history.

This particular period of international tension is identified by Daniel as the period when the matter under discussion comes to its destined end. In the last verse of this chapter (7:28), Daniel writes 'Hitherto is the end of the matter' (*AV*), which can be more literally translated 'Here is the conclusion of the subject-matter' (*SP.*). The matter being discussed is the close of the period of Gentile domination of Israel when the saints enter the everlasting Kingdom (7:26–27). This is the first time in the book that Daniel speaks of 'the end'. From this point to the close of the book he will refer to 'the end' or 'the time of the end' no less than seventeen times (7:28; 8:17,19 (twice); 9:26 (twice); 11:6, 27, 35, 40, 45; 12:4, 6, 8, 9, 13 (twice)). The 'end' is clearly the closing years of Gentile rule on earth and its replacement by the reign of the Son of Man as set forth in this chapter. This is clearly the end of the 'times of the Gentiles, of which the Lord spoke (Lk. 21:24).[34] In chapter 2 this is the time period depicted in the image. The commencement of the period is the capture of Jerusalem in 606 BC. The course of the period is shown as under four empires. Finally, the close of the period is shown to be the smiting of the image on the feet by the stone. Now Daniel is to be given more detail of the end of the period, as shown in the feet and toes of the image just before the stone arrives to destroy the image. The image symbolises – dominion! First, the dominion is in the hands of men from earth; then the dominion, by Divine judgement (v. 26), is to be placed in the hands of 'the Son of Man'. G.H. Lang agrees as he writes:

> Thus the vision of the beasts shows the political movements by which the feet and the toes of the image will develop. It is not repetition of the whole image, but an expansion in detail of that final stage of world-empire which is to be the culmination of 'man's day' and is the chief subject of prophecy.[35]

To identify this time of the storm generally as the very end of the 'times of the Gentiles' is vital to the correct understanding of what is unfolded here. Yet the focus needs to be sharper still. To bring that time into sharp focus it is necessary to take a brief glance ahead to Daniel's third vision. It is recognised by all conservative pre-millennial commentators on this book that in this third vision Daniel is given the Divine programme for earth, which is linked by a date to the Person of the Messiah. Since the Church was not in existence until after the cross of Calvary it is not the subject of prophecy and the Church age is not included in that earth-centred programme. In the study of the seventy weeks prophecy (9:24–27, see comments), it will be shown that there must be a very

[34] See Appendix 7, 'The Times of the Gentiles'.

[35] Lang, *The Histories and Prophecies of Daniel*, p. 84.

considerable time gap between the sixty-ninth and the seventieth week. The cross takes place after the close of the sixty-ninth week and the whole period of the Church age follows – from Pentecost down to the present time. It will be argued (*in loc.*) that the Church will be removed from earth before the seventieth week commences. The seventieth week of that prophecy has therefore a very special significance – it measures the time as seven years from the signing of a covenant with Israel until the Son of Man (7:13) takes the Kingdom. These years are, without question, a time when an unprecedented storm will break upon earth (see Rev. 7:1). The Lord spoke directly both of the storm and its setting when He said:

> For then shall be great tribulation, such as was not since the beginning of the world to this time, no, nor ever shall be (Mt. 24:21).

Again, He spoke of that same time and the storm when He said:

> And Jerusalem shall be trodden down of the Gentiles, until the times of the Gentiles be fulfilled. And there shall be signs in the sun, and in the moon, and in the stars; and upon the earth distress of nations, with perplexity; the sea and the waves roaring; men's hearts failing them for fear, and for looking after those things which are coming on the earth: for the powers of heaven shall be shaken. And then shall they see the Son of man coming in a cloud with power and great glory (Luke 21: 24–27).

So this is the time period that closes the 'times of the Gentiles' – the seven-year storm called the Tribulation. The storm closes the period and the consummation is the coming of the Son of Man.

The present day international situation points inescapably to the imminence of the Lord's coming for His Church. When this glorious hope of the Church is realised and the Lord comes and removes the believers, the way will then be open for God's end-time programme. It is suggested that this is the period in time to which Part 2 of Daniel (ch. 7–12) refers. Daniel makes reference to this same period in the phrase the 'time of the end'. This 'time of the end' includes the period of seven years called the Tribulation which, it is suggested, would be the reality behind the symbol of the storm in this chapter. After the Lord has removed the Church from earth (see comments at 9:26), and with the Church the final restraint upon the actions of men (2 Thess. 2:5–7) has gone, there is no question but that the present unrest in many nations will spread and deepen round the world. Stormy conditions will exist in the political world, the industrial world, the financial world and the social world. Then, a pseudo-peace having been agreed in Israel, the confirmation of a covenant opens the seventieth week of Daniel's prophecy. In John's picture from heaven, this is the moment when the Lamb takes the book from the hand of the Throne Sitter (Rev. 4:1–5:14). Once the Lamb begins to open the seals on the book, the Tribulation begins on earth. What a storm will then rage through the earth! It is suggested that as believers of that day survey the political scene with Bible in hand they will be able to identify and name these four end-time kingdoms without any doubt. The actions of these nations will make the news headlines on a daily basis. The four empires will be on the scene together.

When it is recognised that the vision is focussing on the end-times, and not on the history of the past, the whole perspective changes. This chapter is saying that in those end-times four kingdoms or empires will emerge from the world conditions of unrest then existing; empires that will carry world authority. They are successive empires as to their appearing, but they all exist contemporaneously – notice the preposition 'before' (v. 7), which should be interpreted with location – not time – in view. Then the fourth kingdom, absorbing features of the first three (Rev. 13:2), yet leaving those nations still in existence, is to be destroyed by the 'one like the Son of man' (v. 13) as He is given 'dominion, and glory, and a kingdom' (v. 14). In chapter 2 what was prophetic to Daniel, in the kingdoms symbolised in the metals, has already become history. In this chapter it is not history but prophecy that is in view. These four kingdoms have yet to appear together on the world stage.

From many indications of Scripture and society around us it is clear that we are close to the end of the Church age. With the coming of the Lord to the air for His Church impending, it would be no surprise if the end-time stage was already being set, with nations arranged for action after the Church has been raptured. Should we not be able to see at least the shadow of coming events – like the emergence of alignments amongst the nations that could come to maturity in a very short time once the Church has been called away by her Lord? This is a point used by the Lord Himself when He said, 'when these things begin to come to pass, then look up, and lift up your heads; for your redemption draweth nigh' (Lk. 21:28). The emphasis falls on the word 'begin'. So, without any *a priori* assumption that these four animals must represent the empires foreshadowed in the metals we see a completely different picture emerging; a picture that does not require any twisting of history – for it is still prophecy and yet to be fulfilled.

In reaching an interpretation of these four beasts, it is necessary to be clear that there is no licence to be given to our imagination nor must there be any question of trying to read our times into the Scripture. Expositors must not become prophets. This has happened often in the past to the embarrassment of many a well-meaning commentator. Scripture must be allowed to speak for itself, and inferences drawn from our present conditions treated with considerable reservation. Of false prophets there have been enough!

However, having set the time frame as the end of the 'times of the Gentiles', climaxing in the seven-year Tribulation, which precedes the Coming of the Son of Man, we might ask: are there any indications of what empires we, near the close of the Church age and from our perspective of history, might see as possibly foreshadowed in these four beasts? I suggest that once these indications are expected they are clearly to be seen. I trust the following suggestions may be considered.

A Suggested Identification of the Four Beasts of the End-Time

If the Lord should fulfil His promise today (Jn 14:1–3) and 'descend from heaven with a shout' (1 Thess. 4:13–18) to summon to Himself His blood-bought Church, then earth with its peoples and its nations will enter immediately upon the 'day of the Lord' (1 Thess. 5:1–3), of which period the Tribulation is the last seven years before the Christ returns to earth. This 'day of the Lord' is the period under consideration in these prophecies, called by Daniel 'the time of the end'. As shown already it is pictured in the storm in this chapter.

With the 'if' of the previous paragraph in mind – and this prophecy open before us – would it be possible to suggest any nations on the political scene at present which could possibly fill the roles given to the four empires in this prophecy? Consider the following possibilities:

1. 'The First [Beast] was like a Lion, and had Eagle's Wings'

One suggestion, made by Geoffrey R. King over forty years ago, may be worthy of consideration. He suggested that the first beast could well be a representation of the association of Great Britain and the United States of America. At least, the lion has been the symbol for British power for nearly two centuries while the eagle has been the symbol of American presence for over a century. King suggested it may be 'the British lion flying on the wings of the American eagle'.[36] An end-time coalition between Great Britain – the British Lion – and the USA – the American Eagle – is not an unreasonable speculation, and this combination of English-speaking nations could carry weight in those troubled times. Such a coalition, suggested by Sir Winston Churchill in the dark days of 1941, would, perhaps, bring on to the political scene a new empire that would carry considerable authority. In fact, it could possibly do on the political scene what NATO (North Atlantic Treaty Organisation) has done on the military front since 1945. NATO was a new entity that demanded respect in the Cold War years.

When this suggestion is made the usual immediate response opens with a 'but'. But, it will be pointed out very plainly, both Britain and the USA have been on the political scene for many years ahead of this period under consideration. That is certainly true! Over those years both nations have lost their early vigour and, in one sense, are already standing in the wings of the world stage, as each has passed its peak of world authority. Maybe this suggested coalition would be the link that brings a new empire on to the earthly political scene: a new composite world power carrying world authority that emerges from the storm conditions.

The question is often asked, 'Does America come into Bible prophecy?' Taking the traditional interpretation of the four beasts, which focuses attention on the Roman Empire and Europe and the emergence on the world stage of an empire labelled as 'the Revived Roman Empire', the answer is generally in the negative. This leaves the problem of why such a dominant world power, as the USA is at this time, finds no place in Biblical prophecy. Some prophetic students in recent years have speculated that some catastrophe must occur that leaves the mighty USA powerless and a mere spectator in the end-time. It has been suggested that such a catastrophe might be either: (a) a moral implosion as a result of the present culture of drugs and depravity; or (b) an overwhelming military blow, which could occur either in a nuclear attack or an electromagnetic pulse (EMP) attack.[37] Even should some such

[36] King, *Daniel*, p. 119.

[37] Rhodes, *The End Times in Chronological Order*, p. 36.

catastrophe hit the USA perhaps the suggestion made above could then come into the picture and the old British lion and the American eagle find it vitally necessary for survival to join in this coalition. This new empire could then become one of the ten horns (Dan. 7:7–8; Rev. 13:1), and one of the ten toes (Dan. 2:42) from which, it will be recalled, the end-time ruler emerges. Any such discussion is, and must remain, purely speculative, but if this suggestion is accepted it becomes clear that the USA does have a key place in the end-time but in a new role.

The change in this beast needs interpretation. It could well indicate that a shattering blow, maybe a military setback or a political misstep early in the development of this western coalition, brings about this change. Something along the lines of the Vietnam catastrophe for the USA, the Afghanistan debacle for the USSR, or the Suez catastrophe for the UK could bring this about. It is also not outside the range of possibility that one of the disasters mentioned above for the USA could hit this new coalition and result in this change. As a consequence this empire would begin to show, instead of the brutality of military force of previous years, a more humanitarian face in world affairs. This is suggested as a possible explanation of the statements that follow: (a) '[Stood] upon the feet as a man' may mean that this new coalition took a more humanitarian stance than either the 'lion' or the 'eagle' – both implacable predators – would have taken in their past; (b) 'A man's heart … given to it' – a uniting of their wills – notice the singular number – 'heart'. The set intention to devour the prey is replaced with an impulse to move to the aid of the distressed nation. Perhaps this humanising process becomes the weakness factor, since it is replaced on the world scene by the brutal bear.

There are other possibilities of interpretation, and if our time frame is correct this is prophecy and not history. The believers who see it on the world stage will know, from this Scripture, what is taking place and thank God for the preservation of this vision to Daniel.

2. 'Another Beast, A Second, like to a Bear'

The Rapture of the Church has opened the 'day of the Lord' (1 Thess. 5:1–3) and another nation will be readily identified as aspiring to world dominance. This nation is symbolised by the bear. Identification of this nation offers little problem today – unbelievers do it readily. A present-day website states, 'The Russian

Bear is a national personification for Russia, used in cartoons and articles and dramatic plays at least since the seventeenth century, and relating alike to Tsarist Russia, the Soviet Union and the Russian Federation.'[38] This encyclopaedia continues, 'After the collapse of the Soviet Union, there was some support in the Russian Parliament for having the bear as the new Russian coat of arms – with the proposers pointing out that "Russia is always identified in the world with the bear"'.

In this twenty-first century, when the recent history of Russia is examined, three matters of interest come to light that help in the identification. These are:

(a) Union – in the early twentieth century very different states were forcibly united to form the USSR (Union of Soviet Socialist Republics) under the banner of communism. Would the expression 'made for itself one dominion' have any relevance? (See comments on v. 5). There is no question in the minds of politicians of the nations today that the present leadership in Russia could be even more forceful than its predecessors in its compulsion to control neighbouring nations.

(b) Satiation – communism demanded expansionism and many nations were engulfed by the USSR immediately after World War II.

(c) Voracity – Russia is back on the world stage after its virtual disappearance from it. Perhaps it is now a state more economically voracious than ever it was communistically or militarily. Could the cry 'Arise, devour much flesh' still be an ironic challenge by the angelic supervisors of the nations to the bear to display its true nature and show itself ripe for the coming judgement, as it steps out in a new role on the world stage?

3. 'And Lo Another, like a Leopard'

In the interpretation of these beasts as nations prominent in 'the time of the end' there emerges a third great beast that catches Daniel's eye. This beast has the appearance of a leopard – but differs from the natural leopard in that it has four wings and four heads. First, there is the lion with eagle's wings, which is clearly western in origin, and may represent Anglo-American power. This is followed by the bear, which is clearly a northern power (probably Russia); there appears a third world power, which is obviously from the east. The link with the east comes from the identification of the leopard.

[38] Wikipedia, accessed 20/09/2011.

The leopard and tiger (incidentally, not mentioned in the Bible) come under the same generic name in Hebrew and the comment by Wilson is interesting: 'a panther, leopard, so called from its spots. This animal is remarkable for swiftness and for watching its prey; [it] cannot be tamed. Not improbably the tiger was also comprised under this name, as the Hebrews had no specific word for that animal.'[39] Is it not relevant to consider that the leopard (tiger) is an eastern animal and has a long association with China? The national symbol for Singapore, where the population is almost eighty per cent Chinese, is the tiger. So a third world power comes onto the world stage, from the east. The speed of the leopard is inherent and self-explanatory; this world power moves quickly across the world stage. As pointed out previously, the wings are not the wings of the eagle but the wings of the fowl, and may contribute little to speed but more to shelter. The word 'four', in Hebrew thinking, always suggests universality; thus the four heads indicate universal dominion. Perhaps, if China eventually fulfils this prophecy in the end-time, its control over its ethnic peoples, scattered through many nations, will give the nation a global significance. Also, the peripheral location of this world power, on the borders of the previous powers, has already offered sanctuary to neighbouring peoples seeking protection from tyrannous regimes and may offer safety and security to many a persecuted refugee from the empire of the fourth beast.

4. 'And Behold a Fourth Beast'

The first three beasts are clearly on the scene together and seem to form a group from which Daniel turns as his eye is caught by a fourth beast. The repetition of the verb 'I was looking' (imperfect) and the note of special interest in the repeated 'behold' draw attention to this beast, as if it is expected to be different from those who preceded it onto the stage. It most certainly is very different – both in appearance and in actions. The very arrival of this beast seems to make the others shrink back from its eye as it surveys those 'before it' – a preposition that contextually indicates location – they were standing before the fourth beast. It is to be noted that: (a) there is no suggestion of one kingdom replacing the one before it, as the metals in the image replaced each other. All the four beasts are on the world-stage together; (b) there is no suggestion that the fourth

[39] *OTWS*, p. 248.

beast destroys the first three beasts: the devouring and destroying (v. 7) is of other enemy nations; the other three are still there after the fourth has been destroyed (v. 12).

The special features that make this fourth beast stand out are noted by Daniel:

(a) 'Dreadful and terrible' – the words are virtually synonyms; 'dreadful' means 'fear-inducing'; 'terrible' means 'terror-inspiring'. The sheer size of this beast plus its forbidding appearance so impress that no comparison is available from the beasts known on earth, so no name can be given to it. This is a factor in the terror the beast induces! A name given means the animal has been observed before. Nameless, it inspires fear. A fear-inspiring beast!

(b) 'Strong exceedingly' – the size makes any other predator hesitate. Men fear it; other beasts are frightened to come near to it. It is a frightening beast!

(c) 'It had great iron teeth': it devoured and brake in pieces and stamped the residue with its feet. This action is not against the other beasts already in the picture but shows its appetite for devastation and destruction of all others opposed to it. Teeth and feet involved show its ferocity. The actions of this beast mark it as ferocious! There is no suggestion that it attacked the other beasts in the vision.

(d) 'Diverse from all the beasts that were before it'. This is not just a matter of degree. The word 'diverse', used five times in this chapter (vv. 3, 7, 19, 23, 24), comes from an Aramaic verb that means 'to be changed'.[40] This does not suggest that this fourth beast is more ferocious, or more voracious than the others. It is not the degree of destructiveness but the very nature of the beast that makes it different from the others. It is not just a bestial nature. This beast supersedes the natural; it is something more dreadful than a normal beast. When Divine interpretation is given (v. 19) the reason for such a difference will be seen. The three present participles show the continuing activity of this beast – devouring, breaking, stamping – as if to utterly destroy all that opposes it. This is the symbolic representation of constant military campaigns to conquer more territory and destroy every enemy.

(e) 'It had ten horns'. This beast when it first appears has ten horns. 'Horns', when used metaphorically in Scripture, always signify 'kings' and this chapter interprets them in the usual way –

[40] *OTWS*, p. 129.

'And the ten horns out of this kingdom are ten kings that shall arise' (v. 24). So ten kings will be seen to represent powers, nations or empires that are united under one political leader. This is one mark of distinction from previous empires and, on this point alone, the attempt to link this beast with the Roman Empire historically must be abandoned. All authorities, with surprising unanimity, agree that the old Roman Empire never had a time when it comprised ten discrete kingdoms, or when ten kings united under the Caesar. This is clearly a unique feature of the final empire ruling on earth when Christ takes the Kingdom.

This end-time fourth empire of Daniel's vision has much in common with the end-time empire of the book of Revelation (Rev. 13:1–8). Both come from the sea and both have ten horns. With the given time frame at the end of the age as indicated these two passages must present the same fourth and final empire on earth before the Son of Man comes. John adds two additional facts that highlight the difference already seen between this and previous empires:

(a) The other empires already present in Daniel's vision are reflected in this fourth and final empire. John's description reads: 'And the beast which I saw was like unto a leopard, and his feet were as the feet of a bear, and his mouth as the mouth of a lion' (Rev. 13:2). This unnamed beast representing the fourth world power to dominate this end-time scene will not destroy the empires that have preceded it on to the world stage, but it will incorporate some of their distinctive features – suggesting that, while they still exist, they are under the domination of the fourth beast. The distinctive colouring and the muscular build of this beast remind John of the litheness and speed of the leopard. The feet, disproportionately large, remind him of the feet of the bear and reflect the tenacity that refuses to let go the prey. The mouth of the lion reminds him of the ferocity of the carnivore.[41] There is no doubt that celerity in movement, tenacity of purpose and ferocity in action will be seen in this empire.

(b) The second additional factor that John sees may be the reason why this kingdom is so 'diverse' from the others. John adds the fact that the emergence of the beast is supervised by the dragon himself – almost as if this empire is favoured by Satan himself. Note the reading, 'he stood upon the sand of the sea' (Rev. 13:1, *RV*), where

[41] Allen, *What the Bible Teaches, Revelation*, p. 327.

the antecedent of the 'he' is the 'dragon', overseeing the emergence of this kingdom. This is emphasised by the explicit statement, 'and the dragon gave him his power, and his seat ('throne', *RV*), and great authority' (Rev. 13:2). This empire is the product of direct satanic action and power moving amongst the nations at this time. It should also be said that Scripture, particularly in the book of Revelation, sometimes speaks of an empire as represented by the emperor who rules it. History does exactly the same for the Pharaoh and Egypt and for the Caesar and Rome. Satanic power in a special way is behind this final empire and final emperor on earth.

The distinctive features noted in this final empire on earth before the Son of Man arrives in glory show that it will be an empire very different from all the empires that have preceded it. Perhaps the closest parallel may be seen, not in the United Nations, but in the concept of the European Union. Could the ten most powerful and richest nations from east and west link up to form a new world power charged with keeping peace on earth? This could be driven at first by economic forces already at work in our age; add to this the financial necessity of a single currency for world trade, which would lead inevitably to an economic union of these nations. This, of course, would soon be followed by the emergence of the need for a political union that would bring powerful men to take the stage as world leaders. This new empire would leave individual nations much as they have been but with powers ceded to this new super regime that will promise peace and prosperity – just as power in Europe, under the European Union, has moved from national capitals to leaders in Strasburg and Brussels. This has left the nations of Europe – while still national entities – with no real power. On this European Union pattern this new government would soon require military and security forces answerable only to the new Parliament. This would be supported by a new legal system placing power in the hands of a new executive, from which it would not be difficult to see emerging one specially gifted individual who could well become the superman earth has been awaiting. Could this be the one presented as the Little Horn? The next verse describes such a leader.

Verse 8 The Little Horn

Daniel's gaze is fixed on the horns – 'I was looking' catches the thought of the imperfect tense. Suddenly 'another ... horn' appears among them (literally 'between them'). Called a 'little' (small) horn, as compared to the others at its appearance, it does not remain small for long. Outgrowing the others the Little Horn soon makes room for itself by uprooting three of the original horns so it becomes the eighth horn. It should be observed how the seventh head of the beast becomes the eighth (Rev. 17:9–11).

This king or ruler, interpreting the symbol of the horn in the scriptural way, clearly has three things that mark him as outstanding:

(a) Power – in displacing three contemporaries he has shown inherent power – whether political skill or military might is not explained, but sufficient to assert his authority over fellow rulers.

(b) Personality – whether magnetic, charismatic or satanic is not made clear but it is very real. The word 'behold!' draws our attention to his eyes; 'like the eyes of [a] man' is the description, denoting intelligence beyond what could possibly be expected. Horns do not normally have eyes – but his horn does, and abnormal intelligence it is!

(c) Propaganda – 'a mouth speaking great things' – this could be interpreted as the power of his commanding oratory and the ability to sway men with charismatic speeches. This takes the word 'mouth' literally. Interpreting the word 'mouth' metaphorically, it would be a reference to the voice of a political propaganda machine. This man has the ability to control men by means of his oratory. The 'great things' which he speaks will be considered under verse 25.

These features identify the ruler of the final world empire opposing the return to earth of the Son of Man and the establishment of the Kingdom of God on earth.

This alternative view of the four beasts in this chapter seems to the author to present fewer problems than the generally accepted view linking them to the metals in the image in chapter 2. Agreement with and support from other Scriptures seems conclusive and it is Scripture alone that must decide the case, not present day happenings in the world.

COMMENTARY ON CHAPTER 7:9–28

The Vision (Part 2) Background – The Throne vv. 9–16

vv. 9–12 The Fiery Throne
vv. 13–14 The Future King
vv. 15–16 The Reaction of Daniel

The Interpretation (Part 1)

vv. 17–18 The Four Beasts and the Future Kingdom
vv. 19–22 The Fourth Beast and Final Ruler

The Interpretation (Part 2)

vv. 23–25 Detail of the Fourth Beast and Final Ruler
vv. 26–27 Detail of the Kingdom of God and the King
v. 28 The Reaction of Daniel

Verses 9–12 The Fiery Throne: The Scene in Heaven

Verses 9–10 In these verses, Daniel's gaze is now switched from the sea to the sky; from earth to heaven. As he continues to gaze – 'was looking' better translates the imperfect tense in this sixth repetition of the verb in the chapter – it would seem that the first scene fades as this second scene comes into focus. It suggests that, while on earth beasts are emerging from a storm-tossed sea, matters in heaven are being arranged to deal with the situation. The rise and rule of the final dictator upon earth is paralleled in heaven by the setting up of a court for his judgement.

In responsive reading, the rhythmic balance in the description of the throne is certainly apparent, but is perhaps brought out most clearly in the following translation:

As I looked,
thrones were set in place
    and the Ancient of Days took his seat.
His clothing was as white as snow;
    the hair of his head was white like wool.
His throne was flaming with fire,
    and its wheels were all ablaze.
A river of fire was flowing,
    coming out from before him.
Thousands upon thousands attended him;
    ten thousand times ten thousand stood before him.
The court was seated,
    and the books were opened. (*NIV*)

The Court of Heaven Assembled in Session

'Thrones were cast down' (*AV*) in English lends itself to misunderstanding as it seems to suggest the overthrow of existing thrones. Some commentators take it so and suggest it is the overthrow of the thrones of the beasts on earth. However, while the Hebrew word does mean 'to cast', it never is used in the sense of 'destroying' but in the sense of 'casting down', meaning 'to put or set in place'. What Daniel sees is the setting up of what may be called 'The High Court of the Cosmos', where justice is to be done. Filling the central throne (seat) is One called the 'Ancient of days' – a unique title for Deity – not found elsewhere in Scripture but used on three occasions in this chapter (vv. 9, 13, 22). There can be little doubt that this is the view granted to Daniel of heaven's reaction to the mounting blasphemy of the Little Horn of the previous verse.

There are two scenes in Scripture touching upon this unseen court in heaven. This is the one given to Daniel; the other is the one given to John, the beloved apostle, in the book of Revelation (Rev. 4:1–5:14). Both scenes show Deity acting as Judge. The similarities in the two scenes are so striking and the differences so thought-provoking that it is useful to compare them:

Throne Scene in Daniel 7:9–12	**Throne Scene in Rev 4–5**
(Seen by Daniel in 553 BC)	(Seen by John *c.* AD 97)

1. Dating (Prophetic)

Close of the Tribulation	Commencement of the Tribulation

The context proves this point. The next scene in Daniel is the installation of the Son of Man in His 'dominion, and glory, and a kingdom' (vv. 13–14). The next scene in Revelation is the opening of the seals on the seven-sealed book (Rev. 6). This commences the Tribulation.

2. Judge

Ancient of Days (Eternity)	God on Throne (Rev 7:10) (Sovereignty)

The title Ancient of days and the description of His hair 'like the pure wool' should not be read so as to depict a grey-headed old man marked by advancing age – a common misrepresentation. The literal meaning of 'Ancient of days' points to 'The constant, everlasting One – unchanged by days'; a somewhat similar title to that used of Christ – 'The same yesterday, and today, and for ever' (Heb. 13:8; Heb. 1:11–12). Nations rise, have their day on the world stage, and pass from the stage. In absolute contrast, there is One Who stands outside of time, unchanged by its passing and untouched by its ravages. This is the Wise One equipped to judge. While the eternity of the Throne Sitter is emphasised in Daniel and His sovereignty is implied, in Revelation it is His sovereignty that is stressed and His eternity (worshipped as Creator) that is implied.

3. Executor

One like the Son of Man	The Lamb

The title Son of Man will be discussed under verse fourteen and it will be seen that His authority is to take action so that 'all people, nations, and languages, should serve Him'. In the Revelation scene the executive power is in the hands of the Lamb. With two-fold authority, as Creator and as Redeemer, the Lamb acts to open the seals and, in doing so, deals with and displaces the usurper on earth, and then establishes the Kingdom of God.

4. Associated Authority

Thrones	Four and Twenty Thrones

In this passage thrones are plural and no number is given. Those who filled the thrones are not identified. In Revelation the number is given as twenty-four, answering to the twenty-four courses of the priesthood in Israel (1 Chron. 24:1–18). A weighty case for these individuals being representatives of the raptured and judged believers of the Church age can be set out.[42]

5. Colour

White and Fiery Red	Jasper and Sardine Stone

The white speaks of righteousness, the fiery red of holiness. In the Revelation scene, the jasper and sardine are two precious stones representing the same truths: the jasper is a clear stone like a flawless diamond, while the sardine is a blazing ruby-red colour. The additional colour in the rainbow round the throne in Revelation (significantly described as an emerald (green)) shows

[42] Allen, *What the Bible Teaches, Revelation* p. 167.

that while the Tribulation is about to begin there can still be grace for the individual through the gospel preached. At the end of the Tribulation the time for grace is over and only judgement remains. There is no mention of the rainbow in Daniel. Grace has given way to judgement.

6. Fire

Throne, Wheels, Stream	Seven Lamps of Fire

Daniel is shown a 'throne flaming with fire', with 'wheels all ablaze' sitting at the apex of 'a river of fire' – while John sees 'seven lamps of fire burning before the throne'. Fire ever speaks of the holiness of God and what Daniel and John see is the execution of the demands of holiness from the throne. In Revelation the agent is, of course, the Holy Spirit as the agent of holiness. Here it is seen objectively and pictured in the fire flowing from the throne over the earth. The speed of its movement through the earth is seen in the wheels. Swiftly and as surely as a mighty river sweeps all before it, so the uncleanness of earth is swept away from the presence of the Holy One on that holy throne.

7. Attendants

Thousands upon thousands and ten thousand times ten thousand	Ten thousand times ten thousand and thousands of thousands

Attending the throne in both scenes, charged with the execution of the sentences once they are delivered, are innumerable angels. Thousands upon thousands and ten thousand times ten thousand (Rev. 5:11) – often translated 'myriad myriads' – earth's numbering system is inadequate to calculate the numbers involved. They wait upon the throne and execute its edicts.

8. Books

Books were opened	A Book Sealed with Seven Seals

In Daniel's vision, 'the judgment was set', simply sums up the stage reached and could be translated 'the court was seated' (*NIV*), meaning all was in order for the case to be heard. The 'books were opened' tells us the next stage of the judicial process has arrived – the hearing of the evidence comes first, then the consideration of the evidence, and finally the passing of sentence. A similar statement is emphasised in connection with the great white throne (Rev. 20:12) – the final court before which all sinners will stand who have not been judged before the court at the end of the Tribulation, described as 'the throne of His glory' (Mt. 25:31–46). The books indicate that all the necessary evidence is on record and will be placed before the court of heaven when required. This seems to suggest the special court before the throne of His glory on earth at the end of the Tribulation to deal with a particular situation and particular men. This may well explain why the Beast and the false prophet are consigned directly to the lake of fire; there is no record of their appearance before the great white throne (Rev. 19:20).

Verses 11–12 Removal of Earth's False Ruler: The Beast with the Little Horn

Verse 11 The seventh and the eighth repetition of the verb 'I was looking' occur in this passage. Between the two occurrences is the word 'because', which, grammarians insist, in this context should be translated as 'due to'. The implication is clear. From the time that the Little Horn with the 'mouth speaking great things' (v. 8) uttered such blasphemies Daniel's eyes were fastened upon it. He is clearly engrossed and awaits, we might say with bated breath, the reaction of the throne to such impiety. He had not long to wait. As he watched, the beast was slain. This prophetically takes us to the very end of the Tribulation period described in detail in the Revelation (Rev. 19:20–21). There the Beast, as an individual, seen contextually here as the Little Horn (v. 8), was seized as a person and cast alive into the lake of fire. The military forces of his empire supporting him are destroyed – if John's light is added, they would be destroyed at Armageddon (Rev. 19:21). Here the statement 'I beheld even till the beast was slain' covers the personal judgement of the Little Horn – slain as earth sees it – and the consequent destruction of those who followed him. The fiery stream from the throne engulfs all who have given allegiance to the Little Horn in this fourth and final empire of earth. In the Revelation the imagery is different but the outcome is similar. The holiness of God, seen here in the fiery stream, is seen there in the sharp sword of the King of kings and Lord of lords (Rev. 19:21). Clearly it is the same scene described from different prophetic angles. The fourth empire of the end-times is destroyed with its ruler.

Verse 12 Attention is turned now to the three beasts who outlive the fourth. This verse offers clear confirmation of the alternative interpretation of the four beasts from the sea given in the opening paragraph of this chapter (vv. 1–8). These beasts were seen as four contemporary kingdoms of the end-time appearing in succession and remaining on the scene until the fourth and final empire appears. These empires are not the Gentile empires of chapter 2, each of which had been replaced by its successor down the ages (Babylonian, Medo-Persian, Grecian and Roman). The three empires on which the spotlight of heaven now fastens had lost their dominion – their right to rule – to the fourth beast so terrible it remains without a name. This beast had brought the first three beasts under his control without destroying them. He left them in existence but helpless, without power. 'They had their dominion taken away' is the scriptural description but they still existed under their old names. This is surely the same beast as that described as the beast from the sea (Rev. 13:1–8), and it incorporates features of the first three beasts. This beast has the body of a leopard, interpreted previously as China – an eastern empire (v. 6); the feet of a bear, interpreted as Russia – a northern empire (v. 5); and the mouth of a lion, interpreted as a UK-USA confederacy – a western empire. These features are not interpreted in the text but will be clearly recognisable as the fourth beast steps on to the earthly stage and people realise this is an unbelievable coming together of financial control, military force and political propaganda in a unique empire. Features of the preceding empires are discernible in this fourth empire but it stands out distinct in its own right.

To suggest that earth's final empire would include aspects of the Babylonian, Medo-Persian, Greek and Roman empires, all empires long disappeared from earth, seems to stretch credulity to the limit without any Scripture to support such a thesis. To put a name on this empire and call it the revived Roman Empire may satisfy our sense of continuity but it is not used in Scripture nor does it make the suggestion any more plausible. Clearly the peoples and their cultures of the preceding three empires, while absorbed by the fourth empire, still existed at this point and would exist even after the destruction of the fourth empire. How could this be said of kingdoms that have long disappeared into history? Accepting such a premise, it must be explained how these long-disappeared kingdoms are still in existence as the fourth beast is slain. In fact this text speaks of their lives prolonged 'for a season and time' beyond the destruction of the fourth beast. Wood at least faces this fact and offers an explanation as he writes:

> Whereas the fourth empire and its closing ruler were fully destroyed at the time of the divine judgment, the other three had been given an extension of time. That is, when each of the previous three had been brought to an end by the beginning of its respective successor, it had continued in some sense that was not true for the fourth.[43]

Wood continues: 'Each of the three previous empires would be continued, by this reduplication of self in people and culture, in their respective successors; but the fourth would not be.' I am afraid this will not do: it does not answer to history, nor should we play word games to escape a difficulty brought into the passage by faulty interpretation. It is perfectly plain that the fourth empire (beast) took dominion from the preceding three but, while under his nominal control and contributing manpower to his armies, they still held to their old names.

As suggested earlier in this chapter, they present the world empires subdued by the mightiest empire and emperor the world has ever seen, but as the military power of this fourth empire is smashed at Armageddon the earlier kingdoms still have an existence for 'a season and time'. Remnants of a western empire (UK and USA?), a northern empire (Russian?) and an eastern empire (Chinese?) outlast that destruction, even if their armies have been destroyed at Armageddon. Scripture says, 'their lives were prolonged for a season and time'. Wood (*ibid*) tries to sweep this vital statement under the carpet. While admitting there is a difference in the meaning of the words, he continues: 'Here, however, they seem to be used quite synonymously.' This is not so – as with the Greek words so with the Hebrew – the word 'season' draws attention to the character of the period, as does our English word when we speak of the 'winter season'; the word 'time' refers to the chronology of the period – the counting of days, months or years. So these nations, as such, could continue until a new 'season' comes in with the new 'dominion' (the same word 'dominion' as in vv. 12 and 14) of the Son of Man referred to in verse 14. Perhaps the chronological 'time' referred to is the period from the destruction of the Beast and the armies gathered round him (Rev. 19:20–21) until

[43] Wood, *A Commentary on Daniel*, p. 191.

Gentile rulers (4:22). In the sovereignty of God, dominion was granted to the kingdoms mentioned for a time (vv. 6, 12) but all failed most miserably. Now we learn that dominion is withdrawn from failing men and entrusted to a real Man – a Man Who cannot fail. Thus, this Man is granted 'an everlasting dominion'; a dominion that will never be taken from Him neither will He pass it to another.

(b) Glory speaks of that honour and manifest excellence that must be seen in such an endowment of dominion (rule) that 'all people, nations, and languages' bow to His authority. Nebuchadnezzar may claim such dominion (see the same terms used by him in 3:4, 7, 29) as permitted of God, but only the Son of Man will know the fulness of that glory, when all peoples bow to His rule. Zechariah spoke of Him when he cried 'and he shall bear the glory, and shall sit and rule upon his throne' (Zech. 6:13). His dominion will encompass the world and His glory will fill the earth. The basic meaning of the verb 'to serve' is 'to pay reverence' and it is used negatively in the refusal of the three Hebrew boys to bow before Nebuchadnezzar's idol (3:28). Though sometimes translated 'to serve' (3:12), the basic meaning suits this context. All peoples on earth will give to this One the reverence that is given only to Deity.

(c) Kingdom speaks of the administration over which the King presides. It is clear that the four kingdoms that precede this one were literal earthly kingdoms, characterised by a certain kind of rule. No indication is given that this Kingdom is any different in those respects, but it is most certainly very different in the quality of the rule. This is the monarchical rule of the King acknowledged by the Ancient of days and thus it will be a perfect rule under the perfect Ruler – the One identified as Son of Man.

There is no question that this is the rule of Christ in a literal Kingdom ruling from Jerusalem to ends of the earth. This Scripture speaks of the chronology of His Kingdom as it fits into the prophetic picture. There are many Scriptures that will fill in the detail of that Kingdom, long expected, as expressed when the Son of Man welcomes His subjects into that Kingdom at the end of the Tribulation: 'Come, ye blessed of My Father, inherit the kingdom prepared for you from the foundation of the world' (Mt. 25:34). That a period of one thousand years (Rev. 20:1–6) is placed on the earthly aspect of this Kingdom is not to deny that it is an 'everlasting dominion'. The earthly aspect is but a time corridor that leads into the heavenly aspect (Rev. 22:1–8), which is timeless and therefore eternal.

Verses 15–16 The Reaction of Daniel

These two verses are the link between revelation and interpretation. Clearly overwhelmed at the import of what has been shown to him, Daniel admits to being inwardly distressed and mentally alarmed. A spirit 'grieved' means a spirit 'in pain', as if constricted within its 'sheath'. [45] 'Sheath', the word translated 'body', is used metaphorically here; as sheath and sword are related so body and spirit are similarly related. The word for 'troubled' is very strong and, while used sparingly in Scripture, is used eight times in this book (4:5, 19(twice); 5:6, 9, 10; 7:15, 28). It is defined at length:[46] 'to be in great perturbation of mind, as by the intelligence of some unexpected calamity; to be suddenly seized with fear, to be amazed and confounded'. As the implications of the visions granted to him begin to dawn on his heart he is thrown into a terrible maelstrom of conflicting thoughts.

To relieve the turmoil within his mind Daniel seeks clarification on what he had seen and turns to 'one of them that stood by'. These are not casual bystanders, as the English language may seem to suggest, but, according to Zechariah (Zech. 3:7), they are those selected to have the special privilege of standing close to the throne before Jehovah. It would seem that these are not always angels. That some may be men is a logical deduction from the promise to Joshua the high priest in Israel, 'And I will give thee places to walk among these that stand by' (Zech. 3:7), and the privilege granted to John to converse with the elder (Rev. 5:5; 7:13). The word for 'truth' (or 'true meaning' *NIV*) could be translated 'certainty' (*Newberry*). From his previous experience of interpretation of dreams Daniel could possibly have interpreted the symbols, but in such tremendous events he clearly felt that he dare not rest on human intelligence alone. He desired absolute certainty from the One Who gave the visions. Since symbols were used in the vision Daniel knew that behind the symbols were realities that must be taken literally; he wanted to be assured of those realities. The one who stood by the throne was quite willing to respond to the request of Daniel.

[45] *OTWS*, p. 202.
[46] *OTWS*, p. 454.

Verses 17–18 The Four Beasts and the Future Kingdom Interpretive Summaries

Verse 17 Interpretative Summary of Verses 2–8

Four matters need to be observed in this verse:

(a) The unusual word order in the text places the emphasis upon the number of the beasts: 'these great beasts, which are four, are four kings, which shall arise out of the earth'. They are seen as a group, with no mention of succession – one displacing the other.

(b) The interpreter translates the beasts as kings who clearly are outstandingly mighty men and dominate the empires they represent. Those empires do come into the picture, as the interpretation has already shown, and that emperor and empire are interchangeable is clear from verse 23 – where the fourth beast is identified as a kingdom. If these are four end-time kingdoms, as suggested in this commentary, then we can look for a 'king' figure in each empire. It will be remarkable if any one of these men will be addressed in their time as 'king'. More likely each will have a title such as President, Prime Minister, Secretary-General or Chairman – a man in each case who outranks all contemporaries in his nation. The title 'emperor' is comprehensive enough to cover all these rulers.

(c) The tense of the verb is imperfect and normally translated into English as a future – 'shall arise'. This rules out, in one statement, the interpretation of this vision as paralleling the four empires symbolised in the four metals of chapter 2. Nebuchadnezzar, by the time of this vision, had been dead nine years and the mighty Babylonian Empire was in terminal decline. To meet this difficulty in that interpretation Wood writes: 'The history of the four empires, however, is taken as a unit, which is incomplete until the fourth empire is destroyed, and the form of the verb can only be imperfect, even though one aspect of the history has begun well before.'[47] This rather savours of special pleading on a recondite point of grammar. These empires will be on the scene together at the end-time, as already explained.

(d) That the four beasts 'came up from the sea' (v. 3) but here (v. 17) are said to 'arise out of the earth' is readily explained. In the symbolic picture the sea pictures the conditions in the nations of the time of their arrival. In the interpreted picture their character is

[47] Wood, *A Commentary on Revelation*, p. 196.

in view – they are from the earth, in other words, earthly in their origin and thus standing in contrast with the fifth and final Kingdom, which is from heaven.

Verse 18 Interpretative Summary of Verses 9–14

Now, in contrast to earthly kingdoms, there is introduced a new company, called 'saints' or 'holy ones' (there is no definite article in the Aramaic language) who 'receive the kingdom' (*RV*). Mentioned six times in this chapter (vv. 18, 21, 22 (twice), 25, 27) these are a different company from the 'watchers' and 'holy ones' (4:17), who have been shown to be angelic beings with responsibility for nations and their rulers. This new company consists of those who are associated with Christ in the Kingdom; in fact, those who enter that Kingdom with Christ. The word 'saints' therefore has the NT meaning of the saved ones of earth, set aside for God by the Spirit of God and, as such, fit to enter the Kingdom. During the Tribulation, believers in Christ are called by this name thirteen times in the book of Revelation. In that book the Beast is said to 'make war with the saints, and to overcome them' (Rev. 13:7), which is simply the language of verse 21 of this chapter: 'I beheld, and the same horn made war with the saints, and prevailed against them.' So there is an identification link between the Little Horn of this chapter and the Beast out of the sea. At the close of the Tribulation, from the throne of His glory the Son of Man addresses the sheep: 'Come, ye blessed of my Father, inherit the kingdom prepared for you from the foundation of the world' (Mt. 25:34). These would be of the same company as those seen here who, in association with the Son of Man, take the Kingdom. Lest it be thought that the saints take the Kingdom as Darius took Babylon (Dan. 5:31), by strategy and armed conflict, the clearer translation is 'shall receive the kingdom' (*RV*). They receive it in association with Christ and go in to experience its delights so different from those offered by earthly kingdoms. And the most glorious of all truths concerning this Kingdom is that it never ends – 'for ever, even for ever and ever'. This is a superlative form of expression that emphasises the endurance of this Kingdom: no invader will ever overthrow it. It stands in contrast to all previous kingdoms: no dark clouds of impending destruction will ever darken the horizon. This is clearly showing that, though the millennial reign of Christ on earth is limited to one thousand years (Rev. 20:1–6) by Divine purpose, this millennial age runs into the eternal state. The Millennium is but the prelude to eternal bliss.

Verses 19–22 The Fourth Beast and the Final Ruler

Verse 19 Recognising the unique character of the fourth beast, different from the others in so many features, Daniel is constrained to ask about the 'truth', or, to use his language, the 'certainty' of it. This fourth beast, on the pattern of interpretation of the earlier beasts, must symbolise a unique and most remarkable kingdom or king (v. 17) – this latter thought makes king and kingdom interchangeable in these verses. Five features in particular contribute to the uniqueness of this final empire of earth. See comments at verse 7, where these features are described in somewhat less detail, but Scripture has always a reason for repetition.

(a) 'Exceeding dreadful'. Awe-inspiring ('most terrifying', *NIV*) is the only way to describe this animal; the hearts of men would begin to sink as they gazed upon this animal without a name. Named, it would not have been so terrifying; men had no past experience to draw upon when this nameless beast appeared. Appearance – terrifying!

(b) 'Whose teeth were of iron' – which term, as in v. 7, draws attention to the fact that what the beast used to devour flesh will not wear out. Since this beast has the 'mouth of a lion' (Rev. 13:2) it is marked by an insatiable appetite from its emergence until its destruction. The tools it uses in this symbolic picture are not normal teeth but iron teeth. These of course would never wear out, as ordinary teeth would tend to do. There may be here a suggestion that the armies of the Beast remain undefeated until the Son of Man deals with them at His coming. Any link with the iron of the fourth empire of Nebuchadnezzar's image is difficult to support, but it might just suggest that the way this final empire will treat its subjugated peoples is reminiscent of the way the Roman Empire treated the nations it conquered – as slaves. Appetite – insatiable!

(c) 'His nails [were] of brass', or it can be translated 'bronze claws' (*NET*). This feature is not mentioned in v. 7, but the feet of a bear (Rev. 13:2) do have remarkably powerful claws. The bronze in the claws may suggest something of the tactics the army of Alexander the Great used in bringing nations under his control. Animosity – implacable!

(d) 'Which devoured, brake in pieces, and stamped the residue with his feet'. As in verse 7 the three participles – devouring, breaking, stamping – indicate continuous action; this was the very character of the beast. There is no suggestion in the passage that it was the first three beasts that were so attacked. As suggested in verse 12, it would seem these empires, in giving acceptance to this beast on its arrival, had their dominion taken away but still existed as empires while other nations were ruthlessly brought into subjection. Activity – unceasing!

(e) 'The ten horns that were in his head'. It is clear that these ten horns symbolically represent ten world powers or kings who have acknowledged the supremacy of this empire and emperor. The fact that this is not history but prophecy is to be noted. When John sees the beast in the book of Revelation (Rev. 17:12) he is told: 'And the ten horns which thou sawest are ten kings, which have received no kingdom as yet; but receive power as kings one hour with the beast.' These two beasts, Daniel's unnamed beast and John's beast from the sea (Rev. 13:1), must be the same empire viewed from different perspectives since there can only be one such empire. Thus when this fourth empire arrives it will have the support of ten kings from all over the earth. As suggested earlier (see under vv. 1–7) this must be a union of ten major world powers to make a new super empire, which will be the means of presenting the final world ruler to the place of supreme authority over earth. This world union would be on the pattern of the European Union rather than on the pattern of the United Nations; authority and power would eventually be within the grasp of one supreme emperor, who would eventually be the world ruler. Authority – unchallengeable!

These five features combine to make this final empire different in appearance, appetite, animosity, activity, and authority. No empire could ever approach it in size, scope or strength; it dominates the world! From this world empire emerges the world emperor who will challenge the Son of Man for His Kingdom.

It should be pointed out at this point that this empire of necessity takes features of the Roman Empire, which in its day was world-dominant in size and scope and strength. This empire stands in this heritage yet Scripture does not speak of it as the 'revived' or even 'restored' Roman Empire. It is an empire that will be far greater than the Roman Empire ever was – in the territory controlled, in the population embraced, and in the power centred in it. As the Roman Empire stood behind the cross as earth rejected Christ, this empire, with features of Rome, yet very much greater, stands behind the armies of earth, gathering to Armageddon (Rev. 16:13–16) to resist the Christ as He claims the crown.

Verses 20–22 The Final World Emperor

The features that set apart the leader of this world empire have been mentioned earlier (v. 8) but are here emphatically re-stated. Men will readily recognise this man who claims world dominion. His distinguishing features are impossible to miss:

(a) His Power. Appearing later than his fellows (v. 8), there was an arrogance about this horn noted by Daniel: 'whose look was more stout than his fellows' (v. 20). Daniel records that arrogance in two statements: 'before whom there were three of the first horns plucked up by the roots' (v. 8) and 'before whom three fell' (v. 20). Both records show the ruthless removal of three of his contemporaries. He thus becomes the eighth horn. In John's vision, this eighth horn is identified as the eighth head of the 'beast out of the sea' in John's vision (Rev. 13:11; 17:9–11). The mention of the 'eighth' suggests resurrection – not of an empire but an emperor!

(b) His Perspicuity. This is made clear in the statement – '[had] eyes like the eyes of man' (v. 8), while here (v. 20) it is put simply '[he] had eyes'. No-one expects eyes in a horn, so their unexpected appearance in this horn indicates unexpected abilities and, as the eyes of man reflect insight and intelligence, there is no question that perception, to a most remarkable degree, will lift this man above his fellows. While still only a man, he will be politically shrewd, militarily skilful and socially gifted in a most remarkable way – he can read and respond to every situation.

(c) His Propaganda. 'A mouth speaking great things' is stressed each time this man is described and becomes an identifying feature of him:

v. 8 'A mouth speaking great things'
v. 20 'A mouth that spake very great things'
v. 25 'And he shall speak great words against the Most High'

Note also the link with the end-time ruler described in the NT: 'And there was given unto him a mouth speaking great things' (Rev. 13:5).

Powerful oratory has been a feature of world leaders from time immemorial: Alexander the Great, Hitler, Mussolini, and a multitude of other men, in their overweening pride, have boasted of their power and what they planned to do. With skilful oratory these men could sway the crowds. Now, with all the present-day technology behind him and the media under his control, the power of this man will be virtually unlimited. By use of his mouth he will be able to bring the world to his feet – a charismatic orator!

(d) His Purpose. 'Made war with the saints, and prevailed against them'. These are the saints mentioned (v. 18); saved through the preaching of the gospel worldwide (Rev. 14:6–7), they bear testimony to Christ. In this Tribulation period they are the people hated by this dictator and he plans their total annihilation. Encompassed by this hatred are not only those who have believed the gospel of the Kingdom – the message of the coming King – but also the remnant of Israel who will not accept his claim to Deity. This is a further link with the 'beast out of the sea' (Rev. 13:7) and shows that Daniel and John saw the same personage in their respective visions.

(e) His Period. The word 'until' (v. 22) tells the story. This man is allowed to continue just as long as God permits and no longer. 'Until the Ancient of days came' gives the boundary of time for this man – that is, until God steps into the picture and takes action, so that 'judgment was given to the saints of the Most High'. This does not mean, as some commentators seem to think, that the judgement of this man was placed in the hands of saints (1 Cor. 6:2 is used to support the principle), but rather that the Ancient of days gave judgement in favour of the saints of the Most High. Shown to be unfit to rule, this dictator would be replaced by the Son of Man and the saints associated with Him would possess the Kingdom. The sense of the word 'possess' is that they would enter the Kingdom and enjoy it to the full.

Verses 23–25 Detail of the Fourth Beast and Final Ruler

The final paragraph of this chapter describes, with some repetition and some significant additions, the fourth kingdom and its final emperor – the Little Horn. There is no suggestion that this empire falls and is revived – it has been on the scene since its arrival. Subsequent revelation will reveal that the final ruler of this kingdom had such an experience (see Rev. 13:3) but that must be interpreted, in the context, as the person of the beast. It must also be noticed that first the fourth beast fills the picture (v. 19–24), then the focus shifts to the ten horns and finally the Little Horn (v. 25 ff.) – an individual. It is in the reign of this man that time runs out and the judgement of the Ancient of days takes effect. As the result, the Kingdom passes to the saints of the Most High.

Verse 23 The Fourth Kingdom

Stage 1. This fourth kingdom is the background power in which the mightiest of earth rulers emerges. This unique kingdom embraces the previous three kingdoms. They are assimilated but not destroyed, while this fourth kingdom achieves a dominion that becomes worldwide. For the first time it is said of it: '[it] shall devour the whole earth', which suggests the assimilation of nations and kingdoms, so that politically, financially, and militarily there is but one world power. That this empire is far greater than the Roman Empire is clear from this statement alone. If it embraces the previous kingdoms then its eastern border must be beyond the Indus River, while at its very greatest extent the Roman Empire eastern boundary never reached beyond the River Euphrates. Any dissident nations or peoples are ruthlessly suppressed; graphic terms are used to express this domination – 'tread ... down' and 'break ... in pieces'.

Verse 24 The Little Horn

Stage 2. Within this kingdom are ten kings. This is the interpretation of the ten horns on the beast and, noting the future tense in the verb, it could be that these kings will arise one after another after the Rapture of the Church and before the peace covenant with Israel is confirmed. They will be apparent in the latter days as they willingly place themselves under this man to form an empire.[48] Then 'another' horn arises whose character and career has already been considered (vv. 20–22). Attention has been drawn to his power, perspicuity, propaganda, purpose and the limit set to his period of rule.

Verse 25

Stage 3. Four matters are mentioned as the arrogance of this man is exposed:

(a) The words he speaks. His speeches catch our ear and are described: 'great words against the Most High' and these are defined in the case of the Beast from the sea: 'and he opened his mouth in blasphemy against God, to blaspheme His name, and His tabernacle, and them that dwell in heaven' (Rev. 13:6). No clearer identification of the Little Horn of Daniel with the Beast from the sea of Revelation could be given.

[48] See Rev. 17:12–14 for further elucidation.

(b) The war he wages. The activity of this man is described: 'and shall wear out the saints of the Most High'. The verb 'wear out' carries the thought – 'to persecute with the purpose of entire annihilation'.[49] In explaining the use of the word a commentator[50] points out that it describes constant rough usage that wears out garments, wineskins and sandals. The verb is used both negatively – something that does not wear out (Deut. 8:4) – and positively (Josh. 9:4–5) – something that does wear out. To 'wear out the saints' means to harass them continually, so that legislation discriminates against their business, their family, and their faith; injustice denies them education and freedom to proclaim the gospel. This constant opposition ends in the seizure of goods and persons, with martyrdom the ultimate sanction.[51] The believers of this age will find life virtually impossible under this tyranny, and many will be put to death. This statement should be compared with the declared purpose of the Beast out of the sea, revealed to John: 'it was given unto him to make war with the saints, and to overcome them' (Rev. 13:7). For two persons so similar in so many ways to operate in the same period would be most unlikely. These two pictures identify the same person as at war with believers worldwide.

(c) The work he undertakes. His inward thoughts are disclosed as he would 'think to change the times and the law' (*RV*). The use of the word 'think' would suggest that this evil man, with the most evil intention, was still not able to do what he wanted to do. The *NIV* translates 'think' as 'try', which interpretative translation would indicate a limit on the power allowed this man – he was certainly not omnipotent – even if he did claim Deity (2 Thess. 2:4). In this context what he wanted to change is understood by some commentators to be the timing of Jewish festivals under the ceremonial Law (notice the singular number in 'law'). That this will be within his powers is clear from chapter 9, where it is observed that 'he shall cause the sacrifice and the oblation to cease' (9:27) – an action that links the later vision of the Coming Prince (9:26–27) with this Little Horn in chapter 7. It would seem, however, that this man tries and fails to do something more fundamental than interrupt the practice of the ceremonial laws of Judaism. It would suggest, in this context, that he attempts to change a law perhaps

[49] *OTWS*, p. 476.
[50] Wood, *A Commentary on Daniel*, p. 201.
[51] See Rev. 6:9 11; 15:2–4.

incorporated in creation. For example, a natural law of the universe is the seven-day week, established for the good of mankind (Gen. 2:3). Is it not remarkable that the atheistic leaders of the French Revolution tried to do exactly this when they demanded a ten-day workweek in keeping with their metric scheme? This did not succeed in the eighteenth century; neither will this man be successful in changing any of God's laws in a future day. In the area of moral law, even before the Ten Commandments, marriage was a Divine institution going back to creation and, while atheism has made many attempts to displace or replace this institution, it still survives. This arrogant claimant to Deity attempts to do what God alone can do, and he fails miserably.

(d) The writ he is permitted. In Divine purpose this man is allowed certain latitude for a time described as 'they shall be given into his hand until a time and times and the dividing of time'. The only antecedent for the 'they' that makes grammatical and contextual sense is the people defined as the 'saints of the Most High' of the same verse. Thus, in Divine purpose and by Divine permission, this man is allowed to persecute the people of God. God is working out His plan for His own, and that includes this testing and painful time, as a time of disciplinary preparation for His saints. That which makes it endurable for them is that God has placed a strict limit on the period – it is for a time (singular) and times (plural) and the dividing of a time (half-a-time). Since the word 'time' in Aramaic indicates a unit of time and therefore can refer to a day, a week, a month or a year, the most reasonable of these units in the context is a year, and thus the time period is three-and-a-half years. This understanding of the unit of time as a year agrees with the other occasion the Aramaic word is used in this book: in chapter 4 it is used to measure the period of Nebuchadnezzar's discipline – given as seven 'times' (4:16, 23, 25). It has already been shown (see comments *in loc.*) that this period must be seven years. The equivalent phrase in Hebrew is 'a time, times, and a half' (12:7), which in the context of that chapter demands that it be interpreted strictly as three-and-a-half years. Since the prophetic year is 360 days, which is twelve months of thirty days, (see comments at 9:24) this means the three-and-a-half year period equals 1,260 days. This is perfectly in keeping with the two periods mentioned further along that passage in chapter 12 – 1,290 days (v. 11) and 1,335 days (v. 12), as these are clearly meant to be extensions of the given period of 1260 days to complete the Divine purpose (see comments *in loc.*).

In the book of Revelation the period of three-and-a-half years is referred to on five occasions and in three different ways as follows:

(a) Forty and two months – 11:2; 13:5;
(b) A thousand two hundred and sixty days – 11:3; 12:6;
(c) A time and times and half a time – 12:14.

Since the seventieth week (seven years) of Daniel's prophecy (9:25–27) is divided into two parts by the reference to 'the midst of the week' this means that either half of the week could be referred to as a three-and-a-half year period. This means that where one of the above phrases occurs in the Revelation it must be determined from the context whether it refers to the first half of the week or to the second half. When this contextual study is carried out[52] it is suggested that only one of the five references – that related to the period of testimony of the two witnesses (Rev. 11:3) – refers to the first half of the seventieth week; the other four all make reference to the last half of the seventieth week. It is suggested that this is the same period referred to in this verse – the last half of the seventieth week of Daniel (9:24–27) and the period of rule of the Coming Prince (9:26), the Little Horn (7:8), the Man of Sin (2 Thess. 2:3–4), and the Beast from the sea (Rev. 13:1–8). This is, indeed, the same person reigning for the same period. The different names indicate the different angles from which he is viewed in prophetic Scripture.

Verses 26–27 Detail of the Kingdom of God and the King

The heavenly court in session from v. 10 with the Ancient of days on the judicial throne now acts:

Verse 26 To End the Rule of the Little Horn

The judgement executed previously in verse 11 has dealt summarily with the Beast. It was suggested that the summary statement included both the person and the empire – one sent directly to the lake of fire and his empire, as represented in its military forces, wiped out at Armageddon. The Little Horn is the subject of vv. 24–25 and, as an individual who has been used by Satan as a puppet (Rev. 13:1–8) is judged as an individual responsible to God for his own actions, has been sent directly to the lake of fire (Rev. 19:20);

[52] Allen, *What the Bible Teaches, Revelation*, p. 282.

his army has been destroyed at Armageddon (Rev. 19:21); here dominion is taken from the empire he ruled and given to others. Neither the kingdom he controlled, nor the king who ruled it as Satan's regent, will ever trouble men again. The expression at the close of this verse, 'unto the end', carries the idea of 'forever' (*NET*) and would apply both to the dominion and to the dictator who ruled. Such an empire and emperor will never be allowed again to dominate earth as this one has done.

Verse 27 To Establish the Rule of the Saints

Satan's puppet prince having now been judged, the way is open for the establishment of the rule of the saints. In place of the previous kingdom another Kingdom comes into view. The majesty, magnificence, and the might of this new Kingdom far outshine its forerunner. The new Kingdom will have a Sovereign, in prophetic Scripture called 'Son of Man' (7:13; Mt. 24:30), 'His Anointed' (Ps. 2:2), 'The Messiah' (9:25), 'The LORD my God' (Zech. 14:5), 'The Word of God' (Rev. 19:13), and 'King of kings and Lord of lords' (Rev. 19:16). His dominion will be absolute dominion over all of earth which, conferred by the Ancient of days (vv. 13–14), means it is from God and that the submission is universal. The scale of this Kingdom outranks every preceding kingdom; there is a special greatness about the sovereign, the state, and the saints who share with the Sovereign the rule of this everlasting kingdom. The antecedent of 'whose' is the 'saints of the Most High'; while they rule with God's Sovereign they also submit, as do all in the Kingdom, to 'serve and obey him'. He is the supreme One.

There can be little doubt that the first glimpse that Daniel had of this Kingdom of Christ, so frequently and eloquently set forth by earlier prophets, was in the vision of the image given to Nebuchadnezzar and pictured as the 'stone ... cut out of the mountain without hands' (2:44–45). This stone, after breaking and consuming the previous kingdoms, then 'became a great mountain, and filled the whole earth' (2:34–35). It has already been noted (see comments *in loc.*) that the stone actually smote the image 'upon his feet that were of iron and clay, and brake them to pieces' (2:34). It is perfectly clear that in that action is seen the end of Gentile rule, and while only the feet are mentioned, the ten toes in the image must be seen to be a first glimpse of the ten rulers Daniel now sees as ten horns on the beast. Much more detail is given here, but the same crisis in earth history brings the same Christ into the picture in chapter 2 as 'the Stone' and in this chapter 7 as the 'Son of Man'. Associated with Him is a literal worldwide Kingdom; it is this Kingdom of which Zechariah speaks: 'And his dominion shall be from sea even to sea, and from the River even to the ends of the earth' (Zech. 9:10).

Verse 28 The Reaction of Daniel

Two main statements divide this verse. The first statement, 'Hitherto is the end of the matter', is spoken by the interpreter, one of those close to the throne, whom Daniel had approached for the interpretation of the visions (v. 16). This attendant upon the throne has been speaking from verse 23, and on reaching the unfolding of the Kingdom closes his story at this point. The final end for earth, as seen in this vision, is the Kingdom glory of the reign of the Son of Man on earth. The interpretative authority given to this attendant goes no further than this glorious reign. As far as this passage is concerned this is the final outcome for earth. The Revelation given to John brings him to this point in Revelation 20:1–6. John, however, is permitted to see further stages in Divine purpose that run beyond time and into eternity, in the final chapters of the Revelation.

The second statement is made by Daniel as he introduces himself into the narrative for the second time (see v. 15). Daniel confesses he is still 'troubled' – he uses the same word again. On the previous occasion (v. 15) it was the visions that troubled him – threw his mind into turmoil – clearly because he could not interpret them with absolute certainty to himself. In this verse it is his 'cogitations' (*AV*), a word that would be better translated 'thoughts', that are causing the turmoil in his mind. There can be no question that he has very solid reasons for his troubled thoughts after what he has seen of the rise and fall of kingdoms, the persecution of saints, and the judgements falling upon world rulers and yet, through all this gloom, a great King and a glorious Kingdom are in prospect. Daniel would scarcely be human if a multitude of questions had not arisen in his mind – 'how', 'when', and why'. When no answers are apparent he is affected in mind and body. A mind perplexed and shocked by what had been revealed would be reflected in the pale face and furrowed brow of Daniel; he acknowledges that 'my countenance changed in me'. Though so troubled, Daniel shows no sign of rejecting what had been revealed or even questioning it. In fact, the very reverse is true, for he states 'but I kept the matter in my heart'. The verb 'to keep' used here is an unusual word and is given by Wilson[53] to mean 'to keep the eye intently fixed, as upon an object of care'. Daniel can be seen as one pondering the different facets of the visions and carefully guarding each element of them as he awaited events. The statement may also imply that he could not, or maybe would not, share the vision with anyone. Few in Babylon would believe him; he was clearly afraid to trust even his own people. It may well be that the faithful companions of former years – Shadrach, Meshach and Abed-nego, who have not been mentioned from chapter 3 – have died, and this lonely man of around seventy years continues to ponder over what God has given him.

[53] *OTWS*, p. 236

Chapter Note

Does Scripture speak of the United States of America in end-time prophecy?

The answer to this question by students of prophecy is generally a firm NO! There is no Scripture that speaks of such an empire directly! Many commentators of sound premillennial orientation, when they face the issue, seem to agree with this verdict. John F. Walvoord whose prophetic insights are highly valued by many, and has been quoted frequently in this study with appreciative approval, has this to say: 'Although conclusions concerning the role of America in prophecy in the end time are necessarily tentative, the scriptural evidence is sufficient to conclude that America in that day will not be a major power and apparently does not figure largely in either the political, economic, or religious aspects of the world.'[1] Many commentators and prophecy students agree with this assessment. Yet as the political world is viewed in the twenty-first century, with the Rapture evidently so near, this seems very hard to believe. The only logical conclusion is that something unexpected and catastrophic looms large for the USA; something that will remove this powerful nation from the leading place in the world to the side-lines of world power or, indeed, off the world stage completely.

Many have speculated as to what kind of happening could befall such a great power to reduce its status on the world stage so drastically. Mark Hitchcock has gone very thoroughly into the possibilities and presents his conclusions in a recent book.[2] He decides there could be three major areas in which failure in any one could be the cause of catastrophic collapse of the mightiest empire on earth at present. The three main possibilities presented by Hitchcock with supportive evidence are certainly worth consideration in light of the present world conditions and, singly or together, they present a very plausible case. The three possibilities are:

(a) Moral Meltdown – the direct judgement from heaven as God 'gives them up' (Rom. 1:24, 26, 28) to the out-working and total disintegration of a drink-sodden, sports-mad, sex-obsessed society resulting from the acceptance of open sexual immorality and federal

[1] Walvoord, *The Nations in Prophecy*, p. 175.
[2] Hitchcock, *Iran and Israel*, p. 91.

approval of homosexual behaviour. These are the very evident hallmarks of the doomed empires of the past – Babylonian, Medo-Persian, Greek and Roman.

(b) Military Attack – A more terrible blow than the Islamic attack of September 11, 2001. This time more deadly and widespread, backed by one of the powers already threatening attack: Pakistan, North Korea or Iran. Hitchcock writes 'Either of these scenarios [a 'dirty' bomb or nuclear device] would cause untold loss of life and economic catastrophe, not to mention the lingering psychological effects that may leave the nation in a state from which it will be unable to recover.'[3]

(c) Money Matters – the debt-ridden American economy could readily implode in a spectacular stock market collapse that could bring the world financial markets to a standstill. Or America, facing financial collapse, judges the cost in being the police force for the world too high. As Korea, Vietnam, Iraq, Afghanistan are recalled and now Syria and Iran loom on the horizon, there is the possibility of the USA reverting to an old isolationist policy. That would mean the passing of power to later arrivals on the political scene like the European Union. In either case the USA would be off centre-stage of world politics.

As already set out in the study of this chapter there is most-assuredly a place for the USA in end-time prophecy. The suggested interpretation of the four beasts leaves three of the empires represented on the end-time scene until they are absorbed in the fourth and final empire. If the interpretation of the 'lion with eagles' wings', suggested in this study, is correct then, in spite of, or maybe because of one or all of the three disaster scenarios happening to the USA, the union of the UK (the British lion) with the USA (the American eagle), presents to the world a new powerful empire. It is interesting to recall that in the dark days of the Second World War Winston Churchill suggested such a union and discussed it with President Roosevelt privately. His first reference to it publicly was in the House of Commons in August 1940.[4]

It has also been suggested that the final empire of ten powers is not Europe-based but world-based with its financial capital in the re-built Babylon on the Euphrates. The European Union may well be one of the ten powers. It is also clear that the combined UK-USA

[3] Hitchcock, *Ibid.*, p. 99.

[4] House of Commons 20th August 1940. HC deb Vol. 354

power will feature as one of the ten-power Federation with Russia a possible third. If this is so the interesting question that arises will be – does this mean that Britain leaves the European Union? Believers in Holy Scripture have a privileged standing as we view a troubled world through prophetic truth and, best of all, we know the end of the story

CHAPTER 8

INTRODUCTION

A. A Note on the Change of Language in this Chapter

THIS CHAPTER RE-OPENS the Hebrew language section of the prophecy. The Aramaic language has been used from chapter 2:4–49 to chapter 7:1–28. Now, without any warning, Daniel resumes his use of the Hebrew language. It has already been pointed out that when Aramaic is used the subject matter is the relationship between the nations of earth and Israel. So it will be of interest to notice that the opening and closing chapters of the Aramaic section stand in contrast to each other. Both chapters show Israel under Gentile nations but with a time difference thus:

Chapter 2:4–49	The four nations who hold dominion over Israel as the 'Times of the Gentiles' commence.
Chapter 7:1-28	The four nations contemporary with independent Israel as the 'Times of the Gentiles' close.

Another contrast should be observed in connection with the two language sections side by side:

Chapter 7 is the final chapter in the Aramaic section and presents a world leader called:

A Little Horn – The leader of a ten-power empire
Gentile – Presents himself as Anti-God.

Chapter 8 is the first chapter in the reopened Hebrew section and presents the leader in Israel:

A Little Horn – The leader in Israel
Jew – Presents himself as Anti-Christ.

B. A Note on the Prophecy in this Chapter

God is about to give Daniel information in connection with the empires that follow Babylon and their treatment of his people Israel. In doing this he shows the clear time break already noticed between the commencement and the close of the period of subjection of Israel to Gentile power. This time break in the chapter is marked by the words 'and in the latter time of their kingdom' (v23). So it is to be noticed:

Verses 1–22 set out prophecy concerning the near future.
Verses 23–26 set out prophecy concerning the distant future.

It will be noted that for Daniel both parts of the chapter are prophetic – they lie in his future. For the present age, the passage down to verse 22 has now become history while verses 23–26 are still prophecy.

C. A Note on the Little Horn in this Chapter

In chapter 7 an end-time ruler, identified as the 'Little Horn' (7:8), is to emerge from the fourth empire. Winning control of the ten-power kingdom he will lead the world in rebellion against God. This man will be shown to come from the west (9:26) and will be a Gentile.

In the first part of this chapter (vv. 1–22) another bearing the title 'Little Horn' is to arise from the Greek Empire of Alexander the Great who died in Babylon in 323 BC. Out of the Seleucid dynasty established by Seleucus I, one of the four generals of Alexander who divided the Grecian Empire between them, would arise a king who would bring terrible distress to the nation of Israel. Since this part of the prophecy has now become history this 'Little Horn' has been readily identified as Antiochus IV Epiphanes (175–164 BC).

In the second part of the chapter (vv. 23–26) shows that, in addition to the political oppressor of chapter 7 a Gentile arising from the nations, Israel will a religious oppressor, who rises within the nation. This man, following the pattern and using the same tactics as Antiochus Epiphanes did, will seek to destroy the nation of Israel. To gain democratic acceptance, this man must be a Jew, even if he has Greek citizenship. He is identified here as 'a king of fierce countenance'. This charismatic Jew, reflecting Antiochus Epiphanes by his attributes and activities, earns by his actions different names. The Lord Jesus spoke of him when He said 'I am come in my Father's name, and ye receive me not; if another shall come in his own name, him ye will receive (Jn 5:43). This will be the man who acting as leader of the 'many' (9:27) in Israel takes the place of a prophet for Israel but, indeed, a false prophet. When he introduces the 'abomination of desolation' (Dan. 12:11), as Antiochus Epiphanes did, he will be acting in priestly fashion for the 'Coming Prince'. Thus, usurping the offices of Christ to the nation of Israel, he becomes prophet, priest and king – earning rightly the NT designation of 'Antichrist'. The prefix 'anti' is to be understood in its primary meaning of 'instead of' – this man is the replacement Christ. See Note A above.

D. A Note on the Link with Revelation 13

In this book Satan is not mentioned by name but unseen forces, antagonistic to the purposes of God (10:13), are shown to be at work behind earth's scenes. The prophet Zechariah identifies the director of these forces as Satan (Zech. 3:1–2), who, though unseen by men, is symbolised in Scripture as a dragon (Rev. 12:3). In the book of Revelation, a dramatic scene shows the dragon standing on the sand of the sea (Rev. 13:1 *RV*) and supervising the arrival of two beasts. The first verse of chapter 13 reads: 'he stood upon the sand of the sea' (*RV*), obviously to supervise the arrival of his princes – the Beast from the sea (Rev. 13:1) and the Beast from the earth (Rev. 13:11). These two beasts symbolise the two satanic princes or puppets that arise in the last days – the days of which these chapters in Daniel speak. The Beast from the sea (Rev. 13:1–8) is to be identified as the Little Horn of chapter 7 – the Gentile world ruler, emerging from the ten-power kingdom and identified by his actions as the Man of Sin. The Beast from the earth (Rev. 13:11–18) is to be identified as the king of fierce countenance of chapter 8 – a Jew emerging from the land of Israel and, by his actions, to be identified as the one coming in his own name (Jn 5:43) claiming to be a prophet, a priest and a king; he is the Antichrist.

THE OUTLINE

Section A

Prophecy Concerning the Near Future vv. 1–22

Introduction vv. 1–2

(a) The Vision vv. 3–4 The Ram with Two Horns
(b) The Vision vv. 5–8 The He-Goat with the Notable Horn
(c) The Vision vv. 9–14 The Little Horn

Interpretation vv. 15–22

Section B

Prophecy concerning the Distant Future vv. 23–26

(a) Character of the King vv. 23–24
(b) Condemnation of the King v. 25
(c) Command to the Prophet v. 26

Reaction of Daniel v. 27

SECTION A

Verses 1–22 Prophecy Concerning the Near Future

Verses 1–2 Introduction 551 BC **Daniel is 72 yrs**

Verse 1 Significance of the Date The Period

This chapter is dated in the third year of King Belshazzar, two years after the first vision (chapter 7), and thus in the year 551 BC. Daniel would be seventy-two years old. The significance of the date lies in the political issues of that year. The deciphering of the cuneiform text of *The Chronicles of the Chaldean Kings*,[1] by D.J. Wiseman, in 1956, shows that within the city there was tension and within the empire there was trouble. Since the death of Nebuchadnezzar (562 BC) tension had mounted, with treason and murder in the royal family. Evil-Merodach (2 Kgs 25:27; Jer. 52:31), the son of Nebuchadnezzar, had held the throne for less than two years when he was murdered and replaced by his brother-in-law, Neriglissar. His reign ended after less than four years, when he died rather mysteriously in 556 BC. He was replaced by his young son, called

[1] See Appendix 2. History of Neo-Babylonian Empire. The translation of *The Chronicles of Chaldean Kings* by D.J. Wiseman 1956. Quoted from an article 'Nebuchadnezzar and the Last Days of Babylon' in *Christianity Today*. Nov. 25, 1957.

Labashi-Marduk, who survived for three months, until another brother-in-law, called Nabonidus, was installed as king by a group of conspirators who had awaited their opportunity. Nabonidus, the man who was placed on the throne of the empire, was not of the royal family, but a general in Nebuchadnezzar's army, whose claim rested on the fact that he had married a daughter of Nebuchadnezzar. The city remained tense. While it is clear that, according to *The Chronicles of the Chaldean Kings*, mentioned above, King Nabonidus was a usurper, supported by an influential military cartel, he had much to commend him both as a military leader and as a man. However, he was not a worshipper of Marduk, the patron saint of Babylon, and was thus viewed with considerable suspicion. According to the same record,[2] three years after his accession to the throne (553 BC) he made his son Belshazzar co-regent with him in the empire. These *Chronicles* further show that two years later, indeed in the very year of this vision, King Nabonidus left Babylon in charge of his son and set out with an army into Arabia to deal with a trouble spot where an insurrection, stirred up by Median infiltrators, was causing unrest. Cuneiform records confirm that Belshazzar was addressed as King of Babylon[3] – a point denied by liberal criticism of earlier years. Formal inscriptions do refer to Nabonidus as the last king of Babylon but these records do vindicate the accuracy of Daniel.

Trouble in the empire stemmed from Babylonian weakness and the rise of the Median Empire, which was growing in power year by year. With the marriage of Cyrus, a Persian prince, to a Median princess, there were signs of unrest in the eastern provinces. In the nine years since the death of mighty Nebuchadnezzar, the assassinations and usurpations around the royal family had shown the weakness of the leadership of the Babylonian Empire. More ominous still was the military skill of this Persian prince called Cyrus, the son of King Cambyses of Persia. Politically and militarily, he was uniting two strong kingdoms – Media and Persia – into one formidable world power. The combined might of such an empire was already casting dark shadows over even mighty Babylon. The decade that follows this prophecy (551–541 BC) will see the increasing

[2] From The Chronicles of the Chaldean Chronicles, quoted in Walvoord, *Daniel: The Key to Prophetic Revelation*, p. 179.

[3] Montgomery, *The International Critical Commentary*, *Daniel*, p. 66.

power of this new Medo-Persia Empire until, in 539 BC, its armies are laying siege to the city of Babylon (5:30–31).

Verse 2 Significance of the Location The Place

In the Palace in Shushan, Elam

Two years after his first vision (7:1–28), Daniel is granted a second vision. In this case there is no mention of 'dream'; it would seem this is a supernatural vision during daylight hours. In the vision he recognises the place – geographically he was in the province of Elam, and in the capital city, called Shushan, and in the palace in that city. Immediately the question arises: was Daniel transported bodily to this city or was it simply a vision experience? Commentators are divided. Some think the language demands an actually physical bodily removal of Daniel to the palace in Shushan.[4] The majority, however, of both conservative and liberal scholars, support the view that, while Daniel remained physically in Babylon, in the vision he was transported 350 miles east. This latter view seems to fit the context better and finds support in Daniel's physical reaction to the vision (v. 27). Daniel's experience would seem to echo that of Ezekiel who, while physically still in Babylon, visits the Temple in Jerusalem (Ezek. 8:1–3).

'*Shushan*' is a Hebrew word meaning 'lilies' and the city was named after the abundance of these beautiful flowers that grew in the neighbourhood. Some translations read 'Susa' (*RSV*, *NIV*), which is the Greek equivalent and the name used by archaeologists. In modern times it is called Shush. Shushan is located about 350 miles east of Babylon; 150 miles north of the Persian Gulf; and mid-way between Ecbatana and Persepolis. It had a notable past under the old Babylonian Empire and it was in this city that the stele bearing the Code of Hammurabi was uncovered, in 1901. The city was taken from the Assyrians by the Chaldeans in 645 BC and thus became part of the Babylonian Empire (Ezek. 32:24).

Why should this city and palace come into this vision given to Daniel?

Shushan at the time of Daniel was but a very ordinary provincial city, even if it was the capital of the province of Elam (see Gen. 14:9),

[4] Josephus, *Complete Works*. p. 227. Keil and Delitzsch, *Commentary on the Old Testament*, Vol. 9, p. 285.

without any special claim to prominence, and, as far as available records are concerned, had no very distinguished buildings and no palace. So in his vision Daniel is transported about a century ahead of his own time (551 BC), into a palace not yet built in the capital city of an empire just emerging on the world stage, and allowed to glimpse at what lay ahead for Israel under the empire that would replace Babylon as the world power.

But change was on the way for this very city at this very time of Daniel's vision. When the Babylonian army, under king Nabonidus, father of Belshazzar, was defeated by Cyrus, just before the fall of Babylon, the whole of this area, including Shushan, became part of the growing Medo-Persian Empire. Nothing changed until King Darius I (522–486 BC) rebuilt the city and included a splendid palace to mark it as a royal city – the capital city of the province of Elam. Endowed and enlarged by the kings who followed, it became the residence of the kings of the Medo-Persian Empire, who saw it as a testimony[5] to their wealth and power. This coming kingdom had already been foretold in the image, in the symbolic language – 'his breast and his arms of silver' (2:32). One could wonder if the palace to which Daniel is now transported is possibly the very palace in which Nehemiah will be cup-bearer to the Persian King Artaxerxes Longimanus[6] (Neh. 1:1), in the years 446–445 BC. This could also be the palace – mentioned twelve times in the book of Esther – that forms the background to the drama in that book, under King Xerxes I (485–465 BC), the son of Darius I.[7]

Daniel's location in Shushan is 'by the river of Ulai', translated 'the Ulai Canal' (*NIV*). While the word used for 'river' is unique to this chapter (vv. 2, 3, 6), there seems no reason to question its identification as the river, in modern times called Eulaeus, that flows past Shushan to the north. In this city Daniel is given the vision concerning the two empires that would succeed Babylon as world powers.

Verses 3–4 The Vision – The Ram with Two Horns

As Daniel views the scene, his gaze falls upon a lone ram standing by the river Ulai. Majestic in posture, this magnificent animal surveys its domain. In this picture something catches the eye of

[5] *UBD* p. 1023, for description of the wealth and splendour of Shushan.
[6] See Appendix 1.
[7] See Appendix 3.

Daniel. Two large horns might have been expected on this remarkable beast, but something strange is taking place. The two horns are still growing, but not at the same rate: the fresh looking one is outgrowing the older looking one. One, slower than the other at first, then eventually outgrowing the horn that appeared first, becomes the taller of the two. 'Most unusual!' – Daniel must have thought. Then, as he watched, the ram began to push – first westward, then northward, and finally southward. It is in keeping with the picture to translate the verb 'to push' as 'to butt', as depicting the aggressiveness of the ram. It appears as if the ram was clearing the whole area of any competitor so he could stand alone in majestic solitude – monarch of all he surveyed. No beast can oppose him; they flee before him. No hunter dare approach this two-horned ram; he has the whole domain under his absolute sway. The picture is clear but surely Daniel must have wondered why the ram pushed in three directions only, and not four. Why did that ram not butt towards the east?

As we have the Divine interpretation given to Daniel (v. 20), there is no argument. The following translation makes it clear: 'The ram which thou sawest that had the two horns, they are the kings of Media and Persia' (RV). The features noted by Daniel in the symbol are readily observed in the empire that took the place of Babylon on the world stage after 539 BC. The Medes and the Persians had become one empire. In the early part of the sixth century, the Medes were a major world power in competition with Babylon when Persia was but minor province. Cyrus, son of a Persian father and a Median mother, on the death of his father (Cambyses I) was crowned king over the small Persian province of Anshan (c. 557 BC). By the year 550 BC he had taken over the whole Median Empire and forged a Medo-Persian Empire which, by the time of his death, in 530 BC, ruled the world from the Nile to the Hindu Kush, from Macedonia to the Sahara. His successors in the Persian Empire controlled this area for two hundred years, until Alexander the Great led an army into Asia in 333 BC to attack what had become a mighty empire under Darius III.

Thus, the order in which the horns developed had its fulfilment in the rise of Cyrus – the Persian who took over the Median Empire. It is interesting to note that the order in which Cyrus brought the nations under his sway is foreshadowed in the butting of the ram. Having consolidated his Median and Persian Empire he then marched his army westward, first through northern Babylonia, to bring the mighty Syrian kingdom, and then the wealthy Lydian kingdom, under his authority. Then he moved back toward his base but laid siege to Babylon on the way. Having conquered Babylon, his next move was northward to subdue Armenia and the kingdoms around the Caspian Sea. His final move was southwards to bring mighty Egypt and Ethiopia into this worldwide kingdom. The remarkable thing is that, in keeping with the prophetic Word, he never had to campaign to the east. This is most likely a consequence of his Median heritage, which gave him nominal control of these lands, and no rebel arose to question that right. How accurate is the prophetic Word! Those who followed Cyrus would have to bring much more pressure on these eastern lands but Cyrus never had to move an army eastwards.

Scripture is, as always, accurate – no nation was able to stand before Cyrus. A skilful diplomat with a strategic mind; an able military leader with tactical skill; there was simply none who could meet him on the field of battle with any hope of success. Scripture states: 'he did according to his will, and became great' (v. 4). The epitaph 'great' was given to Cyrus in his own day and it aptly reflected his stature on both the political and the military scene. In Scripture, his name occurs twenty-one times in historical settings (2 Chron. 36 (three times); Ezra (fifteen times); Dan. 1:21; 6:28; 10:1 (three times). But the interesting point is that Isaiah the prophet mentions him two hundred years before he appears on the world stage. Jehovah speaks through Isaiah and calls him 'My Shepherd' (Isa. 44:28). Again, Jehovah speaks of him as His 'anointed': 'Thus saith the LORD to His anointed, to Cyrus, whose right hand I have holden, to subdue nations before him' (Isa. 45:1). These Scriptures allow us to see God at work amongst the nations of the world who, while they think they are doing their own will, are simply working out the purposes of God. This is the king who, having captured Babylon in 539 BC, shortly afterwards issued the decree that allowed the captive people of Israel to return to their own land – the result was the return under Zerubbabel, in 536 BC. This was a landmark in the purpose of God – a most significant step in light of the coming of the Messiah (9:24–27).

Verses 5–8 The Vision – The He-Goat with the Notable Horn

Verse 5 His Crusade

As Daniel is absorbed with the ram and the implications of the vision, suddenly (notice the 'behold') he is startled to find another beast in the very area dominated by this imperious ram. Until now, no beast seemed able or willing to stand up to the ram. This new animal on the scene is a he-goat, literally, a 'buck of the goats', and its belligerent intention is made clear to Daniel from when it first appears. It comes from the west, out from the sunset, and with a very definite target in front of it – the ram. It is not its strength that startles Daniel, but its speed – it almost seems to be flying –'without touching the ground' (*RSV*). What catches Daniel's eye is that, instead of the usual two horns of a he-goat, this particular goat has only one, and right between the eyes. It is called a 'notable' or 'great' horn (v. 21). Strangely the word 'notable' is connected with sight and some render it a 'horn of vision'[8] or, interpreting this in the passive sense, it could be called a 'prominent' horn (*NIV*); one that cannot fail to catch the eye.

Gabriel interprets for Daniel again (v. 21) and identifies the he-goat as 'Grecia' and the great horn that is between his eyes as the first king. The ram has been shown (see comments at 7:5) to be generally accepted as symbolising the Medo-Persian Empire. In the same way the goat is the universally-acknowledged symbol of Greece; so this he-goat symbolises Greece as a national entity, while the horn, described as 'great', is identified as symbolising the first king.

The background of this next world empire is sketched symbolically but precisely. So cruel had been the repression meted out to the rebellious city-states of the Greek mainland and islands by the Medo-Persian Empire that for the first time there was a real movement by the very independent-minded city-states of Greece to unite against the common enemy of Medo-Persia. Philip of Macedon had used this common feeling amongst the most warlike of the city-states to get them to stand together with him against Persian might. By skilful diplomacy, and the judicial use of his small but well-trained army as a threat to the more reluctant states, plus a series of strategic marriages amongst the leading families, he had managed to unite many of the states under his banner. This had allowed him to dispatch a small invading force to test the military

[8] Wood, *A Commentary on Daniel*, p. 209.

might of Persia.[9] His son Alexander was born in 356 BC and at the age of twenty was called suddenly to fill his father's place, as King of Macedon. Philip was assassinated in 336 BC by one of his own bodyguards.[10] Immediately the army elected Alexander to the throne and notified the ruling council in Macedonia of their action; an action that was ratified by the council. Alexander's one ambition was to follow in his father's steps and lead the crusade mounted by the Greek States to attack the Persian Empire. He achieved this by demanding, within weeks of his accession to the throne, a meeting of the Hellenic League of Corinth. His sheer audacity, backed by the threat of war against any dissident state, won the day and he was confirmed as Captain-General of the anti-Persian crusade. Alexander was a crusader in the full meaning of the term. Life had no other meaning for him. He lived to deal with the Persian Empire.

Verse 6 His Coming

Without any prior warning, this crusader arrived suddenly on the scene. In symbolic terms the scriptural statement is terse: 'And he [the he-goat] came ... and ran unto him [the ram] in the fury of his power.' The people of the Persian Empire, under King Darius III, could not believe what they first heard and then could see. The tiny Greek states, usually in constant and bitter conflict one with another had now united under one, virtually unknown, young Macedonian king and were, even now, preparing to attack Medo-Persia. Inconceivable! What nonsense! His father, Philip II of Macedon, they would have conceded, was a renowned warrior who had earned his reputation on many battlefields; him they would have treated with respect, but this young fellow! The great Darius III treated the ambassadors of Alexander of Macedon with total contempt.

That attitude of disbelief was fine until, in March 334 BC, Alexander crossed from Europe into Asia with around fifty thousand infantry and five thousand cavalry in his mainly Macedonian army to attack the mighty Medo-Persian Empire. It was then that Persia felt 'the fury of his power'. By the time he died, in Babylon, reputedly of malaria, on June 10, 323 BC, he had smashed this mighty empire. His realm stretched from the River Danube to the River Indus and from Macedonia to the River Nile. Even at this stage, despite the rebellious mutterings of his veterans, he had plans to

[9] See article on *The League of Corinth* in *OCD*, p. 375.
[10] See Appendix 3, History of the Grecian Empire.

attack empires to the west; he had his eye upon Rome and even as far as Carthage. Already orders were in place for the gathering of an army in Cilicia and for the building of a fleet of over four hundred vessels to invade North Africa and get a foothold in the Mediterranean area. Alexander died just before his thirty-third birthday. In the short span of ten years he had destroyed the mighty Medo-Persian Empire and laid the foundation of a Greek Empire that would endure for nearly three hundred years. Crowned King of Macedonia in 336 BC, he reigned just twelve-and-a-half years (336–323 BC).

Verse 7 His Crown

How aptly Alexander the Great fits the picture of the 'great' or the 'notable' horn and his identification as the first king of the Grecian Empire – there was no Grecian Empire before him. His father had been King Philip II of Macedon and he became Alexander III of Macedon. In November 332 BC he had himself crowned King (Pharaoh) of Egypt at Memphis. It was not until 323 BC that Greek envoys, arriving in Babylon just before he died, acknowledged him King of Greece and offered him divine honours. How accurate is Scripture: Alexander the Great was the first King of Greece.

The expressions used by Daniel to describe the attack of the he-goat on the ram depict graphically Alexander's attack on the Persian Empire (v. 7). These seven expressions tell a dramatic story, as Daniel watched the drama unfold stage by stage. Daniel says, 'I saw':

(a) 'I saw him come close unto the ram' – Alexander drove his small force right to the heart of the empire. Crossing the Hellespont with a total force of about fifty thousand warriors, in the spring of 334 BC, he routed the army of Darius III at the Battle of Granicus River. Ancient capitals fell before him – Ecbatana, Persepolis, Babylon, Jerusalem, Tyre, and Memphis (Egypt), until the final battle with a Persian army was the Battle of Issus, in November 333 BC. There were other battles with Persian auxiliary forces, and some historians[11] date the end of the Persian Empire with the Battle of Gaugamela, in October 331 BC, where the major part of the army opposing Alexander was auxiliaries. Alexander's bitterness towards Persia was seemingly satisfied with the death of Darius. The body of Darius was dragged into the presence of Alexander but, to the surprise of his officers, he ordered a dignified funeral befitting a king. However, Scripture reveals, in the next phrase, the bitter

[11] Cartledge. *Alexander the Great*, p. 108.

animosity that drove Alexander relentlessly to pursue Darius in something like a personal vendetta. He had boasted he would kill Darius. God did not allow this but he was permitted to arrange his funeral! With his bitterness of heart satisfied, Alexander's attitude towards the Persian people changed remarkably; he married a Persian princess and ordered his generals to do the same. Naturally all were not too happy about this change of treatment of the enemy.

(b) 'He was moved with choler against him' the word 'choler' means 'fury'. All the bitterness of a subjugated and humiliated Greek people lay behind the initial fury of Alexander and his Macedonian veterans in the army. The cruelty and humiliation with which Darius had treated Greek cities, on many occasions in the past, had driven Alexander and his army to excesses of rampage and cruelty.

(c) 'Smote the ram, and brake his two horns'. Both the Median states and the Persian states in the once great Medo-Persian Empire alike succumbed to the fury of Alexander's relatively small army.

(d) 'There was no power in the ram to stand before him'. From the moment Darius hesitated to attack the recently-landed forces of Alexander, in the spring of 334 BC, and the consequent rout of his army at the Battle of the Granicus River, the Persian king was never able to take the offensive; he was constantly in flight. Darius did face Alexander at the head of his army and gave battle, but he lost every battle – there was no power to stop this conqueror. The different strategies and tactics used by Alexander have afforded lessons in military campaigns down the centuries. He was a master tactician.

(e) 'But he cast him down to the ground'. Figuratively, the empire was thrown to the ground and broke into pieces. Literally, Darius the King was thrown to the ground. He met an ignominious death as he was literally dragged out of a farm cart and thrown to the ground under the knives of his own inner counsellors, in July 330 BC.

(f) 'And stamped upon him'. Alexander gave Darius a burial befitting his rank but the empire he figuratively stamped into the ground. The Medo-Persian Empire was finished and it would never rise again in this form.

(g) 'There was none that could deliver the ram out of his hand'. It was a military and political reality of the time that Alexander had faced the major world power. Having won that battle there was no other power left, either to the east or to the west, that had the ability to bring aid to the Persian Empire in its hour of need.

Verse 8 His Conqueror

There was no empire on earth at this time to challenge the might of the Greek Empire under Alexander the Great. He had the world at his feet. All the eastern lands, from the Indus River at least, paid tribute to Alexander. The Phoenicians might well have had thoughts of sending help to Persia, on whom their trade depended, but the memory of Alexander's might and savagery in the siege and eventual destruction of Tyre, in the first six months of 332 BC (see Zech. 9:1–8), was too bitter a memory. Egypt had crowned him king at Memphis in November 332 BC. Scripture is accurate: 'there was none that could deliver the ram out of his hand'. No-one before his time had reached such greatness in so short a time.

Suddenly it was all over. Scripture again is clear and concise: 'the great horn was broken'. In little over a decade Alexander had built an empire spread over 1·5 million square miles stretching from the River Danube, in Europe, to the River Indus, in Pakistan. Then in early 323 BC Alexander brought his army back to Babylon. His weary men were on the verge of exhaustion; his inner counsellors and senior officers were seething with resentment and bitterness at some of his recent favours to local Persians. Nevertheless, Alexander had little thought of recuperation or rest, far less any thought of return to Macedon. He summoned shipwrights and boat builders from ports around the empire to prepare a maritime fleet of over four hundred vessels to scout the coast of Libya and North Africa.[12] He dispatched Craterus, a trusted official from his inner circle, with a large detachment of his veterans under orders to return to Macedonia. Ostensibly they were on the way home, but unaccountably had already been delayed in Cilicia for two months. It may have been no coincidence that Alexander was in process of preparing a main base there for operations westward. He had plans to move through North Africa and build a Mediterranean Empire. The prophetic Word, here given to Daniel, becomes a Divine sentence – the great horn was broken! Suddenly, with but a few days' warning, Alexander the Great was gone. A trip down the Euphrates, a mosquito bite, a raging fever, a drunken orgy, and the mighty commander who had never lost a battle had fallen before the last enemy. Murder, involving poison, has been suspected but never proven; no-one ever claimed or admitted such treachery.

[12] O'Brien, *Alexander the Great: The Invisible Enemy*, p. 217.

When the announcement of his death was made, the veterans who had followed him across a continent through mountains, over rivers, and across desert sands, forgetting any resentment, stood in tears; Alexander the Great was dead! Their world fell apart! The date was June 10, 323 BC. A few days into July and he would have been thirty-three. Scripture records his passing tersely: 'the great horn was broken'.

For the final statement of this verse the following translation is helpful: 'and instead of it there came up four notable horns toward the four winds of heaven' (*RV*). Alexander had shown himself to be an outstanding tactical genius on the battlefield. On occasions, he had displayed great administrative skill, yet Alexander failed totally in the creation of a unified empire. Satraps (rulers of the provinces), governors of cities, and, indeed, any official appointments, were all at his personal whim; there was no common structure or pattern of administration, either in the empire he built or the rule he imposed on the conquered lands. Alexander left no will; one that appeared four years after his death was an obvious forgery and unveiled for political advantage. On his deathbed, when pressed to name his successor, he was reputed to have said 'the strongest'.[13] The story is judged apocryphal by most historians, but it reflects his Macedonian culture. The ensuing murderous chaos endured for over twenty years. Within a short time four possible heirs were murdered and this was followed by the bitter personal rivalries of his generals leading to war after war. Even the treaty agreed between them, called the 'Peace of the Dynasts', in 311 BC, was only a temporary armistice. It divided the heritage of Alexander into four warring empires that eventually produced four men on the pattern of Alexander with the same war-like features – just as Scripture states: 'four notable ones'. These four were to be 'toward the four winds of heaven', but it took twenty years of bitter warfare before this end was achieved. The eventual division of the spoils of Alexander left four regions, under four successors who emerged from the empire of Alexander. These may be shown thus:

[13] Green, *Alexander the Great*, p. 259.

'littleness' of this horn, a background that fits Antiochus perfectly. Though in the Seleucid line, he was not the rightful heir. His older brother, Seleucus Philopator, was on the throne and his son Demetrius, the rightful heir, was being held as a hostage in Rome. Antiochus by skilful use of flattery and bribery (see comments at 11:21) succeeded in usurping the throne of his nephew. As soon as he was crowned, he assumed the name 'Epiphanes' – the word itself means 'illustrious' but it was associated in general usage with the 'outshining' of Olympic gods and in later life Antiochus seems to have used it this way. But first he set about earning his title by military conquest. This Scripture speaks of him as 'waxing great' as he marshalled his armies and first moved 'toward the south' – with one quick campaign he brought Egypt under his control. His next move was 'toward the east', where lands once under the rule of Alexander were swept into this new empire. His final move was 'toward the pleasant land'. The word 'pleasant' carries the thought of 'beauty' and in some translations is given as 'the glorious land' (RV, RSV *inter alia*) or more literally 'the Beautiful Land' (NIV). This is scriptural language for the land of Israel (11:16, 41, 45; Jer. 3:19; Ezek. 20:6, 15; Mal. 3:12) as God intended it to be. In *The Cambridge Biographical Encyclopaedia* the entry under Antiochus IV Epiphanes (215–163 BC) is brief yet pointed and helpful with reference to this Scripture: 'Seleucid king of Syria, the son of Antiochus III. He succeeded his brother in 175 BC, then fought against Egypt and conquered a great part of it. He twice took Jerusalem, provoking the Jews to a successful insurrection under Matthias and his sons, the Maccabees.' This brief synopsis does not mention his move to the east. Perhaps the reason for this omission of this well-substantiated invasion[16] is that it did not end in a war but with a peace agreement that gave Antiochus nominal control over all the eastern territories of Alexander. Despite his early conquest of Egypt, the main threat to Antiochus was still King Ptolemy, in Egypt. In any campaign to deal with Egypt Israel lay in his path (see map, p. 683) and so, for military reasons, he had to keep this land in total subjection. Antiochus hated the Jews for their stubborn resistance to his Hellenisation programme for the empire and their frequent attempts to rebel against his rule. But there was a deeper reason for his animosity, touched upon in the next statement, which lies at the root of all anti-Semitism.

[16] See OHCW, pp. 323–325.

Verse 10 (a) Religious Persecution against Israel

'It waxed great, even to the host of heaven.'

Having already identified this Little Horn as Antiochus IV of Syria, eighth king in the Seleucid dynasty, who had inherited the antipathy of the Seleucid kings for the Ptolemaic dynasty in Egypt, it has been stressed that to keep his armies safe on his Egyptian campaigns, Israel had to be kept in total submission. Every time Antiochus moved southwards with his army to deal with Ptolemy in battle, he had to be sure that Israel was not able to sabotage his supply line. He found the Israelites a very stubborn people and soon came to recognise that their recalcitrance and stubbornness were due to their consciousness of being a chosen people, having a Divine revelation based on the Holy Scripture, and a worship expressed in sacrificial offerings presented in a Holy Sanctuary. To stamp out their racial identity and their exclusive monotheism he decided to compel the Jews to embrace his Greek gods. Antiochus seemed to reason that if the other nations in his empire did not object to adding another idol to their pantheon, the Jews could not be allowed their Jehovah God. So he banned the distinctive features of Judaism – circumcision, the Sabbath, the sacrifices and the Scriptures. The penalty for disobedience was instant death. A quotation, even if a little lengthy, from Maccabean times, gives an idea of his purpose:

> And king Antiochus wrote to his whole kingdom, that all should be one people, and that each should forsake his own laws. And all the nations agreed according to the word of the king; and many of Israel consented to his worship, and sacrificed to idols, and profaned the Sabbath. And the king sent letters by the hands of messengers unto Jerusalem and the cities of Judah, that they should follow laws strange to the land, and should forbid whole burnt offerings and sacrifice and drink offerings in the sanctuary; and should profane the Sabbaths and the feasts and pollute them that are holy; that they should build altars, and temples, and shrines to idols, and should sacrifice swine's flesh and unclean beasts; and that they should leave their sons uncircumcised, and that they should make their souls abominable with all manner of uncleanness and profanation (1 Macc. 1:41–48, *RV*).

Verse 10(b)

> *'It cast down some of the host and of the stars to the ground, and stamped upon them.'*

The Jews in their stubbornness stood in the way of his ambitious plans for a united empire and culture under his Hellenisation programme. But it was much deeper than this: when he added 'Epiphanes' (illustrious) to his name, he was actually claiming to be the 'outshining' of deity – a blaze of glory from the Greek Mount Olympus, home of the gods. It is to be recognised that, in his mind, the uncompromising monotheism of the Jews became to him a personal insult. His immediate reaction was to destroy the Jews. Of course, he did not realise that in doing so he was attacking a people chosen of God for a purpose. Antiochus did not know that to Abraham, the patriarchal progenitor of the Jewish race and a man who believed God, had been given a promise that linked Israel with astronomy. God commanded Abraham: 'Look now toward heaven, and tell the stars, if thou be able to number them'; then God promised, 'So shall thy seed be' (Gen. 15:5). This link between the nation of Israel and the stars is repeated to Abraham after the sacrifice of Isaac (Gen. 22:17), and repeated again at the Exodus, when Israel is spoken of as 'the hosts of the LORD' (Exod. 12:41). The metaphor of the 'star' is used in this book of Daniel to describe the appreciation of heaven for faithful testimony in dark days: 'They that be wise shall shine as the brightness of the firmament: and they that turn many to righteousness [shall shine] as the stars for ever and ever' (12:3). When viewed collectively 'stars' and 'saints' are both spoken of in Scripture as a 'host', and it is worth recalling that in the OT God is often spoken of as 'The LORD of hosts'. So, when it is recorded that 'it waxed great, even to the host of heaven', the 'it' must be the Little Horn, which has been interpreted as Antiochus IV. Having identified the actor then the action follows – 'cast down some of the host and of the stars to the ground, and stamped upon them' – the word 'and' in the sentence can be rightly translated as the appositional 'even' – and the explanation becomes perfectly clear. 'Some of the host' describes faithful persons of Israel whom Antiochus ruthlessly cut down. Among those who perished were those who had witnessed clearly and faithfully for Jehovah; they were the 'stars' who, like the Maccabean family, would accept no compromise and died for their faith. Many passages from the Maccabean writings witness to the cruelty of this Syrian king. One may be quoted:

> And on the fifteenth day of Chislev, in the hundred forty and fifth year [of the Seleucid dynasty, 167 BC], they builded an abomination of desolation upon the altar, and in the cities of Judah on every side they builded idol altars. And at the doors of the houses and in the streets they burnt incense. And they rent in pieces the books of the law which they found, and set them on fire. And wheresoever was found with any, a book of the covenant, and if they consented to the law the king's sentence delivered him to death. Thus did they in their might unto Israel to those that were found month by month in the cities. And on the five and twentieth day of the month they sacrificed upon the idol altar, which was upon the altar of God. And the women that had circumcised their children they put to death according to the commandment. And they hanged their babes about their necks, and destroyed their houses, and them that had circumcised them. And many in Israel were fully resolved and confirmed in themselves not to eat unclean things. And they chose to die, that they might not be defiled with the meats, and that they might not profane the holy covenant; and they died. And there came exceeding great wrath upon Israel (1 Macc. 1:54–64, *RV*).

This was genocide on a terrible scale.

Verses 11–12 Blasphemous Policies and Practices

> *'Yea, he magnified himself even to the prince of the host, and by him the daily sacrifice was taken away, and the place of His sanctuary was cast down.'*

The 'he' of this verse interprets the symbol of the Little Horn. The 'yea' introduces a note of deep shock that a man could go so far as this. That a man could go so far in his blasphemy against God as to:

(a) oppose one spoken of as 'the prince of the host';
(b) take away the daily sacrifice ('the continual burnt offering', *RV*); and
(c) cast down the place of his sanctuary.

So in his bitter hatred of Israel, the people of God, this man:

(a) claimed superiority over against a special Person in this theocratic state of Israel;
(b) stopped a scriptural practice in that nation; and
(c) destroyed a sanctified place in that same land.

(a) A Person Defied

Most commentators are clear that the host must be the host of Israel, the people of God that would be regathered to Jerusalem in anticipation of the coming Messiah. Differences arise over the interpretation of the 'prince of the host'. Some commentators interpret this person as the high priest in office at this time, a man called Onias,[17] regarding him as the representative of Jehovah. While this is certainly possible within the context, yet it is suggested that this is too narrow a view. A clearer picture is presented when it is seen that, in so mistreating the people of God, Antiochus was magnifying himself in blasphemous opposition to God Himself. Thus to understand the 'prince of the host' as God presents no problem and fits the context perfectly. It will then be observed that the title 'Prince of princes' (v. 25) must be interpreted as Christ – of Whom the Scripture speaks: 'God was manifest in flesh' (1 Tim. 3:16). The very title Antiochus claimed for himself – 'Epiphanes' – implies a manifestation of deity and this is exactly what he claimed as he demanded worship and set himself against both God and Christ. In this he becomes a portrait of one who will appear in the end-time and has already been identified as the Antichrist.

(b) A Practice Denied

The next statement is: 'it took away from him the continual burnt offering' (*RV*) or, reading a translation that makes the matter even clearer, 'from whom the daily sacrifice was removed' (*NET*). The 'it' of the *RV* must be interpreted as the Little Horn. This is the one who stopped the morning and evening sacrifices and thus robbed God of that which symbolised and expressed the worship of His people. These sacrifices had been observed since Israel had become a nation (Exod. 29:38; Num. 28). God was being robbed of the worship of His people and Israel was being robbed of their special identity.

[17] See Appendix 1, History of Judah.

(c) A Place Destroyed

The Little Horn now attacks a specific place. The statement is pointed: 'and the place of His sanctuary was cast down'. It is interesting that a Hebrew scholar points out that 'the word used here for 'place' is used specifically elsewhere of the place (habitation, dwelling) of God (Exod. 15:17; 1 Kgs 8:13, 39, 43)'.[18] This points directly to the Temple in Jerusalem, which, in 551 BC, no longer existed – Nebuchadnezzar had destroyed it on his third invasion of Judah, in 586 BC. This passage therefore anticipates the rebuilding of the Temple under Zerubbabel, who would return to Jerusalem in 536 BC with about fifty thousand of his people to build the sanctuary. This rebuilding of the Temple was completed by 516 BC. The Temple was refurnished under Ezra, who returned with all the vessels of the sanctuary in 458 BC. Nehemiah, charged with the rebuilding of the city, led another company back to Jerusalem in 445 BC. This rebuilt and refurnished Temple is the one defiled by Antiochus. The verb 'cast down' in English generally means the physical levelling of a building, but the Hebrew root is much wider and includes a mental attitude to the act of destruction. A Hebrew scholar translates it 'to cast down, away, out; to be cast down, in a neglected, abandoned condition; it often implies contempt and disgust'.[19] The careful accuracy, in the use of this particular verb, is seen in the fact that, while Antiochus did not physically destroy the rebuilt Temple, he so desecrated it that even the Jews viewed it with contempt and disgust. They could no longer regard it as the place where God dwelt; it was cast down from its sacred status in the eyes of the people. The record of the Maccabees is sad: 'Her sanctuary was laid waste like a wilderness, her feasts were turned into mourning, her Sabbaths into reproach, her honour into contempt' (1 Macc. 1:39, *RV*). To sacrifice a pig on the brazen altar and sprinkle its blood over the holy place and the holy vessels was the work of this blasphemer.

(d) A People Defiled

The following translation, which is better identified as a paraphrase, clarifies the meaning: 'Because of rebellion, the host of the saints and the daily sacrifice were given over to it' (*NIV*). The 'it' is the Little Horn. The word 'host' must carry the same meaning as above

[18] Wood, *A Commentary on Daniel*, p. 215.
[19] *OTWS*, p. 68.

(v. 11) and points to the people of Israel given into the power of the Little Horn. However, the use of the article suggests that, while the whole nation was affected, there was a remnant that refused to bow to his dictates and, out of this company, a further remnant that escaped death by his agents. Antiochus went very far, indeed, but was not allowed to wipe out the whole nation of Israel. There is not the slightest doubt, as the history of that time is examined, that Antiochus intended genocide on a national scale, but God had set limits to his evil work. Nevertheless, the wording demands unbelievable cruelty and carnage.

The mention of the 'daily sacrifice' points to the evening and morning burnt offerings offered daily at the brazen altar in the Temple. These were banned by Antiochus. The explanation is given – 'by reason of transgression'. This poses the problem – whose transgression? At first sight, it would seem that it must be the transgression of Israel in turning to idolatry. This would explain why God permitted such happenings to His saints and to His sanctuary – these happenings are the Divine discipline because of the sin of Israel. There is truth in this and it can be supported by many other Scriptures. However, the context, and specifically the repetition of the word 'transgression' in the next verse, where it can only refer to the transgression of Antiochus, leave little question that the 'overstepping' (transgression) is that of the Little Horn. The next statement supports this interpretation. In these actions the Little Horn 'cast down the truth to the ground'. Truth is always found to be in God and His revelation of Himself. At the time when this prophecy was fulfilled, the truth of God was coming through a people (saints regathered), a place (a sanctuary rebuilt), and practices (sacrifices re-commenced), all based on Scripture. These were the very things attacked by this 'transgressor' Antiochus Epiphanes, who was prepared to throw down and stamp upon a people (Israel), a place (Temple in Jerusalem), and practices (daily sacrifice) that were each so dear to the heart of God. Antiochus tried to stamp on these holy things and replace them with a lie – the idolatry of Greece, seen in the image of Jupiter Olympus placed in the Temple.

The horrific actions of this blasphemer have been recounted and are now summed up in one verb: 'it practised' (*AV*) or 'it did' (*RV*); so heaven's judgement would be expected to fall upon this Little Horn. It is with surprise, even shock, that we read 'it ... prospered'. Success seemed to attend the actions of Antiochus against Israel and there appeared to be no possibility of any successful rebellion against his domination. For exercised hearts in Israel who knew their God this must have been very difficult to understand.

Verses 13–14 (a) A Limited Period

'Unto two thousand and three hundred days'

There can be no doubt that Daniel was much affected by the fact that not only was Israel, at this very time, under Divine discipline, as seen in his present servitude in Babylon, but there was a further period of discipline to come, under another Gentile king, far more evil than a Belshazzar. However, at this very dark moment, Daniel is permitted to overhear a conversation in heaven that brings the first glimmer of light in the darkness. He learns there is a period set for this persecution under the Little Horn; which persecution would not go on indefinitely. It would even be shorter than the seventy years servitude in Babylon he had endured; it would be counted in days. This must have been a comfort for him personally as he identified himself with Israel; it would also be a beacon of hope for Israel in these dark days to come.

Daniel is privileged to be so close to heaven that he 'overhears' two 'saints' chatting together as the attention of heaven and earth is focussed on the actions of the Little Horn. This individual had emerged from one of the four segments of the divided empire of Alexander the Great, and now shows himself to be a belligerent, blasphemous dictator, of Greek background. This is the man who, with satanic energy, persecutes the people of Israel, pollutes the sanctuary and puts an end to the sacrificial system that was instituted by God in view of the coming Messiah. Daniel's attention is caught by other voices, and the first voice puts in a very relevant and urgent question that must have been uppermost in his own mind. The question is: 'How long ...?' The grammatical structure is complex but students of Hebrew[20] seem assured that it does not mean 'How long until these things happen?' but 'How long will it be until the daily sacrifice is restored again?' The answer is clear: from the stopping of the sacrifice until the restoration of the sacrifice will be 'two thousand and three hundred days'. Both the sanctuary and the host have the same meanings as given above (vv. 11–12). The rebuilt Temple in Jerusalem is the sanctuary and the restored

[20] See the following *in loc.* Wood, *A Commentary on Daniel*; Walvoord, *Daniel: The Key to Prophetic Revelation*; Miller, *New American Commentary, Daniel.*

remnant of the nation of Israel is the host (the saints) who await the Messiah.

The word 'saint' is simply 'holy one'; a designation that can be used equally correctly of saints on earth (Hos. 11:12) or saints in heaven (7:18). However, it is also used of angels (Deut. 33:2), and on this basis some have argued that the interpreting angel is Gabriel (see v. 16) and the questioner is a fellow-angel seeking enlightenment from the angel responsible for the vision. This is very appealing, but it is unlikely that Gabriel should be introduced without being named at this point. It is more fitting, in the context, to see these two onlookers, not as angels (*contra* most commentators) but as saved men, from earth and now in heaven. These have already been shown to be associated with the throne (7:18) and vitally interested in and now discussing the happenings on earth; they are asking the questions any saved one on earth would ask. This interpretation seems to fit the context. The answer is said to be 'unto him' – which is the Spurrell translation, based on the Septuagint; this suggests it is the other saint in heaven who receives the answer. However, most translations (*AV*, *RV*, *JND*, *NET*) read 'unto me'. This is the Hebrew reading and seems to indicate that Daniel is the one informed. Indeed, the specific recipient makes no difference as both Daniel and the other saint hear the reply.

Few verses in this book have stirred up such debate and controversy as the time reference in this text. Yet the strange thing is that, when the text is allowed to speak for itself, and keeping closely to a basic rule of scriptural hermeneutics often quoted as *The Golden Rule of Interpretation*,[21] which has been summarised by one writer as 'When the literal sense makes good sense then seek no other sense, lest you end up with nonsense',[22] it is abundantly clear that the period when Israel would suffer death and destruction and defilement from the power and policy of this Little Horn would be exactly 2,300 literal twenty-four hour days. The fact that the word 'day' is the composite word 'evening-morning' (Newberry marg.) has led some expositors to think that this referred to the actual number of sacrifices missed, so that the actual time in view is

[21] Suggested some years ago by Dr D.L. Cooper and quoted in T.F. LaHaye, *The Revelation of Jesus Christ*, p. 4: 'When the plain sense of Scripture makes common sense, seek no other sense; therefore take every word at its primary, ordinary, usual, literal meaning unless the facts of the immediate text studied in the light of related passages and axiomatic and fundamental truths indicate clearly otherwise.'

[22] Allen, *What the Bible Teaches, Revelation*, p. 9.

halved, to 1150 days. It is to be feared that this is a suggestion designed to try to make this period the same as the period of the Little Horn in the previous chapter (7:25), which has been shown to be three-and-a-half prophetic years, or 1260 days. These could be set in parallel thus:

> 7:25 'until a time and times and the dividing of time' shown already to be 1260 days (see comments *in loc.*). This time period was another link between the Little Horn (of 7:8) and the end-times. This period is defined again when there is mentioned the 1290 days (12:11) where the midpoint of the seventieth week is given as 1260 days plus an added 30 days to reach a particular goal.
>
> 8:14 'unto two thousand and three hundred days'. This period does not answer to the period of the Little Horn of chapter 7, nor can it be adjusted to fit. This is a period unique to this man and fulfilled in history.

Set thus in parallel, any such link is patently wrong. Even if we were to adopt the suggestion that the number refers to the morning and evening sacrifices and therefore should be halved to 1150, there is still a difference of 110. Keil[23] has answered the argument most ably by pointing out the reasons for his refusal to accept this interpretation: No Hebrew reader would understand the expression to point to half-days because (a) 'evening' and 'morning' in its earliest usage (Gen. 1:5, 8, 13 etc.) meant a whole day of twenty-four hours and not half-a-day; (b) the expression 'forty days and forty nights' (Gen 7:4, 12), paralleling this expression, meant forty days of twenty-four hours each and not twenty full days; (c) 'three days and three nights' Jon. 1:17; Matt 12:40) does not mean thirty-six hours but three full days.

Thus, this statement must mean a literal period of 2,300 twenty-four-hour days.

Verse 14 (b)

'Then shall the Sanctuary be cleansed'

The simple reading of the text marks a closing date, when the sanctuary was cleansed. Following the line of interpretation already

[23] Keil and Delitzsch, *Commentary on the Old Testament*, Vol. 9, p. 304.

has been stressed that the period under consideration in this book is the period when the people of Israel, because of their sin, are under Gentile dominion – the period spoken of by the Lord as the 'times of the Gentiles' (Luke 21:24). It becomes clear that this period, by Divine purpose, ends with the darkest and most difficult time that Israel has ever known, identified by the Lord when He spoke to the disciples: 'then shall be great tribulation, such as was not from the beginning of the world to this time' (Matt. 24:21). Thus, Daniel becomes aware that the suffering of Israel is not over yet. Their continued rebellion against God means that the darkest days of all will be the days just before the dawn of the new day. Thoughts of this kind, weighing heavily upon his mind, had begun to affect his body.

Still in the same location by the side of the River Ulai, which loops around Susa and flows into the Euphrates River, Daniel is searching for the meaning of the vision, probably comparing it in his mind with the dreams he had interpreted in earlier years. Suddenly he is arrested, even startled – the ejaculation 'behold' alerts us. A man stands by the riverside and a voice speaks from above the waters. The voice, ruling out any consideration of a Theophany, identifies the man as Gabriel – an angel appearing in the form of a man. In the exercise of their ministry (Heb. 1:14) angels have appeared as men on occasions in the past. This voice will come again in the last vision (10:1–12:13) but from above the river Hiddekel (Tigris). While the speaker is not identified it can hardly be other than the voice of Deity (or the pre-incarnate Son) since no other could give a direct order to the angel Gabriel. It is to be noted that Gabriel appears as a *Geber*. The Hebrew word means 'strong man', and his name, Gabriel, echoes this, for it means 'Strong-One of God'. On the occasions when angels have been sent as messengers to earth they are invariably seen as men, both in OT times (e.g. Gen 19:1) and in NT times (e.g. Acts 12:7–8). Gabriel is seen only on three occasions in Scripture and on each occasion he is the bearer of a vitally important message. In this book of Daniel (8:16; 9:21) he announces the prophecy of the King (9:24–27); in Luke's Gospel he announces the Person of the King, first in the coming of the herald, John the Baptist (Luke 1:19), and then the Person Himself (Luke 1:26). Divine messengers of the standing of Gabriel are not dispatched on minor missions. This is an important development with respect to the kingdom. The only other angel named in Scripture is Michael (10:13, 21; 12:1; Jude 9; Rev. 12:7), who carries the title of 'Archangel' (Jude 9), and his particular responsibility is the welfare of the nation of Israel (12:1).

Verses 16(b)–19 The Introduction to the Interpretation

Verse 16(b) The Person Commissioned

'Make this man to understand the vision'

As Gabriel approached Daniel in response to the Divine command, it is clear that not only is Daniel awestruck but panic-stricken ('I was affrighted', *RV*). Daniel, with no thought of worship, but gripped by a very understandable terror, prostrates himself before Gabriel. Realising that he is in the presence of the Holy and Divine, and overwhelmed with a sense of his own sinfulness and worthlessness, Daniel does what men normally do when confronted with God – he falls on his face (Rev. 1:18; 19:10). However, Gabriel's mission on this occasion is not government but grace; to reveal to Daniel the meaning of the vision he has been given. To be addressed by Gabriel as 'son of man', for the only time in the book, must have brought back the memory of a previous vision to Daniel (7:13) and shown him how heaven has both evaluated and appreciated his testimony in Babylon up to this point. At this late stage, with the whole picture before us, it can be seen that Daniel was entrusted with the unfolding of earth's relationship with the Son of Man in time, spanning the period from His first coming, as Messiah the Prince (9:25), until His second coming, as Son of Man. Ezekiel in the book under his name is addressed by this same title on ninety-three occasions.

Verse 17 The Period Considered

'At the time of the end shall be the vision'

Before he unfolds the interpretation, Gabriel reminds Daniel of an important point – the vision relates to 'the time of the end'. It has been pointed out (in the commentary on 7:3–8) that there are seventeen references to 'the end' or the 'time of the end' in this book (7:28; 8:17, 19(twice); 9:26 (twice); 11:6, 27, 35, 40, 45; 12:4, 6, 8, 9, 13 (twice), but the full expression 'time of the end' in this verse occurs but four times in this Hebrew language section (8:17; 11:35, 40; 12:4). Both expressions point to the final days of Gentile rule over Israel and the earth and the replacement of man's rule with the eternal Kingdom from heaven (7:18). For earth's empires and their emperors, it is the end-time. This is the ultimate time in prophecy, when the rebellion of man, Israel included, will finally come to a climax and God will act to place the rule of earth in the hands of the One already introduced as the Son of Man. The capture of Babylon by Cyrus the Persian (539 BC), the defeat of Darius III at the Battle of Issus by Alexander the Great (331 BC), and the appearance of the Roman legions in Alexandria (4 BC) marked world-empire changes on earth, but any relief for Israel was only temporary. There is, however, a day coming that will blaze with unending glory, when this Son of Man is given the dominion and the glory in the Kingdom of God (7:14). A redeemed Israel with the redeemed of every nation will enjoy the earth liberated from every usurper (Rev. 20:1–6).

Verses 18–19 The Point Confirmed

> *'For at the time of the end shall be the vision'* or
> *'The vision pertains to the time of the end'* (v. 17 *NET*)

When Daniel heard again of 'the time of the end', such was the impact on his mind that, pushed emotionally beyond normal limits, he fainted. The verb translated 'I fell into a deep sleep' (*RV*) is related to the verb used in v. 27 translated 'fainted'.[25] Emotionally drained, Daniel falls on his face before the angel. However, one touch from Gabriel and Daniel is awakened to full consciousness and made to stand on his feet. Two vital matters remain to be communicated to him: (a) There is to be a very definite end to the period called 'the indignation'; it does not continue indefinitely or just fade away – it is brought to a definitive end. Daniel will be instructed so that he recognises what this means; (b) This end is brought about by God and it fits into His timetable; men cannot change this timetable – it 'shall be' – it states what will become a fact.

The word 'indignation' should really be translated 'fury'. It has, in its etymology, the idea of a person physically sorely hurt or wounded so that he flies into a rage.[26] It is used in the OT of those periods when God showed His anger with Israel for their sin and, in His outrage at their hurtful behaviour, allowed invaders like Assyria

[25] *OTWS*, p. 154, (faint) and 399 (sleep).
[26] *OTWS*, p. 227.

and Babylon (Isa. 10:25; 54:7–8) to move against them. It is used here of the period already set (v. 14) for the domination of Jerusalem by Antiochus Epiphanes and it will be used again for the terrible period of tribulation that still lies ahead for Israel and for the nations of earth (11:36). These periods are allowed of God and He sets the timetable for their closure – 'the end' as it is called here. It is important to see 'the end' of each period of indignation within its own context. The end in connection with the Babylonian 'indignation' was the capture of Babylon by Cyrus. The end of the Antiochus 'indignation' was the confrontation with Rome, the defeat of his armies and his subsequent death. The end of the tribulation under the satanic princes will be at the appointed time with the coming of the Son of Man to claim the Kingdom, with the arrest of the leaders and the destruction of their gathered armies (Rev. 19:20–21). God can use events in history to foreshadow greater events in the future. The indignation brought on Israel by Antiochus Epiphanes was for Daniel prophetic. From our vantage point, we read the history, but recognise that such happenings foreshadow a darker time, when Israel will suffer under a crueller foe than Antiochus Epiphanes. That time still lies ahead.

This interpretation is fully supported by the translation of this verse by Keil and Delitzsch (both Hebrew scholars), which can be accepted as touching on the nuances of meaning buried in the grammar and would seem to be closest to the text. This reads: 'I will show thee what will happen *in the last time of the indignation* for it relates to the appointed time of the end.'[27] The italicised phrase is rendered similarly by the *NET* translation: 'in the latter time of wrath'. This clears away any mist of uncertainty, and it is abundantly clear that the story of earthly kingdoms will be closed by a severe period of 'indignation' – in NT language it should be read 'tribulation' – and the end of this period is already appointed by God. In the visions to follow, Daniel will be made aware of the length of the period of indignation (9:27) and, in addition, will be trusted with greater detail of its dramatic close.

Verses 20–22 The Interpretation

The interpretation by Gabriel has already been used in comments on the early portion of this chapter (vv. 1–8). This can be summarised thus:

[27] Keil and Delitzsch, *Commentary on the Old Testament*, Vol. 9, p. 311.

(a) The ram symbolises one empire composed of two peoples, the Medes and the Persians, who were united since the time of Cyrus the Great under one king. Historians agree that Daniel's history is absolutely accurate as he shows there was only one empire – a unique merging of Media and Persia – in his time. Under the able leadership of Cyrus the Great it marched to world dominion and Babylon fell before it in 539 BC.

(b) The he-goat is identified as the 'King of Grecia', literally 'King of Javan' – an Ionian word by which Jews identified Greece (Gen. 10:2, 4; Isa. 66:19; Ezek. 27:13). Comment has been made with respect to the identification of Alexander the Great as the interpretation of this symbol; Greece is linked traditionally with the goat. Four features are noted of the goat: (i) Attention is drawn to the fact that it is a 'he-goat' or 'a buck of goats' – the male of the species; (ii) He is identified as the first King of Grecia and this is exactly how history presents him (see comments at v. 5); (iii) He is spoken of as a 'notable' horn or 'horn of vision', here interpreted for us as a 'great' horn. The horn is eye-catching; (iv) He is described here as 'rough' – a word meaning 'shaggy' or 'hairy'. The only other time this word is used in Scripture is to identify a false prophet (Zech. 13:4). This is interesting because very recent historical research has brought to light[28] something that surprised many historians: an insistent demand for worship sought by Alexander, especially in the last year of his life. This megalomaniacal pride, allied to his manly presence, his monarchical pre-eminence, and his military prowess, combine to make him an outstanding figure in history. He had begun to think that men owed him worship.

(c) The breaking of the great horn (323 BC) and its replacement with four others has been shown (v. 8) to have been fulfilled in the sudden death of Alexander and the eventual dividing up of his empire into four empires covering the four points of the compass around the nation of Israel (see comments at v. 8). The hostility and animosity of these four kings kept the world in turmoil for twenty years, 332–311 BC. Even after a peace agreement was reached between the four 'successors' of Alexander, in 311 BC, bitterness still rankled and Syria, under the Seleucid dynasty, and Egypt, under the Ptolemaic dynasty, were constantly at war. These antagonists will be identified in Daniel's third vision as 'the king of the north' – Syria (11:6) – and 'the king of the south' – Egypt (11:11). These

[28] Cartledge, *Alexander the Great: The Hunt for a New Past.*

warring nations both used Israel as a staging post in their campaigns (see chapter 11), and both kept the world of their day in turmoil, until Rome moved onto the world stage and by the might of its legions settled all disputes – mainly on the field of battle. History shows that Macedonia and all Grecian lands fell before the Roman legions led by Sulla, in 86 BC. In 64 BC Pompey ended the Seleucid monarchy and also the nominal independence of Judaea, which Rome had allowed to exist from the end of the Maccabean rebellion in 143 BC; on this date, without a battle, Rome simply annexed Judaea. In 30 BC Rome ended the Ptolemaic dynasty by annexation of Egypt. Alexander's empire had been replaced on the world-stage.[29]

Up to this point in the chapter most conservative commentators will agree on the general picture presented here. They will also agree that the details given here of the Little Horn point, without any serious question, to the historic figure of Antiochus IV, self-styled '*Epiphanes*' (the 'glorious' or 'outburst of glory'). The megalomania of Antiochus was treated with scorn by many contemporaries; some changed one letter in his name and spoke of him as '*Epimanes*', readily translated as 'madman'. This man ruled the Seleucid Empire, based in Syria. This was that part of Alexander's Empire that had been allocated to Antigonus, who was displaced almost immediately by another general, called Seleucus, who was crowned as King Seleucus I Nicator ('the Conqueror') in 311 BC. He became the founder the Seleucid dynasty, in which dynasty Antiochus Epiphanes was the eighth ruler. He was a usurper, who seized the throne from the true heir, his nephew, in 175 BC. The actions of this Syrian king against Israel during his reign (175–164 BC)[30] fit exactly the detailed prophecy given to Daniel as the portrait of a supreme oppressor of Israel. The detail is too explicit to fit any other. While features of his treatment of Israel will be reproduced in future rulers, this part of the prophecy, up to this point, has already been fulfilled. No further fulfilment is required or to be expected. The accuracy of the detail with which the prophecy has been fulfilled gives the reader due warning that for any prophecy as yet unfulfilled the same level of literal accuracy is to be expected.

[29] *OHCW*, pp. 850–853.
[30] *OCD*, p. 105.

SECTION B

Verses 23–26 Prophecy concerning the Distant Future

From this point in the chapter commentators differ. There are two major views concerning the person here described:

View 1 – Some commentators see this paragraph as giving more detail of The Little Horn (vv. 8–14), the man already identified in history as Antiochus IV Epiphanes.[31] It will be shown in the comments that this is too restricted a view to meet the statements that follow.

View 2 – Other commentators take the view that, while Antiochus Epiphanes still stands in the background, the person that Scripture now presents is an eschatological figure to appear in the end-time (v. 23), of whom Antiochus Epiphanes is only a portrayal. For a number of reasons that will come to light in the study, this second view is, by far, the more satisfactory way of interpreting the picture here presented.

The first point to be considered is the time frame for the person emerging. A chronological gap after what has gone before is demanded by the first statement of the verse: 'the latter time of their kingdom'. This statement would take us down historically to the end of Grecian rule. It was the arrival of the Roman power on the world stage that brought all four of the Hellenistic kingdoms to an end.[32] The next vision, in chapter 9, will show, in the dating based upon it, that 'Messiah the Prince' (9:25) will arrive and be presented to the nation when Israel is ruled by the Roman Empire.

The second statement envisages a further chronological gap and takes us down further centuries to the time 'when the transgressors are come to the full'. This omits the Church age entirely and moves to the end of the 'times of the Gentiles'. This is the time when God deals with the transgressors both in Israel and the nations of earth – all united to oppose the taking of the Kingdom by the Son of Man. The man described in these verses will be one of the transgressors

[31] Young, *The Prophecy of Daniel*, p. 178.

[32] *OHCW*, pp. 850–853. Macedonia and all Grecian lands fell before Roman legions under Sulla in 86 BC. In 64 BC Pompey ended both the Seleucid monarchy and the nominal independence of Judaea – permitted by Rome from the end of the Maccabean rebellion in 142 BC – now Rome simply annexed Judaea. In 30 BC Rome ended the Ptolemaic dynasty with the annexation of Egypt. Alexander's Empire had been totally replaced on the world-stage.

with whom God will deal in judgement. This moves the fulfilment of this prophecy to the end of the Divine timeline. This is the end of the seventieth week of Daniel's prophecy (9:27), which seven-year period in the NT is called the Tribulation. The last three-and-a-half years of this period are spoken of as the Great Tribulation – compare 12:1–2 with Matt. 24:21. It is at that climactic point of earth history that this 'king of fierce countenance' will be 'broken without hand' (v. 25).

A chronological gap, as noticed here between verses 22 and 23, is not uncommon in prophetic Scripture, when God wishes to lift the eye from a historical present to an age yet future, to which the prophecy points. Condensed prophetic statements can be noticed in quite a number of Scriptures, but two examples, taken from Isaiah's ministry, will suffice at this point: (a) Consider the words of Isaiah, 'For unto us a child is born, unto us a son is given: and the government shall be upon His shoulder' (Isa. 9:6). There is a gap of over two thousand years, somewhere in the verse, between the first and second comings of Christ to earth. Depending on our interpretation, it could fall between statements one and two or between statements two and three, but it must come at some point. This could only be seen in the light of history; (b) It is to be noted how the Lord stopped His reading of Isaiah's prophecy (Isa. 61:2) in the synagogue in Nazareth (Luke 4:16–21) in the middle of a connected statement, to distinguish what was being fulfilled – 'the acceptable year of the Lord' – from what lay ahead – 'the day of vengeance of our God'. Again, the time gap can only be seen in the light of history. See comments at 9:26–27 for further examples of this time gap in prophetic statements. So it is suggested that the break in this chapter between verses 22 and 23 moves the prophetic eye from Antiochus IV Epiphanes forward to another man, in the end-time, who is the subject of this part of Daniel's vision.

A King of Fierce Countenance

Verses 23–24 Character of the King

The difficulty facing the expositor is very simple. If this is not Antiochus Epiphanes the question has to be raised as to the identity of this person. To consider what is said of him it might be useful to present the statements of Scripture in tabular form:

TABLE 1

Comments on Table 1

1. When the eight statements listed in Table 1 are examined carefully it becomes clear that, while there are some statements that could, in a superficial way, reflect the actions of Antiochus IV Epiphanes from the past, the majority of them point to someone far more skilled in perfidy and blasphemy than he ever was.

2. In at least two of the points, Antiochus IV must be ruled out of the picture completely. Both of these (the first and seventh points) have to do with a time far down the centuries from Antiochus IV.

In OT history God waited four hundred years for the right moment to act in judgement against the Amorite idolaters of Canaan – 'for the iniquity of the Amorites is not yet full' (Gen. 15:16). When this point was reached God had His people out of Egypt and ready to enter Canaan. Thus, the judgement on sinners and blessing for saints came at the same point in God's timetable. It will be the same in a future day, when lawlessness has reached a climax and two satanic puppets lead the rebels of earth in rebellion. This is the very moment when the Son of Man takes the Kingdom (7:14). God even permits one of these satanic princes to carry out a pogrom, even to the genocide of the nation of Israel, as noted in this passage.

Conclusion of the Study of Table 1

Antiochus Epiphanes clearly portrays someone after him in time; someone who would answer to Antiochus as the substance does to the shadow. When this someone appears, he will be a deceiver and a destroyer of Israel in a way far more deceitful and more destructive than that of Antiochus Epiphanes. Let us examine what the Scripture presents:

Verse 23 His Period

(a) '*The latter time of their kingdom*'
(b) '*When the transgressors are come to the full*'

These two statements point far beyond Antiochus IV, to one who will appear at the end-time. In this verse the time period when this individual comes to the fore is identified by two statements:

v. 23	Period	(a) Latter time of their kingdom	The end of the rule of all four successors of Alexander with the arrival of Rome on the world stage
		(b) When transgressors are come to the full	The Tribulation period marks the time when transgressors come to the full
	Person	(a) A king of fierce countenance	'Fierce' means 'strong', or 'bold'.
		(b) And understanding dark sentences	Dark sentences' is the same word used in its Aramaic form as 'riddles' (5:12)
v. 24	Power	(a) His power shall be mighty but not by his own power	The power source is not identified here (*cf.* Rev. 13:12)
		(b) He shall destroy wonderfully, and shall prosper and practice	What Antiochus did (v. 12) – yet on a much larger scale
		(c) Shall destroy the mighty and holy people	A more complete genocide than Antiochus ever achieved
v. 25	Policy	By his policy shall he cause craft to prosper in his hand	'Policy' is better translated 'cunning'; 'craft' should be translated 'deceit'
	Pride	And he shall magnify himself in his heart	'In his heart' reflects what he thinks of himself. Much magnified from reality -'in his own opinion' – Pride marks him
	Peace	By peace shall destroy many	'By peace', translated in *RV* 'in their security' or in *NIV* 'When they feel secure'. He takes action to bring peace through the 'covenant' (9:27). But it is a false peace. It is a plan for genocide
	Purpose	He shall also stand up against the Prince of princes	Not the 'Prince of the host' (v. 11), but the 'Prince of princes'. This is Christ on the pattern 'Lord of lords' and 'King of kings'
	Passing	But he shall be broken without hand	Direct Divine action, not human action, brings his death

(a) 'The latter time of their kingdom'. The empires of the four kings ('their kingdom') who succeeded Alexander the Great controlled between them the greater part of the known world east of Rome. Rome, having conquered the west, now moves east, and, step by step, takes over all four of these empires and closes each of the four dynasties from the time of Alexander the Great. This is the end of what is known as the Hellenistic Age (323–30 BC). From this point Rome becomes the mightiest empire this world has known up to this date. This brings us to the time of the fourth empire of the image of Nebuchadnezzar's dream (2:31–32), represented by the metal iron.

(b) 'When the transgressors are come to the full'. Daniel will learn in his next vision (chapter 9) that the chronology of earth is fixed by the coming of the Messiah. The closing stage of this Divine timetable is shown to be a period of seven years (the seventieth week of the seventy weeks prophecy), when the leader of the nations described as the Coming Prince (9:26) moves to a confrontation with heaven, called the consummation. This is the time period when the transgressors are come to the full. Already it has been shown that the Little Horn (7:8, 20–25), the leader of the ten-power kingdom on earth, is to be identified by his actions as the Man of Sin (2 Thess. 2:3–4). It is suggested that these titles identify the same person – a Gentile from the West. This world leader of the nations against God has a worthy aide in ruling the nation of Israel, identified in this passage as the king of fierce countenance. These two transgressors have come to the full, in both numbers of adherents and depth of their antagonism against God, and are leading Israel and the nations to a confrontation with heaven (9:25; Ps. 2:1–6).

His Person

'King of fierce countenance, and understanding dark sentences'
'*A stern-faced king, a master of intrigue*' (NIV)

As this man appears on the scene, two things make him stand out:

(a) His appearance. The word 'fierce' describes that hard, determined look that reflects the unyielding character of his person and pronouncements. No-one can stop this man doing as he wishes once he has decided on a course of action. The expression is taken from Deuteronomy, when God threatens His people with 'a nation of fierce countenance, which shall not regard the person of the old, nor shew favour to the young' (Deut. 28:50). In verb form the word is used of a harlot: 'she strengthened her face' (Prov. 7:13)[33] – absolutely impudent. Just one of that race will do Israel untold damage at this time. He wears this face; no matter what form the opposition takes, he confronts it. Whatever the scandal alleges, he refutes it. No-one dare answer him back.

(b) His ability. Beyond the normal political acumen of the first-rate brain of a very clever and able man, there is something sinister about his skills. The corresponding word for 'hard sentences' is used in Aramaic by the queen (5:12). In Hebrew it is used of Samson's riddle (Judg. 14:12); translated 'hard questions' it covers the matters the Queen of Sheba put to Solomon (1 Kgs 10:1). When used of this man it suggests that he is in touch with occult powers and spirit forces who have behind them satanic knowledge for the deception of mankind. It suggests that the 'working of Satan' (2 Thess. 2:9–11) has brought this man to prominence in various areas in society – he has solved their problems.

Verse 24 His Power

> *'And his power shall be mighty, but not by his own power: and he shall destroy wonderfully'*
> *'His power shall be great, and he shall cause fearful destruction'* (RSV)[34]

Behind the personality of this man there lies another power. This, in context, can only mean the power of Satan. This is in full agreement with the NT statement in connection with the Beast from the earth: 'And he exerciseth all the power of the first beast' (Rev. 13:12). The source of the power of the first Beast is clearly defined in the words of Paul: 'Even him, whose coming is after the working of Satan with all power and signs and lying wonders' (2 Thess. 2:9). Thus, the power behind each of these satanic princes is Satan in person – they are simply satanic puppets (Rev. 13:1, *RV*). The links between the king of fierce countenance and the second Beast, the false prophet (Rev. 13:11–18), should be noticed. The Saviour disdainfully refused outright the satanic offer of the kingdoms of earth (Lk 4:5–8). As a usurper, Satan had not the slightest right to make such a proposal, yet the satanic deceit brings dire consequences on earth through his puppet; and such power is used for destruction. The word 'wonderfully' is best taken

[33] Young, *The Prophecy of Daniel*, p. 179.
[34] *RSV* marg. includes a note: 'Theodotion and Beatty papyrus of Gk. Hebrew repeats '*but not with his own power*' from v.22.

here as an adverb, modifying the verb 'destroy', as in the translation 'he shall cause fearful destruction' (*RSV*). This able man, as a tool of Satan becomes a destroyer of good – both men and institutions – as in the next statement.

His Prosperity

'And shall prosper, and practise'

The next two verbs go together – 'prosper and practise'. The word 'prosper' comes from a root word meaning 'to go through', and it is used of a person going through every difficulty to reach the goal set. It is used of Christ in the words of Isaiah: 'the pleasure of the LORD shall prosper in His hand' (Isa. 53:10). This man has different goals but, for a while, he will be successful in all areas as he moves to world dominion. This is supported by the word 'practise' – which is defined as 'to be busied therein'[35] but should, according to other authorities in Hebrew, be rendered here 'accomplish'.[36] He accomplishes the things he sets out to do. Some of these things will come to light in the prophetic Scripture as the stages of his leadership of Israel come before us. He is to be seen as:

(a) One of whom the Lord warned when He spoke: 'if another shall come in his own name, him ye will receive' (Jn 5:43);

(b) One of whom Daniel will write in the next vision who would lead the majority of the nation to confirm a covenant (Dan. 9:27) with the Coming Prince; this is the covenant that the prophet Isaiah calls 'a covenant with death' (Isa. 28:15);

(c) One who would lead the nation of Israel into worship of the first Beast and suggest the making and worship of his image as well as the acceptance of his number (Rev. 13:11–17).

These actions are the accomplishments of this man as he leads his people to utter destruction. This is the very nation that suffered so much under Antiochus Epiphanes and throughout the Maccabean times. This is the nation from whose people come names that embellish the honour roll of heaven (Heb. 11:36–38). But the man identified here will be the agent in Satan's hand to bring a most terrible time to that same nation. He deceives them and then betrays them into the hand of the Man of Sin (2 Thess. 2:2–4), who has already been identified as the Little Horn (7:8), the Coming

[35] *OTWS*, p. 321.

[36] Wood, *A Commentary on Daniel*, p. 227.

Prince (9:26–27), and pictured as the Beast out of the sea (Rev. 13:1–8). This world-leader and arch-deceiver at the midpoint of the seven-year Tribulation stuns the world. He drops the veil and seats himself in the Temple in Jerusalem and proclaims himself God (2 Thess. 2:4).[37] Thus he summons earth to his crusade against God – anti-God!

The willing colleague of this arch-deceiver is this man in Israel – the king of fierce countenance. At this point he displays his betrayal of his own nation and his allegiance to the deceiver in the making of an image of this man and placing it on the wing of the Temple (Mt. 24:15) for witness and for worship (Rev. 13:11–18). This action reveals his calculated betrayal of his nation and opens the purpose of his heart: '[he] shall destroy the mighty and the holy people.' The 'mighty' and 'holy' people are the saved people of that day, who have believed the gospel of the Kingdom (Mt. 24:9–14). There will still be others who, while not believers in the Lord Jesus Christ, will not accept idolatry in the Temple of God and will be the object of his animosity. Besides Israel, there will be millions from the nations worldwide, who have believed the gospel of the Kingdom, are waiting for the coming King (Rev. 7:9–17), and are now subjected to the same persecution. In this context it is worth noting that 'mighty' carries the thought of being able to 'overcome that which opposes'; the word 'holy' simply means 'set apart' for God. Is it not strange that, for His own purposes God allows this man 'power' to make war with His saints (Rev. 13:7) and to overcome them – His 'holy ones'? This king of fierce countenance, in seeking to put to death all who will not bow to the image, becomes the tool of Satan in his crusade to destroy Israel, as pictured in the persecution of the woman by the dragon (Rev. 12:13).

Verse 25 Condemnation of the King

His Policy

'Through his policy also he shall cause craft to prosper in his hand'
'He shall magnify himself in his heart'
'By peace shall [he] destroy many'

[37] In the quotation (2 Thess. 2:1–12) note that the verb 'revealed', meaning 'to drop the veil', is used three times – in vv. 3, 6, and 8. It is the 'apocalypse' – the unveiling of the Man of Sin. He has had his '*parousia*' (appearing, v. 9) at the commencement of the Tribulation as he moved unto the world stage with the confirmation of the covenant; now in this action at the midpoint of the week he is revealed for what he is – the claimant to Deity, in fact the anti-God.

Verse 26 Command to the Prophet

'Shut thou up the vision'

This second vision has taken a full day; both 'the evening and the morning' have been occupied with it. Gabriel would see the effect the vision had upon Daniel – a man in his seventies. The strain would show on his face. However, before he closes his message, Gabriel gives Daniel two matters to ponder:

(a) An Assurance – The Vision is True

Daniel had very real concerns. On the political scene, dark thunder clouds were gathering; war was on-going with Medo-Persia and the siege of Babylon was inevitable. There were few positive signs of spiritual recovery in the captives from Israel; they were too much at rest in Babylon now. The recent visions gave him added burden of soul. Yet the heavenly messenger gave him a word that must have set his heart aglow. One thing upon which Daniel could depend without fear; one thing about which he could be absolutely sure – the vision is true!

Far down the stream of time Peter assures the saints that the prophetic Word is to be treated with similar assurance today, as he writes: 'We have also a more sure word of prophecy' (2 Pet. 1:19). With utter conviction he gives the reason for such assurance: 'But holy men of God spake as they were moved by the Holy Ghost' (2 Pet. 1:21). Daniel was writing in 551 BC, three-and-a-half centuries before any shadow of Antiochus IV Epiphanes appeared on the world stage (c. 215–164 BC). Daniel could rest in the assurance that God would keep His Word and deliver His people.

As we look back from our vantage point and see how accurately every prophecy concerning Antiochus Epiphanes has been fulfilled to the letter, it brings fresh assurance that the Word of God that has stood the test of history will stand the test of time to come. The details of this future world leader, of whom Antiochus Epiphanes is but a faint picture, will be fulfilled just as minutely and as literally. God's Word is true!

(b) An Instruction – 'Wherefore shut thou up the vision'

In light of the assurance of the truth of the vision, this instruction may be somewhat surprising. Two things are balanced. The truth of the vision, which belongs to it inherently, must be balanced against the date of its fulfilment. This latter lies far ahead in the counsels of God, so in the meantime, lest it be misunderstood or misapplied, Daniel is given instruction: 'shut thou up the vision'. This verb is used only in this book and only on two occasions (here and, in the same context, at 12:4). Its meaning is generally interpreted as 'to stop' or 'to shut up', with the thought of a writing not to be divulged or published, but rather concealed from view. This is the meaning given by Wilson,[39] supported by Baker and Carpenter.[40] However, some linguistic authorities, by reading the word with different Masoretic pointing (which has no claim to inspiration), understand it to mean 'preserve'. Wood writes: 'The thought is not, however, to shut the vision up in the thought of keeping it secret; but in the sense of preserving it.'[41] There is no doubt that the meaning translated 'to preserve' seems to fit into a similar context on each occasion of its use in this book. The explanation of this somewhat strange instruction is given in the next statement: 'for it belongeth to many days to come' (*RV*). In other words, do not misapply it to some occasion in your immediate future – it is to be preserved until, in its fulfilment, men will see the meaning very clearly and understand that God has foreseen it. In fact, the vision is going to leap centuries, first to Antiochus and then further centuries to the time of Antichrist; it is only as time brings certain conditions to light that the relevance and the importance of this prophecy will be fully understood. Daniel is advised not to worry but to wait.

Verse 27 Reaction of Daniel

'I Daniel fainted, and was sick certain days'

For the third time in the chapter (vv. 1, 15, 27) Daniel draws attention to himself to let us see what a powerful, emotional impact the vision has had on him; an impact not unexpected as we begin to glimpse just what is in store for his people, Israel. His response – again Daniel has fainted (*cf.* v. 18) – but this time there is no angelic touch to revive him. He is sick for some days. When emotionally disturbed the human body has mechanisms for its preservation but they take time to operate. His responsibility is still to the king –

[39] *OTWS* p. 392.

[40] Baker and Carpenter, *The Complete Word Study Dictionary*, p. 792.

[41] Wood, *A Commentary on Daniel*, p. 228.

even if it is Belshazzar. Daniel is a man of over seventy years, yet still he feels responsible to get back to work as quickly as possible. God has given him a place and he must fill it for God. There is no biblical record of what office he filled under Belshazzar. Daniel must still have held some post in the Babylonian administration, even if not such a prestigious one as he had held under Nebuchadnezzar. Before he returns to work he gives us a little insight into his thinking – 'I was astonished' shows the shock it must have been to him. The next phrase, 'but none understood it', shows he did not feel the instruction he was given from above precluded his sharing the vision with others. Even with Gabriel's interpretation, the significance and implication of what he had seen continued to escape all who were consulted – 'none understood it'. With the full light of Scripture now upon the vision, a relevant question for each reader would be – do we understand it any better today?

Excursus

'Then shall the sanctuary be cleansed'

The simple reading of the text suggests a definite date in history when the defilement brought into Israel by Antiochus IV Epiphanes, through his programme of enforced Hellenisation, would be at an end. This would result in the cleansing and rededication of the Temple in Jerusalem. As historical records stand, this date is not difficult to find. The history recorded in 1 Maccabees is quite definite that, under Judas and his brethren, the defeat of the Syrian armies enabled the Maccabees under Judas to retake Jerusalem. The Maccabean chronicler writes first of their determination: 'But Judas and his brethren said, "Behold, our enemies are discomfited: let us go up to cleanse the holy place and to dedicate it afresh." And all the army were gathered together and they went up to Mount Sion.' (1 Macc. 4:36–37, *RV*). He follows this with a description of what they found: 'and they saw the sanctuary laid waste, and the altar profaned, and the gates burned up, and shrubs growing in the courts as in a forest or as on one of the mountains, and the priest's chambers pulled down; so they rent their clothes, and made great lamentation, and put ashes upon their heads.' (1 Macc 4:38–39). After much mourning they took action:

'and they cleansed the holy place, and bare out the stones of defilement into an unclean place' (1 Macc. 4:43). After much rebuilding, repair and renewal the record continues: 'And they rose up early in the morning, on the five and twentieth day of the ninth month, which is the month *Chislev*, in the hundred and forty and eighth year' (1 Macc. 4:52, *RV*).

This passage gives us a date for cleansing of the sanctuary that is well documented in the Maccabean Chronicles as quoted and supported by Josephus. It is noted as the twenty-fifth of the month *Chislev* in the one hundred and forty-eigth year of the Seleucid dynasty. Translating this date into our chronology, and using 312 BC as the commencing year of the Seleucid dynasty, it becomes December 25, 164 BC. This date has been woven into Jewish history as the Feast of Dedication, of which the Maccabean records speak and Josephus[42] tells at length. It is meant to be a happy and joyous feast that is still observed in Judaism on the same date, from the time of the Maccabees.

Note: The Seleucid dynasty is dated from 312 BC

After the death of Alexander the Great, in 323 BC, Seleucus, one of his generals, gained the satrapy of Babylonia, which formed the core of his kingdom, but he was ousted by a certain usurper, called Antigonus, and Seleucus fled to Egypt. He regained the kingdom of Babylonia with a small task force in a most spectacular exploit in 312 BC and added other kingdoms, until he ruled the greater part of Alexander's empire, except for Egypt and Macedonia. The commencement of the Seleucid dynasty is reckoned from this date of regaining his kingdom – 312 BC. Counting regnal years by the Babylonian method, the one hundred and forty-eighth year would be 164 BC. The 20th *Chislev* becomes in the Julian calendar December 25.[43] This date becomes the base line (*terminus ad quem*) for the count of 2,300 days.

Dates important to the Maccabean chronicler are set out in the table on the following page with corresponding dates in our chronology.

The quotations from 1 Maccabees are as follows (all quotations from *RV*):

[43] We now use the Gregorian Calendar.

1 Macc. 1:10–11 – 'And there came forth out of them a sinful root, Antiochus Epiphanes, son of Antiochus the king, who had been a hostage at Rome, and he reigned in the hundred and thirty seventh year of the kingdom of the Greeks. In those days came there forth out of Israel transgressors of the law, and persuaded many, saying, "Let us go and make a covenant with the Gentiles ..."'

1 Macc. 1:14 – 'And they built a place of exercise in Jerusalem according to the laws of the Gentiles';

1 Macc. 1:15 – 'And they made themselves uncircumcised, and forsook the holy covenant, and joined themselves to the Gentiles, and sold themselves to do evil'.

1 Macc. 1:20–21 – 'And Antiochus, after that he had smitten Egypt, returned in the hundred and forty and third year, and went up against Israel and Jerusalem with a great multitude, and entered presumptuously into the sanctuary.'

1 Macc. 1:54 – 'And on the fifteenth day of *Chislev* in the hundred and forty and fifth year, they builded an abomination of desolation upon the altar, and in the cities of Judah on every side they builded idol altars.'

1 Macc. 4:52–56 – 'And they rose up early in the morning, on the five and twentieth day of the ninth month, which is the month *Chislev*, in the hundred and forty and eighth year, and offered sacrifice according to the law upon the new altar of burnt offerings which they had made. At what day and at what time the Gentiles had profaned it, even on that day was it dedicated afresh, with songs and harps and lutes, and with cymbals. And all the people fell upon their faces and worshipped and gave praise unto heaven which had given them good success. And they kept the dedication of the altar eight days and offered burnt offerings with gladness and sacrificed a sacrifice of deliverance and praise.'

The exact number of days is given so that Daniel, and, through him, the saints who would be facing those terrible days, would know and be able to mark the days off, one by one, knowing that their God, as shown in the careful numbering, cared about each pain.

TABLE 2

DATES FROM THE MACCABEES

The Seleucid dynasty is dated from 312 BC[44]

Reference	Seleucid Date	Julian Date	Event	
1 Macc. 1:10–11	137th year	175 BC	Antiochus Crowned	First Hellenists appear in Jerusalem
	138	174 BC	Jason as high priest	
	139	173 BC		
	140	172 BC		
1 Macc. 1:14–15	141	171 BC	Building of Greek Gymnasium	
1 Macc. 1:15	142	170 BC	Made themselves uncircumcised and forsook the holy covenant	Menelaus high priest +114 days
1 Macc. 1:20	143rd year	169 BC	Enters sanctuary on return from Egypt	+[365 days + 1]
	144	168 BC		+[365 days]
1 Macc. 1:54	145th year	167 BC	Abomination on altar	+[365 days]
	146	166 BC		+[365 days + 1]
	147	165 BC		+[365 days]
1 Macc. 4:52	148th 20th *Chislev*	164BC Dec. 25	Sanctuary cleansed	+[359 days]
			Total	**2,300 Days**

The commencing date for them would be no problem – they would know exactly when the sanctuary was defiled and faithful Israelites could no longer worship there. Their interest would be fastened on the end of the period. Looking at the historical records, the

[44] For the importance of this date see *ODCW*, p. 690.

complexity of this Hellenistic age, and the paucity of historians, make it difficult to determine the exact date for the commencement of the 2,300 days. The main sources available to us are the Books of the Maccabees, Josephus, Herodotus, and the records of the nations involved, as well as the data obtained by archaeology, from inscriptions on monuments and tombstones.

If the date given in the Maccabean record is accepted (most authorities, including Josephus, agree with it) then the closing date can be ascertained, as shown, to be December 25, 164 BC. This enables us to track back, as shown in Table 2, to the date for the opening of the period, characterised by the defiled sanctuary. From the table it is clear that this must fall somewhere in the month of September 170 BC. There is an uncertainty about leap years, which could alter this figure within a day or so. If the figure of 114 days is correct, as required to make the 2,300 days, this would take us to September 22.

If weight is placed on the verb 'cleansed', it can be clearly seen that the emphasis falls on the period when the Temple was first defiled and not on the later episode of the 'abomination of desolation' that followed inevitably. Thus the search is for the date when it became impossible for the faithful to recognise the Temple as the House of God. As shown in Table 2, the date when Antiochus entered the tabernacle (169 BC) and the date when he placed the idol on the altar (167 BC) are both too late to fit the timetable. It is suggested that this took place after the accession of Antiochus to the throne (175 BC), which excited the Hellenist party in Jerusalem. In 172 BC Jason[45] (the brother of the godly high priest Onias III), who led the Hellenists in Jerusalem, bribed the always poverty-stricken Antiochus Epiphanes with 360 talents of silver to appoint him (Jason) as high priest in place of his brother (Onias). He promised to reorganise Jerusalem as a Greek city-state and call it 'Antiocheia', of which he would provide the register of citizens, and also establish a training school for young male citizens. Antiochus took both the money and the opportunity to Hellenise Judaea from the inside and did as he was asked. The Maccabean record is clear – Jason did as he promised: 'He brought in new customs forbidden by the law; for he eagerly established a Greek place of exercise under the citadel itself; and caused the noblest of young men to wear the Greek cap. And thus there was an extreme of Greek fashions, and an

[45] Errington, *A History of the Hellenistic World*, p. 270.

advance of an alien religion, by reason of the extreme profaneness of Jason, that ungodly man and no high priest; so that the priests had no more any zeal for the services of the altar; but despising the sanctuary and neglecting the sacrifices, they hastened to enjoy what was provided in the *palaestra*.' (2 Macc. 4:11–20, *RV*). A '*palaestra*' is a wrestling, or more generally, an athletics school or hall.

The appointment of Jason as high priest seems to have taken place in 174 BC.[46] The Maccabean record tells of a surprise visit that Antiochus made to Jerusalem: 'Antiochus, learning [through his agent Apollonius at the Egyptian court] that Ptolemy had shewn himself ill affected toward his state, took thought for the security of his realm; wherefore, going by sea to Joppa, he travelled on to Jerusalem. And being magnificently received by Jason and the city, he was brought in with torches and shoutings. This done, he led his army down into Phoenicia' (2 Macc. 4:21–22). Taking place in 171 BC, this encouraged the treachery of Menelaus who, sent the next year (170 BC) to carry the yearly tribute to King Antiochus in Antioch, bribed Antiochus with a promise of three hundred talents of silver more than Jason. Antiochus accepted this extra bribe and Menelaus was appointed high priest in place of Jason. On his return to Jerusalem, with the army garrison at his command, Jason was displaced and fled the city. To pay the money promised in the bribe Menelaus entered the Temple and stole the golden vessels from the Temple to present them to Antiochus (2 Macc. 4:32), when he marched past Jerusalem in the autumn of 170 BC, as he opened what is known in history as the Sixth Syrian War between Syria and Egypt.[47] This may well mark the total desecration of that which had been the Holy Sanctuary in Israel. There is no record found in the historical records as to a specific day. The faithful in Israel would have no question in their minds – they would know exactly and, if they believed Daniel, their faith would bring much hope and consolation. In just such a way, believers in the Tribulation period will know the date of their relief from the trials and tears at the coming of the Son of Man.

It is suggested that the commencement of the period of desecration of the sanctuary, the *terminus a quo*, is a day in early autumn 170 BC.

[46] Bruce, *Israel and the Nations*, p.234.

[47] *OHCW*, p. 850.

CHAPTER 9

INTRODUCTION DATE 538 BC DANIEL IS 85 YRS

BABYLON HAS FALLEN to the Medo-Persian army under Cyrus in October of the previous year; it is the year 538 BC. Daniel is now eighty-five years old. In the previous years he has received two disturbing visions. The first one, received in 553 BC and recorded in chapter 7 (in the Aramaic language) had left him mentally perplexed (7:28); the second one, received two years later, in 551 BC, and recorded in chapter 8 (in the Hebrew language) had left him physically prostrated (8:27). Now, deeply burdened as to what lay ahead for the exiles of his people, Daniel prepares his heart to seek the face of his God. Responding to his concern, God graciously entrusts His servant with a further vision. Since he makes no comment on any mental or physical tension as result of this vision, it is tempting to assume that Daniel has had some of his perplexities and questions, arising from the two previous visions, answered in this prophecy. It will be a useful exercise to notice how God answers the unacknowledged concern that must have been in the mind of Daniel.

Each of the previous visions has dealt with the same period – the close of the 'times of the Gentiles'. The focus in each vision can be summarised from the previous discussion as follows:

Chapter 7

The Leader	*NT Titles*	*His Judgement*
The nations will rally behind a Gentile leader pictured as the 'Little Horn' (7:8).	'Man of Sin' (2 Thess. 2:3); 'beast from the sea' (Rev. 13:1–8).	'They shall take away his dominion, to consume and to destroy it' (7:26).

Chapter 8

The Leader	*NT Titles*	*His Judgement*
Israel will rally behind a Jewish leader called 'king of fierce countenance' (8:23).	'False prophet' (Rev. 16:13); 'beast from the earth' (Rev. 13:11–17); 'Antichrist' (1 Jn 2:18).	'He shall be broken without hand' (8:25).

Having pondered on these matters for the last thirteen years, amidst a changing political scene, with armies marching and cities falling, Daniel watches, possibly with some trepidation, the approach of a crisis date in the history of his people. With a bowed heart and Scripture open before him, he is found before his God in prayer and supplication. In answer to his exercise God gives this third vision to Daniel. There is no doubt this Divine revelation settles for Daniel some of the perplexities and problems arising out of the previous visions; for Daniel this is the key vision.

With surprising unanimity, prophetic students would agree with this judgement and see in this chapter the timeline along which God will act to fulfil His promises to Israel. This means that God unveils here the purpose that lay behind the sovereign choice of the nation through which He would bring into the world the promised Redeemer – called in this chapter 'Messiah the Prince'. For this reason the emphasis must fall on:

(a) The key nation on earth: the people of Israel, through whom the Messiah comes to earth;

(b) The key land on earth: the land of Israel, with its capital Jerusalem, is the key place, to which the Messiah comes;

(c) The key Person coming to earth: in this chapter identified as Messiah the Prince.

The final important matter dealt with in this vision is the date of the coming of the Messiah to earth. Daniel learns this and much more. He is given the Divine timetable for the Messiah-Redeemer that will involve the revelation of the Messiah on earth followed by His rejection ('cut off'), and His consequent return to earth. For the first time in prophetic truth, these are brought into a time relationship with each other. This timetable will set the stage for the emergence of the figures mentioned in these two chapters.

With the added light of the New Testament, it is clear that these two individuals are identifiable in the book of Revelation as the princes of Satan, who come onto the world stage under his supervision when we read 'and he [the dragon] stood upon the sand of the sea. And I saw a beast coming up out of the sea' (Rev. 13:1, *RV*). Again John speaks, 'And I saw another beast coming up out of the earth' (Rev. 13:11, *RV*). They are identified as:

(a) The 'beast from the sea' (Rev. 13:1–8) – the Gentile – the 'Coming Prince', arising from the nations;

(b) The 'beast from the earth' (Rev. 13:11–18) – the Jew – the leader of the 'many' in the nation of Israel at this time.

Now Daniel will understand that in this sacred programme there is not only coming a very special Person, identified by the title 'Messiah the Prince', but a specific period of 490 years 'have been determined' (*NET*), cut out of the timeline of history, within which period God will fulfil the promises made to Abraham concerning the land of Israel, and to David concerning the throne of Israel. In Messiah the Prince, the promises concerning King and Kingdom will all be realised.

Preliminary Questions

Question 1

Why is the Nation of Israel the Key to History and Prophecy?

The answer is very straightforward. God, in Divine sovereignty, chose this nation of Israel to be the nation through which He would bring in the promised Redeemer for sin-ruined men. Any review of history makes it clear that nations were arranged sovereignly by God, so that He could bring in this promised Redeemer through the right person, in the right place at the right time. The information given to Daniel in this chapter serves to identify this Redeemer, called here 'Messiah the Prince'.

The story begins after the fall of man in the Garden of Eden. God gave a promise concerning the seed of the woman (Gen. 3:15), which, as the purpose of God unfolded in history, was limited to the seed of Abraham (Gen. 22:18). In the working out of the plan of God the seed of Abraham was narrowed to Isaac, then to Jacob, then to Judah and finally to become the Seed of David (2 Sam. 7:12–16). The expected One would thus have claim to both the land of Israel (through Abraham) and the throne of Israel (through David). God had chosen the nation and the ancestral line through which the promised Redeemer, His Son, would come into manhood. Thus from Scripture it is clear that the chosen nation for this purpose was the nation of Israel (Mt. 1:1). Attention was drawn to the unique advent of this expected One by the prophet Isaiah when, at a crisis point, it seemed that the Messianic line hung upon one living person (Hezekiah), he cried, 'Behold, a virgin shall conceive, and bear a son, and shall call his name Immanuel' (Isa. 7:14). This promise was realised, centuries later, when Mary held a babe in her arms and obeyed the sacred instruction 'Thou ... shalt call His name Jesus' (Lk. 1:31). It can now be recognised how important a place the nation of Israel held, and still holds, in the counsels of God. God had ever before Him what is enshrined in the opening words of the Gospel of Matthew: 'The book of the generation of Jesus Christ, the son of David, the son of Abraham' (Mt. 1:1). This blessed Person, as the gospel records prove beyond question by word and work, was not only the son of Abraham, and the son of David, but 'declared to be the Son of God with power, according to the Spirit of holiness, by the resurrection from the dead' (Rom. 1:4). This One is both the Messiah of Israel and the Redeemer of mankind. Deity incarnate would be revealed in this Messiah, Who would come to earth through the nation of Israel. As Daniel considered, with bowed knee in the presence of his God, a captive nation, a ruined Jerusalem, a desolated land, he had every reason to wonder as to the reliability and viability of those ancient promises to Abraham and David. This prophecy is the answer to the exercised mind as to how God will keep those promises in Messiah the Prince. The important point in this passage is the 'when' of his coming; Daniel is given a date.

Question 2

Why is this Chapter the Key to Prophetic Revelation?

In the prophetic programme of God this chapter fills a vital role. So crucial to the understanding of prophecy is this chapter, and very particularly the last four verses (vv. 24–27), that it is often referred to by students of prophecy in words that seem to have been used first by Sir Edward Denny. He called these final four verses 'The Backbone of Prophecy'.[1] The matter of supreme interest lies in the fact that this is the only prophecy in all Scripture that links the coming of Christ to earth with an identifiable date in secular history. This particular date, as will be shown in the commentary on verse 25, can be ascertained from Scripture and, when secular history is examined, it stands as a witness to the God Who knows the future. Thus assured, the believer recognises the beginning of the countdown to the coming of the Messiah. In this Scripture God announced the date centuries before Christ appeared in history. So there was absolutely no reason why the nation of Israel, from this Scripture alone, should not have known the time of the Messiah's

[1] Tatford, *Daniel and His Prophecy*, p. 151. He gives no reference for the statement and it may have been taken from a public address.

sojourn on earth. The gospels clearly show that some did know and believe and were awaiting the Christ.[2]

For the believing Israelites much more information was open to them, through other prophetic voices. Prophets foretold (a) the place of His birth (Mic. 5:1–3); (b) the identification of the forerunner (Isa. 40:3–5); (c) the place of His opening ministry (Isa. 9:1–2); (d) the exact date of His presentation to the nation (v. 25). As a consequence the exact day of His death should have been known. It will be seen from the Gospel records that, while the majority of the religious leaders of Israel were unbelievers, there were individuals, perhaps not a few, in the nation who believed. Amongst others it is very clear that Mary of Bethany stands out as one who believed that Christ was to die at that particular Passover. In light of this knowledge she had made preparation. The Lord acknowledged her faith (Jn 12:7).

After the introductory verses (vv. 1–2), this chapter readily divides into two sections:

Section 1	**The Appeal of the Prophet**	**vv. 3–19**
Based on	(a) National Confession	(vv. 3–14)
	(b) Scriptural Claim	(vv. 15–18)
	(c) Personal Cry	(v. 19)
Section 2	**The Answer From Heaven**	**vv. 20–27**
Based on	(a) Dispatch of the Messenger	(vv. 20–23)
	(b) Declaration of the Messiah	(vv. 24–27)
	(The Prophecy of the Seventy Weeks)	

Verses 1–2 The Crisis and the Condition of the Nation

The careful wording of the first verse gives the date – a date that has a vital role in this exercise of Daniel. The year is 538 BC and even Babylon, under its new administration, must have taken a lesser place in Daniel's thoughts, as this date weighs upon his mind and brings its challenge. The challenge that Daniel faced, it is clear, arose from his consideration of the date in light of Scripture. It

[2] Amongst those who believed would be Simeon, who 'was waiting for the consolation of Israel' (Lk. 2:25); Anna, who was amongst those 'who looked for redemption in Jerusalem' (Lk. 2:38); and Joseph of Arimathaea, 'who also himself waited for the kingdom of God' (Lk. 23:51).

brought such deep concern that it led to a changed priority in his life, summed up in the expression – 'I set my face unto the Lord God'. Affairs of the mighty Medo-Persian Empire had to take second place as Daniel faced the issue in the presence of his God. This is 'the first year of Darius the son of Ahasuerus, of the seed of the Medes'. World-shaking events had taken place in recent months. Babylon had fallen to the Medo-Persian army, under Cyrus, some months before. A new empire dominated the world scene; Darius the Mede was the new king in Babylon, appointed personally by Cyrus the Persian. Daniel had already faced the new conditions in his experience amongst the lions but something of more importance weighed upon his heart and brought him to his knees in the presence of God.

Thirteen years have passed since the last vision (551–538 BC). World hegemony has changed hands; Babylon has changed rulers; Judaean captives are facing changed conditions. Daniel has come through two major crises:

(a) A National Event. The fall of Babylon was a world-shaking event. God had permitted Daniel a part to play when He used him to announce heaven's verdict (5:17–30) on Babylon, the 'golden city'. The decline of Babylon's power and the growing might of Medo-Persia under Cyrus were climaxed on that October night of the previous year (539 BC), when Babylon fell and King Belshazzar was slain. Daniel would call to mind the image of Nebuchadnezzar's dream and the change of metal from the head of gold to the breast and arms of silver (2:32). He would, doubtless, wonder afresh at the exactness of the Word of the Lord – he knew, and the world knew, that gold was a fitting symbol associated with Babylon, while Medo-Persia was always linked with silver. One major issue that concerned everyone in the empire was that the taxes imposed by Cyrus, from his capital, Susa, had all to be paid in silver. Each day now he handled that metal.

(b) A Personal Experience. Daniel's first experience of oligarchic rule in the Medo-Persian Empire had been very trying, but the outcome was a testimony to the power of Daniel's God. His experience in the lions' den (6:16–23) had shown how God can deliver those who trust Him – a comfort for tested saints in any age. The lesson was plain: the most egotistical of rulers, and the most corrupt of administrations, may only go as far as God permits in their attacks on the people of God. In His own time, God will deliver His people and destroy their enemies. This experience of

Daniel gave a clear warning as to the character of the new Medo-Persian rule; at the same time it also gave persecuted believers amongst the Jewish captives an assurance of the ability of God to deliver His own.

Note 1: The Timing of Chapter 9 in Relation to Chapter 6 – Personal

Since this vision was given in the same year as Daniel was thrown to the lions, some argue that the vision came first. This is a possible sequence and some expositors support it.[3] However, three considerations favour placing this vision after the lions' den experience:

(a) The title – 'greatly beloved' – with which Gabriel addresses Daniel (v. 23) suggests the esteem of heaven for a tested saint who has already come through a very severe test with flying colours. The term 'greatly beloved' is more accurately translated as 'greatly desired' or possibly 'greatly delighted in' (Newberry *in loc.*). This bears testimony to heaven's evaluation of a man who had already faced the ultimate test of loyalty to his God; now God can entrust to him one of the great prophecies of the coming Messiah.

(b) The calm – there is no suggestion in this chapter that Daniel is worried about disaffected colleagues or plots against him. Daniel is free to concentrate his mind on the condition of his people rather than concern about the plotting of disgruntled courtiers. That trouble appears to have been settled and he is free to face the real issue on his heart – the date!

(c) The date – since Darius was appointed by Cyrus before he left Babylon in the winter of 539 BC, the first year of Darius, according to the Babylonian method of calculating regnal years, would begin at *Nisan* 538 BC, which leaves room for Daniel's promotion, the jealousy of his colleagues, and the night with the lions before this vision.

Note 2: The King – Darius – Political

Darius is not a personal name but a dynastic name and there are a number of Medo-Persian kings who bear this name. This is the same Darius as Daniel introduced into this record after the fall of Babylon (5:31; 6:1).[4] This Darius was 'made king over the realm of the Chaldeans'; a most unusual way to describe the receiving of a kingdom unless it is to indicate that behind him was a higher

[3] Walvoord, *Daniel: the Key to Prophetic Revelation*, p. 202.
[4] See Appendix 2.

earthly authority who put him there. This fits the circumstances of the man suggested in the comments on chapter 5:31 since it is clear that Cyrus, before the end of 539 BC, installed Darius as viceroy in Babylonia, with the title of king. In both passages (6:1; 9:1), Darius is identified as of the Medes; the significance of this lies in the contrast with Cyrus, who was of Persian origin. The conciliatory policy towards a defeated foe, adopted by Cyrus throughout the empire, brought into his government able men from the Median Empire – a policy that succeeded in keeping peace and pre-empting the rise of a rebellion under an able man. Two points need clarification:

(a) The realm over which Darius was made king is called 'the realm of the Chaldeans'. The term 'Chaldeans', as shown in comments on their first appearance in this book (1:4, see also 2:2), is used in two different ways. One sense describes a special group of the wise men, ethnically Chaldeans, but with special skill and learning in both astronomy and astrology. The second sense is strictly ethnic and refers to the descendants of the race originally inhabiting part of southern Babylonia (prior to 1000 BC), known then as Chaldea. Abraham came from Ur of the Chaldees. This is the way the term is used here. So the realm over which Darius was made king, including Babylon as its capital city, extended over the ancient territory of Chaldea, in southern Babylonia.[5] This was certainly an extensive empire but only a fraction of the great Medo-Persian Empire over which Cyrus ruled from his capital city, Susa.

(b) It should also be pointed out that this Darius is called 'the son of Ahasuerus' – a man unknown beyond this single reference either in Scripture or in any known historical record.[6] The date shows that he is not the same Ahasuerus as the king who took Esther for his wife (Es. 1:1); this latter king reigned half a century later and is identified by his other name, Xerxes I (485–465 BC). This is one of the matters that may be clarified by further archaeological research and the decipherment of further cuneiform documents.

Note 3: The Cause of Daniel's Spiritual Concern – Preparation

Daniel, as the most senior executive in Babylon, would have the date always under his eye. For Daniel, its significance is not

[5] Recent excavations and recently discovered inscriptions point to the inclusion of 'The Realm beyond the River' in the realm controlled by Darius. This would make his realm indistinguishable from the previous Babylonian Empire.

[6] See Appendix 3.

political but arises from Scripture, as he records: 'I Daniel understood by books'; a literal translation stresses the article before 'books' – pointing specifically to particular scrolls, indeed the sacred records from Israel's past. The five foundational books (the Torah) had come down from Moses, whom God used to deliver the nation from Egypt. To the sacred books – the Pentateuch – had been added the sacred histories from the times of Joshua and Samuel. The writings of prophets accredited of God were acknowledged as part of this sacred lore. It is a remarkable fact that, though the nation of Israel refused to obey the word of the Lord through the prophets, in this case specifically from Jeremiah, they still preserved and revered their writings. King Jehoiakim may cut Jeremiah's scroll into pieces and burn it (Jer. 36:22–23), but God saw to its replacement, so that His word would be preserved (Jer. 36:27–28). No council adjudicated on the canonicity of the writing of a prophet, but from an accredited prophet, as Jeremiah was, his writings were accepted as 'the Word of the Lord' from the time they were written down. Reverence, Israel was prepared to give to the Word; but obedience – that was another matter entirely! The writing that Daniel had before him (Jer. 25:10–11) is the written record of a message that God gave to Jeremiah, who first preached it in Jerusalem in the year 606 BC (Jer. 25:1). This was the terrible year when Nebuchadnezzar captured Jerusalem, and Daniel, with a band of young men from the leading families in Judaea, was carried off as a captive to Babylon. This was the year that the storm of Divine chastisement burst upon Israel for their disobedience to the Word of God and their defiance of the prophets God had raised up to warn them. Amid unsparing exposure of their sin, Jeremiah offers just a glimpse of consolation for an exercised Israelite. While Babylon had been allowed to invade and enslave the nation of Israel, this captivity was not to be open-ended but for a specified period. The period was set by Jehovah as seventy years. This limit did not offer much consolation to the disobedient generation, who had incurred the discipline, but it did offer hope to a repentant Israelite. Repentance offered the prospect of restoration and a hope for their families. The word of the Lord was clear: 'And this whole land shall be a desolation, and an astonishment; and these nations shall serve the king of Babylon seventy years' (Jer. 25:11). Recalling the tears of deportation, followed by the years of desolation, Daniel could draw consolation from the assurance that God had set a time limit on their years of subjugation to a Gentile nation. Now an old

realisation seems to burst upon him that, with the period of discipline almost over, there can be a national restoration. An exercised heart will ask – what is to be done? What does believing God demand? Reading on in Jeremiah's neglected letter (Jer. 29: 1–28) Daniel discovers a message for him – placed there for his direction, sixty years before this date. Not, of course, for him alone, but for every heart in Israel burdened in the same matter. Ezra's record shows there must have been quite a number of such believers (Ezra 1:5–6). The message for such hearts is plain and very pointed: 'For thus saith the LORD, "That after seventy years be accomplished at Babylon I will visit you, and perform My good word toward you, in causing you to return to this place"'(Jer. 29:10). The closely following words bring the challenge 'Then shall ye call upon Me and ye shall go and pray unto Me, and I will hearken unto you.' Daniel is obedient – now he has the promise of his God for this very situation. In light of this Daniel makes his personal commitment – 'I set my face unto the Lord'. A deliberate action – just as deliberate as his refusal to eat the king's meat (1:8); just as deliberate as opening his window toward Jerusalem (6:10) – but this time it is not in testimony to men, but a definite longing to see the promise of his God fulfilled to his people. Daniel deliberately turned away from any earthy distraction to consecrate time and person to this purpose. The affairs of an earthly empire take second place now!

Note the following features of Daniel's prayer:

(a) The Person Addressed. Daniel records carefully that it was the 'word of the LORD [that] came to Jeremiah' (v. 2), where the word for 'Lord' is 'Jehovah'. This is the first time the word 'Jehovah' has been used in the book and, in fact, this is the only chapter in which it does occur and it occurs seven times (vv. 2, 4, 10, 13, 14 (twice), 20). This clearly implies that the covenant relationship between Israel and their God is in view. Taking his stand on that covenantal relationship, Daniel sets his face and addresses the Lord God (*Adonay ha'Elohim*). Both of these titles are plurals, the Hebrew plural of intensity in each case. Absolute sovereignty is stressed in *Adonay* (means 'master') – the One to be obeyed; *Elohim* stresses the awesomeness of majesty – the One to be worshipped. Daniel is conscious that this Majestic Sovereign holds absolute sway over creation (*Elohim*) and over the creature (*Adonay*). However mighty the empires of earth may appear they do the will of Daniel's Lord God – no-one can overrule Him!

(b) The Plea Expressed. The verb 'to seek' suggests a definite object before the mind of Daniel. However, with a consciousness deserving of our emulation, he recognises that certain matters have first to be faced. Transgression, sin, and iniquity that have caused the present condition cannot be ignored. These matters must be admitted and confessed before his request can be presented to a holy God. In fact, it is only at the very end of his prayer that Daniel allows the cry from the heart to be put into words: 'O Lord, hear; O Lord, forgive; O Lord, hearken and do; defer not, for Thine own sake, O my God (*Elohim*).' The thrice repeated 'Lord' in this cry is the word '*Adonay*' – the Sovereign One (the title used here and in vv. 7, 8, 9, 15, 16, 19). The matter lies in His hands.

(c) The Practice Evidenced. Two words convey the essentials in his attitude before God as he seeks the goal he had before him; he uses *'prayer'*, a word that embraces 'intercession'. An essential word – the people have sinned and an intercessor is demanded; *'supplication'*, a word that can be translated 'entreaty', and this embraces the thought of mercy – sin demands punishment; mercy withholds what sin deserves. A plea for preservation from deserved punishment demands reality before God. Reality for Daniel demands positive action – the very necessities of life take second place: food gives way to fasting, normal clothing is replaced with sackcloth, and the usual unguents used on the head are replaced with ashes. In the culture of that day, these were the signs of a contrite heart in the presence of God (Ezra 8:23; Neh. 9:1; Es. 4:1; Job 2:12; Jon. 3:5–6). The petitioner has become a penitent.

Verses 4–14 Confession of Departure

Verse 4 It is instructive to note with what reverence Daniel draws near to God. He acknowledges that in a land dominated by dead idols he has personal dealings with the living One (6:20); this living One, through his experience with the lions (6:21–22), has been proven by Daniel to be 'my God (*Elah*)'. He can now address Him as the Almighty (*Adonay Elohim*); but, as an indication of that which lies heavily on his heart, he engages with Him using the sacred covenantal name 'LORD' ('*Yahweh*', Hebrew) translated 'Jehovah'.[10] This is the covenantal name that God used to reveal Himself to Abraham, to Isaac and to Jacob; it was the name by which God

[10] See *NET, in loc.*

Almighty introduced Himself to Moses as the Deliverer of the nation:

> I have also heard the groaning of the children of Israel, whom the Egyptians keep in bondage; and I have remembered my covenant. Wherefore say unto the children of Israel, I am the LORD [Jehovah] and I will bring you out from under the burdens of the Egyptians' (Exod. 6:2–8).[11]

It is the covenantal name used with the nation of Israel.

The first part of Daniel's prayer is simply confession (vv. 4–14). It is a personal burden as he acknowledges in his opening words – 'made my confession'. Yet it is very soon apparent that he is embracing the sin of the nation as his own. This becomes very clear as we hear that burdened cry from a troubled heart: 'we have sinned'. Repeated four times (vv. 5, 8, 11, 15), each cry throws light on another feature of the sin that has wrought such havoc in Israel. In this Daniel has left a pattern. Godly saints down the ages have followed his example and identified themselves with the sin of their people in the same way. Scriptural examples are to be found in the prayer of Ezra in 458 BC (Ezra 9) and of Nehemiah in 445 BC (Neh. 9) as they sought the recovery of their people.

Daniel approaches God with becoming reverence and fear: 'O Lord, the great and dreadful God' tells of the awe in which Daniel holds his God; not a trace of unbecoming familiarity. 'O' is a particle that in English introduces a plea and becomes almost 'please'. 'Lord' is '*Adonay*' – a plural of sovereignty – and is followed by a word from the root 'to fear' that is best translated 'one to be feared' or – in one word – 'awesome' (*NIV*). Daniel is well aware of the distance between Deity and mere humanity.

Awesome He is! Yet He is known in the experience of His people for His faithfulness. No failure can be attributed to this God – keeping 'the covenant and [the] mercy'; both nouns carry the article and point to the double link between God and this people. There are the promises in the covenant that speak of His presence, His provision, and His protection. At the same time, behind the promises there lies the passion involved in the word 'mercy' (*chesed*), which means 'covenantal loving-kindness'. The word

[11] The difficulty of linking the covenant name, Jehovah, with Abraham, Isaac and Jacob is cleared up when it is grasped that the word order demands a question mark at the end of the (rhetorical) sentence – 'But by my name Jehovah was I not known unto them?' See lengthy discussion under Exod. 6:3 in *NET*.

'mercy' (*chesed*) is sometimes translated 'loving kindness', but to draw out the uniqueness of the word a better translation would be 'steadfast love'. So committed is God that even failure on the part of His people does not turn away His love. God does not fail – His love is steadfast; God loves them still. On the other hand, His people fail, and His righteous character demands judgement – yet so committed is this God that He will search for grounds to forgive them. The failure of this nation, the object of His covenantal love, to repent under prophetic rebuke has led directly to the captivity. Even now, it would seem, Daniel cannot detect any clear signs of true repentance in those so deeply indebted to a gracious God. Its absence is of deep concern to the exercised heart of Daniel. He knows that for forgiveness and recovery to take place repentance is absolutely vital. This is now his burden.

Verse 5 Confession of Disobedience

Disobedience to the Scriptures – God's Precepts

This consciousness of the necessity of repentance leads Daniel to identify with his people and cry 'we have sinned'. In deep concern he exposes sin in its many guises. In doing this he uses four different verbs in a climactic way – the shades get darker in each verb: (a) 'Sinned' – the verb comes from the field of archery and means 'to miss the mark' – failure to reach the Divine standard; (b) 'Committed iniquity' – refers to the treatment of others, to treat others unjustly or to pervert or twist what is good to a wrong purpose – to do harm; (c) 'Done wickedly' – means with open eyes and with deliberate intent to go against what is known to be right, an evil action with intent to harm; (d) 'Rebelled' – reveals that rebellion against God in the hearts of men is the root of the trouble. God's people would not obey God's 'precepts' and 'judgments', or we might say 'accept His commandments and acknowledge His decisions'. They refused to obey the Word of God or, to use the OT term, the Law of God. This verse can be summed up in one statement – Israel had the Scripture and would not obey it.

Verse 6 Confession of Defiance

Defiance of the Servants – God's Prophets

As well as disobedience to the written word Israel added defiance of the spoken word through the prophets whom God sent for their recovery. Refusal to obey Scripture led God in grace to send His servants the prophets to speak words that witnessed to His unchanging love, unchallengeable righteousness and unsullied holiness. The door was always open for repentance and recovery, but Israel closed their ears and refused to listen to the prophets sent by God down the years. Divine discipline had to follow. This verse may be summed up in the statement – Israel had the prophets and would not listen to them.

Verses 7–8 Confusion of Face

Defiance of Sinners – God's People (by profession)

The claim of the covenant disobeyed, and the call of the prophets defied, the condition of Israel now stands in sharp contrast to the character of the God they professed to know. Righteousness belonged to God but shame was their portion. 'Confusion of faces' is better translated 'shame of face' (as in Ps. 44:15) or paraphrased as 'covered with shame' (*NIV*). It is used twice in the paragraph. First it is used nationally and geographically of the whole nation (v. 7) whether 'they are near' or 'afar off'. Shame must be upon every single Israelite – even the men of Judah (especially those of Jerusalem) – and including all the men of Israel. Their present captivity (shame) is a result of their own conduct, called their transgression – a wilful stepping over the Law. Their faces should be hidden in shame! In the 'us', Daniel links himself again with his nation. Secondly, the expression 'shame of face' (v. 8) is used to emphasise that all classes in the nation must feel this shame – none are excluded. Shame 'to our kings, to our princes, and to our fathers' – all must accept the shame attached to the captivity and acknowledge the cause – 'we have sinned against Thee'. Notice the first person plural pronoun again, as Daniel accepts his share of responsibility and confesses it in the presence of God. Daniel is surely recalling the shame:

(a) 'to our kings' – King Jehoiakim was imprisoned in Babylon for thirty-seven years (2 Kgs 25:27); King Zedekiah had his sons slain before his eyes then, his eyes put out, he was carried to Babylon, in 586 BC (2 Kgs 25:7);

(b) 'to our princes' (see 1 Kgs 4:1–6) – the local leaders whom God raised up in Judah in the monarchy. The record of Jeremiah shows how they were shamefully treated by their Babylon overlords;

(c) 'to our fathers' – not the national fathers but the responsible leaders of households, men who had seen their households torn apart and their sons and daughters carried into slavery. Daniel himself must have felt the shame most keenly.

Verses 9–14 Claim to Grace

The nation has no claim to any blessing. In fact they fully deserved 'the curse' (v. 11) now upon them. Daniel recognises that his nation lies under that comprehensive curse imposed by God upon disobedience to the Law, spelt out so carefully by Moses (Deut. 28:15–68). Any claim for restoration must rest upon the character of their Sovereign God (*Adonay Elohim*). It is to be noted how gladly Daniel turns from the condition of Israel and unfolds the only ground of hope – the character of their God. If 'righteousness' was His sole attribute there was no hope (v. 7), but another attribute did offer a genuine hope. He is a God to Whom belong '[the] mercies and [the] forgivenesses' (v. 9) – both words have the article and both are plurals – most likely the Hebrew plural of intensity. The 'mercies', or 'compassions', is a different word from that used previously (v. 4); in a physiological context it would be translated 'bowels', but here it is used metaphorically of the inward longings and pity of a God Who would go to any righteous length to withhold from the guilty what is richly deserved. The word 'forgivenesses', used only of God, appears to be coined to spell out what an offended God can do – bestow what cannot be deserved or earned[12]: mercies withhold what we deserve; 'forgivenesses' bring what we never could earn. The heart of Daniel bows before the richness and fulness of the forgiveness that is found alone in the character of the God of Israel.

The charges are clear and concise. The rebellion of the nation was the result of disobedience. The root of the word 'disobedience' is in the verb 'to listen'. Failure to listen to the prophets led to going their own way (Isa. 53:6), which is rebellion against God. The repetition of the name 'the LORD' (Jehovah) displays the ingratitude of a disobedient people to their covenant Lord. Grace lay in the covenant love of Jehovah, but even when the 'voice of the LORD' was heard through the prophets, they still persisted in defiant disobedience until grace had to be replaced by government.

[12] *OTWS*, p. 174.

Israel not only 'transgressed' (v. 11), a word meaning 'to pass or step over' the Law, but when Hosea, Isaiah and Jeremiah laid its demands explicitly before them they still 'departed' – they put as great a distance as they could between the prophet and themselves. 'Departed' is translated 'turning aside' (*RV*), and suggests a desire to hide from the challenge of the Word. This invites the curse spelled out so carefully by Moses (Deut. 28:15–68); a curse confirmed by the oath of God, conveying the awful solemnity of what has overtaken the nation. Disobedience leading to departure has brought the doom promised in the Law. Daniel recognises that he himself is under that very curse when he prays: 'therefore the curse is poured out upon us'.

The cause of the whole situation was the sin of the nation; the curse is the consequence of that sin; the consequence of the curse is the 'great evil', which here can be translated 'calamity' (*NET*) or 'disaster' (*NIV*). That disaster was the Babylonian invasion and the captivity they were presently enduring. There was no possible defence. Isaiah had warned that the enemy would come in like a flood (Isa. 59:19). Few listened and the army of Nebuchadnezzar swept the nation away (2 Chron. 36:17–21). Jerusalem was left as a testimony to Divine judgement. Daniel invites himself to scan history and scan the nations ('under the whole heaven') – Jerusalem stands unparalleled as a symbol of a judged city. The great 'evil' (vv. 12, 13, 14) – the capture and desolation of Jerusalem, because of the disobedience and departure of his people, has been 'brought' (vv. 12, 14) and has 'come' (v. 13), in spite of the warnings of Moses and the prophets. Against 'us' – again Daniel identifies with his people – and against 'our judges' – present leaders of the nation – and against 'our kings' – those in places of national leadership – the judgement has come. And yet one can almost hear the break in the voice of Daniel as he strikes the saddest note of all! The Divine discipline has brought no response from that guilty people. There is: (a) no penitential prayer being made in the presence of the Lord (the fourth time 'Jehovah' is used in the chapter); (b) no pointed plea asking for a change of direction ('might turn from our iniquities') in the nation; and (c) no painful perception of the misunderstanding (of Divine 'truth') that did not allow sin and its sentence to be clearly linked in their spiritual understanding.

In confession before God, Daniel has already acknowledged His righteousness (v. 7); the calamity upon Israel is fully deserved. God's mercies and forgiveness (v. 9) can be their only ground of recovery.

Now Daniel bases his claim upon the justice of Jehovah (mentioned in vv. 14 and 16). When he says, 'the LORD our God is righteous in all His works', it carries the thought of 'Jehovah El is just'. His righteousness demanded punishment for sin. Now, that same righteousness that demanded the execution of the sentence will not allow the curse to continue indefinitely. Justice will set a just limit to the judgement. He will assess the measure of the pain and select the moment when righteously 'the evil' (the captivity) can be lifted. It is for this moment of deliverance that Daniel is praying.

Verses 15–19 The Cry of the heart

Verse 15 In the previous verses (vv. 4–14), Daniel has used the name Jehovah five times. Now he addresses the 'Lord our God' (Adonai Elohim). This is the sovereign God Who acts amongst the nations of earth. For Israel as a nation, there stands the record of their deliverance from the bondage of Egypt, which bore testimony to the power of Jehovah. Daniel speaks of it and recognises that in it his God 'hast gotten Thee renown' (*AV*) or 'made thee a name' (*RSV*). Testimony to the power of Jehovah was borne throughout the world. By implication, Daniel awaits another deliverance, from Babylon, so that the name of the Lord would gain fresh renown throughout the earth. Just as God smote the gods of Egypt (Exod. 12:12), so in the experience of Daniel all the gods of Babylon had already been smitten (2:47; 3:28; 4:37; 6:26–27), and now was the moment for Jehovah to display His power in rescuing His people from bondage once again. He bases this plea for Divine intervention on the acknowledgement by the nation of their sin. With brevity and simplicity, he confesses in his prayer for the nation for the third time – 'we have sinned, we have done wickedly'.

Verse 16 Petition 1 – Realise the Sanctification: 'Thy Holy Mountain'

At this point of confession a cry rises from the heart of Daniel for Israel and for Jerusalem. With the thought of the just God (v. 14) in mind, Daniel asks relief for his nation that has suffered so much, and so justly. He cries 'Let Thine anger and Thy fury be turned away' – the sin of Israel has resulted in calamity. God's settled displeasure – 'Thine anger' – has resulted in outbreaks of sweeping judgement –'Thy fury' – because of their refusal to listen to the voice of the weeping prophet, Jeremiah. It is suggested that Daniel is possibly thinking of the three particular invasions by Babylonian forces as judgements on Jerusalem – in 606 BC, in 597 BC and in 586 BC. This interpretation can be supported by the fact that Jerusalem, as the capital city, bears the guilt of the past, and now, in the present, bears testimony to the government of God – it stands a ruin! The city that was intended to bring delight to the heart of God now brings only shame – 'a reproach to all that are about us', or 'are mocked by all our neighbours' (*NET*). Daniel cries specifically for 'Thy holy mountain' – Mount Zion, in Jerusalem. At that moment it stood a monument to Divine judgement – defiled, desecrated, and destroyed! Amazing to think that here it is still called 'holy'. It is so, because God, from King David's day, had set that city apart for Himself. This purpose stands unchanged and unchangeable while earth endures. At the very mention of 'holy', the consciousness of Israel's sin bears upon the conscience of Daniel and a further confession bursts from his lips – 'our sins, and ... the iniquities of our fathers'. It would seem as if Daniel has grasped the truth concerning his God. Righteous yet forgiving, the God Who brought desolation is the very same God Who, on the ground of repentance, can grant deliverance.

Verse 17 Petition 2 – Rebuild the Sanctuary: 'Thy Sanctuary'

This truth of the God of recovery moves Daniel to fresh prayer and even more urgent supplications – note the plural – for the Lord's people, the Lord's city, and the Lord's sanctuary, remembering that this will be 'for the Lord's sake'. The Name *Adonay*, used four times, stresses the absolute rights of God amongst the nations – He is Sovereign. All prayer from believing hearts on earth must be directed, not to their selfish interests, but to the glory of the Sovereign Lord Who works out His will amongst the nations of earth. Daniel acknowledges that the removal of the curse, the restoration of the city and the rebuilding of the Temple is not primarily for their blessing but 'for the Lord's sake'. His honour demanded the removal of this testimony; His honour demands its restoration. Directed to the Sovereign Lord, the cry of Daniel is 'cause Thy face to shine upon Thy sanctuary that is desolate'. The 'face to shine' is an idiomatic way of expressing favour towards an object. Blessing must follow the favour. Such is the thought in the priestly blessing (Num. 6:25) echoed in the prayer of the psalmist: 'Turn us again, O God, and cause Thy face to shine; and we shall be saved' (Ps. 80:3). That sanctuary, destroyed in 586 BC, would be rebuilt for the Lord's glory[13] and consecrated afresh in 516 BC. The seventy year 'desolations' (Jer. 25:9) had in Daniel's time yet to run their course.

Verse 18 Petition 3 – Restore the City: 'Thy City'

The cries of Daniel seem to mount in intensity as his eye sweeps over the desolation that sin has wrought and moves from the Temple Mount to the city. The same word – 'desolation' – describes that city which, once the joy of the whole earth (Ps. 48:2), lies at this time desolate (v. 2). He cries to his God from an anguished heart to 'incline Thine ear'; as if God is bending low to catch the sob of the saint. He cries to his God to 'open Thine eyes'; as if calling upon God to look carefully at this total ruin of the city. These anthropomorphic expressions graphically picture Daniel's desire that God will hear the sob, and respond to the sight of the misery of His people. This is no ordinary city but the sacred city, 'called by Thy Name'. In the light of its present condition – 'desolations' is the plural of intensity – Daniel is saying, 'Can our cry be denied and Thine honour remain undiminished?' This petition for restoration is not made on the grounds of their conduct but on the grounds of the character of their God. 'For our righteousnesses (pl.)' cannot be the ground for our appeal – we have none – our plea rests on the character of God; 'for Thy great mercies (pl.)' – they are many. Unable to meet Divine standards, we look to Thee – for mercy – that which withholds what we deserve; and for grace, that which bestows what we never could have deserved or earned.

Verse 19 Specific Petition

Now, as Daniel comes to the close of his petition before this Sovereign Lord (*Adonay*), his words are brief and ejaculatory: 'O Lord, hear; O Lord, forgive; O Lord, hearken and do'! Then there comes the request that climaxes his prayer. The earlier cries have been preparatory. Daniel knows what his people need at this point. On the positive side – they need to be 'heard' – their petition listened to; they need to be 'forgiven' – their sins pardoned. Now Daniel adds the negative 'defer not'. The 'doing' required is for the Lord to wait no longer; the captivity has lasted from 606 BC to 538

[13] The history is clear: the Temple was rebuilt in the years 536–516 BC. The foundation was laid under Zerubbabel (536 BC) and the Temple finished under the ministry of Haggai and Zechariah (520–516 BC).

BC – sixty-eight years have passed; the seventy-year period is moving to its close. Babylon has been replaced by Medo-Persia as the world empire. The Scripture awaits fulfilment; the saints think of repatriation; all await political action, and this must come from the Sovereign Lord. Daniel, as he closes his prayer, views the priorities correctly: (a) 'For Thine own sake, O my God'; (b) 'For Thy city; and (c) '[For] Thy people'. We might paraphrase the last note of his prayer: 'Both the city and the people are called by Thy Name and it is in Thine interest and for Thy glory to restore them to Thy land'. Release of His people and their return to the land God had given them would be the first step to the rebuilding of the sanctuary and the restoration of the city.[14]

Section2 The Answer from Heaven vv. 20–27

(a) Dispatch of the Messenger vv. 20–21

These four verses give the background setting for the important prophecy of the seventy weeks. That setting unfolds very simply as follows:

Verse 20 The Appeal of the Penitent

Daniel had reached a very definite point in his concern for his nation at this crucial time politically for earth. Another day was well gone; it was drawing near the time of the evening sacrifice (three o'clock in the afternoon) and he had just reached the critical moment, when he felt he could put into direct speech the burden of his heart before his God. The cry had come – 'defer not' – and clearly he was about to tell his God what to do without delay! The hours had slipped away as, without mealtimes, he had been occupied 'speaking', 'praying', 'confessing my sin and the sin of my people Israel' and 'presenting my supplication'. These activities, defined by the same four verbs as in the earlier verses (vv. 1–19), were just about to be climaxed by the cry of his heart – when he was suddenly interrupted. Daniel had been engaged with 'Jehovah Elohim' – the covenant-keeping God of Israel. Jehovah (the covenantal name) is used here for the seventh and last time in the chapter. Jehovah's people and Jehovah's 'holy mountain' (Zion) were burdening the heart of Daniel; both had come under Divine

[14] When God fulfilled this petition – the first wave of people returned in 536 BC under Zerubbabel, the Temple was rebuilt by 516 BC and the city rebuilt by 396 BC (Malachi's ministry).

discipline for sin and desolation reigned. The date too was important and Daniel could see that God was about to act, but in what way? About to put his burden of heart into words, he was interrupted. A Divine messenger touched him.

Verse 21 The Angel and his Appearance

Even after thirteen years Daniel recognised the man who had interpreted the previous vision for him and, when he had fainted, had awakened him with a touch of his hand (8:15–19). The touch this time is not to awaken the sleeper but to alert the supplicant. His prayer had been heard in heaven. The word 'man' (Hebrew '*ish*') does not deny his angel status, but draws attention to the form angels adopt when on missions on earth, and links him directly with the interpreter of the previous vision. 'At the beginning' does not refer to the first vision (7:1) for Gabriel only appears in the second (8:15), but points to the first appearance of Gabriel to Daniel. The verb translated 'to fly swiftly' has given expositors much trouble since it can be traced to two different roots: one means 'to fly swiftly' (*AV*) and the other 'to be weary'. The etymological argument may be followed in Wood[15] but, since weariness is the last thing that one would associate with an angel, the *AV* translation has been generally accepted. However, the latest edition of the *NET Bible* (2009) has a very interesting translation: 'the man Gabriel ... was approaching me in my state of extreme weariness'. In this case, the translators refer the extreme weariness, not to the angel, but to Daniel – which presents a more likely picture, and is most probably correct. To assume from this verb that angels have wings seems too weighty a deduction and lacks support from other Scriptures. These considerations would suggest that Gabriel is present in human-like form and not merely in a vision. The reference to 'vision' (v. 23) is best understood as referring to the vision in chapter 8, on which Gabriel will now throw further light. This would be one of Daniel's regular daily prayer times (6:10) but this time, in the dress of a penitent, he reaches the climax of his supplication. If conditions had been normal, in his homeland he would have been listening for the sounding of the ram's horn, from the Temple in Jerusalem, that heralded the evening oblation. That evening sacrifice was a perfect male yearling lamb, offered as a burnt offering, with the accompanying meal offering, and the appropriate drink offering. In

[15] Wood, *A Commentary on Daniel*, p. 245.

this oblation was prefigured the complete and sufficient sacrifice of the coming Messiah – the great subject of this prophecy. But things were far from normal. He was in Babylon – a captive. There was no oblation, no ram's horn, no Temple, and Jerusalem was desolate. Then the touch of an angelic hand aroused him!

(b) Declaration Concerning the Message vv. 22–23

Verses 22–23 Announcement and Authority

Gabriel has been dispatched from heaven to meet the need of Daniel. That need is summarised by Daniel himself: 'he informed me, and talked with me'. The first verb is better translated 'he instructed me', or paraphrased, 'caused me to understand'. Daniel already had information but he needed some further data to understand its implications – just as a university tutor would go over the previous lectures with his student to make sure the undergraduate had understood the relationship between the data he had and that which was freshly given. The second verb, 'talked', indicates the method employed by Gabriel. This was to use simple, straightforward verbal communication – no further vision would be used. This is how the statement 'a word went forth' (*RSV*) is to be understood. In answer to Daniel's intercession, the decision was made in heaven, to communicate directly with Daniel. As a consequence Gabriel is charged with bringing to Daniel the verbal communication of vv. 24–27. This is the 'word' (Heb. '*dabar*'), from the Lord through Gabriel to Daniel.

Gabriel's definition of his mission supports this interpretation: 'I am ... come ... to give thee skill and understanding.' Both 'skill' and 'understanding' are related to 'wisdom', which can be defined as 'acting wisely in light of what you have seen or known'. The word 'skill' suggests an overall view that allows someone to act with dexterity,[16] while 'understanding' suggests wisdom that allows one to separate and distinguish different viewpoints.[17] These are the insights that Daniel needed to understand what had been given in vision form. No-one can deny that they are still essential to the student of these prophecies.

Daniel's exercise had caught both the eye and the ear of heaven from the beginning of what are called here 'thy supplications' – that period when, leaving all else aside, he adjusted his priorities to

[16] *OTWS*, p. 398.
[17] *OTWS*, p. 461.

enable him to spend time in the presence of his God. His burden for his people resulted in those special petitions reaching the very throne. As a consequence, Gabriel is dispatched to communicate a message verbally to Daniel. The reason for this disclosure thrills the soul. Daniel is addressed from heaven as 'thou ... greatly beloved',[18] and this explains why Gabriel is by his side. Almost seventy years in Babylon, Daniel had long ago caught the eye of heaven, as now his supplications have caught the ear of heaven. Gabriel addresses him as 'greatly beloved', which means, literally, 'one desired, counted precious'.[19] The rendering of Newberry is expressive and helpful: 'greatly delighted in'! What a testimony from heaven for a man in Babylon. Now it becomes clear why Daniel can be trusted with one of the most vital of the Messianic prophecies! Gabriel uses three different verbs to cover the revelations made to Daniel. The following translation makes those verbs stand out: 'I have come to tell it to you, for you are greatly beloved; therefore consider the word and understand the vision' (*RSV*). With the mind engaged, truth is conveyed through eye-gate and ear-gate. The 'matter' may refer to chapter 7 (see 7:28), and the 'vision' may refer to chapter 8 (see 8:27); both have troubled Daniel down the intervening years. Now they are to be understood and considered, in light of what Gabriel is about to communicate. The (more literal) translation of the *RSV* brings out a useful point: the verb 'tell' and the noun 'word' indicate a verbal communication. This communication comes in the next four verses (vv. 24–27). The unfolding of the Divine programme that centres on Christ, including the date given of God, will bring all the previous revelations and visions into a time-related perspective for Daniel – and, incidentally, for us, the later recipients of this prophecy.

The Seventy Weeks Prophecy vv. 24–27

Verse 24 Two points require immediate clarification:

(a) The meaning of 'weeks'. Hebrew scholars agree that the word 'weeks' is a generic term meaning 'sevens' without specifying whether 'days', 'weeks', 'months' or 'years'. A better translation would be 'heptad', which simply means something made up of seven

[18] One cannot forget another like Daniel – who was called 'the beloved disciple', and who at an advanced age, in exile, was given visions of the Divine programme for the end-times – John the apostle.

[19] Wood, *A Commentary on Daniel*, p. 246.

identical parts. Since the matter on Daniel's heart was the seventy years of the captivity and he receives an answer that sets forth 'seventy sevens' – the *a priori* assumption is that the subject is still years. This means that attention is to be concentrated on this limited and selected period of 490 years. To assume it means either 490 days or weeks or months makes little sense in the context. Even liberal scholars have conceded that any Israelite accustomed to the tradition of the seven sevens of the Jubilee year calculation making forty-nine years would be immediately aware that seventy sevens was 490 years. Nothing else makes any sense, yet it is surprising that even some very conservative scholars would try to make the 'seven' a perfect but unspecified period.[20]

(b) The length of the year. Scripture is perfectly clear that a luni-solar year comprises 360 days. This is the year used in the first book of the Bible in the days of Noah and selected by the Spirit of God to convey prophetic truth. This can be seen in a comparison of the dates in Gen. 7:11 and Gen. 8:3–4: the beginning and the end of the flood, where the months are clearly reckoned to be each thirty days. This answers readily to the division of the circle into 360 degrees. It is interesting to consider whether the flood, which brought so many changes to the cosmos, may have altered the period of the earth's rotation around the sun, giving us the slightly longer year. The last book in the Bible is equally clear that three years and a half are reckoned as forty-two months or 1260 (42 × 30) days (Rev. 11:2,3; 12:14; 13:5). This period of 490 years will have to be reckoned with this luni-solar year in mind. It is an interesting fact of history that the Babylonians in their records used this same length for the year.

The next point needs careful examination. The verb translated 'are determined' (*AV*) or 'decreed' (*RSV*) comes from a root meaning 'to cut', or, comparing its Aramaic translation, it could mean 'cut off'.[21] It suggests that God has acted to 'cut' or 'cut off' a certain period of time from the general stream of history, in which to accomplish a certain purpose – just as if a businessman has decided that one particular aspect of his work was so vital that he was going to cut out a portion of his time and devote all his energies to this task until it was done. So God is going to complete a work for Israel within a set time period – seventy weeks of years – 490 years. Daniel has been praying for 'Thy people' and 'Thy city' and may still be on

[20] Keil and Delitsch, *in loc.* and Young *in loc.*

[21] *OTWS*, p. 248.

his knees as the angel brings this message concerning Daniel's people (Israel) and Daniel's city (Jerusalem). Now he is going to hear what God has in mind for Israel.

1. The Scriptural Purpose

This nation now identified with Daniel and called 'Thy people' is, of course, the nation of Israel, whom God had disowned during the captivity period in keeping with the solemn message through Hosea: 'Then said God "Call his name Lo-Ammi: for ye are not My people, and I will not be your God"' (Hos. 1:9). During these captivity years God never addresses Israel as 'My people' (see Hag. 1:2). The city is, of course, Jerusalem, the only city to bear the title 'holy' in Scripture (Neh. 11:1, 18; Isa. 48:2; 52:1; Mt. 4:5; 27:53; Rev. 11:2), yet now, because of sin, allowed of God to be under the heel of a Gentile invader, it is still spoken of as 'holy city'. The possessive adjective makes it seem as if the city belonged to Daniel and not to God. Transgression, sins and iniquity had alienated a holy God from people and city, so that He could not publicly identify with them – yet He still speaks of the city as 'holy' – set apart by God. He has not abandoned His purpose for them despite their sin. But as God seeks to recover His people, the sin that caused the alienation must first be faced. So if the purpose of God is to be reached through the nation of Israel in the specific period of seventy weeks, the first matter to be put right is their sin. Once sin in every form is dealt with righteously then blessing follows. The burden of sin of the nation (that has driven Daniel to his knees in real confession) is shown to be dealt with first – transgression, sins and iniquity. Sin having been thus dealt with and removed, the promised Sovereign arrives to take the throne. In this Sovereign will be fulfilled all the promises given to Abraham and to David. The Sovereign of God's appointment reigns in Jerusalem.

The purpose of God for this people and this city involves six statements: the first three deal with the problem exposed – the removal of sin. The last three deal with the Person expected – the residence of the Sovereign.

A. The Problem Exposed: Removal of Sin

Since this lies at the root of all the problems of individuals and nations, it must be dealt with righteously and completely before any blessing can be enjoyed personally or nationally. So here, before salvation for the nation can be introduced and enjoyed, sin must be faced. It is not given to Daniel to unfold the righteous basis on which God can forgive sin.[22] That ministry has been given to the prophet Isaiah who, nearly two hundred years before this time, had spoken of the One Who would undertake this tremendous work. Isaiah had spoken: 'Behold, a virgin shall conceive, and bear a son and shall call his name Immanuel' (Isa. 7:14; see also Isa. 9:6), Who would appear on earth as the Servant of Jehovah' (Isa. 42:1–8 *et al.*) and would die as the vicarious sacrifice for sin (Isa. 52:13–53:12) to enable God to cleanse and forgive guilty men. Isaiah's ministry showed that through this Person the issues of 'transgression', 'sin' and 'iniquity' can be justly dealt with and forgiven (Isa. 53:5). Upon confession of faith in this person the possession of pardon and peace and a place in God's Kingdom was assured. Individuals enter upon this now, and individuals in such numbers from the nation of Israel will accept this work that in a day yet to come it will be as if a nation was born 'at once'. Isaiah had preached, 'Who hath heard such a thing? Who hath seen such things? Shall the earth be made to bring forth in one day? Or shall a nation be born at once?' (Isa. 66:8). From the scroll before him containing the ministry of Isaiah, Daniel knew how God could forgive sinful men on the basis of the sinless sin-offering. Further, neither was it given to Daniel to show how and when this Messiah would be embraced by the nation of Israel – that awaited the ministry of Zechariah (520 BC). Zechariah spoke of the nation in confession of sin (Zech. 12:10–13:1), followed by confession of the Saviour, in the words of Isaiah, 'But He was wounded for our transgressions, He was bruised for our iniquities: The chastisement of our peace was upon Him; And with His stripes we are healed' (Isa. 53:5). Daniel's ministry is to show what the result of faith in the Messiah will mean on a national scale. Three statements expose the state of the sinner, the substitution by the Saviour, and the salvation that is available in the Messiah of this chapter.

(a) To Finish Transgression. The noun 'transgression' comes from a verb which is translated 'to rebel'. The root idea is a breach of relationships, civil or religious, between two parties. The verbal form designates a casting off of allegiance – 'a rebelling against

[22] Perhaps the timing of this revelation – 'the time of the evening oblation' (v. 21) has significance for Daniel.

rulers'.[23] The history of Israel was of rebellion against God; they broke His Law, they refused His prophets, and even seventy years in Babylon taught them few lessons. This message must have cheered Daniel. The inherent rebellion of this nation was to be 'finished' forever. 'Finished' is a valuable translation and it should be understood in the sense of 'brought to an end'. Alternative meanings come from examples of usage, when the verb can have an extended meaning – 'to shut up' or 'to restrain' – and this gives a graphic picture of a 'beast shut up'. Transgression has been so dealt with that the inherently rebellious nature of the nation can never break out again. The picture is fascinating, but in theological terms the closer translation reads 'put an end to' (*NET*). The rebel nature of the nation would be dealt with in such a way that there can be no expression of this nature again. It is a new life manifest. The wilful and wayward hearts would be brought into line with the will of God. The first term of the New Covenant states, 'I will put My law in their inward parts, and write it in their hearts' (Jer. 31:33); when applied to Israel it means that the disobedience and defiance, which had resulted so frequently in rebellion in the past, would never recur again. This is the work of grace shown to men as applied to the nation. To understand how this will be on a world scale through the gospel, it would be necessary to study the subject of how men are made new in the Epistle to the Romans (Rom. 5:1–8: 39).

The picture in the verb is – a beast is shut up – never to be released.

(b) To Make an End of Sins. The root of the verb 'to make an end' means 'to seal', and it refers to the authentication of documents and decrees that carried official imprimatur (1 Kgs 21:8, Est. 3:12; 8:8, Dan. 6:17–18). That which lay under a seal was securely enclosed; scriptural examples are: a book (Dan. 12:9), or a treasure (Deut. 32:34), or one's transgression (Job 14:17). While in general usage the verb implies that the sealing has in view a future opening, that thought is not in this context. Here the idea of sealing is that the record of Israel's sins has been sealed so that no further sins may be added. The list is closed; Israel has done with sinning. In simple language, Israel will sin no more. The word 'sin' carries its normal picture of 'missing the mark', and the fact that it is the plural draws attention to the variety of actions in daily life that stem from the

[23] *OTWS*, p. 451.

in their national experience. The land promised to Abraham and his seed will be fully possessed (Gen. 15:18–21); the throne promised to David and his seed will be filled by a Son of David (2 Sam. 7:12–16). In the purpose of God, His King and Kingdom have been established through the One to be identified as Messiah the Prince. Three things follow:

(a) To Bring in Everlasting Righteousness. In His first coming to earth, the Messiah, though rejected by the national leaders of Israel, dealt with sin through the suffering of the cross, as the prophet Isaiah had announced (Isa. 52:13–53:12). Satisfaction for sin having been made before the throne, God could now 'be just, and the justifier of him which believeth in Jesus' (Rom. 3:26). What God could do for the individual sinner, He could do on a national scale for Israel. The second coming of Christ to earth brings, for believers, the realisation of the blessings entailed (1 Pet. 1:6–7). To unbelievers, this second coming to earth brings the judgement deserved (2 Thess. 1:6–10). The Holy Spirit working throughout the Tribulation days in individuals brings the nation of Israel to repentance and confession of sin (Zech. 12:10–13:1). True repentance and confession lead to the Saviour Christ. This time they give Him the crown denied on His first coming; the coronation of the Sovereign follows in Jerusalem (Ps. 24:7–10). In this acceptance and acknowledgement of their King, 'everlasting righteousness' is brought in. 'Righteousness' is singular and 'everlasting' is plural and could be translated 'ages'. This indicates that the standard of behaviour seen formerly in heaven, then in Christ on earth, is now seen in men on earth. From this point in time onwards, righteousness marks the ages to come. Isaiah speaks of this time: 'Behold, a king shall reign in righteousness, and princes shall rule in judgment' (Isa. 32:1). This is the same King of Whom Jeremiah speaks:

> Behold, the days come, saith the LORD, That I will raise unto David a righteous Branch, And a King shall reign and prosper, And shall execute judgment and justice in the earth. In His days Judah shall be saved, And Israel shall dwell safely: And this is His name whereby He shall be called, 'The LORD our Righteousness' (Jer. 23:5–6).

With the fulfilment of the promises to Abraham and to David, a King rules throughout the land of Israel from the capital city Jerusalem. This is the establishment of the millennial reign of

Christ (Rev. 20:1–6). That reign is not confined to Israel, but embraces the nations of earth as Zechariah records: 'and he shall speak peace unto the nations: and his dominion shall be from sea to sea, and from the River to the ends of the earth' (Zech. 9:10, *RV*). Christ dealt with sin in His first coming; now, in His second coming, He brings in righteousness – universally and eternally. The use of the word 'everlasting' emphasises what has already been shown with respect to sin: sin has been dealt with permanently, so this is no temporary restoration. Often in Israel's past, when repentance led to recovery under good kings such as Hezekiah or Josiah, there was blessing, but it was only temporary. The same cycle began again – rebellion and retribution, followed by recovery. Not this time – this Kingdom is forever! As pointed out already, the millennial Kingdom is but an avenue that leads directly into the eternal state. We recall that Christ is spoken of as 'the great King' (Ps. 48:2).

(b) To Seal up the Vision and Prophecy. The idea of 'seal up' in this context is not affixing a seal as a guarantee of authenticity, but the idea in the verb is to 'close up' so as to restrain from activity. As defined by Wood[25] it means 'to enclose something authoritatively, hiding it from view and showing that its functions are completed'. God introduced these two methods of communication with men – vision and prophecy – in days of departure and failure. Now, with those days past forever and the Kingdom of God manifest on earth, these means of recalling men to their responsibilities are no longer required. With the arrival of the Kingdom the visions and prophecies have all been fulfilled; the Kingdom stands as a record of their veracity and accuracy, but their function is no longer needed. Face to face communication belongs to this new realm, and the old indirect methods are obsolete; they are sealed up. The prophet is redundant now as Christ reigns, and He is still the Word of God (Rev. 19:13). When the Son arrived in time in humble guise the last prophetic voice fell silent (Heb. 1:1–2); when the Son of Man arrives back on earth and takes His seat on the throne of His glory (Mt. 25:31) it will be absolutely clear that no other means of communication between God and men is required. No other voice will be heard; no former vision will be required.

(c) To Anoint the Most Holy. Most commentators and translators agree that it is a place that is anointed. The reading 'the most holy'

[25] Wood, *A Commentary on Daniel*, p. 250.

(*AV*) is somewhat ambiguous; the *RV* translates similarly but with the marginal reading making the translators' view clear – 'a most holy place'. The Newberry marginal reading supports the thought of a place with the translation 'holy of holies'. The term 'most holy' is never used of persons in the OT but always refers to 'things' or 'places'. This suggests a place on earth consecrated to God. Christ is already the Anointed One (Ps. 2:2) – a Man in the presence of God awaiting the moment to publicly claim His Kingdom. There is no scriptural record of any further anointing. The plural 'holiest' is best translated 'Holy of Holies', and when used with the article in the OT it points to the innermost sanctuary in the Tabernacle or Temple, where the ark of God rested (e.g. Exod. 26:33). When used without the article, as in this passage, it can include the Temple complex and even articles within the complex (e.g. Ezek. 43:12). As holy vessels were anointed in Israel's economy (Exod. 29:36; 30:26–28), and the Temple of Solomon was set apart for God by the presence of the Shekinah (1 Kgs 8:11), so the phrase here suggests the consecration of the millennial Temple as seen by Ezekiel (Ezek. 40–48). This Temple will be anointed, not by a literal anointing with oil, which procedure was ever but a figure, but set apart by the very real and manifest presence of God (Ezek. 43:1–5). We recall the words of the psalmist: 'The LORD hath sworn, and will not repent, "Thou art a priest for ever after the order of Melchizedek"' (Ps. 110:4).

Messiah is Prophet, Priest and King!

While the basis for these prophetic happenings is laid in the first coming of Christ to earth and in the cross, the fulfilment of all six events awaits the return of Christ to earth at the second advent. Then the nation of Israel, regathered in their own land, repentant under the ministry of the Spirit (Zech. 12:10–14), will receive their once-rejected Sovereign, to become the 'nation ... born at once' (Isa. 66:8). This new birth brings a new life – rebellion is now forever gone, their sins are forever removed, reconciliation is their portion, neither prophet nor vision will ever again be required, and their King reigns in righteousness. Truly the prophetic word thrills the heart – 'And His dominion shall be from sea even to sea, And from the River even to the ends of the earth' (Zech. 9:10). Daniel is made aware that, despite their terrible failure, there is a great future for his nation and its capital city, Jerusalem. The promises to Abraham and to David are not abrogated, but simply postponed, until the

One already identified on earth as 'Jesus Christ, the son of David, the son of Abraham' (Mt. 1:1) sits upon the throne in Jerusalem.

2. The Specified Period

Verse 25 It has been shown that the expression 'seventy weeks' in this context can only have one interpretation. The 'seventy sevens' are of years – a period of four hundred and ninety years. This is the specific time span for the completion of this Divine programme. The verb 'determined' is not used elsewhere in Scripture. It has the root 'to cut' and indicates that this selected period has been 'cut out' or 'isolated' from the course of history to achieve a distinct and stated purpose. That purpose has been shown in the previous verse as the six objectives achieved when God has worked through the Divine programme and accomplished His purpose. Sin will have been removed and the Sovereign will reign in Jerusalem. Other Scriptures will fill in the detail of blessing throughout the world but Daniel is focussed on Israel. This is God's plan for that nation. The commencement, the course and the close of this specific period are clearly indicated.

At this point two verbs claim consideration. The *AV*, catching the nuances of the Hebrew grammar, gives an excellent translation of both verbs, which are in the imperative mood – 'know' and 'understand'. Readers are to give their minds to this prophetic revelation: first to know the facts, but secondly to 'understand' – and it should be pointed out that this verb is the root word from which the noun 'wisdom' is derived. Thus the facts of history, when understood in the light of Scripture, give wisdom as to how the believer should react. Daniel sums up the implication later when he writes, 'but the wise shall understand' (12:10). The variety of interpretations offered for these verses over the years makes plain that not enough consideration has been given to this exhortation.

A. The Commencement of the Period

'From the going forth of the commandment to restore and build Jerusalem'

A careful consideration of the wording of this statement would have preserved from many errors of interpretation. This is the point from which the specific period of the seventy weeks commences. Commentators call it 'the beginning point' – in more technical writing it is designated '*terminus a quo*' (point from which) – of the seventy weeks period. Since it will set the date for the coming of the Messiah this is one of the most vital dates in prophecy.

First, we must be clear as to what is to be looked for as the starting point of the seventy weeks. The text speaks of a 'commandment' (Hebrew '*dabar*', meaning 'word') – the question must be asked: does this 'word' come from God or from an earthly monarch? Some expositors[26] contend that, since the same word is used two verses before this in the statement 'the commandment (*dabar*) came forth' (v. 23), where it is clear that God is the Author, it must be the same in this verse. This is a mistake – such an interpretation fails to note the change of subject. Daniel's exercise (vv. 3–19) having touched the throne of God, the 'commandment', or 'word', comes forth from that throne that Daniel is to be shown and made to understand what lies ahead. The word comes from the throne of God and the subject is the nation of Israel. The subject here (v. 25) is Jerusalem. God in disciplinary action has allowed this city to come temporarily under the authority of a Gentile monarch, so the 'word' must come from the throne of the Gentile monarch. An argument in support of this statement is found in that men would never have known about the 'word' in v. 23 if Gabriel had not revealed it. Now God reveals that the earthly power permitted to control Jerusalem would issue a historic decree for the rebuilding of the city. Such a vital date would necessarily be recorded in Scripture. This points the reader, not to the records of earth, but to the record of Scripture, where it should be found. It will be a landmark decree, issued by an earthly monarch to whom God has, temporarily, allowed authority over Jerusalem. The action of this king is to authorise the restoration and the rebuilding of Jerusalem. Men cannot search the records of heaven but they can search the record of Scripture.

When such a search is carried out Scripture reveals that there are four separate edicts issued by Persian monarchs connected with the restoration period, thus:

(a) A decree of Cyrus (2 Chron. 36:22–23 repeated with fuller detail in Ezra 6:3–5) in the first year of his reign. The date for the issue of the decree was in 538 BC. The result of this decree was seen when Zerubbabel led the first company of Jews back to Jerusalem, in the year 536 BC.

[26] Young, *The Prophecy of Daniel*, p. 201.

(b) A decree of Darius Hystaspes (Ezra 6:6–12) reaffirming the decree of Cyrus. This decree is in connection with the ministry of Haggai and Zechariah and is thus dated 520 BC.

(c) A decree of Artaxerxes (Ezra 7:12–26) issued to Ezra as he led the second company of exercised Jews back to Jerusalem in 458 BC.

(d) A decree of Artaxerxes (Neh. 2:1–9) issued to Nehemiah as he led the third company back to Jerusalem in 445 BC.

When the first three decrees are examined closely the subject of the reconstruction in each case is seen to be the 'house of your God', pointing to the 'Temple of the LORD', in Jerusalem. There is not a single mention of the city of Jerusalem or any reference to its rebuilding. This may seem strange, but it is neither a mistake, nor an oversight on the part of the Persian kings concerned. Unlike their Babylonian predecessors, the Medo-Persians, with their liberal religious policy, allowed their subject nations the right of religious freedom. This is what they gave to the Jews and why the focus is the rebuilding of the Temple. While there was certainly partial re-occupation of the city by the people working on the Temple (Hag. 1:4), there was no question of them authorising the rebuilding of a city. For a Medo-Persian king to authorise the rebuilding of Jerusalem would have been, in real terms, to recognise a political entity – a state called Israel. No Persian monarch would have been prepared to do this at this early date. It is to be noted that this is the very charge, false though it was, that the Samaritan adversaries used against the returned exiles to bring the work to a standstill in the time of Ezra. Their charge is recorded in the letter to the king: 'Be it known unto the king, that the Jews which came up from thee to us are come unto Jerusalem, building the rebellious and the bad city, and have set up the walls thereof, and joined the foundations' (Ezra 4:11–16). This false claim concerning the city brought the work on the Temple to a standstill. It was only the fourth decree in the above list that allowed the Jews, in the time of Nehemiah (ninety-one years later, 536–445 BC), to rebuild the city and the walls and set up the gates.

Decree of Artaxerxes (Longimanus)
Commandment to Rebuild Jerusalem – Nehemiah – 1st *Nisan* 445 BC

As already noted, the only decree relating to the city is the fourth decree, given by Artaxerxes I (485–424 BC), known as Longimanus ('Long-handed'), in the twentieth year of his reign (Neh. 2:1–9). When Nehemiah, the king's cupbearer, in his interview with a recently-returned delegation from Jerusalem, made enquiries as to the welfare of the returned exiles and the condition of Jerusalem he was totally shocked. The exiles had returned to Jerusalem in 536 BC and it was now 446 BC so they had been there over ninety years, into the third generation from the return. Nehemiah was told: 'The remnant that are left of the captivity ... are in great affliction and reproach: the wall of Jerusalem also is broken down, and the gates thereof are burned with fire' (Neh. 1:1–3). Deeply exercised by this condition of things in Jerusalem, Nehemiah took no hasty action but waited for God to open a path for him. He patiently waited from the month '*Chisleu*' (November 446 BC) until challenged by King Artaxerxes (Neh. 2:1–8) as to the reason for his sadness of face at the New Year celebrations at the month of '*Nisan*' (March), in the twentieth year of the rule of King Artaxerxes (445 BC). He had waited four months. The king must have feared that such an unusual sadness in the face of a senior official at a time of celebration indicated trouble, of which he had not been told, somewhere in the empire. Following the explanation of Nehemiah, King Artaxerxes authorised Nehemiah to return to Jerusalem with a mandate to rebuild the city (Neh. 2:5). Nehemiah carried 'letters' (Neh. 2:7) to the governors of the surrounding territories beyond the river (Euphrates); these letters made three matters very clear: (a) The appointment of Nehemiah as Governor of Judaea; (b) The authorisation for the rebuilding of the city of Jerusalem, even to its wall (Neh. 2:8); (c) The order to the officials of the neighbourhood to supply the materials for that rebuilding.

In this decree, by permitting the rebuilding of the city, the Persian king recognised the reality of the state of Israel. It was not independence, for Israel was still under the overlordship of the Persian throne, but it was virtually dominion status, under a governor. This permission for Israel to take her place on the political map of the day, by the rebuilding of her capital city, was the reason for the bitter animosity shown by the neighbouring people to Nehemiah's presence in Jerusalem (Neh. 2:10). This marked a major turning point in the history of the nation of Israel.

The incident that resulted in this commandment is carefully dated as occurring in the month *Nisan* in the twentieth year of Artaxerxes. This king, we know from historical records, reigned from 465 424 BC. This date is so vital that Scripture marks it carefully as 'the twentieth year of King Artaxerxes'.[27] Using the Babylonian method of counting the regnal years,[28] that year becomes the year 445 BC in our chronology. The question was looked at some years ago by Sir Robert Anderson as to which method of counting regnal years Daniel used. His answer was to look at the passage in Nehemiah (Neh. 1:1–2:9), and it is worth recording. He writes: 'As Nehemiah mentions '*Chisleu*' (November) of one year [Neh. 1:1], and the following *Nisan* (March) [Neh. 2:1] as both being in the same year of his master's reign, it is obvious that, as might be expected from an official of the civil court, he reckons from the time of the king's accession *de jure* [sanctioned by law], that is from July 465 BC. The twentieth year of Artaxerxes therefore began in July 446 BC, and the commandment to rebuild Jerusalem was given in the *Nisan* following. The commencement of the Divine programme for the coming of Messiah is thus fixed in the month *Nisan* of the year 445 BC.'[29] Anderson goes on to point out that since the wall was completed on the 25th day of the month *Elul* (the sixth month in the Jewish calendar), then Nehemiah must have arrived in Jerusalem not later that 1st *Ab* (the fifth month), and possibly a few days earlier (Neh. 2:11). It was a four-month journey from Babylon to Jerusalem (see Ezra 7:9), so Nehemiah must have set out within the first few days of *Nisan*. In keeping with international practice of the day, the commencement of this special period – the seventy weeks prophecy – dated from the issue of a Medo-Persian official document must be reckoned from the first day of the month of issue. This gives the precise date for the commencement of the seventy weeks prophecy as 1st *Nisan* 445BC.[30] As shown by Anderson[31] this date corresponds to March 14, 445 BC (Julian calendar), and if the interval is sixty-nine prophetic years this would mean, in days, 69 × 360 = 173,880 days, from the commencement (*terminus a quo*) of the sixty-nine weeks to Christ (*terminus ad quem*), which in the Julian calendar is April 6, AD 32. This becomes, in the Babylonian calendar, 10th *Nisan* AD 32. It should not be forgotten, in this examination of dates, that Daniel received this prophecy in 538

[27] Secular historians agree with this date. See J.M. Cook, *The Persians*, (London: Folio Society, 1983) p. 186.
[28] As discussed under comments on 1:1.
[29] Anderson, *The Coming Prince*, pp. 64–66. Note his brackets [ ] are interpolations for easy reference.
[30] Anderson, *The Coming Prince*, p. 122.
[31] Anderson, *Daniel in the Critics Den*, p. 120; See also Appendix IV.

BC – that is ninety-three years before the event that marked the official recognition of Israel on the world stage.[32] Since Daniel died *c.* 530 BC, he did not see this prophecy fulfilled.

We are indebted to Sir Robert Anderson for the calculation given above; the full details are set out in his book *The Coming Prince*.[33] It can be said that the majority of present day conservative commentators are in general agreement with Anderson, while admitting some have problems with the accuracy he demands – down to the very day Christ was presented to the nation. However, J.F. Walvoord puts the case in a very balanced way on behalf of those who hesitate when he writes:

> That Sir Robert Anderson is right in building upon a 360 day year seems to be attested by the Scriptures ... the conclusions reached by Anderson, however are quite complicated in their argument and impossible to restate simply. While the details of Anderson's arguments may be debated, the plausibility of a literal interpretation which begins the period in 445 BC and culminates just before the death of Christ, makes this view very attractive.[34]

It should be said on the positive side that the able commentator Mr Alva McClain gives Anderson full support.[35] The main problem of John F. Walvoord, which, it must be said, is a problem shared by several commentators, is that Anderson's calculations show the date of the cross as falling in the year AD 32. While there has been a lot of uncertainty about the exact date of the cross and while scholars still debate the matter, the weight of scholarship would make that date one or two or even three years earlier than AD 32 – depending on the understanding of the date given by Scripture for the commencement of the ministry of John the Baptist (Lk. 3:1). Walvoord goes on to admit: 'There has been a tendency, however, in recent New Testament chronology to consider a later date for the death of Christ, and no-one today is able dogmatically to declare that Sir Robert Anderson's computations are impossible.'[36] Indeed, a most detailed study by Harold W. Hoehner, an acknowledged

[32] See Prophetic Note below and chart, pp. 678–679.

[33] Anderson, *The Coming Prince*, p. 119.

[34] Walvoord, *Daniel: the Key to Prophetic Revelation*, p. 228.

[35] McClain, *Daniel's Prophecies of the Seventy Weeks*, p. 20.

[36] Walvoord, *Daniel: The Key to Prophetic Revelation*, p. 228.

chronologist, presents his case for the cross being as late as AD 33.[37] It is not possible to examine every claim made on the subject, but it is sufficient to say that, based squarely on Scripture, as they are, the calculations made by Sir Robert Anderson are most convincing, and should be given close attention. They have never been seriously challenged, as they stand on clear Scriptural statements.

Prophetic Note

It may be of interest to point out that the remnant of the nation of Israel were back in their land ninety-one years before the Divine programme was scheduled to begin and the prophetic clock began to tick for the count-down of sixty-nine weeks to the first coming of Messiah the Prince to earth (536–445 BC). This time gap will have significance for us and for the future when it is pointed out that the remnant of the nation of Israel have been back in their own land as an independent state and a factor in world politics since May 14, 1948, but the prophetic clock does not commence to tick until the peace treaty is confirmed in Israel. In May 2013, the sixty-fifth anniversary of the return was celebrated. How close we must be to the Rapture! This will be followed by the 'covenant' (v. 27) that begins the countdown of the final seven years to the second coming of Christ to earth. The question that must be asked in light of these studies is a simple one – When does the end-time of our study commence? The answer to this question will colour the thinking towards many passages of Scripture that formerly were judged to belong to the Tribulation or even Kingdom times. See Chapter Note A, at the end of chapter 11.

B. The Course of the Period

The whole period of seventy weeks is divided into three:

(a) A period of 7 weeks – 49 years (on the interpretation already discussed at v. 24)

(b) A period of 62 weeks – 434 years

(c) A period of 1 week – 7 years.

Total: 70 weeks– 490 years

Three matters must be noted:

(a) That the first two periods are clearly indicated as running consecutively, without interruption, to the end of the sixty-ninth

[37] Hoehner, *Chronological Aspects of the Death of Christ*. See Note 39.

week (483 years). While there is no suggestion of any time break between the two periods, there must be some reason why the first seven weeks are marked off from the remaining sixty-two weeks.

(b) That the sixty-nine weeks conclude with the identification of a person. Using technical language, as used in v. 25, this person is the *terminus ad quem* (the end to which the timeline moves). This Person, central to the prophecy and, in fact, the culmination of the prophecy, is identified as 'Messiah the Prince' (*AV*) or, as it is translated, 'the anointed one, the prince' (*RV*). The term 'anointed' in the OT marked out those who were set apart for special and sacred service in Israel. Kings were anointed (1 Sam. 10:1; 16:13 *inter alia*), priests were anointed (Exod. 29:7) and prophets were anointed (1 Kgs 19:16); in their separate offices each pointed to One Who would be, pre-eminently and outstandingly, 'His Anointed' (Ps. 2:2) – the Anointed of Jehovah. This One would be a Prophet, worthy of more glory than Moses (Heb. 3:3) in His ministry to Israel while on earth, a Priest now in the presence of God 'after the order of Melchisedec' (Heb. 5:6), and the King Whose 'dominion shall be from sea even to sea, and from the River even to the ends of the earth' (Zech. 9:10). The word 'prince' has the basic idea of 'one who stands above the crowd', or 'one who goes before', and is used frequently in the OT of outstanding leaders. The corresponding Greek word is '*archegos*', used four times in the NT and only of Christ (Acts 3:15 ('prince'); 5:31 ('prince'); Heb. 2:10 ('captain'); 12:2 ('author'). The word used here, 'Messiah', or 'Anointed', points to the long-awaited Priest-Prophet-King expected in Israel down the centuries from Moses. Isaiah had spoken of this One before the captivity, as the anointed One (Isa. 61:1–3) through Whom 'the sure mercies of David' would be secured to the nation (Isa. 55:3–4); Psalms had echoed to the same anticipation (Pss. 2:1–6; 110:4). Now, it is simply in keeping with this Divinely-given prophecy that the time of His appearance in the nation should be announced. In other words, the sixty-nine weeks of this prophecy would come to an end in the time of Christ – the Messiah – the Anointed.

(c) There is clearly a gap between the sixty-ninth and the seventieth week. After the sixty-ninth week, Messiah is cut off, and following this the city and sanctuary are destroyed – this action is after the sixty-ninth week but not in the seventieth week. There must, of necessity, be a time gap between the sixty-ninth and the seventieth week.

(a) A Period of Seven Weeks
7 weeks of 7 years each = 49 Years

The last sentence of this verse makes it very clear that the first period of forty-nine years is associated with the building of the city – 'the street shall be built again, and the wall, even in troublous times'. Since the decree was issued in 445 BC, seven weeks of seven years (forty-nine years) bring the date to 396 BC. These were the years that followed the return of Nehemiah, when the walls were built and the gates of Jerusalem put in place (Neh. 3). In the following years serious construction took place throughout the city, until Jerusalem became a capital city worthy of the recovered national status of a restored nation of Israel (Neh. 12:40–43). The word for 'street' (Heb '*rehob*') refers to an 'open place' (Gen. 19:2) or 'broad place' (Neh. 8:1, *New.*) and is often used of a square or market place, where civic or public gatherings took place. By metonymy, it essentially defines the re-establishment of city life. The word for 'wall' is not the usual word and is best understood as 'the scarped rampart',[38] which, while including the idea of a wall, goes further and is often used of the defensive works that surround the city. The *RV* translates the word as 'moat', which is generally understood as a 'defensive ditch' forming part of the fortifications. While there is something to be said for this translation, the English word could mislead.

Two reasons may be suggested for the separation of these seven weeks:

(a) Since the city itself is the focus of the prophecy, a key date would be the completion of the restoration of the city as a functioning entity. The story of the rebuilding, even in troubled times, is given in the book of Nehemiah. Much to the consternation of the Moabites, Ammonites and Arabians, this city, once judged by God, rises again out of the ashes. No doubt this very prophecy was a great source of strength to the returned exiles doing battle with their adversaries;

(b) With the completion of the city and the restoration of the Temple sacrifices in light of the arrival of the Messiah, God sends His final message through the prophet Malachi, before the prophetic voice falls silent for almost four hundred years. That

[38] Tatford, *Daniel and His Prophecy*, p. 155.

silence is broken when John the Baptist stands on bank of the river Jordan and announces the arrival of the Messiah (Mt. 3:1–17).

Thus the two reasons suggested for the distinction between the seven weeks period and the sixty-two weeks period are:

(a) The time required for the city of Jerusalem to be rebuilt and recognised as capital of Israel once again, and,

(b) The final prophetic voice to be heard before the arrival of Messiah. It is of interest that Malachi's last message is dated in 396 BC – exactly forty-nine years from this commandment in 445 BC.

(b) A Period of Sixty-Two Weeks
62 weeks of 7 years = 434 years

It has already been noted that some distinction must exist between period 1 (49 years) and period 2 (434 years). Could it be that the first period deals with the preparation of the place to which Messiah comes and the second period deals with the preparation of the people to whom He is to come? The important point is that the two periods make a total of 69 weeks, or 69 × 7 = 483 years. The end of this period is clearly marked by the phrase 'unto Messiah the Prince', or, as another translation reads, 'unto the anointed one, the prince' (*RV*). As discussed, the use of the title 'Messiah' points to the long-awaited Priest-Prophet-King expected in Israel down the centuries – from the patriarchs to the monarchy. Now the moment has come to announce the date of His coming to the nation of Israel. In other words, the sixty-nine weeks of this prophecy would come to an end with the Christ amongst His people Israel.

The statement 'unto Messiah the Prince' does not identify what event or stage in the life of Christ is in view. Commentators have discussed and scholars have argued as to what particular event in the life of Christ would mark the terminus of this sixty-ninth week. The possibilities are really only three, and commentators are still divided on the issue. Some have argued that it must point to His birth; some have insisted it points to His baptism, at the beginning of His public ministry; or some argue for the date of His triumphal entry into Jerusalem, just before He was crucified, this latter being the occasion when Christ rode into Jerusalem on the ass and John records:

> On the next day much people that were come to the feast, when they heard that Jesus was coming to Jerusalem, took branches of palm trees, and went forth to meet Him, and cried,

> 'HOSANNA: BLESSED is THE KING OF ISRAEL that COMETH IN the NAME OF the LORD' (Jn 12:12–13).

One event that it cannot be is the crucifixion, since the next verse shows that the cutting off of Messiah only takes place after the close of the sixty-ninth week. Since whatever event is in view must be identified by the 483 years from 1st *Nisan* 445 BC, the question really becomes: which event, if any, fits the time span? That only one of these events can be correct is shown by recognising the time differences between them. Thus between the birth of the Messiah and His baptism there are thirty years (Lk. 3:23) of His private life, and between His baptism and the triumphal entry into Jerusalem there are the three-and-a-half years of His public ministry, so only one of the three possibilities mentioned can fit the date. Taking the *prima facie* case first, it could readily be assumed that what is implied in the expression 'unto the Messiah the Prince' is some public presentation of Christ to the nation of Israel. This would rule out His birth – a family matter – and His baptism – a local matter – and suggest that, without question, one of the most public events in the Messianic ministry – a national matter – was the morning when Christ rode into Jerusalem on the back of the ass – the triumphal entry. But this event would have to be shown to have taken place on the final day of the period of 483 years.

It has already been discussed and demonstrated that much light has been thrown on this point by the researches of Sir Robert Anderson (1841–1918), who began his studies with the basic assumption that Scripture is accurate and means literally what is stated. If Scripture states '483 years' then it does not mean 'about' or 'around' 483 years, no matter what unbelief says. Taking Scripture literally means that 483 years with 360 days to the year gives the total in days as 483 × 360 = 173,880 days. Taking into account the solar year of 365 days (including leap years) then the period, counted from the *terminus a quo* – 'from the going forth of the commandment' – to the *terminus ad quem* – 'unto Messiah the Prince' – should be exactly 173,880 days. Sir Robert Anderson has shown, in calculations that have never been seriously challenged, that the 483 prophetic years include exactly 173,880 days (483 × 360 = 173,880 days).[39]

[39] The most competent challenge to Sir Robert Anderson's calculation is presented by Harold W. Hoehner in his book *The Chronological Aspects of the Life of Christ*. Hoehner insists that new evidence since Sir Robert Anderson's time has changed the date of the 20th year of

To present the argument it is necessary to use Sir Robert Anderson's figures, which are as follows:[40]

- The 1st *Nisan* in the twentieth year of Artaxerxes (the edict to rebuild Jerusalem) was 14 March, 445 BC.
- The 10th *Nisan* in Passion Week (Christ's entry into Jerusalem) was 6 April, AD 32.
- The intervening period was 476 years and 24 days (the days being reckoned inclusively, as required by the language of the prophecy, and in accordance with the Jewish practice).

  But 476 × 365 = 173,740 days.
  Add (March 14 to April 6, *both* inclusive) 24 days.
  Add for leap years 116 days.
  Total 173,880 days

- But 69 weeks of prophetic years – each of 360 days is 69 × 7 × 360 = 173,880 days
- Thus 173,880 days commences on the 1st *Nisan* 445 BC and closes on the 10th *Nisan* AD 32.

The vital point then is to establish the date of the day when the Messiah made His triumphal entry into Jerusalem upon the ass.[41] As is only to be expected the importance of this event in the life of Christ is marked by the fact that there is a record of it in each of the gospels. A further significant point, in light of the importance of this date, is the fact that the Gospel of John seems to draw attention to the date – it happened on the morning after the Sabbath that

Artaxerxes Longimanus from 445 to 444 BC (p. 137) and, taking this into account, using the same methods as Anderson he dates the cross on Friday 14th *Nisan* in AD 33, thus making Monday 10th *Nisan* the day Christ rode into Jerusalem on the ass. Whichever account is accepted in interpretation the Scripture stands unchanged. The Messiah arrived on time on the date expected. My difficulty with the conclusion arrived at by this author is that to reach it, he has, on occasions, interpreted Scripture in the light of secular data drawn from Rabbinic sources, secular historians like Josephus and Philo, and astronomical data, instead of giving Scripture its full authority.

40 Anderson, *The Coming Prince*, p. 127 ff.

41 Anderson, *The Coming Prince*, p. 127 ff. Sir Robert Anderson's calculation will repay careful study. He shows that the scriptural dates of 1st *Nisan* 445BC and 10th *Nisan* AD32 correspond to the Julian dates (we now use the Gregorian calendar) of March 14, 445 BC and April 6, AD. 32 . When the days between these dates are counted inclusively the total is exactly 173,880 days.

begins the week in which the Passover would be celebrated. In keeping with Jewish custom Christ was present at each Passover since He had moved into His public ministry about His thirtieth birthday (Lk. 3:23). As detailed in the Gospel of John, that public ministry encompassed four Passovers. Coming to Jerusalem for this fourth Passover, in this year AD 32, it is recorded: 'Then Jesus six days before the Passover came to Bethany' (Jn 12:1). Since the Passover was always celebrated on the 14th *Nisan*, Jesus arrived in Bethany on the 8th *Nisan*, which in this year was a Friday. Jesus would rest on the Sabbath day, which would be the 9th *Nisan*. After sunset He attended the supper in the house of Simon the leper (Mt. 26:6; Jn 12:1–9). It was at this supper that Mary showed her clear apprehension of that which lay ahead for her Lord. We read:

> Then took Mary a pound of ointment of spikenard, very costly, and anointed the feet of Jesus, and wiped His feet with her hair: and the house was filled with the odour of the ointment (Jn 12:3).

Many have pointed out, that on His person and on His clothing, the Lord must have carried the smell of that anointing into Jerusalem the following day. The next day (Jn 12:12), the first day of the week, the 10th *Nisan*, Christ presented Himself officially to the nation of Israel as 'the Messiah the Prince'. The religious world recalls this as 'Palm Sunday'. Zechariah was given a prophetic foreview of that moment and could challenge the nation:

> Rejoice greatly, O daughter of Zion;
> Shout, O daughter of Jerusalem:
> Behold, thy king cometh unto thee:
> He is just, and having salvation:
> Lowly, and riding upon an ass,
> And upon a colt the foal of an ass (Zech. 9:9).

This event is carefully and fully recorded by each evangelist (Mt. 21:8–11; Mk 11:7–10; Lk. 19:35–40; Jn 12:12–15). Three matters marked this unique event: (a) The deliberate choosing of the ass by Christ as the transport of a king coming in peace; (b) the spontaneous spreading of the garments and the palm fronds along the way; and (c) the cry of the multitude, which ensured that the nation knew that a claimant, with all the credentials of the Messiah, was presenting Himself to the leaders of their nation. It was the heralding of a royal ascent as the crowd cried exultingly:

> HOSANNA to the Son of David:
> BLESSED is HE THAT COMETH IN the NAME OF the LORD;
> HOSANNA in the highest (Mt. 21:9).

Messiah the Prince had arrived on time, as Scripture had said, and as one would expect, since the timing was not human calculation but given of God through His prophet Daniel. Messiah had arrived on schedule – a schedule that proved accurate to the very day. There can hardly be a question but that it is the dates in this prophecy that alerted Mary, Joseph of Arimathaea and Nicodemus, and they were prepared.

Verse 26 (a) 'And after the three score and two weeks (*RV*)

1. The Stated Period Re-emphasised

The first two periods of weeks – the seven week period (forty-nine years) and the sixty-two week period (434 years) – with a total of sixty-nine weeks (483 years) have reached the *terminus ad quem* – their goal – a Person called Messiah the Prince has arrived in Jerusalem on schedule. Now there is a time break introduced into the text and indicated in the words 'after the threescore and two weeks' (*RV*). The inclusion of the article (*RV*) is important as signifying the particular threescore and two weeks period; it is the period already mentioned. Two events, mentioned as taking place after the sixty-ninth week has ended and before the commencement of the seventieth week, are given in the next verse (v. 27). The word 'after' lays stress on the closing of the sixty-two week period, before these next events can take place. No indication is given as to the period that intervenes before they occur. It is important to stress this fact, plainly incorporated in the text, for many commentators refuse to acknowledge that a very lengthy time break must come into the programme at this point. The reason for this time break and its purpose will become clear as the exposition proceeds. For the moment, it is enough to stress that the text demands it.

After the sixty-ninth week has closed two connected events are prophesied for Jerusalem:[42]

[42] It is necessary to keep in mind that that which was prophecy to Daniel is now history for us. Thus the very authenticity of the prophetic word must be answered by historical accuracy.

Verse 26 (b) 'Shall the anointed one be cut off and shall have nothing' (*RV*)

2. The Special Person Rejected

Presented to the nation as the Messiah on the 10th *Nisan* (Sunday morning); before sunset on the evening of the 14th *Nisan* (Thursday) He died on a cross. As Israel's Lamb He had been kept for the four specified days (Exod. 12:6) and then, in the words of Isaiah, 'He was cut off out of the land of the living' (Isa. 53:8). The word 'cut off' has its root in a physical act, as in cutting off, or amputation, of a part of the body (Exod. 4:25), or the cutting down of a tree or an idol (Judg. 6:25), but in such Scriptures as Genesis 17:14, Exodus 12:15 and Leviticus 7:20; 17:10 it can be nothing less than the equivalent of the death penalty, reached by a judicial process. Its basic meaning is 'to root out, to eliminate, remove, excommunicate, or destroy by a violent act',[43] the decision having been made by a recognised authority. The Anointed of God was violently cut off as the nation accused Him of blasphemy against God; He was 'cut off' both in the judicial sense, from the nation of Israel, and in the very physical sense of dying in the vigour of His manhood. While the Roman authority was actually responsible for the crucifixion of Christ, the moral guilt behind the act is charged to the nation of Israel (Acts 2:23; 4:10).

The translation 'but not for Himself' (*AV*) is not literal enough. The word 'not' is absent from the Hebrew text and a noun is present that is best translated as 'nothingness'.[44] The more literal translation 'and shall have nothing' (*RV*) is to be preferred. His Messianic entitlements were all denied Him. Instead of a throne He was nailed to a tree; instead of a crown He was given a cross. An Israelite with every Messianic credential has been 'cut off out of the land of the living' (Isa. 53:8). An Israelite, in the prime of His manhood, of Whom the prophet had mourned, crying 'who shall declare His generation?' (Isa. 53:8), has died nailed to a cross, disowned and dishonoured by the responsible leaders of His own nation. The cross of Calvary stands out in history as the greatest miscarriage of justice of all time.

This point will be stressed again in the final paragraph of this chapter, under the subtitle 'Summary of Chapter'.

[43] *OTWS*, p. 106.

[44] See *NET*, *in loc.*

Yet believers now know, with the light of resurrection and the NT Scriptures falling on it, that in this cross rests the secret of every blessing mankind will enjoy. The blessings that flow from the cross of Calvary are enshrined in words that rejoice the heart – words like propitiation, redemption and salvation. This cross is the source of all life and all hope; it is the sowing of the seed from which would spring the harvest that would fill heaven (Jn 12:23–24); it is the yielding of the Son that many sons could be brought to glory (Heb. 2:10), who would serve God eternally (Isa. 53:10; Rev. 22:3). That sinless silent Sufferer, vindicated in His claim to be Son by the resurrection from the dead (Rom. 1:4), is fitted to be the Saviour 'able to save ... to the uttermost' (Heb. 7:25) and to be 'that great Shepherd of the sheep' (Heb. 13:20) – the flock He is taking to glory. Yet to Daniel, who had no direct knowledge of the glorious outcome of the cross, the fact of the Messiah 'cut off' must have been totally inexplicable – a tragedy beyond what he could conceive, both unbelievable and incomprehensible. The Messiah had 'nothing' – no dominion, no glory and no kingdom. It is of interest to study what Daniel had been told of the Messianic hope in an earlier vision (7:14).

Verse 26 (c) 'And the people of the prince that shall come shall destroy the city and the sanctuary'

3. The Sacred Place Razed

The responsibility for the rejection of the Messiah must be placed squarely upon the nation of Israel – the people to whom Christ was sent in fulfilment of the Scriptures they had known from childhood. The leaders had examined those claims, rejected them as inadequate, and sent the Claimant to the cross as a 'blasphemer'. When presented to them by Pilate, the Roman Governor, in the words 'Behold your King!' (Jn 19:14), the leaders of Israel cried, 'Away with Him, crucify Him.' Upon the generation that had acted in this way Divine retribution must fall. In this verse it is announced in the clearest of terms that 'the city' and 'the sanctuary' are to be 'destroyed'. There can be no doubt that 'the city' is Jerusalem, over which Christ wept (Lk. 19:41–44), and 'the sanctuary' is the magnificent Temple, built by Herod the Great, in whose courts Christ had preached frequently and did so many miracles. Now these two particular places, which held so special a place in the heart of every Jew, were placed under the sentence of destruction.

It will be kept in mind that this is the same city and the same sanctuary over which so much spiritual exercise would take place amongst Daniel's people during the captivity years; over which battles had been fought by Assyrians and Babylonians; over which the Medo-Persian Empire had held sway and been involved with:

(a) Repatriation of the people – under Zerubbabel (536 BC); decreed by Cyrus (538 BC);
(b) Rebuilding of the sanctuary – under Haggai and Zechariah (520 BC) and Ezra (458 BC); decreed by Darius I (521 BC);
(c) Rebuilding of the city – under Nehemiah (445 BC); decreed by Artaxerxes Longimanus (445 BC).

All this still lay in the future for Daniel but he would readily understand (from v. 25) that this must take place in preparation for the coming Messiah. But it must have been a dreadful shock for him to realise that this very people of Israel, having returned to their land, and having rebuilt the city and the sanctuary, would then reject the very Messiah they were expecting. With every Messianic credential, and having presented Himself to the nation on the exact date indicated in this prophecy, they would refuse Him. Daniel must have waited with trembling heart to receive the next statement from Gabriel, knowing that it must be judgement. The sentence of heaven upon this city and this sanctuary comes as no surprise to us, yet to Daniel the shock must have been severe – this rebuilt city and this rebuilt sanctuary were marked for total destruction.

There is remarkably little dissent amongst conservative commentators that the destruction mentioned here is that carried out by the Roman General, Titus Flavius Vespasianus, in AD 70, exactly thirty-eight years from the crucifixion of Christ. In AD 67, Titus was sent from Rome to aid his father, Vespasian, in the crushing of a very serious rebellion in Judaea. Titus took control of the Fifteenth Legion and in the following campaigns showed so great personal courage and military competence that when, after the death of Nero, Vespasian returned to Rome, he left the army in charge of his son Titus. Under Titus, the Roman legions moved inexorably to stamp out the rebel armies of the Jews, until only Jerusalem and the fortress at Masada were left. After a year-long siege of Jerusalem the last defences fell before the Roman assault and the city was captured, the defenders massacred, and the Temple burnt. It made no difference that Titus had given explicit orders that the Temple was not to be burned; nor did his personal intervention to try to stop the burning accomplish anything.[45] God had already spoken, through Gabriel to Daniel, in 538 BC, of its destruction, and a greater than Daniel had said, thirty-eight years before, 'There shall not be left here one stone upon another, that shall not be thrown down' (Mt. 24:2). City and sanctuary were totally destroyed, as this prophecy foretold.

It seems inexplicable, but some expositors have difficulty in accepting that there is a time break in the prophecy at this point. For example Mr G.H. Lang[46] goes to considerable lengths to insist that the destruction of the city is not the destruction of AD 70 but the destruction still future, under the Antichrist (Zech. 14:2). This cannot be so, since the opening of the seventieth week does not take place until after the destruction of city and sanctuary. It is certainly true that there are historical parallels, where history seems to be repeated, but the history of Jerusalem makes it abundantly clear that this prophecy was fulfilled by the Roman legions under Titus, in AD 70.

The agent of this destruction is very carefully identified as 'the people of the prince that shall come'. Notice that it is 'the people' and not 'the prince' who is the subject of the verb 'destroy'. In other words, the prince must be someone different from Titus, but from amongst the people whom Titus led there would arise in the future another prince. This prince is qualified by the participle as 'coming': he has not yet arrived. The presence of the article before the participle means the literal reading would be 'prince, the coming one'. Two things are clear: (a) This cannot be Messiah the Prince, of the previous verse: in the date line of this prophecy Messiah has already come; this second prince is yet to come; (b) It cannot be Titus, since he too has arrived and gone but this prince is yet awaited and must arise from the people represented by the armies (legions) with Titus. The 'people' who actually destroy Jerusalem are clearly the Roman legions; they are the tool used in the destruction of the city. Thus it seems a reasonable inference that an able leader, identified as a 'prince', will arise from the western peoples represented in the Roman legions who destroyed Jerusalem. This person will be of sufficient importance in prophetic terms to

[45] Josephus, *Complete Works*, p. 580.
[46] Lang, *The Histories and Prophecies of Daniel*, p. 135.

be designated 'the Coming Prince'. No information is given as to the time of his arrival on the world scene. It will be shown that the prophetic clock stopped at the presentation of the Messiah, at the end of the sixty-ninth week of this prophecy, so no date can be deduced. All that can be said, at this point, is that this prince comes after the Messiah has been rejected and the city and sanctuary have been destroyed by Titus and the Roman legions. His appearance on the world scene must be at some point in the gap between the sixty-ninth and seventieth weeks. The qualification on the time of his appearance is that it must be close to the end of the gap-period, because it is his action with regard to the covenant that marks the commencement of the seventieth week. It is suggested that he will appear in the 'time of the end'[47] (11:35), from the western world empire, and be contemporary with the self-willed king in Jerusalem (11:36–39).

This offers further support for the time gap that has already come to light between the sixty-ninth and seventieth week of this prophecy. That the Roman army, representing the power of imperial Rome, from the west, destroyed the city and the sanctuary is a matter of history. In this statement is foreshadowed the coming onto the world stage of a far greater prince than Titus ever was and representing a western power far more imperial in its world control than Rome ever could be. The article that marks out this one as 'the' Coming Prince, by the usual rule of grammatical reference, would suggest that it points to someone who has already appeared in the story. Scanning the previous prophecies it is clear that the only personage that fits this pattern is the one foreshadowed in the Little Horn (7:8, 24–25) arising out of the ten-power world kingdom of the end-time. Already quite a lot has been revealed of his emergence politically on the world scene, as well as something of his career, his character and his confrontation with heaven. Since chapter 7 and this chapter 9 are focussing on the same period – 'the time of the end' – it would be most unlikely that there would two world rulers of such pre-eminence amongst the western nations. So there is a *prima facie* case for serious consideration to be given to the suggestion that both titles, 'Little Horn' and 'Coming Prince', are describing the same person. The 'Little Horn' title links him with the empire he controls, while the 'Coming Prince' title describes the emperor himself. A point of comparison arises that should not be

[47] For a discussion of 'time of the end' see Excursus after chapter 11.

overlooked; it is how heaven reacts to such a mighty man. The Divine condemnation of the Little Horn, this supremely arrogant dictator, is stated (7:26): 'But the court will convene, and his ruling authority will be removed – destroyed and abolished forever' (*NET*). It is to be noticed that his empire is stripped from him. With respect to the Coming Prince, the judgement is such that 'even unto the consummation, and that determined, shall wrath be poured out upon the desolator' (v. 27, *RV*), or, as another translation reads, 'until the decreed end is poured out on the one who destroys' (*NET*). It is to be noted that in connection with the title 'Little Horn' the empire is judged; in connection with the title 'Coming Prince' the emperor himself is judged. Thus empire and emperor are simply the two sides of one composite picture.

With this background picture of the arrival and status of the leader of a world-dominating empire understood, it will now be possible to see the significance of the action he takes to confirm the covenant (see v. 27).

Verse 26 (d) The Sentence upon the City of Jerusalem

The history of Jerusalem from this point is summarised in three solemn statements:

(a) 'And the end thereof shall be with a flood';
(b) 'And to the end there shall be war' (*RSV*);
(c) 'Desolations are determined'.

The statement 'the end thereof' is more literally translated as 'its end' (*RSV*), where the antecedent of 'its' is clearly Jerusalem. The word 'flood', as used by the prophets, describes in metaphorical language an invading army sweeping through the land (Isa. 28:2; Jer. 46:7–8; Amos 8:8; 9:5; Nah. 1:8). This is exactly how the Roman army of four veteran legions under Titus swept through Judaea, culminating in the destruction of Jerusalem in AD 70, followed by the seizure of the fortress at Masada, where the Jewish forces made their last stand. The night before the final Roman assault, the remaining warriors and families committed suicide. Since that time the people of Israel have endured much, and their capital city has suffered 'war'. On many occasions it seemed as if the 'flood' would sweep the nation entirely off the map. If Titus left a ravaged city in AD 70, and he certainly did,[48] then there are scarcely words to describe what the Emperor Hadrian did to Judaea and Jerusalem in

[48] Josephus, *Complete Works*, p. 586.

AD 142, after the Jews rebelled again, under Simon bar Kochba. Exasperated with Jewish resistance, Hadrian vowed total genocide and got close to success. Every Jew was banished and thousands died; Jerusalem was razed to the ground and the site was covered with salt.[49] More than one invading army ('flood') in the following centuries swept over this rebellious city. It is suggested that the first occurrence in the verse of the expression 'the end' refers to the destruction under Titus, and that the second occurrence, in the expression 'to the end', refers to the eschatological use of 'the end', considered more fully in the chapters to follow (ref. 11:35, 40; 12:1, 4, 9), and points to the future. Though Jerusalem will not be completely destroyed under its end-time ruler, mentioned in the next verse, it will suffer very sorely indeed (Zech. 14:1–2; Rev. 11:2). It is possible to see the whole history of Jerusalem, from the time of Titus to the time of the Antichrist, summarised in one prophetic statement – 'desolations are determined'. The word 'determined' is different from that used earlier (v. 24): this word would be more accurately rendered 'decreed' (*NIV*, *NET*, *RSV*), since it defines the Divine sentence upon Jerusalem. It seems almost as if God has written this word over Jerusalem. This statement shows that the fate of Jerusalem arises, not alone from the anti-Semitism stirred up by Satan (Rev. 12:13), but it is allowed by God as Divine judgement for sin. Jerusalem has to reap what has been sown in the rejection of its Messiah. Daniel had already observed 'desolations' (v. 18) in the Jerusalem of his day. Down the ages since then Jerusalem has been besieged twenty times, and it has been totally destroyed by an invading army[50] on seventeen occasions. The prophetic word has been truly written: 'there will be destruction' (*NET*). This will persist right to the close of the Tribulation, until the time arrives when, with repentance and confession of sin, that Messianic city will welcome the Christ, crying, 'Blessed is He that cometh in the Name of the Lord' (Mt. 23:39; Ps. 118:26). The first time He came, the nation of Israel gave Him a cross; when this moment arrives they will reverse the previous decision and will gladly give Him a crown.

[49] See Appendix 1, History of Judah.
[50] Montefiore, *Jerusalem – the Biography*, is useful for overall view of the history of Jerusalem.

The Parenthesis between the Sixty-ninth and Seventieth Weeks

1. Existence of the Time Gap

It is very clear that the message of Gabriel to Daniel anticipates a parenthesis between the sixty-ninth and the seventieth week. This is necessarily so, since both the death of the Messiah and the destruction of the city come after the sixty-ninth week has ended, with the presentation of the Messiah to the nation (v. 26), and before the commencement of the seventieth week (v. 27). The final decree of the verse, embracing war and desolations on Jerusalem, implies that the time gap would be substantial. The destruction and restoration of a city takes some considerable time, and there is the clear implication, in the plural number used, that there would be a number of these occasions.[51] A failure or a refusal to see this time gap has led commentators[52] into all kinds of interpretations of the seventieth week. Some commentators continue to think in terms of the past history of Israel and search for a parallel of the covenant in some local peace agreement made with some nation against Rome. It is hardly necessary to say any such search has always been in vain; nothing of this nature can be found in history.

Other commentators, abandoning the literal method of interpretation, try to spiritualise the statements and make them apply to the death of Christ and the New Covenant. It is here that, surprisingly, it is necessary to stand apart from such an able Aramaic scholar as E.J. Young. Young considers the arguments for the gap between the sixty-ninth and seventieth week, presented in his day by men like Alva J. McClain, A.C. Gaebelein, and J.F. Walvoord, to be unconvincing, and insists that the covenant refers to the New Covenant that Christ makes, through His cross, at the midpoint of the week. According to Young, this causes the sacrifices of Judaism to cease. Since they did not cease literally at that point, Young brings in the Hebrew epistle to show that, consequent upon His death, their efficacy was gone – the typical had given way to the real; since the veil in the Temple was rent in twain the way into the holiest[53]was now open.

[51] See Appendix 1, History of Judah.

[52] Montgomery. James A., *The International Critical Commentary, Daniel*, p. 386. He links the covenant back to Antiochus Epiphanes followed by his interruption of the sacrificial system in Jerusalem of about three years. He excuses the lack of accuracy by writing 'of the chronology of which we are ill informed'.

[53] Young, *The Prophecy of Daniel*, pp. 213–216.

Such an interpretation abandons two basic principles of Scriptural hermeneutics: first, that 'where the literal sense makes good sense, seek no other sense, lest you end up with nonsense'; second, that the context must decide the interpretation; thus if the sixty-nine weeks already considered are rooted in the history of a literal Jerusalem, this seventieth week must be of the same kind. Thus it is a period of seven years that, finding no parallel in the past history of Jerusalem and no suggestion in the context of a spiritualised interpretation as amillennialism suggests, must necessarily await fulfilment in the future. Viewed with these two principles in mind, this alternative view scarcely deserves consideration. The amillennial position is based on the assumption that the seventieth week must follow the sixty-ninth week without a break. This is totally untenable, for reasons already stated but which are summarised as follows:

(a) In the text the seventieth week is treated as a separate entity;

(b) Two events follow the closure of the sixty-ninth week, which are not in the seventieth week;

(c) There is no scriptural way in which the seventieth week can be applied to the New Covenant or the ministry of Christ in heaven. There is no support for spiritualisation of the week or any stretching of it into an indefinite period. It must be as literal as the previous sixty-nine weeks;

(d) Christ spoke of the 'abomination of desolation' (v. 27) as still future in His day (Mt. 24:15) – thus indicating that the fulfilment of the whole verse lies in the future;

(e) To the student of prophecy, gaps in the timelines come as no surprise. Many condensed prophetic statements demand such gaps. While unrecognised when first given, history shows their presence. The following are but a few examples:

Time Gaps in the Timeline of some Prophetic Statements

(a) 'For unto us a child is born, Unto us a son is given: And the government shall be upon His shoulder' (Isa. 9:6). There is a time gap of at least two thousand years between the fulfilment of these two statements. This could only be seen in the light of history.

(b) 'The Spirit of the Lord GOD is upon Me; Because the LORD hath anointed Me to preach good tidings unto the meek; He hath sent Me to bind up the broken hearted, To proclaim liberty to the captives, And the opening of the prison to them that are bound; To proclaim the acceptable year of the LORD, And the day of vengeance of our God' (Isa. 61:1–2). While reading this passage in the synagogue in Nazareth (Lk. 4:16–21), Christ stopped His reading after 'the acceptable year of the Lord' and sat down. He knew that the next statement, 'and the day of vengeance of our God', would have moved the picture forward in time, over at least two millennia of gospel preaching, to the time of the Tribulation. This particular Scripture still awaits fulfilment. Again the time gap can only be read in light of history.

(c) Already Daniel has been presented with a time gap: 'And in the latter time of their kingdom, when the transgressors are come to the full, a king of fierce countenance, and understanding dark sentences, shall stand up' (8:23). Daniel is instructed to cross the centuries to link the kingdom of Alexander the Great (died 323 BC) with a man yet to arise in the world. Another time gap will appear in the next vision of Daniel (see comments on 11:35–36).

While these time breaks would not be recognised when the prophecies were first given, they are Divinely placed, so that when other prophetic Scriptures have been given and the full programme of heaven is revealed, it will be abundantly clear that only Divine superintendence could have prevented utter confusion. It becomes evident that the Divine programme fits perfectly together.

It is essential to our understanding of the situation that events between the sixty-ninth and seventieth week of the prophecy be dealt with in some detail. Prophetically, it is vital to see that today we are still in this major time gap. Historically, it has now lasted for almost two thousand years. This is the day of grace, when the message of the gospel is sounded out and salvation proclaimed to all men – Jew and Gentile alike.

2. Events within the Time Gap

When the full revelation of NT truth is taken into account, it is abundantly clear that within this time break between the sixty-ninth and seventieth week there lie:

(a) The Setting Aside of the Nation of Israel

The Lord stated as He left the city of Jerusalem: 'Behold, your house is left unto you desolate. For I say unto you, Ye shall not see Me henceforth, till ye shall say, "Blessed is He that cometh in the name of the Lord"' (Mt. 23:38). The 'house' here is not the 'Temple', but is used metaphorically of the nation of Israel. From that which followed the presentation of Christ on the 10th *Nisan*, it is clear that the leaders of the Pharisees and the Sadducees in the Sanhedrin had already taken the decision to reject Him. After the final 'sign' to the nation, in the raising of Lazarus, there was a decision taken by a caucus in the Sanhedrin at that point: 'Then from that day forth they took counsel together for to put Him to death' (Jn 11:53). This is when Jesus withdrew with His disciples to Ephraim (Jn 11:54), where He remained until He returned to Bethany on His way to His last Passover. He arrived in Bethany 'six days before the Passover' – Friday the 8th of *Nisan* (Jn 12:1). Having rested on the Sabbath, the 9th *Nisan*, after sunset He attended the supper in the house of Simon the leper. Next morning, Sunday morning, the 10th *Nisan*, He entered the city of Jerusalem on the ass to the acclamation of the crowd. Daily He preached and ministered in the city, retreating every evening to the haven of Bethany. On the Tuesday afternoon, the 12th of *Nisan*, He preached His final message (Mt. 23:1–39) to the multitude, revealing the hypocrisy of the scribes and Pharisees, the national leaders, and pronouncing the eight 'woes' upon them. He then left the Temple court for the last time. As they went, the disciples, seemingly unconcerned at the warnings in His ministry, pointed out the magnificence of the Temple buildings. In reply, the Lord authenticates Daniel when He announces: 'There shall not be left here one stone upon another, that shall not be thrown down' (Mt. 24:2). Seated on the Mount of Olives, His disciples around Him, as evening drew on, the Lord explained the significance of His withdrawal from the Temple and answered their questions. The Lord knew well that within two days the prophecy of Daniel demanded that Messiah would be 'cut off'. Further, He knew that within forty-eight hours He would die on a cross, on the 14th *Nisan*.

That cross reflected the attitude of the nation of Israel, as shown in their leaders, to the claims of Jesus of Nazareth to be the Messiah. The title on the cross would read: 'Jesus of Nazareth the King of the Jews'; the leaders of Israel would have liked it to have read: 'He said, "I am King of the Jews"' (Jn 19:19–22). They absolutely refused His claim.

From the fourteenth day of the month *Nisan*, AD 32, it is clear that Israel, as a nation, in the Divine timeline has been set aside: in the Divine purpose they are under Divine discipline (1 Thess. 2:16). Further action towards the completion of God's programme through that nation has been suspended. The record of Scripture concerning this matter is given thus: 'Blindness in part is happened to Israel, until the fulness of the Gentiles be come in' (Rom. 11:25).

To use a metaphoric figure, it might well be said that the clock of prophecy stopped! We can be sure that when Israel, as a nation, is taken up again in the Divine timeline, then the clock of prophecy will be restarted. The moment when the prophetic clock is re-started is indicated in the next verse of this chapter (v. 27). Israel as an independent nation will be seen again on the world stage – supported by a world figure who will outrank the Caesar of Rome.

(b) The Preaching of the Gospel and the Calling-out of the Church in the Day of Grace

This age, marked by the preaching of the gospel, heralding the grace of God to all men, began on the day of Pentecost and will close when the Church is caught up to meet the Lord in the air (1 Thess. 4:13–18). To this latter event believers give the name 'Rapture', to distinguish it from the Lord's second coming to earth. The word 'rapture' comes into English via the Latin Vulgate, which translates the Greek word *harpagesometha* ('snatch away') as *raptus*. The Church having been removed from earth, this opens the way for God to take up the nation of Israel again and work out His purpose. This resumption of Divine purpose with that nation recommences, not with the removal of the Church from earth (the Rapture), but with the confirmation of a covenant in Israel that must follow the Rapture. During this interval of grace, men hear the good news of the gospel and grace flows out to all mankind, bringing blessing to individual souls – both Jew and Gentile – who believe the message. The message is based upon the death, burial, and resurrection of Jesus Christ, the Son of God. The Lord made sure that the disciples understood that His coming for the Church would be uniquely for them – hence the teaching in the upper room (Jn 13–17), where the eleven disciples are seen as representing believers of the Church age. In the upper room He promised: 'I will come again, and receive you unto Myself' (Jn 14:3). Deliberately setting no date for His return for the Church, the Lord meant that coming to be 'imminent' from the moment of His going; it was to remain 'impending', or 'overhanging', during the whole period of His absence. No event could ever be cited as necessarily to take place before His return to the air. As He was leaving (Acts 1:9–11) another promise was put in place for the Church; heavenly messengers announced: 'this same Jesus, which is taken up from you into heaven, shall so come in like manner as ye have seen Him go into heaven.' Without a mention of armies or angels or astronomical signs, the manner of His going back to heaven would be 'the manner' of His coming out from heaven for His own. The manner of His going was bodily, 'this same Jesus', visibly to His own, yet silently as far as the world around was concerned. Jerusalem, two miles around the hill, continued uninterruptedly with its religious, political and social life. Thus will it be at the Rapture, as the Church is called into the air to meet her Lord.

(c) The Rapture of the Church

The Church does not come into the prophetic picture until the nation of Israel is set aside. It is to be noticed that the seventy weeks prophecy given to Daniel has no mention of the Church; this was hidden in the counsels of God until the Lord first revealed it (Mt. 16:18), as a consequence of His rejection by the nation. Note the dates:

Presentation to the Nation as Messiah the Prince
  10th *Nisan* AD 32 Sunday
Cross of Calvary
  14th *Nisan* AD 32 Thursday
Resurrection. Feast of Firstfruits
  17th *Nisan* AD 32 Sunday
Ascension – 40 days later
  Thursday
Feast of Pentecost – 10 days later
  Sunday

This Day of Pentecost marks the incorporation of the Church (Christ and His Church become one) and the commencement of its witness. It is perfectly clear that the Church is neither a continuation of Israel under another name, nor is it a replacement of Israel in testimony on earth. The judgements and promises of the OT both belong to Israel, and will be as literally fulfilled in the future as they have been in the past. Neither judgements nor promises, on any fair exegesis, can be transferred to the Church without distorting the Word of God. The Church is a completely new entity, standing in contrast to the nation of Israel. The Church stands distinct from Israel in its calling, composition, character and destiny. Since the Lord made it plain that His return to the air for the Church was always to have the character of 'imminent', or 'overhanging', during His absence, setting a date for His return is both futile and dishonouring to His name. Ever mindful of the 'imminence' of His return for the Church, He did not give any direct prophecy for the Church age. Instead, in the letters to the seven selected local churches of the Roman province of Asia (Rev. 2–3), the Lord makes us aware that He knew what would happen down the ages of Church testimony: the conditions faced (see the letter to Smyrna), the compromises made (see the letter to Pergamum), and the corruption that would follow (see the letter to Thyatira), do not take Him by surprise. It is a joy to believers in this age to know that the Lord was aware of that which they would face in the days of Church testimony. His messages, of course, were prophetic, but with the proviso that they could only be read as such in the light of history. The fact that believers now can see the complete seven-stage history tells us that we must be very close to the close of Church testimony – the Rapture.

Since the Church did not come into the prophetic picture until Israel was set aside, simple logic would lead one to expect that the Church must be removed from earth before Israel can come back into the prophetic timeline. God would not have two witnesses to Himself on earth at the same time – that would be utter confusion. Therefore, before Israel comes back into the prophetic timeline a safe deduction demands that the Church be removed from earth. This is the point where the return of the Lord to the air for the Church comes into the prophetic programme. Since the Church as an entity is not included in any prophetic Scripture in the OT, nothing is said in this prophecy about the commencement or the close of the Church age. It can be seen that the Church age is allowed for in the gap between the sixty-ninth and seventieth week, but the truth itself was retained in the Divine counsels until the Son of Man was rejected by the nation. Neither the commencement of the Church age, announced by the Lord in the promise 'I will build my Church' (Mt. 16:18), nor the close of Church age, again announced by the Lord, in the promise given within hours of the cross, when He said, 'If I go ... I will come again, and receive you unto Myself' (Jn 14:3) were known to Old Testament saints. Once the Church has been removed from earth the way is open for God to take up the nation of Israel again.

3. End of the Time Gap

The removal of the Church does not bring Israel back into the Divine timeline, but it opens the way. That moment is reached when the Coming Prince confirms the covenant mentioned in this verse. With the confirmation of the covenant, which is for seven years, Israel is back on the prophetic timeline. The clock of Daniel's prophetic seventy weeks is restarted for the final week. This is the seven-year countdown until the Lord comes back to earth. As the leader in Israel is a party to this covenant, the nation of Israel must be back in their own land as an independent nation before the covenant can be confirmed. This is what makes the date of the establishment of the nation of Israel on May 14, 1948 of such prophetic interest to believers in the present time. At that point there was again on the international scene an independent nation that had not been amongst the nations since 606 BC – a period of 2,554 years. This independent nation, despite the bitterness of its many enemies and three major wars, has been established at this present time (2013) in their land for over sixty years and their earnest longing is for a peace treaty or covenant[54] to guarantee peace between Israel as a nation and the Palestinians, which must be underwritten by a person or authority respected by both sides. Until now every such effort has failed. One day, to the amazement of world nations, a man will succeed in bringing about this peace accord. That man will be hailed as a super-man!

Some will raise objection to this interpretation of Ezekiel 37 on the ground that it infers that Israel returns to the land in unbelief. When considered carefully, this is exactly what the chapter presents as the first step to national blessing.

It must be remembered that the ministry of Ezekiel, as well as that of Daniel, was to a people who, feeling the heel of the oppressor, were arguing that their existence as a nation was finished. In this message (Ezek. 35:1–37:28), Ezekiel shows that in contrast to other nations – particularly Edom in chapter 35 – Israel has a future. That future is given in outline in chapter 37.

That outline in Ezekiel 37 has three steps which may be set out as follows:

(a) A national return of the people of Israel to their own land (37:1–6). This chapter uses resurrection symbolically, as explained within the chapter, as a picture of national revival. It pictures dead

[54] With the hindsight of history, it would not be an unjustified assumption that the nation of Israel was readmitted to the political scene with the Declaration of Nationhood on May 14, 1948. This is the first time the nation of Israel has stood absolutely independent since 606 BC (2,554 years). The stage seems to be set for the signing of a peace agreement of some kind. The Roadmap to Peace, backed by the USA, the EU, Russia and China is still on the table at the United Nations. It demands a man who carries world authority for its implementation.

bodies coming out of graves. The graves are symbolic of the nations in which the people of Israel had been buried for so many centuries. It is suggested that this is the stage represented by the return of Israel to their land in 1948. Indeed, a real miracle of national revival, but only a preliminary step in God's dealings with them. There will follow in due course –

(b) A spiritual rebirth by the Spirit of God (37:7–10). The consequence will be –

(c) A reunion of the divided nation (37:11–23). This will mean that they way is opened for the establishment of the millennial Kingdom that follows (37:24–28).

To restate what has been set out, for clarity: since the Church is not in OT prophecy, the removal of the Church from earth, at the Rapture, cannot signal the re-instatement of Israel in the prophetic programme and the restarting of the prophetic clock. It is the confirming of the covenant, mentioned in this verse, that signals that Israel is back in the Divine timeline as a witness to the resumption of God's programme. This is surely the reason behind the conversion and commissioning of the 144,000 witnesses (Rev. 7:1–8). This must take place just before the covenant is signed. Every one of these witnesses is of Israel and identified by tribe; now saved and sealed, they are sent as witnesses to herald the good news of the coming King. This is surely evidence that the Church has gone and God is taking up His ancient people as His witness once again. So, while the day of the Lord commences with the removal of the Church (clearly set out in 1 Thess. 5:1–5), there is no indication given as to the period of time between the Rapture and the confirming of this covenant in Israel. Speculation has ranged from days to months and years. While dogmatism would be unjustified and most unwise where Scripture is silent, it would seem to be a fair inference that this period of time is part of the generation of which the Lord spoke when He said, 'This generation shall not pass till all these things be fulfilled' (Mt. 24:34). It suggests very plainly that the generation of which the Lord spoke would be the generation between the Rapture of the Church and the return of Christ to earth with His saints. Since the seventieth week is the last seven years before the return of Christ to earth, there must lie a time interval between the signing (or confirmation) of the covenant that opens the seventieth week and the Rapture (see chart, pp. 678–679). Within this period, it is clear certain events must take place, which precede the signing. Thus, the opening of the day of the Lord, signalled to earth by the catching away of the Church, becomes a warning to men on earth that the judgement of heaven is about to burst upon them. There is a clear parallel here with what happened in Noah's day; a parallel drawn by the Lord Himself (Mt. 24:34–42). The taking away of Enoch, who preached of a coming Lord (Jude 14–15), was a warning to that very generation – Methuselah's generation (Gen. 5:25–27) – upon which the flood would burst. So the taking away of the Church, as pictured in the taking away of Enoch, will be the warning to the generation upon which the Tribulation will burst. Believers, among whom will be the 144,000 witnesses and their innumerable converts (Rev. 7:9–17), safe in Christ, will pass through the dark days of the Tribulation, as pictured in Noah and his family going through the flood.

PROPHETIC LINK A

A. Prophetic Links with the New Testament

(With respect to events before the commencement of the seventieth week)

It has been made clear that this seventieth week in the prophetic calendar is opened by the public endorsement of a peace covenant in Israel by the leader of the ten-power empire – identified by Daniel as the Coming Prince. This event is but the culmination of events and happenings that may well have been in their initial stages even before the Church was removed. Some of these indeed may be ongoing as the covenant is signed and await completion in the early part of this seven-year period. Consider the following:

(a) The Expectation of Earth – The Coming of a Man

The Peace in the Middle-East
Link with Matthew 24:5; 2 Thessalonians 2:9

It is suggested that the signing of this peace covenant marks the emergence of the Coming Prince on the world stage as the Man of Sin. He is not on the world stage when the Church is on earth, but after the departure of the Church[55] there is the 'coming' (Greek word is *parousia*) of this Man of Sin (2 Thess. 2:9). This is very likely his emergence on the world stage by both his willingness and his ability to guarantee or underwrite a peace treaty between the nation

[55] 2 Thess 2:3–4. If the noun '*apostasia*' is translated literally as in all early English translations it would read 'departure' and refer to the Rapture.

history of Israel, already in the past before Zechariah's time. The next four visions deal with the conditions in the time of Zechariah, conditions among the returned remnant. The last two visions deal with the future. In the seventh vision Zechariah sees a large basket called an *ephah* – generally accepted as a symbol of commerce, and closed within the basket a woman named as 'wickedness'. A talent of lead keeps the basket closed while it is being rapidly transported back to Babylon; the wings of the women and the 'wind in their wings' emphasise the speed with which the action takes place. The purpose is given – 'to build it a house in the land of Shinar', and 'it shall be established, and set there upon her own base' (Zech. 5:5–11). What is suggested in the picture is the rapid return of world commerce to its home base in Babylon.[59] What Israel knew of the wickedness of commerce, she learned in Babylon – the golden city; and Israel carried the same ruthless, unethical, and immoral practices, learned in Babylon, round the world. Now, as Israel is in such tribulation, the dishonesty and the deceit inherent in the ruthlessness and selfishness of big business is symbolically carried back whence it came. It will be judged there. The Coming Prince will bring back to Babylon, as he makes it his financial centre, something of its past splendour, as he from this centralised capital of world commerce controls the finances of earth.

(d) The Evangelisation of Earth – Commission of the Messengers

The Preparation of the 144,000 Witnesses
Link: Matthew 24:14; Revelation 7:1–3

In the book of Revelation, John is shown (7:1–8) that the commencement of the Tribulation period – in Daniel's view the seventieth week of this prophecy – was delayed, by direct Divine order for a period, to allow the saving, sealing and sending forth of the 144,000 witnesses from the tribes of Israel. Their mission was to announce the coming King. Saved by direct Divine intervention, possibly on the pattern of Saul of Tarsus on the Damascus Road (Acts 9:1–16; 1 Cor. 15:8), this delay implies an indefinite period of time between the Rapture and the commencement of the Tribulation. There can be no doubt but that this evangelistic company will be ready to enter upon their mission as soon as the covenant is signed.

[59] See Appendix 2.

The above considerations agree with the suggestion of a 'generation', however long this may be in years, between the Lord coming to the air for the Church and His coming to the earth at the close of the seven-year Tribulation. Thus the generation that saw the beginning of the 'signs', which, it is suggested, is the Rapture of the Church, would see the last of the signs, which, it is suggested, is the Return of the Son of Man to earth (Matt. 24:30).

Verse 27 Period 3 – The Seventieth Week

Since this week is the final week of the seventy it must be of the same character as the others that have preceded it – it must be a week of 7 prophetic years of 360 days (7 × 360 = 2,520 days). It will be useful to consider this verse under three headings:

A. The Commencement of the Seventieth Week

This is a key point in the prophecy and is marked by the confirmation of a covenant between two major figures on the world stage. The first party is spoken of simply as 'he', and the second party is described as 'many', which, in the context, must refer to 'many' in the nation of Israel. If paralleled with its usage in chapter 11:39, it may be translated as 'the many', which suggests a majority within the nation. The identification of these two parties will clarify our understanding of this prophecy.

The First Party to the Covenant: The Identification of the 'he'

Within the context, the verb indicates the action of the last person mentioned; this is the 'Prince that shall come' of the previous verse. The adjectival participle translates as the 'Coming Prince', the term used by Sir Robert Anderson (*inter alia*). The repetition of the word 'prince' (v. 25 and v. 26) suggests that, while distinct from 'Messiah the Prince' in character and conduct, this man will make claims or allow claims to be made on his behalf that are reminiscent of the Messiah. The charisma is so clearly manifest in his personality and in the power he wields that men view him as the long-awaited superman – the messianic figure. Since the true Messiah was rejected on earth this imposter will fit the messianic picture drawn by men.

Since it was the power of the Roman legions that destroyed Jerusalem in AD 70, this prince must come from the west and must be the leader, whatever formal title he may use, of a world power that will show features of the old Roman Empire. The Roman

Empire has long disappeared from earth. The western Roman Empire disappeared when the city of Rome fell to the Goths in AD 476. With the fall of Constantinople to the Turks in 1453 the eastern Empire was gone at last. However, it has already been pointed out (7:23–25) that the final empire on earth, before the Son of Man takes the Kingdom, is a ten-power world kingdom whose dominion will be vastly greater than the old Roman Empire. In fact the whole European Union may just be one of the ten constituent nations of that empire. This empire has been pictured already in the fourth beast of chapter 7 (7:23–24).

The 'emperor' in control of this empire has already been identified in chapter 7 as the Little Horn (7:8) – a title pointing to his origin and his sudden emergence in the world of national politics. This is this same person in this chapter but now called the Coming Prince because of both the personal charisma allied with the political acumen that he has already shown on the world stage. This man promotes this covenant as the solution to the long-time Middle-East trouble spot – the bitter animosity existing between the State of Israel and the Palestinian people. The achievement of this peace will confirm his credentials as the peace-maker of earth and open the way for his NT identification as the 'beast from the sea' (Rev. 13:1–8), both in his 'coming' (*parousia*) at the commencement of this week (2 Thess. 2:9) and the 'Man of Sin' at the midpoint of the week when the veil is dropped (*apokaluptō*) (2 Thess. 2:8). This empire, foreshadowed by Rome headed up in the Caesar, will manifest a complete world dominion under this mighty ruler, but it will also display two additional factors that Rome never possessed. First, ten world leaders will be federally united under one man – represented by the toes of the image (2:4) and the ten horns of the Beast (7:7). Rome never had this federal feature. Further, while Rome had many enemies they generally lurked on the periphery of the empire, as did the Gauls, the Aryans, and the Parthians. This end-time empire has a weakness running through every constituent nation. This is presented in the image as 'clay' running through the feet and toes of the image (2:41–43). Comments on that passage (see *in loc.*) have already suggested that the clay may represent the cultural divide running through all the ten constituent nations of this empire as a result of the rise of Islam – from the seventh century AD to the present day.[60]

The Second Party to the Covenant: The Identification of the 'many'

The other party to this covenant is identified simple as 'many', which, in context, must identify a company within the nation of Israel. Studying the usage of this term (see 11:39; 12:2) it would be a reasonable deduction that the term indicates a majority of the nation. While not stated explicitly, this prophecy very clearly demands: (a) that the Jewish people are back again in their own land as an independent nation; (b) that they have the political power to make an alliance or enter into a covenant of this nature; (c) that they are a nation organised on democratic principles. Such, it is suggested, are true of Israel since May 1948. While the phrase 'the many' stresses individual culpability yet it still leaves room for an autocratic leader. At this juncture this will assuredly be the one of whom Christ has spoken: 'I am come in My Father's name, and ye receive Me not; if another shall come in his own name him ye will receive' (Jn 5:43); this is the one in whom 'the many' in unbelieving Israel put implicit confidence and trust.

Daniel has already been told of just such a dictatorial leader in Israel. In this man it is easy to see the features of the 'king of fierce countenance' (8:23–26) already introduced. This king is evidently endowed with a remarkable and strange charisma. He shows a power clearly derived from another – 'not by his own power' (8:24); a prosperity that allows him to buy supporters and with a policy that encourages underhand dealing of all sorts ('craft') to prosper in Israel. Most important he has the answer to the conflict in the land of Israel – he is offering 'peace'. The statement of his activity, 'by peace shall destroy many' (8:23–25), points to the signing of this covenant. His personality demands that the nation follow his lead and accept this peace, which will prove so disastrous.

This leader of the democratic majority of Israel, with his mind set on peace, has a purpose before his mind. This becomes clear when he is seen finally in this prophecy as the 'king that shall do according to his will', often spoken of by commentators as 'the wilful King' (11:36–40). In this personage are seen the very same features as the 'king of fierce countenance', but with an additional

[60] For further detail see Excursus on the term 'Revived Roman Empire' at the end of this chapter.

factor – he is an apostate – he turned from the 'God of his fathers' to honour the 'god of forces'. This is a clear reference to his rejection of Israel's God and the reception of the claims of the 'Coming Prince' of this chapter, who in the NT is called the 'Man of Sin' (2 Thess. 2:3–4).

The apostasy, followed by the deception practised by this king as he utilises a power that is evidently satanic (8:24) to achieve the confirmation of this covenant, will be fully displayed when, in the middle of the 'week' as discussed below, he breaks the covenant. His apostasy will be clearly manifested when he assumes a priestly role and demands worship for the image placed on the wing of the Temple, described here as 'the overspreading of abominations'.

To keep the full picture before us it should be pointed out that in the book of Revelation this same person is called the 'false prophet' on three occasions (Rev. 16:13; 19:20; 20:10). On behalf of his mentor – the blaspheming claimant to Deity – this man becomes spokesman and herald from the midpoint of the Tribulation. He thus plays the part of a prophet to a false deity and, supported by the attendant miracles expected of a prophet, 'deceiveth them that dwell on the earth' (Rev. 13:11–17). First seductively, then threateningly, he leads men in the worship of the 'Man of Sin'. Thus Scripture describes this false prophet so accurately – 'he had two horns like a lamb and he spake as a dragon' (Rev. 13:11).

There can be little question that this man arising in Israel to lead his people into this disastrous covenant will have the features of a prophet, a priest and a king. In this he is best fitted to bear the title **'Antichrist'** (1 Jn 2:18). This time the prefix 'anti' is to be understood in its full substitutionary meaning – 'in place of' or 'instead of' – thus he takes the place of the Messiah to Israel. This is the man who leads the nation of Israel into the most unholy alliance of all time before which the Israel-Assyria alliance of Isaiah's day fades into insignificance. It is clear that at this time in the prophetic picture Israel has few friends. The Palestinian cause is supported with the full might of the surrounding Muslim nations. A fire-breathing Iran stands ready to wipe Israel off the map even using nuclear power if necessary. With these threats in mind, it is easy to understand that this man persuades the majority of his people to enter into a covenant of peace with the Palestinians. The assurance he gives is that this covenant will be guaranteed to hold firm, unlike all the previous covenants, because it is to be underwritten by the charismatic leader of the mightiest political power earth has ever known – greater even than mighty Rome in its heyday.

It is not simply that this man deceives the nation – they know exactly what is at stake and enter into the covenant gladly. As pointed out, Isaiah heard the boast in that earlier day:

> We have made a covenant with death and with hell are we at agreement; when the overflowing scourge shall pass through it will not come unto us; for we have made lies our refuge and under falsehood have we hid ourselves (Isa. 28:15).

God answered the complacency with the plain message through Isaiah: 'your covenant with death shall be disannulled, and your agreement with hell shall not stand; when the overflowing scourge shall pass through ye shall be trodden down by it' (Isa. 28:18). The same answer will apply in this still future day.

These two men on the world stage, placed there as satanic princes or puppets (Rev. 13:1, *RV*), from the moment of the confirmation of this covenant, have the key roles to play in leading the rebels of earth into confrontation with heaven at Armageddon (Rev. 16:12–16). From this moment there is but seven years until the arrival of the Son of Man.

The Confirmation of the Covenant

The literal translation of the next statement points to the action by this Prince that ensures his prominence on the world stage. In fact, it may herald his 'arrival' on the world stage – notice the word 'coming' (*parousia*) used in connection with this same personage in the NT (2 Thess. 2:9). The action he takes at this time reads literally, '[he] shall cause a covenant to be strong'.[61] A covenant is generally made 'strong' or 'sure' by the authority of the signatories. The verb itself carries no suggestion of the ratification of an existing covenant. To use the verb in that way requires the article to qualify 'covenant' – which article is missing here. However, the context does allow the 'making strong' to refer to the value of the covenant in the eyes of the public, and may point to a public signing of a covenant personally brokered by this 'Prince' between the Israeli leader and the representatives of Islam. This will surely include representatives of the Palestinian people. This will allow the Israeli leader to present this covenant, now publicly endorsed by earth's mightiest leader, to his nation as 'firm' or 'strong' or indeed 'unbreakable'.

[61] Wood, *A Commentary on Daniel*, p. 258.

These two mighty men will doubtless endorse such a covenant in the most public way possible. This will likely take the form of an announcement before an international gathering in Jerusalem in the glare of the world media. Earth's nations cannot believe that such a peace, after so many years, has, at last, been brokered. This world-dominating figure, head of the ten-kingdom empire, lends his authority to a covenant bringing peace to the Middle East. For the first time since 1948 there is peace between the Israelis and Palestinians. This seeming impossibility has been brought about, and now publicly guaranteed, by this mighty man. The secret of his power, from the world's viewpoint, is that this man not only has the support of the military potential of the best equipped forces of the western nations but he has also the confidence of the major Arab states with their oil and wealth, along with more moderate brand of Islam.

The achievement of such a peace not only ensures the hailing of the western leader as the 'peace-maker' of all time but delivers Israel from the threat of Islamic invasion from the north. There can be little question that, by this time, Israel will have lived under such a threat for many years. Iran has been the source of the threat, but having the support of the militant Islamic majorities in lands to the north (some in Russian territory and many under Turkey) such an invasion would sweep through the land of Israel 'as a flood'. Scripture envisages such a northern invasion (*cf.* 11:40–45 and Ezek. 38:1–6).[62] In the twenty-first century it hangs threateningly over Israel, awaiting the moment when, its nuclear ambition achieved, Iran decides to fulfil its threat and wipe Israel off the world map. Israel has outlived such threats before – the War of Independence in 1948–49, the Six-Day War in 1967, and the Yom Kippur War in 1974. Compared to this northern invasion these would appear somewhat minor skirmishes. The immediate result of the peace covenant is a world-acclaimed acceptance to the solution of the world's most insoluble problem. It would seem that, with this covenant, the Middle East problem has, at long last, been resolved; peace is assured for seven years between Israel and the Palestinians with the support of the moderate Islamic nations.

[62] See comments on the northern invasion under 11:40–45. It will be shown that Russia is drawn into the conflict because of its Islamic populations and their commitment to militant Islam. That moderate Islam is against Iran was exposed in a leading article in the *Daily Telegraph* of July 11, 2013, where it was revealed that the missiles in the storage silos of Saudi Arabia are targeted on Jerusalem and on Tehran.

In this action this Prince has 'come' – has 'arrived' on the world stage. Such an unbelievable and unexpected diplomatic triumph as the peace in the Middle East has marked his 'coming' (Greek – '*parousia*', 2 Thess. 2:9) – he has shown himself to be the man whom earth has long awaited.

B. Prophetic Links with the New Testament

(With respect to events after the commencement of the seventieth week)

In the overall prophetic picture it is necessary to point out that the confirmation of this covenant on earth and the taking of the seven-sealed book by the Lamb from the hand of the throne Sitter in heaven must coincide (Rev. 5:7) – they must be synchronous. Both actions, one in heaven and the other on earth, signal the commencement of the Tribulation period – the last seven years of earth history prior to the coming of the Son of Man and the setting up of the Kingdom.

In Daniel (9:27) – the seven-year Tribulation is covered in this one verse. The commencement has been shown to be the covenant signed in Israel. The crisis occurs 'in the midst of the week'. Then the focus moves directly to the close of the week, which it speaks of as the consummation.

In Revelation (6:1–19:10) – the seven-year Tribulation is given in 234 verses. Details of events in these same seven years are given from heaven's viewpoint in the book of Revelation; from the opening of the first seal (Rev. 6:1) until the opening of heaven (Rev. 19:11) covers the same time as Daniel's one verse but with much more detail. The seven seals are opened, the seven trumpets are blown and the seven bowls are poured out. The close of the seven years is marked by the cry from the throne: 'it is done'. At that moment the heavens are opened and John says, 'I saw heaven opened and behold a white horse and him that sat upon him was called Faithful and True' (Rev. 19:11). Daniel has already identified Him as the Son of Man but John goes further and speaks of Him as 'The Word of God' made manifest as 'King of kings and Lord of lords' (Rev. 19:11–16). This final week of the seventy weeks prophecy will see the consummation of the programme of heaven in the person identified as Messiah the Prince.

The Crisis in the Midst of the Seventieth Week

This week is divided into two parts by a crisis that arises at the midpoint. Without explanation, the next statement informs us that 'he shall cause the sacrifice and oblation to cease'. The antecedent of the 'he' must be the prince who confirmed the covenant. The 'sacrifice and oblation' are terms that refer technically to the two types of offerings in the sacrifices in the OT ceremonial Law – the blood sacrifices and the non-blood offerings. Along with the permission to rebuild the Temple, it would seem the sacrificial system has been re-established as a result of the covenant now in place. Muslim objections and Arab protests seem to have been overruled; perhaps hidden concessions, or possibly hidden promises, have been given to the Muslim world. Now, for some reason not stated in this prophecy, the prince orders all these religious observances to cease immediately. It is generally accepted that this happens in spite of all the promises he has made; in other words, he breaks the covenant. Since the NT makes it plain that both these men are deceivers of the highest order, it might well be that this cessation of the Jewish ceremonial observances is not the breaking of the covenant, as is generally assumed, but the implementation of a secret codicil to the covenant that was included to satisfy the Muslim world at the time of the signing. Now the covenant is implemented in full and the previously hidden clauses come to light. It could well be that this deception was part of the plan from the beginning, to lull Israel into a false sense of security – a suggestion lent some weight by the fact that the Jewish leader does not seem to have made the slightest protest over the cessation of the sacrifices; he remains the non-protesting faithful supporter of the Prince during the last half of the week. In fact, it could be argued from the very ambiguity of the antecedent of the 'he' that both men are guilty of this blasphemous act. They seem to have acted almost as one in this matter. It will be recalled that Antiochus acted through his appointee – Menelaus, the high priest in Jerusalem who betrayed his people in 167 BC.

The very language used concerning the sacrifice and oblation must have recalled to the mind of Daniel the prophecy given to him thirteen years previously in connection with the Greek Empire and recorded for us in his second vision (8:8–14). This prophecy has already been considered in detail (see comments *in loc.*), and shown to have been fulfilled in a successor of Alexander the Great called

Antiochus IV Epiphanes, who reigned over the eastern division of Alexander's Empire from his capital city, Antioch, for twelve years (175–163 BC). In 167 BC he defiled the brazen altar in the Temple in Jerusalem by the sacrifice of a pig, desecrated the holy place with the pig's blood and placed the idol of *Jupiter Capitolinus* within the sacred precincts of the Temple – thus bringing the daily sacrifice in Judaism to an end. He carried out this action with the total support of the 'many' in Israel under the leadership of the high priest, Menelaus, who bribed Antiochus to appoint him and ruled Jerusalem from 171–161 BC. This prophecy was given to Daniel in 'the third year of the reign of King Belshazzar' (551 BC) and was fulfilled to the letter by Antiochus IV Epiphanes some 384 years after the prophecy of Daniel. For Daniel it was given as prophecy; for us it is seen as history.

In these four visions, Daniel is given details of the pollution of the sanctuary in Jerusalem on two occasions. The first occasion, as has been mentioned, is in his second vision (8:9–14), where Antiochus Epiphanes is seen as the 'Little Horn', and the question is asked and answered, 'How long shall be the vision concerning the daily sacrifice and the transgression of desolation' (8:13). In his fourth vision (11:21–31) Daniel is allowed to speak of the same Antiochus Epiphanes, but seen as a 'vile person', acting in the same way – 'And arms shall stand on his part and they shall pollute the sanctuary of strength, and shall take away the daily sacrifice, and they shall place the abomination that maketh desolate' (v. 31). The same king is clearly in view. The figure 'the Little Horn' infers the unexpected power with which he acted; the epithet 'vile' implies the deception and perfidy of this contemptible person. These passages fasten on the one despicable blasphemous action of betrayal that is copied by the Coming Prince in this passage. The word used in each case is 'abomination', since it was basically an act inspired by idolatry, and it left an unforgettable mark on Israel.

For the Lord Jesus this was history, as it is for us. So when the Lord speaks as he did to His disciples (Matt. 24:5): 'when ye therefore shall see the abomination of desolation, spoken of by Daniel the prophet, stand in the holy place' (Matt. 24:15), He is not speaking of that which is in the past but of something future to Daniel, in this year 538 BC, and something still future in the time of the Lord. It is clear that the Lord understood that the blasphemous action of Antiochus Epiphanes would be the pattern of a far more powerful and perfidious figure than Antiochus could ever be. This passage speaks, as does the next and final vision (see comments at 12:11), of a time, future to Daniel and still future to us, when a blasphemous idolatrous action by two men – and both must share guilt – will bring about the cessation of the animal sacrifices in Judaism, which had been reinstituted as a result of the peace covenant in Israel. This is the midpoint of the seventieth week.

That the cessation of the Jewish sacrifices was but the prelude to a far more blasphemous action is seen in the next strange statement: 'for the overspreading of abominations he shall make it desolate'. Most Hebrew scholars (Gesenius *et al.*) are agreed that the word 'overspreading' should be translated 'wing', but here agreement ends and interpretations are many. The translation with most textual support reads: 'on the wing of abominations will come one who destroys' (*NET*). It would also seem that the most justifiable interpretation is to interpret the 'wing' as 'the wing of the Temple', or, as it is called in the Gospels, the 'pinnacle of the Temple' (Matt. 4:5). Here Satan sought to tempt Christ to make a dramatic claim to Deity by casting Himself down from it. Of course, Christ utterly refused the devil's offer. Perhaps the idea is that this Prince, with the aid of his miracle-working prophet, will do what Christ refused to do and give a miraculous public demonstration of his claim to Deity. Such would catch world attention and encourage him to the supreme act of blasphemy, of which Scripture speaks thus: 'so that he as God sitteth in the Temple of God, showing himself that he is God' (2 Thess. 2:3–6). While he seats himself there initially, and since he cannot be there all the time, it would seem that his colleague in Israel, the false prophet, comes again to his aid, and suggests that an image be made that men may be able, constantly and publicly, to show their allegiance to this blasphemer (Rev. 13:14–17). Thus, the 'abomination of desolation' would be the image placed on the Temple pinnacle in Jerusalem at the midpoint of the seventieth week. Those who accept this blasphemous claim will share the judgement of this false claimant to Deity.

C. Prophetic links with other Prophetic Scriptures
(Events around the Midpoint of the Seventieth Week)

It must be clear that this particular event has a background from which it arises as well as consequences that flow from it. The complete picture demands consideration of both OT and NT

Scriptures centred upon the midpoint of the seventieth week. The order of events as given below is but suggestive:

Events Leading up to the Midpoint of Seventieth Week

1. The Muslim Invasion. It does seem that the very thing Israel feared and had entered into this covenant to avoid must befall that land. It would seem that the invasion of the land of Israel by militant Islam (see comments on 11:36–45) takes place just before the midpoint of the seventieth week, when Israel has been at peace for almost three-and-a-half years, with the subsequent run-down of their formidable security forces. Led by Iran (called by its old name, Persia), Sudan (called by its old name, Ethiopia) and Libya (which still bears this name, Ezek. 38:5), and drawing in the nations that have been under Russian control (Ezek. 38:4), because their populations are predominately Islamic, this treacherous attack will take Israel completely by surprise. The Prince in this passage, the leader of the western ten-power kingdom, makes a very feeble protest (Ezek. 38:13). Most likely, he raises the matter in the Security Council, or, possibly, makes a protest on the floor of the United Nations or some similar body but he refuses any direct military involvement in coming to the aid of his colleague in Jerusalem – his word is seen to be valueless. It is only because God steps in and destroys the invading armies (Ezek. 38:18–23) that Israel is preserved from total destruction. Yet the leader in Israel – the Antichrist, and the western leader – the Prince, seem able to keep faith with each other through this crisis, possibly even claiming some diplomatic skill in handling the situation.

2. The Assassination/Resurrection Scene. The covenant remains in place and it is possible that perhaps some public celebration is arranged to both celebrate the deliverance of Israel and to warn the moderate Islamic nations not to repeat the error of the Islamic militants. Some sort of celebratory gathering may be the background for the 'assassination' and 'resurrection' of this coming Prince. This is where the Prince in this passage – whose 'coming' (the Greek word is '*parousia*') is linked with the commencement of the covenant. At the midpoint, one of the heads of the 'beast from the sea' (Rev. 13:1–8) is 'wounded to death', yet 'his deadly wound was healed' (Rev. 13:3–4). As one claiming resurrection from the dead, he is worshipped by men: 'and they worshipped the beast saying 'who is like unto the beast? And who shall make war with him?' (Rev. 13:7). Encouraged by such adulation, this man takes that final blasphemous step that identifies him as the Man of Sin who enters the Holiest – 'the Holiest' is a reference to the most sacred place in Judaism: 'so that he as God sitteth in the temple of God, shewing himself that he is God' (2 Thess. 2:3–4). At this midpoint the veil is dropped and 'the Man of Sin' is revealed – the Greek verb is '*apokalupto*' meaning 'the uncovering; the unveiling'. This can be seen as almost his second coming; from this point to the end of the week, he demands the worship of earth (see comments at 11:40–45).

3. **The Setting up of the Image.** Suggested by the Beast out of the earth (Rev. 13:11–17) to represent the Beast from the sea, this is placed on the Temple wing. A breathing, speaking image demands that the worship of earth be directed to the Man of Sin – the final display of Babylonian idolatry symbolised in the image of Nebuchadnezzar (chapter 3).

Events Following the Midpoint of the Seventieth Week

4. **The Martyrdom of the two Witnesses.** Having endured their ministry for the first half of the Tribulation period, the Man of Sin seizes his moment to destroy them (Rev. 11:7–13). Their ministry to Israel finished and their Divine protection withdrawn, they are killed by the security forces of the Man of Sin. Their bodies lie in the street of Jerusalem until the fourth day. Their resurrection and rapture to heaven give eloquent testimony to the authenticity of their ministry and, for just a moment, bring reality to rebel earth.

5. **The Destruction of the Harlot.** It is at this point that the Man of Sin, who had supported the harlot (apostate Christianity) up to this point, decides that she is no longer of value to him so he, with his ten kings, destroys the harlot utterly. The detail of this world-shattering action is described in detail in the Revelation (Rev. 14:8; 17:1–18). The Man of Sin will allow no other form of religion to divert attention from the worship that he claims for himself. Judaism has been destroyed; apostate Christianity has now been dealt with and this leaves but one world religion to contest his claim. Islam will soon be on the move again. The armies from the east are mobilising for Armageddon (Rev. 9:13–19).

6. **The Flight of Israel.** All those in the land of Israel who will not accept the claims of the Man of Sin will have to flee for their lives.

The Lord warned of this (Matt. 24:15–24) and John saw it symbolised in the flight of the woman (Rev. 12:6). This launches the greatest act of genocide in all history. The nation of Israel is to be wiped out to the last individual that can be found by the security forces of the Beast. Anyone who shelters, supports or supplies these fugitives could pay with their lives (Matt. 25:34–40). This is why the faith of true believers in Christ is recognised in this way – their response to the need of Christ's brethren. This action is a follow-up to the relentless war to the death against all who have professed to believe in Christ (Rev. 12:17; 13:7).

These actions show that the western prince has achieved total dominance in all areas of life; he is politically and militarily unassailable, commercially, through his financial wizardry, he has established a Babylonian-type empire with its rebuilt commercial centre on the banks of the Euphrates. Religiously, he has destroyed apostate Christianity ('the harlot') and apostate Judaism, and now the final Babylonian idolatry is unveiled as he claims Deity for himself. This claim has been supported by the image placed on the wing of the Temple in Jerusalem. No wonder the word 'abomination', which in the OT is the contemptuous designation of idolatry, is used here. This blasphemy will render the Temple an 'abomination' to God and this iniquitous man will be the very instrument of desolation. The antecedent of the 'he' is this same person; 'shall make it desolate' is a spiritual description of the result of his action. He is described in the final sentence as 'the desolator' (*RV*). In fact, this man is the reason why God allows Divine judgement to fall upon the Temple and the city, as well as engulf the apostate people of Israel associated with him during these final three-and-a-half years – forty-two months (Rev. 11:2) – of the Tribulation.

The Consummation of the Seventieth Week

The last half of this seventieth week, which corresponds exactly with the three-and-a-half years of 'great tribulation' (Rev. 7:14), is when Jerusalem is 'trodden underfoot' (Rev. 11:2) for forty-two months and all Israelites who will not bow to the image are put to death – an anti-Semitic genocide that will surpass the Holocaust (when six million Jews perished). The final statements of this verse point onward to the consummation of this period in two world-shaking events:

(a) 'Until the Consummation and that determined'. The word 'consummation' (Heb '*kala*') means 'full end' and it suggests that the desolation that has been taking place from the midpoint of the seventieth week, because of the image on the Temple pinnacle, will have its 'full end', indeed its 'consummation', when the time period runs out on the last day of the seventieth week. From our link with the book of Revelation, it can be seen that this will be when two things occur simultaneously. First, the seventh vial brings the shattering earthquake (Rev. 16:18) and then heaven opens to allow earth to see the Rider on the White Horse (Christ in conquest (Rev. 19:11). The word 'determined' is the same word as used above (v. 26) and means 'decreed'. Heaven has passed its judicial sentence upon the city and the nation, and this will be executed completely.

(b) 'Shall be poured upon the desolate' or compare the *RV* reading: 'shall wrath be poured out upon the desolator'. The *RV* supplies the missing subject for the verb in the *AV* translation, and this is supportable from the context. On good manuscript authority, it also changes the object of the wrath from 'the desolate' (*AV*) to 'the desolator' (*RV*). These last three-and-a-half years see the wrath of God poured out upon the rebellious men of earth. When the term 'wrath of God' is used in Thessalonians (1 Thess. 1:10; 2:16; 5:9) and in Revelation (11:18; 14:10; 16:19; 19:15) it must be understood as pointing directly to Tribulation times. The word 'desolate', changed to 'desolator' (*RV*), points unequivocally to the prince in this prophecy, also described as the 'beast out of the sea' (Rev. 13:1) and 'the Man of Sin' (2 Thess. 2:3–4). This is the desolater who has brought such desolation to Israel through his agent the Antichrist, also described as the false prophet (Rev. 16:13) and the Wilful King (11:36). That desolation will be complete on the return of Christ to earth. John records what happens:

> And the beast was taken, and with him the false prophet that wrought miracles before him, with which he deceived them that had received the mark of the beast, and them that worshipped his image. These both were cast alive into a lake of fire burning with brimstone (Rev. 19:20).

This prophecy clears the way for the revelation of the Christ in Kingdom glory.

EXCURSUS

Why does Scripture make no reference to a Revived Roman Empire?

The image in Nebuchadnezzar's dream (2:31–45) shows that only four world empires fill the historical period called by the Lord the 'times of the Gentiles' (Lk. 21:24), which defines the period when the nation of Israel is subjected to a Gentile power; in fact, from the time that King Nebuchadnezzar captured Jerusalem to the coming of Christ to take the dominion of earth. The Coming One in that programme is seen as 'the stone'. Christ, at His coming in glory, will smash all earthly political power. Nebuchadnezzar is identified by Daniel as the head of gold (2:38). The two empires that followed the Babylonian are identified in Daniel's vision in chapter 8 as Medo-Persia (2:39; 8:20), symbolised as the ram; and as Greece (2:39; 8:20), symbolised as the he-goat. The fourth empire, significantly enough, is not named but history tells us it was the Roman Empire, which took world dominion from the Greeks. In the time of the Roman Empire Christ came and died on a cross. It has already been argued in the comments on this chapter that, at the end of the sixty-ninth week, and the presentation of Christ to the nation, the prophetic clock stopped. The rejection of the Messiah and His subsequent death on the cross follow the stopping of the prophetic clock. That the cross of Calvary is the first event in the time break that must occur between the sixty-ninth and seventieth week of this prophecy has already been presented.

As already discussed, there must be a time break in each of the timelines – the seventy weeks prophecy and the image picture. Since there can only be one time break in each timeline it must be the same in both cases. The time break in the seventy weeks prophecy begins at the close of the sixty-ninth week when Christ is presented to the nation of Israel. This has already been shown to be 10th *Nisan* AD 32. In the image picture, this must come just below the thighs, near the commencement of the iron part of the image, early in the Roman Empire (see chart, p. 676). If the prophetic clock stops at this point then this means that the subsequent history of the Roman Empire after AD 32 is irrelevant from the prophetic viewpoint. Even the east-west division into two empires with capitals in Rome (Western Empire) and Constantinople (Eastern Empire), which might be suggested as represented in the two legs of the image, cannot be in view.[1] So, to look for two divisions of the Roman Empire or the coming together of ten separate kings in one federal state under the Caesar is futile – point on which Roman historians would agree – there is no such development in the history of that empire. In fact, the Roman Empire has long since left the stage of world history. The Western Empire was invaded by the Goths and the city of Rome fell to these invaders in AD 476. The Eastern Empire, later spoken of as the Byzantine Empire, was taken over by the Ottoman Turks after the capture of Constantinople in 1453.

It is a strange fact that the Roman Empire is never mentioned in prophetic Scripture, neither here in Daniel, nor elsewhere in the OT. It comes into the history of the NT as it must, but from a strict scriptural view, Christ is put to death under the fourth empire in Nebuchadnezzar's dream image. Doubtless, the Roman Empire had features, as already set forth, that will be fully developed in this fourth empire, but the empire remains nameless in Scripture. So, there is little point in speaking of the Roman Empire prophetically, never mind a 'revived Roman Empire'. Based on the statement of John concerning the Beast, 'I saw one of his heads as it were wounded unto death' (Rev. 13:3), many have seen the fall of the Roman Empire, either with the fall of Rome in AD 476 or with the fall of Constantinople in 1453 – it makes no difference. In the next statement, 'and his deadly wound was healed', they see the 'revival' of the old Roman Empire in the last days. Those who accept this line of teaching look diligently for the old boundaries of that empire; they look for the common language link, the common law link and other links that remind us of the unity imposed by the old Roman Empire. All this is unnecessary and based on a faulty interpretation of the wounding of the Beast. This must be interpreted as the fall, not of an empire, but of a person; in the same way the recovery must be of that person, not an empire. The assassination / (pseudo) resurrection fits the picture much better. It is to be observed that in the Revelation, after the wounding and healing scene, the Beast is called the 'beast out of the abyss'. As G.H. Lang writes succinctly: 'In what conceivable sense can an *empire* or a *city* or political *system* go *there*, and come thence again?[2]

[1] It should be remarked the Scripture never stresses the numbers either in the case of the *two* legs or of the *ten* horns.

[2] Lang, *The Histories and Prophecies of Daniel*, p. 150, italics in original.

As the timeline in the seventy weeks prophecy is taken up again with the focus on the final week, so must the focus in the image be upon the feet and the toes of the image. This is where the 'stone' smites the image (2:34), as the first action in the setting up of the Kingdom of God is the destruction of the whole image. So, the timeline in the image must be taken up again when an empire is present on earth that includes the former territory of Rome,[3] but goes far beyond its boundaries in all directions – it is no longer centred round the Mediterranean Sea, but touches the continents of earth. A second feature is that, while it copies Rome, being under the control of one man, in this case, the final emperor will far outrank any Caesar. He will carry an authority that no Caesar ever commanded. Other features will reflect Rome in a common language expected and a common policy for trade, education, law and finance that seeks to bridge culture differences – perhaps with limited success. Globalisation will have gone as far as it can to unite men of earth.

Two points on which this empire will certainly differ from the Roman Empire are: (a) It will be composed of ten nations whose leaders willingly agree to put their nations under the control of the charismatic figure who now rules earth; (b) Through many of these nations, if not all, there is a culture that cannot be assimilated into the empire – the cultures are so distinct in basic outlook that to unite with others they cannot. Like clay and iron they will not cohere. It has already been suggested that this indicates Islam and its failure to bind with other peoples and other cultures. This becomes the inbuilt weakness of this mighty empire (see comments at 2:40–43). On the chart on page 676, the horizontal band will show the time gap as applied to the image. It can be seen that when the Church is removed from earth at the Rapture there will exist, or very soon after the Rapture come into existence, a mighty empire that will have features that reflect the uniqueness of the Roman Empire. It will have the world domination seen in Rome on a small scale, and it will have as Emperor a man of such charismatic personality who will outrank Nebuchadnezzar, Cyrus and Alexander the Great, on the pattern of a Caesar, but far outranking any Caesar. In its scope and its sovereignty it features the Roman Empire, but the territorial extent of this empire goes far beyond

[3] Could the European Union be one of the nations represented in the ten toes? Or could the Anglo-American Union or Confederacy be one of the ten toes? Time will tell.

Mediterranean shores. This is the kingdom existing when Christ comes as Son of Man to claim His Kingdom. The question might be asked – why not use the term 'revived', 'restored', or 'reconstituted' to qualify the coming empire?

Since Scripture does not use the term 'revived Roman Empire' it is better not to use it. Unless carefully defined it may cause problems in our thinking. As has been pointed out, the assassination/resurrection scene belongs to an individual, not to a nation. The mighty USSR, torn apart in 1991, has re-emerged on the world scene in the last decade and has caused some diplomatic stir and headlines in a few newspapers but no-one thought of worshipping the empire. In the absence of Scriptural reference, it seems to be importing an unnecessary term into prophetic teaching that has caused problems in our view of the timing of events. The features of the Roman Empire are clearly reflected in the final phase of Gentile rule over Israel and show the fulness only after the clock of prophetic truth is restarted by the signing of the covenant for the commencement of the seven years of Tribulation.

CHAPTER 10

THE LAST THREE CHAPTERS of the book of Daniel record the fourth and final vision given to Daniel. The relative dates of the four visions are important and should be noted:

Ch.7	First year of Belshazzar	553 BC	Daniel aged 70	Vision 1
Ch.8	Third year of Belshazzar	551 BC	Daniel aged 72	Vision 2
Ch.5	Final year of Belshazzar	539 BC	Daniel aged 84	
Ch.6	First year of Darius	538 BC	Daniel aged 85	

(Notice there is a gap of thirteen years between chapter 8 and chapter 9)

Ch.9	First year of Darius	538 BC	Daniel aged 85	Vision 3
Ch. 10	Third Year of Cyrus	536 BC	Daniel aged 87	Vision 4

It should be noticed that the third year of Cyrus is also the third year of Darius, who was made king over Babylon in the year Cyrus captured that city (539 BC). Cyrus was the Persian overlord of Darius the Mede. It will also be noticed that the first two visions were given to Daniel in the first and third years of the last ruler in Babylon (Belshazzar), while the last two were given in the first and third years of the Medo-Persian Empire, which followed the Babylonian Empire in history.

After the climactic and dramatic unfolding of world-shaking events in the earlier visions, this one seems almost an anticlimax. However, there are aspects to it that mark it as vitally important and absolutely unique in character. A glance at some of these features would prepare us for the study.

Special Features that distinguish this Final Vision

The final revelation given to Daniel is overshadowed by a unique Theophany (vv. 4–9) that left Daniel prostrate on the ground in the presence of Deity. A figure, described as 'a certain man clothed in linen' (v. 5), stands over the river Hiddekel, as if overseeing this final vital vision given to Daniel. At the end of the vision, in answer to

Daniel's direct question, He speaks with unquestionable authority (12:5–7) and, when requested, reveals with Divine assurance the timing of the events disclosed. Pictures of the Messiah (Christ) have already been presented in the earlier chapters. Seen as the Stone (2:35), He destroys the corrupt political systems (kingdoms) that have held dominion over the earth. Described by a pagan king as the One 'like the Son of God' (3:25), Christ accompanies His people in the furnace of persecution (3:24–26). Entitled 'Son of Man', He introduces the everlasting Kingdom (7:13–14) and takes His place as King. Identified as 'Messiah', this same One is timetabled into earth history (9:24–27) for the working out of the Divine programme. Now, in this final vision, there is unveiled a glimpse of this same glorious Person. Despite the hesitation of some expositors[1] there can be little question: Daniel is granted the rare privilege of a Theophany (a pre-incarnation revelation of Deity). This makes the final words of this awesome Figure most weighty. As the book is closed it reveals Him awaiting the day when, the Divine programme complete, He takes His place with His people in the Kingdom that will never be superseded. He announces: 'Blessed is he that waiteth, and cometh to the thousand three hundred and five and thirty days. But go thou thy way till the end be: for thou shalt rest, and stand in thy lot at the end of the days' (12:12–13). The waiting believer joins the waiting Christ in anticipation of the coming Kingdom.

Prophetic Link

The final note of this chapter may be compared with the closing words of the book of Revelation. The same Person Who spoke to Daniel for Israel spoke to John for the Church and announced 'Surely I come quickly' (Rev. 22:20). Saints in this present age await their coming Lord to close this part of the Divine programme and open the way for the proclamation of the Kingdom, when saints on earth will await their coming King.

Another vital point must not be missed. With this vision, the perplexity that has filled the mind of Daniel from previous revelations is resolved. From this fourth vision he will have an 'understanding' that he did not previously enjoy (v. 1). In the previous paragraph, one aspect has been clarified – understanding of prophecy centres on a Person – the Messiah; without Him at the

[1] Paisley, *This Daniel*, p. 156.

centre, prophecy cannot be understood. But a second vital point arises, around the time of the coming back again of this Messiah, which, necessarily, involves the timing of events among the nations of earth. The 'man clothed in linen', having taken the oath (12:7), immediately focuses attention on the vital period, identified as 'a time, times and an half'. We have already encountered this time span in Part 2 of this book (7:25; 9:27). It is in this period that evil comes to a climax under one spoken of here simply as 'he' in the statement 'when he shall have accomplished to scatter the power of the holy people, all these things shall be finished' (12:7). The repetition of the same period as 1,260 days allows Daniel to place the period as the moment in earth history just before the Son of Man takes the Kingdom. There can be little doubt that Daniel can now see the programme fall into place with respect to dates previously given in the seventy weeks prophecy (9:24–27).

The central theme of all four visions is a sacred Person, and linked with Him is a special period, when all the prophetic programme focuses upon the replacement of Satan's man with God's Man. With this focus, all the previous visions fall into place and we have a full picture. Failure to grasp this truth means the picture is distorted. As emphasised in earlier discussion, the key lies in placing the time break correctly in each chapter. It would seem that at this point Daniel saw this and was content to 'rest' (12:13), now that the picture for him has been focussed. Centuries have rolled away but we may still rest, as Daniel did, in the assurance that Scripture is 'true' (10:1), and that God's programme will be worked out on earth on the exact dates given.

Once the focus of the prophecy is grasped then the shadows that exist in history fall into their true perspective, as just shadows, even as the substance casting the shadow becomes ever more sharply clear. The climax allows God's Man to confront Satan's man and take the Kingdom in keeping with the Divine programme. This permits, for the parenthetic and preparatory periods, such detailed prophecies of events to take place on earth as could never have been foreseen by man. The happenings on earth become pictures of persons and events in the end-time. A perfect example is found in chapter 11:2–35. Such a catalogue of historical happenings, involving circumstantial and minute detail, running down history from the arrival of Alexander the Great in Asia, and his overthrow of the Persian monarchy under King Darius III at the Battle of Gaugamela (Oct. 13, 331 BC) to the time of Antiochus IV Epiphanes (215–164 BC), has been fulfilled in history so exactly as to stamp this passage as direct Divine revelation.

The fulfilment of these prophecies in history, now open to us, is so exact and precise that believers are assured it is God Who gave the prophecies. It can now be seen that such prophecies have a triple function: (a) These Scriptures would be a source of strength to the exercised believers who had returned to Jerusalem in 536 BC to rebuild the testimony for God in preparation for the Messiah. These faithful saints endured long years of trial and tears, climaxing in the oppression of the time of the Maccabees (167–37 BC); (b) These Scriptures, which were given to prepare hearts before the first coming of the Messiah to earth, would foreshadow the end-times prior to the second coming of the Messiah. Prophecy would become history, and this history would foreshadow prophecy of the end-time – which, of course, still lies ahead; (c) These Scriptures tell out an omniscient and omnipotent God, Who foretells the future accurately. Scripture, down the ages, has ever presented, and still presents, atheism with questions for which it has no answer.

This last point is the one denied by liberal critics, who reject the idea of a God Who can foretell the future. Instead of giving God thanks for His accurate prophecy, they use these very detailed prophecies in this fourth vision to insist that the record must have been written after the events. This is the main passage (11:1–35) used to support the late date for the writing of this book, in the second century BC.[2] Liberal critics place it in the Maccabean period (168–63 BC), written by some writer, unknown to history, who wrote history as prophecy after the events foretold here had taken place. To claim credibility this writer used the name of 'Daniel'.

However, for those who believe that the God Who knows the future can foretell it, the precise fulfilment of these prophecies comes as no surprise. Their accuracy, when read as history, is an assurance that the prophecies still awaiting fulfilment will, in their own proper time, be fulfilled just as literally and just as precisely as the earlier ones. History in this case has a purpose – authentication of the prophetic voice!

[2] See Introduction, Section 2 A.

THE FOURTH VISION

There are 4 Sections to Vision 4:

Section	Portion	Subject
1	10:1–11:1	Prologue: The Man Clothed in Linen The Central Figure
2	11:2–35	Prophecy (1): The Near Future for Daniel (538–164 BC)
		The Scriptural Time Break (From Antiochus IV Epiphanes to Antichrist)
3	11:36–12:4	Prophecy (2): The Distant Future: The End-Time
4	12:5–13	Epilogue: The Man Clothed in Linen The Consummation

SECTION 1

CHAPTER 10:1–11:1 – PROLOGUE: THE MAN CLOTHED IN LINEN

The length of this prologue (twenty-two verses) reflects the importance of this fourth revelation given to Daniel. The length of the special soul exercise of this godly man (twenty-one days) underlines the same fact. These facts suggest there is something very crucial about this final vision given to Daniel.

Verses 1–3 The Prophet and his Preparation

This revelation is dated 'in the third year of Cyrus king of Persia'. A century ago liberal critics delighted to point out that this particular title for Cyrus had never once been found in contemporary inscriptions and thus suggested that Daniel could not have been contemporary with Cyrus or he would not have made such an elementary mistake. However, Robert Dick Wilson, the noted archaeologist, in 1917 put this particular canard to rest by uncovering a number of inscriptions, dated from the sixth century BC, using this very title for Cyrus.[3] Once again, Daniel's record has proved to be accurate and reliable. Scripture uses the title frequently in the historical books – Chronicles and Ezra.

Some have wondered about the date of 536 BC since it seems to be in conflict with chapter 1, where it is recorded: 'Daniel continued even unto the first year of king Cyrus' (1:21) – as if that verse marked the death of Daniel. This is not so. Most authorities agree that the

[3] Wilson, *Studies in the Book of Daniel*, p. 145 ff.

available evidence points to the death of Daniel in or about the year 530 BC. The verse simply underlines the fact that Daniel was in Babylon for the whole length of the captivity under the Babylonian Empire. It shows, further, that he outlived that empire and held the high post to which he was promoted under Darius in Babylon (6:28).

The timing of this revelation to Daniel is significant. Daniel had his previous vision (in chapter 9 – the third in this series of four) in 538 BC, which was the first year of the reign of King Darius and also could be called the first year of Cyrus King of Persia – his overlord. Following the deep exercise of his heart (9:1–23) and the subsequent revelation through the angel Gabriel (9:24–27), Daniel could rest in the assurance that his people were to be restored to the land, the Temple would be rebuilt, and, eventually, a decree would be issued for the restoration and rebuilding of the city Jerusalem (9:25). This must have bowed his heart in thanksgiving to his God. Subsequently Daniel would have known of the edict of Cyrus, issued in his first year (538 BC), to allow the Jews to return to their homeland. He may even have been consulted by Cyrus on the wording of such a decree. Daniel knew this was Jehovah's doing, as the chronicler makes clear:

> The LORD [Jehovah] stirred up the spirit of Cyrus king of Persia, that he made a proclamation throughout all his kingdom, and put it also in writing, saying, 'Thus saith Cyrus king of Persia, All the kingdoms of the earth hath the LORD God of heaven given me; and he hath charged me to build him a house in Jerusalem, which is in Judah. Who is there among you of all his people? The LORD his God be with him and let him go up' (2 Chron. 36:22–23; see Ezra 1:1).

This Scripture makes clear that it was the Lord working on the heart of Cyrus, and not just a benevolent foreign policy linked to his own political future, as some historians would argue, that lay behind this proclamation. It would have been natural and easy for Daniel to relax, assuming his work was done. But Daniel, above all else, was a man in touch with his God and he knew there was trouble ahead for the Lord's people. Hence his present exercise.

Daniel introduces this final vision in a unique manner. He highlights the reality and the authority of this fourth vision in a way that he has not done for any previous vision. He speaks abruptly, almost staccato, as if the words are drawn from him:

(a) 'and the thing was true';
(b) 'but the time appointed was long' (*RV* translates 'even a great warfare');
(c) 'he understood the thing';
(d) 'had understanding of the vision'.

(a) The word 'thing' appears twice in the first part of the verse but most translations give the translation as 'word'. Most Hebrew scholars, including E.J. Young, agree with this interpretative translation.[4] So this 'word' – the vision he was about to receive, as recorded in the next two chapters – is 'true'. Such startling revelations are made in this vision that God has left a special emphatic note regarding their verity. This highlights the veracity of Deity contrasted with human incredulity – our slowness to believe God. The word order[5] places 'true' before 'word' for emphasis. God has put a stamp on this word – it can be relied upon with absolute assurance.

(b) This assurance of reliability is needed as a second point is emphasised. The translation 'even a great warfare' (*RV*) is supported by seven other translations consulted. The introductory word 'even' should be accepted as concessive – 'even though'; so that the meaning would seem to be that the revelation is certainly true – even though a great battle is involved. The key Hebrew word (*tsaba*) has several meanings, including 'army' or 'host', but the usual translation is 'warfare', 'conflict' or 'trial'. Perhaps the following translation is closest to the meaning: 'and concerned a great war' (*NET*), where the war involved is the spiritual conflict in the vision (10:1–11:1). It suggests that the revelation about to be given to Daniel involves such a conflict in the unseen spiritual realm that it needs this Divine stamp of authenticity given here.

(c) Since the word 'thing', translated 'word', describes this fourth vision, the difference with the previous visions is remarkable: at the close of the first vision Daniel confessed, 'my cogitations much troubled me' (7:28); at the end of the second vision he acknowledged, 'none understood it' (8:27); this time he speaks of himself in the third person and states without hesitation, 'he understood [it]'. This vision clarifies some very important questions that have arisen in the mind of Daniel, as will be shown.

[4]Young, *The Prophecy of Daniel*, p. 223.
[5] Wood, *A Commentary on Daniel*, p. 265.

(d) Daniel uses the noun from the verb 'to understand', saying he 'had understanding of the vision'. This particular word for 'vision', used in this chapter five times (vv. 1, 7 (twice), 8, and 16), differs from the usual word (used in v. 14) in that it adds the thought of Divine instruction to visual apprehension. Newberry draws attention to the word change by his marginal translation, 'appearance'. This supports the thought suggested above – that through this vision (appearance), with the interpretative oral communication from the 'man clothed in linen', came the understanding required to interpret correctly the previous visions.

This fourth vision came to Daniel on the twenty-fourth of the first month, so Daniel's preparation of mind and body must have begun on the third day of the month following the two-day celebration of the new moon. The religious new year in Israel was the first day of the month *Nisan* (Aramaic name), known earlier as *Abib* (Exod. 23:15); in the Gregorian calendar this month falls in the spring (March-April). Since the time of the monarchy (1 Sam. 20: 18–34) the new year had been traditionally welcomed with a two-day festival. If Daniel began his fast on the third day of the month, then his exercise continued over the fourteenth day, when the Feast of the Passover took place, then over the seven-day Feast of Unleavened Bread, to the Feast of Firstfruits. After the discipline of three complete weeks, God gave Daniel this final vision on the twenty-fourth day of the month.

For the fifth time in the book, Daniel directs attention to himself by using the phrase 'I Daniel'. He seems burdened to make plain that these were not second-hand stories but intensely personal experiences. Daniel speaks of these three weeks as a time of 'mourning' (compare the similar period in 9:3). Why Daniel mourns at this time is not explicitly stated. The sin, transgression and iniquity of his people have been dealt with before the Lord (9:3–19). In answer, God has moved the heart of Cyrus, and exercised saints have left for Jerusalem. It may well be that relatively few exercised saints (just around fifty thousand, out of possibly several million captives in Babylon) had responded to the challenge and returned to Jerusalem. Maybe reports of how slowly things were moving in the building of the Temple in Jerusalem and the opposition from the enemies around (Ezra 4) has alerted Daniel to the fact that there was something wrong. There seemed to be forces stirring up opposition to the holy exercise of the people of God. Is it the consciousness that the returned remnant of Israel must have Divine help that has brought him on his knees again before his God? The answers granted to Daniel in this vision seem to suggest that this was his special burden at this time.

The period of Daniel's exercise is expressed clearly, so there could be no confusion with the 'weeks of years' dealt with in the previous chapter – the word 'weeks' is the same, meaning 'sevens', but here the stress falls on 'days'. Three sevens of days is simply twenty-one days. During these days he:

(a) ate plain food – all the delicacies of Babylon to which he would be accustomed as his usual fare were set aside;

(b) refused flesh – he became a vegetarian for three weeks – going back to the herbal and vegetable diet enjoyed when, with his three fellow teenagers, he had resisted the idolatry of Babylon (1:8–12);

(c) refused wine – even the celebrated Median wines of rich vintage, available to him as normal accompaniment to meals in Babylon, were refused;

(d) did not anoint himself – anointing was practised as protection from the effects of the sun (Ps. 104:15), but it also signified a joyous occasion and abstinence was normal when in mourning (2 Sam. 12:20; 14:2).

Not that there was anything wrong with these things in themselves, but there could be no trifling with such everyday trivialities when higher issues were at stake. Not that abstinence from these things bought Divine favour. It did no such thing nor ever could – but it did underline the vital interest and serious concern that so absorbed Daniel at this time that everything else was excluded. He had on his heart the welfare of the people of God.

Verses 4–6 The Prophet and his Location

It is clear that between the proclamation of Cyrus in his first year (538 BC), which allowed Jews to go back to their homeland, and this final vision granted to Daniel (535 BC), the first company of returning exiles of around fifty thousand under Zerubbabel had already reached Jerusalem (normally a four-month journey) and had begun to rebuild the Temple of the Lord (Ezra 1–2). Since Daniel is still in Babylon in this third year of Cyrus it is clear he did not accompany them. Reasons may be suggested for Daniel's decision to remain in Babylon. First, a natural reason – his advanced years (about 88 years) would have made that journey of around six hundred miles difficult if not impossible. Second, a logical reason – the high and honoured position of Daniel in the government under

Darius would suggest that his presence at the seat of world power would make him more valuable to his people in Babylon than in Jerusalem. Third, and most importantly, a spiritual reason may lie in the character of Daniel. Doubtless, his heart was with the exiles in their return to the land of their fathers but, as Daniel had practised for a lifetime, he would await direction from his God. His twenty-one-day exercise at this point suggests that he knew that God had not closed the page of Divine revelation as yet – so he was prepared to remain in Babylon. Thus God allows the same man, who had been so close to the throne of the Babylonian Empire, to remain close to the throne of the great Medo-Persian Empire. He is still to be used by God. That continuity is underlined by the use of Daniel's Babylonian name – Belteshazzar (1:7). God can still trust this man who has witnessed so faithfully throughout a lifetime in captivity. On Daniel's part, he has still work to do for his God in receiving this final vision.

The spiritual exercise of Daniel over the three-week period is now complete (notice the word 'fulfilled' in v. 3) and, on the twenty-fourth day of the first month (*Nisan*), he is waiting upon his God in the quietness of the riverside. Daniel seems to have chosen a quiet secluded spot for meditation by the river Hiddekel (known to us as the Tigris). The Hiddekel is the eastern boundary of the great alluvial plain known as Mesopotamia (the land between the rivers), of which the river Euphrates is the western boundary. It rises in the Zagros Mountains to the north-east of Babylon and flows 1,150 miles southward to the Persian Gulf. The two rivers follow roughly parallel courses with distances between them ranging from three hundred miles at the widest part to sixty miles at the closest point. At this nearest point Babylon stands – just sixty miles from the river Hiddekel. Somewhere along the bank of the Hiddekel – where exactly is not given – Daniel has found a quiet place to wait before his God. As he seems to have remained here for some length of time, it is not likely that he was on official business, a possibility some commentators suggest in spite of his age. Possibly he has chosen this quiet place to wrestle with the spiritual problems considered earlier. Daniel is here in the body; there is no suggestion that he had been transported here in the vision, as when he had been transported to Shushan and found himself in the palace (8:1–2). That there were others with him is clear (v. 7) – whether bodyguards, or court officials, or friends, is not evident.

Suddenly Daniel is arrested and he recalls the shock as, finishing his prayer, he lifted up his eyes and records: 'I ... looked'. Perhaps the verb would be better translated as 'stared' – he could not tear his gaze away. The next word is 'behold' – take a look at this! A Man fills Daniel's gaze – a Man Who, he later reports, 'was upon the waters of the river' (12:6). At this moment the appearance of this Man holds his gaze, and well it might.

A Certain Man (Heb. '*ish*')

The garment of pure white linen is girdled around the loins with a belt of pure gold. These are but background for the unforgettable features of this man. These may be shown thus:

(a)	His Body	like beryl
(b)	His Face	as the appearance of lightning
(c)	His Eyes	as lamps of fire
(d)	His Arms and Feet	like in colour to polished brass
(e)	His Voice	like the voice of a multitude

Viewing the whole scene (from vv. 4–14), it is clear that this dominating figure stands on the waters in the middle of the river with his attendant angels – one on either bank (12:5). Daniel's companions did not see 'the Man' but, aware of a Divine presence, they fled terror-stricken (v. 7) to find a hiding place from the supernatural. Daniel, however, has two attendant angels who minister to him as he receives this Divine visitation. The first angel appears and touches him (v. 10) to wake him up and give him the strength to stand before his Divine Visitor. The second appears and touches his lips (v. 16) to give him the courage to speak to his Divine Visitor. These attendant angels are distinct from the 'man clothed in linen' standing on the river waters Who has responsibility for the communication of the revelation to Daniel.

The confusing of one of these angels with the Man on the river has led many commentators to understand that the Man is just a mighty angel. The hand that touched Daniel is clearly seen to be the hand of the interpreting angel and not the hand of the Man. This interpreting angel is also the one who required the help of Michael to deliver his message. Further, most commentators are agreed that this Man cannot be Gabriel since Daniel would recognise Gabriel from the earlier visions (8:15–19; 9:20–23). When Gabriel first appeared to him Daniel was, very naturally, overcome but on the second occasion Gabriel was welcomed as a friend. If this Man was

Features

4. 'His face as the appearance of lightning'. With what brilliance does that flash of lightning illuminate the night scene! It cannot be gazed upon without interruption, but it dispels the darkness. So before this One darkness flees or the light is outshone by this brilliant flash of illumination. John writes of the Son of Man: 'His countenance was as the sun shineth in His strength' (Rev. 1:16). The comparison is inescapable. Neither lightning nor sun can be gazed upon without interruption; both illuminate, but lightning does it spasmodically, as glimpses of Christ are seen in the OT, the sun permanently, as Christ is seen now in glory and forevermore.

5. 'His eyes as lamps of fire'. Even through the lightning flash His eyes stand out as 'lamps of fire' or, better, 'flaming torches' (*RSV*), which denotes the penetrative insight of One Who cannot be deceived by any outward show. In his description of the Son of Man John says 'His eyes were as a flame of fire' (Rev. 1:14).

6. 'His arms and his feet like in colour to polished brass'. The body parts not covered by the white linen have the sheen of 'beryl', denoting perfect health, but the arms and legs, used in service for the Master, are the colour of 'polished brass'. This was the bronze alloy fashioned in the fire (see Ezek. 1:27), which was used for making armour for the military forces. The only other clear reference to the use of this brass lies in the description John gives of the Son of Man – 'His feet like unto fine brass, as if they burned in a furnace' (Rev. 1:15). This Person has the power to execute the purposes assigned to Him no matter how far He would have to travel – His feet; or how hard He would have to labour – His hands. These will never wear out.

7. 'The voice of his words like the voice of a multitude'. Notice the repetition of the word 'voice': when He speaks it is in unison with all the voices on the side of Deity. His voice, covering every audible frequency, carries absolute authority; no conflicting voice can be heard: no false prophet can compete once this One speaks. Is not this the same Person as John heard speak on the Isle of Patmos and said: 'and his voice as the sound of many waters' (Rev. 1:15)? The metaphor changes but the overwhelming authority of the spoken word is the same in each presentation. In John's picture, the voice is the middle feature of the seven, as if it was the most important – it takes pre-eminence. In Daniel's picture, it is the seventh and last in the list, because now he is to hear the voice – this glorious One

speaks. Daniel's physical reaction to the voice of awesome authority is immediate: consciousness fades and he falls prostrate on his face to the ground (vv. 7–9).

A Man Reflects Features of Deity

The closer the examination of these two pictures, the closer the identification of the two Persons becomes. This is especially so if it is remembered that one view is taken from an OT perspective and the other from a NT perspective. Each view presents a Priest-Judge Who, with absolute Deity and therefore absolute authority, is about to act for the furtherance of the purposes of God on earth. Any lingering thought that this One is merely an angelic messenger of high rank is ruled out when the context that follows is carefully examined. William Kelly writes: 'He, of whom we have so magnificent a description in verse 6, and whom Daniel alone sees, does not appear to have been a mere angel. He may have been seen in some features of angelic glory; but I conceive this is One, who often appears both in New and Old Testament history – the Lord of Glory Himself. He appears now as a man – as One who had the deepest sympathy with His servant upon earth.'[9]

That the appearance of this Person is a Theophany – Jehovah revealing Himself to men as a Man – is supported by facts incidental to the story:

(a) The singular effect upon Daniel, which leaves him totally prostrated;

(b) In the Theophany to Ezekiel (Ezek 1:26–28) there is a Man presented with similar features captured in the colour, the fire, and the brightness. Ezekiel reacts in exactly the same way as Daniel did – falling prostrate to the ground;

(c) As has been set forth above, the revelation of Christ as Son of Man, acting as Priest-Judge for God in the midst of the seven lampstands representing the seven churches of Asia, reproduces the same features of this glorious One;

(d) This Person is clearly in control of the vision, through supporting angels. There are at least four angels present, two with Daniel on one side of the river and two in attendance upon this majestic Figure (12:5). That this One has the full understanding of the prophecy is seen when questions are put to Him (12:6) and He replies with unhesitating certainty and absolute authority.

[9] Kelly, *The Great Prophecies of Daniel*, p. 168

Many commentators insist that this must be an angel because he claims to have been sent when Daniel began his prayer three weeks before, and subsequently having been delayed, due to the opposition of the prince of the kingdom of Persia, with the result that he needed the aid of Michael, one of the chief princes, before he could deliver fulfil his responsibility to Daniel (vv. 12–14). The deduction is perfectly valid, for Deity could not be withstood in this way. However, this is no problem when it is observed that the angel who ministered to Daniel (v. 10) is not the 'man clothed in linen' but the angel whom God was using to communicate with Daniel, his interpreting angel, who needed the aid of Michael to get through to Daniel (see comments at vv. 10–11 and at v. 13).

Verses 7–9 The Prophet and his Reaction

The reaction of Daniel and those who were with him at this time underlines the fact that it was an actual experience by the side of the Tigris River. It is made very clear that the actual appearance of the 'man clothed in linen' was for Daniel alone, but the awesomeness of the whole experience so gripped the hearts of the others present that they fled to hide themselves. They recognised instinctively that something supernatural was taking place and they trembled with fear. Those who were travelling with Saul of Tarsus had a very similar experience when he met the Lord on the road to Damascus (Acts 9:3–7). The fear of those who were with Daniel confirms, in an incidental way, the interpretation that sees the vision as including this Divine Theophany. The word used five times in this chapter (v. 1, v. 7 (twice), v. 8, v. 16) for vision is not the usual word for night vision (used twice – 10:14; 11:14) but another Hebrew word (*mereh*), which the Newberry margin translates as 'appearance' and which points directly to the 'man clothed in linen'. He is the focus of the chapter.

Daniel had experienced a real reaction to the supernatural when Gabriel first appeared to him (8:16–18), but this time the experience is even more severe. Notice his weakness – strength is mentioned twice in verse 8. The first verb, 'there remained no strength', shows strength 'draining' from him; the second verb, 'I retained no strength', shows him trying desperately to hold onto his strength. He cannot do this and as the Man speaks to him the last of his strength slips away and he faints – to lie helplessly on his face, a picture of absolute weakness. Between the two references to strength is the statement 'my comeliness was turned in me into corruption'. This presents a contrast between 'before' and 'after'. Before the experience he had the appearance of health – the glow, the sheen and the vigour of health – comeliness was seen in him.[10] After the experience, what marked him was corruption – all was 'marred', 'spoiled', 'lay in ruins'[11]; instead of being the picture of life he was the picture of death. A graphic picture of man totally overwhelmed in the presence of Deity.

Verses 10–11 The Prophet and his Reassurance

In the presence of revealed Deity, Daniel is totally overwhelmed and falls prostrate. The 'deep sleep' carries the same thought as on the previous occasion (8:18) – Daniel has fainted and fallen prostrate on his face. There seems to be a pause here as the Man speaks to Daniel but no further information is given as to what the Man said to him. This is personal communication, for Daniel alone.

The next thing that Daniel is aware of is the touch of a hand. The interpreting angel comes back into the picture at this point. Daniel felt the touch of a hand, and, while startled out of his faint, is no longer terrified as before. Daniel had felt this touch and heard this voice before (8:18). Startled but unafraid, we note again his exclamation of surprise – 'behold'! So, physically exhausted by the emotional reaction to the appearance of such a glorious Person, Daniel needs physical assistance to get up on hands and knees and eventually to stand, somewhat tremblingly, to his feet. This interpreting angel has been there throughout but, in the presence of the Theophany, had faded into the background. Now he comes forward and, in keeping with his Divine commission, gives Daniel the physical strength he needs to take in the revelation. However, more importantly, he is to give Daniel spiritual understanding of the vision. It must have encouraged Daniel very much to be addressed as Gabriel had addressed him in the earlier vision (9:23), as 'greatly beloved' or 'greatly delighted in'. This term, denoting the Divine favour in which Daniel was held, must have dispelled much of his weakness as Daniel realised the double privilege granted to him, of first the vision and now the interpretation. He needed strength – 'stand upright' is the command, but he needed mental alertness – 'understand the words that I speak unto thee' is the order. In other words, the angel is saying, 'Let me have your full

[10] *OTWS*, p. 86.
[11] *OTWS*, p. 97.

attention.' The aged prophet does his best to comply and writes one graphic sentence that tells the whole story – 'I stood trembling'.

Although no name is given to this angel, many scholars identify him as Gabriel. There are arguments for and against this identification. On the 'against' side, since Gabriel is named in the previous two visions (8:16; 9:21), it seems strange he is not named here. On the 'for' side, he addresses Daniel as 'greatly beloved', the title used elsewhere only by Gabriel (9:23). Nothing major hangs on the identification so it may be best to leave him simply as a mighty angel commissioned to interpret this word to Daniel.

There is now opened to Daniel, by the interpreting angel, an unseen world where Satan uses agents under his command to oppose the purpose of God in the history of Israel and the nations. In the exercise of his concern for his nation's future through prayer (9:3–19) Daniel, unwittingly, had thus become involved in this age-old conflict on the side of God's people. In response to this exercise, he is now to be given a special 'vision' or 'word' (see comments on v. 1) with respect to the future of his people. The incidental uncovering of this unseen realm, hinted at in Scripture (Isa. 24:21–23; Ps. 82:1–8) but never previously described, will show to Daniel quite clearly that, despite all the powerful satanic opposition, the will of God will triumph and the purpose of God will be carried out. All opposing forces will be defeated, so that what is revealed to Daniel can be relied upon with absolute confidence – it is 'the scripture of truth' (v. 21).

Verses 12–13 The Prophet and Satanic Power

Satanic opposition to the passing on to Daniel of this prophecy is an indication of how seriously Satan regards prophetic truth. In this passage is disclosed, for future ages, something of the unseen spiritual conflict in which the exercised believer shares a part as he understands from Scripture what God is doing on earth. This is why a study of the prophetic Word is so vital and valuable for the believer. This is the reason why Satan seeks to keep books like Daniel and Revelation closed to believers by suggesting they are too difficult. Without some understanding of the prophetic Word, there cannot be any insight into the Divine programme and our praying becomes 'without understanding'. In the study of the prophetic Word the believer soon begins to grasp certain basic truths, such as the following:

(a) Satanic antagonism to the nation of Israel. This hatred is implacable and unchanging. Satan knows that Israel is the nation chosen of God, through which He would bring the Seed of the woman (Gen. 3:15), the Redeemer of mankind, with consequences for himself. This is the origin of satanic anti-Semitism, which underlies so much of history (Rev. 12:1–5).

(b) Saintly dedication is demanded even in the study of the Word, as Satan hates to see believers researching his doom in Scripture. For this prophetic Word to reach us, it cost Daniel much as a target for the agents of satanic power.

(c) With the opened prophetic Scripture in hand, saintly intercession will arise in the heart of a believer, thus, with intelligent prayer each believer begins to play an important role, just as did Daniel, in the great cosmic battle. This is a special aspect of the lifelong war in which each saint is engaged from spiritual birth (Eph. 6:10–18). In this conflict, 'the whole armour of God' is essential.

(d) Scriptural prophecy is truth, even if it is not understood; it is the Word of God, in which the believer can put full and unreserved confidence. This prophetic Word may come through the human channel – even a Daniel – but it is truth (v. 21). This Word will stand when all deceivers and deceptions have been removed (2 Thess. 2:11).

The introductory words of the angel – 'Fear not, Daniel' – would relieve him of the natural reaction to a supernatural manifestation. Daniel must have wondered whether, with this introduction, the next words would reveal Divine approval or disapproval of his intercession. Had his importunity, over the last three weeks, pleased or displeased heaven? Will he be rebuked for his ignorance or commended for his understanding? It very soon becomes clear: the angel explains that heaven is delighted that a man on earth is concerned about the people of God. When the angel assured him – 'thy words were heard' – Daniel's heart must have lifted. The next remark must have thrilled him: 'I am come for thy words.' A man prays on earth and an angel arrives from heaven!

When told that his prayer was registered and action had been taken from the very beginning ('the first day') of his exercise of three weeks duration, Daniel must have wondered at the distance between heaven and earth. The response of heaven is only reaching Daniel three weeks later. A message takes such a time – Daniel must have wondered! The look on Daniel's face allows the angel to explain to Daniel that, in this fallen world, there is a powerful enemy at work: an enemy who has his agents in every land. The angel explains to Daniel that there is a realm ruled by Satan that is totally opposed to God and opposed to His people and to His purposes. This mighty angel, dispatched from the throne of God, had a mission *en route* that involved the kingdom of Persia, under whose authority Daniel had now lived for three years (since Babylon's fall, in 539 BC). Satanic resistance to his mission to Daniel delayed his arrival for three weeks, as Daniel prayed and fasted. The resistance came from one described as 'the prince of the kingdom of Persia'. The word 'withstood' has the idea of literally 'standing up to block the way', as was indeed intended, to prevent the angel fulfilling his revelatory mission to Daniel. This resistance, a refusal to allow him to execute his mission, went on day after day for twenty-one days, as Daniel continued to fast and pray. Then to the angel came unexpected aid – notice the 'lo' (or, better, 'behold'). Michael, identified as 'one of the chief princes', arrived to assist him. With the help of Michael, the opposition was speedily dealt with, and the angel could now complete his mission to Daniel and move to help the King of Persia. This interpretation of the angel's words is based on the verb 'I remained there' (Hebrew root '*yather*'), which can be translated 'left over, remain'.[12] Many a victorious general has used this very word as he has surveyed the battlefield with the enemy in full retreat. The satanic enemy had fled and left the field – the angel could get on with heaven's business.

Several matters need explanation:

(a) The title 'Prince of the kingdom of Persia' indicates that, while having some relation to Persia, this is not the king in normal terms – at this time the king was Cyrus (v. 1). Some older commentators have tried to interpret this reference as indicating Cambyses, the son of Cyrus, but the full context rules this out completely;

(b) This one is not just an heir to an earthly throne. His effective opposition to this mighty angel, who, as has been shown, could well be Gabriel, indicates that he belongs to the senior ranks of the powers of evil. Supporting this is the fact that he could only be subdued by the aid of Michael, who is called 'one of the chief princes'.

This enemy prince must be of high angelic status in the hierarchy of satanic power, opposed to God. The link with Persia is to indicate his area of responsibility, assigned, doubtless, by his satanic master. The 'Prince of Grecia' will be similarly identified (see comments at v. 20).

[12] Wood, *A Commentary on Daniel*, p. 273.

Thus, there is opened here to Daniel's understanding, and indeed to all subsequent readers of this book, that there is a realm, unseen by men, where evil powers and persons, under the control of Satan and in bitter opposition to God, try to control matters and men on earth. The national and political figures on earth are influenced, or even controlled, by these dark forces. When Daniel was exercised about the Divine purpose for the people of God he found himself wrestling 'not against flesh and blood, but against principalities, against powers, against the rulers of the darkness of this world, against spiritual wickedness in high places' (Eph. 6:10–13). That spiritual realm is under the control of Satan, where, clearly, he assigns areas of responsibility to trusted emissaries – angels charged with opposing the purposes of God generally, but with bitter hatred for the nation of Israel, through whom the Redeemer would come. There can be no doubt that had this Prince of Persia had his way Cyrus would never have issued the decree to allow Israel to return to their land. Doubtless also, the one here called 'the Prince of Grecia' is the satanic agent assigned to stir up Antiochus Epiphanes of the Seleucid dynasty in Syria to wipe out the nation of Israel. It is significant that it is Michael who comes to the aid of the interpreting angel on his way to Daniel with the timetable of the Redeemer. Michael, whose name means 'who is like God', is called here 'one of the chief princes'. This indicates the place he holds and the power he wields and is reflected in his NT title of 'archangel' (Jude 9). His responsibility is defined at the end of this vision, when he takes action on behalf of the persecuted nation – 'Michael … the great prince which standeth for the children of thy people' (12:1). Michael's duties would include seeing to the confirmation of the covenant and its implementation, giving permission for the release of the captives of the nation of Israel.

Verse 14 The Prophet and Scriptural Purpose

The final announcement to Daniel gives the essence of the mission on which the angel has been sent. It was to give Daniel an understanding of 'what shall befall thy people in the latter days'. Prophecy still focuses on Israel, the nation chosen to introduce the Messiah to earth. Of particular interest to Daniel would be what would follow the Babylonian and Medo-Persian Empires that he has known. Of course, in the back of his mind must be the question of how long it would be until Israel entered upon the full enjoyment of the promises God had given with regard to the Kingdom.

The angel answers the unarticulated question of Daniel by deliberately focussing attention on the period when these promises would come to fulfilment, at a time given as 'the latter days'.[13] The meaning of this term in Scripture is first to refer to times later than that of the writing; see for example the expression 'in the latter times' (1 Tim. 4:1), which must be interpreted in this way. Here the term is restricted by the context and must be very much narrower for it is clearly focussed on the breaking of Gentile dominion, under which Daniel and Israel were still suffering, and the realisation of the promises God has made to Israel with respect to the Kingdom of God on earth. From the use of the term in the Hebrew Epistle ('in these last days', Heb. 1:1–2), 'the latter days' period must begin with Christ's first coming to earth and close with His second coming, to establish the Kingdom. In this period, the nation of Israel is still the focus of history and other nations are dealt with as they treat Israel. The particular 'vision' that is mentioned here, and for which understanding is to be given to Daniel, is that which is unfolded in the next two chapters and therefore is necessarily concerned with the interval between the first coming of Messiah to earth – His cutting off – and the consequent second coming of the Messiah, to break Gentile dominion and establish the Kingdom of God on earth. From our viewpoint, this is the end-time, especially focussing on the Tribulation and the moment of the arrival of the Messiah. At this point a necessary caution is given to Daniel – 'for yet the vision is for many days'. There is actually no adjective qualifying 'days' – 'many' is missing in the Hebrew – but the translators (*AV* and *RV*), in an attempt to clarify the syntax, have added the word 'many' – which only serves to obscure the issue. The wording is simple: 'for yet the vision is for days'; when interpreted contextually its meaning is clear, when we understand these 'days' to be the days just mentioned – 'the latter days'. In other words, this particular prophecy has to do with days far distant from Daniel's time. The *RSV* translates it 'for days yet to come'; while possibly the thought is best caught by 'the vision pertains to future days' (*NET*). It will be seen, as the study unfolds, that, stage by stage, the prophecy tells of events that move toward the climactic crisis moment of history, when Christ will return to end the Gentile dominion of the 'times of the Gentiles' and set up His Kingdom as the Son of Man. All Scripture focussing on the key nation in earth history points to this crisis moment; the prophetic clock will be set to count down to this moment.

[13] See Chapter Note at the end of this chapter.

Verses 15–21 A Personal Interlude

Verse 15 Daniel has not spoken throughout the vision but now, standing with head bowed and face toward the ground, he cannot speak; overwhelmed and overawed he records: 'I became dumb', where the passive form of the verb indicates that the power of speech has gone from him. Isaiah (Isa. 6:5) and Ezekiel (Ezek. 3:26) had similar trouble with their vocal cords in the presence of God – Daniel stands humbly in the presence of the Holy in total silence.

Verses 16–17 Divine intervention startles him, introduced as ever by the word 'behold'. One described as 'like the similitude of the sons of men', which simply means who looked like one of the genus 'mankind', touched his lips (*cf.* Isa. 6:6–7). This is either the interpreting angel or Gabriel himself (see comments at v. 10), most likely the latter, who restores Daniel's speech. Strength was given to Daniel and his first words are an explanation of his weakness and confession of his own worthlessness. With the deepest respect Daniel speaks. The form of address, 'my lord' (Hebrew *adoni*, used three times in vv. 16–17 and again in v. 19), is a term of respect, equivalent to our 'Sir', used for persons of higher rank, but not a term of reverence for Deity. He is speaking, of course, as becomes clear, not to the 'man clothed in linen', but to the angel who had touched him. Overpowered by the 'vision' (appearance) – the Theophany (vv. 4–6) – Daniel explains 'my sorrows are turned upon me' (*AV*); the word 'sorrows', or 'anguish' (*NIV*), is a strange word to use since it is used primarily of a woman in labour – 'the writhing of a woman in travail' (see Isa. 13:8; 21:3 and 1 Sam. 4:19). The mental and emotional turmoil engendered by the vision has had its result in physical and bodily pain. It was an interesting word to use in light of the 'travail' of the nation of Israel before Christ comes (Mt. 24:8; 1 Thess. 5:3; Rev. 12:2). Drained of all strength, Daniel is totally exhausted. Overawed by the dignity of the exalted angelic messenger, but above all by the Theophany, he feels a total worthlessness. The literal Hebrew is translated: 'How is the servant of this my Lord able to speak with this my Lord?'[14] Feeling so weak and unworthy, Daniel is so overwhelmed he seems to find it hard to breathe – 'neither is there breath left in me'.

[14] *NET*, Dan. 10:17, Note 35.

Verses 18–19 The first touch of the angel has restored speech to Daniel. Now the second touch of this same angel, described 'like the appearance of a man', restores strength. This is the third time Daniel has been touched in this chapter (v. 10, v. 16 and v. 18). As physical strength flows into him again, spiritual strength is imparted by the use of heaven's title: 'O man greatly beloved' (9:23; 10:11). Fear is immediately banished ('fear not'), peace embraces him ('peace be unto thee'), and he is mentally challenged ('be strong, yea, be strong') – Divine enablement invites human cooperation. The result is first inward and then outward as Daniel records: 'I was strengthened, and said'. Now, instead of overwhelming weakness, there is an overwhelming willingness to listen to the Divine messenger. With renewed capability, Daniel is ready now to receive this most important vision.

Verses 20–21 The rhetorical question – 'Knowest thou?' is designed to make Daniel realise afresh just how important this prophecy is – and how vital his correct apprehension of this word of prophetic truth. A cosmic battle has already taken place to bring this prophecy to him. Satanic forces implacably opposed to the purposes of God were at work behind the scenes. His message delivered, this mighty angel would return to the battlefront. A prince of Satan, defeated on one field of battle (v. 13) would use all his powers to stir up the kings of Persia against the people of God (Israel). Already a crucial edict has been issued (2 Chron. 36:22–23) favourable to the purpose of God, but this enemy was indefatigable and would attack again and again, through later kings of Persia.

History subsequent to this date (536 BC) will show that Satan almost succeeded in wiping out the major part of the nation in the days of Esther, during the reign of Xerxes I (reigned 485–465 BC). No wonder they needed this mighty angel, as well as the help of Michael the archangel, for their preservation. In the other part of the nation – those who had returned to Jerusalem – their difficulties were many (Ezra 4:3–4). Nevertheless, they were preserved and without question this mighty angel, supported by Michael the archangel, played a full part in their preservation.

Many of their problems, as recorded in Ezra and Nehemiah, were traceable to the vacillation of Persian kings who, under pressure from the satanic prince, would seek their destruction. This would continue, as hinted by the angel to Daniel, over a period of two hundred years (536–334 BC) until, with the arrival of Alexander the Great (334–323 BC), another satanic prince comes into the picture. The Scripture presents certain aspects in the history of Persian power over Israel. For easy reference these are listed in the table below.

This mighty angel now takes a moment to explain to Daniel that his post of duty is the palace where the king of Persia is, and it is urgent that he leave as soon as he has delivered the revelation to Daniel. Further, his period of duty is the time when the Persian king is world ruler. The phrase 'when I am gone forth' uses a verb that, both in historical documents and in Scripture, means 'to go forth to war' (See 2 Kgs 11:7). Its use here shows that this mighty angel, who in guarding Divine interests has already put one enemy, the Prince of Persia, to flight, has to return to face another enemy on the same battlefield – this time the prince of Grecia.

King of Persia	Reign	Relevant Date	Reference
Cyrus the Great	539–529 BC		
Edict to allow Israel's return to Jerusalem		538 BC	2 Chron. 36:22–23; Ezra 1:1–4
Cambyses	529–522 BC		
Pseudo Smerdis	522–521 BC (7 months)		
Darius I (Hystaspes)	521–486 BC		
Ahasuerus (Xerxes I)	485-465 BC		Est. 1:1
Artaxerxes (Longimanus)	464–423 BC		
Ezra permitted to return to rebuild Temple		458 BC	Ezra 7:9; 8:31
Nehemiah permitted to return to rebuild city		445 BC	Neh. 2:1–8

The full list of Medo-Persian kings is given in Appendix 3.

When Medo-Persia lost world dominion, which it did in the defeat of Darius III by Alexander the Great, at the Battle of Issus, in October 333 BC, a new enemy would appear on this unseen battlefield. This new enemy is called 'the Prince of Grecia' and is the angel to whom Satan had entrusted the ordering of affairs in the Grecian kingdom in his interests. This battle will continue throughout the ages, until a major turning point sees Satan and all his angels (called 'princes' in this book) expelled from heaven, at the midpoint of the seventieth week (9:27) in preparation for the consummation of the Divine Programme (see Rev. 12:7–9). The close of the battle will be on earth at Armageddon (Rev. 16:16; 19:11-16) when, the forces of Satan routed, Christ takes the Kingdom and is acknowledged over all the earth as 'King of kings, and Lord of lords' (Rev. 19:16).

There is an implied urgency in the next statement, introduced by the 'but'. In spite of the cosmic battle taking place in the unseen realm, the angel has an urgent responsibility to discharge – 'I will tell thee that which is inscribed in the writing of truth' (*RV*). It is 'the writing of truth' because it is the writing down, through the agency of the already Divinely-prepared prophet, of that which will assuredly come to pass, because it comes directly from the God Who is truth. This refers to what is unfolded in the two chapters that follow. Daniel need not have the least fear – dark happenings there will be, some specially designed for the discipline of the people of God, but the final outcome is that the will of God is done. Since God is great, good and gracious, the worked-out will of God will mean blessing for all from mankind who willingly bow before the Theophany – the manifestation of Deity in OT terms. In the NT the Messiah, Christ – God manifest in flesh (1 Tim. 3:16) – is the Lord before Whom 'every knee should bow ... and ... every tongue should confess that Jesus Christ is Lord' (Phil. 2:9–11).

The weight of scholarly opinion will not allow the chapter division at this point; that comes at the end of the next verse (11:1). This is both grammatical and logical. Grammatical, because the verb 'shew' (*AV*) of the last verse of chapter 10 is repeated in chapter 11:2 and grammarians call this an '*inclusio*' (bracketing related matters), with the matters between the verbs being closely linked. Logical, because the subject is unchanged – the cosmic battle that surrounds the Word of God. The issue is a simple one – is the will of God to be carried out amongst the nations or not? The will of God, made known through His Word, causes all the forces on God's side to cooperate with Him. This is exactly what this mighty angel has been doing as he engages in this war centred on the nation of Israel, through whom the Messiah will come. In their interests, this mighty angel generally acts alone, but in emergencies he can call upon, and count upon, the willing help of Michael, who has special responsibility for Israel. That cooperation between God's agents is mutual and, in the recent great crisis, just two years previous, 'in the first year of Darius the Mede', this mighty angel came to the aid of Michael. The angel recalls: 'I ... stood to confirm and strengthen him'. The verb 'to confirm' is used in participle form and means 'one causing another to be strong'.[15] The word 'to strengthen' should be translated as a noun – thus 'stronghold' – meaning he provided strength and shelter for Michael in the battle. God's mighty angels are mutually supportive as they engage in this cosmic battle. This is the year for the issue of the vitally important decree from Cyrus (538 BC), the implementation of it falling to Darius, as the man in charge of the release and repatriation of the captives of Judah. Only at this point are we made aware of the titanic struggle in the heavenly places before the issue of this decree. Of course, the agents of God won the battle, the decree was issued, and the Word of God was literally fulfilled. The prophecies awaiting fulfilment, as of now, will yet be fulfilled, just as exactly and just as literally.

It could be that this chapter should be closed by the first statement in chapter 11:2 – 'And now will I shew thee the truth'. That cosmic battlefield is the background against which God will show what will happen to the people of Israel in the days ahead. This record is 'The Truth'.

[15] Wood, *A Commentary on Daniel*, p. 278.

NOTE

THE MEANING OF THE TERM 'IN THE LATTER DAYS'

This term is used on two occasions in this book:

(a) 2:28 – 'maketh known to the king Nebuchadnezzar what shall be in the latter days'; (b) 10:14 – 'what shall befall thy people in the latter days'.

The first of these was given to King Nebuchadnezzar in the Aramaic language since it concerned the Gentile nations, while the second was given to Daniel in the Hebrew language since it concerned Israel. Both expressions will be shown to refer to the same period of time.

Both terms agree with the definition already given of 'the latter days': firstly, they are days that must lie ahead for the recipient from that point. Secondly, when these phrases are seen in the prophetic context they mean much more: they define the days preceding the return to earth of the rejected Messiah. From the study of the Scriptures they had, the faithful in Israel could see virtually two distinct persons presented as Messiah, depending on which Scriptures they studied. They could readily see a rejected Messiah in certain Scriptures (e.g. 9:26), but immediately this was accepted, other Scriptures presented a reigning Messiah (e.g. Isa. 11; Zech. 14). How to put this together was a problem. Yet, the very problem was solved by the prophet Isaiah in one Person – the Servant of Jehovah (Isa. 52:13–53:12). When He came to earth and to the nation of Israel the first time, He would be the rejected One and be 'cut off'; yet this same Person, Who would accomplish redemption, would be received and reign on earth from the time of His second coming. There is a multitude of phrases used of this period in the OT; a few may be noted, as, for example, the following: 'the latter days' (2:28; 10:14), 'time of the end' (8:17), 'end of the days'(12:13), 'the latter years' (Ezek. 38:8), 'in the latter days' (Hos. 3:5), 'those days, and in that time' (Joel 3:1). Consideration of these expressions shows that they have nothing whatever to do with the imminent end of the world, as sometimes imagined. The expressions all fasten on a particular stage of prophetic anticipation: the days immediately preceding the coming of the Messiah Who, previously rejected, now comes back to reign. The result of His first coming and consequent rejection was the destruction of Jerusalem (9:26) and the scattering of the nation of Israel through all nations (AD 70), as Jehovah had threatened under Moses (Lev. 26:31–33). They were the unbelieving nation; and they so remain in this age of grace – as a nation. Putting together all the expressions quoted, it is perfectly plain that this same nation will be regathered in its own land, the city of Jerusalem rebuilt, and the independence of the nation restored, before the second coming of their Messiah. A most significant point is that this is to be effected while they are still the unbelieving nation: Ezekiel's vision of the valley of dry bones is a fitting prophecy and description of their spiritual condition (Ezek. 37).

It is the suggestion of this chapter that this is very evident today in the re-establishment of the nation in Israel in May 1948. Their independence as a nation, the retaking and rebuilding of Jerusalem, and their defences of this freedom from the hostile world around them, have been accomplished in their unbelief. Few nations have closed their borders so effectively against the gospel. This regathering in unbelief is an evident indicator that the 'last days' are upon us now. This further explains: (a) the almost paranoiac rejection of the Name 'Jesus' – their refusal to believe. It is glad evidence of the unchanging grace of God when an individual Israelite gets salvation; (b) the unbelievable Islamic hostility to the nation of Israel – one can readily see that Satan, at least, believes the Scripture concerning the coming of the Saviour. In an effort to frustrate that coming he would wipe out the people to whom Messiah is coming, knowing that that coming will be his own undoing. Thus the Arab-Israeli War (1948–49), the 'Six-Day War' (1967), and the 'Yom Kippur' War (1972), and yet God preserves them. The return of the nation of Israel to their own land while still unbelieving, and their Divine preservation through the subsequent wars, means that the stage is being set for the programme of heaven.[16]

[16] A valuable aid to the study of 'the last days' has been published in an English translation from the German. It is called *Are We Really Living In The Last Days?* The author is a respected academician called Dr Roger Liebi and it is published by Christlicher Medienvertrieb Hagedorn, Germany (2012).

CHAPTER 11:1–20

VISION 4

Section	Portion	Subject
1	10:1–11:1	Prologue: The Man Clothed in Linen: The Central Figure
2	11:2–35	Prophecy (1): The Near Future for Daniel (538–164 BC)
		The Scriptural Time Break (From Antiochus IV Epiphanes to Antichrist)
3	11:36–12:4	Prophecy (2): The Distant Future :The End-Time
4	12:5–13	Epilogue: The Man Clothed in Linen: The Consummation

SECTION 2

CHAPTER 11:2–35 PROPHECY (PART 1): THE NEAR FUTURE 538 BC TO 164 BC

Verse 1 It has already been pointed out in connection with the first verse of this chapter that the majority of conservative commentators are agreed that it should be read as the closing verse of chapter 10. They do this in spite of the fact that most English translations place it as the opening verse of chapter 11 and this position has the support of both the Septuagint and the Masoretic text. It is easy to see why it has been so positioned. The sequence of the preceding chapters, as dated in the first verse of each, is readily followed (7:1; 8:1; 9:1; 10:1) and each one opens with a date. Hence, in the same sequence the chapter division falls into place at 11:1. However, the reasons for recognising this verse as closing chapter 10 are convincing. It is clear that the date is given, not to date the vision, which has already been dated in 10:1, but to date a particular event in the spiritual warfare of the preceding chapter. There are three reasons to support this conclusion. The first is a grammatical reason – the verb 'I will shew' from 10:21 is repeated in 11:2, making the intervening material a grammatical *inclusio* – as if placed in parenthesis as an explanatory note – distinct from the flow of thought. This *inclusio* dates a point in the cosmic warfare when even Michael needed help, and the date is given as that vital point for Israel, 'the first year of Darius the Mede'. Secondly, there is a logical reason – the repetition of 'the truth' (11:2) from 'the scripture of truth' (10:21) means the subject already introduced is taken up again for expansion, now that the *inclusio* has explained a detail of the cosmic battle. Thirdly, there is a contextual reason – while the dates mentioned earlier in the first verse of each of the chapters 7–10 all introduce new visions, it is perfectly clear that chapter 11 is not a new vision but a part of the fourth vision, already dated (10:1). So it is clear that this verse should close chapter 10.

There has been much scholarly speculation over the issue, or issues, that caused the angelic conflict here described. But there is not the slightest doubt that this first year of Darius (538 BC) was a crucial time for the world powers, after the fall of mighty Babylon to Cyrus, in October 539 BC. That crash had shaken the world of that day to its political roots. Israel could, doubtless, hear echoes of the voice of Isaiah foretelling the doom of Babylon (Isa. 13–14) two hundred years before. Jeremiah (Jer. 50–51) sixty years before had warned of its capture and rejoiced at its downfall. Now, the Judaean captives in Babylon had lived to see mighty Babylon, 'the glory of kingdoms, the beauty of the Chaldees' excellency' (Isa. 13:19), humbled before the might of Medo-Persia. It was an unforgettable moment in history for the world, a critical moment in history for Israel, and a vital moment for the purpose of God, Who was going to bring the Messiah into the world through this nation of Israel. This is one of the moments that prepared the world for the 'fulness of the time' (Gal. 4:4), when God would send His Son as Redeemer into the world.

Events around that critical moment in history can be summarised thus:

(a) The replacement of the world empire of Babylon by the Medo-Persian Empire. In those preparatory years – from the death of Nebuchadnezzar (562 BC) to Babylon's fall (539 BC) – exercised believers like Daniel would be on their knees before their God as they waited for God to move among the nations. Their patience must have been sorely tried as licentious and corrupt Babylon, under King Belshazzar, awaited the final blow by Cyrus. Eventually, on the night of October 13, 539 BC, Babylon fell to the armies of Cyrus (5:30–31).

(b) The appearance on the world stage of Cyrus, King of Persia, already named two hundred years before this by the prophet Isaiah (Isa. 44:28; 45:1). This king becomes so vital in God's purpose at this critical time that He calls Cyrus 'My shepherd' and '[Mine] anointed'. Consciously or not, he was the instrument that God used, at this critical moment in history, in the working out of His will for Israel.

(c) Darius the Mede was appointed by Cyrus to be king in the city of Babylon, since Cyrus needed to return to his capital, at Susa, before the end of that year. Darius proved to be a most remarkable man who, despite his egoistic pride, which God graciously humbled, was strong enough, when aided by the unseen powers mentioned here, to execute the decree of Cyrus and allow the Jewish exiles to return to Jerusalem. This was despite the bitter anti-Semitic feeling amongst his senior satraps (see 6:1–9). Daniel, after the lion's den experience (6:1–28), as senior president over the satraps and responsible directly to Darius, must have played a major part in the drawing up and implementation of that decree of Cyrus.

(d) This was the critical year following the issue of the decree that allowed captives from Israel to return to their homeland (2 Chron. 36:22–23; Ezra 1:1–4). Now came all the logistics necessary for the safe transport of over fifty thousand exiles over six hundred miles of virtual desert from Babylon to Jerusalem, under Zerubbabel.

(e) The humbling of the pride of Darius, the removal of the satraps who hated the Jews, and the testing of Daniel in the den of lions all took place before the vital prophecy of the seventy weeks was entrusted to Daniel (9:24–27). This vital prophecy, which links the date of the coming of the Messiah to earth history, was the climax of a most important year.

Each of the matters listed above would, doubtless, have been the subject of controversy and conflict in the heavenly realm, between the mighty angels furthering Divine interests and the angels under satanic control, implacably opposed to the Divine purpose (9:24–27).

It is thus against the background of the revelation of cosmic conflict involving angelic powers that this final vision is given to Daniel. It allows believers, who accept the 'truth' given in the Word of God, to realise that behind all the movements, machinations and motives of men, rulers and governments of earth, dark satanic powers are at work. Yet, despite all the might of Satan, God works out His purpose – God is sovereign. This purpose of God has at its centre a Man, One already identified as 'Messiah the Prince' (9:25).

Under God's Man dominion will be taken out of the hands of mere men, who so readily become the puppets of Satan, and placed in the hands of One 'whose kingdom is an everlasting kingdom, and all dominions shall serve and obey Him' (7:27). This points to the period of the blessing on earth under God's King that is later spoken of as the time when 'the kingdoms of this world are become the kingdoms of our Lord and of His Christ; and He shall reign for ever and ever' (Rev. 11:15). Indeed, God's Man and God's King, identified already as Messiah, and in future revelation shown to be both Son of Man and Son of God, will display dominion in the Kingdom that lasts for a thousand years (Rev 20:1–6), when the blessing anticipated in the benediction at the close of this vision will be a reality: 'Blessed is he that waiteth, and cometh to the thousand three hundred and five and thirty days' (12:12). That waiting will see the programme outlined by God in this book completed on the specified day in earth history and the establishment of a literal Kingdom in real time. Many Scriptures speak of this Kingdom and its ruler. Isaiah speaks with a note of wonder: 'Behold, a king shall reign in righteousness' (Isa. 32:1). Zechariah joins in the anticipation: 'His dominion shall be from sea even to sea, and from the River even to the ends of the earth' (Zech. 9:10). Men are impatient but God will fulfil His programme in His own time. It would resemble the Hebrew day, where the 'evening' comes before the 'morning'. Believers of that future time will wait for the dawn of Kingdom glory through the evening and night of Tribulation gloom. The evening shadows will deepen to the midnight darkness of the Tribulation, but the believer's hope, like a ray of light through the gloom, will rest in the promise of Malachi: 'But unto you that fear My name shall the sun of righteousness arise with healing in His wings' (Mal. 4:2). The Kingdom will assuredly come – the 'truth' has been revealed to Daniel.

Verse 2 The Medo-Persian Empire 539–331 BC

'The breast and arms of the Image'
The Metal – Silver (2:32) Commerce and Wealth
The Animal – Ram (8:3–4, 20) Conquest and War

The introductory words, 'And now', mark the opening of the final angelic mission to Daniel. Already granted a Divine visitation in the Theophany (10:4–6), he is now reminded that what is to be revealed is 'truth'; the word 'truth' is repeated for emphasis. Daniel will have the grave responsibility of conveying this truth to men. First given a view of history from the standpoint of heaven, now he is charged with putting on record portraits of the men who will move across the world stage and fill their appointed roles in days to come. So Daniel is summoned, almost peremptorily, by the mighty angel to 'behold'; to allow his eye to fasten on the Medo-Persian throne. The abrupt summons seems to suggest that in spite of his surprise, even shock, he must look closely at what God reveals. This mighty, all-conquering empire of Medo-Persia, which has replaced Babylon in Daniel's time, is not here to stay, but suddenly and dramatically, at the very height of its power, it will be replaced by another.

Daniel, on account of his responsible position, would be in daily contact with the men in power in Babylonia – a semi-independent realm within the Medo-Persian Empire. He must have pondered at length what the future held for his people under Cyrus – his appointees in the present and his successors. Now, in one brief sentence, he is given an encapsulation of the Medo-Persian rule far beyond his time. He is told: 'there shall stand up yet three kings in Persia'. With Cyrus presently on the throne (10:1) – both the 'yet' and the future tense in the verb 'shall stand up' show that these three kings will succeed Cyrus – he is not included. Since Daniel died in 530 BC, just months before Cyrus was killed in a minor battle, he may have had some knowledge of Cambyses, the oldest son of Cyrus, but not the others. The prophetic word to Daniel has been fulfilled in history exactly as he said. For clarity and easy reference an outline summarises this section:

Verse 2 The Medo-Persian Rulers

Cyrus died	530 BC
(1) Cambyses, son of Cyrus	530–522 BC
(2) Pseudo-Smerdis	522–521 BC
(3) Darius I Hystaspes	521–486 BC
(4) Xerxes I Ahasuerus	486–465 BC

A time gap is seen between verse 2 and verse 3

The death of Xerxes I Ahasuerus	465 BC
To the death of Darius III (after the Battle of Issus)	331 BC
Time gap is 135 years	

above. If the numbers given by Herodotus, the Greek historian, are accepted this would be the largest army ever put in the field and the largest maritime force ever assembled. Even if recent scholarship would divide the army figure given by Herodotus by ten, the resulting figure of over three hundred and sixty thousand fighting troops still presents a very formidable army. Scholars reckon that the maritime force cannot have been less than one thousand triremes with three thousand supporting craft – a huge force for that day.[2] King Xerxes had used his wealth to raise and equip large auxiliary forces from the different satrapies, as well as build the warships of the day – the mighty triremes, with the bronze ram fixed on the prow at the waterline. Each trireme carried 170 oarsmen, 10 marines, 4 archers and 16 sailors and had a speed of nine knots. When one thousand of these were in full sail it must have been quite a formidable sight. Pride must have filled the heart of the king.

(c) War – 'He shall stir up all against the realm of Grecia'

In the verb 'stir up' the AV translation has caught the right note – the root from which it comes is 'to be hot' or 'ardent'. King Xerxes seems to have had that charismatic personality that inspired his army with his burning zeal to recoup the losses incurred by the defeat of his father's army and to revenge the humiliating insults hurled at his empire by those same triumphant Greeks. In this use of revenge and retaliation as a principle of unification of the disparate peoples of his empire he was outstandingly successful: it was a totally dedicated, if somewhat unwieldy, invasion force that Xerxes led to a pyrrhic victory at the Battle of Thermopylae (August 480 BC).[3] While he was left victor on the battlefield, the number of Persian dead far exceeded the number of Spartan dead. The delay caused by the heroic defence of the pass by Leonidas and the three hundred men of his bodyguard, who fought until the last man fell, contributed to the total destruction of the Persian naval armada at the Battle of Salamis (September 480 BC). This invasion left a burning resentment in the Greek cities and provinces, particularly in Macedonia.

[2] Cook, *The Persians*, p. 167ff.

[3] The Spartan defence of this pass through the mountains has come down in legend: a handful of brave men held the pass against an army. They perished to the last man.

Verses 3–4 The Grecian Empire 333–64 BC

(See summary at the beginning of Section 2)
'His belly and his thighs of brass'
The metal – Brass (2:32, 39)
The animal – He goat (8:5, 21)

In Daniel's vision the great Medo-Persian Empire that dominated the world for just over two hundred years (from 539 BC to 333 BC) is covered in one sentence. It is no surprise, therefore, to discover that the history of the next empire is summed up in two verses. This is the Greek Empire that burst upon the world scene under Alexander the Great. He and, particularly, his successors kept the near-eastern world in turmoil from 333 BC to 64 BC, a period of 269 years. The date 64 BC marks the end of the Seleucid dynasty, when the northern division of Alexander's empire came face-to-face with the expanding Roman Empire, which will be the fourth empire seen in the image of Nebuchadnezzar's dream. The portrait of one called 'a mighty king' is brief but memorable and unmistakeable. This is notable when it is recalled that this prophecy was written two hundred years (535–333 BC) before Alexander the Great appeared so unexpectedly and dramatically on the world scene. In Daniel's time Macedon was a minor province of little importance amongst the great city-states of Greece. Yet from this land, not even mentioned in this Scripture, arose a most remarkable man, whose meteoric rise and fall flashed across the earth stage over a brief period of only twelve years. His fall was as dramatic as his rise – in 336 BC, within a day, after his father's assassination, he was raised to the throne of Macedonia and to fame. In 323 BC, after three days of illness, as a young man of 33 years, he died and in his dying laid down the crowns of three kingdoms. Yet in that short lifetime the world was changed. This remarkable man is called 'Alexander the Great'. Three scriptural statements present King Alexander III of Macedon (356–323 BC):

1. His Charisma – Impressive – 'shall stand up'

Historians still find facets of the personality of Alexander to discuss and admire. His simple charisma marked him out in any company. In the home, around the council table, but especially on the battlefield, he was the centre of attention. That word 'impressive' describes him rightly in various ways:

(a) In physical stature – he stood head and shoulders above most. From earliest days, he was a leader on the field of battle;

(b) In intellectual power – Aristotle had guided his educational development for three crucial years, until he acknowledged his work finished. In debate, he could handle most arguments clearly and concisely;

(c) In battle – he proved absolutely fearless on the battlefield, learning battle tactics by the side of the acknowledged military genius of the day, Philip II of Macedon – his father;

(d) In personality – he attracted friends of the best character. Indeed, a group of friends known as 'companions' remained virtually unchanged throughout the whole campaign in Asia. These men were recognised on battlefields by their sheer courage and in council chambers by their wise counsel. Thus they acted both as a bodyguard for Alexander and an inner cabinet for counsel.

As a young man of only twenty years, but already the veteran of several campaigns, on a beautiful day in June 336 BC he stood by the side of his father, King Philip II of Macedon, at the head of a procession moving into the great stadium outside Aegae, the capital of Macedonia. On the other side of King Philip stood another Alexander, King of Epirus (a neighbour state of Macedon), his new son-in-law, who had just married Cleopatra, the sister of Alexander, the previous day. This was a day for the celebratory festival to be opened with a great pageant of games in the stadium. At dawn, every seat in the great stadium had already been filled. As the sun rose higher, the magnificent procession moved into the stadium. In the lead were priests carrying the images of the twelve Olympic gods, followed by a thirteenth priest, with an image of Philip. Immediately behind came King Philip and the two men named Alexander. Assured of his popularity, Philip had ordered his bodyguard, which normally surrounded him, to follow behind him. Just through the gate, the king paused. Suddenly one of his own bodyguards, a man called Pausanius, drew a short-bladed Celtic sword from his tunic, dashed forward, and plunged it into King Philip. He died instantly. As the assassin rushed for the gate, where horses awaited him, he tripped and three courtiers of the king killed him on the spot.[4]

As soon as King Philip's body was removed and order restored Antipater, the Regent of Macedonia, presented Alexander to the

[4] O'Brien, *Alexander the Great: The Invisible Enemy*, p. 36 ff.

army, which at once acclaimed him as king.[5] This was in keeping with Macedonian custom, and the council ratified the action and proclaimed their support. Alexander's rise to real power amongst the Greek city-states was rapid. In two months (July-August), at the head of the Macedonian army, Alexander had won the allegiance of all the Greek states; most were won by skilful diplomacy, but, at the same time, there was always the formidable Macedonian army ready to assert the will of their king. With this success, he summoned the League of Corinth (representing all the Greek states) to elect him, in his father's place, as plenipotentiary and Captain General of all the Greek forces to be gathered to invade the Persian Empire. The Greek states did exactly as they were told. With the highly trained veterans of the Macedonian army ready to view any hesitation as betrayal, they had little choice in the matter. Thus in the late summer of 336 BC there was opened to Alexander the real possibility of carrying out the lifelong ambition of his father. That ambition, which was nothing less than the complete destruction of the Persian Empire, he made his own. Under the successors of King Xerxes I (486–465 BC), who had led an army bent on rampage through the Greek mainland, the Persian Empire had continued this war policy and was skilled at isolating a Greek city-state and then destroying it. The Persian leaders had shown a special hatred, arising possibly from fear, of Macedonia, and had carried out many atrocities. The people of Macedonia never forgot, and certainly never forgave, their terrible deeds. Alexander wanted their blood.

2. His Dominion – Immense – 'shall rule with great dominion'

If the word 'dominion' in this verse is restricted to the size of the empire Alexander established then it must be pointed out that it was far greater territorially than either Babylon or Medo-Persia. It was Alexander's charismatic, dynamic personality that kept his small army of Macedonian veterans intact as they marched and fought from the Hellespont to the Indus River, in India, and back to Babylon. In the set pieces of battle he displayed such military skill and tactical adaptability, using the famous Macedonian phalanx, with deadly variation from battle to battle, that he is rated as the top military strategist of all time. He never lost a battle. As a result, from

[5] Antipater had already been appointed as Regent of Macedonia with power to run the country in the name of Philip II during the time of his absence anticipated when he would lead the Greek invasion into the Persian Empire supported by the League of Corinth (coalition of the Greek city-states).

Babylon as his capital city his dominion stretched from the River Danube, in Greece, as its northern border, right across the known world: southwards to Alexandria (which he founded), near the mouth of the Nile; west and south to the border of the Sahara Desert; and then sweeping eastwards and including all the lands formerly under Babylon and Medo-Persia. The eastern boundary of Alexander's empire was the Indus River, in India. Alexander brought the world to his feet in eight major battles and in just over ten years (January 334 BC to June 323 BC). (See map, p. 683).

3. His Self-Will – Implacable – 'do according to his will'

This comment of Scripture is forthright and accurate. It would be difficult to find in history a man who showed such self-confidence, such self-belief and such self-assurance that, at strategic moments, he would overrule his battle-hardened veteran commanders, including even General Parmenio, who had led campaigns by the side of his father, Philip. An example occured early in the campaign before the key battle that took place on the banks of the Granicus River. There his generals counselled caution and waiting to see what Darius would do. Alexander ignored all the cautious advice, threw his army across the river, as originally planned, and was proven right on the battlefield the next day. He could single-mindedly pursue his personal vendetta against King Darius III (Codomannus) and put his army at risk. Instead of appointing reliable men to administer the newly-won kingdom and moving on, he rejected the cautious policy of his companions and stayed to train auxiliary troops from a conquered people, for his invasion plan for the neighbour state. Instead of listening to sensible voices round the council table, he simply did his own will. That stubborn will would not yield even to the recall summons of the Macedonian government. On two occasions, he received direct orders to bring home his Macedonian troops. He simply ignored the order and demanded further troops. When bluntly parliament refused him reinforcements to fill the gaps in his army, Alexander simply recruited more auxiliaries. Neither did he listen to appeals of his wife, Olympia, for his return. In the Hindu Kush, he faced down his war-weary Macedonian veterans when they mutinied and refused to go any further. They had to pick up their kit, fall into line, and march. His will carried the day, even to the secret building of ships for the invasion westwards, when he lay dying. It would be very difficult to find another man in history exhibiting such self-will.

Thus the prophetic Scripture marks out a man; history points to its accuracy.

The grammatical construction in the next verse indicates both the unexpectedness and the suddenness of the fall of the kingdom established by this self-willed man. He had just reached the high point of his life: (a) He was a young man of almost 33 years with a battle-hardened army of veterans behind him; (b) He had an empire at his feet, stretching from the banks of the River Danube, in Europe, to the River Indus, in Asia; from Alexandria, on the mouth of the Nile, to Susa, on the banks of the Tigris River; (c) He had plans to extend his empire, at the point of the sword, westwards into the Mediterranean, with Carthage and Rome as his goal. And suddenly, within a few days, Alexander the Great was dead!

A great banquet was held in Babylon on the night of May 29, 323 BC. At the close of the feast, Alexander was challenged to drink a goblet of 'unmixed' (undiluted) wine; he did so, collapsed, and was put to bed. The next day he had a high fever, yet by the afternoon was back at his desk, arranging army affairs. He attended another banquet the next night, and the following day he was seriously ill with a terrible fever. Taking to bed on June 5, he grew weaker by the hour, until, in the late hours of June 9, King Alexander's senior officers gathered round their leader's bed. An authority on Greek history, Peter Green, paints the scene:

> At this the King's friends gathered round his bedside; they asked him – it was after all, a vital question – to whom he bequeathed his kingdom? Weakly Alexander whispered 'to the strongest'. His last all-too-prophetic words were 'I foresee a great funeral contest over me'. Early in the morning of 10th June 323 BC his eyes closed forever. [6]

One of earth's mighty men had gone!

The words used by the angel concerning the kingdom of this mighty king are simple yet graphic – 'broken' and 'divided toward the four winds of heaven'. The political power was certainly broken instantly; never again would the direction of this kingdom lie in the hands of one man. In his dying moments, Alexander had passed his royal ring to Perdiccas, a friend from boyhood, now his chief of staff. Before dawn the next morning, Perdiccas summoned the council of army generals and asked for a decision on the successor

[6] Green, *Alexander the Great*, p. 259.

to Alexander. Under the Macedonian constitution, the army was entitled to do this, and then forward the name of the chosen one to the senate in Agaea for confirmation. Finally, after days of acrimonious bickering, it was agreed that two of the 'heir apparent' group should share the throne, but under regents appointed by the army. Regents were essential since one of the candidates was Philip Arrhidaeus – a mentally deficient half-brother of Alexander. The supporters of this claimant were already addressing him as Philip III. The other was the child of Alexander, expected within weeks, by his latest wife, a Persian princess called Roxane – if it was a boy. The child was born in August of that year (323 BC), three months after his father's death, and named as Alexander IV. However, bitter controversy and open conflict raged in the army council over the appointment of the regents. It was here that real power and patronage would lie. Again, bitter wrangling, to the point of fisticuffs, preceded the appointment of the chief of staff, Perdiccas, as sole regent for the two kings. This arrangement satisfied most of the army, but only for a time. Other claimants made bids for power. One of the most notable was an illegitimate son of Alexander, called Hercules, by his mistress, Princess Barsine – a daughter of Darius III. The child was just four years old. However, Scripture is explicit in ruling out any of Alexander's family – 'not to his posterity'. Philip III, half-brother to Alexander, was murdered in 317 BC; in 310 BC the young Alexander IV was put to death, and in the following year (309 BC) Hercules, his illegitimate son, was also murdered.

Following the death of Alexander the next forty-two years (323–281 BC) have been called 'one of the great forgotten wars of history' by Robin Waterford, a notable historian writing of this period. He goes on to say: 'It took more or less forty years after the death of Alexander the Great for his heirs (the *Diadochoi* – the Successors) to finish carving up his vast empire. These years, 323–281 BC, were filled with high adventure, intrigue, passion, assassinations, dynastic marriages, treachery, shifting alliances, and mass slaughter on battlefield after battlefield.'[7] Daniel's prophecy becomes history again, as, after this period of turmoil Alexander's successors, four generals from the Macedonian veterans succeeded in reaching relative stability, with the empire divided into four, as Scripture said (8:8, 22), the four parts being related geographically as the four winds are related – North, South, East and West. The verb 'plucked

[7] Waterfield, *Dividing the Spoils*, p. ix.

up' points to an uprooting by force; battle after battle did exactly this. 'Nor according to his dominion' means not one of his heirs wielded a fraction of the authority that marked Alexander – they were lesser men in smaller kingdoms; merely provinces of the once so great empire.

While borders changed rapidly as the four kingdoms vied and fought with each other for territory during this extended period, the borders of 311 BC are reasonably typical – after the agreement called 'The Peace of the Dynasts' was accepted by each:

	Area	Alexander's Commanders[8]	Location
1	Babylonia and North Syria	Seleucus I Nicator	North
2	Egypt	Ptolemy I Soter	South
3	Macedonia	Cassander	West
4	Thrace and Bithynia	Lysimachus	East

It will be observed that the centre of the geographic direction is taken from neither Babylon (capital of the Babylonian Empire and the *de facto* capital for the Grecian Empire) nor Susa (capital of the Persian Empire), but Jerusalem. God, through Daniel, is focussing upon His people and their capital city, Jerusalem, which He uses as God's geographic centre of earth.

Verses 5–12 The Seleucid and Ptolemaic Dynasties

The peace treaty between the four generals of Alexander's army led to the separate kingdoms acknowledging their leaders as 'kings' and these leaders being allowed to pass the throne to their family heirs. Thus in 312 BC Seleucus accepted the title of King over the realm of Babylonia in northern Syria with his capital in Antioch. He is therefore the first king of the Seleucid dynasty, who is called in this chapter (v. 6) 'king of the north'. Similarly, when Ptolemy took over Egypt, in 323 BC, he was addressed as Ptolemy I, the founder of the Ptolemaic dynasty, in Egypt, having its capital city Memphis, and called in this chapter (v. 5) 'king of the south'. The other two empires, Macedonia (Greece), under Cassander, and Thrace and Bithynia, under Lysimachus, have no major roles to play in

[8] These men must have been around the age of very late teens or early twenties when they had command under Alexander. Alexander was around twenty-one when he led the Greek Army into Asia.

scriptural prophecy at this point, so they can be omitted for the moment.

Summary

From the death of Alexander (323 BC) until the commencement of the reign of Antiochus IV Epiphanes (175 BC), who is the eighth king in the Seleucid dynasty, is 148 years. The information given to Daniel is to strengthen the nation of Israel for the turbulent times ahead at the hands of the two warring enemies named above, so that, in difficult days, the exercised in the nation would know how to react to these two invaders of their land. Not having learned the full lesson from their captivity years, some of their leaders would again be drawn into idolatry – this time Hellenistic idolatry, and discipline from the hand of God must follow. However, as this is the nation through which the Messiah will come, there will still be a faithful remnant to hold the truths of Scripture. This prophecy will be a stay to the faithful in difficult times.

Living through the Babylonian captivity period and into the Medo-Persian Empire, Daniel has had personal experience of the first two empires of the 'times of the Gentiles'. In the preceding verses (vv. 2–4) he has learned how the Persian Empire would lose world dominion and be replaced by the Grecian Empire, established by Alexander the Great. After the carrying away to Babylon God had seen to it that, while still a captive people, Israel was preserved through dark years, until the decree of Cyrus (538 BC) permitted the return to their homeland of those who were exercised to go.

(a) Israel under Persian Rulers

As a result, under the leadership of Spirit-moved men there was a remnant of Israel that returned to Jerusalem to rebuild the Temple and re-establish a testimony for God. The history of those early years is recorded in the books of Ezra, Nehemiah, and Malachi. The first company came up under Zerubbabel (536 BC), the second company under Ezra (458 BC) and the third under Nehemiah (445 BC) – the last prophetic voice is heard in Malachi, in 396 BC, ministering to the returned exiles in Jerusalem. The voice of John the Baptist will break the silence of four hundred years when he cries on the banks of the Jordan River: 'Prepare ye the way of the LORD, make His paths straight' (Mk 1:3), and later, after Divine accreditation: 'Behold the Lamb of God' (Jn 1:29, 36).

There can be little question that, despite the problems recorded in Ezra and Nehemiah, the Medo-Persian Empire was, on the whole, favourable to the struggling congregation of returned exiles in and around Jerusalem. The action of King Artaxerxes Longimanus, in 445 BC, to permit and encourage the rebuilding of the city of Jerusalem becomes a landmark in the prophetic programme (9:25). A point of great interest will be to see how the new world power, under Alexander the Great, will treat this re-established nation.

(b) Israel under Hellenistic Rulers

While this prophecy gives no direct assurance of preservation of that remnant, the fact that it is accepted as still in existence in the prophetic centuries ahead is sufficient. There is a faithful testimony for God existing in Jerusalem throughout these years. For exercised hearts God, through the prophet Zechariah, in 520 BC, sixteen years later than this prophecy, gives a clear promise of Divine preservation for Jerusalem. In the autumn of the year 332 BC (188 years after Zechariah's prophecy) the outlook for Jerusalem was very bleak. The all-conquering army of Alexander was moving towards Jerusalem. Syria fell and Damascus was virtually wiped out; Egypt offered little resistance and crowned Alexander as Pharaoh; Tyre had fallen, after a bitter siege, as Ezekiel had said it would (Ezek. 26:15–21), and its island fortress was destroyed. Now Alexander is free to deal with Philistia and Judaea. Zechariah tells that Alexander's triumphal march would capture and destroy the Philistine cities of Gaza, Ashkelon, Ekron and Ashdod (Zech. 9:1–7). As Alexander fulfilled these prophecies and moved towards Jerusalem the whole city trembled. Scripture gives no further detail but the story recorded by Josephus is fascinating. The governor of Judaea, a Samaritan called Sanballat, appointed by King Darius III, refused to recognise Alexander's claim to the Persian Empire. As a result, he refused to pay the annual tribute to Alexander, instead sending it to Darius. Exasperated at such stubbornness, Alexander marched towards Jerusalem with every intention of wiping it out in his rage and, at the same time, promising unrestricted looting to his war-weary veterans. Knowing that an enraged and ruthless enemy was approaching, Jaddua, the high priest, claiming to have received guidance in a dream, gave detailed instructions for the reception of Alexander. He himself, in the splendour of his high-priestly robes of glory and beauty, led a great procession issuing from the city gate; he was followed by all the priests, in their white linen garments; behind them came the whole populace of the city, robed in white. The record in Josephus reads:

> For Alexander, when he saw the multitude at a distance, in white garments, while the priests stood clothed with fine linen, and the high priest in purple and scarlet clothing with the mitre upon his head, having the golden plate whereon the name of God was engraved, he approached by himself and adored the Name and first saluted the high priest. The Jews also did all together, with one voice salute Alexander and encompass him about.[9]

Josephus goes on to record how, when he showed Alexander the prophecy dealing with the destruction of Darius, he was much impressed by Daniel's God. Josephus records his reaction: 'and when the book of Daniel was showed him wherein Daniel declared that one of the Greeks should destroy the empire of the Persians, he supposed that he himself was the person intended.'[10] While historians point out that other records make no reference to this incident, there is a high probability that it is authentic. A minor incident in a war of conquest, given the erratic actions of Alexander, even with regard to clemency on many occasions, would be of little interest to other nations, while it meant a lot to the Jewish historian. Also, in the Greek records the list of cities destroyed is carefully noted, in honour of Alexander, and there is no question that Jerusalem was spared. There must have been a reason for this sparing by an often-ruthless Alexander. It should be remembered that God had spoken through Zechariah (520 BC) in the very context of Alexander's conquests: 'And I will encamp about Mine house because of the army, because of him that passeth by, and because of him that returneth: and no oppressor shall pass through them any more' (Zech. 9:8). The record of Josephus shows how God, in spite of the failure of Israel, works out His own purposes with regard to His people.

While the historical records show that Alexander personally favoured the Jews and spared Jerusalem, there would be amongst his successors in the Hellenistic world those who, for weighty reasons, as they judged, would seek the destruction of the nation of Israel. The reason would vary from reign to reign. On occasion a

[9] Josephus, *The Complete Works*, p. 244.
[10] Josephus, *The Complete Works*, p. 245.

neighbouring power – either north or south of Israel – would want support in its war and Judah was weak enough to have to agree. So there would be at times a political reason for their going to war. Again, since the main highway between Europe and Asia passed through Israel, there was often a geographical reason for Israel to be drawn into wars that were not of its making. However, behind the obvious, there was often a religious reason at the root of the animosity against Israel. Idol-worshipping nations did not readily accept the uncompromising monotheism of an Israel professing to believe in a holy God. Since this meant that Israel, when in obedience to prophetic ministry, showed an uncompromising rejection of both idolatry and the consequent immorality associated with it, heathendom hated Israel and would take every opportunity to attack her. Again, behind these national enemies there lay the animosity of the hierarchy of satanic powers who, as shown in the previous chapter, were at work to destroy Israel. Satan knew this was the nation of the promised Redeemer and his interest and intention (see Rev. 12:1–5) has always been to wipe Israel off the world map. This is the reason why this section is given for our instruction, as it moves across prophetic history and closes with the reign of Antiochus IV, who embodies a portrait of the age. That the relatively minor figure in world history of Antiochus IV Epiphanes should have such a prominent place in prophetic Scripture is the result of two things: (a) He was the embodiment of the hostility of the age, promoted by the unseen satanic powers, to the coming Messiah; (b) He becomes, in history, the portrait of the most terrible enemy that Israel would ever face. This last mighty king of the end-time will lead the nations of earth, under satanic direction, in opposition to the second coming of the Messiah. This end-time king is the man who will come perilously close to doing what Antiochus Epiphanes tried and failed to do – wipe out the nation of Israel entirely.

Verses 5–6 Founders of the Dynasties

The Ptolemaic Dynasty – King of the South

Verse 5 The word for 'South' (*Negev*) generally means the literal desert to the south of Israel. Here it is used in a wider sense and points to the nation directly south of Jerusalem; thus it is seen as Egypt, which became historically one of the major satrapies of Alexander's empire; an inheritance from the Medo-Persian Empire.

This deduction is confirmed explicitly in the context (v. 8), where Egypt is named as receiving the spoils of war. The terms 'King of the South' and 'King of the North' indicate the predictive character of this prophecy and allow history to fill in the specific names at any given time. The north and south directions can only be with reference to Israel generally, and Jerusalem specifically. This supports what has already been suggested – prophecy relates to God's chosen nation, Israel; other nations come into the picture as they relate to Israel. Egypt, an ancient enemy, lies directly south of Israel; directly north of Israel lies 'Aram' (Num. 23:7) – the same Hebrew word is translated 'Mesopotamia' (Judg. 3:10) – and then 'Syria' (Judg. 10:6). Syria is an abbreviated form of 'Assyria' and came into common use about the time of Alexander the Great.[11] In modern times Syria, directly north of Israel, is only a fraction of the size it was in the old Seleucid Empire.

In this verse the King of the South can be readily identified as King Ptolemy I, called 'Soter' (Saviour). He was a Macedonian and a childhood friend of Alexander. During Alexander's years of conquest, he proved himself a dependable and very able general. Immediately after Alexander's death, in 323 BC, he was appointed 'Satrap' of Egypt. '*Satrapy*' was the Persian word for province, retained for convenience by Alexander when he seized the Persian Empire. Ptolemy was the first of the four 'successors' of Alexander to feel secure enough to call himself 'King', in 304 BC, and thus he became the founder of the Ptolemaic dynasty. He proved an able administrator and put the country on a sound financial standing, backed by a well organised army. To honour Alexander he moved the capital of Egypt from Memphis to the newly founded Alexandria. This city, with its royally founded library and museum, became the chief centre of learning for the whole Mediterranean area. Most unusually for these times, he abdicated, in 285 BC, and passed the throne to his son, who reigned as Ptolemy II Philadelphus. The angel describes him as 'strong'- an adjective from the verb 'to hold fast, to bind fast' and describes things made fast by binding them together. This was true of him personally, as he lived to the age of 83/4. It is a word too that very accurately reflects his rule in the formerly much troubled land of Egypt. For the first time in many years, Egypt had a strong and stable government.

[11] *UBD*, p. 1055.

The Seleucid Dynasty – King of the North

The second statement in the verse points to a prince who for a time was a reliable man at the court of Ptolemy II. A more literal translation makes the matter clearer: 'but one of his princes shall be stronger than he and his dominion shall be a great dominion' (*RSV*). This person is clearly identified in history as Seleucus I Nicator (Conqueror), another of Alexander's Macedonian generals, who had been first appointed as 'satrap' over the northern kingdom of Babylonia, in 321 BC. When Antigonus, a fellow general in Alexander's army, who had been designated as satrap in Phrygia, Lycia and Pamphylia, called himself 'King of Asia' and seized Babylonia, Seleucus fled to Egypt and served under Ptolemy I. In 312 BC, after the defeat and death of Antigonus on the battlefield, Seleucus returned to his former satrapy as Seleucus I where, with a much stronger army behind him, he brought all Babylonia, Syria and Media under his control and ruled an empire that stretched from the Hellespont to India – the largest acreage of the four divisions of the empire. After this success, he was acknowledged as 'King' and he added the word 'Nicator' (meaning Conqueror) to his name. This return to the throne in his kingdom is the date accepted by historians for the commencement of the Seleucid dynasty. In 300 BC he moved his capital to Antioch, in Syria. 'His dominion shall be a great dominion' is a fitting description of this Seleucid Empire, with the most extensive territory of the four 'successors' of Alexander the Great.

Verse 6 The opening words of verse 6 should read: 'after some years' (*RSV*), thus another time break is envisaged, which refers to the period of bitter animosity when these two nations (Syria, under the Seleucids, and Egypt, under the Ptolemies) waged war after war against each other. Eventually they decided a mutual peace would be beneficial for both lands. Scripture records the reconciliation thus: 'they shall make an alliance' (*RSV*). From 304 BC to 250 BC historians find two periods of conflict, referred to as two Syrian Wars; the first is dated 274–271 BC, between Ptolemy II (King of Egypt) and Antiochus I (King of Syria), and the second is dated 260–253 BC, between Ptolemy II and Antiochus II. The second Syrian War ended with an agreement between the two kingdoms that was to be sealed with a dynastic marriage – the daughter of Ptolemy II (Egypt) was to be married to King Antiochus II (Syria) – a

The whole episode was such an unmitigated disaster that Scripture sums it up in four brief statements:

(a) 'She shall be given up' – no Egyptian armies were dispatched to the aid of this beleaguered princess;

(b) 'And they that brought her' – clearly all those that had come from Egypt to attend her in Syria perished;

(c) 'And he that begat her' – while her father did die just at this time, the reference here is more likely to be to her child, the infant put to death by Laodice. In defence of this latter interpretation Wood points out that many of the versions read 'child', as does the *RSV* and *NET*, by omission of the Masoretic pointing;[12]

(d) 'And he who got possession of her' (*RSV*) is her husband, Antiochus, who had entered most willingly into the intrigue to further his own hidden purpose – the union of two kingdoms under his own rule. It resulted in the deaths of the main figures involved with the original immoral marriage.

This brings the timeline at verse 6 down to 246 BC.

Verses 7–9 In the year 246 BC new monarchs come to the throne in both Egypt and Syria. This is also the date given by historians as the date of the Third Syrian War (246–241 BC),[13] as history records the renewal of hostilities between these kingdoms after the broken agreement. There is no doubt about the bitterness in ruling circles in Egypt concerning the betrayal and death of Princess Berenice. The son of the betrayed King Ptolemy II Philadelphus, crowned in Egypt as Ptolemy III Euergetes (246–221 BC), was enraged. Scripture makes sure the link with Berenice is observed, and, incidentally, the cause of the war, by speaking of this king as 'a branch from her roots' (*RSV*). The word 'branch' (Hebrew '*netser*') means a 'sprout' or 'a shoot' – coming from the same root as Berenice – this is quite clearly her brother. In retaliation for his sister's murder Ptolemy III launches his armies against Syria (King of the North). The death of Antiochus II has brought to the throne in Syria his son by Laodice, crowned as Seleucus Callinicus (246–226 BC). Arriving in Syria with a battle-hardened army, Ptolemy III found little opposition, since Seleucus had prudently withdrawn his forces to the eastern region of his empire. Scripture foretells what history confirms almost three hundred years later:

[12] Wood, *A Commentary on Daniel*, p. 285.

[13] *OHCW*, p. 847.

(a) '[He] shall enter into the fortress of the king of the north'. Ptolemy invaded Syria and moved quickly to capture and loot the fortified capital city – Antioch. The young king refused to meet him in open battle so Ptolemy ravaged at will;

(b) '[He] shall deal against them, and shall prevail'. Ravaging Syria as he marched, hastily-mustered Syrian forces were quickly dealt with and the western part of the Seleucid Empire was laid waste. He dealt with the vindictive Laodice by putting her to death;

(c) '[He] shall also carry captives into Egypt their gods, with their princes, and with their precious vessels'. There is no doubt the booty carried to Egypt was huge. The items detailed tell of the utter subjugation of a people: even 'their gods, with their molten images' (*RV*) were carried down to Egypt. Some of these gods had doubtless been carried to Syria from Egypt when Cambyses first brought Egypt under Medo-Persian rule. Now they were repatriated and, significantly, the Babylonian idols were carried away as well. The gesture was partly symbolic, since it announced the defeat of Syria's gods. Few scholars question that the word 'princes' (*AV*) should be translated, as in the majority of translations, 'molten images'. 'With their precious vessels of silver and of gold' – in the context this is to be interpreted as the precious vessels associated with the idols and their worship. In the wider context, it speaks of the great booty that Ptolemy brought back to Egypt. So great was that booty that Egypt conferred on their king the title 'Euergetes', meaning 'Benefactor'.

The final statement about this king – 'He shall continue more years than the king of the north' – is somewhat ambiguous and has been interpreted in several ways. At first glance, the thought would seem to be that not only did Ptolemy out-fight Seleucus, but he would out-live him as well. He did this, not by some remarkable longevity, but indeed by only six years (Seleucus II died in 226 BC and Ptolemy III in 221 BC), which makes this a somewhat strange remark in the context. An alternative reading: 'and for some years he shall refrain from attacking the king of the north' (*RSV*) is a possible translation, especially as a peace treaty was agreed between Ptolemy III and Seleucus II in 240 BC. Keil translates it 'continued to stand' and suggests that the phrase simply means that the supremacy of the King of the South stood for years.[14] Though there was the peace treaty agreed (240 BC), the King of the North (Seleucus II Callinicus) did make an attack upon the King of the

[14] Keil and Delitzsch, *Commentary on the Old Testament*, Vol. 9, p. 437.

South (Ptolemy III), but this was easily repulsed. In fact Keil draws attention to the statement that follows (v. 9) in support of his interpretation: 'And he shall come into the realm of the king of the south, but he shall return into his own land' (RV). Keil offers the best explanation when he remarks (*ibid*): 'by the mention of an expedition of the king of the north into the kingdom of the king of the south, from which he again returned without having effected anything, the way is opened for passing to the following description of the supremacy of the king of the north over the king of the south.' This is a very valid insight into a complex period of history.

Verses 10–19 The Ascendancy of the King of the North

From Seleucus II to Antiochus III the Great 227–187 BC

Verse 10 When Seleucus II Callinicus, the King of the North, attacked Egypt in defiance of the peace treaty, he was repulsed and returned a much-chastened man to his own land. This verse notes the reaction of his two sons. The verb 'stirred up' recognises the anger that motivated both of them to raise armies to avenge the disgrace of their father's defeat in Egypt. Both raised armies but the older brother, Seleucus III Ceraunus, inheriting the kingdom, wished to deal first with unrest in the Asian provinces. He raised and led an army there and was killed in battle (223 BC). His younger brother, just eighteen years old, on accession to the throne became Antiochus III and had a long reign, of thirty-six years. The accuracy of the prophecy is seen again. It is to be noted that the plural 'sons', used in the first statement, becomes a singular in the next: 'and one shall certainly come, and overflow, and pass through'. It was Antiochus III who led the northern armies in a number of incursions and campaigns to push Egypt out of Syria. This was done quickly and with overpowering force. The verb 'overflow' invokes the imagery of a river overflowing its banks and sweeping all before it. Antiochus swept down from the north, through the land of Israel as far as Gaza, then across the Jordan. In this action the ruler of Egypt, the King of the South, was stripped of all his conquered territories and pushed back to his own borders. Antiochus was successful mainly because of the indolence and incompetence of Ptolemy (Philopator) (221–203 BC). These conquests won for Antiochus III the surname 'The Great'. This was accomplished over several campaigns, which, as the final statement (v. 10) shows, brought him territorial gains right up to the very border of Egypt.

Verse 11 Even the luxury-loving King Ptolemy IV (Philopator) was roused from his self-indulgent lifestyle by this real threat to the heartlands of Egypt. 'Moved with choler' at these reverses in the war with Syria, he gathered a mighty army and marched to oppose Antiochus the Great, the King of the North. His army is described here as 'a great multitude'. Polybius records that this army was composed of over 70,000 infantry, 5,000 cavalry, and 73 elephants.[15] The armies met at Raphia – a border fortress (Heb. 'stronghold') in Egypt. Ptolemy IV, accompanied by his sister-wife, Arsinoe, led a mighty army to face Antiochus IV. According to reliable historical records[16] Antiochus had managed to muster a powerful army of around 62,000 infantry, 6,000 cavalry, and 102 elephants. At Raphia a major battle took place (217 BC). At the first clash it appeared that the forces of Antiochus would add Egypt to their empire but a tremendous rally late in the day by native Egyptian auxiliaries, in defence of their homeland, saved Ptolemy's Egypt.[17] The result of the battle is recorded in one brief sentence in Scripture: 'but the multitude shall be given into his hand'. There could be some ambiguity about the antecedent of 'his' in this sentence, but history knows no doubt of the victor. Ptolemy's army, most unexpectedly, comprehensively defeated the forces of Antiochus. Antiochus lost his entire army, barely escaped capture himself and fled northward, a defeated and disappointed man. The multitude given into Ptolemy's hand was the army of King Antiochus, who in this defeat suffered a devastating blow to his grandiose plan to reunite Alexander's empire by the sword under his own rule.

Verse 12 There is no dispute about the scriptural assessment of the character of Ptolemy IV. An extremely proud king, this victory added enormously to his already inflated ego. His arrogance was insufferable, as the repetition from verse 11 shows – he treated his captives without mercy. The following translation gives a clear picture of this arrogant and ruthless ruler: 'When the army is carried off, the king of the South will be filled with pride and will slaughter many thousands' (*NIV*). Polybius claims he killed ten thousand infantry, three hundred cavalry, and five elephants, and took four thousand prisoners.[18] The words of Scripture sum up this

[15] Young, *The Prophecy of Daniel*, p. 238. Note his quote from Polybius.
[16] Jerome. *In Danielem Prophetem*, Ed. Migne 1865, XXV, 124.
[17] *OHCW*, p. 849.
[18] Wood, *A Commentary on Daniel*, p. 288, quotation from Polybius V: 86.

campaign with a sobering note on his subsequent reign: 'but he shall not be strengthened by it'. A man of this character never learns from experience. After the battle, Ptolemy went back to his life of indolence. The self-indulgence and depraved appetite of Ptolemy turned his people against him. In fact, this victory so fostered his self-esteem that he thought he was invincible and acted foolishly. Instead of pursuing his advantage over Antiochus he simply chased him northwards, but making little show of a determined pursuit, leaving this veteran fighter his freedom to gather another army. He annexed Judaea, and, instead of acting as a deliverer from bondage, he immediately enraged the Jews by his profanation of the Temple. Trying to force his way into the holy of holies, he collapsed speechless. Sobered, he agreed to an ill-considered truce with Antiochus that was intended to lead to a peace treaty. Such a treaty was never agreed and his implacable enemy was allowed time to recoup his losses. In Egypt, his disillusioned subjects rebelled against his imperious rule and profligate lifestyle. Incensed by the recalcitrance of the Jews in Jerusalem, he put thousands of Jews to death when he returned to Alexandria. Most of the Jewish population fled the country; it is calculated that less than three hundred were allowed to retain any civil rights. Unexpectedly, things changed in one night. Ptolemy IV (Philopator) and his wife (Arsinoe) both died, suddenly and mysteriously, in 203 BC, and the leaders of Egypt, both civil and military, seem to have accepted this with varied degrees of thankfulness. There were, most remarkably, very few questions asked about their sudden deaths. They were buried quietly with little fuss and their five-year-old son was crowned as Ptolemy V Epiphanes.

Verse 13 Defeated at the Battle of Raphia (217 BC), on the Egyptian border, Antiochus III (The Great) was absolutely determined to subdue his Egyptian enemy. Still, he had learned some lessons – particularly concerning the preparation and provision of an adequate force to meet the enemy. 'After certain years' is the scriptural interval and it is readily seen in history as the years 217–203 BC. These fourteen years, from the defeat at Raphia (217 BC) to the next Syrian invasion of Egypt, identified by historians as the outbreak of the Fifth Syrian War, were years that showed the growing power of Antiochus. In these years, Antiochus campaigned very successfully into lands eastwards, going as far as the Caspian Sea and even to the borders of India, recovering much of the lands subdued initially by Alexander the Great. This gave him not only an army bigger numerically than his previous army, but a better-equipped and a better-trained army. Scripture had foreseen these very features in the invasion force: '[He] shall certainly come ... with a great army and with much riches'. The word used for 'riches' means 'possessions', 'property', 'substance';[19] in fact, the plunder from conquered territories. Antiochus had used these years effectively, to develop and to train his army, but at the same time to accumulate phenomenal riches to subsidise the invasion of Egypt, his old enemy. How precise are the words given to Daniel. Antiochus had his army ready by 201 BC and, indeed, made several incursions southwards, probing the Egyptian defences before launching his major offensive. This is where Israel comes again into the world picture.

Verse 14 Other factors weighed with Antiochus III as he awaited the right moment to invade Egypt. These are highlighted in the words of this prophecy: 'In those times there shall many stand up against the king of the south'. By 204–203 BC a number of factors suggested the moment was right for the King of the North to make his move. Note the political scene:

(a) King Ptolemy IV (Philopator) and his sister-wife (Arsinoe) both died suddenly and mysteriously in 203 BC. Rebellion was brewing in Egypt because of the licentious lifestyle of the royal couple. Their sudden and unexplained death opened the way for the crowning of their five-year-old son, in Alexandria, as Ptolemy V Epiphanes, under a regent from the army. Rebels proliferated in Egypt. One major group, led by a man called Agathocles, made an attempt to overthrow the regency and dethrone or murder the infant king. The attempt failed but with a regency rule in place and a restive population ripe for rebellion, it seemed to Antiochus to be just the right time to invade Egypt;

(b) Other enemies of Egypt were ready to stand up, as the prophecy indicates: 'And in those times there shall many stand up against the king of the south'. One of these was Philip V of Macedonia, the western region of Alexander's empire, who by his links with Hannibal, the Carthaginian enemy of Rome, needed the support of Antiochus against Rome. Philip and Antiochus had already entered upon an agreement to divide the spoils of the

[19] *OTWS*, p. 355.

Egyptian Empire between them. In explicit terms, Philip agreed to support Antiochus now, if Antiochus would agree to support him against the growing power of Rome in the days ahead;

(c) In the preservation of the newly renascent Israel, some of their priestly leaders were tempted to take the side of Antiochus at the price of faithfulness to Scripture. This is indicated by the words 'also the children of the violent among thy people shall lift themselves up to establish the vision' (*RV*). The reference to 'thy people' makes plain the link with Daniel and the re-established and growing nation of Israel in Jerusalem. The emotive word 'robbers' (*AV*) would be better translated 'children of the violent' (*RV*); Leon Wood translates it 'sons of breaking'.[20] The interpretation is that some of the priestly leaders in Israel, in their desire to achieve some measure of political independence, were ready to abandon without scruple the practices of Judaism. The Ptolemaic dynasty in Egypt had ruled Judaea from the break-up of Alexander's empire – except for the brief interlude under Antiochus himself fourteen years previous – and these kings had, on the whole, treated them well. The exception had been Ptolemy IV on his last expedition, after the Battle of Raphia (217 BC), when he had enraged them by his profanation of the Temple. Fortifying a building near the Temple in Jerusalem, this same Ptolemy had left a garrison there under an Egyptian general, Scopas, to guard his interests. In his recent probing excursion Antiochus had been approached by a number of Jewish leaders who were prepared to support him against Egypt. They promised him aid if he would attack and wipe out the Egyptian garrison in Jerusalem. The expression 'shall exalt themselves' seems to indicate the coming to the fore of men who, without any mandate but their own and tired of Israel changing conquerors every few years, wanted the Jews to support Antiochus wholeheartedly against Ptolemy and drive out the Egyptian garrison in Jerusalem. Josephus writes of Jerusalem welcoming Antiochus at this time and supporting him with provisions for his army and the care of the elephants[21];

(d) The purpose of the men mentioned above may well have been the laudable desire to see Scripture fulfilled. This is implied in the statement 'shall lift themselves up to establish the vision' (*RV*). The vision is a reference to the Divine Word through the prophet Isaiah

[20] Wood, *A Commentary on Daniel*, p. 289.

[21] Josephus, *Complete Works*, p. 251.

and the judgement pronounced against Egypt (Isa. 19:1–17). This pro-Syrian party could see themselves playing a key role in these plots against Egypt. Their reward would be that a grateful Antiochus would surely replace the godly leaders in Jerusalem and put them in charge. However, the book of Daniel was written over three hundred years before these priestly leaders would have known of these events. The character of this Greek king, whom they were willing to support, had already been exposed by Daniel (8:9–14). This rebel group should have heeded the warning of the terrible danger in such an alliance. If that was not sufficient, then surely the very next statement in this verse should have caused them to think again: 'but they shall fall' – where the verb is better read as 'fail' (*RSV*) or 'falter' (*NET*). With the best of motives, these men could not accomplish what they were endeavouring to do. No lasting peace could come in Israel by an agreement with such a man. By aligning themselves with Antiochus III and attacking the Egyptian garrison under General Scopas they probably hoped to gain national independence by the favour of Antiochus. Not only were their hopes dashed, but also this unscriptural alliance opened the way for Seleucid dominance, under the next king – Antiochus IV Epiphanes – the man who would almost wipe out the nation of Israel. Most of these self-willed priestly leaders would perish in the wars that followed this alliance.

Verse 15 After the parenthetic verse just considered (v. 14, to show why Antiochus chose this time to declare war on Egypt), the repetition of the opening phrase of the paragraph (v. 13) goes back to the invasion of Antiochus III into Egypt, in 203 BC. General Scopas had recovered a lot of territory for Egypt, including the rich lands of Coele-Syria – the southern and economically valuable part of Syria running into Judaea and down as far as the Phoenician coastal cities. Approaching through Judaea, Antiochus attacked and recovered these valuable parts of the Syrian Empire. After several skirmishes between the Syrian and the Egyptian forces (under General Scopas), they confronted each other at Panium – a town in the northern part of Judaea, where Caesarea Philippi would stand in a later day. In the battle that followed (199 BC) the Egyptian forces were totally routed and a small remnant of the Egyptian army took shelter in Sidon, which is indeed a 'most fenced' city; in fact it was a fortress. Antiochus immediately besieged it, as indicated in the phrase 'cast up a mount', where 'mount' would be more clearly translated as 'siege works'. The city surrendered in 198 BC and the remaining Egyptians fled back to Egypt. Antiochus, King of the North, was left in complete control of the 'liberated' lands, including Israel and Phoenicia as far south as Gaza. The comprehensiveness of the defeat of Ptolemy is described in three sentences:

(a) 'The arms of the south shall not withstand'. The reference in the word 'arms', or 'forces', indicates that there was no cohesive army left to take the field; nor was there any source from which such an army could be gathered to face Antiochus again;

(b) 'Neither his chosen people'. In the context, this cannot refer to Israel as the chosen nation, but draws attention to the desperate effort that Ptolemy made to relieve the siege of Sidon. He dispatched specially trained reserve troops, under the command of his three most able and most experienced generals. They too were soundly beaten;

(c) 'Neither shall there be any strength to withstand'. With the main army, under General Scopas, totally routed and the reserves wiped out, King Ptolemy faced catastrophic defeat – he had neither army nor resources to oppose the Syrian invader.

The timeline in the chapter has reached 198 BC. The defeated king is the King of the South, Ptolemy V Epiphanes; the triumphant king is the King of the North, Antiochus III, The Great.

Verse 16 Antiochus III had brought the greater part of the land area of Alexander's empire under the Seleucid throne. He would henceforth be known as 'Antiochus the Great'; people in his day could not fail to catch the implications of the title. Keeping in the context, 'he that cometh against him' is to be identified as the King of the South, whose defeat has just been described (vv. 13–15). Antiochus has certainly imposed his will on the Egyptian armies and they are out of the picture. Now he has the freedom to impose his will on all the newly subjected nations torn from the suzerainty of Egypt. No nation or people is able to resist his terms, and these terms are soon made clear. 'None shall stand before him' is possibly a side glance at Rome, who is watching this empire-builder carefully, viewing his recent movements with grave suspicion. Rome is afraid of his motives but is not fitted nor equipped to deal with the threat just yet.

One of those recovered lands brought back under Seleucid control is called 'the glorious land' (8:9; 11:41; Ezek. 20:6), which must be understood as the land of Israel. Anyone who expected magnanimity from Antiochus must have been bitterly disappointed. His treatment of the land of Israel is summarised in this Scripture: 'which by his hand shall be consumed'. This is an excellent translation and reflects accurately what Antiochus did to Israel. This land had already suffered much from the transit of armies moving through it to the various battles north and south. Now that Antiochus had won this latest war those in Israel who had betrayed Ptolemy and supported Antiochus might reasonably have hoped for independence or, at the very least, fair treatment by the conqueror. Far from it; now they were subjected to a far worse despotism than they had ever faced. The land had suffered great desolation, as already explained, but now Antiochus made it the bridgehead and a base, in case of any further trouble with Egypt. He stationed an army there to live off the land. Is it any wonder the prophet uses the word 'consumed'? This accurately describes what Antiochus did in Israel. Some translations do use the word 'destruction' (*RV*) but in this context 'consumed' is better. Antiochus did not destroy the land of Israel at this time – he did devour it.

Verse 17 While Antiochus had retaken all the empire of Alexander east of Egypt, he recognised that if he attempted any westward move Egypt would always be a threat. To Antiochus, Greece had always been a tempting prize just about within his reach. With its many city-states, often at war with each other, he calculated it would be an easy prey to the army he now commanded. However, he knew full well that, for him to make such a move, Egypt must be appeased. The expression 'he ... set his face' indicates that his mind was made up; peace must be made with Egypt, whatever the cost. So Antiochus confronted his defeated enemy once again; not this time on the battlefield, but around the diplomatic table. Not only had Antiochus a purpose; he had a plan – and behind it the 'strength of his whole kingdom'. The presence of his army, very naturally, overshadowed the peace discussions; it certainly gave his arguments a special weight. According to the text (*AV*) he had also with him some counsellors, called 'upright ones'. Some commentators explain this term as 'men who could be trusted', and some go so far as to suggest that the king is accompanied by Jews who had proven their loyalty to him. It is more in keeping with the context to accept that the reading should be 'equitable conditions' (as in *RV* margin).

In other words Antiochus is presenting to Ptolemy a plan backed, as he would claim, by his whole kingdom and presenting such reasonable terms that a defeated enemy cannot afford to reject them. Antiochus is not deceiving Ptolemy. In this matter at least he is prepared to keep to the proposed terms: Scripture says 'thus shall he do'. In simple terms, so determined is Antiochus to get his vital peace treaty into place that he will go to any limit to get it.

The limit to which Antiochus III will go is, indeed, a major step – to the length of another dynastic marriage. He will give his daughter Cleopatra[22] in marriage to Ptolemy V Epiphanes. The unusual designation 'daughter of women' is probably to highlight her status as the outstanding lady of her day; she was the royal princess, the daughter of Antiochus the Great. F.A. Tatford takes a different view of this expression.[23] He points out that Cleopatra must have been quite young and still under the tutelage of both mother and grandmother; the implication is that this explains the plural 'women'. Since no authority quotes her age, it is suggested that the first explanation is better suited to the context. The reasoning behind this marriage on the part of Antiochus is very obvious, if it is recognised that the burning ambition of Antiochus was to keep Egypt quiet when he attacked Greece. Even if this long term ambition was delayed, Antiochus is placing his daughter in a strategic position to make sure her husband, and thus Egypt, did not interfere when Antiochus moved against Greece. Even when he made his move to attack Greece and Rome did move against him, Antiochus must have calculated that his daughter, wielding influence in Egypt, would make Rome think carefully at least. There is no doubt Antiochus intended to make his move in the very near future (see v. 18). This offers a possible explanation of the next term: 'corrupting her'. Instead of allowing the girl to give undivided allegiance to her husband, her father was priming her to further his interests instead of those of her husband. The alternative reading, 'to destroy it' (*RV* marg.), or 'to destroy the kingdom' (*RSV*), goes further in the thought of corruption. Commentators who accept this reading suggest that Antiochus had ordered his daughter to use every means at her disposal to act contrary to her husband's interests, and the interests of Egypt generally, so that when the time

[22] Montgomery insists that this was the first woman in the Ptolemaic line to bear the name Cleopatra (*Daniel*, p. 441). The Cleopatra associated with Julius Caesar and Mark Anthony lived much later (69–30 BC).

[23] Tatford, *Daniel and His Prophecy*, p. 190.

was ripe he, on the strength of his relationship to her, could march in and lay claim to a chaotic kingdom. There is no doubt that Antiochus had world dominion on the scale of Alexander's wildest dream before him, and either translation leads to the same end. This treaty and the accompanying dynastic marriage confirming it were agreed between Syria and Egypt in 197 BC.

While the terms were agreed in 197 BC, the marriage only took place four years later, in 193 BC, when Ptolemy V had reached seventeen years of age. The marriage took place at Raphia, on the border of Egypt. Antiochus promised as dowry the total income for a year from the wealthy, recently conquered states of Coele-Syria, Phoenicia and Israel. As a matter of interest, this dowry was never paid in full. Antiochus kept back half of it as a deduction for the cost of administration.[24] Still, the strategy was a complete fiasco; in fact it became a total disaster for Antiochus. Scripture puts it in plain language: 'but she shall not stand on his side, neither be for him'. The young queen, with a mind of her own, would not betray her husband as her father expected, but gave him her total loyalty and whole-hearted support. This will be seen in the history that follows. Egypt remained stable even when Antiochus moved to invade Greece and, as a consequence, Rome emerges onto the world stage. Egypt aided the Romans to the embarrassment of Antiochus. His strategy was a complete failure.

If Antiochus III had been content at this stage (197 BC) there is no question that his title 'The Great' would have been acknowledged worldwide and he would have gone down in history as one of the great military leaders of the ancient world, on the pattern of his illustrious predecessor Alexander the Great. However, the overruling ambition of his life, namely to bring Greece into his empire, had driven him throughout his life and now, it seemed, was within his grasp. Tempted by the weakness of the Greek states, he launched his armies into Europe and met total failure. The last ten years of his life (197–187 BC) brought disaster, defeat, disappointment, despair and eventually an ignominious death. This is the record of Scripture.

Verse 18 Advance of Antiochus III The Great

The expression 'turn his face', repeated in verse 19, means to 'focus all his interest upon' and marks the moment subsequent to the

[24] Tatford, *Daniel and His Prophecy*, p. 190.

marriage of his daughter in 193 BC when Antiochus decided that the time was ripe to invade Greece. This would fulfil his lifelong ambition, to rule where his hero Alexander had ruled. The word 'isles' means 'coastlands' and refers to any land beside the water – a good description of the Greek Islands in the Aegean Sea. At first all went well for Antiochus who, having gathered a large fleet of over three hundred vessels, captured Rhodes, Samos, Colophon, and many others. Landing on the eastern side of Greece, they built a fortified army base at Thermopylae, the key pass through the mountains to mainland Greece. The prophetic forecast was fulfilled to the letter: 'he … shall take many'. Significantly he was now joined by Hannibal from Carthage. Hannibal was the great military strategist army leader who had humbled Rome so spectacularly a few years before, but had been decisively defeated at the Battle of Zama (202 BC) by the Roman general Publius Cornelius Scipio (Scipio Africanus), and had returned to Carthage to become a senator and a diplomat. Out-manoeuvred by the 'peace party' in the senate at Carthage, Hannibal was forced to lead Carthage into a peace on Rome's terms at the close of the Second Punic War (218–201 BC). However, knowing he would certainly be betrayed by the Carthaginian leadership, who blamed him for taking them into war with Rome, Hannibal fled to Greece hoping to rally King Antiochus to his 'anti-Rome' banner. Antiochus had already adopted an anti-Roman stance, when he welcomed Hannibal to his forces with a royal banquet in 192 BC. It hardly needs to be pointed out that Rome hated the man who had humbled their most able generals for years. His every move was watched, and the antipathy now focussed upon the Syrian king who sheltered him. So the presence of Hannibal in the Syrian army was a very mixed blessing – his experience could be useful, but his enemies now became their enemies. Rome had decided that the 'reproach', or 'humiliation', heaped on them by this attack on Greece, which they claimed as part of the Roman Empire, had pushed their forbearance beyond the limit. Rome reacted quickly. The senate dispatched immediately to Greece Lucius Cornelius Scipio (Scipio Asiaticus), a very able general and the brother of Hannibal's nemesis, Scipio Africanus. His arrival added three Roman legions to the Greek forces. The following translation (from *NET*) seems best to convey the scriptural Hebrew: 'But a commander will bring his shameful conduct to a halt; in addition, he will make him pay for his shameful conduct.' Another translation supports this: 'a commander shall put an end

CHAPTER 11:21–35

THIS CENTRAL SECTION of the chapter is taken up with one particular king of the Seleucid dynasty in Syria that followed the break-up of the empire of Alexander the Great on his death, in 323 BC. This is the eighth king of the line; the history and conflicts of his predecessors have been touched upon in the previous sixteen verses (vv. 5–20). Now fifteen verses (vv. 21–35) are devoted to this one Seleucid Greek ruler, called Antiochus IV. The self-given name 'Epiphanes', meaning 'The Manifest One', or 'The Illustrious One', is a title (in this Hellenistic age) reserved for deity. The full title is '*Theos Epiphanes*', meaning 'God manifest'[1] – and shows the arrogance of this man who craved the adulation of his fellows. Heaven's name for this same man, given to Daniel, is arresting – he is called 'a vile person' (*AV*), 'a contemptible person' (*ASV*), or 'a despicable person' (*NET*). As his history is studied his immoral life, untrustworthy character, and implacable hatred of Israel testify to the truth of this descriptive God-given word. His contemporaries assessed him in less restrained language when, in absolute contempt, they changed 'Epiphanes' by one letter to make it 'Epimanes', which translates as 'madman'. It might well be asked why such prominence is given to this king, who displayed such impiety, idolatry and immorality, allied with military incompetence and political naivety, and who ruled for only twelve years (175–164 BC), in a relatively small nation that was no longer a world power. In historical records, he seldom receives more than a brief footnote, but here, in this prophetic book, his history takes fifteen verses. There must be a reason for such scriptural notice.

In prophetic Scripture it is recognised that heaven values things differently from earth. Nations and their leaders come into the prophetic picture, not because of their political prominence or military power, but as they relate to Israel, the key nation through which the purposes of God are worked out on earth. This can readily be observed in the empires seen in the image in Nebuchadnezzar's dream (2:31–35). The first empire is the Neo-

[1] Bruce, *Israel and the Nations*, p. 135.

Babylonian Empire but Nebuchadnezzar only appears on the page of Scripture when he attacks the nation of Israel and Jerusalem (2 Chron. 36:17–20). In the long history of the Medo-Persian Empire –the second world empire of the image – King Cyrus comes into Scripture when he captures Babylon, with its Jewish captives. The Greek Empire, founded by Alexander the Great, opens the long history of the Hellenistic age, attracting world attention, but the mention in Scripture of any one of the kings of this time is due to their relationship with Israel.

Daniel, in this year, 536 BC, is given forewarning concerning what lay ahead for his people. The early verses (vv. 2–20) have covered the years from the time of Daniel (536 BC) down to the death of Seleucus IV, in the year 175 BC. We read it now as history. More detail is given about the next king than any of his predecessors and the question has to be asked as to why such a relatively obscure king should hold such a place in Scripture. There are two reasons for the prominence given him:

(a) A Prophetic Warning

It has already been shown that this figure can be readily identified in history as Antiochus IV Epiphanes, of the Seleucid dynasty of Greece. For Daniel and his contemporaries he lies 350 years in the future. Daniel is given such a detailed coverage because believing souls would need the forewarning given here if their faith was to be preserved through the terrible days of turmoil that this king would bring to Israel before Messiah arrived. From our viewpoint it can be said that this prophecy was a major stimulant to faith, as Antiochus by his actions provoked the Maccabean revolt, with all the terror of those difficult years. We know that a faithful remnant of the nation came through those dark days and were awaiting the Messiah in the land when He arrived on earth the first time.

(b) A Prophetic Witness

The character and conduct of this Antiochus IV Epiphanes towards the nation of Israel was of such a nature that the Holy Spirit (2 Pet. 1:20–21) would use them as a portrayal of a future ruler to appear in the end-times who would be the cruellest of despots towards Israel. Thus rooted in history for us are lessons for the time of tribulation on earth; a time when hard-pressed saints will be awaiting the Messiah when He arrives on earth the second time.

So Antiochus IV Epiphanes of the Seleucid dynasty of Greece is given detailed coverage because in his cruel and ruthless treatment of the nation of Israel he becomes a picture of a far more ruthless man yet to come. From verse 5 this chapter is centred upon Antiochus IV Epiphanes. Concerning him Daniel is shown:

The Predecessors	vv. 5–20
The Portrait He Presents	vv. 21–35
The Person he Portrays	vv. 36–45

If the sixteen preceding verses (vv. 5–20) provide the background out of which King Antiochus emerges; these fifteen verses (vv. 21–35) describe him in character and conduct. The next ten verses (vv. 36–45) will lift the focus to the final man – a king who in character and conduct will be the actual person of whom Antiochus is but a portrait. Through this final man Satan will come closer to his aim – the wiping out of Israel – than he came when he used the Antiochus Epiphanes of history (Rev. 12:17). Antiochus was the man used by Satan to attempt to destroy Israel in light of the first coming of the Messiah; he portrays the man who will be used by the same power to attempt to destroy Israel in light of the second coming of the Messiah.

It will be readily recalled that an individual has already appeared in this prophecy, under the title of 'Little Horn'. This is a king, who arises in the latter days of the Medo-Persian Empire (8:9–14, 23–25), has certain characteristic features, set forth in that chapter. He is a king with: (a) considerable military power in certain areas; (b) a compelling religious purpose – the Hellenising of the empire; (c) and a corroding hatred of the faithful Jews in Israel because of their devotion to Jehovah. Notice his character, conquests, and career, but pay particular attention to the mention of: (a) a sacred place and its pollution (the sanctuary); (b) a special people and their persecution (the saints); and (c) a singular period, when his introduction of 'the transgression of desolation' (8:13) and 'the abomination that maketh desolate' (11:31) cause the interruption of the sacrificial system for a specified period.

When the above matters are considered fairly, only one conclusion is possible: these are two portraits of the same man – Antiochus IV Epiphanes, King of Syria. Both portraits show the same person emerging in the end-time. In chapter 8, stress falls upon his power and he is called 'the little horn'. In chapter 11, stress falls upon his personality and he is called the 'vile person'.

Verses 21–35 Antiochus IV Epiphanes (175–164 BC)

Verse 21 When Seleucus IV Philopator (187–175 BC) died suddenly and mysteriously in 175 BC, the expected and legitimate heir to the throne of Syria was his son Demetrius I Soter. He was a boy of eleven years of age at this time and a hostage held by Rome to ensure that his father observed the terms of the Treaty of Apamea (188 BC). This treaty had been agreed by his father, Antiochus III the Great, whose invading army on the Greek mainland had been routed by the victorious Roman legate, Lucius Cornelius Scipio (Scipio Asiaticus). In this treaty Antiochus III pledged never again to land forces in Europe or move an army westwards beyond the Taurus Mountains. Greece was now virtually a Roman colony. To ensure Syrian compliance, the Roman legate took as hostage to Rome his younger son – also called Antiochus. When Seleucus IV (older brother of Antiochus the captive in Rome) came to the Syrian throne, Rome demanded he accept the terms of this same treaty. To ensure his compliance, Rome replaced Antiochus (his younger brother) with his own son and heir, Demetrius, as hostage for his good behaviour. But Antiochus, the released hostage, did not return directly to Antioch, the Syrian capital, where his older brother reigned, but stopped in Athens, where his licentious behaviour and profligate ways would pass unremarked and where, incidentally, he made many friends. He remained there until his older brother died.

Scripture makes three statements with reference to this successor to Seleucus IV, which explain why he is called 'vile' (*AV*) or 'contemptible' (*RSV*) in Scripture:

(a) 'To whom they shall not give the honour of the kingdom'. It is made clear that this person is not the rightful heir to the throne. As explained, the rightful heir was Demetrius, his nephew, who was expected to become Demetrius I. Seleucus had another son, just weeks old, but this child was murdered, in Antioch, soon after his father's sudden death. Suspicion pointed plainly to the recently freed Antiochus through an agent in Syria, whose name history gives as Antigonis. This man was himself assassinated a short time afterwards. Antiochus, uncle to the rightful heir, Demetrius, had absolutely no claim to the throne of Syria. The statement goes further and shows that no party in the nation wanted him, neither did any group invite him to accept the crown – he seized it.

Furthermore, he accomplished this seizure of the throne not with an army behind him but by something far more subtle.

(b) 'But he shall come in peaceably', which is rendered 'but he shall come in time of security' (*RV*) or, perhaps a clearer translation, 'he shall come in without warning' (*RSV*). As pointed out earlier (see comments at v. 19), the man under suspicion for the sudden death of Seleucus IV was Heliodorus, his own prime minister, who, within hours of his death, had himself proclaimed king. This would have been impossible without the compliance of the courtiers around the throne; some historians would suggest that 'connivance' would be the more accurate word. Immediately, this claim of Heliodorus to the throne was disputed by Ptolemy VI Philometor, King of Egypt, who claimed the throne of Syria on the ground that he was a nephew of King Seleucus IV. Ptolemy VI had been a boy of six years when his father died, in 181 BC, and he became king under the regency of his mother – Cleopatra, who was the sister of the dead king (see v. 17 and comments *in loc.*). So war over the succession to the throne of Syria loomed large. However, Rome was watching the situation with eagle eye, and for the sake of the balance of power was prepared to back a third claimant to the Syrian throne. The third claimant was Antiochus the younger brother of Seleucus and uncle to the rightful heir – Demetrius. As already discussed, Antiochus, the released captive, had tarried by the fleshpots of Athens. When the news reached him of his brother's sudden death he set out *post haste* for the palace in Antioch, the Syrian capital. On his arrival he immediately had himself proclaimed king. This seems to have taken place so suddenly that Heliodorus and his co-conspirators were taken completely by surprise. They had thought themselves secure in their seizure of power but, without any preliminary warning, their new government is challenged – just as this prophecy foretold. Antiochus, as a royal hostage, had moved freely in Rome and was well known to many key figures, where his liberality, allied with his profligacy, had won him many powerful friends. Rome, with its policy of maintaining a balance of power between Syria and Egypt, was prepared to support his claim rather than see those two major powers united under one king. That union would have posed a challenge to the growing power of Rome. So it was apparent that Antiochus was doing this with the support of Rome.

(c) 'And obtain the kingdom by flatteries'. 'Flatteries' is literally 'slippery places'[2] (Ps. 35:6; Jer. 23:12), and here it means 'underhand plots, slippery actions, intrigues'. Little did the first group of conspirators, around Heliodorus, know that a more able plotter had already laid the ground-work for his claim to the throne. First in Rome, where during the hostage years he had made many powerful friends, and then he did the same in Athens, where he made his home after his release. He did the same in Pergamum, a prosperous and war-like city allied to Athens, which he took care to visit while living in Athens; King Eumenes and his brother Attalus were flattered that a Syrian prince would spend time in their small province. So Antiochus, backed by imperial Rome, intellectual Athens (an important Greek city-state), and a belligerent Pergamum, with a well-trained army, came in unexpectedly and seized the throne using flattery, bribery and intrigue. His supporters could supply both the military forces he needed to threaten opponents and the finance he required to bribe key people in Syria. Heliodorus and his fellow-conspirators were taken completely by surprise; he was arrested and put to death immediately, while his supporters simply disappear from the record. Nothing more is heard of them. Antiochus took the kingdom. The rightful heir was left in captivity in Rome. Rome was prepared to make a blatant concession to injustice, for the sake of her balance-of-power policy in relation to Syria and Egypt.

Antiochus became Antiochus IV. He consolidated his position by: (a) flattery of the King of Pergamum; (b) promises of clemency to suspected traitors – at home and abroad; (c) taxation reduced for Syrian nationals; (d) a promise to Rome to make up the arrears of tribute; (e) a further promise to Rome to continue the annual tribute if Rome granted him the same terms as his father had received under the Treaty of Apamea (188 BC); and (f) a most lavish donation to Rome conveyed by a Royal Ambassador from this new Syrian King. So, in keeping with Scripture, this usurper came in 'peaceably', but he certainly excelled in that which was to manifest itself as characteristic of his reign – 'flatteries'.

Verses 22–23 The following translation makes the meaning of the text very clear: 'Armies will be suddenly swept away in defeat before him' (*NET*). An interpretive paraphrase by Leon Wood supports this

[2] Wood, *A Commentary on Daniel*, p. 295.

translation: 'and before him shall invading armies be overwhelmed and broken'.[3] Quite correctly, both translations interpret the 'flood' (AV) as an invading army, in keeping with many scriptural references (Isa. 28:2; Jer. 46:8; 47:2; Dan. 9:26). Translated literally the text reads: 'arms of the overflow shall be overflowed', which points to the overthrow of an invading army. This describes exactly what happened in the following year, when King Ptolemy VI Philometor of Egypt, incensed at the usurpation of the Syrian throne by Antiochus IV, and stirred up by unwise counsellors who had replaced the wise Cleopatra as regents, launched a tremendous attack against Syria through the land of Israel. With the aid of his Grecian allies from Pergamum, led by King Eumenes and his brother Attalus, the Egyptians were routed at the Battle of Pelusium, in northern Egypt.[4] 'Swept away in defeat before him' is a dramatic description of the Syrian victory. King Ptolemy VII, a boy of only fifteen years, was taken prisoner and his army destroyed. Antiochus seized the boy-king as a hostage; he had plans for this Egyptian boy.

The next statement describes the defeat of one called 'the prince of the covenant'. The word 'prince' is defined as 'a captain, a person raised, eminent and conspicuous, one that goes before'.[5] Many expositors interpret the covenant as the holy covenant of God with Israel and thus identify 'the prince of the covenant' as the high priest in Jerusalem at this time. His name was Onias III and he had been a leader of the pro-Egypt party amongst the Jews in Jerusalem and had already had dealings with Ptolemy. Expositors who take this view suggest that Antiochus, when he passed through Israel on his return journey, dealt summarily with these rebels and replaced Onias III, the high priest of the Temple in Jerusalem and the leader in the theocracy, with his brother Jason. This suggestion has merit but there are two problems. The first problem concerns the date. The dismissal of Onias III and his subsequent murder by his brother is generally linked to a later expedition of Antiochus, in 171 BC, while this action must have taken place about 174 BC. However, a most respected commentator has suggested a correction to this date, to 174 BC, and this can be made to support this interpretation.[6] The second problem becomes serious when it is seen that there are

[3] Wood, *A Commentary on Daniel*, p. 295.
[4] Tatford, *Daniel and his Prophecy*, p. 193.
[5] *OTWS*, p. 327.
[6] Bruce, *Israel and the Nations*, pp. 137, 234.

no grounds contextually for equating the covenant here with the 'holy covenant' of the later verses (vv. 28–30). In these later verses the context and the use of the adjective 'holy' demand the 'covenant of the LORD' with Israel. It is much more satisfactory to allow the context in this passage to link the 'covenant' with the 'league' (v. 23) recently agreed. Taking this view, the 'prince' is Ptolemy VI Philometor of Egypt, who entered into the peace agreement with Antiochus IV. The wily Antiochus completely deceived his young relative with totally false assurances of his peaceful intentions. F.A. Tatford explains the situation clearly:

> Feigning friendship for Ptolemy, the Machiavellian Antiochus made a treaty with the youthful monarch. His deceitful character was at once manifested. Ignoring the terms of the treaty, but with profuse protestations of friendliness, Antiochus immediately began a scheme to overreach his royal ally. With a very small army, he proceeded up the Nile as far as Memphis and besieged it. Although his army was very small, it was sufficient to be the base of great military power. Scripture speaks 'for he shall come up and shall become strong with a small people'.[7]

This Scripture was fulfilled to the letter. Memphis was the old capital of Egypt and, using the deceit of the covenant promises, Antiochus seized its treasures and wealth. This foreshadows a covenant to be made in a day yet to come between the 'Coming Prince' and Israel (9:26–27). In this there is a picture of the darker figure whom Antiochus portrays.

'He shall work deceitfully' aptly describes the attitude and actions of Antiochus toward Egypt from the moment the treaty was signed. He was not content with a peace agreement with Ptolemy that allowed him to slip a small army into Egypt without opposition, saying it was to consolidate the young king on his throne. It is probable that he also promised that he would fulfil the dowry terms of Cleopatra by ceding, as his father had promised, the provinces Coele-Syria and Israel to Egypt. At first, in the general euphoria of the peace settlement, Antiochus won the interest and good will of the young king, Ptolemy. However, it can be shown that in 170 BC Antiochus reneged on this promise and, as will be noted shortly, he reinforced his garrisons in those lands as he went up to attack Egypt

[7] *OTWS*, p. 195.

(v. 25). From an insignificant beginning he had now become strong; with 'only a few people [the tiny kingdom of Syria] he will rise to power' (*NIV*). At this point Antiochus controlled the greater part of the united territories of the Seleucid and Ptolemaic kings. Rome could not allow this new threat on its eastern boundary to get any stronger. Steps would have to be taken to deal with Antiochus.

Verse 24 The unique strategies of this ruler are outlined in this prophetic verse. They may be noted thus:

(a) Peace. 'He shall enter peaceably'. A similar expression is used of his coming to the throne of Syria (v. 21; *cf.* also 8:25). As already shown with respect to Egypt, he preferred to offer friendship first, then betray or out-manoeuvre those he claimed as friends. With Antiochus a peace treaty was invariably false, setting out terms he never meant to fulfil, and promises he never meant to keep; it was simply a political tool to achieve his own ends. Professing undying friendship to his young nephew, he brought a small army into Egypt and, before Ptolemy was even aware of it, had captured town after town, until he had seized 'the fattest places of the province'. The most fertile and wealthiest parts of Egypt were plundered by Antiochus. Having won the Battle of Pelusium (v. 22), in northern Egypt, and subdued Galilee *en route*, he had the most fertile areas of the Egyptian Empire under his control. Antiochus had achieved by craft what none of his forerunners had been able to achieve by force. He had taken control of Egypt; its fertile lands were in his hands; its prestigious treasures were at his disposal.

(b) Policy. 'He shall scatter among them the prey'. Having the wealth of Egypt at his disposal, Antiochus could now do something else that was part of his character – buy friends, or, more accurately, bribe his foes. The 'them' is generally thought to be his cronies, as in the translation 'He will distribute plunder, loot and wealth among his followers' (*NIV*). But since this is what victors generally did, and his ancestors did too, this cannot be the meaning. The 'them' must be viewed as his enemies, or, at least, those who had held back from supporting him; he used the bounty arising from his stripping of the wealthy areas to bribe the poorer areas to yield to his control. The Maccabean record tells of this very policy in operation (1 Macc. 3:27–31).

(c) Power. 'He shall devise plans against strongholds' (*RSV*). As he moved through the conquered lands he took pains not to leave any fortified town in his rear. He was very careful of this, even in his own land, where he was well aware that a defensible strong point could soon become a centre of rebellion. Antiochus was outstandingly successful in this policy of control, and eventually he had only one stronghold to bring into subjection – the city of Alexandria. It was while seeking to conquer this city that he was brought to a stop. The last phrase of the verse sets a Divine limitation on his conquests – 'even for a time'. God was still in control. In terms of the politics of earth, two matters stayed his triumphal march. One was 'tidings out of the west'. The senate of Rome sent a direct order for him not to besiege Alexandria, and to leave Egypt. In such messages from Rome there was always the implied threat – 'or else' – the Roman legions stood menacingly in the background. Since his father, Antiochus the Great, had been so decisively defeated by a Roman army, under Scipio (Asiaticus), at Magnesia (189 BC), Antiochus had great respect for the power of the Roman legions. A second thing that stopped this man was that a false report of his death had spread through Judaea and caused jubilation there. Angered by this, Antiochus resolved to teach Jerusalem a lesson and publicised this intention as his reason for leaving Egypt.

Verses 25–26 History records at least five invasions of Egypt by Antiochus Epiphanes; this verse refers to the fourth one, dated in 171 BC. If this reading of the confused history of these years is correct then the king in Egypt is no longer Ptolemy VI Philometor, but his younger brother Ptolemy VIII Euergetes,[8] who was later given the nickname 'Physcon' because of his bloated appearance.[9] Since the defeat of Egyptian forces by Antiochus at Pelusium, in 170 BC, the younger brother of Ptolemy had staged a palace coup against Ptolemy VI and, with support of palace officials, claimed the throne of Egypt. Judging that the sudden withdrawal of Antiochus from before Alexandria indicated a weakness to be exploited, this usurper decided to try to turn this to his advantage. If he could quickly gather his forces and reclaim the rich areas that the Syrian king had seized in Egypt as well as Coele-Syria and Judaea, then his claim to the throne would be bolstered and his popularity with the people of Egypt greatly increased. These lands were part of his mother's dowry and, by this time, it was clear Antiochus had no

[8] Feinberg, *Daniel*, p. 167.

[9] Wood, *A Commentary on Daniel*, p. 298.

intention of handing them back to Egyptian control – in spite of the peace treaty and his protestations of good will. With rebellion against Antiochus in view, Ptolemy VII gathered an army.

When such news reached the Syrian capital, Antiochus was thoroughly aroused. The verb to 'stir up', in its root meaning, is to be awakened from sleep. The Syrian kingdom had dozed off to sleep after the previous successes against Egypt. Now comes this news and Antiochus stirs the nation to action. First, his 'power' – which term points to the military forces at his disposal; these were alerted to move quickly southward! Beyond that, he stirred up the 'courage' (AV), where the word should be translated 'heart'. Unlike in western thought, in eastern minds the heart is viewed as the organ of decision, in other words 'the will'. Antiochus, a skilled rhetorician, as shown in earlier debates, could, readily and easily, stir the war-like spirit of his nation to fever pitch. Playing on the twin themes of disloyalty to the throne and insult to the nation he would point to the Greek culture, in which they had all been reared, and warn that it was about to be swallowed up by the imposition of an Egyptian life-style. Whatever arguments he used, they were very successful, for he soon put in the field a 'great army' to launch a disciplinary attack against the king of the south, who, as shown above, was Ptolemy VII Physcon, the younger of the two sons of Cleopatra, and his own nephew.

The reaction was immediate: the army of Antiochus was described as 'great', but that of Ptolemy was greater still, as support gathered to his banner from out of the many subject peoples in the Syrian Empire. The prophetic Word describes what was to become history: 'with a very great and mighty army'. The summary words of Scripture describe the clash of arms in one graphic sentence: 'but he shall not stand'. What an epigraph for a devastated army! The 'he' is interpreted by history as the King of the South. Ptolemy VII suffered total defeat by Antiochus Epiphanes. The reason for this terrible defeat is given: 'for plots shall be devised against him' (RSV). Ptolemy did not lead a united nation; his recent usurpation of his brother had left him in the power of advisers not to be trusted, many of whom were engaged in various intrigues. The result was total disaster. The following translation is helpful: 'Even those who eat his rich food shall be his undoing; his army shall be swept away, and many shall fall down slain' (RSV). The rich food was the perk of counsellors (1:5, 8) who fed from the king's table; the deadly treachery arose in the innermost court circle. The king had around him few counsellors he could trust; even in his own family circle some remained faithful to his older brother and were prepared to betray him. The result for Ptolemy VII Physcon was an utter catastrophe – his great and mighty army was routed. It had seemed so impressive: 'shall overflow' pictures the army as a tide sweeping all before it, but the end is sudden – 'many shall fall down slain'. Many died on the battlefield and the young Ptolemy was taken captive.

Verse 27 There is apparently an interval for readjustment within Egypt to the imposition of Syrian rule and the re-emergence of Ptolemy VI (Philometor) as king under the dominion of Syria. The two kings who sit at the same table here are Antiochus Epiphanes and his young nephew Ptolemy VI (Philometor). They are both under pressure from different sources: Ptolemy is uncertain of the total allegiance of his court and government, given the attempt to replace him by his younger brother; Antiochus has to keep a wary eye on the reaction in Rome, where he knows his conquest of Egypt will be viewed with grave suspicion. So while each protagonist offers many a profession of family affection, this uncle and nephew have very different political agendas. Ptolemy VI needs his uncle's support to re-establish his control of Egypt after the recent coup by his younger brother. At the same time Antiochus knows that time is running out for Syria, as the patience of Rome is near breaking point. Rome has gone beyond encouraging the Greeks to stand against him and is contemplating action to stop the expansion of the Syrian Empire. Time, in a sense, is on Egypt's side. On the other hand Antiochus, while prepared to offer Ptolemy his support in regaining control in Egypt, cannot allow him to be strong enough to challenge his rule, or even strong enough to invite Rome to take a hand in this political game. So, with mischief in their hearts and lies on their lips, these two men eat at the same table. To the eastern mind, to indulge in deception while eating at the same table is absolutely despicable. The character of each of these men is revealed. Compromises were worked out. In the final outcome, Antiochus was left in control of Memphis, the old capital, so here Ptolemy VI renewed his kingship while allowing his rebellious younger brother (Ptolemy VIII) control of Alexandria, which had resisted all the efforts of Antiochus to capture it. Antiochus was satisfied at the 'great riches' he had acquired. This was the booty he had seized from a ravished land and it served, at least, as a salve for his wounded pride. The Maccabean chronicler writes: 'And they [the Syrian army] got possession of the strong cities in the land of Egypt; and he took the spoils of Egypt' (1 Macc. 1:19, *RV*). Two Scriptural comments are vital: (a) Heaven's comment on the past (the new treaty) is brief but conclusive: 'but it shall not prosper'. A divided Egypt was weak, and such a weakness Antiochus could not leave indefinitely – it would be exploited by Rome. The wealth acquired by Antiochus would soon be used up; the question then would arise as to the replenishment of his coffers; (b) Heaven's comment on the present is equally brief and conclusive: 'for yet the end shall be at the time appointed'. The obvious deduction from this statement is that the deceitful plots of these two men would not achieve the publicised goal – peace in the nation (Egypt) and peace between the nations (Egypt and Syria). That goal (true peace) would only come 'at the time appointed' – in God's time, under God's Man! Thus, prophetic anticipation is written into these statements that now are clearly history!

Verse 28 Returning to his capital city, Antioch, in Syria, his army laden with booty from Egypt, Antiochus had to pass through Judaea and Jerusalem. The year was 171 BC. Having aroused the ire of Antiochus on a previous occasion, when they had rejoiced at the rumour of his death, certain changes had taken place amongst the leaders in Judaea. The pious Onias III had been removed from office and replaced by his ungodly brother Jason, who had given Antiochus a huge bribe to agree to this replacement. Menelaus, another brother in the same priestly family, and a still more evil man, murdered Onias. This same Menelaus gave Antiochus a far larger bribe and was appointed high priest, replacing his brother Jason. To get the cash for his huge bribe Menelaus sold many of the gold and silver vessels of the Temple in Jerusalem. The link in this chain of depravity was a senior Syrian officer appointed by Antiochus. The result was that the Jews were in arms against Menelaus and the Syrian representative – who now called for the intervention of Antiochus as he passed through the land. This was perfectly acceptable to Antiochus, whose 'heart [was] against the holy covenant'. The prophets in Israel had made plain that the nation of Israel stood in a special relation to Jehovah – they were His holy people. God had given them a holy land, with its holy city; He had established there a holy sanctuary with a holy service and a holy priesthood. This whole concept was utterly alien to Antiochus

know that a Roman army, under the command of a Roman consul, Gaius Popillius Laenas, had just defeated Perseus, King of Macedon, in a battle on the west coast of Greece at Pydna, near Thessalonica (June 168 BC). More crucially, Antiochus did not know that as soon as the Egyptian ambassadors had reached Rome, the senate sent orders for their consul Laenas to take ship, with his victorious legions, to Alexandria, and give whatever aid Ptolemy required against the invasion of Antiochus. The fleet conveying the Roman army had, of course, come from the west, from Greece and past Cyprus, to land in Alexandria, as Scripture has said. The ships of 'Chittim' had arrived and Roman legions were already under arms and in camp just outside Alexandria.

When he reached Alexandria and no opposing army met his forces, Antiochus made camp and contacted the palace. It must have been an unbelievable blow to learn that Roman forces had arrived in Egypt. He thought of sending officers but finally decided to convey his greetings himself to the Roman Consul. F. A. Tatford gives a clear and graphic account of this momentous meeting between King Antiochus and the Roman consul:

> Antiochus heard that delegates from the senate had arrived at Alexandria and he went to salute them. At Elusia, four miles from Alexandria, Popillius Laenas met him and presented the decree of the senate that he and his army should forthwith evacuate Egypt and cease to interfere with his nephews. Antiochus replied that he would consult his friends, but the Roman instantly took his staff and drew a circle in the sand around the spot where Antiochus stood and haughtily declared that Antiochus should not step out of the circle before he had given his specific assurance to conform to the senate's decree. Mortified and humiliated, the thoroughly intimidated Syrian submitted and withdrew his forces from Egypt with no more ado and retired to his own country.[12]

Rome was moving rapidly to world domination – thus becoming the fourth world empire of the image of Nebuchadnezzar's dream (2:33). The iron fist of Rome stopped Antiochus Epiphanes in his purpose.

The humiliation for Antiochus was absolutely devastating. He had to retreat with as much dignity as he could muster, and lead his undefeated army back to Syria. He knew full well he dare not take

[12] Tatford, *Daniel and His Prophecy*, p. 197.

any other course. He could not risk war with Rome, for he knew his armies could not stand before its disciplined legions. He would readily recall the might of Carthage and its fall before the shattering power of the Roman legions. He would recall the fate of the man who had got so far as to besiege Rome itself – Hannibal. History carried too many warning notes where Rome was concerned. That he was 'grieved' (v. 30), as the verb translates into English, is very much an understatement. The word describes a defeated, disheartened, disappointed man retracing the route he had travelled with such anticipation some months before. But grief soon gave way to an incandescent rage as news began to reach him that those rebellious, intransigent Jews were giving his puppet ruler, Menelaus, fresh trouble in Jerusalem. The first verb 'return' in the verse refers to his leaving Egypt and heading homewards, on his usual route through Israel. With this news of trouble from his puppet regime in Jerusalem, Antiochus camped near the city, determined to deal with these troublemakers, who are identified as linked to the holy covenant (see comments on v. 28); in fact, the faithful in the nation of Israel, who would stand up for their God. The word 'indignation' means 'overflowing anger', or 'rage', that breaks in bitter animosity against the Jews who will not accept his Hellenising programme. The next phrase: 'so shall he do', a repeat of the phrase from verse 28, is given in the *RV* as '[he] shall do his pleasure'. Immediately he launches his forces to ravage Jerusalem. According to Josephus, forty thousand Jews were put to death and forty thousand led to captivity and slavery; the city was burned and Temple worshippers put to death. This second use of the verb 'return' points to his onward journey to Antioch, but not with the triumph and treasure as on the previous occasion, but humbled and humiliated before the power of Rome. But this time Antiochus is intent on leaving in Jerusalem only those who have forsaken the holy covenant. Thus he ensured that Menelaus, the leader of the Hellenising party in Jerusalem, was totally in control. This was the party whose members, having apostatised from true faith in Jehovah, wished to turn the whole land into a secular Greek state, in keeping with the ambition of Antiochus. This unholy alliance is seen in the statement '[shall] have intelligence with them that forsake the holy covenant'. Menelaus, the apostate high priest, and his party willingly cooperated with Antiochus in the total destruction of all that set Israel apart from the nations around. The Law of Moses was robbed of its authority, the rite of circumcision was denied to the males, and the Temple was openly defiled by the introduction of idols. Every distinctive mark of Judaism was to be erased. Those recalcitrant Jews who talked about holy Scriptures, a holy sanctuary, and holy saints, and rejected the Hellenisation programme, were to be put to death. The records of the Maccabean times remind us of the dreadful period faced by the nation of Israel in those troubled years. Part of that record can be studied in 1 and 2 Maccabees.

Verse 31 The consequence of the Antiochus assault and his support for the high priest, his appointee, the apostate Menelaus, is summarised: 'And arms shall stand on his part'. This, in its somewhat literal reading of the Hebrew, indicates that the agents of Menelaus, assured of the support of King Antiochus, took action to:

(a) 'Profane the sanctuary, even the fortress' (*RV*) – the added words 'even the fortress' indicate that Antiochus had already fortified part of the Temple. Having made it a fortress (1 Macc. 6:7) and no longer a sacred religious building, Antiochus, with the agreement of Menelaus, set about to reduce its standing still further in popular opinion, and, to the absolute horror of the faithful, had a pig slain on the brazen altar and its blood carried into the holy places and sprinkled there (2 Macc. 5:15–21). To every Jew who would be faithful to his God, the Temple was now a forbidden place.

(b) 'Shall take away the daily sacrifice'. While the reference is to the daily burnt offering, the action in defiling the sanctuary made impossible the continuation of any of the ceremonies associated with the whole ritual of the Jewish sacrificial system. According to Josephus, Antiochus had declared all Mosaic ceremonies illegal.[13] Special laws were directed against the rite of circumcision. Those who practised this were to be put to death immediately. The record of such deaths makes very sad reading (see 1 Macc. 1:60–61).

(c) 'And they shall place the abomination that maketh desolate'. Antiochus ruled that the Temple in Jerusalem should be consecrated to Zeus Olympus,[14] the supreme Greek god, who ruled from Mount Olympus. He ordered that an image of this god be placed on the brazen altar. Thus, the Hellenisation of Judaism could be judged complete – if it had not been for those religious fanatics who were prepared to lay down their lives for the Word of the Lord.

[13] Josephus, *Complete Works*, 429–430.

[14] The Roman name for this god was Jupiter.

Abomination and desolation have already been met in the third of Daniel's visions (9:27). In keeping with this historical situation, the word 'abomination' is used here, in chapter 11, in the singular number. 'Abomination' means 'a detestable thing' and is the word used by God for 'something or someone that makes a false claim'; a good word for a 'nothing', an 'idol'. But this idol brings something with it. The word 'desolation' is a participle that can be understood either passively – 'made desolate', or actively – 'making desolate'. Once Antiochus had set up the idol of Zeus Olympus on the brazen altar and brought the suspension of the daily sacrifice, he issued a second order that idol altars were to be built in every city of Judah (1 Macc. 1:45–54). He went even further than this and associated himself with that worship; in this indirect way claiming deity. From the context here, the participle should be understood in the active voice, as carrying desolation before it. And the singular 'abomination' instead of the plural used in 9:27 indicates that but one nation is in view in this passage. That nation is of course Israel, under the iron rule of Antiochus Epiphanes.

Note on Verse 31

It is worth noting, for future reference, that the mention of the 'abomination of desolation' in this passage has already been fulfilled and passed into history with Antiochus Epiphanes. Therefore, when the Lord spoke of 'the abomination of desolation' as yet to come in His day (Matt. 24:15), the reference cannot be to this passage but to the later reference in this book (12:11).

Verses 32–35 The Final Issue

Verse 32 The actions of Antiochus in 167 BC caused bitter division in Israel. The defilement of the sanctuary, the stopping of the sacrifices, the encouragement to disobey Scripture (10:21), and the challenge of the idol, was a deliberate programme intended to destroy Judaism and leave the way open for complete Hellenisation of Israel. The actions of Antiochus are described by the verb 'corrupt', or 'pervert' (*RV*), and Wilson[15] explains: 'to pervert it to the purposes of craft and deceit; moral corruption implies the loss of integrity and virtue'. Judaism was to be stripped of all that gave it spiritual power and moral integrity, as well as removing from the nation all the distinctive marks that set it apart from other nations.

[15] *OTWS*, p. 97.

Israel would lose the authority of Scripture, the attraction of the sanctuary, and the availability of the sacrifice, and with the loss of these things they could not be a witness for, and would soon lose the hope of, a coming Messiah.

The programme of Antiochus brought clearly to light the two parties in Israel. The first party is described by the plural participle 'such as do wickedly against the covenant'. This party has come to the fore already and been described as 'them that forsake the holy covenant' (v. 30); forsaking the covenant was but the first step; now they are acting wickedly against it. These were the many in Israel who at this time followed the puppet high priest Menelaus in his subservience to Antiochus and colluded with: (a) disobedience to Scripture, in accepting the new laws of Antiochus; (b) defilement of the sanctuary by the blood of unclean animals; and (c) deification of Antiochus, with the introduction of the idol. Antiochus, of course, bought the subservience of this party by 'flatteries'. This is the same word used in verse 21 to describe the methods he used to get the throne – sweet talk and lavish bribes. In the same way at this point, he used personal flattery, public promotion to high office, and promises of wealth to those who, having abandoned the covenant already, would give their full support to his Hellenisation programme. Sadly, many in Israel accepted these blandishments. The issues were made plain when Antiochus issued his infamous decree (167 BC) commanding all the peoples in his empire to conform to the religion of their sovereign, on pain of death.[16] This was easy for all others (who simply had to add another idol to their pantheon) except for the faithful in Israel, who believed in the sole God of Creation, revealed in their Scriptures.

On the other hand, there were many in Israel who, despite all the blandishments of the tempter to choose an easy path, remained faithful to Jehovah and refused to bow before the demands of Antiochus and his puppet regime in Jerusalem. Described in the participle 'the people that do know their God', these faithful ones were prepared to stand apart from their present leaders and become objects of hatred and scorn and to die rather than betray the God they had come to know. It is said of these faithful ones that they 'shall be strong, and do exploits'. Their spiritual strength being drawn, as it must ever be for spiritual men and women, from obedience to the Word of God, these faithful saints refused to

[16] *UBD*, p. 675.

defile themselves by eating unclean meat, by entering the defiled sanctuary, or by denying their sons the rite of circumcision. They chose rather to die, and many did. The Maccabean chronicler speaks: 'And many in Israel were fully resolved and confirmed in themselves not to eat unclean things. And they chose rather to die, that they might not be defiled with meats, and that they might not profane the holy covenant' (1 Macc. 1:62–63, *RV*). Others who did not die immediately 'did exploits' – a verb that covers many remarkable happenings in the life of many saints at this time. At this point comes in the stirring story of the Maccabean uprising, recorded as commencing in the time of Antiochus, in 167 BC, when he issued the decree mentioned above.

The historical records in the First and Second Book of the Maccabees, in the Apocrypha, do not carry the stamp of inspiration, and therefore are not authoritative for doctrinal or moral issues, but they are valuable, eye-opening, and heart-stirring accounts of what the faithful ones suffered under the rule of Antiochus Epiphanes.[17] The Maccabean rebellion led eventually, after the death of Antiochus, to the intervention of, and the confrontation with, the fourth empire in the image of Nebuchadnezzar's dream. It is at this point that the Roman Empire (the metal iron in the image) comes into prophetic Scripture.

Verse 33 The faithful in Israel, described as 'the people that do know their God', are given a further identification as 'they that understand among the people' (Hebrew '*maschilim*'). The participle could be translated as 'teachers', in light of the verb to follow. Those who stood apart from the 'state religion' imposed by Antiochus were anxious to instruct others and maintain a faithful testimony in obedience to the Word of God in a hostile environment. It is at this time that Mattathias Maccabeus comes to the fore, a man already advanced in years, a father of five sons, and a priest. A priest of the house of Aaron, he belonged to the course of Jehoiarib, the first of the twenty-four courses established in the time of Solomon (1 Chron. 24:7). Now retired, Mattathias lived quietly with his family at Modin, a little town near Jerusalem. In the presence of the Syrian ambassador, he was called to sacrifice on a heathen altar but refused. A priest from the Temple coming forward to offer in his place, Mattathias, in zealous defence of the honour of Jehovah,

[17] See Appendix 6, A Short History of the Maccabees.

killed him on the spot, overthrew the pagan altar, summoned all the faithful to follow him, and fled with his five sons into the wilderness. Many in Israel, from all parts of the land, rejoiced at his defiance of paganism and joined him in the desert, so that the rebellion swept through the province. However, the cost was very high. Daniel is warned of this when he is told that many 'shall fall' – where 'fall' must be taken, in light of the following statements, to mean dying for their faith.

Faithful souls died: (a) 'by the sword'. This expression could mean either by judicial execution, through the legal process, or simply summary execution on the spot. Those who joined the rebels in the early stages were those with unshakeable convictions about obedience to the Word of God. This can be seen in their refusal even to defend themselves or their families on the Sabbath day. The Books of the Maccabees bear witness to this and tell how, when the security forces of Antiochus realised that the Jews would not fight on the Sabbath day, made sure they attacked the hideouts of the Maccabees on a Sabbath, knowing there would be little resistance (1 Macc. 2:31–38); (b) 'by flame' – the same records show that many of the faithful in these times were burnt at the stake or roasted before a fire to extract information (2 Macc. 7:1–23); (c) 'by captivity' – other records show men and women imprisoned for their faith for long periods; (d) 'by spoil', which suggests that many were sold into slavery as mere chattels. The time span of 'days' ('many' is in italics) seems to make the period short but when it came and faithful men and women endured pain day after day, it seemed a very long time. From a cold-blooded onlooker's viewpoint the relatively short period covered just over three years, from 167–164 BC. Limited help could be had from the shelter, support, and supplies available from sympathisers when not directly under the eye of the security forces (1 Macc. 2:44) – a very similar situation to that in the Tribulation period, when there will be those who will provide help for persecuted believers (Matt. 25:37–40). But even this limited support is qualified by the necessity to be wary of the insincere or time-servers. Some of these individuals will use 'flatteries' – the same word used earlier in the chapter (vv. 21, 32) of Antiochus himself, and now of his followers. It would suggest that some would 'cleave', or 'adhere', to the Maccabees, using bribery and intrigue, either to escape the reprisals the Maccabees meted out to those they called 'compromisers', or to find out the identity and location of the Maccabees; knowledge they could use to betray friends and buy their own security. It is clear that, as the protest movement grew within the nation, there was attached a certain pride in letting the neighbours know you belonged to this honoured band. Strange as it may appear, it was a useful thing to have that honour amongst the people. At times, it was almost a popular thing to belong to the Maccabees. Some would even use intrigue to join it and then, when under pressure, use this knowledge to buy their safety by betraying former friends (2 Macc. 7:21).

It is clear that this section of the chapter is describing the same person called the Little Horn in chapter 8:9–14. It is also focusing on the same period, when Antiochus invades the land of Israel. However, the main focus in chapter 8 is the place: the sanctuary, and the period of its defilement. In this chapter the main focus is the people: the saints, and the period of their distress. Thus it is to be noted that the period of the defilement of the sanctuary began with the accession of Antiochus (175 BC) and the first appearance of the Hellenising party amongst the priests in the Temple in Jerusalem (see Excursus at the end of chapter 8), while the most intense period of distress of the faithful stemmed from the issue of the uncompromising edict of Antiochus for the Hellenisation of the empire (167 BC). Thus this second period is much shorter than the first. The defilement of the sanctuary ends with the historical cleansing and rededication after the Maccabean rebellion (164 BC), so the way is cleared for the first coming of the Messiah. It would be quite correct to say that the Maccabean testimony opened the way for a people to be ready for the first coming of the Messiah, and there were those faithful in Israel who did respond to the preaching of John the Baptist and were awaiting the Messiah. However, it is more in keeping with the contextual statements concerning the 'time of the end' and the 'time appointed' to see the closing verse of this passage (v. 35) as looking on to the end of the Tribulation and the second coming of the Messiah.

Amongst the testimony bearers down the ages listed in Hebrews 11:1–40 there is a group of unnamed individuals, placed after the prophets (vv. 33–40), who can readily be shown to have borne testimony in the period from the captivity of Israel in Babylon unto the coming of the Messiah. Certain experiences of saints recall Babylon, as in the statements: 'stopped the mouths of lions' – and chapter 6 of this book is recalled; 'quenched the violence of fire' – and chapter 3 comes to mind; 'escaped the edge of the sword' – and chapter 2 is revisited, when four young believers await the death penalty. The scriptural statements that follow offer an interesting and rewarding exercise to trace, both in Scripture and historical records, examples of such triumphs of faith. There is no question that in the time of the Maccabees there were many who suffered severely yet kept the flag of testimony high before the world. The parenthetic statement in the Hebrew list is certainly true of the Maccabean heroes – 'of whom the world was not worthy' (Heb. 11:38).

These terrible days had an unexpected result, in that, while many suffered and died for the testimony, those who came through the tears and the trials had a firmer faith and a sharper focus in their testimony. God permitted this dark day to try His own people. The word 'try' means generally 'to refine' and is a word used in metallurgy to describe the smelting process to obtain pure metal from an ore. This process is used for the noble metals gold and silver, to remove the dross (Mal. 3:2–3). Thus God allows the fires of persecution to bring out the true believers amongst His people. 'To purge' means to separate the pure from the impure. It repeats the thought in the word 'try' but this time water is the agent, not fire, but the result is similar – whatever is left is 'pure'. 'Tried' – it has come through the fire and impurities are gone; 'purged', or 'made white' – it has passed through the waters and the defilement is gone. In this context the words 'white' and 'pure' are almost synonymous. As a result, coming through this testing time will be those who know their God (v. 32) and who understand His Word (v. 33) and are now ready to welcome the Messiah.

This truth, applicable to the Lord's first coming to earth, will be equally applicable to His second coming to earth. The Tribulation, in days yet future, will be allowed 'to try them that dwell upon the earth' (Rev. 3:10). The Maccabean persecution was but a foreshadowing of this troubled time to come, under the despotic rule of a man of whom Antiochus Epiphanes was but a portrait. An important lesson for believers in any age is inherent in these times of trouble: God permits the testing of His people for a purpose, but He always limits the period of the testing. Thus any time of tribulation has a Divine purpose and a strictly limited span.

The phrase 'time appointed' is used earlier in the book (8:19) and now three times in this chapter (vv. 27, 29, and 35). Wilson points out that the word 'appointed' used on these four occasions is distinct from the word 'appointed' used elsewhere in the book of

Daniel (1:5, 10; 5:21; 10:1).[18] The normal meaning of the word used here is 'to appoint a time' – in a forensic sense. Wilson uses the word 'forensic' in its strict sense, meaning as 'sanctioned by law', pointing to an order in a law court when the judge appoints a set time for the court to reassemble. So 'the time of the end', when the final decisions will be given, is already 'appointed' by God. The happenings detailed so far in this chapter anticipate a reality that will close at the time already set by God, when all the actors in the end-time drama come together for the final session of the court and to hear the verdict. This understanding is vital, as it is recognised that the time break between history and prophecy comes at this point in the chapter. After such a clear statement with respect to the 'time appointed', it is difficult to believe that some expositors see no time gap and continue to try to find in the following verses (vv. 36–45) further reference to Antiochus Epiphanes. The most exacting historical scrutiny of the remaining years of the life of this Seleucid king fails to unearth any correspondence whatever, never mind correspondence on such an exact pattern as that which has already been found in this Section 2 (vv. 21–35). In fact, some expositors have found in these first thirty-five verses of the chapter 135 prophetic statements all now fulfilled.[19] Surely this forms an impressive backdrop to the prophetic statements not yet fulfilled. Is it not also an absolute guarantee that just as the prophetic Word has been fulfilled literally in the past, so the remainder will, just as literally, be fulfilled in the future?

It has been pointed out on different occasions in the study that this is one of the passages used by liberal-minded critics to insist that the book of Daniel must have been written after the events, by a pseudo-Daniel in the second century BC. This conclusion is the result of disbelief that the God Who knows the future can reveal the future. Further, it denies the reality that the prophetic statements coming from God by His chosen servant Daniel were absolutely trustworthy. This has been shown, without the slightest doubt, in the first thirty-five verses of this chapter, where prophecy has already become history and we can read it. It will be seen in a future day, when what we see now as prophecy will again be read as history. The testimony of believers will be that the God of Daniel is absolutely dependable and worthy of the confidence of believers in every age.

[18] *OTWS*, p. 18.

[19] Walvoord, *Daniel the Key to Prophetic Revelation*, p. 269.

v. 40	**Period**	Almost mid-point of the Tribulation – Northern Invasion	
vv. 41–43	The Northern Invader		Victorious
vv. 44–45	The Northern Invader		Vanquished

CHAPTER 12:1-4

v. 1 (a)	Midpoint of the Tribulation (*cf.* 2Thess. 2:3–4)
v. 1 (b)	The Great Tribulation – the Time of Jacob's Trouble (*cf.* Mt. 24: 21; Rev. 7, 14)
v. 2	The Resurrection of OT saints and Martyrs of the Tribulation (*cf.* Rev.11:18)
v. 3	The Entry to the Kingdom
v. 4	Instruction to Daniel

It might very reasonably be asked if the history of Antiochus Epiphanes up to his death in 164 BC is not continued in these verses. The historical records come to our assistance at this point and make it abundantly clear that this is not so. Having introduced the 'abomination that maketh desolate' in Jerusalem (v. 31), his history, as far as this record is concerned, is closed. The verses that follow (vv. 32–35) tell of the response in Israel to his programme of Hellenisation, which led directly to the Maccabean rebellion. It might have been expected that the story would include his death, and, indeed, some liberal commentators would try to read it into this passage. While there is a 'coming to his end' of a king in the passage (v. 45), it is certainly not the death of Antiochus as history records it. Antiochus returned to Antioch, his capital city, in Syria in 167 BC, where he resumed his life of luxury and licentious depravity, until this was ingloriously cut short in 164 BC. Because of his lifestyle he was always short of money, and it appears he was killed while attempting to rob a temple in Media. Even those liberal commentators who want to interpret this passage as a depiction of Antiochus have to admit there is not the same accuracy here as in the statements of the previous section (vv. 21–35). James A. Montgomery, a leading liberal commentator, agrees that to see the death of Antiochus in this section needs a very liberal interpretation of Scripture.[1]

Most conservative expositors are agreed that a very clear break occurs in the prophecy at this point and that the ten verses that

[1] James A. Montgomery, *The International Critical Commentary, Daniel*, p. 465.

close the chapter focus on a personality who appears in the 'time of the end', of whom Antiochus IV Epiphanes is only a portrait. His prominence in biblical prophecy is due to the fact that his character and conduct show features that are used to warn the wise of earth (12:3) of an infinitely more sinister personality who will appear at 'the time of the end' (11:35).

To read on at this point as if there was no time break is impossible to any reader sensitive to prophetic nuances. To miss the hints of a changed time scene in verse 35 might suggest that some preconceptions have engendered some degree of spiritual myopia. The very tenor of this passage is different from what has gone before. The king is not identified in the text as either the King of the North or the King of the South. Since both these kings attack him (v. 40) he must be distinct from both. Questions must be asked, but it is essential that they are answered from Scripture. The weighty contextual evidence, the main points of which are considered below, will be seen not only to allow a time break, but, when all the evidence is weighed, demand it. The secret of this section lies in the identification of the sovereign introduced at this point.

The time period is already fixed by the two expressions in verse 35. These are:

(a) 'The time of the end'. The expression of verse 35, repeated in verse 40, is a term that on each occasion of use in the last half of this book (8:17; 11:35, 40; 12:4) points to the immediate period preceding the coming of the Son of Man to earth to establish the Kingdom. It has already been made clear that this period begins with the signing of the covenant in Israel, at the beginning of Daniel's seventieth week, seven years before the coming of the Son of Man.

(b) 'For a time appointed'. The other time breaks, in the earlier verses of this chapter, are relatively short, as already noted.[2] However, this time break has extended from Antiochus Epiphanes right down to the present time. Even at this point, this age of grace and gospel preaching still awaits closure by the Rapture of the Church. With the Church removed from earth the next time mark is the confirmation of the covenant, which begins the seventieth week of Daniel and the seven-year Tribulation. In previous discussion it has been shown that this expression, on each of the four occasions of its use in the last half of the book (8:19; 11:27, 29, 35,

[2] The short time breaks in the chapter are: (a) between v.2 and v.3 there are 135 years (465–336 BC), (b) between v.4 and v.5 there are 12 years (323–312 BC).

see comments *in loc.*), points to the appointed time for the coming of the Son of Man. This is, of course, the climax of the 'times of the Gentiles', when the final Gentile kingdom will be shattered by the 'stone' (2:45). The stone destroys the whole image, beginning with 'the feet' (2:34–35), and then fills the whole earth. This is the scriptural imagery for the coming of the Son of Man and the establishment of His Kingdom. God has fixed that very date – the ultimate goal of OT prophecy. Our study thus far points to the period in view as being the seven-year period of Daniel's seventieth week. However, to fix the time period exactly, there must be a closer look at what the passage presents.

The invasion of Israel described in this section takes place when the nation of Israel are already enjoying the false peace (the beginning of the Tribulation) that their leader, the self-willed king here mentioned, has led them into, through his confidence in the ability of the western prince to defend Israel. But the information given concerning the invader fixes the time even more exactly. The destruction of the invader is given to Daniel in terrifyingly simple language: 'yet he shall come to his end, and none shall help him' (v. 45). Omitting the (uninspired) chapter division, the very next verse reads: 'And at that time shall Michael stand up' (12:1). This action by the archangel indicates the mid-point of the week (Rev. 12:7–9), when he moves to the defence of Israel, the nation for which he bears special responsibility. The reason for identifying the mid-point lies in the next statement, when Daniel is told, 'and there shall be a time of trouble, such as never was since there was a nation'. This is the commencement of the last three-and-a-half-year period of the Tribulation – called the Great Tribulation.

For further confirmatory scriptural support see Note A at the close of this chapter.

As to location, it has been noted throughout this study that the interest of heaven is centred on the people of Israel and the land that God gave them. It has been recognised that the King of the North (Syria) and the King of the South (Egypt) are so identified because of their geographic relation to Israel. Thus, when we are told concerning this end-time king that 'at the time of the end shall the king of the south push at him: and the king of the north shall come against him like a whirlwind', it is perfectly logical, as well as scriptural, to see this king as king in Israel – the land lying between two bitter political enemies. This has been true in the past, as has been shown from the study of the previous verses (vv. 2–35), which have already become history. So the context points to Jerusalem as the place where this king reigns when Israel is invaded.

As already observed, some liberal commentators argue that there is no break in this passage and the story of Antiochus Epiphanes continues. This has been shown on historical grounds to be completely invalid. The context too, as shown above, demands a different time period from the second century BC. The person introduced at this point is designated 'the king', and attention must be called to the presence of the definite article. Antiochus is never spoken of like this. From Seleucus, the first king identified, as 'King of the North', each king in the Seleucid dynasty bears this title and Antiochus, by right of succession, would bear it too. However, it is to be noted that the only time he is given the title 'king' in Scripture is to distinguish him from the King of the South (v. 27).

The definite article marks this king as different from all the kings introduced in the earlier verses. This distinction is confirmed by the simple fact that both the King of the North and the King of the South attack this man (v. 40), so identification with either is ruled out. This is incidental contextual justification for seeing a break in the chapter at this point. This is a different person from any who have appeared in this vision before him. Yet the problem is that the presence of the article suggests that this king has appeared in the record previously.

Since the period under consideration is the seven-year Tribulation this must be the king pictured in Antiochus. In chapter 8 the one in the lineage of the Little Horn reflecting Antiochus is called the King of Fierce Countenance (8:23). In this passage the king patterned on Antiochus is described by the phrase 'the king shall do according to his [own] will'; he may for convenience be spoken of as the 'Wilful King'.

Contextual studies in the two chapters show that each of these kings, reflecting the pattern of Antiochus IV Epiphanes seem to be ruling from the same place – Jerusalem – and in the same period of time – the Tribulation. The logical conclusion seems inevitable – it is the same person observed from two different aspects. In chapter 8 where he is spoken of as the 'King of Fierce Countenance', the emphasis falls on actions against the nation of Israel – he is the puppet of Satan, the destroyer of Israel. In contrast Christ is the deliverer of that same nation (Rom. 11:26). In this chapter where he is called the 'Wilful King' the emphasis falls on his relationship to God. Again the contrast with Christ is clear. In Gethsemane on the way to Calvary Christ bowed before His God and said 'not what I will, but what Thou wilt' (Mk. 14:36).

This Scripture shows plainly that at the midpoint of the Tribulation period a leader will have already emerged in Israel who will claim the rights of royalty – in other words, he sees himself as a king, entitled to the loyalty and fidelity of the people of Israel. The Lord Jesus Christ spoke solemnly to the nation of Israel in His day in memorable words: 'I am come in My Father's name, and ye receive Me not: if another shall come in his own name, him ye will receive' (Jn 5:43). The false claimant to the throne of Israel has now arrived and been received. Other Scriptures deal with the same time and place and person. The following summary is helpful:

Identification of the End-Time Ruler in Israel

(1)	The King of Fierce Countenance (His personal background)	8:23:25
(2)	The leader of the Many (His democratic claim)	9:27
(3)	The Wilful King (His religious aspiration)	11:36

For the NT identification see Chapter Note B at the end of this chapter.

Verses 36–45 The Revelation of Satanic Power

This short section of ten verses reveals, as perhaps no other passage of Scripture does, both the power and the perfidy of one who is not even named in this book – Satan. Through Daniel God has allowed us to see the way in which this murderer would treat the people of God if allowed by God to do so. We have just studied the fiery furnace (chapter 3) and the lion's den (chapter 6). Also made absolutely clear is the utter indifference shown by Satan and his powers even to those who are his agents – we remember what was designed for all the wise men of Babylon (2:12–13) and what happened to the guards used by Nebuchadnezzar to throw the Hebrew youths into the furnace (3:22). We also recall what befell the satraps who, as the agents of Satan, accused Daniel (6:24). We learn from these records the utter indifference of Satan and his cohorts to the fate of those who follow him. In this very vision (10:20–21) we are allowed a glimpse behind the scenes and behind the earthly monarchs to see how Satan, through his angelic agents, seeks to control nations and men. In these verses is set before us an unparalleled example of Satan the deceiver working with Satan the destroyer to the utter ruin of all. Not only are those who oppose him destroyed, as far as he can go, but it is not always recognized that those who follow him are led to utter ruin. This record shows what those who follow him may expect. Yet in the midst of the whole dark picture, in the darkest days of the Tribulation, God preserves His people.

There are two sections in the passage:

vv. 36–39	Satan revealed as the Deceiver
	His Puppet Ruler of Israel – Antichrist
vv. 40–45	Satan revealed as the Destroyer
	His Political Rule of the Nations

Verses 36–39 His Actions and his Character

Verse 36 It is very clear that a very major end-time personality is on the scene now and in power in Jerusalem. Arrogance and pride unite in a self-confidence that goes far beyond the egotism of Antiochus Epiphanes. The very first comment defines both his character and his conduct – 'shall do according to his will'. As he comes to power one thing alone counts: what he wants – his will has to be done. Christ, the pattern for all believers, spoke to His Father in Gethsemane acknowledging the rule of His life – 'not what I will, but what Thou wilt' (Mk 14:36). This man stands in absolute contrast. Pride leads to presumption and his second character trait comes into the picture – 'and he shall exalt himself'. Presumption leads to profanity and the third character trait comes to light – this man will 'magnify himself above every god (*El*)'. He is not going to allow any god to dictate his path, direct his life or demand his worship. This goes beyond even Antiochus who, while he demanded worship as a god, was quite willing to worship the gods of Greece and demand that the Jews do likewise. He placed the idol representing Jupiter Olympus on the altar of burnt offering in the Temple in Jerusalem. In contrast, this man will not allow any of the old gods to claim his allegiance. Strange it is to record that this self-proclaimed atheist will bow before another man on earth, and give to him that which should be given to God alone.

In his self-indulgent, self-exalting, arrogant pride he is quick to speak 'marvellous things', or 'unheard-of things' (*NIV*); an expression which suggests that this man has a unique form of derision and blasphemy, peculiar to himself. He blasphemes against the 'God of gods' – this is the God of Daniel, the true God.

Arrogant pride and atheistic presumption hardly seem the basis of prosperity, but God allows him to prosper for a time. Popularity, possessions, and power reward this man, until he appears unassailable and unconquerable. But it is just for a time; God has already marked out his boundaries in the phrase 'till the indignation be accomplished'. The word 'indignation' has been met previously (8:19) and shown, in the context, to point to the end-time outpouring of the wrath of God upon sinful men in the seven-year Tribulation period – the seventieth week of Daniel's third vision (9:24–27). Until that period is accomplished God allows this evil man to prosper; the will of a man is executed in Israel. But the period is limited; God has allowed the display of what man can do, but God has the final word: 'for that that is determined shall be done'. From this point, the timetable is already set and God, through Daniel, has made it known. A sovereign God will bring the Son of Man (7:13–14) to receive the Kingdom on schedule.

Verse 37 The pride and arrogance of this man know no bounds; unnatural and unrestrained, he defies all the normal aspirations and limitations of mankind. Three matters are highlighted that set this man apart from others:

(a) 'Neither shall he regard the God of his fathers'. He will give no respect to what has come down to him through his ancestry. Commentators worthy of the highest respect[3] point out that here the word used for 'God' is 'Elohim' and not 'Jehovah'. This means that, in their judgement, the phrase would be translated more accurately as in the *NIV*: 'the gods of his fathers'. In the judgement of such commentators, this man is not necessarily a Jew, but could be a Gentile, even a Greek national (based on 8:23). These commentators also point out, quite rightly, that the usual expression to describe the God of Israel is 'LORD God (*Jehovah Elohim*) of your fathers'. Used first in Exodus (Exod. 3:15–16), it is repeated more than thirty times in the OT books. However, while taking these arguments into account, the fact that Daniel himself uses this title in thanksgiving before his God (2:23) should carry a lot of weight – especially when it is realised that the nation is out of fellowship with its covenant LORD (Jehovah) at this time. Accepting these latter arguments and agreeing that the title refers to the God of Israel, means that this man is an apostate Jew, who has

[3] Wood, *A Commentary on Daniel*, p. 306: Walvoord, *Daniel*, p. 272.

deliberately rejected the God of Abraham, Isaac and Jacob. He may well have Greek citizenship (taking 8:23 into account), but assuredly a Jew by birth, and – brought up in the land of Israel – a Jew nationally, yet denying the God of his fathers, he looks very like one to whom reference has already been made, of whom the Lord spoke as quoted above: 'I am come in My Father's name, and ye receive Me not: if another shall come in his own name, him ye will receive'. An apostate Jew in the land of Israel, disdaining and defying the God of his fathers, he claims the authority of a king.

(b) 'Nor the desire of women'. He will give no respect to 'the desire of women'. This phrase has had a wide variety of interpretations. Some commentators think it marks him as a homosexual, disdaining the normal male desire for a woman. Others think he disowns the pagan worship of female deities, such as the Greek Artemis or the Babylonian Astarte. However, in the context of the interpretation of the previous verse, the simplest explanation is to see it as the natural desire of a Jewish mother to become the mother of the Messiah, promised as the seed of the woman (Gen. 3:15). The same Hebrew grammatical construct is seen in the ministry of Haggai: 'I will shake all nations, and the desire of all nations shall come' (Hag. 2:7), where the phrase must be objective. So Haggai must be read as 'the desired of nations'; in the same construct this passage should be read as 'the desired of women'. Both statements must point to the Messiah. This king disdains the God of his fathers and despises the desire of any mother in Israel. The past of his people he rejects, and the prospect of his people he refuses. In fact, none of these religious notions has any appeal whatever for this totally materialistic ruler. His religious outlook is very simply defined: he does not regard any god. None of the idols of the past can claim worship from this man – all these religious ideas are anathema to this rationalistic ruler. He worships himself; he regards himself alone as worthy of acknowledgement as a deity. While Antiochus did show this inclination to demand worship, even he did not go so far as this man. He is prepared to 'magnify himself above all'; he wants the whole nation of Israel to bow before his claims; he expects to be viewed through the magnifying glass of his own self-importance.

Verse 38(a) This atheistic king will revere a deity called 'the god of forces'. Another translation makes this transfer of worship obvious: 'But in his place shall he honour the god of fortresses' (*RV*). The word for God is '*Eloah*', which presents God as the 'one supreme object of worship, the adorable One' (*TN*). Instead of his heart being filled with the true God, alone worthy of adoration, this man has his heart taken up with one called 'the god of fortresses'. It is tempting to see in the word 'fortress', already used four times in this chapter (vv. 7, 10, 19, 31), a reflection of the military forces he commands, which make him simply a worshipper of military might. The difficulty with this interpretation is that this makes him very little different from others who have gone before – many before him had placed their confidence in military might and huge armies. The next statement rules this out completely – 'a god whom his fathers knew not shall he honour'. There is only one possible alternative view. This is to see this king in Jerusalem accepting as his god a man claiming Deity! A man who can guarantee his safety! To him this man offers the security and the sense of safety as of a fortress. This man had appeared only recently on the world scene, yet his promotion has been unbelievably fast. A financial wizard, he had come to world notice when he solved the world's financial problems; then his political skills have brought a ten-power confederation under his control. Without doubt he is now the most powerful man on earth. With an empire behind him greater than Rome ever had, and wielding a power greater than any Caesar, he had western roots and, unlike Titus, had not come to destroy Jerusalem but to offer his protection. He has been identified already in this prophecy as 'the prince that shall come' (9:26). But he already had an earlier title that stressed another side of his character. His two titles may be compared:

1. The Little Horn (7:8) – arising from, and then controller of, a ten-power empire (Political and Military identification).

2. The Coming Prince (9:26) – a Gentile leader of world empire status (National and Personal identification).

For further identification see Chapter Note B at the end of this chapter.

Verse 38(b) The honour paid to pagan idols was measured in costly gifts: precious stones, precious metals and valuable things were donated for use of the god; images were made of them in valuable materials – stone, iron, silver and gold. This god is to be honoured 'with gold, and silver, and with precious stones, and pleasant things'. 'Pleasant things' means 'desirable things' and, if the train of thought in the list shows increasing value, it could mean 'jewels'; if the phrase is used antithetically, it simply means that gold, silver and precious stones are the desirable things; if the use is summative, it should be translated 'anything valuable'.[4] This man finds that the service of his god is costly; especially draining are the wars necessary to guard his interests. Nevertheless, in such worship he is prepared to sacrifice much that men hold dear.

Verse 39 The aid of this strange deity, revealed as the world ruler, gives this king the confidence to attack every bastion of religious activity and bring all under his absolute control. The following translations make his objective clear: 'He will attack mighty fortresses, aided by a foreign deity' (*NET*), or 'He shall deal with the strongest fortresses by the help of a foreign god' (*RSV*). He has sufficient confidence in this leader of the western world to count on his support as he seeks to bring all in Israel under his religious control. He is prepared to attack any 'fortress'; which term is to be understood metaphorically, as of 'any organisation or system refusing him allegiance'. Three things are offered as bribes to buy followers who will acknowledge him or 'to those who recognize him' (*NET*). These bribes are:

(a) Promotion. 'Those who acknowledge him he shall magnify with honour' (*RSV*). He promises to a follower a more prestigious position than he presently holds – there will be promotions.

(b) Power. 'He will place them in authority over many people' (*NET*). Their responsibilities will be increased as he gives his adherents wider fields of duty, with the delegation of increased authority, over more persons. In fact, they will share real power in the nation.

(c) Property. 'And shall divide the land for gain', or 'He will parcel out land for a price' (*NET*) – this man begins to use this sacred land that was given of God to the nation of Israel, as if it was his own property. This usurper grants leases, or sells sub-divisions, and even whole areas, 'for development'. This will likely be his excuse to cover his thefts. The main beneficiaries of this policy will be himself and his cronies. Those he can trust to support him will share the profits and thus become the sycophants and yes-men required to give him the electoral support essential for his position. These men will be amply rewarded for their allegiance by faster promotion, increased power and a growing property portfolio.

[4] Wood, *A Commentary on Daniel*, p. 306.

These bribes enable this leader in Israel to, first, claim leadership of the greater part of the nation and, then, maintain it over those who are spoken of as 'the many' (9:27). It should be clear that this man has bribed his way to a secure an electoral mandate in Israel. This throws a fascinating light on the condition of the nation at this time. The first statement in the verse indicates some strong opposition to his leadership. The word translated 'strong holds' (*AV*), or 'fortresses' (*NET*), indicates that different factions in the nation oppose him for different reasons, and he moves against them. 'He shall deal with the strongest fortresses by the help of a foreign god' (*RSV*). For further suggestions on this theme see Chapter Note C at the end of this chapter.

Verses 40–45 Satan's Political Rule of the Nations

The Time of the End

Verse 40 The expression 'time of the end' is repeated from verse 35 to indicate that this is the critical point in the vision. It has been shown in the previous discussion that this can be identified, without question, as the midpoint of the seventieth week – the last seven years of the prophetic programme given to Daniel (9:24–27) in the third vision. The whole seven-year period has already been shown to be the Tribulation. The week is divided into two parts by the interruption of the sacrificial system in Jerusalem through the 'abomination of desolation', when the image is placed on the wing of the Temple. The Lord calls the first half of this week 'the beginning of sorrows' (Mt. 24:8) and names the last half of the week 'the great tribulation' (Mt. 24:21–23; Rev. 7:14). Since this period has very special relevance to Israel it is also called 'the time of Jacob's trouble' (Jer. 30:7).

It is at this point that Israel, under the king already described in the previous verses (vv. 36–39), who has been identified as the Antichrist, is attacked by two enemies. The King of the South shall 'push at him'. The language itself suggests a kind of half-hearted affair but it triggers a far more serious attack by the King of the North. Since the signing of the peace covenant, over three years before, the nation put their confidence in the great leader of the mighty ten-power kingdom in the west. This alliance will lull them into a false sense of security, which may well have far-reaching implications for her military preparedness. Israel may have allowed her defence forces to be cut back, her renowned intelligence department to be disbanded, and perhaps also the great security wall dividing the nation to be removed. The material resources released by these measures, poured into development plans, may have brought progress and prosperity. The future for Israel looked good. Suddenly, without warning, their peace is shattered.

Little did this king in Israel realise that his acceptance of the peace had opened the way for a tremendous, devastating military attack – in fact, a full scale invasion of Israel. The language is simple, but the results are devastating. After a kind of false alarm from the south, there is a full-blown assault from the north. The King of the North 'shall come against him like a whirlwind'. Up to the time break in the chapter (between v. 35 and v. 36) the 'King of the South' always means the king of Egypt;[5] thus the first signal of trouble for Israel arises from their old enemy, Egypt. The immediate response to this action is by the King of the North, who with a mighty army sweeps into the land of Israel. In the earlier verses the 'King of the North' has been identified as the king of Syria. Again there is no valid reason to change this identification, except to remember that the peoples occupying the land area may have changed down the centuries or a nation may have changed its name. The use of the term points to Syria still, but the major part of the old Seleucid Empire is now Iran. So, interpreting the picture as it stands, unbelieving Israel, under the Antichrist, having been supported by the given word of the leader of the mightiest empire on earth, and enjoying their peace, are suddenly disturbed by a probing or provocative attack by Egypt into the southern parts of Israel. This attack is quickly contained, but it triggers a full scale invasion of Israel from the north – the area that is now called Iran.

The simile used in the 'whirlwind' emphasises the suddenness and the unexpectedness of this invasion of this land at peace. The language is meant to convey the idea of the irresistible, overwhelming force of a full scale military invasion carrying all before it. The language describes a mighty army. This is readily

[5] In Egypt the Ptolemaic line ran from Ptolemy, one of the generals of Alexander the Great – who proclaimed himself king in 304 BC – to Cleopatra, the last of the Ptolemaic blood-line, who committed suicide in 30 BC. She and her consort, Anthony, were faced with humiliation in Rome after their army was defeated at the Battle of Actium (31 BC); they both committed suicide (30 BC); he with his sword and she with an asp. The name King of the South has, down the ages and up to the present, been identified with Egypt. This tells us that Egypt has some part to play in triggering this end-time invasion.

interpreted by any later age. That this invader comes: (a) 'with chariots' would indicate the mobile armour of the day; (b) 'with horsemen' would point to the cavalry of the day, or with whatever has replaced the horse on the battlefield – perhaps in our day tanks or aircraft are indicated; (c) 'with many ships' can be easily interpreted as the warships of the day. The language shows an overwhelming military attack of an invasion force launched over the border of Israel from the north. This attack has only one objective – to wipe Israel off the political map of the world.

The 'whirlwind' is interpreted for Daniel, as he is told the invader 'shall enter into the countries, and shall overflow and pass over'. Any efforts to stop this invader are in vain. All countries (note the plural) who try to oppose him are simply swept out of way; they are irrelevancies: his target is Israel.

Who is this Invader from the North?

Suggestion 1

Some expositors link this invasion with the army of two hundred million mobilised at about this same point in time (Rev. 9:13–19 – the midpoint of the seventieth week). The problem is that, while mobilisation takes place, it appears to be located east of the Euphrates River and no hint is given in that passage as to the purpose of the mobilisation. It would seem that, while it was gathered just after the midpoint of the week, it only begins to move at a later date. It is surely one of the armies crossing the Euphrates River, three years later moving towards Armageddon (Rev. 16:12–16). Two reasons therefore make it impossible to link that army with this invasion just before the midpoint of the week. These reasons are: (a) The direction from which the attack comes. In this chapter the main invasion comes directly from north of Israel; the invasion in Revelation comes from east of Israel; indeed from east of the River Euphrates (Rev. 16:12–16); (b) The time of the invasion. In this chapter the invader and his army are destroyed by God, on the mountains of Israel (Ezek. 38:18–23), before the midpoint of the Tribulation. The invasion from the east is mobilised at the midpoint of the Tribulation in the sixth trumpet (Rev. 9:13–21), but only moves towards Jerusalem and Armageddon in the time of the sixth vial (Rev. 16:12), at the very close of the Tribulation period, when Christ is revealed as 'King of kings, and Lord of lords' (Rev. 19:11–16).

It is quite evident that these two invasions are distinct and not to be confused. They take place at different times, are led by different enemies, and come to different ends. The only thing they have in common is their target – Israel. They each set out to wipe out that nation.

Suggestion 2

Light from Ezekiel: The Invasion of Israel from the North

As Scripture is searched for some help in the understanding of this invasion, much light is thrown by the prophecy of Ezekiel. The ministry of Ezekiel reveals, in unsparing detail, the failure and disobedience of Israel and the consequent judgement from God on their sin, by their banishment from the land. Against this, Ezekiel shows that, despite their present condition, they still have a future, when all the promises of God will be fulfilled in their national blessing in their own land. Two passages in Ezekiel deal with this millennial blessing: 36:1–38 and 39:21–29, which is further expanded in detail in the following chapters (40–48). Notice particularly that these two passages that speak of Divine blessing enjoyed nationally in their own land under a true covenant of peace are divided by an interpolated section, from chapter 37:1 to chapter 39:16. This section sets out the means that God will use for the recovery of His people. There would be two main steps in their national recovery. First, there would be permitted, at a future time, a remarkable regathering of the nation of Israel in their historic national homeland. This is not the result of a spiritual exercise but a practical response to the longing of a displaced people to return to the land from which they, or their ancestors, had been ruthlessly torn and the politics of the day and an answer to the anti-Semitism of the nations amongst whom the Jews had been forced to live. They are not believers in Christ, as indeed is shown in chapter 37, where the regathered company is seen as a 'valley which was full of bones' (v. 1); they were dead, but under a human voice the bones came together (vv. 7–8). They had life but it was not Divine life. To bring Divine life to this nation God would have to pour out His Holy Spirit for their regeneration, that they may enjoy millennial blessing. The point of interest, in light of this prophecy of Daniel, is that in the disciplinary process to bring the nation of Israel to a consciousness of their sin and leading to their repentance, confession, and cleansing, there lies the description of a devastating and unexpected invasion of Israel from the north. The timing of this invasion shows that it must occur within the Tribulation period that ends in the coming of the Son of Man and entry to the Kingdom. Notice particularly the placing of this invasion. It is placed between two passages speaking of millennial blessing – Ezekiel 37:15–28 and Ezekiel 39:21–29. The detail of this northern invasion is given between Ezekiel 38:1 and Ezekiel 39:20. It is suggested that this is the same invasion as that seen in the timeline given to Daniel.[6] The headlines of these two chapters in Ezekiel are:

(a) Deceit of the northern invader (Ezek. 38:1–12);

(b) Delay of the western powers to come to the aid of Israel (Ezek. 38:13–16); and

(c) Destruction of the invader (Ezek. 38:17–39:20).

Unbelieving Israel would learn: first, the perfidy of the man they had trusted to aid them (in his failure to keep his word); and, second, the fact that their God, despite their unbelief, had yet a purpose for them, and so He delivered them as He has done so often in their history. There is no record of any impression made on the nation of Israel through the invasion; not a single indication of any national repentance. Some individuals could have been reached through the gospel being preached. Preachers would very likely use this invasion as a text, warning of judgement and yet mercy. Those who believed would become part of the remnant. Little impression seems to have been made on the majority, who still continue to accept 'the lie' centred on the Antichrist, as they continue to reject 'the truth' in Christ.

A detailed comparison of these two invasions – the one in Ezekiel (Ezek. 38–39) and the other here in Daniel (Dan. 11:40–45) – will support the identification: (a) Each invasion has as its target the same nation – the nation of Israel; (b) Each invasion takes place at the same point in the prophetic timeline – in Ezekiel, at a time of peace in Israel; in Daniel, at the middle of the seven-year false peace of the Antichrist; (c) Both invasions show contextually that each is a necessary preparation of the nation for the Coming of the Son of Man and the Kingdom; (d) Both invaders are wiped out by a signal display of God's direct intervention on the mountains of Israel.

It will be suggested that this identification helps in the understanding of events that follow in the second half of the Tribulation and, most notably, may offer a possible answer as to the

[6] See an examination of the details in the Note D at end of this chapter.

reason for the setting up of the idol in Jerusalem at this time. Further details of the examination and confirmation of this link are summarised in Chapter Note D at the close of this chapter.

Verses 41–43 There is no change of antecedent for the 'he' of this verse, so it must still be the invader from the north, moving as a conqueror in total victory. Indeed, his triumph over those intervening nations complete, he moves swiftly into the 'glorious land' – already identified as Daniel's name for Israel (see 8:9 and 11:16). In this conquest it is, particularly, the Jewish people who are the target of his hatred. This is supported by the next statements: 'And tens of thousands shall fall, but these shall be delivered out of his hand: Edom and Moab and the main part of the Ammonites' (*RSV*). Those who die are Jews, deliberately targeted and wiped out by this psychopathic murderer. Those who escape are the Palestinians, described by their ancestral names – descendants of Esau (Edom) and of Lot (Moab and Ammon). These are the ancestors of the Palestinian people and, while they have been, in general terms, more open to the gospel than their Jewish neighbours, the majority have imbibed a militant form of Islam (Shi'ism), which, with the bitter inheritance of anti-Semitism from their forebears, and adding the fact that they claim to have been displaced from their land, makes them implacable enemies of Israel. The Arabs trace their ancestry to Ismail, brother of Isaac, and have never been generally as antagonistic to Israel as the Palestinians. Probably this invader will claim that he comes as liberator of the displaced Palestinians, with the promise of recovery of their land lost to the Israelis in the previous wars. However, this liberator of the Palestinian people (of the mixed origin suggested) is of such militant character that he has no time for any Arab government, except his own, and states like Jordan, Iraq and Kuwait cease to exist, as he sweeps south as far as Egypt.

This land of Egypt, while an enemy of Israel many times in the past, at this point is of a more moderate Islamic culture than the invader and has just annoyed him considerably. Egypt had dared to challenge this invader (Iran) for leadership of the Arab world – by the premature attack on Israel (see v. 40). Egypt needed to be taught a lesson. He does this by seizing its wealth. The expression 'he shall have power over' is more clearly translated 'he shall become ruler of the treasures of gold and of silver, and all the precious things of Egypt' (*RSV*). In this triumph for 'Militant Islam' it seems nothing is impossible, especially when the two most fanatical of Islamic nations are 'at his steps', or 'in his train' (*RSV*); they support him, and this spreads his dominion from north to south: from northern Russia, through the Middle East, to embrace North Africa. The two supporting nations are identified as, first, 'Libyans', and the name Libya still covers the same territory today; then the 'Ethiopians', and this land is known today as Sudan. It is to be noticed that in each case it is not the state *per se,* but the people, that are mentioned. Is it of significance that today each of these lands has suffered a violent overthrow of a previous regime, and in each case a more militant Islam has gained a more dominant role in the state?

Verse 44(a) However, very suddenly and unexpectedly, news reaches this man that something that has been on the horizon of the world leaders for nearly three years has suddenly taken place. The world empire established by the union of western and Arab nations in the ten-power federation that is now controlled by the Coming Prince, the unabashed supporter of Israel and her king, has been watched uneasily by a mighty nation in the east. Knowing full well the cause and character of this invasion by militant Islam led by the old King of the North (once Syria, now Iran) into Israel, China has concluded that the forces of the western powers will move to the aid of Israel and, in doing so, inevitably, they will clash with the trading empire China has built up in the Middle East and North Africa. China decides to mobilise her military forces and even to begin a search for bases west of the Euphrates. Events now unfold very rapidly indeed.

The picture is clearly painted for us at the midpoint of the seven-year Tribulation period. That the time frame is correct is supported by the opening verses of the next chapter (12:1–4), which should not have been separated by the (uninspired) chapter division. An invasion of Israel from the north, led by Iran or other militant Islamic power out of the old Seleucid Empire, and supported by all the militant Islamic peoples now living in previously Russian territories, has been unbelievably successful. Israel has been overrun and many Jews have died; Palestinian people have been 'liberated' with much rejoicing; some moderate Islamic states have been dismantled and puppet regimes installed. From Russia, through the Middle East, right to North Africa, runs the power of militant Islam. So suddenly has this come about that, it would appear, the mighty western leader of the ten-power kingdom has been so shocked at the speed of events that he seems virtually to have been paralysed. In any event, he has taken no positive action, except to register a very feeble protest. Perhaps the peace in Israel had led to such complacency in western lands that there had been the demobilisation of military forces for economic reasons. This could be part of the reason for the slow response to this northern blitzkrieg. It would appear that these happenings have taken place very quickly – within days and weeks rather than months.

This invader at the peak of his triumph enjoys the wealth and luxury of Egypt – the history of the Roman Empire and the actions of Mark Anthony could profitably be recalled here – suddenly, news breaks that causes alarm. This news comes 'out of the east and out of the north'. For any invader relying on military might to hold down his conquests, the news that an army clearly much superior to his own had been mobilised would cause him some measure of alarm. Scripture speaks of only one such a force at this time. This is the mobilisation of the army revealed in Revelation (Rev. 9:13–19). John records: 'And the number of the army of the horsemen were two hundred thousand thousand', or, in our figures, two hundred million men (Rev. 9:16).[7] Such news, at this point, must have been shattering to this invader of Israel. That the mobilisation takes place at the midpoint of the seven-year Tribulation is clear when it is observed that it takes place under the sixth trumpet judgement (Rev. 9:13–21). The seventh trumpet (Rev. 11:15–18) really covers what follows in the second half of the seven-year Tribulation – this includes the 'vial judgements', which only take weeks to pour out, in the very closing stages of the Tribulation. It is in the sixth vial that an army from the east crosses the dried-up Euphrates River, clearly heading for Jerusalem. So between the mobilisation and the movement of this army there is the better part of three years. The numbers in such a mobilisation and the timing would cause the invader deep concern, but it may be assumed that what would give him the greatest worry was the location. The news that reaches the invader in Egypt comes first from the east and then from the north. The greatest power in the east in the end-time will, from the viewpoint of the present, be China. No reason is given in the book of Revelation for the mobilisation, so any suggestion must be speculative and viewed with caution. One possible reason for such

[7] At the height of mobilisation in the Second World War it is calculated there were 70 million persons under arms.

drastic action is that China, as the number two trading power in the world, with massive financial investments in both the Middle East and the North African nations, would fear that this invasion will either take them over, or, by inviting the intervention of the western empire, bring her operations to a close. China wants to be ready for either of these eventualities and she readies herself with this very public mobilisation of her military forces. This may also mean that China has begun the search for operational bases west of the Euphrates, which can be used later. Suddenly it must have occurred to this invader that some of the nations he has so recently subdued have close racial and religious ties with China, and some, like Israel, have trade agreements with eastern nations. He fears that the nations just subdued, including Israel, and placed under his puppet governments, may see this action as their opportunity to call for help to regain their liberty. The invader must act quickly and decisively.

This devastating news and the shock to his plans throw this northern invader of Israel into a rage – 'great fury' is the expression used. It would be clear to him that he had made serious misjudgements. While he had been correct in his assessment of the weak-kneed response of the West, he had misjudged the depth of militant Islam. He had led the fanatical Muslim nations and peoples into this action against Israel. However, moderate Islam had stood aloof and refused to support him with either arms or resources. Some Arab states, with their sales of oil dependent on the West and their wealth invested there, refused to act. Other Arab states shared government with western powers in the ten-power world empire and had no power to stop the western leader supporting Israel.[8] Perhaps he could now see that his most serious mistake was to leave out of his calculations the result of his actions on the world's second largest economy – China. This great nation must have been rudely made aware that this man now controlled, through his militant Muslim hordes, an empire encroaching on her borders. His actions in Egypt had robbed China of many rich markets. It was time to stop the invader, and the decision is taken to mobilise its military forces – China would be one of the few nations on earth

[8] Over fifty years ago when such a suggestion could scarcely be envisaged, Mr J. M. Davies (India) pointed out to the author that if Nebuchadnezzar's image stood in Babylon, would it not suggest that the five toes of each foot indicated an East-West division in the ten-power kingdom?

who could possibly put two hundred million men under arms. So an immense army is mobilised (Rev. 9:13–19).

Although mobilised and ready to go, it would seem the movement of this mighty army is delayed for some reason. The mobilisation takes place under the sixth trumpet, which places it about the mid-point of the week but this army is not mentioned again until under the sixth vial judgment it crosses the dried-up River Euphrates (Rev. 16:12–16) moving towards Armageddon. This is almost at the end of the week.

This time the invading forces are described first as those of 'the kings of the east' (Rev. 16:12) but soon, by satanic power they are joined by others described as 'the kings of the earth and of the whole world' (Rev. 16:14). It would appear that the Muslim hordes of China, Indonesia, Malaysia, India, and Pakistan in their initiation of *jihad* are joined by many other nations as they move to attack Israel and her western supporter.

The reason for this is that suddenly and dramatically the whole political picture has changed – as with one tap the picture in a kaleidoscope is changed. At first, militant Islam's victory over Israel is so swift and complete that the moderate Islamic *jihad* reckons it is not needed; Israel has been subdued. But, almost overnight, this is reversed; the destruction of this invader on the mountains of Israel by Divine action, the resurgence of Israel with the aid of the western prince, the assassination-resurrection drama, and the consequent world adulation leaves the world almost breathless. China and the supporters of moderate Islam judge they have no option but to pursue the *jihad* path once again. This time they intend to wipe out both Israel and the western power supporting her. This is why they are found moving to Armageddon for the final confrontation (Rev. 16:1–16).

Verses 44(b)–45 In a furious rage the invader retraces his steps, with one objective – that objective is defined by two verbs: (a) 'To destroy': his intention is to wipe out whatever armed forces the western leader has been able at last to get there to support his protégé; (b) 'Utterly to make away many', or to 'wipe out many' (*NET*): his ambition is to wipe out the Jews – to put to death every remaining member of the Jewish race.

In the execution of his aims the northern invader acts very quickly. This summary verse gives the impression of speed. First, he abandons an Egypt robbed of her wealth. Then he moves back to

Israel to 'plant the tabernacles of his palace between the seas in the glorious holy mountain'. The more literal reading gives 'pitch his palatial tents between the sea and the glorious holy mountain' (*RSV*), or, as given by another translation, 'pitch his royal tents between the seas toward the beautiful holy mountain' (*NET*). Ancient conquerors, including Alexander the Great, had splendid tents that were carried by the army and pitched nightly in a suitable location to use as army headquarters when on the march. This readily became a temporary administration centre for a conquered territory, until more permanent quarters could be arranged or built. This conqueror intended to stay here until every Jew was wiped out, so he pitched his palatial tent (with every comfort available to the leader) between the seas. This must be between the Mediterranean Sea and the Dead Sea. In between these seas was the city of Jerusalem. The spot he chose is called 'the glorious holy mountain', which would be Mount Zion. So this ruthless and infuriated invader is about to wipe out, finally and forever, the nation of Israel. The sore thing for the nation is that the orders are to be issued from the sacred Mount Zion.

The final statement of the angel to Daniel makes solemn reading: 'Yet he shall come to his end, and none shall help him'. A line drawn by God has been crossed, and now God acts for His people Israel. Having traced the steps of this invader and seen the devastation he has wrought in Israel and Jerusalem, the death he has brought to so many, and now to see him installed in comfort on Mount Zion, is it any wonder that Jehovah speaks to Ezekiel: 'My fury shall come up in My face' (Ezek. 38:18)? When God is furious things happen quickly. In this case they certainly did and Daniel is told very simply that 'he shall come to his end, and none shall help him'. In simple terms it means that God steps into the story, in the preservation of the nation of Israel, and this invader and his army are dealt with by Divine intervention and they perish on 'the mountains of Israel' (Ezek. 39:1–6). The terrible thing is that not a single one comes to his aid. The details of the execution of this decree are dealt with at the end of this chapter, in Chapter Note D.

It is clear that no major nation with military power moves to either resist or assist this invader of Israel. This is the very kind of attack that Israel and the West have dreaded for years. Yet the peace covenant will have deceived them and then the suddenness and completeness of the attack will be a terrible shock. The threat of nuclear retaliation against them by this man gave rise to a fatal hesitation. So the western powers made only a feeble protest, perhaps in the United Nations or its replacement. On the other hand, while in general support of the invader the Arab States live in such fear of their militant minorities that they dare not openly assist this man they would brand as an 'extremist'. It is left to God to defend His people Israel once again – even in their unbelief.

As has been stressed already, this devastating destruction of this northern invader comes just before the midpoint of the Tribulation. All commentators agree that the first three verses of the next chapter are the conclusion of this vision of Daniel. The chapter division has meant that the time element has been largely ignored. The time when Michael stands up for Israel is seen in the book of Revelation to be the midpoint of the seven-year Tribulation (Rev. 12:7–14). This invader is identified as coming from north of Israel, possibly Iran, as the situation would demand today. It is advisable to treat such a suggestion tentatively, but it will be open to the militant Islamic leader of that day to lead his armies against the nation of Israel with intent to wipe them out. Having dragged Russia, however reluctantly ('I will ... put hooks into thy jaws' Ezek. 38:4) into supporting the invasion, the king possibly calculated that other nations, approving of his objective – the wiping out of the Jew – would come to his aid. Realising he had miscalculated, yet still determined to destroy Israel, such is his burning hate that he leaves Egypt and returns to Jerusalem. There God steps in and destroys this blasphemous invader on 'the mountains of Israel' (Ezek. 39:1–6). In this action by God, the whole political landscape changes for the final three-and-a-half years of the Tribulation, before the Son of Man takes the Kingdom, after the confrontation with Satan's man at Armageddon.

Chapter Note A

Time Setting for Daniel's Fourth Vision (11:35)

As already shown, to suggest that there is no time break between verse 35 and verse 36 is spiritual myopia. The time period to which the prophecy switches must be carefully identified. This has been shown in the comments on the text, using the two phrases from verse 35 – 'time of the end' and 'a time appointed' – to be the seven-year Tribulation, with the emphasis moving to the consummation. Contextually these pointed statements demand a time break. In the clearest possible way the interpreting angel has signalled to Daniel that he must change the time frame of the prophecy. This deduction can be fully supported by noticing the attention drawn to the time marks in this final vision. There are four occasions when attention is drawn to time in this final vision:

(a) The First Reference to Time – A General Reference – 'Thy people in the latter days' (10:14)

Daniel has been told that this final vision has to do with 'thy people in the latter days' (10:14). That the expression 'latter days' describes any time beyond Daniel's immediate present must be accepted. The prophecy just studied in the early verses of this chapter (11:2–20) fulfils this condition – it lies just beyond Daniel's time. Nevertheless, the next statement qualifies the 'latter days' with a further statement, 'for yet the vision is for many days', implying that a longer period intervenes before the complete fulfilment of the whole prophecy. There follows the prophetic sequence of events from verse 21 to verse 35, bringing the timeline from the time of Cyrus (539 BC) down to Antiochus Epiphanes (167 BC – his 'abomination of desolation'). It is at this point that the focus shifts again to the time frame already mentioned – 'in the latter days'. So in the phrase lurks the double shift: (a) from Daniel to Antiochus Epiphanes; and (b) from Antiochus to the Antichrist.

(b) The Second Reference to Time – A Specific Reference – 'The time of the end' (11:35)

Now, at this point, after this time period (Cyrus to Antiochus), Israel is in deep trial. The 'abomination of desolation' identifies the reign of one called 'a vile person' – identified as Antiochus Epiphanes. Daniel is told that these trials continue 'even to the time of the end' (v. 35), with the explanatory statement following – 'because it is yet for a time appointed'. The use of the phrase 'time appointed' (see comments at v. 35), repeated in verses 27, 29 and 35, shows clearly that events on earth run to a Divine timetable that men cannot change. The word 'appointed' implies that heaven's court has already set the time for the purpose of God to be completed. At this point, persons and places and events come together for display of that Divine purpose, to the glory of God. It will immediately be observed that in the final use of this phrase (v. 35) it is defined and qualified, as it has not been in the previous cases, by another expression – 'the time of the end'. Thus the Holy Spirit is deliberately shifting the focus from the time of Antiochus to 'the time of the end' – a phrase that now dominates the remaining section and will be repeated (11:40, 12:4, 9). This must be the period made known to Daniel as the final week of the seventy weeks prophecy (9:24–27) and, indeed, the time of the Tribulation on earth that sets the stage for the coming of Christ back to earth. It is suggested that the context demands a time break at this point that moves across the centuries from the tribulation under Antiochus to the Tribulation under the man here described – who will be shown to be the Antichrist of the end-time (1 Jn 2:18). So there must be a time gap at this point. These two men answer to one another as 'shadow' does to 'substance'. Now the 'shadow' of Antiochus changes to the 'substance' of the Antichrist. This time of suffering for Israel has a time appointed for it to end – but that terminus will be reached under the rule of a man of whom Antiochus Epiphanes is but the shadow.

(c) The Third Reference to Time – An Identifiable Reference – 'At the time of the end' (11:40)

A repetition of the expression 'the time of the end' occurs in connection with the military attack upon this king. It is dated thus: 'And at the time of the end shall the king of the south push at him: and the king of the north shall come against him like a whirlwind' (11:40). This surely identifies 'the time of the end' under consideration – and men will recognise it from the movement of two kings whose ancestry are to be seen in the light of prophecy. Present day Syria and Egypt could again be seen to attack Israel, as happened in the past. This must come within the period of Tribulation marked out by God as closing the 'times of the Gentiles' (Mt. 24:3–31).

(d) The Fourth Reference to Time – A Localised Reference – 'And at that time' (12:1)

This statement marks this end-time more precisely still: 'at that time shall Michael stand up ... and there shall be a time of trouble, such as never was since there was a nation' (12:1). This must be exactly the same point of which the Lord spoke: 'For then shall be great tribulation, such as was not since the beginning of the world to this time, no, nor ever shall be' (Mt. 24:21).

Following these four time marks the conclusion is inescapable. From this point to the end of the vision the prophetic picture is focussed on the nation of Israel, gathered back to their own land, settled and at peace, and yet they now face the very darkest moment in their national history, under a despotic ruler of whom Antiochus Epiphanes was but the shadow. It is a time of tribulation for the world generally, and for Israel specifically, as God deals with the 'husbandmen' who slew His Son (Mt. 21:41). These four time marks point to the seven-year Tribulation period in Daniel's seventieth week (9:27), with the final focus falling on the midpoint of that period.

NT Support for the Crisis at the Midpoint of the Tribulation.

It has already been shown that the midpoint in the seventieth week of the seventy weeks prophecy has been marked with the break in the seven-year covenant by the introduction of the idol – the 'abomination of desolation' – into the Temple at Jerusalem. Compare the statements and comments at 9:24–27 and at 12:11. This event marks a crisis point in the Tribulation. This is supported by the NT prophecies:

(a) In the Olivet Discourse (Mt. 24–25) the Lord also divided this seven-year period of the Tribulation into two parts, thus: (1) 'All these are the beginning of sorrows' (Mt. 24:4–8), which covers the first three-and-a-half years; (2) 'And then shall the end come' (Mt. 24:14), followed by the statement, 'When ye therefore shall see the abomination of desolation, spoken of by Daniel the prophet, stand in the holy place' (v. 15). The consequence of this action is the flight of the nation of Israel. The Lord gives the explanation of the flight: 'for then shall be great tribulation' (Mt. 24:21–28), which covers the last three-and-a-half-years, until the Son of Man comes. Jeremiah speaks of this same period when he writes: 'It is even the time of Jacob's trouble' (Jer. 30:7). Again the crisis point is the introduction of the 'abomination of desolation' into the holy place.

(b) In the Revelation. The apostle John, in the book of Revelation, is shown at this very critical point that there is war in heaven and it is stated, 'And there was war in heaven: Michael and his angels fought against the dragon' (Rev. 12:7–13). When the dragon is cast down to earth he turns upon Israel, symbolically presented as the woman who had borne the Man-child, and she flees. Divinely protected, Israel is 'nourished for a time, and times and half-a-time' (Rev. 12:14) – the same three-and-a-half years as mentioned above. Clearly this also coincides with the midpoint of the Tribulation period before us in this passage. This time period is stressed again in the following chapter in Revelation, when the time granted to the supreme ruler at the height of his power is stated: 'and power was given unto him to continue forty and two months' (Rev. 13:5). This Scripture shows that the Great Tribulation follows the moment in heaven when Michael the Archangel stands to his feet. Clearly Michael is about to act for the preservation of Israel.

As Scripture fastens on this critical point, when the 'abomination of desolation' is introduced in the Temple, there is a simple question that needs an answer: Why is this 'abomination of desolation' introduced into the Temple at this time? Reviewing the Scriptures quoted above, it seems strange that no reason seems to be given as to why the king in Jerusalem should choose this particular moment to introduce an idol into the holy place. From this moment things in Israel are completely changed. Israel becomes the very centre of a cosmic conflict, when forces formerly restrained are released (Rev. 9:1–11), and powers on both sides are marshalled, as earth moves towards the final confrontation of Armageddon. The question still stands out – why now? What circumstance lies behind the Israeli leader deliberately introducing an idol into the Temple precincts? The Scriptures quoted simply register the fact without comment. However, as Scripture illuminates Scripture, it will be suggested that the key lies in the invasion of Israel here spoken of and the consequences of the invasion. This will be discussed when the invader has been identified.

CHAPTER NOTE B

NT Identification of Daniel's Prophetic Figures (11:36)

1. Identification of the King of Fierce Countenance

The NT identifies this man from the perspective of the Church age. It will be remembered that the NT adds to the prophetic light of Daniel. It is our privilege to use the full light available to us.

The portrait of this end-time figure is further developed in the NT as:

(a) The one who comes in his own name — Jn 5:43
(b) The beast from the Earth — Rev. 13:11–18
(c) The False Prophet — Rev. 16:13; 19:20; 20:10
(d) The Antichrist — 1 Jn 2:18

2. Identification of the Coming Prince

The NT offers further identification of this remarkable personage who comes onto the world stage at this end-time. Daniel's viewpoint is that of Israel; John's viewpoint is the world. It is our privilege to see the complete picture. The added titles are as follows:

(a) Beast from the Sea — Rev. 13:1–8
(Political Claim – leader of a world empire)
(b) The Man of Sin — 2 Thess. 2:3–4
(Religious Claim – one to be worshipped)

A number of cross-links can be seen that indicate that these titles describe the same person, but the final statement concerning the Man of Sin puts the identification beyond doubt, as Scripture records:

> And that man of sin be revealed, the son of perdition; who opposeth and exalteth himself above all that is called God, or that is worshipped, so he as God sitteth in the temple of God, shewing himself that he is God (2 Thess. 2:3–4).

Bringing together the revelation of subsequent Scriptures from the NT, it is clear that this king in Jerusalem assures the nation that this man from the west is one who can be trusted. As this invasion takes place just before the midpoint of the seventieth week then the events already discussed (the defeat of the invader, the triumph in Jerusalem, and the assassination-resurrection scenario) follow quickly, and have been made to appear to vindicate that trust. The king in Israel 'suggests' or maybe 'orders' his deification and the making of an image of him (Rev. 13:14). This image placed on a pinnacle of the Temple in Jerusalem is the 'abomination that maketh desolate' (12:11), of which the action of Antiochus (11:31) was but a picture. This image is to be a channel of worship to the man. It will be remembered that the reason for the making and placing of this image was not given to Daniel. This is where the NT light, through the apostle John and the book of Revelation, helps, with the assassination-resurrection picture (Rev. 13: 3–9), as providing the background for this Jew to present this Gentile as worthy of worship. That picture supplies the reason why men were so gullible as to believe such a lie. This is the man who, with all the authority of the ten-power kingdom and its armies behind him, embodies the protection and security of 'the god of forces'. In absolute apostasy, this Jewish king demands that all Israel worship this god on pain of death (Rev. 13:11–18). In doing this, of course, he is acting in complete contradiction to the role of an Aaronic priest in Israel, who presented men to God; this apostate directs worship to a man. In thus directing worship to a man, Babylonian idolatry is restored, bringing men again into bondage. Nebuchadnezzar's image now has its final prophetic fulfilment, in this second half of the seven-year Tribulation.

Chapter Note C

Strongholds Addressed by Antichrist in the Tribulation (11:39)

During the first three-and-a-half year period of the Tribulation there are elements of resistance – speaking metaphorically, they are 'fortresses' that have to be subdued. Including in our presentation the light of NT revelation on the subject, it is suggested that amongst these 'fortresses' will be the following groups of people unwilling to bow to his authority:

(a) **Orthodox Judaism.** Many Jews will refuse to accept the messianic claims of this usurper and, in doing this, immediately become a target of his wrath. In the book of the Revelation (Rev. 12:17) they are identified as those 'which keep the commandments of God'. Acting with the support of his western colleague, this king will put many of his own people to death, and many more will flee.

(b) **Genuine Believers.** Those who 'have the testimony of Jesus Christ' (Rev. 12:17). These are the believers in that day, identified in Revelation as 'the saints' (Rev. 13:7 – the term is used twelve times in Revelation). A tremendous resurgence of evangelical preaching has swept through the land of Israel and, indeed, across the world, in the preceding years (Mt. 24:14). The severest persecution, even martyrdom (Rev. 6:9–11) has not stayed the progress of the gospel nor diminished its power. Indeed, it appears as if the message spread through the very persecution designed to destroy the believers.

(c) **Militant Islam.** This may seem a very strange 'fortress' holding out against the messianic claims of this king. Surely no Muslim would ever accept such a man. However, it must not be forgotten that a division amongst Islamic nations has allowed what might be called 'moderate' Islam to reach accommodation with Israel. Scripture would suggest that some moderate Islamic states are among the ten states that support the western leader already identified as 'the Coming Prince', the 'Man of Sin' and the 'Beast'. This accommodation, reached with Israel on the international front, has allowed the seven-year covenant (9:27) to come into effect. This, in turn, has permitted the re-institution of the sacrificial system in the rebuilt Temple in Jerusalem; all of which have been bitter blows to the Palestinians in Israel and also to the fanatical Muslim nations. 'Militant' Islam, both within and without Israel, had never accepted this compromise at the expense of the Palestinian people. These bitterly disillusioned Muslims, by this

never carried to its intended conclusion. God had given Israel a homeland, but Divine discipline, on account of the rejection of the Messiah, demanded the scattering (*diaspora*) of Israel throughout the world. God had warned very early in their history: 'because thou wouldest not obey the voice of the LORD thy God . . . the LORD shall scatter thee among all people, from the one end of the earth even unto the other' (Deut. 28:62–68). At the same time, God had given many promises of an assured future for the nation restored to their God, ruled by Christ their King, and regathered in their own land. In the study of this book, it has been shown repeatedly that this is the ultimate goal that God has for His earthly people. All the post-exilic prophets show that before the Messiah comes to take the Kingdom there will be a regathering of the scattered people of national Israel. Ezekiel takes special care to show that this gathering will be in unbelief (Ezek. 37:1–10).

There had been the movement of Jews back to their land from around the beginning of the twentieth century, particularly from lands where they were subject to persecution. The real miracle was the vote in the United Nations General Assembly in November 1947, in an aircraft hangar in New York, when, by thirty-three votes 'for' to seventeen 'against' (Britain abstained), the resolution was passed for the establishment of the independent state of Israel. This was to take effect when the British Mandate ended, within six months. The British Mandate closed at midnight on May 13, 1948. On the following day, David Ben-Gurion announced the establishment of Israel as an independent nation. This was an entity not appearing on world maps since 606 BC – a period of 2,554 years.

The history of the nation of Israel in the decades since then is a fascinating story of miraculous preservation through bitter times, when the intense animosity and violent antagonism of the surrounding Muslim nations issued in war after war. There is no question that God preserved this nation through the immediately-declared Arab War of 1948–49, the Suez War of 1956, the Six-Day War of 1967, the Yom Kippur War of 1973, and followed by the '*Intifadas*' – periods of civil disobedience by the Palestinians. Then emerged the terrorist groups like Fatah, the PLO, Hamas, and Hezbollah, some of which are still active and still carry out murderous attacks on Israel. Nevertheless *The Oxford Encyclopaedia of World History* records an interesting fact: 'After 1948 Jewish immigration into Israel took place from over 100 different nations, especially from communist and Arab countries, as well as from

Europe raising the population from 700,000 in 1948 to nearly 5.5 million by 1996.'[2] This period has spoken to the world of Divine preservation. This regathering of the nation has continued until the present. The spiritual condition of that nation is still total unbelief; hardly any other nation in the world is as closed to the gospel as the nation of Israel. The nation is back in the land but spiritually they are in total unbelief – Ezekiel spoke of movement but the 'bones were very dry' (Ezek. 37:1–2). This is the people that God will allow to come under the sway of the Antichrist before they appreciate the true Messiah.

From this situation it can be seen how this plausible and popular miracle worker (Rev. 13:11–17), who has come 'in his own name', is able to persuade the nation (or the majority of it) to place their trust in the world leader from the west. It will be a relief to Israel that a man of sufficient stature has emerged in the west, who carries sufficient authority and charisma to negotiate a peace treaty that satisfies the moderate Muslim world. Of course the world leader does this in cooperation with, or on behalf of, this man in Israel whom Daniel sees here as 'the self-willed king' who leads them into this false covenant – the signing of which marks the commencement of the Tribulation. God uses this Tribulation period to teach the nation of Israel what sin brings, so that they turn and seek the Saviour. This invasion just before the midpoint of that Tribulation period is part of the process. God is not finished with the nation of Israel, even at this point, but God would have them know that everyone entering the Kingdom must have new life through the new birth (Jn 3:3). God acts to preserve the nation with a view to their repentance, followed by remission of sins, that open the way to the regeneration and the restoration in the Kingdom of God. This is the goal to which God is working. This invasion is part of the Divine discipline. Paul could read the situation with spiritual intelligence as he wrote, 'For the wrath is come upon them to the uttermost' (1 Thess. 2:16).

[2] *The Oxford Encyclopaedia of World History*, p. 338.

(2) Invasion of Israel from the North. Links with prophecy given to Ezekiel

(a) The Timing of the Invasion

That the timing of this invasion of Israel can be linked with the timing of the invasion spoken of by Ezekiel (Ezek. 38:1–39:29) is almost self-evident when the following points are carefully considered. Compare the situation here with the prophetic statements from the prophecy of Ezekiel as set out below:

This invasion takes place when the people of Israel (Jews) have returned to their own land again and become a nation recognised by the United Nations (1948) as an independent state. Having rejected the Christ Whom God had sent, they plotted His death on the cross (Acts 2:22–23). God raised Him from the dead and received Him in the glory, and as a result the gospel, in the power of the Holy Spirit, has gone forth to all peoples and nations. Individuals from Israel have believed the gospel based on these facts, but the nation as a whole still refuses Christ and is looking for another. This other, at this point, has been supplied by Satan, as has been shown previously. This man will actually be the 'replacement' Christ – The Antichrist. This false messiah is the man who brought the covenant of peace to this nation of Israel in the time they were still unbelieving. They are enjoying this peace when the invasion comes.

Compare Ezekiel 38:8

Ezekiel identifies the time of the invasion when he addresses the northern invader:

> In the latter years thou shalt come into the land that is brought back from the sword, that is gathered out of many peoples, upon the mountains of Israel, which have been a continual waste: but it is brought forth out of the peoples, and they shall dwell securely, all of them' (*RV*).

It is true that Israel has been re-established in the land as an independent nation since May 14, 1948 but, in all the years since that, Israel has been on a constant war alert. An on-going war and several invasions by the surrounding Arab nations (1948–49, 1967, 1973) have kept defence budgets very high indeed. They have never enjoyed any period of real peace. This invasion clearly takes place when some peace agreement has been reached and the defence forces of Israel are no longer in a state of alert.

Compare Ezekiel 38:10–12

Again Ezekiel speaks:

> It shall come to pass in that day, that things shall come into thy mind, and thou shalt devise an evil device: and thou shalt say, 'I will go up to the land of unwalled villages; I will go to them that are at quiet, that dwell securely, all of them dwelling without walls, and having neither bars nor gates: to take the spoil and to take the prey' (*RV*).

This peace comes when Israel, led by the deceiver called here (in Daniel 11) 'the king', whom they have, in their spiritual blindness, accepted, enters into a peace covenant for seven years (see 9:27). Their security has been guaranteed by the mighty western emperor, ruler of the ten-power empire; a man to whom their king has given absolute allegiance and whom he accepts as god. Israel has been assured that if they should be attacked then a mighty overwhelming force stands ready to defend them. Israel is sufficiently reassured, and defences, so painstakingly put into place over the dangerous years, can now safely be dismantled. Israel, for the first time in its recent history, can now live in peace and enjoy prosperity. Even the more reasonable Islamic nations, once bitterly hostile to Israel, have agreed to the terms. It may well be that Arab states are numbered in the ten-powered kingdom of the western leader, which means that they, too, are committed to the peace of Israel. With moderate Islam in the ascendency, the Palestinian people have little option but to submit. Now, for the first time since the re-establishment of the nation, Israel can say 'We have peace'. But, as shown in the quotation, this invader has other ideas and other plans. Israel gets a very rude awakening.

(b) The Direction from which the Invasion Comes

This invasion takes place from the north. A preliminary move by Egypt in the south triggers the main invasion. Egypt, perhaps as a result of internal political changes, decides to make a gesture towards the leadership of militant Islam, and moves an army into Israel. This does not seem to be in any way decisive – the verb 'push at him' means 'to butt him like a goat' – which suggests more of an annoyance than a full-scale military invasion. Nevertheless, this tentative action so enrages a power north of Israel that he acts precipitately. Scripture says: 'the king of the north shall come against him like a whirlwind'. The antecedent of 'him' must be the king in Jerusalem, the same target as that of Egypt. Clearly this northern enemy will not allow the King of the South to claim any credit for the almost tentative nature of his attack; the King of the North is going to do the job completely; no half-way measures will be tolerated – Israel is to be totally destroyed and wiped off the world map.

Compare Ezekiel 38:15–16

> And thou shalt come from thy place out of the north parts, Thou and many people with thee, All of them riding upon horses, A great company, and a mighty army: And thou shalt come up against My people of Israel, as a cloud to cover the land; It shall be in the latter days, And I will bring thee against My land, That the heathen may know Me, when I shall be sanctified in thee, O Gog, before their eyes.

This northern invasion can only come during the first half of the seven-year Tribulation, since God is going to leave a testimony for Himself on earth when He destroys the invader – this rules out the invasion from the east leading up to Armageddon. It is suggested that this fits Daniel's time frame exactly – since it must take place just before the midpoint of the seventieth week (9:24–27).

(c) The Identification of the Invading Nations

Compare Ezekiel 38:1–6

The leader of this northern invader is spoken of as Gog, generally understood as meaning 'expansion' – who must be an individual (see Ezek. 38:14). The name is found on one other occasion in the OT (1 Chron. 5:4) and once in the NT (Rev. 20:8). He is called the 'chief prince' of Meshech and Tubal. These were two provinces in Asia associated with the Scythians in Roman times. Today the geographical area would be largely lie in Iran and Turkey, touching the southern parts of Russia. Magog is generally accepted as meaning 'extension' and refers to the peoples led by Gog. These people are identified as 'Meshech and Tubal' (Ezek. 38:3), 'Gomer, and all his bands; the house of Togarmah of the north quarters, and all his bands' (Ezek. 38:6). Today, these peoples all live north of Israel, in a sweeping crescent from southern Russia through Turkey eastwards to Pakistan. Today, while these people live in different political states under different regimes, the remarkable thing is that the population of each of the states is predominately Muslim. The vast majority of the Muslims belong to the Shi'ite branch of Islam – recognised as the most militant branch. Nine ethnic peoples are named, crossing several political boundaries, and today they represent, in the name of militant Islam, a very vociferous and a very united bitter opposition to the very existence of Israel.

Compare Ezekiel 38:5

It should also be observed that the allies of this bloc of peoples are named. They are given as Persia, Ethiopia, and Libya. Present day names of these nations are Iran, Sudan and Libya. In recent times it is interesting to note that these nations have been the most virulent and most violent of the nations in their opposition to Israel. In fact at present on the world stage it is abundantly clear that Iran, formerly called Persia, is now the leader in the bitter opposition to Israel.

(d) The Leader of the Invasion

There remains the identity of this 'king of the north' – the leader of this invasion. It is accepted that the King of the North in Daniel's fourth vision has always been the king of the Seleucid line, who ruled the whole segment of the Greek Empire bequeathed to the successors of Alexander the Great at his death (323 BC). The segment secured to Seleucus, hence the Seleucid dynasty, lay to the north of Israel, from the Mediterranean coast to the Persian Gulf. In modern terms it embraced the greater part of Turkey, all of Syria, all Iraq, and most of Iran, down to the Persian Gulf. The capital of the Seleucid Empire was Antioch, lying directly north of Israel. This situation existed until Rome, under Pompey, in 64 BC, brought the Seleucid dynasty to a close, annexed all the lands under its control, and included the land of Judaea in Rome's growing empire. In these opening years of the twenty-first century the most outspoken enemy of Israel is without question Iran:

Aim of Iran President Mahmoud Ahmadinejad (2005–2013) was determined to present himself as leader of the Arab world; indeed, leader of all Islamic nations. What he achieved was to make himself the leader, the main supporter and the wealthy supplier of militant Islamic forces throughout the world.

Ambition of Iran To possess nuclear weapons. In defiance of world opinion, investigators agree that Iran is very close (2013) to developing this ultimate threat. The president made no secret of its purpose – to wipe Israel off the world map. On Arab maps, Israel does not exist – the whole area is called Palestine.

At this point it is necessary to look again at the lead nation of the invader in Ezekiel (chapters 38–39). Older commentators have always pointed out that the terms Magog, Rosh, Meshech, and Tubal are of Russian origin. The peoples mentioned above – nine groups are mentioned – have migrated northwards from the old Seleucid Empire – that which has drawn them together is not the USSR, which, since 1991, no longer exists, but the tighter cords of Islam. In the passage there are statements that have often been generally overlooked. However, in the political scene of the present day, they take on a new significance. The prophetic voice speaks to Gog: 'and I will turn you about, and put hooks into thy jaws, and I will bring you forth, and all your army, horses and horsemen, all of them clothed in full armour' (Ezek. 38:4, *RSV*). These statements indicate that Russia is not the leading nation in this invasion, as many commentators would assert, but Russia is being dragged into this invasion reluctantly by others. Notice the expression 'hooks in your jaws', which indicates the reluctance of Russia, nationally and politically, to get involved; but the Islamic link is decisive. It is suggested that this summons could come from a nation like Iran, announcing an Islamic '*jihad*' and finding an eager ear amongst the Muslim peoples of the northern area, where Russia is in control. Russia would then be dragged in to support the invasion. That, however, is earth politics; heaven's purpose is different. God allows this invasion for: (a) the discipline of His people Israel (Ezek. 39:7, 21–24); (b) a testimony to the world of His power (Ezek. 38:16, 23), when He destroys the invader; (c) the judgement of Gog and Magog (Ezek. 39:1–6), who through the centuries have treated God's chosen nation most cruelly.

If this reading of the passage and identification of this northern invader with Ezekiel's prophecy is correct then an immediate question springs to mind. Recalling the peace covenant with Israel, why does the Man of Sin, the leader of the ten-power empire, embracing the most powerful nations of the earth, not come immediately to the relief of his beleaguered ally in Jerusalem? There is, of course, a protest, as recorded: 'Sheba, and Dedan, and the merchants of Tarshish, with all the young lions thereof, shall say unto thee, "Art thou come to take a spoil? Hast thou gathered thy company to take a prey? To carry away silver and gold, to take away cattle and goods, to take a great spoil?"'(Ezek. 38:13). These protests, possibly through the United Nations, are unbelievably weak and certainly ineffective. In the context, the list of protesters is fascinating, as it indicates that both moderate Islam and the western world power are opposed to it but, for different reasons, take no decisive action. Both world powers deliberately hold back and take no military action in support of Israel. Three protestors are identified in Ezekiel 38:13:

(a) Sheba. Son of Raamah, grandson of Cush (Gen. 10:6–7). Authorities agree he settled on the shores of the Persian Gulf;

(b) Dedan. Brother of Sheba, son of Raamah, grandson of Cush. Also settled around the Persian Gulf. This identification would suggest that a large part of the Islamic world along the Persian Gulf, including the moderate Islamic states of Saudi Arabia, Kuwait, and Dubai, are not in favour of this attack. It is certainly within the scope of prophetic vision that some of the Persian Gulf States may be represented in the ten horns of the Beast and the ten toes of the image. They would represent moderate Islam and would have been a key factor in the peace covenant. Now they would be totally opposed to this invasion of Israel. A possible reason for this is that their leaders are only too well aware of their own vulnerability before extremists in their own lands;

(c) 'Merchants of Tarshish, with all the young lions thereof'. Tarshish is a Phoenician word that had to do originally with the mining of metals. The earliest records in which this word is met go back to the mines in Cyprus. When the mines in Cyprus could not meet the demand for the metal, the industry, and its related vocabulary, moved westwards, to Spain and then to Cornwall. The word included the whole operation to produce the tin – the mining, smelting and refining of the metal. Spain, because of its importance in this trade in early times, was called 'Tartassus'. Reference to 'the merchants of Tarshish' or 'ships of Tarshish' became synonymous with the idea of western power and influence outside the Mediterranean area.

There is no doubt that the western supporter of this king in Israel would protest loudly at this violation of the covenant that has allowed Israel to live in peace for the last three-and-a-half years. However, the western powers, having had their fingers burned badly in Vietnam, Afghanistan and Iraq, would be slow to react militarily. They seem to hesitate to come to the aid of Israel. The result is that the western support upon which Israel has relied will prove totally ineffective. The word of a man in whom Israel trusted has not been kept – he has deceived them. Meantime God acts dramatically in Divine power.

The invading army is 'like a whirlwind' and Ezekiel describes it in words given him by the Lord: 'Thou shalt ascend and come like a storm, thou shalt be like a cloud to cover the land, thou, and all thy bands, and many people with thee' (Ezek. 38:9). Sweeping down from the north, these 'flood' waters overwhelm those who stand in their path – 'countries' (Dan. 11:40) is in the plural. Leaving desolation behind, they sweep towards Israel. Many will be the emergency meetings – the General Assembly and Security Council of the United Nations, or their successors, will be in constant session as this invader sweeps all before him.

This northern invader sweeps into Israel and carries the battle right down through Israel, to Egypt. There he fastens on the wealth of Egypt (v. 43), doubtless in retaliation for its attempt to pre-empt the leadership of the Islamic world by being the first to launch an attack against Israel. They would be angry about the half-hearted attack that had been launched ahead of the northern attack. It is interesting to note that in this record Daniel is told, 'and the Libyans and the Ethiopians shall be at his steps' (v. 43). It will be recalled that three nations were mentioned by Ezekiel: 'Persia, Ethiopia, and Libya with them' (Ezek. 38:5). In the world of today Persia has become Iran. These militant Islamic hordes have no time for any moderate voice in their ranks, so Egypt is subdued at the same time as Israel. This lends support to the suggestion that this northern invader of Israel is the forces of militant Islam, led by the present day king of the north – Iran.[3]

(e) The Judgement of the Invader

Shocked by news from the east and further news from the north received just as he reaches the peak of his conquests in Egypt, the invader returns in great rage to settle his capital of empire in Jerusalem. The final detail is in the summary statement 'he shall come to his end, and none shall help him'. Suddenly, and yet completely and utterly, he and his army are destroyed on 'the

[3] The same area of land has borne the name of Persia, which was replaced by Syria and then by Iran.

mountains of Israel'. The God of Israel has moved to the preservation of Israel. Even in the darkest of times there is still a remnant for which God has a purpose. God uses a variety of instruments to destroy the invader:

(a) The earthquake – 'Surely in that day there shall be a great shaking in the land of Israel' (Ezek. 38:19).

(b) The internal tensions in such a disparate army – 'I will call for a sword against him throughout all My mountains ... every man's sword shall be against his brother' (Ezek. 38:21).

(c) The pestilence – 'I will plead against him with pestilence and with blood' (Ezek. 38:22).

(d) The flood – 'And I will rain upon him, and upon his bands, and upon the many people that are with him, an overflowing rain, and great hailstones, fire, and brimstone' (Ezek. 38:22).

(e) Almost total destruction – 'I will turn thee back, and leave but the sixth part of thee, ... thou shalt fall upon the mountains of Israel, thou, and all thy bands, and the people that is with thee: I will give thee unto the ravenous birds of every sort, and to the beasts of the field to be devoured. Thou shalt fall upon the open field: for I have spoken it, saith the Lord God' (Ezek. 39:2–5).

It takes seven months to bury the dead from this devastating destruction. A valley is named as a testimony to the deliverance of Israel and called 'Hamon-gog' – God has dealt suitably with the 'multitude of Gog' (Ezek. 39:11). The testimony resounds round the earth:

> So will I make My holy name known in the midst of My people Israel; and I will not let them pollute My holy name any more: and the heathen shall know that I am the LORD, the Holy One in Israel (Ezek. 39:7).

2. The Structure of the Chapter

The Close of the Final Vision	vv. 1–3
The Closing Charge to Daniel	v. 4
The Closing Scene and Closing Questions:	vv. 5–10
(a) Question of the Angel	vv. 6–7
(b) Question of Daniel	vv. 8–10
The Coming of the King	vv. 11–12
(a) Realisation of the Throne	v. 11
(b) Realisation of the Kingdom	v. 12
The Closing Benediction	v. 13

Exposition

Verses 1–3 The Close of the Final Vision

With surprising unanimity commentators agree that the first three verses of this chapter complete the fourth vision granted to Daniel. The chapter division interrupts the message of the interpreting angel, which runs from chapter 10:1 to chapter 12:4, with the final verse being a direct instruction to Daniel regarding the revelation given to him. As just pointed out, the opening words of the chapter fully support this link. It is thus at this midpoint of the seventieth week that Michael the archangel stands to his feet.

That Michael stands up is clearly the response to what has happened on earth. The Man of Sin has claimed Deity and the Antichrist, in Jerusalem, has supported him; rebellion on earth against heaven has reached the high point – it can scarcely go higher. Michael's action is his response, as he recognises that Israel, the nation for which he has special responsibility, faces at this point the darkest period in its long and dark history. Michael feels his responsibility for Israel and moves into action.

Daniel has already been shown (10:20–21) that there are spiritual powers at work behind the scenes seeking to direct and control the actions of the nations of earth. In the execution of His purposes God has delegated certain tasks to trusted agents in the angelic realm. Satan, the inveterate and implacable opponent of God, has under his control the angels who followed him into rebellion against God, and he too places his agents strategically amongst the nations (10:13), where they can be most effective in opposition to God – His person, His purposes, and His people.

Michael is one of God's most able angels, named on five occasions in Scripture, listed as follows:

(a) 'Michael, one of the chief princes' (10:13)
(b) 'Michael your prince' (10:21)
(c) 'Michael ... the great prince which standeth [up] for the children of thy people' (12:1)
(d) 'Michael the archangel' (Jude 9)
(e) 'Michael and his angels' (Rev. 12:7)

'Michael' means 'Who is like God?' The only one called 'archangel' in Scripture, not only does he hold the highest rank in the angelic hierarchy, but he is charged with special responsibility before God for the nation central to Divine purpose in the bringing in of the Redeemer. No wonder that as Michael takes action satanic forces respond immediately to something they recognise as a sign of aid for Israel, the special object of satanic venom.[1]

Michael is described here in a literal translation[2] as 'the one standing over the sons of your people'. The idea in the verb is 'to be a guard'. The expression 'the children of thy people' seems to put a difference between the fathers of their nation, who had been so responsive to Divine revelation, and the nation presently in Babylon who are natural progeny but show little evidence spiritually of the faith of their fathers. Their God, while unable to publicly identify with the nation because of their unbelief, still has a place for them in Divine purpose. The very judgements to burst upon them in the Tribulation will testify of a holy God desirous of the recovery of His people.

A time of trouble that surpasses anything that this nation has ever gone through previously is just about to burst upon Israel. As the history of Israel is reviewed, and the dreadful times of persecution they have suffered down the ages are recalled, it makes this period frightening to contemplate. How anything could be worse than the Holocaust, when the genocide policy of Nazi Germany led six million Jews to the gas chambers of Auschwitz and

[1] Only one other angel is named in Scripture. This is Gabriel, mentioned four times:
(1) 'Gabriel, make this man to understand the vision' (8:16);
(2) 'The man Gabriel ... touched me' (9:21);
(3) 'I am Gabriel, that stand in the presence of God; and am sent to speak unto thee' (Lk. 1:19);
(4) 'and in the sixth month the angel Gabriel was sent from God ... to a virgin' (Lk. 1:26,27).
'Gabriel means 'man of God, ambassador'. It can be seen that Gabriel holds a most responsible post as the angelic messenger to deliver God's message to individuals.

[2] Wood, *A Commentary on Daniel*, p. 316.

Buchenwald, is hard to understand. This time of distress is described to Daniel in a way that marks it out as a unique period in history – 'there shall be a time of trouble, such as never was since there was a nation even to that same time'. On the Mount of Olives, on the Tuesday afternoon before the cross, the Lord spoke of this same time when He said, 'For then shall be great tribulation, such as was not since the beginning of the world to this time, no, nor ever shall be' (Mt. 24:21). So both terms, claiming uniqueness, must point to the same unique period – the last three-and-a-half-years of the seven-year Tribulation period. The seven-year period commenced with the confirmation of the peace in Israel, when the king in Jerusalem and the ruler of the ten-power empire in the west signed the covenant of peace in Israel (9:27). The whole period of seven years is called 'The Tribulation' but the last half of that week is distinguished as 'The Tribulation – The Great one' (Mt. 24:21; Rev. 7:14). This latter period begins when the 'abomination of desolation' is set up on the wing of the Temple in Jerusalem (Mt. 24:15) and ends when the Lord's feet stand on the Mount of Olives (Zech. 14:4). It will be exactly 'a time, times and a half' (v. 7; Rev. 12:14); this is 1,260 days (Rev. 12:6). This same period is called by the prophet Jeremiah 'the time of Jacob's trouble' (Jer. 30:7). There can be no doubt that this period will be the darkest that nation has ever been through in all its troubled history. Michael, knowing that this critical period has arrived, and in contemplation of the dreadful years for Israel, and recognising his responsibility, stands to his feet as an indication that he is about to deal with the situation and exercise his protective ministry over Israel.

The action of Michael in rising to his feet implies, in the context, that he is now going to take deliberate and decisive action in the defence and protection of the true Israel. In this day of militant unbelief in the nation, with the Temple defiled, and the image of the world leader standing on the Temple wing, there are still those who stand apart and refuse to bow to the image, or indeed to any of his images in municipal halls or business boardrooms across the nation. This refusal to bow to the image or accept the name, or number or mark associated with the Beast invites denunciation by colleagues, neighbours or family; the penalty is death. For any subjects of the empire of the Beast to aid such a rebel with food, shelter or care of any sort, is to put their own lives at risk (Mt. 25:31–46). The result is that only true believers will dare identify themselves in this way. It will be Michael's responsibility to move nations and individuals to the preservation of the true Israel – now it is just a remnant of the nation that is faithful to God. In the Revelation, the same truth is presented in symbolic terms in the flight of the woman, and her Divine preservation during this dark period of 'a thousand two hundred and threescore days' (Rev. 12:6–17). Behind this preservation there will be the operations of Michael as he fulfils his responsibilities.

As NT light is allowed to shine on this crisis point in the Tribulation the complete picture begins to come into focus. This Excursus is a suggested link-up between this Book of Daniel and the Book of Revelation. It does not interfere with the verse-by-verse exposition but will contribute to the understanding of the brief statements in the text.

Excursus 1 The Midpoint of the Tribulation

War in Heaven (Rev. 12:7-17) – Cause and Consequences

There is no problem in recognising in the scene referred to in Revelation 12 heaven's view of the same point in the history of Israel. However, there is an added factor that is not mentioned to Daniel. As Michael stands up there is an instant reaction from the satanic powers. The result is: 'And there was war in heaven: Michael and his angels fought against the dragon; and the dragon fought and his angels, and prevailed not; neither was their place found any more in heaven' (Rev. 12:7–8). The casting out of heaven of the Devil and his angels makes him turn in rage upon the woman. Since the woman is to be fed secretly for 'a thousand two hundred and threescore days' (Rev. 12:6), we see that the war in heaven takes place at the midpoint of the Tribulation. The flight of the woman (Rev. 12:6) is the moment of which the Lord spoke: 'When ye therefore shall see the abomination of desolation, spoken of by Daniel the prophet, stand in the holy place, ... then let them which be in Judaea flee into the mountains' (Mt. 24:15–16). To make sure the time point has been recognised, the period that follows is mentioned twice:

(a) 'And the woman fled into the wilderness, where she hath a place prepared of God, that they should feed her there a thousand two hundred and threescore days' (Rev. 12:6); and

(b) 'And to the woman were given two wings of a great eagle, that she might fly into the wilderness, into her place, where she is nourished for a time, and times, and half a time, from the face of the serpent' (Rev. 12:14).

It should be clear that Scripture uses the prophetic year of 360 days. The various terms used in prophetic Scripture, both in the OT and the NT, all point to the 360–day prophetic year. The terms are: 'three-and-a-half years'; 'time and times and half a time'; 'forty-two months'; and 1,260 days. Doubtless, when 'days' are used it indicates the sympathy that flows out of a kindred heart, sharing the daily pain of a persecuted people.

From John's account of this war in heaven in the book of Revelation (Rev. 12:7), a hasty judgement might conclude that the movement of Michael to the aid of Israel precipitated the war, and so the expulsion of Satan from his base in the heavenly regions in a rage exacerbates the situation for Israel. Such human reasoning would make Michael guilty of acting either mistakenly or hastily.[3] There is not a shred of evidence to suggest such a conclusion. The opposite is true. From what was happening on earth at this point Michael knew that, in keeping with his responsibilities, he was compelled to act, or the nation of Israel would be wiped out. Satan's reaction, of course, precipitated his own downfall. First he was 'cast unto the earth' (Rev. 12:13), then the second step was 'cast into the bottomless pit (abyss)' (Rev. 20:3), and the third step sealed his doom: finally and forever 'cast into the lake of fire' (Rev. 20:10). Ignominious defeat followed by ignominious dismissal at each stage means that he ends up in eternal death – the lake of fire. Michael moves to the defence of the true Israel on earth, identified as 'the remnant of her seed, which keep the commandments of God, and have the testimony of Jesus Christ' (Rev. 12:17).

It is now vital to see why Michael had to act at this point in the timetable of God. This may best be seen by a review and a summary of events that take place just before, and just after, the midpoint of

[3] The location of this battle is often discussed since it is described as being 'in heaven'. Our risen Lord has 'passed through the heavens' (Heb. 4:14, *RV*), a reference to the aerial and the astral heavens, and having become 'higher than the heavens' (Heb. 7:26) has entered into 'heaven itself, now to appear in the presence of God for us' (Heb. 9:24). The 'third heaven' is identified with Paradise, where God is and Christ dwells (2 Cor. 12:2–4) and where the saved of earth gather (Lk. 23:43) to be with Christ. This cannot be the realm where this battle takes place. Neither has it any reference to the battle in 'the heavenlies' (Eph. 6:10–18), which deals with a different line of truth entirely. It is clear that there was a certain area above, to which all angels had access, and even after his fall Satan still had access (Job 1:6; 2:1), where he was free to accuse the saints. It is from this heavenly base for angelic beings that Satan is expelled at this point and begins that downward path that ends in the lake of fire (Rev. 20:10).

the Tribulation period. There is no doubt that this is the crucial point in the prophetic end-time programme. As both Daniel the prophet and John the apostle are presenting truth for the same period, it will be useful to see the picture that emerges as both Daniel and John are allowed to highlight the same events. Bringing the picture into the timeline enables the whole panorama to be seen, despite the repetition that is required.

Summary and Review for Reference

Just before the Midpoint of the Seventieth Week: (see commentary on verses 36–45)

Israel Invasion of Israel by a northern power (old name Syria, present name Iran) leading a militant Islamic horde; Russia reluctantly drawn in as a result of militant Islamic majorities within her boundaries and nations under her sway (Ezek. 38:1–13; Dan. 11:40–45). This invader moves through Israel, like a whirlwind, as far south as Egypt.

World Protests from western and moderate Arab nations prove futile (Ezek. 38:13).

News from the north (Israel) and from the east (Rev. 9:13–19) trouble the invader as he pillages Egypt.

The invader returns to Israel and plants his headquarters in Jerusalem.

The invading army is wiped out by God on the mountains of Israel (Ezek. 38:14–39:29).

The Sequel Events follow each other in rapid succession. The western leader of the ten-power empire, realising what is at stake, moves quickly to secure his position. Now that the militant Islamic power supported by Russia has had a devastating setback, with its military forces wiped out on the mountains of Israel, there is no other power, except China, to oppose him. While deeply disturbed, China is not yet ready to confront him but, with deadly purpose, begins the mobilisation of the mightiest military force ever assembled (Rev. 9:16–19). This mobilisation will take time and it is towards the end of the Tribulation that these forces of two hundred million men move westwards in battle array (Rev. 16:12). In the modern era this would involve the utilisation of bases already possessed, or possibly leased, west of the Euphrates.

The Sequence We know from various Scriptures the events that are to occur. However, the order in which they occur is not always easily determined and there are widely differing views. The following is simply a suggested sequence that seeks to follow a logical train of thought, yet allows Scripture to carry its full authority in each event:

This swift invasion of Israel from the north is dealt with just as swiftly by God. Following this dramatic intervention by God, the first move, politically, of the western leader, would be to visit the delivered city – Jerusalem. Perhaps he is anxious to explain why he did not come immediately to the aid of his political protégé; he might even claim some credit for his actions in restraining the moderate Islamic nations from joining the invader. Whatever the ostensible reason, both men could well join together in a great show of unity and harmony in a national celebration to mark the overthrow of the northern invader. This suggestion offers a plausible scenario as a background for something that must happen in a very public way: this western leader is assassinated! Bringing the scriptural identifications already met in this study together, this western leader is seen in Daniel as the 'little horn' (Dan 7:8, 23–25) and the Coming Prince (9:26), while in the NT he is called the 'beast from the sea' (Rev. 13:1–8) and the 'Man of Sin' (2 Thess. 2:3). This mighty puppet-prince of Satan is suddenly cut down in a very public way. The scriptural record reads concerning the Beast with the seven heads: 'I saw one of his heads as it were wounded to death' (Rev. 13:3). Out of the crowd steps an assassin with bomb, bullet or knife. In the presence of a horrified world audience provided by the world media coverage, he is assassinated – or it certainly seems so. The doubt as to the reality of his death lies in the scriptural qualification 'as it were' (Rev. 13:3). All may not be as it appears to be, for the very next statement reads simply 'and his deadly wound was healed'. The dramatic and sudden reappearance of this man supports the possibility of a satanic plot. There can be no surprise at how men respond to this supposedly resurrected man, now identified as 'the beast that ascendeth out of the bottomless pit' (Rev. 11:7). The seventh head of this final world empire has become the eighth by a pseudo-resurrection (Rev. 17:9–11).[4] The world has no doubt. They have now, in this man, what men

[4] Allen, *What the Bible Teaches, Revelation*, pp. 424 ff.

have long awaited: a man alive from the dead. This will lend enormous credibility to this man in the eyes of Israel, and they have not a single doubt that the supernatural power displayed by their miracle-working king, in giving this man his full support, demonstrates his prophetic office (Rev. 13:13–16). Israel and the nations respond unreservedly. The reaction is uninhibited – 'the world wondered after the beast. And they worshipped the dragon which gave power unto the beast: and they worshipped the beast' (Rev. 13:3–4).[5]

This assassination-resurrection scenario provides the background for this man to take three dramatic steps:

1. Claim Deity. He takes his seat in the Temple in Jerusalem. This is the moment of his revelation: 'that man of sin be revealed' (2 Thess. 2: 2–3). The word for revelation is *apokalupsis,* meaning 'the dropping of the veil'. Now all deception is over; he is revealed as 'the son of perdition; who opposeth and exalteth himself above all that is called God, or that is worshipped; so that he as God sitteth in the temple of God, shewing himself that he is God' (2 Thess. 2:3–4).[6]

2. Receive Worship. His satanic colleague in Jerusalem acts as a prophet; Scripture acknowledges the term but calls him a 'false prophet' (Rev. 16:13; 19:20; 20:10). He demands that an idol be made to represent this Man of Sin. Scripture highlights his activity:

> And he doeth great wonders, so that he maketh fire come down from heaven on the earth in the sight of men, and deceiveth them that dwell on the earth by the means of those miracles which he had power to do in the sight of the beast (Rev. 13:13–14).

Now, he goes even further and acts as a priest, pointing men to this anti-god (Rev. 13:6), 'saying to them that dwell on the earth, that they should make an image to the beast, which had the wound by a sword, and did live' (Rev. 13:14).

3. Permit the Erection of his Image. The Antichrist, in Jerusalem, erects the image of his 'god' on the wing of the Temple in Jerusalem.

[5] The world saw the US President J.F. Kennedy shot in Dallas on November 22, 1963.The last sight of him by the public was his body, on a hospital trolley, being rushed into theatre. How would that same world have responded if, next morning he had appeared on national TV programmes fit and well?

[6] This is not his coming politically; the word used for this is '*parousia*' (2 Thess. 2:9), when he signs the covenant at the beginning of the seventieth week; his revelation religiously ('*apocalypse*') is the midpoint of the week, when he drops the veil and takes his seat in the Temple.

This is the 'abomination of desolation' (Mt. 24:15; 12:11). Desolation spreads in the wake of this idol worship, which becomes the final form of Babylonian idolatry. The immediate effect of this is felt in Jerusalem, where there is: (a) the cessation of the sacrificial worship of Judaism (9:27); (b) the persecution of Jews who refuse to worship the image (Mt. 24:16–21). As a consequence there is an immediate flight of multitudes of Israel (Rev. 12:6); (c) the introduction of sanctions in Israel, and subsequently in other nations, against all who refuse the mark of the Beast (Rev. 13:16–17). This new religion soon sweeps through politics, commerce, and society in general, over the ten-power kingdom of the Beast, so that his image is reproduced in parliaments, municipal buildings, council chambers, and boardrooms, as men identify themselves with this world emperor. As believers reject the mark of the Beast, they cannot buy nor sell. Believers are penalised commercially for their intransigence in refusing the mark, then ostracised socially for their faith in Christ, and then are soon persecuted officially for their 'rebellion' against the state – this is symbolised in the image. Believers thus become the target of satanic venom, embodied in these two satanic puppets, whose purpose is the complete destruction of Israel and every believer in Christ (Rev. 13:7–8). At this point the world sees them as winning the battle. **(End of Excursus 1).**

Verse 1 It is just at this point that Michael rises to his feet to bring sorely needed relief to the remnant of Israel. Persecution being waged against all refusing to bow to the image puts every Jew under pressure, and Michael's aid will be vital if any are to survive. Other Scriptures show that Gentile believers will also come under that same pressure, but Daniel's focus is Israel. Those who are thus protected and preserved are spoken of as 'thy people'. Each believer, persecuted and harassed as they are, who proves fearless in the declaration of faith in Christ will be as Nathanael was – 'an Israelite indeed' (Jn 1:47). Thus every single genuine believer in Christ will be delivered. This does not mean they will escape death, for many of them will die (Rev. 15:2–4), but these martyrs will share, with their living brethren, in the ultimate deliverance brought by Christ when He appears at the close of the Tribulation (Rom. 11:26–27). With all the pressure upon them, their faith does not fail. This interpretation is supported by the next sentence: 'every one that shall be found written in the book'.

This book stands in contrast to 'the books' mentioned earlier in this prophecy (7:10). Those earlier books have been shown to be the records of history, kept in heaven, but now opened, to show the justice of the judgements to be poured upon people on earth. A comparable situation is seen at the great white throne (Rev. 20:12), where we read: 'And the books were opened ... and the dead were judged out of those things which were written in the books'. Not nations, but individual sinners from the nations, stand at the great white throne and receive their sentence before they go into their eternal abode. Of more relevance to this passage is the next statement in the great white throne scene: 'and another book was opened, which is the book of life' (Rev. 20:12). This is the register of heaven; the list of the names of those who have come to Christ as Saviour during their lifetime on earth. Reference to this book at the great white throne will show that no mistake has been made. No record of their names means that they never got to know the Saviour during their life on earth.

It is suggested that the book in this verse is the same Book of Life – the heavenly register of those who on earth have believed God, received life, and immediately had their names written in God's book. In the two passages in the OT where the 'book of the living' is mentioned (Ps. 69:28, see also Exod. 32:33) it is clear that it refers to the register of those alive on earth at a specific time. 'To blot out a name' from that book is a metaphorical term synonymous with physical death. So this cannot be the book in question here, since many of these saints die physically. Here the term 'found written in the book' acquaints Michael with those who come under his mandate – those whose names are written in the 'Book of life'. There are eight NT references to this Book of Life, seven of them in the book of Revelation (Phil. 4:3; Rev. 3:5; 13:8; 17:8; 20:12,15; 21:27; 22:19; no book is mentioned in Lk. 10:20). This book is the Divine register of the names of all those who, down the ages, have believed in Christ. Now, in Tribulation days, such believers are being persecuted unto death by the Beast and the false prophet. There is no scriptural reason to make any difference between the Book of Life and the Lamb's Book of Life. This verse shows the reality of the faith of these tried believers – whether they live or die, they will share in the deliverance that Christ brings on His return to earth. Since it is clear that many believers die in the Tribulation, the protection afforded by Michael must be preservation of their faith and testimony, even up to and through death.

This one statement is all that is revealed in this book of Daniel of the severe trials befalling believers in Christ and, indeed, all those who will not worship the Beast, in the last half of the seven-year Tribulation period. Daniel's focus is, of course, the people of Israel and why God allows this time of Jacob's trouble (Jer. 30:7). When the earth and the nations of the world are in view the much more detailed picture is given to John, as unfolded in Revelation 4:1–19:11, where, under the different stages of judgement, seen in the seals, the trumpets and the vials, the earth shakes as God deals with rebellious men, led by the Man of Sin and the Antichrist. This enables us to keep the whole picture before the mind. In light of these conditions Michael has a weighty responsibility.

Verse 2 In this verse the focus of the picture moves to the very end of the Tribulation period. In doing this it is, undoubtedly, answering the question of deliverance of saints who die during the Tribulation. It has already been pointed out that Michael's deliverance is afforded to believers who are the special target of satanic animosity. This deliverance does not mean that they are preserved from physical death; many of them do die (Rev. 6:11). This deliverance is much more embracive than mere escape from physical death. Many will die a martyr's death for refusal to take the mark of the Beast (Rev. 15:2–4). The question arises as to what 'deliverance' means in their case. The answer is here in this very passage: death is not the end of their story. After the trial and the tears comes the triumph – resurrection! This resurrection occurs at the end of the Tribulation and before the commencement of the millennial reign of Christ.

It is abundantly clear that there will be two distinct parties in the nation of Israel during these years at the close of the Tribulation. There will be those who 'believe what is false' (2 Thess. 2:11, *NET*) and follow the Antichrist in bowing to the image of the Man of Sin (who claims Deity); eagerly they accept his mark, his number and his name. The second group are those who, having heard the gospel of the Kingdom, through the 144,000 and their converts, have believed it and are awaiting the coming King. They have refused to bow to the image or owe any allegiance to the Beast and are prepared to die for their testimony. When Christ comes to earth in glory (Rev. 19:11), then the living saints from Israel, as well as the unnumbered multitude from the Gentile nations (Rev. 7:9–17), enjoy His triumph – they have a great deliverance (Rom 11:26–27). The problem immediately rises in this context – what of those who have died?

The answer is before us in this verse – the literal, physical resurrection of these saints from among the dead to join with their living compatriots in entering the Kingdom on earth.

Excursus 2 At the Close of the Tribulation The Resurrection of OT Saints

New Testament Scripture: The Resurrection and Reign of Saints with Christ

This agrees perfectly, in context and in timing, with the scene in the Revelation observed by John:

> And I saw thrones, and they sat upon them, and judgment was given unto them: and I saw the souls of them that were beheaded for the witness of Jesus, and for the word of God, and which had not worshipped the beast, neither his image, neither had received his mark upon their foreheads, or in their hands; and they lived and reigned with Christ a thousand years (Rev. 20:4).

Since this is the Kingdom promised, expected, and prayed for down the ages it is submitted that this is the point in the Divine programme when the OT saints will be raised from the grave to enter the Kingdom.

Resurrection is no new truth. Abraham anticipated resurrection when he offered up Isaac (Gen. 22:5; Heb. 11:19). Job, very possibly contemporary with Abraham, saw the truth of resurrection clearly: 'For I know that my Redeemer liveth, and that He shall stand at the latter day upon the earth: And though after my skin worms destroy this body, yet in my flesh shall I see God' (Job 19:25–26). Saints, very likely of Maccabean times, 'were tortured, not accepting deliverance; that they might obtain a better resurrection'. Isaiah, a century before Daniel, spoke of resurrection: 'thy dead men shall live, together with my dead body shall they arise' (Isa. 26:19). The promise of Hosea (a contemporary of Isaiah) is clear: 'I will ransom them from the power of the grave; I will redeem them from death' (Hos. 13:14). Daniel is simply restating the accepted truth of bodily resurrection, and putting it in its time frame, at the close of the Tribulation and the establishment of the Kingdom. This timing agrees with that given to John – at the setting up of the Kingdom, as described thus: 'The kingdoms of this world are become the kingdoms of our Lord, and of His Christ; and He shall reign for ever and ever' (Rev. 11:15). It is just at this point that a vital question must arise as to when these saints are judged. The Judgement Seat of Christ, for the Church, is already past. This passage answers the question and shows that the judgement of these saints follows their resurrection – 'and the time of the dead, that they should be judged, and that Thou shouldest give reward unto Thy servants the prophets, and to the saints, and them that fear Thy name, small and great' (Rev. 11:18). Old Testament saints and the martyred dead of the Tribulation period are judged by the Lord after resurrection, before they go into the Kingdom. This follows a similar pattern to the resurrection of New Testament believers, at the Rapture (1 Thess. 4:13–18) and subsequent judgement at the Judgment Seat of Christ (2 Cor. 5:10). The expression 'the dead in Christ' can only embrace believers of the Church age – from Pentecost to the Rapture. The expression 'they that are Christ's' (1 Cor. 15:23) is a more comprehensive phrase and covers all believers from every dispensation. However, it is explained by the qualifying phrase 'every man in his own order', which implies that the first resurrection has a number of stages.

Some have objected to physical resurrection in this passage on the ground that it seems to teach a general resurrection of saved and unsaved, which is plainly contrary to Scripture (Jn 5:28–29; Rev. 20:4–5). At first glance our text seems to divide the many (the raised ones) into two companies: company A is defined – 'some to everlasting life'; company B is defined – 'some to shame and everlasting contempt'. Hebrew grammarians insist, however, that this does not do justice to the Hebrew text and leads to a wrong interpretation. Amongst those objecting grammarians is S.P. Tregelles, who writes: 'The word which in our AV is twice rendered 'some' is never repeated in any other passage in the Hebrew Bible, in the sense of taking up distributively any general class which had been previously mentioned.'[7] Tregelles translates as follows: 'and many from the dust of the earth shall awake; *these* (the ones who awake) shall be to everlasting life; but *those* (the rest of the sleepers, who do not awake at this time), shall be unto shame and everlasting contempt'. The phrase 'everlasting life' is used here for the first time in the OT, but it carries exactly the same meaning here in Hebrew as it does in the NT in Greek. These saints are raised (leaving the unsaved dead in the grave), not only to enter into the glory of the

[7] Tregelles, *Tregelles on Daniel*, p. 164, italics added.

Kingdom but to enjoy that life eternal already possessed. This fits in with NT teaching exactly as set out in the first resurrection, which is here completed in the saints of the OT with the martyred dead of the Tribulation period, raised together to reign with Christ (Rev. 20:4). The NT statement throws further light on the subject, as it speaks of this same moment at the close of the Tribulation:

> And they lived and reigned with Christ a thousand years. But the rest of the dead lived not again until the thousand years were finished. This is the first resurrection. Blessed and holy is he that hath part in the first resurrection (Rev. 20:4–6).

The term 'first resurrection' implies a resurrection to follow, even if it does not call it 'the second resurrection'. Christ is called 'firstfruits' (1 Cor. 15:20) of the first resurrection, as His resurrection is the pattern for those who follow. Then comes the resurrection of the believers of the Church age, defined as 'the dead in Christ', who are raised and display the power of His resurrection (1 Thess. 4:16). There is no mention of OT saints in this passage; the Church of the dispensation is unique, as the Bride of Christ. Now, at the end of the Tribulation, this great company of resurrected saints (from every age except the Church age) completes the harvest from the sowing of Calvary. Christ will lead His sheep – the living believers, in natural bodies, into the Kingdom (Rev. 7:9–17). But Christ will also have with Him in this triumphal entry to Kingdom glory His resurrected saints, in bodies patterned on His resurrection body (1 Thess. 4:14). What a triumph for Christ! At this point, the first resurrection is finished. No others will be raised with bodies like that of the risen Christ.

The destiny of the second company (those who do not rise) is solemnly described as 'to shame and everlasting contempt'. The word 'shame' means 'reproach' and the word 'contempt' means something 'abhorrent'; indeed, 'something to stand away from'. 'Everlasting' qualifies both substantives and simply indicates that their portion is not temporary, nor will it pass with time – it is eternal punishment (Mt. 25:41; Rev. 20:14–15). These sinners are not raised from the grave at this point, but one thousand years later, at the close of the millennial Kingdom. Then they are raised to stand before the great white throne (Rev. 20:11–15) for judgement. Their end is the 'Lake of Fire' (Rev. 20:15).

In light of this interpretation, a relevant and related question must be raised. Does this resurrection include Gentiles, or is it confined to Israel? The answer is perfectly clear, as Scripture throws light upon Scripture; one Scripture adds detail to a previous revelation. Daniel's focus is Israel; he is concerned only with his own people, and other nations come into the story only incidentally. Yet what he has unfolded allows other Scriptures to bring out the detail. John, in the book of Revelation, amplifies what has been revealed to Daniel. John's focus is Christ and the response of individuals to Him. It is quite clear that this first resurrection (named as such in Rev. 20:5) must include all believers from Adam – those in every age who turned to God, down to men and women, Jew and Gentile, in the Tribulation, who refused to bow to the Beast and were put to death. All believers, other than those of the Church age, are raised at this point; for them it is an 'out-resurrection', leaving others still in the graves. The bodies of the unbelieving dead remain in the soil or the sea until they are called, a thousand years later, to stand before the great white throne (Rev. 20:11). Here their character and conduct are exposed from Divine records, and justice demands banishment to the lake of fire; a judgement confirmed by their intransigent refusal of the call of grace; their names are not in the Book of Life. This unfolding of their rebellion against God and their stubborn rejection of grace in their time on earth will mean shame and contempt, as they pass to their eternal doom – the lake of fire (Rev. 20:11–15).

It is exceedingly strange to note that some of the most able expositors of prophetic truth refuse to see physical bodily resurrection in this passage. A.C. Gaebelein speaks for many conservative, premillennial, commentators when he writes:

> Physical resurrection is not taught in the second verse of this chapter ... we repeat the passage has nothing to do with physical resurrection. Physical resurrection is however used as a figure of the national revival of Israel in that day. They have been sleeping nationally in the dust of the earth, buried among the Gentiles. But at that time will take place a national restoration, a bringing together of the house of Judah and of Israel.[8]

This view understands the phrase 'many of them that sleep in the dust of the earth' to describe a 'national revival' of Israel, using resurrection language figuratively. In other words, these

[8] Gaebelein, *The Prophet Daniel*, p. 200.

commentators are saying that this expression is not to be taken in a physical but in a metaphorical sense, and that it points to the awakening and regathering of the nation of Israel scattered worldwide. It is perfectly true to say that already there is such a recovery and revival, as spoken of by Ezekiel (Ezek. 37:1–28). It is clear from this passage that Israel was to regather in unbelief. Since the close of the nineteenth century Israelites have been regathering in the promised land and on May 14, 1948 they regained national identity without spiritual life. This was the result of United Nations Resolution 181 of November 1947, which divided British Palestine into two states. Their unbelief is patent today, and, using Ezekiel's language, they are 'very many in the open valley; and, lo, they [are] very dry' (Ezek. 37:1–2). Up to the present they reject any gospel approach and in total unbelief still look for 'another', of whom Christ spoke. When the Church has been removed from earth, at the Rapture, Satan will soon meet this need – he will have his man ready – this is where the Antichrist (see above) steps forward and is received.

This is where Michael's work is shown clearly, in the shepherding of true believers through the Tribulation, in spite of the terrible death rate. At the coming of the Son of Man the living saints are delivered, but not without those who have died under the Antichrist sharing the triumph. The deliverance of this company requires physical resurrection in answer to the power of the Antichrist; otherwise how could they share the Kingdom glory? These are joined by the believers of every age who have shared the promise of the Kingdom. The Church has already met her Lord. Any national regathering of Israel before His second coming is in unbelief (Ezek. 37:1–2); any regathering of the nation at His second coming is that of the 'elect' – the already believing Israelites – who are gathered by the angelic messengers of heaven with trumpet blast (Mt. 24:31). There is no reason whatever in the context not to see this awakening as a physical resurrection. Indeed, to fail to take the passage literally, and introduce a figurative meaning, robs the statement of its sweetness and power.

The origin of the spiritualising line of teaching with pre-millennial expositors seems to lie with Mr William Kelly, to whom we are all so much indebted for his generally clear prophetic teaching. In 1897 he published lectures given forty years before (therefore c. 1857) when he had said, and now writes:

> This verse is constantly applied to the resurrection of the body; and it is true that the Spirit founds the figure, which is here used to foreshadow the revival of Israel, upon that resurrection. But it can be shown that it has not the least reference to a bodily resurrection either of us or of Israel.[9]

Some pages later he writes:

> The text shows plainly that this is not the resurrection of the just; because when this takes place, nobody rises to shame and everlasting contempt. The passage has no direct reference to a bodily resurrection; which simply furnishes a figure for the national revival of Israel, who are described as sleeping in the dust, to express the greatness of their degradation.

Following in this line of thought a much later writer, Mr H. Paisley (1972), puts the matter bluntly:

> Physical resurrection is not taught in this solemn verse, but it is simply used as a figure of the revival and rejuvenation of the nation of Israel. Those who teach that physical resurrection is meant in this verse are unable to answer two great questions that arise from such a position.[10]

It is submitted that, from the grammar and context, both of these questions have already been answered in the exposition from the passage itself. Mr Paisley writes again (*in loc.*): 'The first question is "Who are the many?"' The answer has already been given – they are all those who are raised from the dead – who died expecting the King. This includes all OT saints and those believers who have died in the Tribulation. It has been shown many times in this book that, while Israel is Daniel's focus, this does not leave out the nations where they come into the picture. To confine this to Israel makes no sense. Within the context of physical death (v. 1) physical resurrection (v. 2) is demanded. To bring in spiritual revival is to introduce what is foreign to the context. Mr Paisley raises a second question (*in loc.*): 'Secondly, if this passage teaches physical resurrection, then how can the saved and the lost rise together?' It has already been shown that a little consideration of the grammar rules out any such thought; that, in fact, between the two statements 'these' and 'those' stands the thousand years of the

[9] Kelly, *The Great Prophecies of Daniel*, p. 222.
[10] Paisley, *This Daniel*, p. 189.

millennial reign. Exactly the same interval stands between the two resurrections in the NT (Jn 5:29 and Rev. 20:4–5). Therefore there is no case to answer. Rightly understood, the text defends itself. To bring in the spiritual revival of the nation of Israel is to do so without either grammatical or contextual support. Robert Culver, writing on this matter, has this to say:

> The thing so utterly unacceptable about this is that Gaebelein adopts the very spiritualising or symbolising principle of interpretation which our opponents adopt – that in the midst of a passage where everything else is esteemed (by Gaebelein and all Premillennialists) to be literal, not figurative. He does with this passage precisely what the Postmillennialists and amillennialists do with the first resurrection in Revelation 20.[11]

To that statement there is little to be added.

Those who accept the idea of national restoration instead of physical resurrection have a major difficulty with the second statement, since both statements are necessarily the predicates of the same verb, 'awake'. The full statement would read: who 'awake to shame and everlasting contempt'. A question needs to be asked that is never raised or answered by the advocates of the spiritual revival theory. If the verb 'awake' means spiritual revival for the nation of Israel, in what possible sense can it be used of this second company? There does not appear to be an answer to this question.

It would appear that the spiritualising of physical resurrection in this passage by pre-millennialists seems to have arisen from the assumption that the OT saints are raised from the dead with the Church. This means to pre-millennial expositors, since the Rapture must come before the Tribulation, that the resurrection of all believers must come before the Tribulation. Having assumed, wrongly, that the first resurrection is complete at the Rapture (1 Thess. 4:13–18), they cannot allow a physical resurrection at the close of the Tribulation. All such confusion would have been avoided if it had been clearly understood that the expression 'dead in Christ' limits the Rapture exclusively to believers of this dispensation. J. F. Walvoord, a most able student of prophetic truth, sums up the matter concisely:

[11]Culver, *Daniel and the Latter Days*, p. 172.

> Actually, there is no passage in Scripture which teaches that the Old Testament saints will be raised at the time the church is raptured, which is before the final tribulation. It is preferable, therefore, to consider their resurrection as occurring at the same time as the restoration of the living nation with the result that resurrected Israel and those still in their natural bodies who are delivered at the second coming of Christ will join hands and ministries in establishing Israel in the land in the millennial kingdom which follows the second advent.[12]

This is clear thinking that is supported by the last verse of this chapter, which brings us directly into the Kingdom with Daniel.

Other expositors have reached a similar conclusion. After a lengthy discussion of the two viewpoints, F.A. Tatford sums up the matter:

> On the whole, the case for taking the text to mean precisely what it says is the strongest. The plain statement that the eternal future is being described seems to rule out the view that the resurrection in question is only national. Logically, it would appear to refer to the physical resurrection of the individual, and it is appropriate that the ultimate consequences of loyalty and disloyalty should be introduced in close juxtaposition to the description of the hour of tribulation and testing.[13]

This presents the case simply and scripturally. **(End of Excursus 2).**

Verse 3 The coming of Christ to earth closes the Tribulation period and opens the reign of Christ. It is fitting to pause, as the angel does at this point, and consider the link between the two. This link is found in men described as the 'wise' – exactly the same participle that is used twice in chapter 11 (vv. 33–35) and translated 'they that understand', or simply 'the understanding ones'. In the previous chapter it refers to persons who, during the time of Antiochus Epiphanes, knew their Scripture and their God, and were used of God to preserve others from bowing to the claims of the deceiver. Similarly, during the Tribulation these wise ones, using their knowledge of Scripture and their knowledge of God, will preserve many in the nation of Israel from bowing to the claims of the Antichrist – the greatest deceiver of all time. In that dark day, the

[12] Walvoord, *Daniel –The Key to Prophetic Revelation*, p. 287.
[13] Tatford, *Daniel and His Prophecy*, p. 219.

evening of the day of the Lord, these believers will stand out amidst the surrounding darkness just as stars shine against the darkness of the night sky. The promise is that they 'shall shine [forth] as the brightness of the firmament'; the verb and substantive are cognates and describe a blaze of light that automatically catches the eye. They reflect a corporate testimony that cannot be hidden. The next statement is a case of Hebrew parallelism: 'they that turn many to righteousness' describes the effective ministry of 'the wise'. They are seen individually 'as the stars' and their witness runs on 'for ever and ever'. The light they shed in 'the evening' of the day of the Lord, the Tribulation period, will not fade with 'the morning' of the day of the Lord, the Kingdom stage – even though the Sun of righteousness has risen (Mal. 4:2). These stars will never be eclipsed. It is a well-established principle in Scripture that fidelity to God will always be rewarded; the glory of the future will reflect the loyalty of the past.

Summary The message of the angel to Daniel has run without interruption from 10:20 to 12:3. In this vision of the linen-clothed man by the River Tigris has unfolded a prophetic overview of events, particularly related to Israel, from the time of Cyrus and Daniel (539 BC) down to the reign of Christ in the glory of the millennial Kingdom on earth.

Excursus 3 Prophetic Overview of the Tribulation

A prophetic overview of this final vision may be helpful, as it presents a double climax of opposition to this Divine programme. Two crisis points have been observed, when the nation of Israel, through whom God intended to fulfil His purpose, by the bringing in of the Redeemer, was on the point of extinction. The first of these crisis points preceded the Redeemer's first coming to earth; the second will precede the Redeemer's second coming to earth.
The man used of Satan in the first crisis was Antiochus Epiphanes.
The man used of Satan in the second crisis is the Antichrist.

Notice

(a) Antiochus (11:21–35)
The Figure, the Portrait of the Antichrist.
(b) Antichrist (11:36–12:3)
The Fulfilment, the Person of the Antichrist.

In summary, the midpoint of the Tribulation will be:

The end of the first three-and-a-half years of the seventieth week

Marked by:

1. The invasion of Israel from the north
2. The defeat of the invader by God on the mountains of Israel
3. Assassination and pseudo-resurrection of the Beast
4. The Image of the Beast on the wing of the Temple in Jerusalem

Consequences:

(a) Judaism destroyed – flight of the nation of Israel (Rev. 12:13–17)
(b) Harlot destroyed – Mystery Babylon replaced by open idolatry (Rev. 17:1–18)
(c) Two witnesses killed (Rev. 11:3–13)

The Great Tribulation

The last three-and-a-half years of the seventieth week

1. The Seven Trumpets blown (Rev. 8:1–11:19)
2. The Seven Vials poured (Rev. 15:1–16:21)

The Close of the Tribulation

1. Return of Christ to earth (Rev. 19:11–21)
2. Resurrection of OT saints and martyred dead of the Tribulation period (Rev. 20:4–6)
3. Reward in the millennial Kingdom

The Millennium

One thousand years (Rev. 20:1–6)

(End of Excursus 3)

Verse 4 The Closing Charge to Daniel

Having completed his message, the angelic interpreter gives clear instructions as to its preservation. Two verbs are used, and frequently a casual reading has led to misunderstanding.

(a) Daniel is told to 'shut up the words'. As was pointed out when this verb was first met (8:26), it can mean literally 'to shut a door', or 'close from view',[14] but different Masoretic pointing gives the

[14] Refer back to comments on 8:26, where two references are given in support of translating the verb as 'to shut up' – *OTWS*, p. 92 and *WSD*, p. 392, and the suggestion by Wood of translating the verb as 'to preserve': Wood, *A Commentary on Daniel*, p. 228. This alternative translation is in keeping with the context.

meaning of ‘to preserve’. The differing contexts in which this word is found in extra-biblical writings suggest that its most usual meaning is the second mentioned – ‘to conserve’, or ‘to preserve safely’. In the two places where this verb is used in this book (8:26; 12:4) this is the preferred meaning, as it suits the context ideally.[15] God is not given to concealing the truth but to making it known. What the interpreting angel stresses to Daniel is not the concealment of this vision, but rather its preservation. In the first use of the verb (8:26) it is ‘the vision’ that must be preserved, and in the second use, in this verse, the stress falls on the ‘words’ that are to be preserved. Thus, incidentally, is light thrown on the Divine verbal inspiration of Scripture, showing that it lies in the words of the original autographs; these words have been selected by God to convey His message to mankind.

(b) The second direction to Daniel is ‘seal the book’. The verb means ‘seal securely’ and points to the authenticating seal on the cover. The meaning of ‘seal’ here must not be interpreted as the idea of ‘shutting up’, meaning preventing its escaping, but the idea is to put a seal on it for authentication and preservation, as in the case of the sealed company of Revelation (Rev. 7:4). This book is not forbidden. This second verb complements the first verb in that the very text is to be carefully preserved, because the writing carries the seal of Divine authenticity. Daniel is but the human penman. The seal of Daniel secures it from the tampering of any other. These instructions parallel similar instructions in the last chapter of Revelation, where no-one is allowed to add to it or take from it (Rev. 22:18–19). It does not mean that its message is to be hidden away; rather, its message is to be preserved safely down the ages, as it stands, without alteration or emendation, until later ages will so illuminate its page that there will arise a burning desire to search out its meaning. There is absolutely no prohibition in this passage to copying and sending Daniel’s message to the nation of Israel, or, indeed, to any other nation. This should be done, but, at the same time, the original manuscript must be preserved and protected. The use of the word ‘book’ envisages a substantial amount of writing and thus the incipient question in the mind is answered positively. This directive must embrace not only this fourth vision, but the whole of the book of Daniel; it is to be retained as a unit. As he was a man of possibly around eighty-eight years (536 BC) when he was

[15] *OTWS*, 392.

granted this last vision, the prophecy could have been copied and circulated during his lifetime. Tradition says he died *c.* 530 BC, a few months after the death of King Cyrus, in 529 BC. It is a remarkable fact that after two-and-a-half millennia men are still studying this writing of Daniel, to understand what is happening in the world around. It is necessary to remind every heart that Daniel spoke to the 'time of the end'.

This preservation of the Divine revelation in the book is to continue until 'the time of the end'. This phrase has been used twice previously (11:35, 40) and, as has been pointed out already, the time indicated by this phrase in this last vision is the time of the Tribulation; indeed, the time that brings the fulfilment of the prophecy. As features of the time of Tribulation begin to appear in world events the relevance of what had been given to Daniel will become so apparent that great interest will be stirred up. This is indicated in the next statement: 'many shall run to and fro, and knowledge shall be increased'. This phrase is difficult to translate and it has been understood in different ways. Some students interpret the verb figuratively. H. Leupold does exactly this and interprets it as the eye of the reader, running to and fro as it scans Daniel's writing; he translates it as 'diligently pursue'.[16] Leon Wood feels that the usage of this form of the verb is against this figurative interpretation.[17] Yet the same writer insists that the verb does mean 'to move quickly, to run to and fro'. Other commentators take it literally, as meaning the increased travel of men and women in these latter years, and from the verb's usage outside Scripture it is difficult to deny this. There is assuredly more travel in these later years than there has ever been down the centuries past. Emigration and immigration, as well as tourist travel to the remotest places on earth, make this truth plain. However, it is not this kind of general tourist travel that can be in view here, since such has no relevance in the context whatever. Leon Wood understands it in this sense, but limits the travel when he writes, 'the thought is that people would run to and fro trying to find answers to important questions, especially in reference to future events.'[18] This limitation, he suggests, is indicated in the next sentence: 'and knowledge shall be increased'. In the context this must be the knowledge of either

[16] Leupold, *Exposition of Daniel*, p. 534.
[17] Wood, *A Commentary on Daniel*, p. 321.
[18] Wood, *A Commentary on Daniel*, p. 321.

historic or prophetic events – and, further, it must be knowledge coming to light, that only 'the time of the end' could bring. It must be knowledge that depends on either archaeological research on physical sites or archival research in literary records – either or both could illuminate the prophetic Word. The Word of God does not depend on this; Scripture stands alone and needs no support, yet in this case and at this time this knowledge serves as both a reassurance to believers and a testimony to unbelievers of the accuracy and dependability of the Word of God. This brings a warning to all. What God promised in the past, our research shows He carried out exactly as he said – He meant it literally. The warning note to all who discover this is simple – what God has done in the past, He will do again, with respect to the promises and prophecies yet to be fulfilled.

In this very connection there are many examples over the years where archaeological research has refuted the assumptions of sceptical commentators and re-affirmed the accuracy of Daniel.[19] In this lies the scriptural answer to the hesitation of even a believer who harbours doubts about the value of such a prophetic book as Daniel. Prophecies of Daniel have become history for this age, and the deeper we dig in our search for knowledge the more convinced we become that God's Word was literally fulfilled exactly as stated. A good example has been studied in this last vision (11:2–35). At the very least, it shows that our God knows beforehand what will happen. It also shows that the God Who gave the prophecy will ensure that it is literally fulfilled. The final lesson is also plainly set out: God can keep His own people through the darkest of days, when they trust Him. To summarise the final word of the angel in this fourth vision – the preserved book of Daniel will throw much light on the circumstances of the end-time. So much interest will be stirred that men will go to great lengths, even travel the world, to try to discover more. It would be our prayer that, when they do this, they will be prepared to act in light of the clear teaching of the book.

[19] See Anderson, *Daniel in the Critic's Den*.

Verses 5–13 The Closing Scene

Closing Questions

Verse 5 Daniel once more becomes aware of his surroundings; a consciousness marked by the phrase 'I Daniel looked'. As he does so he becomes aware, somewhat to his surprise – note the word 'behold' – that he is still in the same location, on the bank of the River Tigris, as when the vision opened (10:4). The scene, however, is somewhat changed from the earlier one. Two angels are present; one close to him on the bank where he stands and the other further away, on the other bank. Doubtless, their presence reminded him of the interest and role of angels in the execution of God's programme on earth. However, the central figure is still the 'man clothed in linen', Who is seen to be standing upon the waters of the river. Such a stance underlines the Deity and authority of this One, Who has been already identified as having all the features of 'the Angel of the LORD' (10:4–6). The fact that the text has the article before 'linen' points back to the previous mention of the Person. It is the same Person – a pre-incarnate appearance of Deity. One of the executive angels addresses a question to this central figure. The very articulation of the question shows indirectly that: (a) the Person addressed is superior in standing to the angel; and (b) the Person addressed has a knowledge denied the questioner. This underlines the supreme stature of this Holy One.

Verse 6 The Question of the Angel

The question itself arises naturally from the revelation just given, and the answer is vital to the understanding of the vision. Doubtless, Daniel was already wrestling with this same question. Leon Wood is very helpful at this point, when he translates it 'How long shall be the end of the wonders?'[20] It is not a question of the length of time from the present until that time (the end) but, rather, it is a query as to the length of that exceptional and terrible period, 'the time of the end'. 'The wonders' must refer to the things – both 'actions' (8:24) and 'words' (11:36) – that are unique to the last part of the Tribulation. This is in keeping with the fact that the expression 'time of the end' in these chapters (11:35, 40; 12:4) points to the period that closes the Tribulation. In other words, the question is about the length of this unique period; the specific length of time

[20] Wood, *A Commentary on Daniel*, p. 323.

when the Antichrist will be allowed to use such aggressive words and to takc such damaging actions against the people of Israel.

Verse 7 The Answer of the Man Clothed in Linen

The stillness must have been absolute by the riverside, as with awful solemnity that glorious figure standing on the waters of the river slowly raises His right hand, then just as slowly raises His left hand and then swears by the Eternal. To raise the right hand when taking an oath is usual (Gen. 14:22; Deut. 32:40; Rev. 10:5–6); to raise both hands is to draw attention to the absolute veracity and absolute dependability of that which is being handed over. Men can put their absolute trust in this Person, and thus take as absolute truth the pronouncements He makes. The one called upon to witness the oath is the Eternal – 'the one who lives forever' (*NET*). So important is this matter that God commits Himself in absolute sovereignty. It will be recalled that God did the same thing in an earlier day. Before Israel disobeyed Him He warned:

> See now that I, even I, am He, and there is no god with Me: I kill, and I make alive; I wound, and I heal: neither is there any that can deliver out of My hand. For I lift up my hand to heaven, and say, I live for ever (Deut. 32:39–40).

Now Deity gives a similar assurance to close Israel's history of disobedience. There can be no argument, as God pledges Himself (Heb. 6:13), as God calls upon God, in this book revealed as the 'Ancient of days' (7:9). The pledge given here by Deity is the limitation He has, in His counsels, already placed on the length of time His people will be permitted to suffer.

That this understanding of the question is correct can be seen in the answer given by the 'man clothed in linen' with both hands upraised. The duration of this time of trial and tears for the people of Israel is set in the schedule of heaven; it is 'for a time, times, and a half'. The solemnity and singularity of this scene do not allow it to point to any other period but the closing period of earth history just before the Kingdom of God is established on earth. This is the rule of Antichrist over the people of Israel in the last three-and-a-half years of the seven-year Tribulation. The period has been marked out chronologically in the very first vision (7:25); mentioned in the programme of God in the third vision (9:27); and it is now underlined as the introductory preparation for the Kingdom, at the close of the fourth vision. This period when the satanic hatred is released against Israel, as Daniel has been told repeatedly, is limited to three-and-a-half years. In spite of this the angel asks the question. Do angels need the repetition, or is the question raised to emphasise the fact for the benefit of Daniel, and therefore ultimately, those who read this prophecy? Perhaps any one of us could be a slow learner in respect to this vital period. It must be very important indeed.

The oath of this glorious One but re-emphasises a period that has loomed large in the study of this book, here spoken of as 'a time, times, and a half', corresponding to the three-and-a-half years indicated in the earlier part of the book (7:25; 9:27). This is the same period as the book of the Revelation presents as 'forty and two months' (Rev. 11:2); 'a thousand two hundred and threescore days' (Rev. 12:6) and 'a time, and times, and half a time' (Rev. 12:14). This time has been carefully evaluated and set aside by God.

While the first part of this verse gives the length of period, the second part of the verse gives the reason why it had to go on for so long. The toll taken on Israel is horrific. This unrelenting persecution by the Man of Sin and the Antichrist continues until two thirds of the people of Israel are wiped out (Zech. 13:8). It must not be forgotten that this was the chosen nation, through whom God would bring into the world the revelation in Scripture and the Redeemer, in the Saviour. As such a channel, the nation had great privileges but, at the same time, this brought great responsibilities. It is here that failure came in, sin took over, and Israel fell into idolatry and immorality. As a result, the nation rejected the Saviour and gave Him a cross (Acts 2:22–23). Since God still desires their blessing and has made provision for it, the national sin must be faced and repentance sought before they can enjoy forgiveness from God and a future blessed of God. Death being the sentence upon sin, this is exactly what Israel faces in these terrible days.

When the gospel is preached in this age of grace and a sinner is conscious of the sentence he deserves, he can be pointed to Christ and told of the preaching of Isaiah: 'But He was wounded for our transgressions, He was bruised for our iniquities: the chastisement of our peace was upon Him; and with His stripes we are healed' (Isa. 53:5). The sinless One has become the sin-bearer for the guilty so that salvation can be possessed. What is true for the individual is true for this nation; the pain of the Great Tribulation is used of God to bring His people to repentance. The process is described most clearly in the translation of this verse in the *RV*: 'and when they have made an end of breaking in pieces the power of the holy people, all these things shall be finished.' So the whole process is allowed, even designed, possibly weighted, to 'break in pieces', or 'shatter', the power of the holy people. 'The holy people' indicates the desire and design of God in calling them as a nation. He meant them to be a holy people, living in a holy land, ruled from a holy city, and with a holy Temple for worship around a holy God. It is a remarkable fact that often when this adjective 'holy' is used by God it is at a time when men would have no hesitation saying the thing described is 'most unholy'. At this dark hour of the Tribulation, when the nation is under Divine judgement, God still calls them 'holy'; they are still 'set apart' for Him; He has never abandoned His purpose through them. The 'power' must be defined, by its position in the statement, as meaning 'all that would prevent them from feeling the probes of the Holy Spirit searching each heart' as they are brought to repent. Believers in Israel face a very difficult period as they respond to the Spirit and believe the Scripture. Military defences have gone; spiritual leaders have been martyred; even to get a friendly word from a neighbour, a drink of cold water or a meal (Mt. 25:34–40), is a dangerous thing; loneliness, abandonment and isolation break down every thought of self-sufficiency, until they are cast upon God and turn in repentance to Him. God has set a limit, but that limit is linked to the completion of His work of grace in His people. It is at this point that the prophecy of Zechariah comes in: 'In that day there shall be a fountain opened to the house of David and to the inhabitants of Jerusalem for sin and for uncleanness' (Zech. 13:1).

Verse 8 The Question of Daniel

Daniel heard the answer; heard it clearly and fully, as shown in the perfect tense of the verb 'I heard'. The angel's words wrung from him a personal confession. Personal, because the personal pronoun is unusual; it singles him out from others who, by implication, may understand. With a cry to his Lord he confesses (imperfect tense), 'I was not understanding'; try as he might, he could not get a complete understanding of this tremendous subject. If translated literally the text reads 'what is the latter end of these?'[21] And it becomes clear that Daniel's question differs in two points from the angel's question (v. 6). First, he is not asking about the length of the closing

[21] Wood, *A Commentary on Daniel*, p. 325.

period of the Tribulation, but asking as to how the period ends – what brings it to an end, or what kind of event closes it? Second, he is not fastening upon the 'wonders', meaning 'unusual events', during the period, dramatic though they are, but he is asking about the kind of event that brings that period to a close. Perhaps Daniel had in his mind the stone and the dramatic end of the image (2:34–35). Surely, such a terrible period must have a dramatic close, and Daniel is concerned at his lack of understanding. These are two closely related matters that arise in the mind of a believer reading this prophecy. Daniel is allowed to put them to the 'man clothed in linen', his glorious Visitor.

Verses 9–13 The Answer of the Man Clothed in Linen

Verses 9–11 However, strange as it may seem, Daniel receives no further enlightenment. In the reply of the 'man clothed in linen' there is a note of rebuke but, at the same time, there are several notes of comfort. The imperative in the verb 'go', in the command 'go thy way', seems to relate to him mentally rather than physically. It seems to be saying, 'Do not pursue that line of enquiry at the moment: take up present duties and leave further investigation until later and to others. You personally, Daniel, are only the channel; events revealed to you are far down the stream of time and do not affect you. Take up your task.' The task given him in verse 4 is repeated, using the same words, but now in the past tense. Daniel is prepared to close the book and seal it. As shown in earlier comments (see v. 4), this means not the hiding, but the preservation, of the text, until the relevant period arrives. No alterations or amendments are permitted; no deletions or additions are needed. The text must stand inviolate. This reminds the reader of somewhat similar warnings, given over two millennia later, with respect to the text of the Revelation (Rev. 22:18–19). Then, the value of the writing will become evident and the teaching will become clear, through the happenings of the day. The men and women of that day will owe much to Daniel as his prophecy illuminates their circumstances and, in the full light of the Word of God, they will decide their destiny. In that period the question will be whether they are prepared to trust Christ or give allegiance to the Antichrist; whether to worship the Lamb or bow to the image.

The hint of rebuke to Daniel lies in the fact that there is no answer to his request for further information. Did the request arise from a genuine concern for the glory of God or from fleshly curiosity? This is where the line is drawn in all scriptural prophetic study. Maybe Daniel should have read the *terminus ad quem* from the visions already given – the coming of the Son of Man to set up His Kingdom. There could be nothing more dramatic than that glorious moment when the King arrives. But while he must have felt rebuked at the silence, yet he must have been immensely reassured in the statement that follows. Here he is assured that the word conveyed through him would be Divinely effective. Response to the Word of God reveals character. As a result, two different groups would be revealed by their reaction to the prophetic Word. The first group is simply described as 'many'. The substantive is anarthrous – there is no article – and so this must be taken simply in the sense of 'a big number', but not necessarily a majority (compare use of the article with 'many' in 9:27). In this period, illuminated by the word from Daniel, men are enabled to respond positively to the preaching of the gospel of the Kingdom (Rev. 14:6–7) and find themselves 'purified' and 'made white' and 'tried'. These three verbs, each of which can be translated in the passive voice, indicate what is done to them rather than something they do; this is what the gospel does to men. Exactly the same three verbs are used to describe what happened to those in Maccabean days (when Antiochus Epiphanes ruled) who believed the prophets in connection with the first coming of the Christ to earth (11:35). These same three verbs describe what will happen to those during the days of the Antichrist who believe the prophetic Word concerning the second coming of Christ to earth. With perfect legitimacy and grammatical accuracy, the first two verbs may also be read reflexively: 'purify themselves' and 'make themselves white', followed by the passive: 'be refined'. This presents just the same truth except that in this case the responsibility of each person to believe the message is stressed, which responsibility is evident in the statement 'the wise shall understand'. Following faith in Christ, the believer is subjected to the refining fire of the furnace conditions of the Tribulation (Mal. 3:2–3). To 'purify' is 'to make clean, pure, bright by washing'.[22] The Word of God is clear that there is only one cleansing agent for the sin of man and that is spelled out, typically in the OT sacrifices, and in reality in the NT presentation of Christ. The statement stands for all time: 'the blood of Jesus Christ His Son cleanseth us from all sin' (1 Jn 1:7). That this

[22] *OTWS*, p. 333.

precious blood effects the same change in sinners throughout the Tribulation as it does today, is made clear when those coming out of that time are described as having 'washed their robes, and made them white in the blood of the Lamb' (Rev. 7:14). Not only is there removal of the filth; there is the realisation of a righteousness sinners cannot achieve for themselves. This is seen in the second verb – 'made white'. The colour 'white' throughout Scripture generally represents righteousness revealed. In this book the verb 'made white' occurs only twice (11:35; 12:10). Not only are souls who believe the gospel cleansed from their filth; they are cleared from their guilt; they may stand before the Ancient of days, 'whose garment was white as snow' (7:9). Is it any wonder these saints automatically invite the animosity of Satan and his puppets in the Tribulation days and thus are plunged into a fiery trial? In this fire their faith is tried. This is the point made by Zechariah, who makes clear that two thirds of the numbers of Israel perish physically in the flames (Zech. 13:8–9).

If a person refuses to believe the gospel of the Kingdom this leaves such open to believe the lie of the Man of Sin (2 Thess. 2:11–12). These are defined in the next sentence as 'the wicked shall do wickedly' – and there must be the hint of a Divine sentence in that very statement. The word used for 'wicked' means 'lawless' and it is assuredly a fitting word to describe those who, believing the lie of the Man of Sin, bow to the image of the Beast. This is the one identified in Scripture as 'the man of lawlessness' (2 Thess. 2:3, *RSV*). As 'the lawless ones' they have thrown overboard every vestige of the authority of the true God and are abandoning themselves to unconstrained defiance of every vestige of law of any kind – like their master, they simply do as they please. These sinners are taking advantage of the times, as they give rein to every unbridled passion of the human heart. Not even an ethical code; no law of any kind restrains them. Thus they demonstrate their true character. The secret that distinguishes the two groups is very simple: (a) The wicked – 'none of the wicked shall understand'; and (b) The wise – 'the wise shall understand'. Constructs of the verb 'to understand (Heb. root '*bin*'– 'to separate', or 'to distinguish', hence 'to discern')[23] have been used around twenty-five times from the first chapter of this book to these final two references (v. 10). The basic meaning is the ability to distinguish, in the light of the Word of God, between what is true

[23] *OTWS*, p. 461.

and what is false. Action then taken by the individuals will show whether they are 'wise' or 'unwise'. The 'unwise' in response to the revelation of God become the 'wicked' in action and character. The character declares destiny. Daniel's prophecy, preserved down many ages, will be used of God to make many 'wise'. Daniel must have been comforted by this assurance, though he admits lack of full understanding. He is further assured that, in these latter days, believers will have the advantage of historic fulfilments to confirm their faith – an advantage that Daniel did not have.

In spite of Daniel's question (v. 8) being left virtually unanswered, for the reason given, yet in the answer given there is a note of absolute certainty that brings infinite comfort to believers. That assurance lies in the careful accuracy of time periods given in Scripture that many seem unwilling to accept. It is to be recalled that the period in view from chapter 11:36 is 'the time of the end' (11:35), called 'a time of trouble' in Israel (and the world), which begins when the Antichrist (the prophet, priest and king who claims leadership in Israel) sets up the image of the Beast in Jerusalem and demands worship for the Man of Sin (the first Beast, from the sea, Rev. 13:1–8). The final time marks are fixed by this event thus: 'From the time that the daily sacrifice shall be taken away, and the abomination that maketh desolate set up' (v. 11, *cf.* 9:27). This, as previously shown, stands at the midpoint of the seven-year Tribulation period and the event is indicated by the Lord as being still future in His day (Mt. 24:15–16). Now Daniel is told – in effect – 'Look at your calendar! From that crisis point, count, not years, nor months, but days – one thousand two hundred and ninety days.' Knowing, as Daniel did, that from the midpoint of the seventieth week to the day when Christ stands on the Mount of Olives (Zech. 14:4) is 1260 days exactly, his mind would question immediately the reason for the extra month, of thirty days. Perhaps he was afraid to ask, but, wisely, Daniel remains quiet.

It is to be recognised that Christ was accurate to the day in His presentation to the nation at His first coming to earth (see 9:25 and discussion). There is no suggestion that He will be any less accurate when He comes the second time to earth. It will be, without a doubt, on the final day of the one thousand, two hundred and sixty days that His feet will stand on the Mount of Olives (Zech. 14:4). So, with no hint of delay in the context, there must be a very valid reason for the extra month of thirty days. It is clear it must mark the duration of some process that has to take place after the advent of the Messiah (Rev. 19:11) and before the Kingdom is established, though no explanation is offered in the text. So, with Daniel, we are allowed a time to meditate on the arrival of the Messiah and what has to follow. Into that silence there drops an important word of introduction – 'Blessed'!

Verse 12 This is the heritage of the company introduced in this verse who, characteristically, have been awaiting someone or something. They have had their attention gripped by something ahead and every fibre of their being awaits the realisation of their expectation. In the context this must be the realisation of the Kingdom expected down the ages. It is suggested that this parallels the scene of which the Lord spoke on the Mount of Olives when, as King, He would welcome those whom He had identified as sheep, and address them: 'Come, ye blessed of My Father, inherit the kingdom prepared for you from the foundation of the world' (Mt. 25:34). The King is addressing His sheep; those who by their actions in the Tribulation have proven beyond doubt that they were genuine believers. They waited, He arrived; the Judgement before the throne of His glory is over. Now they hear the word they have awaited – 'blessed' – and the Kingdom is opened to them. What they have awaited has arrived with the expected King – the Kingdom! Now the waiting is over and the second verb means reality: 'cometh to' carries the idea of 'reaching', or 'attaining'– this is the realisation of all their hopes! That tremendous moment requires an additional month and a half (forty-five days) in the arrangement of its administration. The final count from the midpoint of the Tribulation is 'one thousand three hundred and five and thirty days' (1,335 days). The stages have been indicated to Daniel thus:

The Close of the Tribulation

(a) Return of the King on the 1260th day from the Midpoint of the Tribulation

The military forces of earth are gathered around Jerusalem for the Battle of Armageddon and the Lord deals with all of these when He comes as the Conqueror on the white horse (Rev. 19:11–21). Time will be needed for the clearing up of the aftermath of the destruction of the armies, stretching from Jerusalem to Megiddo.

This period is possibly involved with the immediate action to clear Jerusalem and the land of the dead from Armageddon, and the arrangements for the setting up of the throne.

A number of associated events during these days of preparation for the establishment of the Kingdom of God must be brought into the full picture. These events may be noted summarily:

(a) The Resurrection of all OT saints (12:2), in company with the martyrs of the Tribulation (Rev. 20:4);
(b) The Judgement of this company before the establishment of the structures of the Kingdom (Rev. 11:16–18);
(c) The Judgement of the nation of Israel (Mal. 3:1–12);
(d) The Coronation of the King in Jerusalem (Ps 24:7–10).

(b) Judgement before the Throne on the 1,290th day from the Midpoint of the Tribulation

Following the clear-up operation throughout the land of Israel, the peoples of all nations alive on the earth will be gathered before the Lord, Who takes His seat on the throne of His glory (Mt. 25:31–46). The King separates the throng of souls gathered before the throne into two groups. One group the King addresses as 'sheep' (believers); the other group he calls 'goats' (unbelievers). The sheep, as addressed above, will enter the Kingdom (Rev. 7:9–17) for which they, along with believers down the ages, have waited. They are the 'Blessed'! On the other hand, the 'Cursed'! The 'goats' are addressed by the King: 'Depart from Me, ye cursed, into everlasting fire, prepared for the devil and his angels' (Mt. 25:41). They had accepted Satan's prince, in the place of Christ, in the Tribulation, so now they must share his doom. With every sinner now removed and banished from the earthly realm, the way is open for the establishment of the Kingdom of God on earth.

(c) Realisation of the Kingdom on the 1,335th day from the Midpoint of the Tribulation

The day when the Kingdom of Heaven is set up on earth.
The day for the establishment of the millennial Kingdom has come.

The word 'Blessed' describes the portion of those who have waited long for the Kingdom. Christ addresses them as they enter the Kingdom under Him: 'Come, ye blessed of My Father, inherit the kingdom' (Mt. 25:34). This is the same company of whom John was instructed to write 'Blessed are they which are called unto the marriage supper of the Lamb' (Rev. 19:9). What a wealth of festivity there will be as this long-expected Kingdom arrives.

Verse 13 As the final vision closes the 'man clothed in linen' gives a final word to Daniel personally. In the very light of the blaze of Kingdom glory Daniel is given private instructions. These are spelt out clearly:

(a) Commendation – 'Go thou thy way till the end'; a statement, with the same implication, repeated from verse 9: 'Leave the matter in God's keeping and take up the daily duties to God and to men that have marked your long life. No alteration is required at this stage.' The 'end' mentioned is not the end of Daniel's life but refers to the 'end' of the Divine programme that has been given to Daniel. Seen in this light, Daniel's obedience to his God and his submission to Scripture, which have marked his course through earth's changing kingdoms, will bring him, assuredly, to the millennial Kingdom, the inauguration of which has just been presented graphically to him.

(b) Comfort – 'For thou shalt rest, and stand in thy lot'. It is plain that 'rest', after all the tests and trials of life, must mean rest as a result of physical death (notice relevant Scriptures, as Job 3:17; Isa. 57:2). This is a word of comfort that is echoed across Tribulation days to struggle-weary saints: 'Write, Blessed are the dead which die in the Lord, from henceforth: "Yea," saith the Spirit, "that they may rest from their labours; and their works do follow them"' (Rev. 14:13). If 'rest' implies death, then over against physical death stands physical resurrection.

(c) Challenge – 'stand in thy lot'. While the grave for the weary servant of the Lord is synonymous with rest, that is not the end of the matter; the grave is not the goal. It should be said, in case of any misunderstanding, with NT light it is clear that on dying the believer passes, immediately and consciously, to be with Christ in glory (Phil. 1:23). Sleep and rest have to do with the body. From Daniel's viewpoint, rest of the body is followed by resurrection of the body, and there is a life that follows resurrection. When the tears have all been wiped away, there is a portion, a possession, pictured in the portion of Canaan allocated to the Israelites by lot on their entry to Canaan (Josh. 14:2, etc.). Studying the apportionment of the land, it could be said that very often the choicest possession required the fiercest fight. Thus Daniel is assured that physical resurrection will bring him into his portion, earned when he awaited the Kingdom.

Then he will share with the Israel of God their place in the millennial Kingdom, when the Son of Man rules and it can be said: 'His dominion shall be from sea even to sea, and from the River even to the ends of the earth' (Zech. 9:10).

The Last Word

As those who believe the prophecies given to Daniel, we learn:

1. Our place in the Divine programme. The Church fits into the interval between the sixty-ninth and seventieth week in the prophecy of the seventy weeks. The commencement of the Church age has been noted as Pentecost, AD 32; the close of the Church age is the Rapture (1 Thess. 4:13–18), which is awaited daily. Since the seven stages of Church history given of the Lord (Rev. 2–3) all exist in Christendom today, we must be very close to the moment of the Rapture. Saints today await the Saviour (Phil. 3:20).

2. Once the Rapture has taken place then a peace covenant is to be signed between a world leader from the west (who is the political head of ten-powered kingdom, worldwide in its scope) and the leader of the political majority in the land of Israel. This begins the countdown to the second coming to the earth of the Son of Man – seven prophetic years, or 2,520 days. Just as He was accurate to a day when He came the first time, so will He be accurate to a day when He comes the second time. Saints in the Tribulation days will await the Sovereign (Mt. 24:14).

3. It would seem that the first main political and military movement against Israel after the peace covenant is signed will be the attack by militant Islam led by the 'king of the north' – the old land of Persia – now Iran. This invasion will be destroyed of God as it reaches Israel, while the western leader hesitates to aid his colleague. This leaves the way open for an eastern power to draw upon the political, financial and military resources of the formerly moderate Islamic nations, as they marshal an army to avenge their fellow-religionists destroyed in Israel. The nations of the world move toward Armageddon.

Can it not be seen very clearly in this twenty-first century that the stage is being set and the actors are moving, behind the curtain, to take their places in this end-time drama? All is virtually ready – it just awaits the going up of the curtain, the Rapture of the Church. With John, the heart of every believer today would say: 'Even so, come, Lord Jesus'!

APPENDICES

APPENDIX 1

HISTORY OF JUDAH

DATES RELEVANT TO THE BOOK OF DANIEL

From King Hezekiah to the Destruction of Jerusalem, 715–586 BC

King	Reign (BC)	Scripture Comment
Hezekiah	715–686 (29 years)	'He did that which was **right** in the sight of the LORD' (2 Chron. 29:2).
Manasseh	697–642 (55 years) (Years of co-regency with his father included)	'But did that which was **evil** in the sight of the LORD' (2 Chron. 33:2).
Amon	642–640 (2 years)	'But he did that which was **evil** in the sight of the LORD' (2 Chron. 33:22).
Josiah	640–609 (31 years)	'He did that which was **right** in the sight of the LORD' (2 Chron. 34:2).

From the Battle of Megiddo (609 BC) Judah was a vassal state to either Egypt, under Pharaoh-Necho, or to Babylon, under Nebuchadnezzar.

King	Reign (BC)	Scripture Comment
Jehoahaz	609 (3 mths)	'The people of the land ... made him king'. Deposed by Pharaoh-Necho and carried down to Egypt (2 Chron. 36:1–4).
Jehoiakim	609–598 (11 years)	Older brother of Jehoahaz called Eliakim placed on the throne by Pharaoh-Necho and his name changed to Jehoiakim (2 Chron. 36:4–6).
Jehoiachin	598–597 (3mths, 10 days)	'He did that which was evil in the sight of the LORD' (2 Chron. 36:9). Carried to Babylon by Nebuchadnezzar.
Zedekiah	597–586 (11 years)	'He did that which was evil in the sight of the LORD' (2 Chron 36:11–16). Made king by Nebuchadnezzar, he rebelled at the instigation of Egypt.

Under the last four kings the final twenty-three years (609–586 BC) of the history of Judah brought total disaster. Nebuchadnezzar closed the history of an independent nation in 586 BC, leaving a devastated city and a deported people.

A. Judah and the Nations

The last thirty years of the existence of the independent little kingdom of Judah, before it was swept into the Babylonian Empire, were years of international turmoil on the world stage. The mighty Assyrian Empire was in rapid decline since the death of its last great ruler – King Ashurbanipal, in 627 BC. The Neo-Babylonian power was, just as rapidly, gaining power under the astute diplomacy and military skill of King Nabopolassar and his son Nebuchadnezzar. As well as the military successes of Babylon on the battlefield, there were uprisings in many areas, as subject peoples began to see the possibility of gaining their freedom. The ruthlessness and cruelty of the Assyrian army were such as to stir up much bitterness in subject peoples. This was the cause of the restlessness in and around the little kingdom of Judah in these closing years of the monarchy. Judah was caught between the waning power of Assyria, the rising power of Babylon, and the driving ambition of Egypt. This is the background that dominates the historical records of Israel in Kings (2 Kgs 22–25) and Chronicles (2 Chron. 34–36). The statements in the book of Daniel fit into the history recorded there. For clarity in a time of turmoil, as well as for ready reference, the major events of that period, with the dates, are set out as follows:

627 BC — Death of King Ashurbanipal and Decline of the Assyrian Empire

The mighty Assyrian Empire, which had dominated the world since 850 BC, was showing signs of terminal decline. The last of its mighty kings was Ashurbanipal, son of Esarhaddon (2 Kgs 19:37; Ezra 4:2; Isa. 37:38) and grandson of Sennacherib, to whom there are thirteen references in the OT, as he moves across the history of Israel and Judah. He died in the year 627 BC. From this point the Assyrian Empire went into a political meltdown that permitted an epidemic of uprisings across the whole empire. So despotic and utterly merciless had been Assyrian rule that subject peoples, embittered by needless cruelty, rebelled at any sign of weakness. Because of such shameful atrocities, the prophet Nahum was used of God to denounce the Assyrians, and especially their capital city, Nineveh, in very plain terms: 'Woe to the bloody city! It is all full of lies and robbery' (Nah. 3:1). Zephaniah joins in this condemnation: 'Woe to her that is filthy and polluted, to the oppressing city!' (Zeph. 3:1).

One major uprising, which gave Assyria its biggest problem, was centred on Babylon. In this city, in 625 BC, the leader of the Chaldean ethnic group, Nabopolassar, proclaimed himself King of Babylon and declared Babylon independent of Assyria. He gathered neighbouring states, one by one, under his banner and made a military alliance with the Medes to march against the capital of the empire – Nineveh.

612 BC Fall of Nineveh

In facing the Assyrian armies sent to deal with the uprising, Nabopolassar had shown great personal courage in battle, which, backed by strategic and tactical skill in handling men on the battlefield, as well as diplomatic skills around the conference table, made him an outstanding leader. He defeated the armies raised to deal with his rebellion, and, with a masterly touch, fashioned an alliance with the Medes and Scythians to attack Nineveh, the capital of Assyria. In August 612 BC, after a siege of two months, Nineveh, that great city, which earlier had repented under the preaching of Jonah (Jon. 3:1–10), fell before Nabopolassar. The ruthlessness and cruelty shown to so many captive peoples over two hundred years were now to be repaid in blood. Not only was the Assyrian army wiped out, but also, once the wall was breached, the whole population of the city, including women and children, was ruthlessly put to death. Animosity and revenge demanded that the city be utterly destroyed. It was left a smouldering ruin in the desert.

B. The Kingdom of Judah

609 BC Battle of Megiddo

King Josiah, placed on the throne of Judah in 621 BC as a boy of eight, was used of God to bring about a spiritual recovery to Judah. This recovery was stimulated by the finding of a copy of the book of the Law of the LORD (2 Chron. 34:14–15) and the personal response of the king in obedience. The weakness now manifest in the Assyrian Empire permitted Josiah, with the support of his professedly restored people, to recover some of his territory lost to the all-conquering Assyrian armies in the previous years (2 Kgs 22:8–13; 23:19). But, sadly, despite solemn warnings from God through the prophet Jeremiah, Josiah, in his self-confidence, over-reached himself. In 609 BC the Egyptians, under Pharaoh-Necho, gave notice to Josiah that Pharaoh-Necho intended to lead an army along the coastal route through Judah to assist the Assyrians against the Babylonian rebels (2 Chron. 35:21). Nabopolassar, accompanied by his son Nebuchadnezzar as crown prince, at the head of his army, was marching through the disintegrating Assyrian Empire intent on seizing what he could. The Egyptians had the same ambition, but, on the pretext of helping Assyria, were intent on helping themselves to whatever areas they could bring within their grasp. Josiah, fearful of Egyptian ambition, raised an army to oppose Pharaoh. The two armies met in the valley of Megiddo (2 Chron. 35: 20–24). Josiah and his army were completely routed and Pharaoh marched northwards to assist Assyria against Babylon. Josiah, fatally wounded in the battle, was carried back to Jerusalem to die and was buried there. Josiah's untimely death remains a testimony to the cost of disobedience to God and the consequent unwise interference in the politics of earth.

609 BC Reign of Jehoahaz, 3 months

The people of Judah replaced Josiah with his son Jehoahaz as king (2 Chron. 36:1). Why they chose Jehoahaz, instead of his older brother, was most likely due to internal politics. It appears that Jehoahaz belonged to the pro-Babylon faction amongst the leaders in Jerusalem. The party that formerly had supported Josiah in his going to the aid of Babylon was now pressing the claim of Jehoahaz against that of his older brother, who favoured Egypt. However, Jehoahaz was king for just three months. Pharaoh-Necho had found Nebuchadnezzar too wily an opponent to face a major battle with Egypt as yet. Frustrated in his purpose, and returning to Egypt, he decided that Judah must be taught a lesson. Having lost its army at Megiddo, Judah had no defensive force to oppose Pharaoh. There was no battle: Pharaoh simply deposed Jehoahaz, and replaced him with his older brother Eliakim, whose name he changed to Jehoiakim. To punish Judah and make the nation feel its subjection he demanded an annual tribute of one hundred talents of silver and a talent of gold.

609–606 BC Reign of Jehoiakim, 11 years

This remained the situation for three years. Judah was part of the Egyptian Empire and King Jehoiakim was the puppet of Pharaoh-

Necho of Egypt and paid annual tribute. In the background is the disintegrating Assyrian Empire, with the powerful King Nabopolassar of Babylon marching through the former Assyrian lands, bringing them, one by one, under his control. However, King Nabopolassar of Babylon was already seriously ill. He placed the crown prince and heir-apparent, his son Nebuchadnezzar, in command of the army. Nebuchadnezzar had been at his father's side for years and shown himself a courageous leader, a brilliant military strategist, and a tactician of the highest quality. Nation after nation fell before the might of Babylon. Finally, Nebuchadnezzar and his army arrived at the gates of Jerusalem.

C. The Neo-Babylonian Empire and Judah

606 BC Nebuchadnezzar captures Jerusalem: First Invasion

(a) The Date of the First Invasion by Nebuchadnezzar

Daniel tells the story: 'In the third year of the reign of Jehoiakim king of Judah came Nebuchadnezzar king of Babylon unto Jerusalem, and besieged it' (Dan. 1:1). Since Jehoiakim was made king in 609 BC, the third year of his reign is 606 BC. This is counting regnal years as simply years, without adding another year with the new religious year (1st *Nisan*). Daniel was counting regnal years, as was done in Babylon; when Jeremiah spoke of this same year he dated it 'the fourth year of Jehoiakim the son of Josiah king of Judah' (Jer. 46:2), since the Hebrew method of counting regnal years was to reckon the period from the actual date of enthronement to the 1st *Nisan* following as one year. Without the slightest reason, except the silence of Babylonian chronicles, of which we only possess fragments, many liberal critics have denied this date for the capture of Jerusalem – claiming it came a year later. Critics base their objection on the fact that the *Chronicles of the Chaldean Kings* make no mention of this particular invasion.[1]

The critics seem to forget that, in the judgement of Babylonian historians, these side campaigns from the main battles were of very minor interest for posterity, and therefore no mention is made of them in the records. There is very weighty support for the view that in the summer of 606 BC Nebuchadnezzar, in subduing the Assyrian Empire, and in the process deposing puppet states of Egypt, did

[1] Wood, *A Commentary on Daniel*, p. 28.

besiege Jerusalem, as Scripture states. Sir Robert Anderson draws upon the evidence of the Babylonian historian Berosus and writes:

> We learn from Berosus that it was as Prince-Royal of Babylon, at the head of his father's army, that Nebuchadnezzar invaded Palestine. And, after recording, how that in the course of that expedition Nebuchadnezzar heard of his father's death, the historian goes on to say that 'he committed the captives he had taken from the Jews to the charge of others while he went in haste over the desert to Babylon'.[2]

Could corroboration of Scripture be more emphatic'?[3] The works of Berosus[4] are now lost, but this quotation comes through Josephus.[5] Scripture supports this (1:1) and shows that Daniel was amongst the first deportees that Nebuchadnezzar had brought to Babylon.

(b) Effects of the First Invasion by Nebuchadnezzar

(1) King Jehoiakim

There is no suggestion of any destruction of the city of Jerusalem on this occasion. Jehoiakim had no forces to muster against Nebuchadnezzar and surrendered quickly to the might of Babylon, and the city seems to have been largely untouched. For King Jehoiakim himself, Nebuchadnezzar first 'bound him in fetters' (2 Chron. 36:6), likely intending to carry him to Babylon. Then that autocratic despot changed his mind, freed Jehoiakim, and placed him back on the throne as a puppet king. What promises were demanded or given is not recorded. For Jehoiakim himself, it was simply a change of overlord – an Egyptian Pharaoh replaced by a Babylonian King.

(2) The Temple

Nebuchadnezzar had to display proof of his victory to Babylon, and so some of the sacred vessels of the Temple in Jerusalem were carried to Babylon. It is to be noted that Daniel very accurately points out that only 'part of the vessels of the house of God' were given into the hand of Nebuchadnezzar.

[2] Anderson, *Daniel in the Critics' Den*, p. 14.

[3] Anderson, *Daniel in the Critics' Den*, p. 17.

[4] Berosus or Berossus (lived *c.*260 BC) was a priest in Babylon who wrote three books (in Greek) of Babylonian history, making use of the archives in the Temple of Bel. Works no longer extant but quoted in Josephus (note 5).

[5] Josephus, *Complete Works*, p. 613

(3) The People

It is made very clear that little destruction took place in the city, little damage was done to the Temple, and few of the people were deported. In his personal story, Daniel refers to a number of young men, selected from the royal and leading families in Jerusalem, who were removed to Babylon at this time (1:3–5). These, as noticed previously, were sent ahead of Nebuchadnezzar himself to Babylon to await his arrival. Daniel was amongst this first group of captives deported to Babylon. This group, distinct from those deported in the later invasions, were not slaves to be sold, but were selected as fit to undertake Babylonian training for service in the administration of the empire. This was a unique quality in Nebuchadnezzar that sets him apart from many other tyrants – he gave some thought to the conciliation of those he must make enemies by his conquests; he carried out this policy throughout his lifetime.

The subjection of Jehoiakim under Nebuchadnezzar only lasted for three years (2 Kgs 24:1) – until 603 BC. At this point, despite the pleading and the prayers of Jeremiah, King Jehoiakim listened to the promises of help from Egypt and the advice of suborned counsellors in Jerusalem, and rebelled against Babylon. While the judgement for this treacherous act did not come instantly, it did come – inevitably and inescapably. The delay was caused by the pressure of world events and the fact that Nebuchadnezzar had first to deal with Egypt.

For the history of the years between 605–597 BC, the date of Nebuchadnezzar's second invasion of Judah, see Appendix 2 – History of the Neo-Babylonian Empire.

597 BC Nebuchadnezzar besieges Jerusalem: Second Invasion

Deportation of the People

While Egypt was finished as a great world power after the Battle of Carchemish[6] (605 BC), she could still stir up lots of problems for Nebuchadnezzar – and she did. There is no doubt that Egypt made many promises of aid to the pro-Egypt party amongst Judaean leaders and thus incited Jehoiakim of Judah to rebel against Nebuchadnezzar. He listened to the promises of the Egyptian Pharaoh and rebelled against Nebuchadnezzar in the sixth year of

[6] See Appendix 2.

his reign, 603 BC (2 Kgs 24:1). While there was plenty of trouble in the following years (2 Kgs 24:2–4), Nebuchadnezzar had so many enemies and so much to contend with that it took a little time for him to deal with this rebellious king. While Nebuchadnezzar was not able at this time to invade Egypt – his real enemy – he could certainly deal with a puny vassal state like Judah, which historians tell us could have fielded an army of no more than ten thousand strong at this time. In 597 BC Nebuchadnezzar gathered a mighty army against rebellious Judah. In this same year Jehoiakim, the rebel, had died and been replaced by his son Jehoiachin (597 BC), who reigned just one hundred days – three months and ten days (2 Chron. 36:9). Then the King of Babylon arrived outside the walls of Jerusalem.

Events followed swiftly:

1. King Nebuchadnezzar besieged Jerusalem (2 Kgs 24:10–12).
2. King Jehoiachin surrendered and was taken to Babylon in chains and remained there for thirty-seven years in captivity. He outlived his captor.
3. The valuable vessels from the king's house and the sacred vessels from the Lord's house were removed to Babylon. All the treasures from Solomon's day were looted – in fact everything of value was carried to Babylon.
4. A total deportation of the people of Judaea to Babylon took place. All the people with any claim to status or with a skill were deported – ten thousand from one area (2 Kgs 24:14) – princes and mighty men, craftsmen and smiths. Seven thousand were deported from another area (2 Kgs 24:16) until Scripture records 'none remained, save the poorest sort of the people of the land' (2 Kgs 24:14). It was at this time that Ezekiel was deported to Babylon.
5. Nebuchadnezzar replaced King Jehoiachin with his uncle Mattaniah, brother of his father Jehoiakim (2 Kgs 24:17) and changed his name to Zedekiah; he ruled for eleven years – from 597 to 586 BC.

586 BC Nebuchadnezzar besieges Jerusalem: Third Invasion

Destruction of Jerusalem

Zedekiah does not appear to have learned any lesson from the plain and sober words of Jeremiah, nor from the sad end of his rebellious predecessors. The history of his reign is a tragic story (2 Chron. 36:11–

21). He shows not a single redeeming feature as he continued to rebel against the Word of the Lord and pursue his disastrous Egyptian policy of rebellion against Babylon. Nebuchadnezzar 'had made him swear by God' (2 Chron. 36:13). Jeremiah had warned Jehoiakim, in 597 BC, of the folly of rebelling against Nebuchadnezzar (Jer. 27:1–11). Later, in 588–586 BC, he repeated the same message, with additional warnings to Zedekiah (Jer. 27:12–22). The Lord spoke clearly:

> And now have I given all these lands into the hand of Nebuchadnezzar the king of Babylon, My servant ... And it shall come to pass, that the nation and kingdom which will not serve the same Nebuchadnezzar ... that nation will I punish (Jer. 27:6–8).

God had been patient; now justice must be done. Nevertheless, given permission of God, there is no question that the fury of Nebuchadnezzar drove him beyond the limit that Divine purpose had allowed. Nebuchadnezzar will bear his own responsibility before God.[7] Patience exhausted, a furious Nebuchadnezzar boded ill for Jerusalem. In fact, it brought about the total destruction of the city.

(a) The people – all using the sword died by the sword: the rebels were virtually wiped out, but the death toll went far beyond this as Babylonian rage spared neither women nor children nor had any mercy on the aged. Jerusalem was literally put to the sword. The whole province, not just the city this time, was systematically depopulated. From outlying areas of Judaea over ten thousand skilled men of various trades were deported to Babylon, with further deportations following (Jer. 52:28–30). Zedekiah was forced to watch the slaying of his sons and was then blinded.

(b) The place – the city and Temple and the palaces were first stripped of any remaining treasures and then burned. The wall around the city was broken down. Nebuchadnezzar's intention was to wipe Jerusalem off the political map.

Note:

Captivity years are dated from the first invasion	606 BC
Desolation years are dated from the third invasion	586 BC

[7] One would wonder if the satanic angel behind Babylon at this time could be one of the four angels 'bound in the great River Euphrates' (Rev. 9:13–14). 'Bound', because they influenced the kings of the nations represented in the image of Nebuchadnezzar's dream to go beyond the limit allowed by God for the chastisement of Israel. There is no question but they would have liked, in the interests of their satanic master, to wipe out Israel completely.

is the first Babylonian invasion of Judah.[2] King Jehoiakim surrenders and Nebuchadnezzar reappoints him as his vassal king. News of his father's death reaches Nebuchadnezzar while in Jerusalem. As a result he sends a small band of captives, including Daniel, back to Babylon under escort, by the normal route – northwards and down the Euphrates. Nebuchadnezzar himself, with a small escort, hurries directly to Babylon across the desert.

605 BC When Nebuchadnezzar, son of Nabopolassar, was acclaimed king in Babylon on the death of his father, he was well aware that as his first priority he had to deal with Egypt, who had supported the old Assyrian Empire against Babylon. By a combination of political acumen in winning allies around the council table and then military skill on the field of battle, he defeated Pharaoh-Necho comprehensively at the Battle of Carchemish (605 BC). This was the name of the town, near the River Euphrates, where, in August 605 BC, these two mighty armies finally faced each other. The Egyptian army of Pharaoh-Necho was utterly routed. There would be further battles and Egypt would still be a source of trouble, but any Egyptian aspiration after world dominance was only a dream. Babylon ruled the known world.

605–562 BC During these forty-three years King Nebuchadnezzar ruled the world of his day from his capital city – Babylon. His relationship with Israel as represented in the tiny kingdom of Judah is dealt with in some detail in Appendix 1, 'History of Judah'. In his final attack on Jerusalem, in 586 BC, he left the city in ruins, the Temple utterly devastated and the vast majority of the population deported to Babylon – the few remaining were placed under a governor – Gedaliah. This book of Daniel has its background in those years, and all important events scripturally are dealt with in the commentary as they arise

562 BC The death of King Nebuchadnezzar. Few details are on record. A fragment of a tablet suggests that Gedaliah (2 Kgs 25:22), the governor in Jerusalem appointed by Nebuchadnezzar, was murdered. Information reaching Babylon pointed to Egypt as the instigator of this rebellious act. This enraged Nebuchadnezzar so much that he gathered a disciplinary force and marched to invade Egypt and teach Pharaoh a lesson. It would seem that he died on the march.

[2] See Appendix 1.

562–560 BC Amel-Marduk (Evil-Merodach) reigned less than two years. The oldest son of Nebuchadnezzar, he was an evil man – without any principles. His profligate lifestyle brought him few friends. One historian writes: 'he was restrained neither by law nor by decency.'[3] It would seem that the solitary decent act in his life is on record in Scripture – the kindly treatment granted to King Jehoiachin (2 Kgs 25:27–30). After reigning less than two years he was murdered in a palace revolution.

560–556 BC Nergal-sharra-usur (Neriglissar) reigned less than four years. This experienced general, who had married a daughter of Nebuchadnezzar, led a very successful and very profitable military invasion of Cilicia. From the booty gained on this invasion, he bestowed much wealth on several temples in Babylon. The circumstances around his death in 556 BC are unclear but there were suspicions of murder.

556 BC Labashi-Marduk reigned three months.
This young son of Neriglissar attempted to assume the throne but the chief officers of state rebelled and he was removed after three months. They placed one of the conspirators on the throne – Nabonidus by name.

556–539 BC Nabonidus reigned seventeen years.
A distinguished and experienced general, who had led armies of Nebuchadnezzar to many a well-deserved victory, he proved to be a skilled negotiator who brought peace to many of the rebellious nations under Babylonian suzerainty. While he had been one of the conspirators who had rebelled against Labashi-Marduk, the son of Nebuchadnezzar's son-in-law (Neriglissar), his claim to the throne lay in the fact that he had married another daughter of Nebuchadnezzar, called Nitocris. While the evidence from the archives is not conclusive, this is suggested as the best interpretation of the information available at present.[4]

A number of things made him somewhat unpopular with the people, as distinct from the court, in Babylon. He himself confessed to being of lowly birth and not connected to royalty – a fatal weakness in Babylonian society even if his marriage gave him some

[3] Oates, *Babylon* p. 131, quotation from Berosus (or Berossus).
[4] See comments in the text at 5:10.

standing. He was also a devoted worshipper of his mother's idol – the god Sin, at Harran. On this idol he bestowed wealth incalculable and tried to force her worship on the Babylonians – which did not make him very popular in a Babylon devoted to the god Marduk. Finally, he became what would be called today an antiquarian – one interested in archaeological pursuits and unearthing past inscriptions on buildings and tombs.

What is of major interest in light of the book of Daniel is that for the last ten years of his reign King Nabonidus was not in Babylon. A Harran inscription reads: 'But I hied myself afar from my city of Babylon ... ten years to my city I went not in.'[5] A number of motives may lie behind this action. It may have been: (a) his unpopularity, as described above – he seemed happier away from the capital; (b) his very genuine interest in the many archaeological sites in Harran, and particularly in the oasis of Taima, in northwest Arabia, where he spent his last years; (c) a real apprehension at the growing power of Persia and his design to place a Babylonian army, albeit with a peaceful objective, in a location where action could be quickly taken against Cyrus. When such action was required, he did take it and led an army to confront Cyrus before he reached Babylon. Roundly defeated, he himself was taken prisoner and, indeed, seems to have been in Persian captivity when Babylon was besieged.

549 BC Nabonidus left Babylon for Taima and placed his son Belshazzar in charge of the city as regent. He gave to Belshazzar the title 'King of Babylon'. Clearly, Nabonidus remained king of the empire and Belshazzar his son was his regent in the city of Babylon.

For many years liberal commentators delighted to point out that the mention of Belshazzar in this book was without any historical support. The name of Belshazzar did not occur on any of the king lists of Babylon. The *Chronicles of the Chaldean Kings* were perfectly clear that Nabonidus was the last king of the Neo-Babylonian Empire, before it fell to Cyrus. It was pointed out very forcefully that the records left no time for the reign of anyone called Belshazzar. Liberal scholarship claimed that Daniel had made a mistake that no sixth-century BC writer could have done.[6] A pseudo-Daniel writing in the second century BC could readily have been mistaken – so liberal scholarship claimed.

[5] Oates, *Babylon*, p. 133.

[6] Anderson, *Daniel in the Critics' Den*, p. 23.

Some conservative commentators had attempted to solve the problem by seeking to identify Belshazzar as Evil-Merodach. Keil follows this line[7] but the difficulties make such identification unlikely, if not impossible. Now a number of freshly deciphered texts from archaeological research have shown that Belshazzar was co-regent with his father of the city of Babylon.[8] The additional suggestion that has altered the picture and helps in the identification of the queen (5:10) is that the wife of Nabonidus is the daughter of Nebuchadnezzar and some name her as Nitocris.[9] Since the mid-nineteenth century various inscriptions have been deciphered and, in particular, the Nabonidus cylinders have been read, and they show, beyond question, that Belshazzar was the eldest son of Nabonidus who, trusting his son completely, possibly as early as the third year of his reign (553 BC) placed him as co-regent. When he left the city, he gave Belshazzar the title 'King of Babylon'. This explains why Belshazzar offered the interpreter of the writing on the wall the position of third ruler in the kingdom – a 'triumvir' (third ruler).[10] Belshazzar himself was but the second.

539 BC On the night of October 13, the annual feast of Marduk, the city of Babylon fell to the might of the Medo-Persian army under Cyrus King of Persia. King Belshazzar died that night (5:30). Daniel was a true prophet.

[7] Keil and Delitzsch, *Commentary on the Old Testament*, Vol. 9. p. 185.
[8] Wood, *A Commentary on Daniel*, p. 131 quotes Smith, *Babylonian Historical Texts, Relating to the Downfall of Babylon*.
[9] Miller, *New American Commentary, Daniel*, p. 160, and note the reference to primary sources at footnote 73.
[10] Wood, *A Commentary on Daniel*, p. 130.

APPENDIX 3

HISTORY OF THE MEDO-PERSIAN EMPIRE

DATES RELEVANT TO THE BOOK OF DANIEL

From Cyrus the Great to Alexander the Great, 559–331 BC

Daniel lived in the crucial years of the decline of the might of Babylon and the emergence on the world stage of Cyrus the Great, who led a rebellion against his Median overlord, King Astyages, and established what historians refer to the Achaemenid dynasty, under which the Persian Empire reached its greatest power and widest extent. Isaiah spoke of this man two hundred years before his appearance (Isa. 44:28; 45:1–7) as one who would play a vital part in the history of God's people – God spoke of him as 'My shepherd' and '[My] anointed'. Coming into the Bible story in the time of Daniel, in the siege and capture of the city of Babylon, he and the kings that followed him played an important part in the history of the returned exiles of Judah to Jerusalem. The history of their treatment of the returned remnant is recorded in the books of Esther, Ezra, Nehemiah, Haggai, Zechariah, and Malachi.

Daniel in Babylon from 606 BC

The Rise of Cyrus the Great to World Dominion[1]

Cyrus was the son of Cambyses I of Persia, who in 559 BC was crowned king of a tiny kingdom called Anshan, in Persia, under King Astyages of the Median Empire. Rebelling against the Median king, he defeated him in battle and in 550 BC began an extensive

[1] *OCD*, p. 407.

series of campaigns in which he conquered the Median kingdom and brought into subjection all the lands of eastern Mesopotamia.

In 546 BC Cyrus launched another campaign and defeated the king of Lydia (modern Turkey), in Asia Minor, to bring under his control the great wealth of that kingdom. A few years later, in 539 BC, Cyrus utterly routed the army of King Nabonidus of Babylon (Nebuchadnezzar's father) and took him prisoner. Nabonidus had led this army into Arabia and based it at Taima in an attempt to curb the rising power of Cyrus, the Persian king. However, Cyrus was unstoppable, and on October 13, 539 BC Babylon fell to his army and Belshazzar was slain (5:30). The history of the Neo-Babylonian Empire was closed. World power passed to the Medo-Persia Empire, under Cyrus King of Persia (10:1).

Daniel under the Medo-Persian Empire 539 BC

The Medo-Persian Empire under Cyrus the Great generally was more accommodating to the subject peoples it inherited from the Babylonian Empire than either Assyria or Babylon had been. Two policies laid down by Cyrus contributed to this more relaxed approach, and are to be seen in the record of Daniel: (a) It was the policy of Cyrus to take capable men from the defeated nation and put them in very responsible posts in his empire. This can be seen in his appointment of Darius the Median to be king in Babylon. There is no previous record of this man (see comments at 5:31); (b) It was also policy for Cyrus to allow captive peoples to return to their own lands if they so desired. This was not always possible or feasible but it can be seen how God could use this man in the furtherance of His purpose for His people. So it is of importance to note:

538 BC Edict of Cyrus concerning Israel (2 Chron. 36:22)
536 BC Return of a remnant of Israel under Zerubbabel to Jerusalem

It is the members of this company who are the focus of scriptural history, for through them would come the Messiah. How they were treated under the Medo-Persian rule is the background for the books of Ezra, Nehemiah, Haggai, Zechariah, and Malachi. The Book of Esther shows the treatment of Jews who did not return to Jerusalem but remained under direct Medo-Persian rule.

Israel under the Medo-Persian Empire from 539 BC

Dates (BC) to mark relations between the returned remnant of Israel in Jerusalem and Medo-Persian Kings:

530 BC	Death of Cyrus	
530–522 BC	Cambyses	Son of Cyrus
522–521 BC	Pseudo-Smerdis	A usurper who reigned only six months
521–486 BC	Darius I (Hystaspes)	Ezra 4:24; Hag. 1:1; Zech. 1:1
485–465 BC	Xerxes I (Ahasuerus)	Est. 1:1–4
465–424 BC	Artaxerxes Longimanus	Ezra 7:1–27; Neh. 2:1–9
424 BC	Xerxes II	
423–404 BC	Darius II	
404–358 BC	Artaxerxes II	
358–338 BC	Artaxerxes III	
338–336 BC	Arses	
336–331 BC	Darius III	

The date of Messiah's coming to earth is the key to the prophetic programme. The key date that fixes this was given to Daniel in 538 BC. The date for Messiah's coming was to be fixed by the action of a Persian king and described thus: 'That from the going forth of the commandment to restore and to build Jerusalem unto the Messiah the Prince, shall be seven weeks, and threescore and two weeks' (Dan. 9:25). It will be shown that this commandment went forth from King Artaxerxes Longimanus in the twentieth year of his reign (Neh 2:1). This date will be shown to correspond to 445 BC, and thus ninety-three years after this writing of Daniel.

The last king, Darius III, was the king so comprehensively defeated by Alexander the Great when he crossed the Hellespont with his Macedonian army in the spring of 334 BC and attacked the Medo-Persian Empire. Three major battles followed: the Battle of Granicus River (334 BC), the Battle of Issus (333 BC), and, finally, the Battle of Gaugamela (331 BC). After this last defeat, Darius III was murdered by his own courtiers and Alexander the Great took control of the empire. Thus, the Grecian Empire moves on to the world stage.

The death of Darius III (331 BC) is generally accepted by secular historians as the date when the Medo-Persian Empire was replaced on the world stage by the Grecian Empire. It is marked in the image of Nebuchadnezzar's dream as the point where the silver of the breast and arms is replaced by the bronze of the belly and thighs.

APPENDIX 4

HISTORY OF THE GRECIAN EMPIRE

DATES RELEVANT TO THE BOOK OF DANIEL

From Alexander the Great to Antiochus IV Epiphanes

From Alexander the Great to the end of the Seleucid Dynasty and the Emergence of Rome on the World Stage
323–64 BC

THE RISE OF ALEXANDER THE GREAT TO WORLD DOMINION

Relevant Dates

336 BC Darius III Codomannus becomes King of Persia
Philip II of Macedon assassinated.
Alexander, son of Philip II, crowned as King of Macedon in his father's place.

Seizing the opportunity, Athens and Thebes immediately rebelled against Macedonian rule. Both cities learned to their cost that Alexander was as able a military commander as his father, Philip, had been: Alexander crushed both cities. As King of Macedon, he was entitled to be head of The League of Corinth, a union of Greek city-states formed to unite the Greek city-states in opposition to the power of Persia as it spread to engulf mainland Greece. As such, Alexander inherited the role of commander-designate of the invasion army that was being mustered to attack Persia.

334 BC Spring – Alexander crossed the Hellespont with a maximum of around fifty thousand Macedonian veterans, now battle hardened, with some additional lightly armed Greek cavalry.

Alexander was leading the Greek crusade against a hated enemy who had humiliated Greek cities in the past. Darius hesitated to attack and Alexander captured Miletus and marched through Lycia and Pamphilia.

334 BC, May – Alexander chose the battleground. The armies met at the Battle of Granicus River. The army of Darius III was defeated and fled the field.

333 BC Alexander took his army through the Cilician Gates and reached Tarsus. Darius crossed the province, and they met in November at Issus, in Cilicia, where Darius III was again completely routed; his queen and their children were taken captive. Alexander refused the offer of Darius of a ransom and a portion of the empire.

332 BC Alexander captured Sidon and Tyre and the Philistine cities, including Gaza. Alexander invaded Egypt with little opposition. He was crowned as 'Pharaoh' in Memphis then founded a new city named after himself – the city of Alexandria. At this point Josephus the Jewish historian gives a most graphic account of the arrival of Alexander with his army before Jerusalem. It is possible that at this point he led an army into Judah and was welcomed in Jerusalem.[1]

331 BC Alexander moved his army into Babylonia. Darius sued for peace for the third and last time. Alexander rejected the appeal, crossed the Tigris, and both Babylon and Susa were captured.

331 BC, October – Battle of Gaugamela. The Persian army was almost totally destroyed. Darius III was murdered by members by his inner council when fleeing after the battle. Alexander gave him an honourable burial.

The Grecian Empire becomes a World Empire

With the defeat of Darius III the whole of the Medo-Persian Empire came under the nominal control of Alexander. He did his very best to make this a reality yet it led to many battles, skirmishes and subsidiary campaigns, as he marched his army as far as the Indus River, in India. Here he was stopped by the refusal of his Macedonian veterans to go any further. This mutiny on the banks

[1] Josephus, *Complete Works*, p. 244.

of the Indus River was in 326 BC, after which he further alienated his veteran officers by marrying Roxane, a Persian princess. In a temper, Alexander divided his army. Sending the larger part back overland, he travelled with the smaller army down the Indus River, subduing pockets of resistance as he travelled. Alexander returned to Babylon, where he immediately put in hand preparations for an attack westwards through the Mediterranean Sea towards Carthage and Rome. It was in Babylon at this time that Alexander, who by the League of Corinth had been appointed commander-designate of the invasion army, now received a delegation from that same authority, conferring on him the right to be called 'King of Grecia' instead of 'King of Macedon'. It had taken the Grecian leaders a long time to accept this but Daniel's prophetic word was true, when in 538 BC (over two hundred years before it took place) he had spoken of him, not only as King of Grecia, but as 'the first king' (8:20–21). The prophetic Word is accurate. By this time, Alexander was not only the first king of Grecia, as Daniel had been told, but he had been crowned as Pharaoh over Egypt, in Memphis.[2] Then, in the place of Darius III, he was installed as Emperor of Medo-Persia. He stands forth as the undisputed head of the greatest empire on earth at that time. His reign was short.

323 BC After a banquet in Babylon on the night of May 29, 323 BC, challenged to drink a goblet of unmixed wine, Alexander did so, collapsed, and was put to bed. The next day he had a high fever, yet by evening was back to ordering the affairs of his army. Another banquet that night, and the next day he was seriously ill with a raging fever. Taking to bed on June 5, he grew weaker by the hour until, in the late hours of June 9, King Alexander's senior officers and close friends gathered round his bed for the closing scene. The historian Peter Green records the scene:

> At this the King's friends, gathered round his bedside, asked him – it was after all, a vital question – to whom he bequeathed his kingdom. Weakly Alexander whispered: 'to the strongest'. His last all-too-prophetic words were: 'I foresee a great funeral

[2] Cartledge, *Alexander the Great*, p. xvii, gives date as November 332 BC. Green, *Alexander the Great*, p. 144, gives the detail.

> contest over me'. Early in the morning of 10th June 323 BC his eyes closed forever.[3]

In his dying moments, Alexander had passed his royal ring to Perdiccas, a friend from his youth and now his chief of staff. Before dawn, Perdiccas summoned the council of army generals and asked for a decision on the successor to Alexander. Under the Macedonian constitution, the army was entitled to do this and then forward the name of the chosen one to the senate in Agaea (the capital city of Macedon) for ratification. These men who had companied with Alexander throughout his campaigns knew well that a number of 'heirs' would soon make their claims to Alexander's kingdom. Amongst these claimants the most important would be:

(a) Philip Arrhidaeus – a mentally deficient half-brother of Alexander. His supporters called him Philip III.

(b) Roxane, the Persian princess and Alexander's only legal wife was with child. A son born posthumously in August 323 BC was named Alexander IV.

(c) Heracles – a four year old illegitimate son of Alexander by his mistress Barsine – daughter of Darius III.

Finally, after days of discussion in the army council, it was agreed that two of the 'heir apparent' group should nominally be recognised as jointly sharing the throne. Ruling out the illegitimate son, whom Alexander had never acknowledged as such, the army appointed the other two claimants as joint-rulers of the empire – Philip Arrhidaeus, half-brother of Alexander, and the unborn child of Roxane – if the baby was a boy. These two – a mentally deficient man and a baby – were to rule Alexander's empire. The real power would be in the hands of two regents, appointed by the army. These arrangements did not auger well for the empire. Undoubtedly, Perdiccas, Alexander's long-time friend and now his chief of staff, was the one who pushed for this strange arrangement. Since he had already control of the army, it seems that he saw himself as the most powerful man in the realm and calculated that he was sure to be appointed as regent. His first responsibility must be to get this appointment.

Eventually, after long wordy battles, he managed to get the council to accept his sole regency, but only after bitter controversy

[3] Green, *Alexander the Great*, p. 259.

in the army council. This spread to various army regiments backing their own candidates, to the point of open conflict. Indeed, lifetime friends were now fighting each other. The army was on the verge of chaos. The Macedonian veteran regiments, weary and homesick, were threatening to leave Babylon and set out for the homeland – Macedon. Eventually the council did appoint Perdiccas as sole regent for the two kings – an agreement that satisfied the army – but only for a time.

It has already been pointed out in the comments on the text that Scripture is explicit on the fact that none of Alexander's family would inherit any part of his empire – Daniel says plainly 'not to his posterity' (11:4). After Alexander's death, there is a terrible record of murder of those related to him:

317 BC Philip Arrhidaeus: named as Philip III. This half-brother to Alexander was murdered.

310 BC Alexander IV: thirteen-year-old son of Alexander's wife (Roxane) was put to death.

309 BC Hercales: illegitimate son of Alexander to Barsine, daughter of Darius III, was murdered.

Scripture is accurate!

323–281 BC In the history of these years it should be remembered that when he died Alexander was a young man of thirty-three years and most of the men who filled senior posts in his army were all personal friends of Alexander from his youth – and all about the same age. Young, ambitious and capable leaders in a veteran army, they were ready to fight to secure the spoils they thought they had earned from their conquests. This may help to explain why these years have been called 'one of the great forgotten wars of history' by a noted historian of this period. He writes: 'It took more or less forty years after the death of Alexander the Great for his heirs (the *Diadochoi* – the Successors) to finish carving up his vast empire. These years, 323–281 BC, were filled with high adventure, intrigue, passion, assassinations, dynastic marriages, treachery, shifting alliances, and mass slaughter on battlefield after battlefield'.[4] The

[4] Waterfield, *Dividing the Spoils*, p. ix.

'Peace of the Dynasts' (311 BC) was only an intermission in the endless feuding and fighting that eventually resulted, as Scripture had prophesied, 'not to his posterity, nor according to his dominion' (11:4). Prophecy became history as, after this period of turmoil, Alexander's 'successors' (historians use this term) succeeded in reaching relative stability with the empire divided into four, as Scripture said (8:8, 22); these divisions being geographically related – north, south, east, and west. The verb 'plucked up' used of Alexander's kingdom (11:4) points to an uprooting by force; battle after battle did exactly this. 'Nor according to his dominion' means not one of the men who succeeded him wielded a fraction of the authority that marked Alexander – they were smaller men in smaller kingdoms – virtually, each of them held just a province of the once-great empire. The four divisions of the Alexandrine Empire are noted.

311 BC Peace of the Dynasts.
Peace Treaty amongst Alexander's Generals.

National borders changed rapidly during this lengthy period (323–311 BC), as squabbles over particular areas continued. Finally, talking face to face in 311 BC, the four successors of Alexander worked out borders that were reasonably satisfactory to all. This agreement is known to historians as 'The Peace of the Dynasts'. They split the empire of Alexander into four regions as follows:

Area	**Alexander's Generals**	**Location**
Babylonia and North Syria	Seleucus I Nicator	North
Egypt	Ptolemy I Soter	South
Macedonia	Cassander	West
Thrace and Bithynia	Lysimachus	East

It will be observed that the centre of the geographic notation is neither Babylon (the Babylonian capital) nor Susa (the Persian capital) but Jerusalem. God, through Daniel, is focussing attention upon His people and their location – Israel, with Jerusalem as their capital city. Two parts of Alexander's empire come into the prophecies in the book of Daniel. The Seleucid Empire and dynasty in Syria, to the north of Israel, and the Ptolemaic Empire and dynasty in Egypt, to the south of Israel, appear in the prophecies of Daniel as:

311 BC	Ptolemy I (Egypt)	Dan 11:5	King of the South
311 BC	Seleucus I (Syria)	Dan 11:6	King of the North

So the gap between the death of Alexander and the appearance on the world scene of the kings mentioned in Daniel 11:4 and Daniel 11:5–6 is nineteen years.

The Kings that Troubled Israel

The Kings of the North

Syria **Capital Antioch**

The Seleucid Kings

312–281 BC	Seleucus I Nicator	'conqueror'
281–261 BC	Antiochus I Soter	'saviour'
261–246 BC	Antiochus II Theos	'god'
246–227 BC	Seleucus II Callinicus	'gloriously victorious'
227–223 BC	Seleucus III Soter	'saviour'
223–187 BC	Antiochus III Megas	'great', Dan. 11:11–13
187–175 BC	Seleucus IV Philopator	'father lover'
175–164 BC	Antiochus IV Epiphanes	'god manifest'
167 BC	Maccabean Revolt	
164–162 BC	Antiochus V Eupator	'a good father'

The Kings of the South

Egypt **Capital Alexandria**

The Ptolemaic Kings

322–285 BC	Ptolemy I Soter I	'saviour'
285–246 BC	Ptolemy II Philadelphus	'love of brother'
246–221 BC	Ptolemy III Euergetes	'benefactor'
221–204 BC	Ptolemy IV Philopator	'love of father'
204–180 BC	Ptolemy V Epiphanes	'glorious'
180–145 BC	Ptolemy VI Philometor	'love of mother'
145–116 BC	Ptolemy VIII Euergetes II nicknamed 'Physcon' ('the belly')	'benefactor'
116–107 BC	Ptolemy IX Soter II with Cleopatra III	'saviour'
107–101 BC	Ptolemy X Alexander and Cleopatra III	
101–88	Ptolemy X Alexander and Cleopatra Berenike	
88–81 BC	Ptolemy IX Soter II (second period of rule)	'saviour'
80 BC	Ptolemy XI Alexander II and Cleopatra Berenike	
80–51 BC	Ptolemy XII Neos Dionysos	
51–30 BC	Cleopatra Philopator	'father loving'

APPENDIX 6

THE MACCABEES AND THEIR TIMES

DANIEL 11:31–35

IN THE EXPOSITION of these verses it has been pointed out that at a point in Israel's history, future to Daniel, an invader, identified in the context as King of the North, would introduce into the Temple at Jerusalem what Scripture speaks of as 'the abomination that maketh desolate' (Dan. 8:13; 11:31). The fulfilment of this prophecy took place in 167 BC, when on the orders of Antiochus IV Epiphanes an idol of Jupiter (Zeus) Olympus was placed in the Temple of the Lord at Jerusalem. This action reveals both the profanity of the Seleucid king and the idolatry still acceptable to many of the priestly leaders in Israel, who had failed to learn the lesson of the captivity. In acknowledging the idol they would lead the nation to disaster.

The Abomination of Desolation

1. Defiled the Place (the Temple). No Israelite faithful to God and to His Word could now be associated with the Temple in Jerusalem. Judaism, as seen in the sacrificial system, was brought to an end. Scripture speaks very plainly: 'they shall profane the sanctuary' (Dan. 11:31, *RV*). The result is made plain in this next statement: '[they] shall take away the daily sacrifice'.

2. Divided the People (Israel). Already sorely divided by the acceptance or rejection of the Hellenisation programme, two very different groups or parties came to light in Israel. Scripture identifies the two parties by their behaviour thus: (a) 'such as do wickedly against the covenant'; and (b) 'the people that do know their God shall be strong, and do exploits' (Dan. 11:32). This latter party is to be identified historically as 'the Maccabees'.

The Maccabean Rebellion, 167–150 BC

The enforcement of the Hellenisation programme of Antiochus IV Epiphanes on the peoples in the empire was a direct result of the humiliation he had suffered at the hands of Rome in his last attack on the King of the South. It was the ruthless application of this policy in Judaea that sparked the Maccabean Rebellion.

167 BC Invading Egypt for his fourth and final time, Antiochus was publicly humiliated by coming face to face with the Roman consul, Gaius Popillius Laenas, who, unknown to him, was on Egyptian soil. Neither did he know that the consul was supported by a fleet conveying Roman legions from a very successful campaign in Greece, where the Macedonian ally of Antiochus had been decisively defeated. Antiochus knew his army had no answer to the might of the Roman legions, so he had no real choice but to withdraw from Egypt and remove all his garrisons. Antiochus vented his frustration and rage on Jerusalem, whose people had recently shown great joy when a false rumour of his death had reached them. So Antiochus sent his lieutenant Apollonius, with an army of twenty-two thousand men, to destroy the city. Taking advantage of the Sabbath day, when he knew the Jews would not take to arms, Apollonius attacked the synagogues first, massacred the men, and took the women and children captive. He burned the city and erected a fort designed to dominate the Temple, while defiling it with the presence of the idol and sprinkling the blood of pigs. The Hellenisation programme decreed by Antiochus was to be ruthlessly enforced in Judaea. This demanded that all countries under his rule must worship his god and no other. So Jerusalem must become a Greek city, with a Greek temple.

Menelaus, the high priest in Jerusalem, was but the tool of Antiochus. He was the man who had bribed Antiochus with a very big bribe to get the job. To get something back, Antiochus stole the gold and silver vessels that were in the Temple and sold them to Greek traders. This action by Antiochus would be the instrument that Menelaus would use against his bitter enemies, the faithful believers who stood obediently by the Word of God. Menelaus was one of the apostates described as 'them that forsake the holy covenant' (11:30). The majority of the priests followed Antiochus, and an image of Jupiter (Zeus) Olympus was erected in the Temple and, to the horror of the Jews, on December 25, 167 BC a pig was sacrificed on the brazen altar and its blood was sprinkled on the holy vessels and in the holy places. Officers, commissioned by Antiochus and backed by troops, moved through the whole land, enforcing the decree of the king. All sacrifices were forbidden, circumcision was outlawed, Sabbath-keeping was disallowed, and the burning of the sacred writings was commanded. Any Jew who refused was to be put to death. This sets the stage for the inaugural action of what became known as the Maccabean Rebellion.

The brief reference in Scripture (11:31–35) opens up a fascinating period of Israel's history. The story that comes down to us, through the history of Israel at this time, displays the unswerving faithfulness of those who believed the Word of God. In this they become a pattern for those who will suffer during the Tribulation period and both will enter into the blessedness of the coming Kingdom. This is confirmed by the NT reference to what can only be the same historic period in the Hebrew Epistle (Heb. 11:33–38). This is the truth that will sustain the believers in the Tribulation period, so it is easy to see how the Maccabean period becomes a picture of the time of the Tribulation yet to come.

Since few details of this historic period are given in Scripture, it is necessary to draw upon extra-biblical sources for the information, and the question arises as to the reliability of these sources. In this case the two main sources are the author Josephus and the author of the First Book of the Maccabees. As the works of these writers are studied for details of the Maccabean period, the following assessments should be kept in mind:

A. Josephus – His Jewish name was Joseph ben Mattathias. He was born in Jerusalem *c.* AD 37. His father was a priest while his mother was linked directly to the princes of the Hasmonean lineage of the Maccabees. Educated in Hebrew and Greek, Josephus had been a Pharisee. As an able man of twenty-six years, he accepted a mission to Rome as a peace delegate to meet the Emperor Nero. Josephus liked Rome and made many friends there. When, in AD 66, the Jews rose in rebellion against the Roman power, Josephus, as the governor of Galilee, was given an army to fight against the Roman legions. In this, he showed tactical skill and great courage. However, he knew full well that any victory could only be temporary and any resistance against the might of the legions of Rome would, in the end, be simply a hopeless gesture costing many lives. The advance of the Roman legions, under Vespasian, was irresistible, and after being besieged in the fortress of Jotapata for forty-seven days, he surrendered the city. He was placed under a kind of benevolent 'house arrest', or 'parole', for three years. He was still with the army of Titus when Jerusalem was besieged; after that, he appears to have resided in Rome and to have survived until after the death of Herod Agrippa II, who died in AD 100. He produced a number of writings, in both Hebrew and Greek, on Jewish history and religion. After his main bias as a Jewish apologist is taken into account, and his tendency to speak well of his Roman patrons, he is generally considered to have used his sources wisely and to have written the history of his own times accurately.[1] In this case, Josephus gives a connected history of the whole period, drawing upon the Books of the Maccabees but bringing in other writings – notably long quotations from the writings of Polybius, of Diodorus, and of Appian. The original manuscripts from which Josephus quoted are no longer available, having long since perished.

Where his facts are open to the cross-checking of history he stands out as quite a reliable historian. Most secular historians give him high marks for accurate recording, even when they take into account his apologetic approach for the Jew and his obvious desire to keep on good terms with his Roman friends. He should be judged by the same standard as other secular historians. When in conflict with Scripture it must be remembered that Scripture is the final authority – Divinely given.

B. The Books of the Maccabees – The Maccabean story is told in two independent narratives written by authors who differ in ability and in emphases. These are two of the fourteen books that make up the Apocrypha. None of the books in the Apocrypha are recognised as inspired documents; they have no claim whatever to be recognised as Holy Scripture; they must on no account be used for the teaching of doctrine. However, that having been made clear, a further statement on the value of these two books can be made as follows:

(a) The First Book of Maccabees is an honest piece of historical writing from the pen of an observer recording events and edicts and happenings within his knowledge. It details, with very little adornment, the happenings throughout this stirring struggle, first for religious freedom and then for political freedom, of the Jews who had returned from the captivity in Babylon to the land of Israel. Serious historians of the period give this first Maccabean

[1] Riggs. *A History of the Jewish People*, p. 4.

chronicle very high marks for accuracy and reliability – just keeping in mind the racial bias of the author and his tendency to glorify the Maccabean heroes.

(b) The Second Book of Maccabees covers much the same ground but is by a much less skilled writer. He shows the absolute superiority of Judaism over any or every pagan religion. He does this superbly but selects rather questionable matter to support his thesis – it becomes a manual of religious instruction in Judaism. In the judgement of historians it carries very much less historical credibility that the first book.

These are the sources from which the story of the Maccabees can be studied.

The story begins in a small village called Modin (present name Modein) about twenty miles north-west of Jerusalem, where an aged priest called Mattathias had retired to live quietly with his five sons. Here the Syrian officers arrived on a day in 167 BC to enforce the Hellenisation policy of King Antiochus IV Epiphanes. They did this by erecting an altar and calling upon the leaders of the local community to make sacrifice to Jupiter (Zeus) Olympus.

The following verses taken from 1 Maccabees 2:15–22 (*RV*) describe the occasion:

> And the king's officers that were enforcing the apostasy, came into the city Modin to sacrifice. And many of Israel came unto them, and Mattathias and his sons were gathered together. And the king's officers answered and spake to Mattathias, saying 'Thou art a ruler and an honourable and great man in this city, and strengthened with sons and brethren: now therefore come thou first and do the commandment of the king, as all the nations have done, and the men of Judah, and they that remain in Jerusalem: and thou and thy house shall be in the number of the king's Friends, and thou and thy sons shall be honoured with silver and gold and many gifts'. And Mattathias answered and said with a loud voice, 'If all the nations that are in the house of the king's dominions harken unto him, to fall away each one from the worship of his fathers, and have made choice to follow his commandments, yet will I and my sons and my brethren walk in the covenant of our fathers. Heaven forbid that we should forsake the law and the ordinances. We will not harken to the king's words, to go aside from our worship, on the right hand or on the left'. And when he had left speaking

> these words, there came a Jew in the sight of all to sacrifice on the altar which was at Modin, according to the king's commandment. And Mattathias saw it, and his zeal was kindled, and his reins trembled, and he showed forth his wrath according to judgement and ran, and slew him upon the altar. And the king's officer who compelled men to sacrifice, he killed at that time, and pulled down the altar. And he was zealous for the law, even as Phinehas did unto Zimri the son of Salu. And Mattathias cried out in the city with a loud voice saying 'Whosoever is zealous for the law and maintaineth the covenant, let him come forth after me'. And he and his sons fled into mountains and forsook all that they had in the city.

Although the name 'Maccabees' has gained wide acceptance, their family name was 'Asmon' or 'Hasmon'. 'Hasmoneans'[2] is therefore the more accurate name for this family but historians generally confine the use of this name to the family descendants after the death of the last son of Mattathias. This family, as explained in the quotation above, was the spearhead of the Judaean revolt. Mattathias died within months of their flight to the hills but he had already advised his sons to place Judas, whose ability and courage on the battlefield had become evident, at the head of the gathering army. At the same time, he advised them to heed the wise counsel of Simon.

There is no doubt that Judas was a very able tactician and skilled military leader. After the early victories he was soon given the name 'Maccabaeus', most probably derived from the Aramaic word 'maqqaba', meaning 'hammer'. This sobriquet seems at times to refer to his crushing military exploits, as he hit the enemy armies with hammer-like blows. On other occasions it seems to refer to his outstanding physical strength allied to the robust mental stamina he showed when things were not going well in the darker days.

The family of Mattathias was joined by many Jews from all over the land, as they retreated into the mountains to wage a guerrilla war against the Syrian authorities. In many places, idolatrous altars were thrown down and the Jewish festivals reintroduced. As the story unfolds, the Syrian authorities reacted quickly, if somewhat casually at the beginning, and the Maccabean rebels were

[2] *UBD*, p. 674.

encouraged in the early stages by many triumphs. The following dates show the progress of the rebellion:

166 BC Both those who stood against the Hellenisation policy on the ground of Scripture and others with a merely political agenda rallied behind Judas. King Antiochus Epiphanes had appointed Apollonius, his former army commander, as Governor of Samaria and thus Jerusalem was under his authority. Apollonius took the matter casually at first, as a minor local affair. Nevertheless, after a few months he had a considerable army in the field and marched toward Jerusalem. He thought the very appearance of his army would cause the rebels to scatter. Instead his army was totally routed. Apollonius himself was killed and Judas appropriated his sword and used it thereafter.

165 BC Another and much larger force was dispatched, under General Seron, by King Antiochus to annihilate the Jewish rebels. This army and the Maccabean army, now well trained and led by Judas 'the hammer', met at Beth-horon, north-west of Jerusalem (1 Macc. 3:13–24). This Syrian army was utterly swept away before the ferocity of the Maccabean zealots fighting for freedom to worship Jehovah. This battle gave the Maccabees hope and these rebels, showing unbelievable bravery and dedication, won battle after battle. So successful were they that the Seleucid king had to sue for peace. However, the price for the people of Israel was very high. This price is detailed very precisely and exactly in Daniel 11:33 – many died on the battlefields ('fall by the sword'); many perished in the flames of reprisal ('and by flame'); many were led into slavery for life ('by captivity'); and many lost everything ('and by spoil'). They found out just how long were the 'many days' – from 167 to 143 BC – around twenty-four years.

As news of success after success of the rebels reached Antiochus in Antioch, he flew into awful rages and vowed to wipe Jerusalem and Judah out of existence. To do this he marshalled a huge army under his ablest general, Lysias. This Syrian army included forty thousand foot soldiers and seven thousand cavalry. Against this mighty army Judas had only about six thousand infantry, and no cavalry. Nevertheless, at the Battle of Emmaus (165 BC) the forces of Antiochus were decisively beaten and the remnant withdrew to their own land (1 Macc. 3:38–4:25). So, after three years of bitter conflict, Jerusalem was recaptured and the Temple purified and rededicated – after the exact period of pollution Daniel had predicted (8:14); an event still commemorated annually in Israel by the Feast of Hannukkah, on 25th *Chisleu* (December).

164 BC Death of Antiochus IV Epiphanes

Even after the death of Antiochus IV Epiphanes, in 164 BC, his successors kept trying to recapture Jerusalem and bring Judaea under their control. The landmarks may be shown thus:

161 BC Judas killed at the Battle of Eleasa.

144 BC Jonathan (nicknamed 'Apphus' – 'the wary') captured at Ptolemais and executed.

143 BC Simon negotiated with the Seleucid king Demetrius II and finally Judaea was formally recognised as an independent state. The wisdom and prudence recognised by his father in his son Simon was vital to their survival (1 Macc. 2:65); he gained the active support of Rome so that for the first time in many years some measure of peace reigned in Jerusalem. Unger[3] quotes an able historian who wrote a fitting tribute[4]: 'The Maccabees inspired a subject people with independence; they found a few personal followers, and they left a nation.' In fact, the family of the Maccabees had played a vital role for God in this critical period and from their experiences will lessons be drawn in a darker day, yet to come, when a man of whom Antiochus IV Epiphanes was but a picture will exercise even greater power and come to a more sudden end.

[3] *UBD*, p. 677.

[4] Ewald, Georg Heinrich August Von, (1803–1875), German biblical scholar and noted as a specialist in the history of Israel.

Appendix 7

The Times of the Gentiles

In the exposition reference will be found to the period called the 'times of the Gentiles' and it has been thought useful to include a short appendix to explain the usage of the term so that this is not required each time it is used.

The Lord used the term once in His ministry when He spoke of Jerusalem – 'and Jerusalem shall be trodden down of the Gentiles, until the times of the Gentiles be fulfilled' (Lk. 21.24). The word 'times' is '*kairoi*', which points to the character of the times rather than their chronology. One inescapable characteristic of this period will be the subjugation of Jerusalem, the capital of the chosen nation of Israel, where Jehovah had placed His Name (Deut. 12:5), to a Gentile power. It is the period when the nation of Israel with its capital city Jerusalem enduring Gentile domination is no longer God's testimony on earth. This period has a commencement and a close.

God had to deal with His disobedient people in discipline and the world-recognised sign of His displeasure is the capture and treading down of Jerusalem by a Gentile power. The first occasion was the capture of Jerusalem by the Babylonian army under King Nebuchadnezzar in 606 BC as shown in this book of Daniel (1:1). This therefore marks the commencement of the 'times of the Gentiles'. The final Gentile king will be the Coming Prince (9:26), who will subdue Israel and Jerusalem during the Tribulation period, as shown in this book (9:24–27). This will bring the close of the 'times of the Gentiles', when the Son of Man comes to take the Kingdom. The period from the first Gentile ruler to the last Gentile ruler is the period spoken as the 'times of the Gentiles'.

This period has been shown in the exposition to be the time period reflected in the image shown to Nebuchadnezzar in the dream and interpreted by Daniel (see chapter 2). Nebuchadnezzar, as the head of gold of the image, when he captured Jerusalem (606 BC) becomes the first Gentile king. During this period four empires are to dominate Israel and continue the desolation of Jerusalem – until the symbolic stone strikes the image and replaces earthly kingdoms with the Kingdom of God; in non-symbolic terms, until the Son of Man sets up the Kingdom of God – a moment that still lies in the future for earth. In chapter 7 the time period, as shown in the exposition, is the end period of the 'times of the Gentiles' that is in view when four empires, different from those of chapter 2, dominate the scene until the final emperor takes control of earth and the time of the treading down of Jerusalem will come to a close with the arrival of the Son of Man.

However, it is shown in the exposition of the seventy weeks prophecy (9:24–27) that there is an interregnum in the timeline of God's programme. At the end of the sixty-ninth week, on the rejection of Christ by Israel, the clock of prophecy stopped. It restarts for the seventieth and final week with the signing of a covenant by world leaders to bring peace to Israel. The purpose of the time gap was hidden in the counsels of God until in the NT His purpose stands revealed as the calling out of the Church by the preaching of the Gospel.

Thus, since Pentecost we are now in the dispensation of grace when the Gospel is freely preached across the world to Jew and Gentile without distinction. For Israel, as a nation, the prophetic clock has stopped (see 9:24–27). While God still rules in absolute sovereignty amongst the nations He is not working now through any particular nation. This period will end when the Lord removes His Church at the Rapture. In light of these facts it is suggested that the period of the 'times of the Gentiles' is suspended during the dispensation of grace – the Church age (see chart on pages 678–679). The 'times of the Gentiles' will recommence when the Church is removed from earth at the Rapture and Jerusalem and the nation of Israel once again becomes the focus of Divine purpose.

It should also be pointed out that the expression – 'the fulness of the Gentiles' (Rom. 11:25) refers not to the Church, as it is often interpreted, but, as the context demands, to the innumerable company of saved Gentiles who, at the very close of the 'times of the Gentiles', are identified as those that 'came out of great tribulation, and have washed their robes, and made them white in the blood of the Lamb' (Rev. 7:14). In another passage the same company is spoken of as 'the sheep' going into the Kingdom (Matt. 25:33–40).

Charts and Maps

IMAGE OF NEBUCHADNEZZAR'S DREAM

606 BC Daniel 2:31-33 Date 603 BC

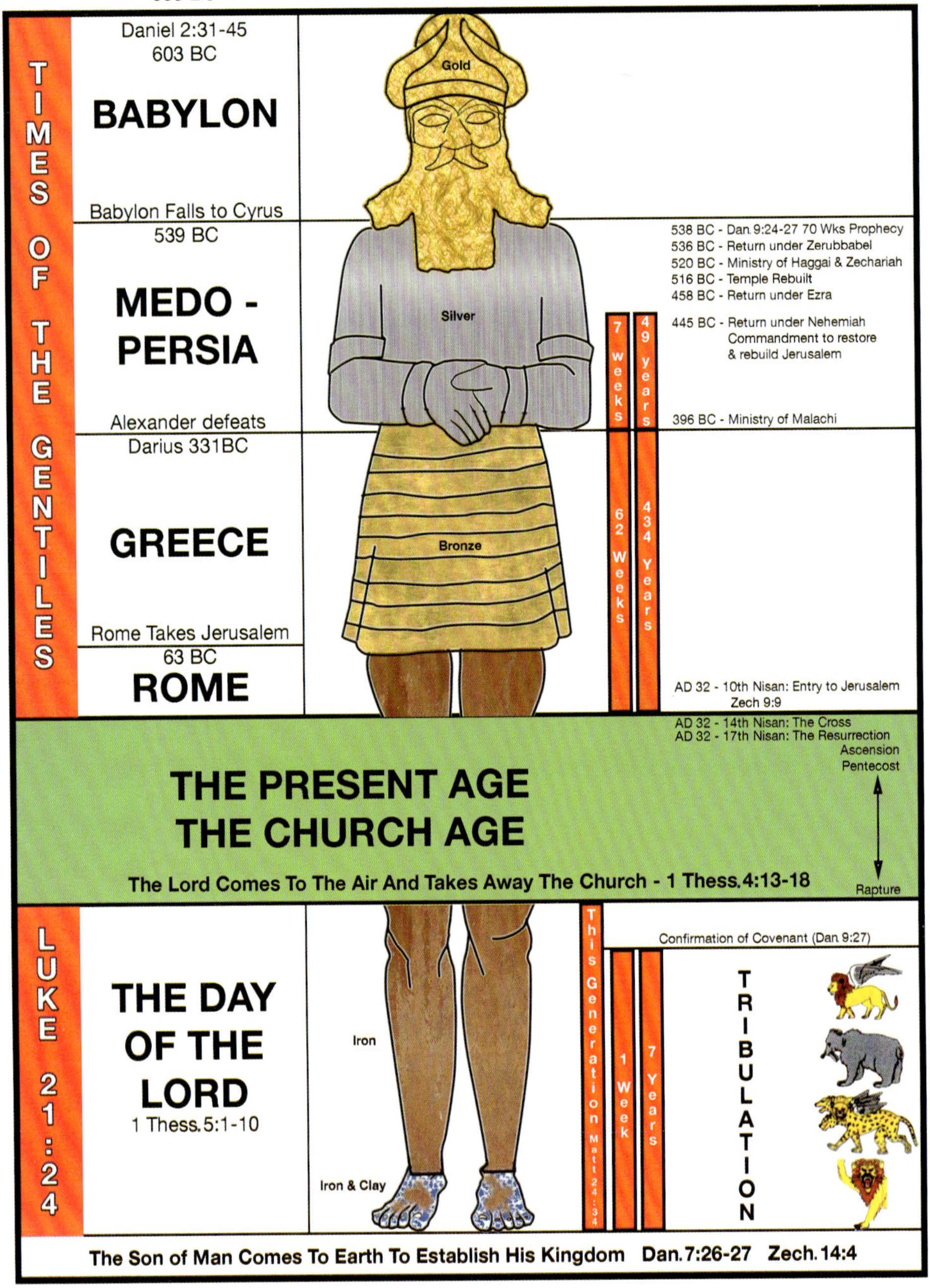

STRUCTURE IN THE BOOK OF DANIEL

Chapter 1	Chapter 2	Chapter 3	Chapter 4	Chapter 5	Chapter 6	Chapter 7	Chapter 8	Chapter 9	Chapter 10	Chapter 11	Chapter 12
Daniel and Friends Tests of Faith			Daniel and Foes Triumphs of Faith			Vision 1	Vision 2	Vision 3	Vision 4		
A King's Demand	A King's Dream	A King's Decree	Nebuchad-nezzar Pride	Belshazzar Profanity	Darius Presumption	FOCUS: Little Horn	FOCUS: King of fierce countenance	FOCUS: Time of consummation	'The Time of the End' (Dan 8:17; 11:35,40; 12:4)		
Hebrew	Aramaic	Aramaic	Aramaic	Aramaic	Aramaic	Aramaic	Hebrew	Hebrew	Hebrew		
HISTORY FORESHADOWS PROPHECY						PROPHECY FORETELLS HISTORY					

Hebrew Indicates chapter written in Hebrew

Aramaic Indicates chapter written in Aramaic

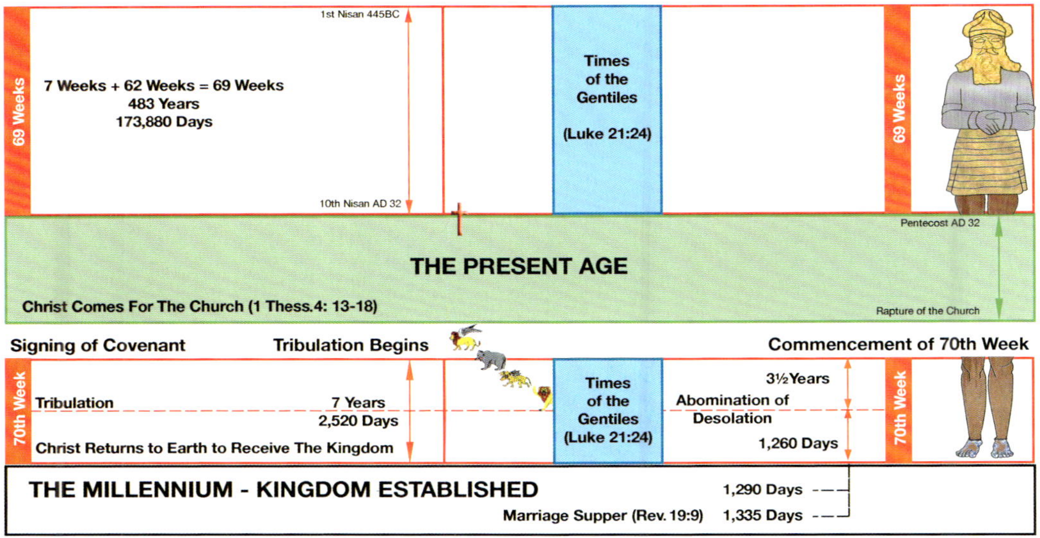

THE SEVENTY

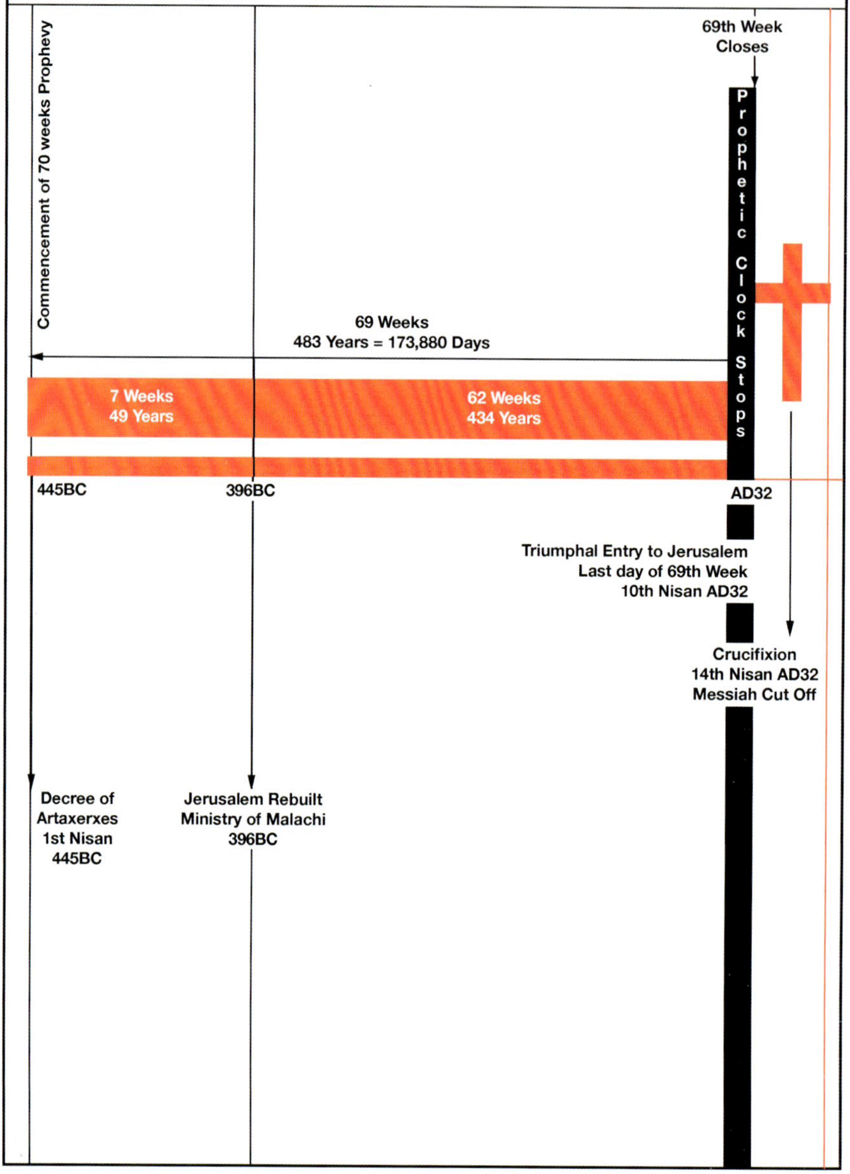
Commencement of 70 weeks Prophevy
69th Week
Closes
Prophetic Clock Stops
69 Weeks
483 Years = 173,880 Days
7 Weeks
49 Years
62 Weeks
434 Years
445BC
396BC
AD32
Triumphal Entry to Jerusalem
Last day of 69th Week
10th Nisan AD32
Crucifixion
14th Nisan AD32
Messiah Cut Off
Decree of
Artaxerxes
1st Nisan
445BC
Jerusalem Rebuilt
Ministry of Malachi
396BC

WEEKS PROPHECY

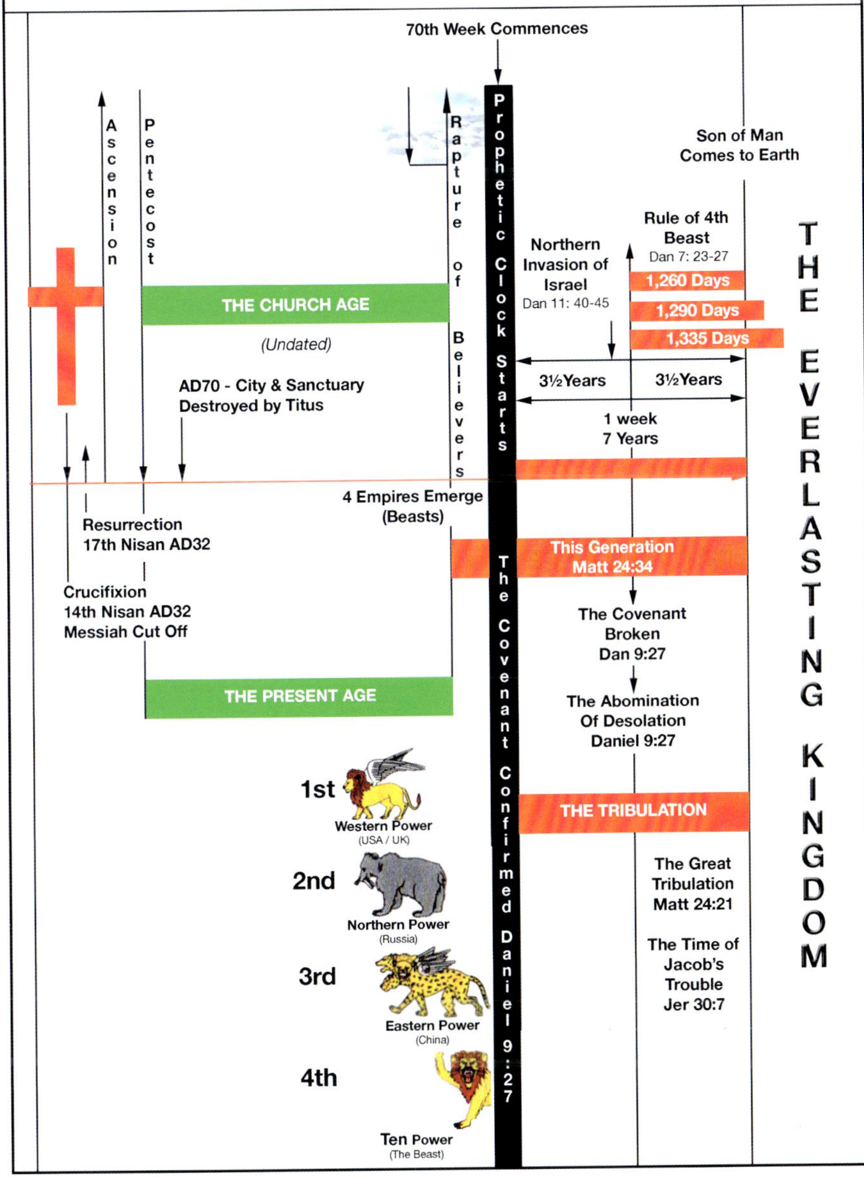

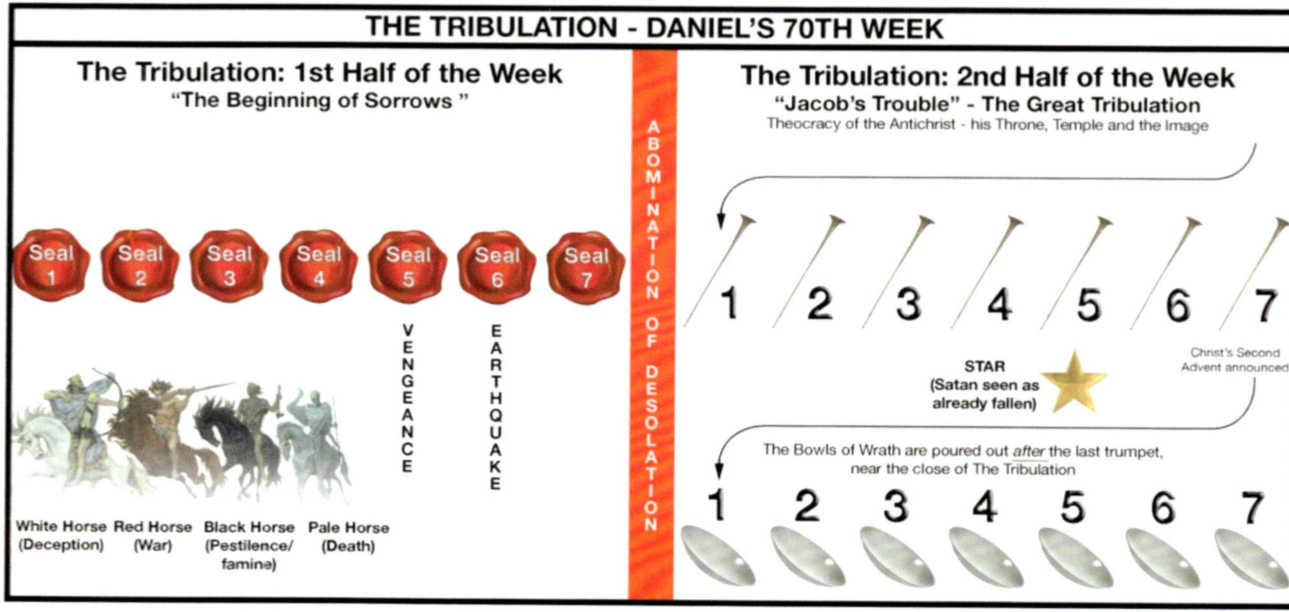

Matthew 24:8 "These are the Beginning of Sorrows"

Deception
War
Famine
Death
Persecution
Earthquake
Invasion of Israel from North (Dan 11:40-45, Ezek 38,39
Destruction of invader by God

Matthew 24:14 "Then shall the end come"

1. Destruction of invader of Israel (Ezek 38:18-23)
2. Desecration of Holy Place ... Man (2Thess 2:3-4) ... Image (Rev 13:11-17)
3. War in Heaven (Rev 12: 7-12)
   Satan cast down to Earth (Rev 12:13)
4. Flight of Israel (Matt 24:15-20, Rev 12:6, Rev 12:13-17)
5. Two witnesses killed (Rev 11:3-12)
6. Destruction of Harlot (Rev 14:8, Rev 17:1-8)

PROPHETIC CHART OF ISRAEL, THE CHURCH AND THE NATIONS

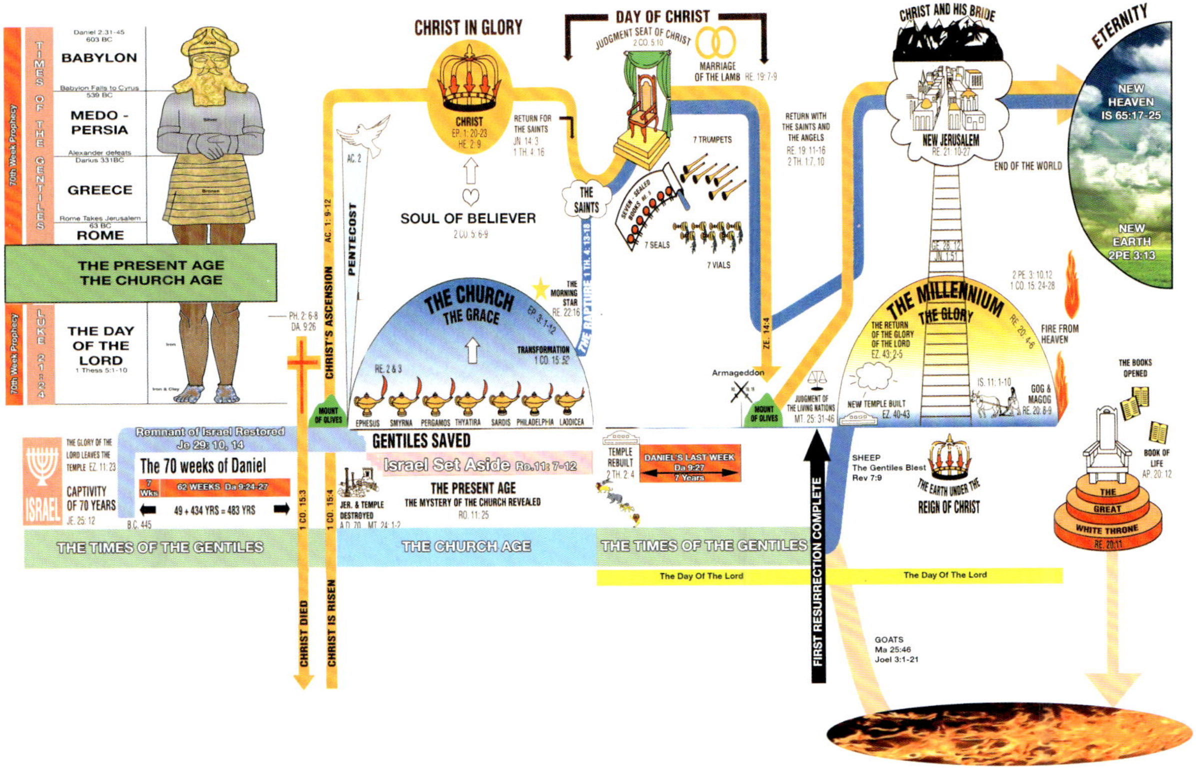

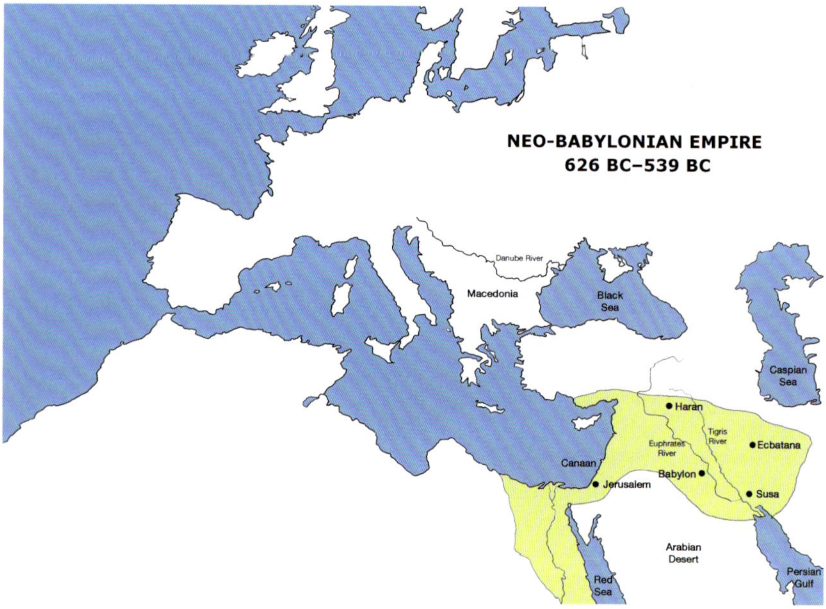
NEO-BABYLONIAN EMPIRE
626 BC–539 BC
Danube River
Macedonia
Black Sea
Caspian Sea
Haran
Tigris River
Euphrates River
Ecbatana
Canaan
Babylon
Jerusalem
Susa
Arabian Desert
Red Sea
Persian Gulf

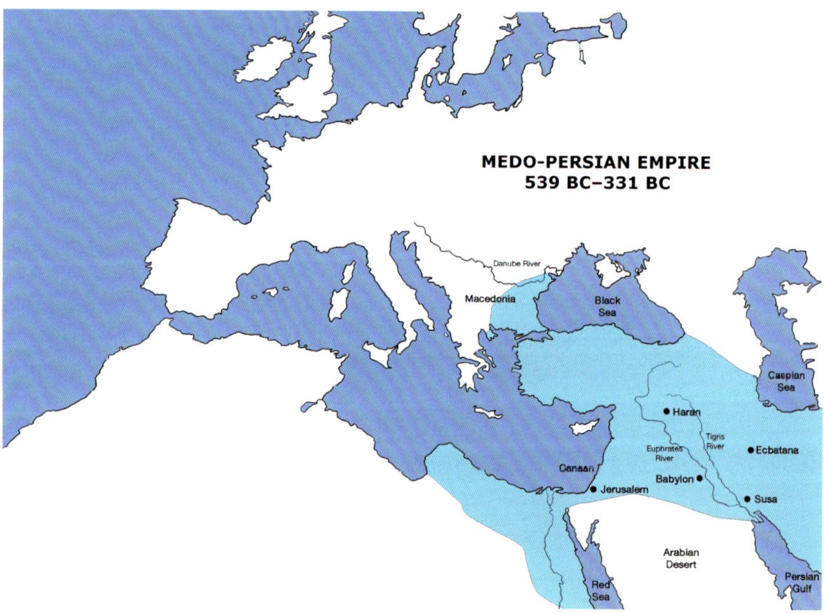
MEDO-PERSIAN EMPIRE
539 BC–331 BC
Danube River
Macedonia
Black Sea
Caspian Sea
Haran
Tigris River
Euphrates River
Ecbatana
Canaan
Babylon
Jerusalem
Susa
Arabian Desert
Red Sea
Persian Gulf

ALEXANDER'S EMPIRE AT HIS DEATH 323 BC
Showing the march of Alexander the Great

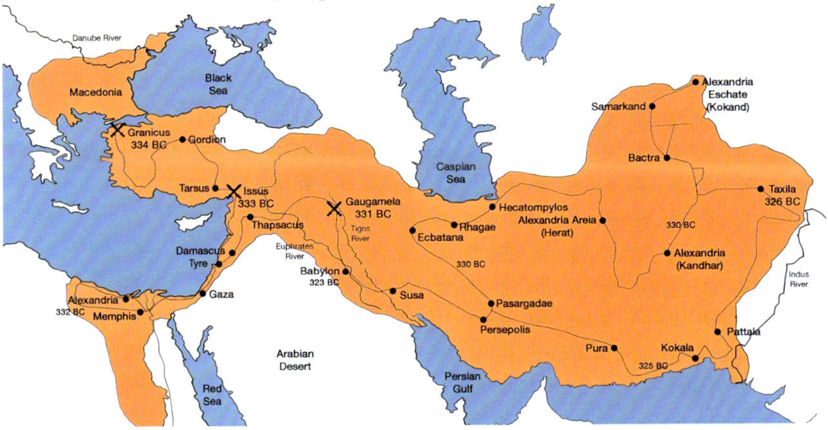

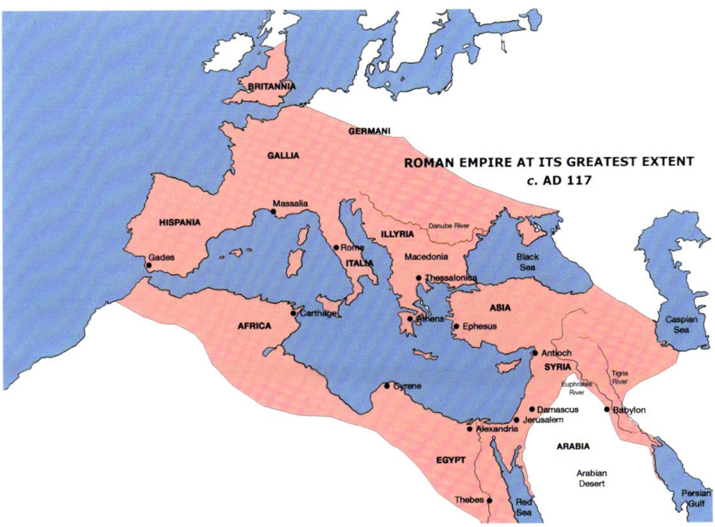

BIBLIOGRAPHY

Authorized Version (*AV*)
English Standard Version (*ESV*)
Revised Version (*RV*)
Revised Standard Version (*RSV*)
New Translation (*JND*)
The NET Bible (New English Translation, First Edition, 1996) (*NET*)
New International Version, 1983 edition (*NIV*)
Spurrell, H (1885) A translation of the Old Testament Scripture (*SP*)

SECTION B – REFERENCE

CRYSTAL, David. *The Cambridge Biographical Encyclopaedia.* Cambridge University Press, 1995.

DOUGLAS, J.D. (ed.) *The New International Dictionary of the Christian Church.* Paternoster Press, 1974.

HORNBLOWER, Spawforth, Eidinow. *The Oxford Classical Dictionary.* Oxford University Press. Fourth Ed., 2012.

MARKET HOUSE BOOKS LTD. *The Oxford Encyclopaedia of World History.* New York: Oxford University Press, 1998.

UNGER, Merrill F. *Unger's Bible Dictionary.* Chicago, IL: Moody Press. Second Edition, 1959.

SECTION C – GRAMMAR AIDS

BAKER and Carpenter *The Complete Word Study Dictionary OT.*, AMG Publishers, 2003.

PICK, Aaron. *Dictionary of Old Testament Words for English Readers.* Kregel Publications, 1977.

WALTKE, Harris, Archer. *Theological Wordbook of the Old Testament.* Moody Bible Institute, 1981.

WILSON, William. *Old Testament Word Studies.* Kregel Publications, 1978.

SECTION D – COMMENTARIES

BAKER, J. *What the Bible Teaches – Daniel.* Kilmarnock: John Ritchie Ltd., 2011.

BALDWIN, J. G. *Daniel.* Downers Grove, IL: Inter-Varsity Press, 1978.

BULTEMA, H. *Commentary on Daniel.* Grand Rapids, MI: Kregel Publications, 1988.

CAMPBELL, D. K. *Daniel: Decoder of Dreams.* Wheaton, IL: Victor Books, 1977.

CULVER, R. D. *Daniel and the Latter Days.* Chicago: Moody Press, 1954.

DAVIS, M. C. *Anticipating the End Times.* Kilmarnock: John Ritchie Ltd., 2010.

DENNETT, E. *Daniel the Prophet.* London: Central Bible Truth Depot Ltd., 1967.

FEINBERG, C. L. *Daniel and the Kingdom of the Lord.* Winona Lake: BMH Books, 1981.

GAEBELEIN, Arno C. *Daniel.* Grand Rapids, MI: Kregel Publications, 1955.

GANGEL, K. O. *Daniel.* Nashville: Broadman and Holman, 2001.

GOLDINGAY, J. *Daniel.* Word Biblical Commentary. Nashville: Thomas Nelson Publishers, 1989.

HARMAN, A. M. *Daniel.* Darlington: Evangelical Press, 2007.

HEADING, J. *The Book of Daniel.* Scarborough, Canada: Everyday Publications Inc., 1982.

ICE, T. L. *Charting the End Times.* Eugene, Oregon: Harvest House Publishers, 2002.

IRONSIDE, H. A. *Lectures on Daniel the Prophet.* Neptune, New Jersey: Loizeaux Brothers, 1911.

IRONSIDE, H. A. *Daniel.* Grand Rapids, MI: Kregel, 1920.

JOHNSON, P. C. *The Book of Daniel.* Grand Rapids: Baker Book House, 1964.

KEIL and Delitzsch. *Commentary on the Old Testament.* Vol. 9. Peabody, MA: Hendrickson Publishers, 1989.

KELLY, W. *Notes on Daniel.* London: James Carter, 1897.

KELLY, W. *The Great Prophecies of Daniel.* Edinburgh: Pickering and Inglis, (No Date).

KING, G. R. *Daniel.* London: Henry E. Walters Ltd., 1966.

LANG, G. H. *The Histories and Prophecies of Daniel.* London: The Paternoster Press, 1950.

LAW, George R. *The Identification of the Mede.* Pfafftown, NC, USA: Ready Scribe Press, 2010.

LEUPOLD, H. *Exposition of Daniel.* London: Evangelical Press, 1949.

MAGEE, J. V. *Delving through Daniel.* Pasadena: Thru the Bible Books, (no date).

MILLER, S. R. *The New American Commentary – Daniel.* Nashville, TN: Broadman and Holman Publishers, 1994.

MONTGOMERY, J. A. *Critical and Exegetical Commentary – The Book of Daniel*. Edinburgh: T & T Clark, 1927.

MOSS, H. G. *Notes on the Book of Daniel*. Belfast: Words of Truth, 1949.

NEWELL, P. R. *Daniel*. Chicago: Moody Press, 1962.

OLYOTT, S. (1982). *Dare to Stand Alone*. Darlington: Evangelical Press, 1982.

PAISLEY, H. S. *This Daniel*. Homewood, Illinois: Essential Truth Publishers, 1972.

PEMBER, G. H. *The Great Prophecies of the Centuries*. London: Oliphants Ltd., 1941.

PUSEY, E. *Daniel the Prophet*. New York: Funk and Wagnalls, 1885.

SEISS, J. A. *Daniel's Prophecies or Voices from Babylon*. London: Christian Herald Office, 1881.

SHOWERS, R. E. *The Most High God*. Bellmawr, New Jersey: The Friends of Israel Gospel Ministry, Inc, 1982.

STRAUSS, L. *The Prophecies of Daniel*. Winona Lake: BMH Books, 1969.

STRONG, L. *Lectures on the Book of Daniel*. London: Yapp and Hawkins, 1871.

STUART, Moses, *A Commentary on the Book of Daniel*. Boston: Crocker and Brewster, 1850.

TAYLOR, W. M. *Daniel the Beloved*. Belfast: Ambassador Productions Ltd., 1997.

TREGELLES, S. P. *Tregelles on Daniel*. London: Sovereign Grace Advent Testimony. 7th Ed., 1965.

VINES, J. P. *Exploring the Book of Daniel*. Neptune, New Jersey: Loizeaux Brothers, 1990.

WALLACE, R. S. *The Message of Daniel*. Nottingham: Inter-Varsity Press, 1979.

WALVOORD, John F. *Daniel The Key to Prophetic Revelation*. Chicago: Moody Press, 1971.

WHITCOMB, J. C. *Daniel*. Chicago: Moody Bible Institute, 1985.

WHITLA, S. W. *Sir Issac Newton's Daniel and the Apocalypse*. London: John Murray, 1922.

WILSON, Robert D. *Studies in the Book of Daniel*. Putnam, NewYork and London: Two volumes, 1917, 'Forgotten Books' Reprint, 2012.

WOOD, L. *A Commentary on Daniel*. Grand Rapids, MI: Zondervan, 1973.

WOOD, L. J. *Daniel – A Study Guide*. Grand Rapids: Zondervan, 1975.

YOUNG, E. J. *The Prophecy of Daniel*. Grand Rapids, MI: William B. Eerdmans Publishing Company, 1949.

SECTION E – HISTORICAL

ABRAHAMS, I. *Campaigns in Palestine from Alexander the Great.* Oxford: Oxford University Press, 1922.

ARRIAN. *The Campaigns of Alexander.* New York: Pantheon Books, 2010.

BRUCE, F.F. *Israel and the Nations.* London: The Paternoster Press, 1963.

CARTLEDGE, Paul. *Alexander the Great –The Hunt for a New Past.* Pan Books, 2004.

CLAYTON, Peter A. and Martin J. Price, *The Seven Wonders of the Ancient World.* London: Routledge, 1989.

COOK J.M. *The Persians.* London: The Folio Society, 1983.

ERRINGTON, R. M. (2008). *A History of the Hellenistic World.* Blackwell.

FOX, Robin Lane. *Alexander the Great.* London: The Folio Society Edition, 1997.

GIBBON, Ernest. *History of the Decline and Fall of the Roman Empire,* London: Strahan and T. Cadell, 1776.

GRANT, Michael. *The Fall of the Roman Empire – A Reappraisal.* Radnor, PA: Annenberg School Press, 1976.

GREEN, Peter . *Alexander the Great.* London: Book Club Associates Edition, 1973.

HERODOTOS, *The History of Herodotos.* Translated by George Rawlinson. New York: Encyclopaedia Britannica Inc, 1984.

JOSEPHUS, Flavius. *Complete Works* translated by W. Whiston. London: Pickering and Inglis with Kregel Inc., 1981.

LAYARD, A.H. *Nineveh and Babylon.* London: Folio Society, , 2011.

LOW, D.M. *The Decline and Fall of the Roman Empire.* Book Club Associates, London, 1972.

MONTEFIORE, S.S. *Jerusalem: The Biography.* London: Weidenfeld & Nicolson, 2011.

OATES, J. *Babylon.* Revised Edition. London: Thames & Hudson Ltd., 1986.

O'BRIEN, John Maxwell. *Alexander the Great: The Invisible Enemy.* London: Routledge, 1994.

PRICE, P.A. *The Seven Wonders of the Ancient World.* London: Routledge, 1988.

RIGGS, J. *A History of the Jewish People.* London: John Murray, 1921.

SAGGS, H.W. *The Babylonians.* London: The Folio Press, 1988.

THIELE, E.R. *A Chronology of the Hebrew Kings.* Grand Rapids, MI. Zondervan Publishing House, 1977.

WATERFIELD, R. *Dividing the Spoils.* OUP Oxford, 2011.

SECTION F – SPECIAL SUBJECTS CONNECTED TO THE BOOK OF DANIEL

ANDERSON, Sir Robert. *Daniel in the Critics Den.* Edinburgh: Pickering and Inglis, (No Date).

ANDERSON, Sir Robert. *The Coming Prince.* Grand Rapids, IL: Kregel Publishing, 1967.

BART, S. E. *The Cycle of Seventy Weeks.* Edinburgh: James Nisbet & Co., (No Date).

BELL, Harry. *Daniel.* Glasgow: Gospel Tract Publications, 1982.

BLAIR, J. A. *Living Courageously.* Loizeaux Brothers, 1971.

BOUTFLOWER, C. *In and around the Book of Daniel.* Edinburgh: McCall Barbour, 1963.

CAMERON, D. C. *The Minor Prophets and the End Times.* Kilmarnock: John Ritchie, 2010.

CRISWELL, W. A. *Expository sermons on the Book of Daniel.* 3 Vols. Edinburgh: B. McCall Barbour, 1968–71.

HAGEE, J. *From Daniel to Doomsday.* Nashville: Thomas Nelson Publishers, 1999.

HITCHCOCK, Mark. *Iran and Israel.* Eugene, OR: Harvest House Publishers, 2013.

IRONSIDE, H.A. *The Four Hundred Silent Years.* First edition. Loizeaux Brothers, 1941.

LEWIS, S. M. *Daniel Trusting the True Hero.* Fearn, Scotland: Christian Focus Publications, 2011.

LIEBI, Roger. *The Messiah in the Temple.* First English Ed., 2012. Translated by Timothy Capes. Dusseldorf.

LIEBI, Roger. *Are We Really Living in the Last Days?* First English Ed., 2012.

MELLISH, N. *The Times of the Gentiles.* Port Colborne: Gospel Folio Press, 2010.

MCCLAIN, D. A. *Daniel's Prophecy of the Seventy Weeks.* Grand Rapids, IL: Zondervan, 1969.

PRICE, Randall *The Temple and Bible Prophecy.* Eugene, OR: Harvest House Publishers, 2005.

RHODES, Ron *The End Times in Chronological Order.* Eugene, OR: Harvest House, Publishers, 2012.

SALE-HARRISON, L. *The Resurrection of the Old Roman Empire.* 12th Edition. Edinburgh: Pickering and Inglis, (No Date).

WALVOORD, John F. *The Nations in Prophecy.* Grand Rapids, MI: Zondervan Publishing House, 1967.